Marianne Angel SMHS
925-2567 x 357

EXTENDED TEACHER'S EDITION

DISCOVERING FRENCH

BLEU

Jean-Paul Valette
Rebecca M. Valette

Teacher Consultant
T. Jeffrey Richards

D.C. Heath and Company
Lexington, Massachusetts / Toronto, Ontario

Merci!

We would like to express our appreciation to the many **French for Mastery** teachers who responded to our surveys and who sent us suggestions for designing this new program. In particular, we would like to thank the following people who carefully read the manuscript as it was being developed and provided us with guidance and encouragement:

Steve Covey
*Sunnyvale Junior
    High School
Sunnyvale, CA*

T. Jeffrey Richards
*Theodore Roosevelt
    High School
Sioux Falls, SD*

Dianne Hopen
*Humbolt High School
St. Paul, MN*

Frank Strell
*LaSalle-Peru Township
    High School
LaSalle, IL*

Patricia McCann
*Lincoln-Sudbury Regional
    High School
Sudbury , MA*

Susan Wildman
*Western Albemarle High School
Crozet, VA*

Director, Modern Languages
Roger D. Coulombe

Managing Editor
Gail G. Smith

Project Editor
Karen Hohner

National Modern Language Coordinator
Teresa Carrera-Hanley

D.C. Heath Consultant
Karen Ralston

Design and Production
Victor Curran, *Design Manager*
Pamela Wing, *Production Coordinator*
Greg Johnson, Richard Curran, *ETE Design*
Gabriella Della Corte, *ETE Design Assistant*

Published simultaneously in Canada
Printed in the United States of America
International Standard Book Number: 0-669-23920-8

Dear French Teachers,

We take this opportunity to welcome you to our new program, **Discovering French**. In fact, this is really your program, for it has taken shape thanks to the suggestions, critiques and encouragement we have received from the many hundreds of secondary school teachers who, over the years, have enjoyed success getting their students to communicate through *French for Mastery*.

As you will see, **Discovering French** stresses communication and interpersonal relationships in meaningful cultural contexts. Some of the key features, which many of you requested, are:

- *An integrated video to accompany each lesson*
  These segments, all shot on location, allow students to hear language as it is spoken in France and share in the lives of dozens of young people, their families and friends.

- *Stronger emphasis on daily life themes*
  The new *Français pratique* lessons in each unit have been especially conceived to develop the students' ability to communicate effectively on common everyday topics.

- *Active encouragement of cooperative learning*
  The many activities designed for pair and small group work incorporate cooperative learning strategies, letting students practice together and come to appreciate each other's differences.

- *Greater opportunity for self-expression*
  The *À votre tour* sections which close each unit in Niveau A and each lesson in Niveaux B and C provide the opportunity for oral and written communication in a broad variety of contexts.

There are, of course, many more new features which you will discover as you look through the book.

In conclusion, we should stress that our program is a *flexible* one which allows teachers to take into account the needs of their students and build their own curriculum focusing on specific skills or topics.

We wish you the best of success with **Discovering French**! It is our hope that for you and your students, teaching and learning French with this program will be an enjoyable as well as a rewarding experience.

Jean-Paul Valette   *Rebecca M. Valette*

EXTENDED TEACHER'S EDITION

Contents

Introduction to DISCOVERING FRENCH–BLEU

Discovering French is a three-level program designed for middle school and high school students.

> *First level:* **Discovering French–Bleu**
> *Second level:* **Discovering French–Blanc**
> *Third level:* **Discovering French–Rouge**

General Characteristics of DISCOVERING FRENCH–BLEU

Key Objective: Building French Proficiency

The key objective of **Discovering French** is to build the students' *French proficiency*. The attainment of this objective requires a focus on:

Communication with accuracy — in an authentic cultural context

The primary aim of **Discovering French** is to teach students to *communicate* in French, both in class with their classmates, and, when the occasion arises, with other French speakers either in this country or abroad. For this communication to be effective, students must learn to express themselves with reasonable *accuracy*, that is, they must "sound French" when they speak and write. The most effective way of developing real French proficiency is to focus on *communication with accuracy*.

The secondary aim of **Discovering French** is to immerse students in an *authentic cultural context*. Through the many conversations in the textbook and the hundreds of additional mini-scenes in the cassette program and the video, students come to know and appreciate a new culture: that of France and the French-speaking world.

Five-Step Approach to Proficiency

Building proficiency in French is very similar to building proficiency in a sport like football. At first, a child is happy to zigzag down the lawn carrying the ball. But soon the young player needs to learn what real football is by:

- watching actual football games (comprehension of authentic material),
- learning the rules of the game (awareness of structure), and
- drilling the skills, such as throwing, receiving, blocking and running (guided practice for building accuracy).

Furthermore, the player needs to gain experience in:

- scrimmage practice (cooperative learning in meaningful context), and
- participating in actual games (opportunity for self-expression).

Clearly a young player who cannot understand the game on television, who cannot catch a pass and who does not know when he or she is "offsides," may have fun "playing football" with friends, but certainly is not "proficient" at the game.

STEP 1
Comprehension of Authentic Language

For students to be able to speak French proficiently, they must first learn to understand French as it is spoken. **Discovering French–Bleu,** with its 39 video modules, each closely integrated to the student text, brings into the classroom the voices, and faces, of dozens of young people, their families and their friends. This authentic language is comprehensible because it introduces useful communicative phrases and expressions in small manageable chunks.

In both the student text and the video, **Discovering French** presents the French language in authentic cultural settings, so that students see French used in real communication situations.

STEP 2
Awareness of Structure

For most adolescent students, learning to communicate in a second language is enhanced when someone explains to them the "the rules of the game". In **Discovering French,** grammar, pronunciation, and spelling patterns are not taught as an instructional goal, but rather are presented to help the students express themselves more clearly and correctly. There is evidently an element of Critical Thinking involved as students begin to analyze how language works, and how French is contrasted with English.

Throughout **Discovering French,** grammar is viewed as a support for accurate communication, but not as the central concern of the program. The emphasis is never on mere manipulation of forms but rather on internalizing high-frequency patterns and using them for comprehension and self-expression.

STEP 3
Guided Practice for Building Accuracy

Once the students can understand new phrases and expressions, **Discovering French** provides numerous opportunities for practice in guided communicative activities. The activities are carefully graded from easier to more challenging, thus letting the students gradually build up accurate language habits. (If French students are confronted with too much new vocabulary or too many new structures at once, they tend to fall back on English speech and pronunciation patterns producing language which native French-speakers have serious difficulty understanding.)

STEP 4
Cooperative Learning in Meaningful Context

Language learning is like a team sport in that it requires cooperative effort. Most of the activities of **Discovering French** have been designed for pair and small-group work so that students can learn together. The focus is always on developing accurate communication skills in meaningful contexts. As students talk with one another about their preferences, plans and activities, they come to appreciate one another's differences while strengthening their command of a new language.

STEP 5
Frequent Opportunity for Self-Expression

For students, the reason for studying the language is to learn to speak French, to have a chance to "play the game." In **Discovering French,** students are given frequent opportunity to express themselves, both orally and in writing. Each video module has speaking as well as viewing activities. In the textbook, the regular **À votre tour** sections provide a variety of communication situations, each structured so that students can express themselves creatively with the language they have learned.

Solid Pedagogical Foundation

The underlying strength of **Discovering French** lies in its carefully crafted basic structure. The authors have drawn on over two decades of pedagogical research and interaction with thousands of teachers around the country to produce a new program in which every element has been painstakingly designed and developed. As with its predecessor **French for Mastery,** each lesson of **Discovering French** has been conceived so that students can readily assimilate the new material and use it for meaningful communication.

The main purpose of a textbook series is to provide a strong linguistic base on which teachers can elaborate curricula to meet the needs of students in their own communities. What sets **Discovering French** apart from other programs is precisely its solid pedagogical foundation.

Special Features

Discovering French has a wealth of special features which facilitate adapting the program to meet specific local needs or district guidelines:

Fully Integrated Video

The **Discovering French Video,** entirely filmed on location, brings people and places from the French-speaking world into the classroom. (See also Section 4)

Authentic Listening Materials

Meaningful listening proficiency is fostered by means of the innovative **Discovering French Cassette Program** which contains hundreds of different voices recorded in everyday situations.

Varied Reading Materials

Reading materials in **Discovering French** range in style from letters, descriptions, dialogues, and narratives to authentic realia from the French-speaking world. Certain selections are accompanied with *pre-reading* and *post-reading* activities.

À votre tour!

Numerous Self-Expression Opportunities

Each unit in Niveau A and each lesson in Niveau B and Niveau C closes with an **À votre tour** section containing numerous proficiency activities enabling students to express themselves orally and in writing.

Total Physical Response Suggestions

Through Total Physical Response (TPR) activities, students are introduced to new vocabulary and structures via listening and demonstrate their comprehension by following commands. (See Section 8)

Cooperative Practice and Learning Activities

Discovering French permits students to work together regularly in Cooperative Learning and Cooperative Practice activities as they strengthen their language skills and develop greater cross-cultural understanding. (See Section 9)

Encouragement of Critical Thinking

Discovering French offers many occasions for the development of Critical Thinking skills. These are signaled in the Extended Teacher's Edition. (See Section 10)

Development of Global Awareness

Through its rich cultural content, especially as brought to life in the video program, and its regular re-entry of geography-related activities, **Discovering French** helps students broaden their global awareness and multi-cultural perspectives. (See Section 14)

Dual Testing Program

In accordance with its objective of fostering *communication with accuracy*, **Discovering French** has a dual testing program. The lesson quizzes focus on accurate mastery of conversational phrases, structures and vocabulary. The unit tests, on the other hand, evaluate proficiency in the four skills of listening, speaking, reading and writing.

Portfolio Assessment

Every unit of **Discovering French** contains specifically designed speaking and writing activities which are appropriate for on-going Portfolio Assessment. (See Section 11)

Teacher Notes

The Extended Teacher's Edition of **Discovering French** contains numerous on-the-page Teacher Notes with suggestions for lesson planning and organization.

Warm-up Activities

Where appropriate, the Extended Teacher's Edition contains ideas for various Warm-up Activities. (The TPR activities also frequently function as warm-ups.)

Cyclical Re-entry and Review

Since the focus in **Discovering French** is on high-frequency language patterns, most of the new material is automatically re-entered in subsequent lessons. However, where needed, there are specific Re-entry and Review activities.

Language Games

From time to time, as a change of pace, the Extended Teacher's Edition of **Discovering French** contains ideas for Language Games. The focus is always on meaningful language use.

Perk Notes

Occasional perk notes in the Student Text encourage students in their study of French.

The components of **Discovering French–Bleu** offer the flexibility needed to respond to the requirements of different types of school systems. Schools may begin with the basic program, and then enhance their curriculum in subsequent years with additional correlated materials.

Basic program

■ **Student Text**
■ **Extended Teacher's Edition**

For schools with limited budgets, the BASIC PROGRAM provides a solid introduction to French language and culture.

■ The **Student Text** contains the basis for effective language acquisition (thematic vocabulary and conversational patterns in cultural contexts, corresponding grammar support, meaningful practice) as well as a broad variety of communication activities (dialogue opportunities, oral and written self-expression, reading comprehension).

■ The **Extended Teacher's Edition** provides creative teacher support. On-the-page side glosses provide teaching hints and suggest appropriate TPR listening comprehension activities, as well as ideas for Cooperative Learning and Practice activities. The side notes also indicate how and when to introduce video and cassette segments. The informative front matter contains a wealth of useful reference material, including a special pedagogical section that introduces topics such as:
• Total Physical Response (TPR)
• Cooperative Learning
• Critical Thinking Skills
• Portfolio Assessment

Enhanced Program

- **Student Text**
- **Extended Teacher's Edition**
  plus
- **Discovering French Audio/Video Program**
- **Student Activity Book**
  and
- **Teacher's Resource Package (TRP)**
- **Achievement and Proficiency Testing Kit**
- **Overhead Visuals**

In the ENHANCED PROGRAM, the material in the Student Text is supplemented with the fully integrated **Discovering French** Audio/Video Program plus the correlated Student Activity Book, thus bringing the sights and sounds of the French world into the classroom.

- The **Discovering French Audio/Video Program**
  - The **Discovering French Video**, filmed on location, consists of 39 modules, corresponding to the 36 lessons and 3 photo essays of the Student Text. Language acquisition is enhanced when students have the opportunity to meet and listen to dozens of French speakers from around the French-speaking world.
  - The **Discovering French Cassettes**, based on the video soundtrack, give the teacher the flexibility of bringing authentic French conversations into the classroom on days when a VCR might not be available. In addition, the Cassette Program contains recordings of the Pronunciation Sections and sample conversations from the *À votre tour* sections of the Student Text.

- The **Student Activity Book** provides additional practice in the four skills of listening, speaking, reading and writing, including worksheets to accompany the video and cassette programs.
- The **Teacher's Resource Package** contains useful supplementary materials, including:
  - the Answer Key to the student text
  - the Video Script and the Cassette Script
  - black-line masters corresponding to the Overhead Visuals
  - a Teacher's Annotated Edition of the Student Activity Book.
- The **Achievement and Proficiency Testing Kit** allows teachers to assess whether the students have mastered the new linguistic material and how well they can use French as a medium of communication. At the lesson level, there are accuracy-based vocabulary and structure quizzes. For each unit, there are proficiency tests of listening, speaking, reading and writing. The kit also contains a complete Testing Manual and Testing Cassette.
- The four-color **Overhead Visuals** contain original drawings as well as selected maps and illustrations from the Student Text and the Video. They may be used for listening comprehension practice (and TPR activities), speaking activities, and building awareness of the geography of the French-speaking world.

Basic Structure

The Student Text contains nine units and three illustrated photo essays which are grouped in three levels or *niveaux*.

CULTURAL PHOTO ESSAY

Parlons français!

CULTURAL PHOTO ESSAY

À l'école en France

CULTURAL PHOTO ESSAY

À Paris

Cultural Photo Essay: *Parlons français!*

NIVEAU A Faisons connaissance!

Unité 1 Bonjour!

Unité 2 Les copains et la famille

Unité 3 Bon appétit!

Cultural Photo Essay: *À l'école en France*

NIVEAU B La vie de tous les jours

Unité 4 Qu'est-ce qu'on fait?

Unité 5 Le monde personnel et familier

Unité 6 En ville

Cultural Photo Essay: *À Paris*

Unité 7 Le shopping

NIVEAU C Les monde des jeunes

Unité 8 Le temps libre

Unité 9 Les repas

INTRODUCTION

Niveau A begins the program immediately by introducing basic conversational skills without any formal presentation of structure.

Topics covered:

- greeting people
- introducing oneself
- talking about friends and family
- ordering in a café

Also:

- numbers 0–100
- telling time
- days of the week
- months and dates
- weather and seasons

CORE MATERIAL

Niveau B provides the linguistic base needed for basic communication skills. Emphasis is on asking and answering questions. (Students should complete these units.)

Topics covered:

- discussing daily activities and leisure pastimes
- talking about people and possessions
- getting around town
- describing where one lives
- shopping for clothes

FURTHER DEVELOPMENT

Niveau C introduces somewhat more complex language functions. (Although it is desirable to present these units, it is not critical to finish them since the material is reviewed and expanded in the first part of *Discovering French–Blanc.*)

Topics covered:

- describing weekend activities
- talking about vacation plans
- planning meals
- shopping for food

Organization of a Unit

Each unit of Niveau A contains four lessons. The first three lessons develop simple conversational exchanges. The fourth, subtitled *Le français pratique*, focuses on a specific communication topic: time, dates, weather. The unit is organized as follows:

UNIT TITLE → **Introduction culturelle** —— Presents unit theme

Leçon [1]

Lesson opener —— Introduces new language patterns (text of the video scenes)

Note culturelle —— Provides cultural background

Leçon [2]

Pour communiquer Activités —— Presents and activates conversational expressions related to the lesson theme

Prononciation —— Practices French sounds

Leçon [3]

Leçon [4] Le français pratique

Lesson opener —— Introduces new language patterns (text of the video scenes)

Pour communiquer Activités —— Presents and activates specific communication topics

À votre tour —— Oral communication activities integrating material from the entire unit

Entracte —— Cultural reading activities

The units of Niveau B and Niveau C also each contain four lessons, but follow a somewhat different format. The first lesson, subtitled *Le français pratique,* introduces expressions and phrases on a specific communication topic. The next three lessons present and practice thematically related structures and patterns. Each unit is organized as follows:

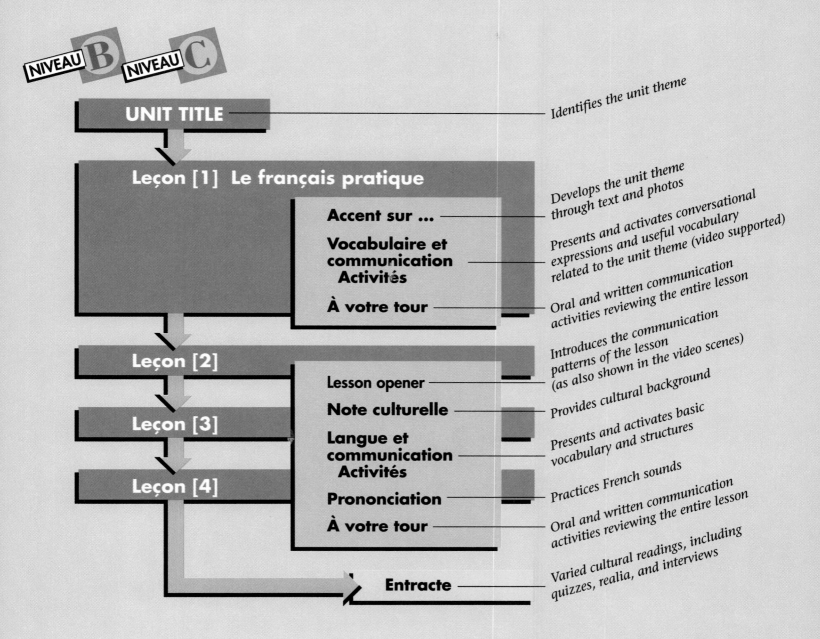

NIVEAU **B** NIVEAU **C**

UNIT TITLE —————————————————— Identifies the unit theme

Leçon [1] Le français pratique ——————————— Develops the unit theme through text and photos

Accent sur ... ——————— Presents and activates conversational expressions and useful vocabulary related to the unit theme (video supported)

Vocabulaire et communication Activités ——————

À votre tour ——————— Oral and written communication activities reviewing the entire lesson

Leçon [2] ——————— Introduces the communication patterns of the lesson (as also shown in the video scenes)

Lesson opener ———————

Note culturelle ——————— Provides cultural background

Leçon [3]

Langue et communication Activités ——————— Presents and activates basic vocabulary and structures

Leçon [4]

Prononciation ——————— Practices French sounds

À votre tour ——————— Oral and written communication activities reviewing the entire lesson

Entracte ——————— Varied cultural readings, including quizzes, realia, and interviews

Scope and Sequence

The students' unit-by-unit progression through **Discovering French–Bleu** is represented on the following Scope and Sequence chart. (The numbers in parentheses refer to the lesson numbers.) This chart identifies the cultural theme of each unit and lists the main communication functions and activities, correlating them with the corresponding communication topics (thematic vocabulary) and linguistic goals (accuracy of expression).

In Niveau A, the emphasis is on oral communication, both listening comprehension and speaking. Grammar is not presented formally, but certain structural contrasts, such as gender distinctions, are pointed out.

In Niveaux B and C, the communication topics are expanded, and the lessons build on the four skills of listening, speaking, reading and writing. In a given unit, the bulk of the thematic vocabulary is presented in the first lesson (**le français pratique**), and then is re-entered and consolidated in the next three lessons as students increase their ability to handle the related communication functions. Grammar patterns are presented formally for reference, but are practiced in functional situations relating to the unit theme.

COMMUNICATION FUNCTIONS AND ACTIVITIES	COMMUNICATION TOPICS	LINGUISTIC GOALS
Comprehension and Self-expression	**Thematic Vocabulary**	**Accuracy of Expression**
■ *Meeting people* • Introducing oneself (1) • Spelling one's name (1) • Asking someone's name (1) • Saying where you are from (2)	• Adjectives of nationality (2)	• L'alphabet (1) • **Français / française** (2)
■ *Greeting people* • Saying hello (1) • Asking how people feel (3) • Saying good-by (3)	• Expressions with **ça va** (3)	
■ *Talking about time* • Asking for the time (4) • Indicating the time (4) • Saying when certain events are scheduled (4)	• Counting 0 to 10 (1) • Counting 10 to 20 (2) • Counting 20 to 60 (3) • Expressions of time (4)	

Unité 2 Les copains et la famille

CULTURAL CONTEXT Talking about people

COMMUNICATION FUNCTIONS AND ACTIVITIES Comprehension and Self-expression	COMMUNICATION TOPICS Thematic Vocabulary	LINGUISTIC GOALS Accuracy of Expression
■ *Talking about other people* • Pointing people out (5) • Finding out someone's name (6) • Saying where a person is from (6)	• People (5)	• **Un garçon / une fille** (5) • **Le garçon / la fille** (6)
■ *Introducing one's family* (7) • Giving their names (6) • Giving their ages (7)	• Family members (7) • Counting 60 to 79 (5) • Counting 80 to 100 (6)	• **Mon cousin / ma cousine** (7) • **Ton cousin / ta cousine** (7)
■ *Talking about dates* • Asking the day of the week (8) • Giving the date (8) • Talking about birthdays (8)	• Days of the week (8) • Months of the year (8)	

COMMUNICATION FUNCTIONS AND ACTIVITIES Comprehension and Self-expression	COMMUNICATION TOPICS Thematic Vocabulary	LINGUISTIC GOALS Accuracy of Expression
■ *Saying you are hungry (9)* • Offering a friend something to eat (9) • Asking a friend for something to eat (9)	• Foods (9)	• **Un sandwich / une pizza** (9)
■ *Saying you are thirsty (10)* • Ordering a beverage in a café (10) • Asking an adult for something to eat or drink (10)	• Beverages (10)	• **S'il te plaît / s'il vous plaît** (10)
■ *Paying at a café in France* • Asking what something costs (11) • Asking a friend to lend you money (11)		
■ *Talking about the weather (12)*	• Weather expressions (12) • Seasons (12)	

Unité 4 Qu'est-ce qu'on fait?

CULTURAL CONTEXT Daily activities at home, at school, on weekends

COMMUNICATION FUNCTIONS AND ACTIVITIES Comprehension and Self-expression	COMMUNICATION TOPICS Thematic Vocabulary	LINGUISTIC GOALS Accuracy of Expression
■ *Describing daily activities* • What people do and don't do (13) • What people like to do and don't like to do (13) • What you want and don't want to do (13)	• Daily activities (13) • Expressions with **faire** (16)	• Subject pronouns (14) • Regular **-er** verbs (15) • The negative **ne... pas** (14) • Verb + infinitive (15) • The verb **faire** (16)
■ *Talking about where people are*	• Places (14)	• The verb **être** (14)
■ *Finding out what is going on* • Asking yes/no questions (14) • Asking information questions (16)	• Question words (16)	• Yes/no questions with **est-ce que** (14) • Information questions with **est-ce que** (16) • Questions with inversion (16)
■ *Inviting friends to do things with you* • Extending an invitation (13) • Accepting an invitation (13) • Turning down an invitation (13)		• Verb + infinitive (15)
■ *Expanding one's conversational skills* • Answering yes/no questions (14) • Expressing approval or regret (15) • Expressing mild doubt or surprise (16)	• Affirmative and negative expressions (14)	

Unité 5 Le monde personnel et familier

CULTURAL CONTEXT People and their possessions

COMMUNICATION FUNCTIONS AND ACTIVITIES Comprehension and Self-expression	COMMUNICATION TOPICS Thematic Vocabulary	LINGUISTIC GOALS Accuracy of Expression
■ *Describing yourself and others* • Physical appearance (17) • Age (17, 18) • Character traits (19) • Nationality (19)	• People (17) • Adjectives of physical description (17) • Adjectives of personality (19) • Adjectives of nationality (19) • Adjectives of aspect (20)	• Singular and plural nouns (18) • Definite and indefinite articles (18) • The expression **avoir... ans** (18) • Adjective formation (19) • Adjective position (19, 20) • Use of **c'est** and **il est** (20)
■ *Describing your room* • What is in it (17) • Where things are located (17)	• Room furnishings (17) • Prepositions of place (17)	• The expression **il y a** (17)
■ *Talking about possessions* • Things that one owns and doesn't own (17, 18) • Whether they work or not (17) • Where they were made (19) • What they look like (20)	• Everyday objects (17) • Color (20) • Aspect (20)	• The verb **avoir** (18) • The negative article **pas de** (18)

■ *Expanding one's conversational skills*
• Getting someone's attention (20)
• Making generalizations (18)
• Talking about regular events (18)
• Expressing opinions (20)
• Contradicting a negative statement or question (18)
• Introducing a conclusion (19)
	• Attention getters (20)
	• Expressions of opinion (20)
		• Use of the definite article:
		  in general statements (18)
		  to indicate repeated events (18)
		• Impersonal **c'est** (20)

OPTIONAL: ■ *Talking about past events (18, 19, 20)*		• Conversational introduction: answering questions in the **passé composé** (18, 19, 20)

Unité 6 En ville

COMMUNICATION FUNCTIONS AND ACTIVITIES Comprehension and Self-expression	COMMUNICATION TOPICS Thematic Vocabulary	LINGUISTIC GOALS Accuracy of Expression
■ *Describing your city* • Streets and public buildings (21) • Places you often go to (22) • How you get around (22)	• City places and buildings (21) • Transportation (22)	• The verb **aller** (22) • Contractions with **à** (22)
■ *Finding your way around* • Asking and giving directions (21) • Indicating the floor (24)	• Giving directions (21)	• Ordinal numbers (24)
■ *Describing your home and your family* • Your address (21) • The inside and outside of your home (21) • Your family (24)	• Neighborhood (21) • Rooms of the house (21) • Family members (24)	• The expression **chez** (22) • Stress pronouns (23) • The construction noun + **de** + noun (23) • Possession with **de** (24) • Possessive adjectives (24)
■ *Making plans to do things in town* • What you are going to do (22) • Asking others to come along (23) • Saying where you have been (23)	• Activities: sports, games, etc. (23)	• **Aller** + infinitive (22) • The verb **venir** (23) • Contractions with **de** (23)
■ *Expanding one's conversational skills:* • Contradicting someone (23) • Expressing surprise (23) • Expressing doubt (24)		

OPTIONAL: ■ *Talking about past events* (21, 22, 23, 24)		• Conversational introduction: answering questions in the **passé composé** (21, 22, 23, 24)

COMMUNICATION FUNCTIONS AND ACTIVITIES Comprehension and Self-expression	COMMUNICATION TOPICS Thematic Vocabulary	LINGUISTIC GOALS Accuracy of Expression
■ *Talking about clothes:* • What people are wearing (25) • Whether the clothes fit (25) • What they look like (25, 27) • What one's preferences are (25)	• Clothing and accessories (25) • Descriptive adjectives (25) • Adjectives **beau, nouveau, vieux** (27) • Expressions of opinion (25)	• The verb **mettre** (26) • The verb **préférer** (26) • The demonstrative **ce** (26) • The interrogative **quel?** (26)
■ *Discussing shopping plans* • Where to go (25, 28) • What to buy (26)	• Stores that sell clothes (25) • Verbs like **vendre** (28)	• The verb **acheter** (26) • Regular **-re** verbs (28) • The pronoun **on** (28)
■ *Buying clothes* • Asking for help (25) • Finding out prices (25, 28) • Deciding what to choose (27) • Comparing items (27) • Talking about what you need and what you would like (28) • Giving advice (28)	• Numbers 100–1000 (25) • Money-related expressions (28) • Verbs like **choisir** (27) • Expressions **avoir besoin de** and **avoir envie de** (28)	• Regular **-ir** verbs (27) • The verb **payer** (28) • Comparisons (27) • The imperative (28)
■ *Expanding one's conversational skills* • Emphasizing a remark (26) • Introducing an opinion (27) • Indicating approval (28)		

OPTIONAL: ■ *Talking about past events* (25, 26, 27, 28)		• Conversational introduction: answering questions in the **passé composé** (25, 26, 27, 28)

Unité 8 Le temps libre

CULTURAL CONTEXT Leisure time activities

COMMUNICATION FUNCTIONS AND ACTIVITIES Comprehension and Self-expression	COMMUNICATION TOPICS Thematic Vocabulary	LINGUISTIC GOALS Accuracy of Expression
■ *Discussing leisure activities* • Going out with friends (29) • Sports (29) • Helping around the house (29) • How you and others feel (30) • Things you never do (32)	• Common weekend activities (29) • Individual summer and winter sports (29) • Household chores (29)	• **Faire de** + sport (29) • Expressions with **avoir** (30) • **Ne... jamais** (32)
■ *Describing vacation travel plans* • Travel dates (29, 32) • How to travel (29) • How long to stay (29, 31) • What to see (31)	• French holidays (29) • Means of transportation (29) • Divisions of time (29) • Periods of future time (31) • Verbs of movement (32)	• The verb **voir** (31)
■ *Narrating what happened* • What you did and didn't do (30, 31) • Where you went and when you returned (32) • The sequence in which you did these things (30) • Remaining vague about certain details (32)	• Adverbs of sequence (30) • Periods of past time (31)	• **Passé composé** of **-er** verbs (30) • **Passé composé** of **-ir** verbs (31) • **Passé composé** of **-re** verbs (31) • **Passé composé** of irregular verbs (31) • **Passé composé** with **être** (32) • **Quelqu'un, quelque chose** and their opposites (32)

Unité 9 Les repas

CULTURAL CONTEXT Food and meals

COMMUNICATION FUNCTIONS AND ACTIVITIES Comprehension and Self-expression	COMMUNICATION TOPICS Thematic Vocabulary	LINGUISTIC GOALS Accuracy of Expression
■ *Talking about your favorite foods* • What you like and don't like (33) • What you can, should and want to eat (33, 34, 35)	• Names of foods and beverages (33) • Verbs of preference (33)	• The verb **vouloir** (34) • The verbs **pouvoir** and **devoir** (35)
■ *Shopping for food* • Making a shopping list (33) • Interacting with vendors (33) • Asking prices (33)	• Quantities (33) • Fruits and vegetables (33)	• Partitive article (34)
■ *Planning a meal* • Asking others to help you (35) • Setting the table (33)	• Meals (33) • Verbs asking for service (35) • Place setting (33)	• Pronouns **me, te, nous, vous** (35) • Pronouns with commands (35)
■ *Eating out with friends* • Ordering food (33) • Asking the waiter/waitress to bring things for others (36) • Talking about people you know (35) • Talking about what others have said or written (36)	• Verbs using indirect objects (36)	• The verb **prendre** (34) • The verb **boire** (34) • The verb **connaître** (36) • The verbs **dire** and écrire (36) • Pronouns **le, la, les, lui, leur** (36)

10 francs le kilo — 2 kilos

18 francs la douzaine — 1 douzaine

12 francs la livre — 1 livre

16 francs la douzaine — 2 douzaines

15 francs la livre — 3 livres

14 francs le livre — 1 livre

12 francs le kilo — 3 kilos

13 francs le kilo — 1 kilo

20 francs la livre — 1 livre

Purpose and Objectives

With the **Discovering French Video**, entirely filmed on location, each lesson of the Student Text is illustrated with images and conversations showing French-speaking young people, their families and friends engaged in a variety of everyday activities. When the video is introduced into the classroom, the study of French becomes a complete cultural and linguistic experience from the very beginning of instruction.

The objectives of the program are several:

- to foster cultural awareness of the French-speaking world and its people, with a special focus on secondary school students
- to develop listening comprehension skills by introducing students to dozens of different voices in varied contexts
- to promote communication skills, especially in proficiency-type situations
- to encourage vocabulary acquisition in context
- to build greater accuracy of expression by having students acquire a "feeling" for what authentic French sounds like

Of equal importance is the motivational aspect: the **Discovering French Video** is a pedagogical tool that will enrich classroom teaching and stimulate students' interest from the first day of class.

Organization of the Video

The **Discovering French Video** consists of 39 modules, one for each of the 36 basic lessons, and 3 Cultural Video Essays which correspond to the three Cultural Photo Essays in the Student Text. The modules vary in length from approximately 4 to 8 minutes.

The chart on the following page lists the title of each module together with the corresponding cultural themes and communication topics. (The Video Script, which accompanies the cassettes, provides the complete transcript of the soundtrack and gives the exact length of each module.)

Description of a Video Module

To enhance student motivation, the format of the video modules varies somewhat from lesson to lesson. Each module is composed of 4 to 7 segments, as shown in the chart at the right.

■ There is always a running time code in the lower right corner of the screen to make it easier to find the beginning and end of each segment.

TYPE OF SEGEMENT	DESCRIPTION	STUDENT OBJECTIVE
Dialogue (type 1): script as presentation text	Video recording of one or several scenes	To watch and listen
Dialogue (type 2): script not in student text	Video recording of one or several scenes	To watch and listen
Mini-scenes: listening	Montage of candid interviews and short scenes focusing on a vocabulary theme or a selected conversational pattern	To listen and observe specific aspects of the French language used in authentic contexts
Mini-scenes: speaking	Structured situations, visually cued, in which students have the opportunity to use the patterns they have been hearing	To answer questions in situational context
Vignette culturelle	Introduction to an aspect of French culture, often accompanied by a brief interview or dialogue	To observe cultural similarities and differences; to watch and listen

Using the Video in the Classroom

The **Discovering French Video** is a flexible pedagogical tool that can be introduced at many different points in the instructional process. In fact, multiple viewings significantly increase its effectiveness.

For every lesson or photo essay in the Student Text there is a corresponding video module. Some of the segments of this module are directly correlated to specific parts of the lesson, while others recombine and occasionally expand on lesson material.

■ **Dialogues.** The main purpose of the dialogues is to develop listening comprehension. Each dialogue is accompanied by an introduction (in English for Units 1 to 6, in French for Units 7 to 9). This introduction functions as an "advance organizer," setting the scene and preparing the students for what they will see and hear. Students will want to view the dialogue several times until they understand it readily. (Or you may have students view it once and then listen to the audiotape version of the conversation on the Cassette Program).

■ **Mini-scenes: Listening.** The listening comprehension mini-scenes consist of from 4 to 10 short video excerpts, mainly from candid interviews, in which different speakers in a variety of situations use specific structures or thematic vocabulary related to the lesson. Each set of mini-scenes is preceded by a brief introduction which focuses the students on what they will be watching. During the second viewing, you may want to stop the video from time to time and have students demonstrate their comprehension by repeating the last phrase they heard.

■ **Mini-scenes: Speaking.** In the speaking segment of the video module, students respond to questions or statements according to pictures or cartoons. You may wish to play each speaking segment with the entire class responding chorally, and then play it again, pointing to individual students to respond. (These activities are also contained in the Cassette Program, and the corresponding illustrations are reproduced in the Student Activity Book.

■ **Vignette culturelle.** The cultural vignettes are presented in English in the early modules, often with corresponding mini-dialogues in French. In the latter part of the program, the vignettes are entirely in French. Students should be encouraged to view these segments critically, looking for cross-cultural similarities and differences.

Description of the Cassette Program

The **Discovering French** Cassette Program is unique in that it brings hundreds of authentic language samples into the classroom. It is important to note that the listening comprehension activities are all based on live recordings derived from the video soundtrack, rather than artificial exchanges recorded in a sound studio. However, the Cassette Program is not simply a reproduction of the soundtrack, but rather a separate ancillary with distinctive listening and speaking activities. It is accompanied by a Cassette Script for convenient reference. A special "cassette" icon in the Extended Teacher's Edition indicates when in the lesson it is appropriate to introduce the specific cassette activities. Note that each Cassette module is accompanied by corresponding worksheets which are found in the Student Activity Book.

The Cassette Program contains the following types of activities:

- **Listening and Repeating.** Recording of the opening presentation dialogue, from the video soundtrack, followed by a paused version for speaking practice. (Where the video dialogue is different from the dialogue in the text, the Cassette Program contains recordings of both dialogues.)

- **Listening Comprehension.** Language samples from the video mini-scenes and dialogues (taken from the soundtrack) in a listening comprehension format with worksheets in the Student Activity Book.

- **Speaking Activities.** Guided conversational activities corresponding to video activities, based on illustrations in the Student Activity Book.

- **Pronunciation Practice.** Repetition exercises corresponding to the **Prononciation** sections in the Student Text.

- **Conversation Models.** Sample dialogues from the À **Votre Tour** sections of the Student Text to be used as models for end-of-lesson conversations.

PART 2

Teaching with DISCOVERING FRENCH–BLEU

 Presenting the Language

All of the basic material of **Discovering French** is presented in the Student Text. (The video and cassette programs provide an authentic audio-visual enhancement, but are not essential to presentation of the basic lessons.)

The Lesson Opener

The opening text of the lesson introduces students to the language patterns of the lesson as spoken by real people in everyday situations. (They can listen to these conversations on the Cassette Program.) Also included are the illustrated **Notes culturelles**.

■ Openers which correspond directly to video dialogues are illustrated with video photographs.

LEÇON **1**

La rentrée

This is the first day of school. Students are greeting their friends and meeting new classmates.

Bonjour! Je m'appelle Philippe.

Et moi, je m'appelle Stéphanie.

«———
—Bonjour! Je m'appelle Philippe.
—Et moi, je m'appelle Stéphanie.
———»

■ The illustrated **Notes culturelles** expand on the cultural content of the lesson opener. (All cultural material is coded in blue.)

■ NOTES ■ CULTURELLES

1 La rentrée *(Back to school)*

French and American students have about the same number of days of summer vacation. In France, summer vacation usually begins at the end of June and classes resume in early September. The first day back to school in fall is called **la rentrée.**

■ Openers which are not directly related to the video are illustrated by cartoons.

LEÇON **4**

Qui est là?

It is Wednesday afternoon. Pierre is looking for his friends but cannot find anyone. Finally he sees Hélène at the Café Bellevue and asks her where everyone is.

Vocabulary and Conversational Expressions

New vocabulary and conversational expressions are introduced in thematic context. (All vocabulary boxes are coded in yellow.)

POUR COMMUNIQUER

How to say hello:

| **Bonjour!** | Hello! | —**Bonjour,** Nathalie!
—**Bonjour,** Jean-Paul! |

How to ask a classmate's name:

| **Comment t'appelles-tu?** | What's your name? | —**Comment t'appelles-tu?** |
| **Je m'appelle . . .** | My name is . . . | —**Je m'appelle** Stéphanie. |

■ In Niveau A, the **Pour communiquer** section groups new conversational patterns by function.

A. Préférences

Est-ce que tu aimes parler français?

How to talk about what you like and don't like to do:

Est-ce que tu aimes . . .?	Do you like . . .?	**Est-ce que tu aimes** parler *(to speak)* français?
J'aime . . .	I like . . .	Oui, **j'aime** parler français.
Je n'aime pas . . .	I don't like . . .	Non, **je n'aime pas** parler français.
Je préfère . . .	I prefer . . .	**Je préfère** parler anglais.

J'aime . . .

| **téléphoner**
to phone | **parler français**
to talk, speak French | **parler anglais**
to speak English | **parler espagnol**
to speak Spanish |
| **manger**
to eat | **chanter**
to sing | **danser**
to dance | **nager**
to swim |

■ In Niveau B and Niveau C, the bulk of the new vocabulary of the unit is presented in the opening lesson, **Le français pratique.**

■ Art is used whenever appropriate, to help the visually-minded students.

■ English equivalents are provided (in smaller print) for those students who feel more comfortable with a new vocabulary item once they "know what a word means."

Expression pour la conversation

How to express surprise or mild doubt:

| **Ah bon?** | Oh? Really? | —Stéphanie organise une boum.
—**Ah bon?** Quand? |

Expressions pour la conversation

Tu parles français?
Oui, je parle français.
Super!

How to express approval or regret:

| **Super!** | Terrific! | Tu parles français? **Super!** |
| **Dommage!** | Too bad! | Tu ne joues pas au tennis? **Dommage!** |

3 **Au téléphone**

When Philippe phones his cousin Michèle, he likes to tell her what his plans are. She asks him a few questions. Play both roles.

J'organise une boum.

Ah bon? Quand est-ce que tu organises une boum?

Samedi.

▸ organiser une boum (quand? samedi)

1. organiser un pique-nique (quand? dimanche)
2. dîner avec Pauline (quand? lundi)
3. dîner avec Caroline (où? au restaurant Belcour)
4. regarder «Batman» (à quelle heure? à 9 heures)
5. jouer au tennis (quand? demain)
6. inviter Brigitte (où? à un concert)
7. parler espagnol (comment? assez bien)
8. étudier l'italien (pourquoi? je veux voyager en Italie)

■ Conversational expressions are usually introduced together with corresponding dialogue activities.

Structures

Since students have different learning styles, **Discovering French** uses a variety of techniques to present the structures of French. (Structure sections are coded in green.)

C. La négation

Compare the affirmative and negative sentences below:

AFFIRMATIVE	NEGATIVE	
Je **suis** américain.	Je **ne suis pas** français.	*I'm not French.*
Nous **sommes** en classe.	Nous **ne sommes pas** en vacances.	*We are not on vacation.*
Claire **est** là-bas.	Elle **n'est pas** ici.	*She is not here.*
Vous **êtes** à Paris.	Vous **n'êtes pas** à Lyon.	*You are not in Lyon.*
Tu **es** d'accord avec moi.	Tu **n'es pas** d'accord avec Marc.	*You do not agree with Marc.*

Negative sentences are formed as follows:

SUBJECT + **ne** + VERB + **pas** . . . ↓ **n'** (+ VOWEL SOUND)	Éric et Anne **ne** sont **pas** là. Michèle **n'**est **pas** avec moi.

Je suis en classe.
Je **ne** suis **pas** à la maison.

■ Sample sentences let students observe how the structure is used in context and arrive at their own deduction.

■ Summary boxes clarify the pattern for students who prefer a schematic explanation.

■ Where appropriate, line drawings are used to depict the structure for students who are more visually minded.

■ Cartoon art is also used to illustrate grammatical distinctions.

ILS or *ELLES?*

The French have two ways of saying *they:*

- **ils** refers to two or more males or to a mixed group of males and females
- **elles** refers to two or more females

Ils sont à Paris.   Ils sont à Bordeaux.

Ils sont à Lyon.   Elles sont à Nice.

INFINITIVE	**parler**	**habiter**	ENDINGS
STEM	**parl-**	**habit-**	
PRESENT TENSE (SINGULAR)	Je **parle** français. Tu **parles** anglais. Il / Elle **parle** espagnol.	J' **habite** à Paris. Tu **habites** à Boston. Il / Elle **habite** à Madrid.	-e -es -e

■ Formal charts help students analyze forms of verbs (and, similarly, nouns and adjectives).

■ Special boxes, entitled "Learning about Language," explain terminology and help students note how language functions.

> ### *Learning about language*
> Verbs conjugated like **parler** and **habiter** follow a *predictable pattern*.
> They are called REGULAR VERBS.

Pronunciation

All basic lessons end with a section entitled **Prononciation**. (Pronunciation sections are coded in violet.)

■ The sound to be practiced is illustrated by a key word.

■ Pronunciation helps are given in English where appropriate.

■ Students practice the sound in single words and then in sentence context.

■ All pronunciation sections are recorded in the Cassette Program.

Prononciation /y/

La voyelle /y/

The vowel sound /y/ – represented by the letter "**u**" – does not exist in English. Here is a helpful trick for producing this new sound.

S<u>u</u>per!

First say the French word **si.** Then round your lips as if to whistle and say **si** with rounded lips: /sy/. Now say **si-per.** Then round your lips as you say the first syllable: **super!**

Répétez: /y/   s<u>u</u>per   t<u>u</u>   ét<u>u</u>die   bien s<u>û</u>r
            L<u>u</u>cie L<u>u</u>c
            T<u>u</u> ét<u>u</u>dies avec L<u>u</u>cie.

9 La boum de Juliette

Juliette's friends are helping her prepare food for a party. Use the verb **faire** to say what everyone is doing.

▶ Je ... une crêpe.

Je fais une crêpe.

1. Nous ... une salade.
2. Tu ... une salade de fruits.
3. Vous ... une tarte *(pie)*.
4. Cécile et Marina ... un gâteau *(cake)*.
5. Christine ... une pizza.
6. Marc ... un sandwich.
7. Patrick et Thomas ... une omelette.
8. Pierre et Karine ... une quiche.

6 Practicing the Language Skills

Discovering French offers students a broad range of opportunities to master practical language skills.

Conversation Skills

The key to developing *communication with accuracy* lies in a careful progression of meaningful activities from structured exercises to more open-ended opportunities for self-expression.

Basic Lesson Activities

There are six types of basic lesson activities which are identified in the Extended Teacher's Edition.

■ **PRACTICE:** Students practice a new structure in a meaningful context.

■ **DESCRIPTION:** Students describe a situation or scene.

8 Un voyage à Paris

A group of American students are visiting Paris. During their stay, they do all of the following things:

voyager en bus

téléphoner à un copain

visiter la tour Eiffel

dîner au restaurant

inviter une copine

écouter un opéra

Describe the trips of the following people.

▶ Jim   Il voyage en bus, il visite la tour Eiffel ...

1. Linda   2. Paul et Louise   3. nous   4. vous

■ **COMPREHENSION:** Students demonstrate their comprehension of a situation or scene by completing sentences or making appropriate statements.

2 Quelle activité?

Describe what the following people are doing by completing the sentences with one of the verbs below. Be logical in your choice of activity.

chanter   écouter   parler   travailler   manger   voyager   regarder   inviter

1. Je ... un sandwich. Tu ... une pizza.
2. Tu ... anglais. Je ... français.
3. Éric ... la radio. Claire ... un compact (un CD).
4. Jean-Paul ... la télé. Tu ... un match de tennis.
5. M. Simon ... en *(by)* bus. Mme Dupont ... en train.
6. Nicolas ... Marie à la boum. Tu ... Alain.
7. Mlle Thomas ... dans *(in)* un hôpital. Je ... dans un supermarché *(supermarket)*.
8. Mick Jagger ... bien. Est-ce que tu ... bien?

34

5 Précisions *(Details)*

Anne is telling Hélène what certain people are doing. She asks for more details. Play both roles.

▶ Alice dîne. (avec qui? avec une copine)

1. Jean-Pierre téléphone. (à qui? à Sylvie)
2. Frédéric étudie. (avec qui? avec un copain)
3. Madame Masson parle. (à qui? à Madame Bonnot)
4. Monsieur Lambert travaille. (avec qui? avec Monsieur Dumont)
5. Juliette danse. (avec qui? avec Georges)
6. François parle à Michèle. (de qui? de toi)

Alice dîne.

Elle dîne avec une copine.

Ah bon? Avec qui est-ce qu'elle dîne?

■ **ROLE PLAY:**
Students play the roles of two French speakers as they interact in mini-conversations.

■ **EXCHANGES:** Students converse with a classmate in a guided situation.

7 Questions

Prepare short dialogues with your classmates, using the information in the illustrations.

▶ —Où est-ce que tu dînes?
—Je dîne à la maison.

où?
à la maison

1. à quelle heure?

2. quand?
en septembre

3. comment?
BONJOUR!
très bien

4. avec qui?
avec Denise

5. à qui?
à mon cousin

6. de qui?
BLA BLA BLA...
de toi

7. pour qui?
pour M. Lambert

9 Non!

One cannot do everything. From the following list of activities, select at least three that you do *not* do.

▶ Je ne joue pas au bridge.

parler espagnol
étudier à Paris
parler italien
habiter à Québec
danser le tango
étudier le japonais
jouer au hockey
nager en hiver
jouer au water-polo
dîner avec le prof
jouer au bridge
travailler dans un restaurant

14 Dialogue

Ask your classmates if they like to do the following things.

▶ chanter?
—Est-ce que tu aimes chanter?
—Oui, j'aime chanter.   (Non, je n'aime pas chanter.)

1. étudier?
2. voyager?
3. téléphoner?
4. danser?
5. parler français en classe?
6. nager en été?
7. nager en hiver?
8. travailler le week-end *(on weekends)*?

■ **COMMUNICATION:** Students express their own thoughts in personal statements or conversations with a partner.

35

The **À votre tour** section at the end of each unit in Niveau A recombines the material from the four previous lessons. For Niveau B and Niveau C, there is an **À votre tour** at the end of each lesson. These thematic activities, which often vary in format from unit to unit, range from guided review to self expression.

■ Activities like **Allô!** focus on comprehension, and call on Critical Thinking skills. (Students can check their work by listening to the conversation on Cassette.)

À votre tour!

1 **Allô!**

Jacques is phoning some friends. Match his questions on the left with his friends' answers on the right.

1 Où es-tu?	a Non, il est au cinéma.
2 Où est ta soeur?	b Oui, elles sont au restaurant.
3 Est-ce que ton frère est à la maison?	c Je suis à la maison.
4 Tes parents sont en vacances, n'est-ce pas?	d Elle est en classe.
5 Ta soeur est avec une copine?	e Oui! Ils sont à Paris.

3 **Conversation dirigée**

Two students, Jean-Pierre and Janet, meet on the Paris-Lyon train. With a partner, compose and act out their dialogue according to the suggested script.

Jean-Pierre			
	says hello	⟶	responds and asks how things are
	says things are fine	⟶	asks him what his name is
	says his name is Jean-Pierre . . . asks her name	⟶	says her name is Janet
	asks her if she is English	⟶	says no and responds that she is American
	asks her if she is from New York	⟶	replies that she is from San Francisco

Janet

■ The **Conversations dirigées** are more challenging because students work together to generate an original conversation from English cues. (A sample dialogue is recorded in the Cassette Program.)

■ Activities like **Faisons connaissance!** give students the opportunity to synthesize the material of the unit in a more extended and personalized conversation.

4 **Faisons connaissance!**
(Let's get acquainted!)

Get better acquainted with a classmate that you don't know very well. Ask questions in French. For instance:

- Where does he/she live?
- Does he/she study much at home?
- Does he/she speak French at home? (with whom?)
- Does he/she watch TV? (at what time?)
- Does he/she like to phone? (whom? [**à qui?**])

10 Qu'est-ce qu'ils font?

Read the descriptions below and say what the people are doing. Use the verb **faire** and an expression from the list below. Be logical.

un voyage   une promenade   une pizza   un match   attention

▶ Madame Dumont est en Chine.
  Elle fait un voyage.

1. Nicolas travaille dans *(in)* un restaurant.
2. Nous sommes en ville.
3. Hélène et Jean-Paul jouent au tennis.
4. Je suis dans la cuisine *(kitchen)*.
5. Marc est dans le train Paris–Nice.
6. Vous jouez au volley.
7. Je suis dans le parc.
8. Monsieur Lambert visite Tokyo.
9. Nous écoutons le prof.

■ Many of the basic lesson activities lend themselves to writing practice. (These are signalled in the Extended Teacher's Edition by the symbol: 📝)

Written Self-Expression

The writing activities of **Discovering French** are also sequenced from more guided vocabulary and structure exercises to more open-ended activities at the end of the lesson.

5 Composition: Personnellement

On a separate piece of paper, write where you are and where you are not at each of the following times.

▶ à 9 heures du matin
  • à 4 heures
  • à 7 heures du soir
  • samedi
  • dimanche
  • en juillet

À neuf heures du matin, je suis en classe. Je ne suis pas à la maison.

■ The **À votre tour** writing activities encourage students to express their own thoughts and ideas.

Listening comprehension

If one of the aims of the program is to teach students to understand French speakers of various ages and backgrounds, then the ideal materials are the hundreds of dialogues and mini-scenes in the video and cassette program. However, if the the class does not have access to these recordings, the teacher can still build effective listening comprehension skills by using the TPR activities suggested in the Extended Teacher's Edition. (See also Section 8)

Reading Comprehension

The opening text of each lesson helps students learn to read new French phrases and expressions. However, it is in the **Entracte** sections at the end of each unit that students have a more structured opportunity to develop their reading comprehension skills.

■ With readings like **Vive la différence!** students read for information, using their skill to learn more about the French-speaking world.

ENTRACTE 4

Vive la différence!
Les activités quotidiennes

Nous sommes américains, français, anglais, canadiens . . . Nos° cultures ont° beaucoup de points communs, mais elles ne sont pas identiques.

Parlons° de la vie quotidienne.° Nous faisons les mêmes choses,° mais souvent nous faisons ces° choses un peu différemment.° Voici plusieurs° questions. Répondez° à ces questions. À votre avis,° quelles° sont les réponses des jeunes Français?°

1 **Quel jour de la semaine est-ce que vous préférez?**
- le lundi
- le vendredi
- le samedi
- le dimanche

Et les Français, quel jour est-ce qu'ils préfèrent?

3 **Voici quatre sports. Quel sport est-ce que vous pratiquez le plus?°**
- Je nage.
- Je joue au basket.
- Je fais du jogging.
- Je joue au football.

Et les jeunes Français,

5 **En moyenne,° combien d'heures° par jour° est-ce que vous regardez la télé?**
- une heure
- deux heures
- trois heures
- quatre heures ou plus°

Et les jeunes Français? Combien d'heures par jour est-ce qu'ils regardent

EN FRANCE

LECTURE ET CULTURE

■ In the **En France** sections, students learn to read and interpret authentic French realia.

À la télé, ce weekend

In France, TV viewers have a choice of six main channels: **TF1, Antenne 2, FR3, La 5, M6,** and **Canal Plus.** (People who want to watch **Canal Plus** need to have a special decoding machine for which they pay a monthly fee.)

Note that in TV listings, times are expressed using a 24-hour clock. In this system, 8 P.M. is **20.00 (vingt heures);** 10 P.M. is **22.00 (vingt-deux heures).**

SÉLECTION DE LA SEMAINE | **VEN** | **SAM**

VEN	SAM
20.30 VARIÉTÉS **SALUT L'ARTISTE** Sketches de **Thierry Le Luron**	**20.35** SPECTACLE **HOLIDAY ON ICE** Mis en scène par **Jérôme Savary**
22.05 DOCUMENT **HISTOIRES NATURELLES**	**22.10** SÉRIE **DANS LA CHALEUR DE LA NUIT**
20.35 SÉRIE **HÔTEL DE POLICE** LE GENTIL MONSIEUR de Claude Barrois avec Cécile Magnet	**20.40** VARIÉTÉS **CHAMPS-ÉLYSÉES** Invités: Elton John, Isabelle Adjani, Tom Cruise
23.20 FILM **ALICE DANS LES VILLES** de Wim Wenders	**22.25** SÉRIE **MÉDECINS DE NUIT**

Entre amis: Bonjour, Patrick!

Qu'est-ce que vous aimez faire? Dans° une lettre, Patrick répond° à cette question. Voici la lettre de Patrick.

Bonjour!

Je m'appelle Patrick Lacaze. J'ai 14 ans. J'habite à Tours avec ma famille. Je suis élève° de troisième.° J'étudie beaucoup, mais je n'étudie pas tout le temps.° Voici ce que° j'aime faire.

J'aime les boums parce que j'adore danser.

J'aime la musique. J'aime surtout° le rock. J'aimerais° jouer de la guitare, mais je ne sais pas.°

J'aime les sports. En hiver je skie et en été je nage et je joue au tennis. (Je ne suis pas un champion, mais je joue assez° bien.) J'aime jouer au basket, mais je préfère jouer au foot. (J'aime jouer au babyfoot, mais ce n'est pas un sport.) J'aime faire des promenades à vélo° le weekend avec mes copains.

J'aime mon école.° J'aime surtout l'anglais parce que le prof est sympa.° (Il s'appelle Mr. Ross, mais il est très gentil.°) Je n'aime pas trop° les maths.

À la maison, j'aime regarder la télé. J'adore les séries américaines! J'aime aussi écouter mes cassettes.

J'aime téléphoner à ma copine, mais je ne téléphone pas souvent. (Mon père n'aime pas ça.°)

J'aime jouer aux jeux° sur le Minitel!

Et vous, qu'est-ce que vous aimez faire?

Amicalement,°
Patrick Laca

■ With the **Entre amis** selections, students learn to read more closely.

■ Pre-reading questions prepare students for the theme of the selection.

■ Post-reading activities encourage students to express themselves on similar topics.

■ The **Comment lire** section helps students strengthen their reading skills.

Comment lire (Reading hints)

GETTING THE MEANING

When you read French, try to understand the meaning. Don't look for a word-for-word English translation for each sentence.

- Sometimes the two languages use different constructions.
  Je m'appelle . . .   (I call myself . . .)   My name is . . .
- Sometimes French uses some words that English leaves out.
  J'aime le rock.   I love rock.
  J'aime jouer de la guitare.   I like to play the guitar.
- And sometimes French leaves out words that English uses.
  Je suis élève de troisième.   I am a student in ninth grade.
- Word order may also be different.
  des promenades à vélo   bike rides

Enrichissez votre vocabulaire

COGNATES

You have already discovered that there are many words in French that look like English words and have similar meanings. These are called COGNATES. Cognates let you increase your vocabulary effortlessly. But be sure to pronounce them the French way!

- Sometimes the spelling is the same, or almost the same.
  la radio   radio
  un champion   champion
- Sometimes the spelling is a little different.
  américain   American

Activité

Read the letter from Patrick again and find five more French-English cognates.

Activité: Une lettre à Patrick

You are writing a letter to Patrick in which you introduce yourself and explain what you like to do. You may tell him:

- if you like music (and what kind)
- what sports you like to do in fall or winter
- what sports you like to do in spring or summer
- what you like to do at home
- whether or not you like French and math
- what you like to do on weekends
- what programs you like to watch on TV

> You may start your letter with the words:
> **Mon cher Patrick,**
> (My dear Patrick)
> and end it with:
> **Amicalement,**

Mon cher Patrick,

Amicalement

7 Pacing Suggestions

General Guidelines

This section answers some of the questions which are frequently raised by teachers using the program for the first time.

■ *At what pace should my classes proceed through* **Discovering French–Bleu?**

There is no single answer to this question. Your optimum pacing will depend on many factors, including the number of contact hours per week, the age of the students, and their language aptitude.

■ *Can you recommend a time budget for classes that meet five times a week?*

The typical school year consists of 180 class days; however, it is more realistic to plan on only 160 full periods of French instruction to make allowance for semester exams and for the less productive days before and after vacations, as well as field days, fire drills, and other unpredictable events.

The chart on pages 42–43 shows three suggested time budgets:

• *Formula 1* for classes that plan to finish the entire book: Niveau A, Niveau B, and Niveau C.
• *Formula 2* for classes that plan to finish Niveau A and Niveau B, plus a light introduction to Unit 8.
• *Formula 3* for classes that plan to finish the entire book and incorporate additional enrichment activities (such as selected readings from Valette and Valette **Panorama 1**).

■ *What is the difference between the three formulas?*

• *Formula 1* is for ninth and tenth grade classes in a standard curriculum where classes meet about 50 minutes a day. Typically these students will be doing some homework on a daily basis. Next year these students will move quickly through the opening chapters of **Discovering French–Blanc** and finish the book by June.
• *Formula 2* is for seventh, eighth and ninth grade students in classes that meet 40 to 50 minutes a day. Students will not always be given daily homework assignments. Next year these students will move more slowly through the opening chapters of **Discovering French–Blanc** and complete three-quarters of the book by the end of the year.
• *Formula 3* is for high school honors classes. Next year these students will move through **Discovering French–Blanc** at a more rapid pace, again allowing for additional enrichment and vocabulary expansion activities.

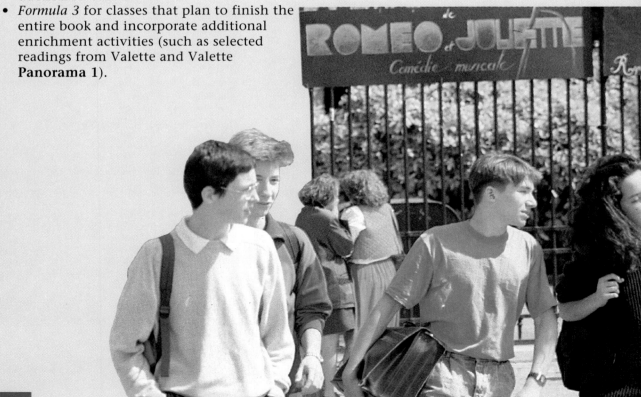

■ *What types of lesson plans fit with these suggested time budgets?*

These time budgets are based on the premise that the typical class lesson plans will include a 5 to 10 minute warm-up (video viewing, TPR activity, communication questions, etc.), a brief presentation of new material, and three to five learning activities of various sorts. It may not always be possible, or even advisable, to do every activity in the program. However, since the emphasis in **Discovering French–Bleu** is on high-frequency vocabulary, structures and conversation patterns, students will always have the opportunity to consolidate their mastery of new material in subsequent lessons.

■ *What if students say the pace is too fast?*

Student performance tends to rise to meet teacher expectations. (If the athletic coach did not push the players to do rapid pushups and running drills, the team would never be in shape to win a game.) By encouraging students to move ahead a bit more quickly, we actually will enhance their sense of accomplishment.

■ *What is the suggested time budget for junior high classes that have daily periods of only 20 to 30 minutes?*

For classes with short periods, you can select either *Formula 1* or *Formula 2* and spread it across two years. For each lesson or section, double the suggested time budget. For example, if the chart suggests 2 days for a given lesson, you would plan for 4 days.

• With *Formula 1*, your students would do Units 1 through 5 in the first year, and Units 6 through 9 in the second year.
• With *Formula 2*, your students would complete Units 1 to 4 (and begin Unit 5) in the first year, and then do Units 5 to 7 (and parts of Unit 8) in the second year.

■ *What about middle school classes that meet only two or three times a week?*

Depending on the age of the students, you may want to schedule **Discovering French–Bleu** over three years. In the first year, the students would complete Niveau A: Units 1, 2 and 3. In the second year, they would do most of Niveau B: Units 4, 5 and 6. In the third year, they would do Units 7, 8 and 9, thus finishing Niveau B and completing Niveau C.

NIVEAU A	Formula 1 (days)	Formula 2 (days)	Formula 3 (days)
CULTURAL PHOTO ESSAY **Parlons français!**	**2**	**2**	**2**
UNITÉ 1			
Leçon 1	2	3	2
Leçon 2	2	3	2
Leçon 3	2	2	1
Leçon 4	2	2	2
À votre tour/ review	1	2	1
Unit test 1	1/2	1/2	1/2
Entracte 1	1/2	1/2	1/2
Unité 1 Total	**10**	**13**	**9**
UNITÉ 2			
Leçon 5	2	2	1
Leçon 6	2	2	1
Leçon 7	2	3	2
Leçon 8	2	3	2
À votre tour/ review	1	2	1
Unit Test 2	1/2	1/2	1/2
Entracte 2	1/2	1/2	1/2
Unité 2 Total	**10**	**13**	**8**
UNITÉ 3			
Leçon 9	2	3	2
Leçon 10	2	3	2
Leçon 11	2	2	1
Leçon 12	1	2	1
À votre tour/ review	1	2	1
Unit Test 3	1	1	1
Entracte 3	1	1	1
Unité 3 Total	**10**	**14**	**9**
NIVEAU A Total	**32**	**42**	**28**

NIVEAU B	Formula 1 (days)	Formula 2 (days)	Formula 3 (days)
CULTURAL PHOTO ESSAY **À l'école en France**	**2**	**2**	**2**
UNITÉ 4			
Leçon 13	4	5	3
Leçon 14	4	5	4
Leçon 15	5	6	4
Leçon 16	4	5	4
Review	1	2	1
Unit Test 4	1	1	1
Entracte 4	1	2	1
Unité 4 Total	**20**	**26**	**18**
UNITÉ 5			
Leçon 17	5	6	5
Leçon 18	6	7	5
Leçon 19	4	5	4
Leçon 20	4	5	4
Review	1	2	1
Unit Test 5	1	1	1
Entracte 5	1	2	1
Unité 5 Total	**22**	**28**	**21**
UNITÉ 6			
Leçon 21	4	5	4
Leçon 22	5	6	4
Leçon 23	4	5	4
Leçon 24	4	5	4
Review	1	2	1
Unit Test 6	1	1	1
Entracte 6	1	2	1
Unité 6 Total	**20**	**26**	**19**
CULTURAL PHOTO ESSAY **À Paris**	**2**	**2**	**2**
UNITÉ 7			
Leçon 25	4	5	4
Leçon 26	4	5	4
Leçon 27	4	4	3
Leçon 28	5	6	4
Review	1	2	1
Unit Test 7	1	1	1
Entracte 7	1	2	1
Unité 7 Total	**20**	**25**	**18**
NIVEAU B Total	**86**	**109**	**80**

NIVEAU C	Formula 1 (days)	Formula 2 (days)	Formula 3 (days)
UNITÉ 8			
Leçon 29	4	3	3
Leçon 30	5	3	4
Leçon 31	4	3	4
Leçon 32	4	—	4
Review	1	1/2	1
Unit Test 8	1	1/2	1
Entracte 8	1	—	1
Unité 8 Total	**20**	**10**	**18**
UNITÉ 9			
Leçon 33	5	—	5
Leçon 34	5	—	5
Leçon 35	4	—	4
Leçon 36	5	—	5
Review	1	—	1
Unit Test 9	1	—	1
Entracte 9	1	—	1
Unité 9 Total	**22**	**—**	**22**
NIVEAU C Total	**42**	**10**	**40**

NIVEAU A, B, C	Formula 1 (days)	Formula 2 (days)	Formula 3 (days)
Total Days	**160**	**161**	**148**

Pedagogical Resource Guide

This part of the front matter focuses on some current educational approaches and indicates how they can be implemented with **Discovering French**. These include: TPR (Total Physical Response), Cooperative Learning, Critical Thinking, Portfolio Assessment, and the French Spelling Reform of 1990.

Introducing TPR into the Classroom

General Background: Questions and Answers

■ *What is TPR?*

TPR (or Total Physical Response) is an approach to second language learning developed by James Asher over twenty-five years ago.[1] The key premise of the TPR approach is that listening comprehension provides the most effective introduction to second-language learning. More specifically, TPR proponents point out that listening activities in which students respond physically in some way (moving around, pointing, handling objects, etc.) are not only excellent ways of establishing comprehension of new phrases, but material learned in this manner is remembered longer. This explains why students learn the parts of the body more quickly by playing "Simon Says" than by repeating the same vocabulary words after the teacher.

■ *How is a typical TPR activity structured?*

In a typical TPR activity, the teacher gives commands to the students, either as a full class, a small group, or individually. Traditionally, the TPR activity consists of four steps:

Step 1. Group performance with a teacher model   The teacher gives a command and then performs the action. The students listen, watch and imitate the teacher. Three to five new commands are presented in this way.

Step 2. Group performance without a teacher model   When the teacher feels the students understand the new phrases, he or she gives the command without moving. It is the students who demonstrate their comprehension by performing the desired action. If the students seem unsure about what to do, the teacher will model the action again.

Step 3. Individual performance without a teacher model   Once the group can perform the new commands easily, the teacher gives these commands to individual students. If an individual student does not remember a given command, the teacher calls on the group to perform the command. It is important to maintain a relaxing atmosphere where all students feel comfortable.

Step 4. Individual performance of a series of commands   When the class is comfortable with the new commands, the teacher gives an individual student a series of two or more commands. This type of activity builds retention and encourages more careful listening.

These four steps are repeated each time new commands are introduced. As the TPR activities progress, the new commands are intermingled with those learned previously.

[1] For a complete introduction, consult James J. Asher, **Learning Another Language Through Actions: The Complete Teacher's Guidebook** , 2nd ed., 1983 (Sky Oaks Productions, P.O. Box 1102, Los Gatos, CA 95031).

How many new commands are introduced at any one time?

Generally three to five new commands are introduced and then practiced. It is important not to bring in new items until all the students are comfortable with the current material. Practice can be made more challenging by giving the commands more rapidly.

Is it necessary to have everyone perform all the commands?

In a regular classroom, it is sometimes difficult to have an entire class performing all the commands. It may be easier to have smaller groups of students take turns coming to the front of the room to learn the new commands and have the rest of the class observe. (Asher found that by actively watching others perform the commands, students would also develop their listening comprehension.)

Must TPR activities relate directly to the content of the lesson?

Since TPR activities develop listening comprehension skills through movement and the use of props, they can be planned independently of the lesson content. Basically there are two kinds of TPR activities:

• *Text-related activities*. These activities introduce material which will be immediately activated in the corresponding lesson of the book. The TPR activity helps students build their listening comprehension before being asked to produce this new material in speaking and writing. Then, when students are presented with this material formally, they can concentrate on details such as pronunciation and spelling because they will already know what all the new words mean.

• *Comprehension-expansion activities*. These activities are designed to expand the students' listening proficiency and introduce vocabulary and structures which will not be formally presented until later in the program. Since TPR is fun, and since the material presented is not formally "tested," TPR can be effectively used for vocabulary expansion and for anticipatory introduction of new material. For example, verbs of movement and classroom objects can be presented via TPR early in the course.

How are TPR activities usually scheduled into the lesson plan?

TPR activities can be planned at the beginning of the hour as a warm-up, or may be introduced in the middle or at the end of the period as a change of pace. It is usually best to use TPR for no more than ten minutes per class period.

How do I prepare for a TPR activity?

Before beginning a TPR activity, it is very important to plan which commands you are going to use and what new vocabulary you are going to introduce. You may want to write these out on an index card or on self-adhesive note paper which you can stick into your textbook. As you lead the activity, you will need to be able to vary the sequence of the commands and give them rapidly and fluidly. If students have difficulty with certain commands, be sure to repeat them frequently.

How and when do I introduce TPR to my students?

TPR activities can be introduced on the first day of class. You will find three initial TPR activities described on the next page.

How do I plan additional TPR activities in the course of the year?

Sample TPR activities for **Discovering French–Bleu** are suggested in the Extended Teacher's Edition and prefaced with the symbol: **TPR**. You may also want to develop activities of your own.[2] A list of sample commands is given on page 47. An illustrated vocabulary listing of common classroom objects may be found on page 83 of the Student Text.

[2] For helpful classroom advice, consult Ramiro Garcia, **Instructor's Notebook: How to Apply TPR for Best Results**, 1985. See also Francisco L. Cabello, **Total Physical Response in First Year Spanish**, 1985. (Both available from Sky Oaks Productions.)

Initial TPR Activities

The following three TPR activities are designed to introduce students to this type of listening comprehension activity.

TPR ACTIVITY 1
Comprehension-expansion: movements

PROPS: Several chairs

- Tell the class: "Listen and see how much you understand of what I am saying. **Levez-vous. Asseyez-vous. Levez-vous. Marchez. Arrêtez. Sautez. Tournez-vous. Marchez. Asseyez-vous.**"
Students will look blank. Then say: "In ten minutes you will understand everything I said."

- Bring out a chair, sit down and instruct the students: "Listen carefully and do what I do. Do not speak. Just try to understand."
"**Levez-vous.**" [Teacher gets up. If necessary, motions to class to get up.]
"**Asseyez-vous.**" [Teacher sits down.]
"**Levez-vous.**" [Teacher stands up again.]
"**Sautez.**" [Teacher jumps in place.]
"**Sautez.**" [Teacher jumps again.]
"**Asseyez-vous.**" [Teacher sits down.]
Repeat the sequence for the class to perform but do not move unless the class seems to need the action modelled again.

- Place several chairs in the front of the classroom and call for volunteers. This time only the volunteers respond while the others watch. Three new commands are added. The teacher models the actions.
"**Levez-vous.**" [Teacher gets up.]
"**Marchez.**" [Teacher walks.]
"**Arrêtez.**" [Teacher stops.]
"**Marchez.**" [Teacher walks again.]
"**Arrêtez.**" [Teacher stops.]
"**Sautez.**" [Teacher jumps.]
"**Tournez-vous.**" [Teacher makes a half turn.]
"**Marchez.**" [Teacher walks back to chair.]
"**Arrêtez.**" [Teacher stops in front of chair.]
"**Tournez-vous.**" [Teacher makes a half turn.]
"**Asseyez-vous.**" [Teacher sits down.]
Repeat the new commands and have the volunteers act them out. Then call on other volunteers. Vary the order of the commands and increase the pace as students show that they understand. For variety, unexpected commands can be given, such as "**asseyez-vous**" where there is no chair and students have to sit on the floor.

- At the end of the TPR activity, read the original list of commands so that students realize how much they have learned.

TPR ACTIVITY 2
Comprehension-expansion: classroom and furniture

PROPS: Classroom furniture

- Begin TPR Activity 2 by reviewing the commands of TPR Activity 1. If necessary, model the actions again.

- Introduce new movements, commanding students to go to the door, to the desk, to the window, etc.
"**Allez à la porte.**"
"**Allez à la table.**"
"**Allez à la fenêtre.**"
"**Allez au tableau.**"

- Tell the whole class to point out the new objects.
"**Montrez la porte.**"
"**Montrez le tableau.**" etc.

TPR ACTIVITY 3
Comprehension-expansion: classroom objects

PROPS: Classroom objects (books, notebooks, pencils, pens, etc.)

Place several objects on a table in full view of the class. Call up two or three student volunteers and tell them to point out and touch various objects:
"**Montrez le livre.**"
"**Touchez le cahier.**"
"**Montrez le crayon.**"
"**Touchez le stylo.**" etc.

- Have students put similar objects on their desks and follow the commands together with the volunteers.

- At the end of the TPR activity, give individual students some simple series of commands drawing from all expressions they have learned so far.
"**Pierre, lève-toi, va à la table et touche le cahier.**" etc.

Note: An illustrated vocabulary listing of common classroom objects is to be found on page 83 of the student text as well as on Transparency 50.

Here is a listing of some sample commands in both the "tu" and the "vous" forms. As a teacher, you have two options:

■ You can use the formal "vous" form for both group and individual commands.

■ You can address the class and small groups with the plural "vous" form and then address individual students as "tu."

MOVEMENTS

Stand up.	Lève-toi.	Levez-vous.
	Debout.	Debout.
Sit down.	Assieds-toi.	Asseyez-vous.
Walk.	Marche.	Marchez.
Jump.	Saute.	Sautez.
Stop.	Arrête.	Arrêtez.
Turn around.	Tourne-toi.	Tournez-vous.
Turn right/left.	Tourne à droite/à gauche.	Tournez à droite/à gauche.
Go ...	Va (au tableau).	Allez (à la fenêtre).
Come ...	Viens (au bureau).	Venez (au tableau).
Raise ...	Lève (la main).	Levez (le bras).
Lower ...	Baisse (la tête).	Baissez (les yeux).

POINTING OUT AND MANIPULATING OBJECTS

Point out ...	Montre (le cahier).	Montrez (le livre).
Touch ...	Touche (la porte).	Touchez (la fenêtre).
Pick up / Take ...	Prends (le crayon).	Prenez (le stylo).
Put ...	Mets (le livre sur la table).	Mettez (le cahier sous la chaise).
Take away ...	Enlève (le livre).	Enlevez (le cahier).
Empty ...	Vide (le sac).	Videz (la corbeille).
Give ...	Donne (la cassette à Anne).	Donnez (le disque à Paul).
Give back ...	Rends (la cassette à Marie).	Rendez (le disque à Michel).
Pass ...	Passe (le stylo à Denise).	Passez (le crayon à Marc).
Keep ...	Garde (la cassette).	Gardez (la cassette).
Open ...	Ouvre (la porte).	Ouvrez (le livre).
Close ...	Ferme (la fenêtre).	Fermez (le cahier).
Throw ...	Lance (la balle à Jean).	Lancez (le ballon à Claire).
Bring me ...	Apporte-moi (la balle).	Apportez-moi (le ballon).

ACTIVITIES WITH PICTURES AND VISUALS

Look at ...	Regarde (la carte).	Regardez (le plan de Paris).
Look for/Find ...	Cherche (la Suisse).	Cherchez (la tour Eiffel).
Show me ...	Montre-moi (Genève).	Montrez-moi (Notre-Dame).

PAPER OR CHALKBOARD ACTIVITIES

Draw ...	Dessine (une maison).	Dessinez (un arbre).
Write ...	Écris (ton nom).	Écrivez (votre nom).
Erase ...	Efface (le dessin).	Effacez (la carte).
Color ...	Colorie (le chat en noir).	Coloriez (le chien en jaune).
Put an "x" on ...	Mets un "x" sur (le garçon).	Mettez un "x" sur (la fille).
Circle ...	Trace un cercle autour de (la chemise rouge).	Tracez un cercle autour de (la jupe blanche).
Cut out ...	Découpe (un coeur).	Découpez (un cercle).

9 Cooperative Learning and Cooperative Practice

General Background: Questions and Answers

■ *What is Cooperative Learning?*

The term Cooperative Learning is used to describe classroom environments where students work together in small groups to accomplish specific objectives. Rather than studying alone and competing for grades assigned on a curve, students help one another attain group goals. In additional to mastering new subject matter, students also acquire social skills and learn to assess how well their group is functioning.[3]

■ *What are the basic elements of Cooperative Learning?*

Although there are several models for Cooperative Learning, they all tend to share the following features:

*   *Mutual goals.* Students in small groups work together to attain a common goal. Each student within a group may have different tasks and/or responsibilities, but they all receive the same reward (grade, certificate, bonus points, etc.) at the end of the project.
*   *Heterogeneous grouping.* Groups contain students of differing abilities. High achievers and low achievers both try to do their best because they are interdependent with one another.
*   *Individual accountability.* Students in the group are also held individually accountable for learning material presented. There may be individual exams or grading of individual assignments.
*   *Social interaction.* By working together, students learn to communicate effectively and to share responsibility.

■ *Can the basic Cooperative Learning model be applied to French classes?*

This is an important question. As has historically been the case with many educational innovations, the research studies in Cooperative Learning have focused on subject matter areas such as math, social studies and language arts, where students communicate with one another in English. Moreover, it is in English that students read material from various reference sources and acquire additional knowledge. In elementary French classes, on the other hand, students are dependent on the teacher to provide the basic instruction. It is the teacher who knows the language, who models the phrases to be learned, who selects comprehensible input (videos, tapes, readings, realia), and who plans activities at the linguistic level of the students.

Since the goal of the French course is to have students communicate in French, the Cooperative Learning model is most appropriate at the advanced levels, once students have the needed linguistic skills. At the early levels, students will tend to interact in English and therefore Cooperative Learning activities must be carefully selected.

The section on page T50 suggests some sample Cooperative Learning activities that can be used effectively with **Discovering French–Bleu**.

■ *Can paired activities and small group work be considered as Cooperative Learning?*

Not really. Paired activities and small group work are usually examples of *Cooperative Practice*.

[3] For an excellent introduction to this topic, see the 1990 monograph by Eileen Veronica Hilke entitled **Cooperative Learning**. This publication (subtitled Fastback 299) can be obtained from the Phi Delta Kappa Educational Foundation, P. O. Box 789, Bloomington, IN 47402-0789 ($.90).

What is Cooperative Practice?

Cooperative Practice is a term used to describe language practice and language acquisition activities in which students interact with one another. These activities take place after the teacher has presented the new material. Cooperative Practice activities are usually much narrower in scope than the traditional Cooperative Learning activities. The group goal may simply be to complete a specific exercise or brief communication task. For certain types of activities, there may be differentiation of tasks. There is usually no group grade given. Individual assessment in the form of a quiz may be delayed until the end of a lesson.

What is the advantage of Cooperative Practice?

The advantage of Cooperative Practice is that students are directly involved in French language activities. Whereas during traditional practice activities, it is the teacher who elicits responses either chorally or individually, during Cooperative Practice, it is the students themselves who ask and answer questions. During Cooperative Practice activities, the teacher can circulate, offering assistance and making corrections privately rather than publicly.

How can Cooperative Practice be incorporated into Discovering French classes?

The section on page T51 gives suggestions for introducing Cooperative Practice activities into the classroom.

This section describes three types of Cooperative Learning activities which can be used effectively with **Discovering French–Bleu**. Further suggestions are found in the Extended Teacher's Edition preceded by the symbol:

Small group homework correction

Students get together in heterogeneous groups of 4 or 5 to check the homework assignment. Each student is responsible for correcting his or her own paper. If the group cannot decide on the right response, they can ask the teacher for help. Students receive full homework credit if all team members have corrected all their errors. Points are taken off for uncorrected mistakes.

Note: To be sure that students do not do their homework during class or copy it from a teammate during the correction activity, the teacher can check that the homework sheets have been completed as the students enter the classroom.

Group homework correction has several advantages:

- Students learn from correcting their own work. In small groups they are more willing to ask their peers for explanations. Since all members of the group have a stake in getting the assignment right, they are not reluctant to request help when necessary.
- By relegating the homework correction activity to the last five or ten minutes of the class hour, the teacher has more class time available for communication activities.
- The teacher's out-of-class homework correction work is reduced to simply glancing over each paper and entering a notation in the grade book.

Team games

Certain sentence-building activities in the Student Text can be easily adapted to Cooperative Learning. The students are randomly divided into teams of 3 or 4. (This may be done numerically by counting off in French, alphabetically by middle initial, sequentially by month of birth, etc.) Each team is given a sheet of paper. When the signal to begin is given, the first student on the team writes a sentence incorporating the suggested phrases. Teammates check to be sure the sentence is correct. Then the paper is passed to the next student who writes the second sentence, and so forth. At the end of the time limit, the team that has the most correct sentences is declared the winner and receives a small reward (such as less homework or extra credit points).

Cross-cultural observation

Students are divided into teams or 3 or 4. The teacher plays a segment of a **Discovering French** video module, and asks the students to look for cross-cultural similarities and differences between what they see and similar situations in the United States. Each team puts together a list of what the members have observed. If time allows, the video may be shown several times. Then the teams take turns sharing the observations they have noted. The team with the highest number of correct observations wins a reward.

Note: To encourage individual accountability, the teacher may give a brief follow-up quiz where students list as many observations as they can remember.

Types of Cooperative Practice Activities

There are many possibilities for incorporating Cooperative Practice into the French classroom. Here are a few guidelines and suggestions. Activities which lend themselves readily to Cooperative Practice are indicated in the Extended Teacher's Edition with the symbol:

Cooperative pair activities

Students each team up with a partner to do the speaking exercises in the textbook.

- For the dialogue activities, each partner plays a role.
- For the practice activities, one person gives the cue and the other supplies the response.
- For personal questions, one student reads the question, and the other student replies.

Halfway through the cooperative pair activity, roles are reversed.

Note: Pair activities work best when students know exactly what is expected of them. Especially with beginning classes, it is often most effective to go over an activity rapidly with everyone, eliciting full-class or half-class choral responses, and then have students practice the entire exercise once more in pairs.

Cooperative practice in trios

In trio activities, students divide into groups of three. Two students engage in a paired speaking activity, such as a role-play exercise or a dialogue. The third student is given a copy of the corresponding answers (taken from the **Discovering French** Answer Key) and makes sure the others respond accurately. Then roles are rotated for the next activity.

Note: In trio activities, students take the responsibility for correcting one another in a supportive way. While two students focus on speaking, the third student practices reading and critical listening skills.

General Background: Questions and Answers

■ *What is meant by the term Critical Thinking?*

Critical Thinking, which some proponents trace back to John Dewey in the early part of this century, is an educational trend that has elicited a great deal of interest in recent years.[4] Typically, the teaching of Critical Thinking is divided into two areas: skills and dispositions.

■ *What are Critical Thinking skills?*

Critical Thinking skills or abilities relate to the cognitive functions of analysis, synthesis and evaluation. Some commonly cited Critical Thinking skills are the ability to formulate questions, to observe patterns, to identify assumptions, to clarify problems, to use logic, and to weigh judgments.

■ *What are Critical Thinking dispositions?*

Dispositions or attitudes constitute the affective aspect of Critical Thinking. They include using one's critical thinking skills, being open-minded, remaining impartial, suspending judgment, questioning one's own views, and recognizing the complexity of the real world and its problems.

■ *How can the teaching of Critical Thinking be incorporated in beginning foreign language classes?*

As one would expect, current educational research has focused on the teaching of logic and the introduction of Critical Thinking skills into subject areas taught in English, such as math, science, social studies, reading and writing. However, even though the main focus of beginning language classes is the acquisition of basic communication skills, students can be introduced to Critical Thinking skills as they make cross-cultural comparisons and as they learn to analyze how language functions. Once their linguistic base is broadened, they can sharpen their Critical Thinking skills while increasing their reading and listening comprehension and learning to express themselves with greater precision in speaking and writing.

■ *How does* **Discovering French** *encourage the teaching of Critical Thinking?*

The manner in which **Discovering French–Bleu** fosters the development of both Critical Thinking skills and dispositions is described in the next two sections. Specific suggestions for Critical Thinking activities are given in the Extended Teacher's Edition preceded by the symbol:

[4] For an informative overview, see Mellen Kennedy, Michelle B. Fisher and Robert H. Ennis, "Critical Thinking: Literature Review and Needed Research" in Lorna Idol and Beau Fly Jones, eds., **Educational Values and Cognitive Instruction: Implications for Reform**, North Central Regional Educational Laboratory, 1991, pp. 11–40. (Published by Lawrence Erlbaum Assoc., 365 Broadway, Hillsdale, NJ)

Strengthening Critical Thinking Skills

Discovering French–Bleu uses four main types of activities to develop Critical Thinking skills. (Since Critical Thinking is an open-ended process, suggestions for these activities are often given in the Teacher's Edition rather than in the Student Text.)

Observing Cross-Cultural Similarities and Differences

With **Discovering French** students have frequent opportunity to observe aspects of another culture with which they are unfamiliar.
- Obviously, the richest point of departure for cross-cultural observations is the **Discovering French Video**. Suggestions for activities of this type are given in the Extended Teacher's Edition.
- In the Student Textbook, the cultural notes and numerous photographs can also lead to reflection and analysis.
- In the *Vive la différence!* readings in certain *Entracte* sections, students answer questions about their own preferences and then compare their responses with those of French students their own age.

Noticing Linguistic Similarities and Differences

The study of a second language helps students think critically about how English works. As they compare English and French, they begin to recognize that concepts exist independently of the words with which they are expressed.
- In *Learning about Language* boxes, students acquire the terminology to talk about language. (See Student Text, p.98)
- Where appropriate, English and French are contrasted graphically to show that there is not a word-for-word correspondence between the two languages. (See Student Text, p.108)

Using Logic

Certain types of activities in **Discovering French** require the students to use logic to arrive at the appropriate responses.
- In *Allô!* activities, students make logical deductions as they match questions with their corresponding answers. (See Student Text, p.126, Act.1)
- In more challenging activities, students are given the responses and are asked to determine which questions were asked. (See Student Text, p.126, Act.2)

- Certain types of completion activities ask the students to think logically as they select an appropriate response. (See Student Text, p.124, Act.10)

Developing Reading Skills

In the *Entracte* sections, students have the opportunity to work with a variety of different types of readings.
- Critical thinking skills are often incorporated into the pre-reading and post-reading activities.
- The *Comment lire* sections encourage students to use critical thinking skills as they learn to read French for comprehension.

Strengthening Critical Thinking Dispositions

Although it is difficult to change attitudes through teaching materials alone, **Discovering French–Bleu**, with the support and guidance of the teacher, encourages students to broaden their views.

Developing a Multi-Cultural World View

Film is a powerful medium for expanding student horizons. Through multiple critical viewings of the **Discovering French** video modules, students will become more open-minded and less judgmental about cross-cultural differences between France and the United States. They will slowly begin to shed a mono-cultural world view and become more accepting of cultural diversity.

Appreciating Linguistic Diversity

As students listen to the more than one hundred different French voices on the the cassette program and see these speakers on the video, they will begin to recognize the diversity of the French linguistic world.

Breaking Away from a Monolingual Mode of Expression

As students learn to observe how the French language works and how it compares to English, they will begin to see that similar concepts are expressed differently in the two languages. Moreover, they will start to realize that to make oneself understood in a second language, one must adopt the characteristics of that language.

11 Portfolio Assessment

General Background: Questions and Answers

■ *What is Portfolio Assessment?*

Portfolio Assessment is a means of evaluating academic progress by collecting the best work a student has produced in the course of the term. This portfolio of material is kept on file in the school to be used as the basis for final grades and other evaluation.

■ *What are the key features of Portfolio Assessment?*

Although the features of Portfolio Assessment vary somewhat from program to program, the following are quite characteristic:
- Students are given clear instructions as to the steps required in the preparation of the portfolio piece or pieces.
- Students maintain a formal log or notebook which contains outlines and early drafts of the written work.
- Students are encouraged to work cooperatively in pairs or teams to edit and polish their final pieces.
- The final portfolio piece is presented in a "formal" format (e.g., written in ink, typed, printed by computer).
- Students often have the opportunity to read one another's pieces.
- Students may be graded on the "process" (that is, how carefully they have gone through the suggested steps in preparing their piece) as well as the "product" (the piece itself).

■ *What are the benefits of Portfolio Assessment?*

Since traditional tests, be they achievement tests or proficiency tests, evaluate performance at a specific point in time, they are often associated with a feeling of pressure which may effect how well a student does. Even if pressure is not a factor, the grades on traditional tests are always subject to Standard Error, that is, some students do better than expected on a test while others do worse.

With Portfolio Assessment, students have longer periods of time to work on the material for which they will be evaluated and feel less overwhelmed. In selecting pieces for their portfolios, they each have the opportunity to interact with the teacher who helps them choose their best work.

The Portfolio itself is of educational benefit. As students compare portfolio pieces done early in the year with work produced later, they see their own improvement and can take pride in their progress. Furthermore, with the Portfolio pieces, the teacher also has a selection of carefully prepared language samples to show families on Parent-Teacher night.

Finally, a system of Portfolio Assessment helps schools evaluate their programs because it provides a basis of comparing learning outcomes over time as well as between classes.

■ *Does Portfolio Assessment replace traditional assessment?*

Usually Portfolio Assessment is used to supplement, but not replace traditional assessment, which usually includes formal tests, quizzes, class participation, homework, and so forth. In classes that have adopted Portfolio Assessment, a given percent of the student's grade is determined by the portfolio pieces.

■ *In what form can Portfolio Assessment be adapted to French classes?*

Traditionally, Portfolio Assessment procedures have been developed for language arts and social studies classes, where students prepare written reports and essays in English. In French classes, Portfolio Assessment would ideally contain examples of both oral and written French since there is an emphasis on speaking as well as writing skills.

Implementing Portfolio Assessment

Although Portfolio Assessment in French classes has traditionally not been introduced until the second or third year, once students have a stronger command of the language, the format of **Discovering French–Bleu** is such that teachers can have students prepare individual portfolios from the beginning of instruction.

For each unit (or every other unit), students can polish one of the *À votre tour* activities for inclusion in their portfolio. For Units 1 to 3, these will be oral conversations. Beginning with Unit 4, the teacher has the option of assigning either an oral or a written piece, or both. Obviously, at this beginning level, the pieces will be brief and limited to known vocabulary and structures. However, over the course of the year, the pieces will become more complex and students will have the satisfaction of seeing how much progress they have made.

Preparing the Oral Portfolio

The preparation of an oral portfolio piece requires careful planning.

- The first step is to decide on format: whether to record the oral portfolio on audiocassette or videocassette. This decision will obviously depend on the audio-visual support available. It is also possible to use audiocassettes for some units and videocassettes for others.
- The next step is the selection of the specific conversation to be prepared and recorded. Depending on the level of the class, you may opt for a structured conversation (such as a *Conversation dirigée* or *Créa-dialogue*, where there is a recorded model in the Cassette Program) or a more open-ended one (for which there is no recorded model).
- The third step is to match each person with a conversational partner. You may let students select their own partners, you may assign them by pairing stronger students with weaker students, or you may determine the pairs randomly by picking numbers.

Once the task has been assigned and the partners selected, the students work together to prepare and record a "preliminary draft" of their conversation. (Even if the final version is to be on videocassette, this preparatory step can be done on audiocassette.)

Then students get together in groups of four and take turns listening to and correcting their two recorded conversations. If they have questions, they can ask the teacher's advice. The purpose of this step is to suggest ways of improving the final portfolio recording which will be graded.

Finally, the students in pairs make their final recordings, which are then placed in the portfolio. (See Student Text, p.31, Act.5)

Preparing the Written Portfolio

The preparation of a piece for the written portfolio is similar, in its general outline, to that of the recorded portfolio piece, but with two major differences: (1) there is no need for audiovisual logistics, and (2) students submit their pieces individually, rather than in pairs.

Beginning with Niveau B, the students learn to express themselves in writing. The *À votre tour* sections, which beginning with Unit 4 appear at the end of each lesson, always have suggestions for written self-expression. For each unit, the teacher will select one topic (or a choice of two or three) for the portfolio piece.

Students prepare their first drafts, and then work in small groups editing and correcting one another's work. If necessary, they may ask the teacher for assistance. (If desired, the students may prepare a second modified draft which is turned in to the teacher for correction.)

Each student then incorporates the suggestions received into a final draft, which is rewritten in formal form and placed, together with the early drafts, in the individual portfolio. (See Student Text, p.105, Act.4)

Sharing the Portfolio Contents

An important by-product of Portfolio Assessment is that students can share their work with others. There are many ways this can be done.

- Video-taped portfolio pieces can be shown to the entire class. If appropriate, classes in a school system can exchange video portfolios.
- Written portfolio pieces can be "published" in a class newsletter. If appropriate, certain pieces can be selected for a school-wide newsletter or a department bulletin board.
- Portfolio pieces can be the basis of pen pal exchanges or class correspondence with a matched school in a French-speaking country.

12 The French Spelling Reform of 1990

General Background: Questions and Answers

■ *Why did the French undertake to reform their spelling system?*

The main impetus for reform in France came from teachers at the elementary and junior-high levels who wanted to make the language easier to write and less confusing for their students.

■ *What is the French spelling reform of 1990?*

In December 1990, the *Journal Officiel* of the French Government published a document authorizing spelling changes in about 1200 words.

This document was the result of months of deliberation by the *Conseil supérieur de la langue française* which had been charged by Prime Minister Rocard to rationalize the French spelling system in five specific areas: the use of the hyphen, the use of the circumflex, the plurals of composite nouns, the elimination of spelling anomalies, and the agreement of the past participle with reflexive verbs. (The last area was considered too complex and was left aside.)[5]

■ *What were the recommended changes?*

The main changes are summarized in the chart on the right.

■ *How were these reforms to be implemented?*

Originally, educational publishers and teachers were to be required to incorporate these spelling reforms into their teaching materials as of Fall, 1991. For general usage, however, both the old and the new spellings would be considered correct.

■ *What was the reaction in France once the reforms were publicized?*

In early 1991, there was such an uproar in France that the *Académie Française* met again to debate the reforms. It was finally decided that the reforms would be recommended, but not required.

■ *What is the present status of the 1990 spelling reform?*

Since there is no longer a mandate to put the new spelling changes into effect by a given date, their adoption will depend on public reaction. Time will tell which of the changes become widely accepted and which do not.

■ *How are the spelling reforms reflected in Discovering French?*

After much deliberation, it was decided to maintain the standard spelling system for the time being, with the exception of the word **weekend** which would drop the hyphen so that the spelling in English and French would be parallel.

■ *How should American teachers react to the proposed reforms?*

Since all the proposed reforms are officially acceptable, it is recommended that teachers not penalize students for spelling words in the new way. For example, students should be allowed:
- to hyphenate all numbers (including **vingt-et-un** and **dix-huit-cent-deux**)
- to omit circumflex accents on the vowels "i" and "u" (as in **diner** and **aout**)
- to leave out hyphens in nouns (such as **piquenique** and **hotdog**)

[5] For a more detailed of the Spelling Reform and its historic antecedents, see Jean-Paul Valette, "À propos de la nouvelle orthographe", **French for Mastery Newsletter,** 18:2 (Spring 1991), pp. 4–5.

LES PRINCIPALES RÉFORMES

■ L'accent circonflexe

Un grand nombre de mots perdent leur accent circonflexe sur le "**i**" ou le "**u**":

île	→	ile
dîner	→	diner
août	→	aout
coûter	→	couter

L'accent circonflexe est cependant maintenu dans les verbes comme **connaître** et **paraître**. Il est aussi maintenu sur le "**a**", le "**e**" et le "**o**".

■ Le trait d'union

Un certain nombre de mots perdent leur trait d'union:

pique-nique	→	piquenique
week-end	→	weekend
blue-jean	→	bluejean
haut-parleur	→	hautparleur
croque-monsieur	→	croquemonsieur
cow-boy	→	cowboy

La disparition du trait d'union s'accompagne d'une fusion lorsque le premier mot se termine en "**e**":

contre-attaque	→	contrattaque

[Les mots soumis à la nouvelle orthographe appartiennent à des catégories très diverses: ils sont d'origine étrangère (**weekend**), composés sur des thèmes "savants" (**audiovisuel**), composés au moyen de préfixes latins ou grecs tel que extra, infra (**extraordinaire, infrarouge**), composés d'une particule invariable telle que contre ou entre (**contrerévolutionnaire, entretemps**).]

■ Les nombres

L'usage du trait d'union est étendu à tous les nombres composés.

cent un	→	cent-un
cent vingt et un	→	cent-vingt-et-un
sept cent mille	→	sept-cent-mille

■ Le pluriel des noms composés

L'usage du "**s**" final est généralisé pour un grand nombre de mots composés:

des après-midi	→	des après-midis
des tourne-disque	→	des tourne-disques
des gratte-ciel	→	des gratte-ciels

■ Les changements d'accent

L'accent aigu devient grave dans certains mots, en conformation avec les règles de prononciation:

céleri	→	cèleri
crémerie	→	crèmerie
événement	→	évènement

■ Autres rectifications

On rectifie l'orthographe de certains mots, en conformation avec les règles générales de l'écriture du français:

chariot	→	charriot
oignon	→	ognon
relais	→	relai
saccharine	→	saccarine
s'asseoir	→	s'assoir

PART 4

Reference Information

 Brief Directory of Useful Addresses

From time to time, classroom teachers of French find themselves in need of professional support. This section gives the names and addresses of selected organizations and the type of assistance they might be able to provide.

Professional Language Organizations

Professional language organizations offer a wide variety of services and support to their membership.

■ AATF (American Association of Teachers of French)

As an AATF member:
- you will receive subscriptions to the *French Review* and the *AATF National Bulletin*.
- you will be able to attend local, regional and national AATF meetings where you can share ideas and meet new colleagues.
- you have the opportunity to apply for one of the many summer scholarships to France and Quebec offered to AATF members.
- you may sponsor a chapter of the *Société Honoraire de Français* at your school so that your students will then be eligible to compete for the ten annual $500 study abroad travel grants and participate in the SHF creative writing contest.
- you can have your students participate in the National French Contest and be considered for local, regional and national awards.
- you can obtain pen pals for your students through the *Bureau de Correspondance Scolaire*.

For membership information, write:
AATF, 57 East Amory Avenue,
Champaign, IL 61820
Phone: (217) 333-2842

■ ACTFL (American Council on the Teaching of Foreign Languages)

As an ACTFL member:
- you will receive subscriptions to the *Foreign Language Annals* and the *ACTFL Bulletin*.
- you will be able to attend the annual ACTFL convention where you can share ideas and meet new colleagues.
- you have the opportunity to apply for one of the ACTFL summer scholarships to France.

For membership information, contact:
ACTFL, 6 Executive Plaza
Yonkers, NY 10701-6801
Phone: (914) 963-8830

The ACTFL office will also be able to let you know whom to contact to join your local state foreign language association, and how you can get information about regional language meetings.

Governmental Organizations

■ Alliance Française

The Alliance Française is a French organization dedicated to the promotion of French language and culture. In addition to language courses, most Alliance Française centers sponsor a variety of cultural and educational events.

To obtain the address of the Alliance Française nearest you, write:
Alliance Française, Délégation générale
2819 Ordway St., NW
Washington, DC 20008
Phone: 1 (800) 6-FRANCE

French Cultural Services

The French Cultural Services are very supportive of French teaching in the United States. For more information, contact the French Cultural Officer at the French Consulate nearest you or write the New York office.

To obtain information about available French cultural materials, write:
Services Culturels de France
934 Fifth Avenue
New York, NY 10021
Phone: (212) 606-3688

Quebec Delegation

The Province of Quebec has official delegations in many of the large cities. Many of these Delegations are eager to work with French teachers to promote the the teaching of French and closer contacts with Quebec.

To obtain the address of the Quebec Delegation nearest you, contact:
Délégation Générale du Québec
Rockefeller Center
17 West 50th Street
New York, NY 10020-2201
Phone: (212) 397-0200

Publications

News from France

News from France is a biweekly English-language publication containing a review of news and trends from France. It is distributed free of charge.

To be placed on the mailing list, write:
French Embassy Press and Information Service
4101 Reservoir Road, NW
Washington, DC 20007

Update

Update is a publication of the Quebec Government which appears every three months. It is distributed free of charge.

To be placed on the mailing list, write:
Délégation Générale du Québec
Rockefeller Center
17 West 50th Street
New York, NY 10020-2201

Journal français d'Amérique

The *Journal français d'Amérique* is a biweekly French-language newspaper published in San Francisco. Special group subscription rates are available to schools.

To receive a sample issue which also contains subscription information, write:
Journal français d'Amérique
P.O. Box 25169
Anaheim, CA 92825-5169
Phone (800) 999-9718

Other Useful Addresses

Sister Cities International

If your town has a Sister City in a French-speaking country, you might want to explore the possibility of initiating a youth or education exchange program. If your town does not yet have a French-speaking Sister City, you might want to encourage your community to set up such an affiliation.

For information on both youth exchanges and the establishment of a sister-city association, contact:
Sister Cities International
120 South Payne Street
Alexandria, VA 22314
Phone: (703) 836-3535

Nacel Cultural Exchanges

If you have students who would like to host a French-speaking student for a month during the summer, or who would themselves like to stay with a family in France or Senegal, have them contact the non-profit organization **Nacel.**

For information on summer homestays, write:
Nacel Cultural Exchanges
Board of Trade #528
301 West First Street
Duluth, MN 55802

KEY
43   = Page number in Student Text
T43 = Reference to teacher's material on page T43 of Extended Teacher's Edition
M 1 = Video module 1
VC 1 = Topic of *Vignette culturelle* of the video module

Topic	Student text page	ETE note page	Video module
Animals			
domestic animals	46, 54	T45, T46, T54, T151	M 7, M 21
wild animals	173, 185		
Arts			
French contributions	7	T7	
la Maison des Jeunes			VC 23
See also: Cinema, Museums, Music and concert halls			
Attitudes and values			
cars	171		VC 20
cinema	42, 235	T307	
cuisine and food	59, 68, 235, 346, 371	T56, T78, T371	
fashion	246, 266, 288		
friendship	34, 37, 136, 161, 180		VC 5
money	66, 136, 275, 290–291, 296		VC 11
music	42, 329	T310	M 32, VC 32
quality of life	296, 307		
school	88	T297	
Birthdays	47, 50, 337		M 8
Cafés	56, 59, 63, 211	T57, T62, T89, T101, T119, T371	M 9, VC 9, M 11, VC 14
ordering beverages	63	T351	M 10, VC 10, M 11
tipping	63		
Cars	171	T171	M 20, VC 20
drivers license	171		VC 20
parking		T146	M 20
Cinema			
French actors and actresses	232, 233	T233	
movies	88, 230, 234–235, 296	T89	M 4, M 29, VC 30
Cities			
Abidjan, Côte d'Ivoire	3, 133		
Angers, France		T189	
Annecy, France			M 29
Bordeaux, France	133, 188		
Bruxelles, Belgium	341	T341	
Chamonix, France	255	T6	
Dakar, Sénégal	118		M-A, M 16, VC 16
Deauville, France	250	T356, T380, T381	M 36
Fort-de-France, Martinique	19		M-A
Genève, Suisse	133		M-A
Grenoble, France	188, 338		
La Rochelle, France	33		
Le Havre, France	342		

Topic	Student text page	ETE note page	Video module
Lille, France	188		M 21
Lyon, France	188	T188, T343	M 21
Marseille, France	188, 392	T188	M 21
Montpellier, France	33, 149	T149	
Montréal, Canada	41, 133, 254	T41, T121, T192, T254, T309	M-A, VC 6
Nantes, France	188		
New Orleans, Louisiana		T206	
Nice, France	188, 255, 338		
Nîmes, France	286	T338	
Orléans, France	33		
Paris, France	33, 119, 137, 188, 199, 236–243	T188, T212, T342	M-C
Québec, Canada	3, 393	T192, T277	M-A, VC 6
Savigny-sur-Orge	76, 77	T77	
Strasbourg, France	149, 188	T149	M 21
Toulon, France	188, 343	T343	M 21
Toulouse, France	2, 182, 188	T182	
Tours, France	130	T190, T199	M 21
Trois Îlets, Martinique	133	T394	
Versailles, France	221	T221	
City life			
apartment buildings	220, 221, 242	T195	M 24, VC 24
châteaux	189, 221		M 21
churches	238	T191	M-A, M 21
libraries			M 21
la Maison des Jeunes			VC 23
neighborhoods	191		
parks	189		M 21
public buildings	189, 191, 199, 236–241	T191, T197	M 21
shopping malls			M 21, VC 27
street names	190	T193	
See also Cafés, Museums, Restaurants			
Clothing and personal appearance			
Fashion	247, 286	T248	M 25, VC 25, M 26, M 27
Shopping for clothes	248–250, 252, 266	T248, T250	M 25, VC 25, M 26, M 27, VC 27
Communications			
le Minitel	132, 189	T132	
post office	189	T189	
telephone		T374, T386	VC 13
writing letters	131, 183		
Concerts: *See* **Music**			
Cuisine			
Creole cuisine	394, 395		
French terminology	348, 371		
making **crêpes**	396–397	T370	VC 35

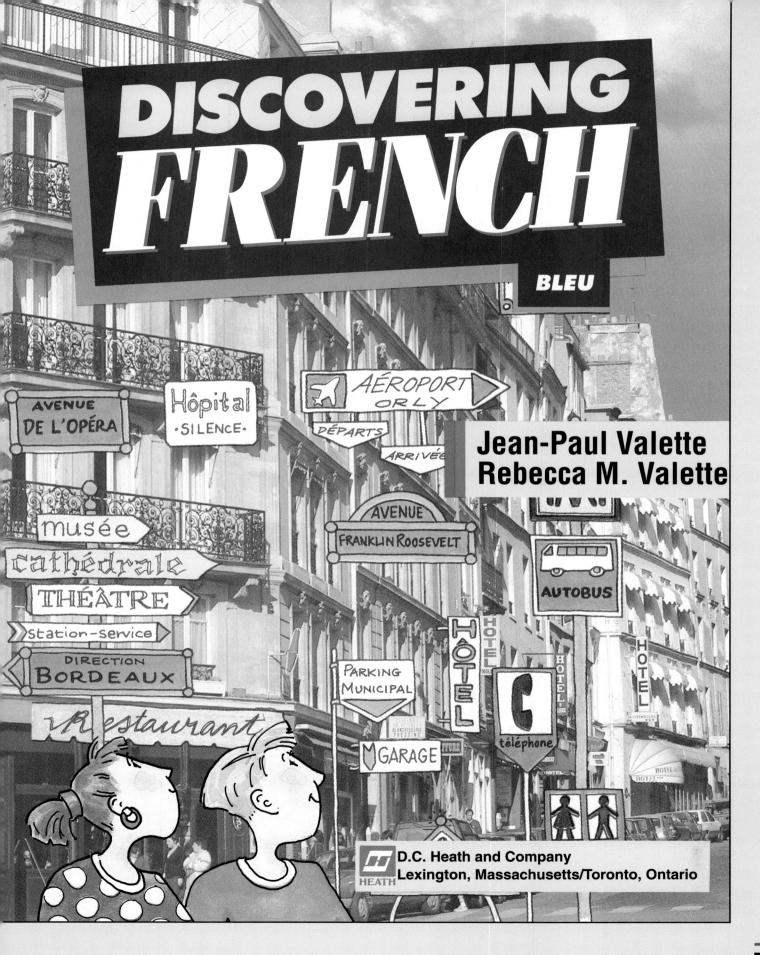

DISCOVERING FRENCH

BLEU

Jean-Paul Valette
Rebecca M. Valette

D.C. Heath and Company
Lexington, Massachusetts/Toronto, Ontario

Teacher Consultants

Steve Covey, *Sunnyvale Junior High School, California*
Dianne Hopen, *Humboldt High School, Minnesota*
Patricia McCann, *Lincoln-Sudbury High School, Massachusetts*
T. Jeffrey Richards, *Theodore Roosevelt High School, South Dakota*
Frank Strell, *La Salle-Peru Township High School, Illinois*
Susan Wildman, *Western Albemarle High School, Virginia*

Director, Modern Languages

Roger D. Coulombe

Managing Editor

Gail G. Smith

Project Editors

Valentia B. Dermer
Gloria A. Ryan

National Modern Language Coordinator

Teresa Carrera-Hanley

D.C. Heath Consultant

Karen Ralston

Design and Production

Victor Curran, *Design Section Manager*
Christine Beckwith, *Designer*
Caroline Bowden, Irene Elios, Tama Hochbaum,
Diana Maloney, Penny Peters, *Design Staff*
Pamela Wing, *Production Coordinator*
Marianna Frew Palmer, *Editorial Services*
Design Five, *Design Concept and Cover Design*
Linda Finigan, *Photo Research*
Studio Goodwin-Sturges, *Art Coordination*

Illustrations

Yves Calarnou
Jean-Pierre Foissy
Elizabeth Schlossberg

Lycée Jean-Baptiste Corot

MERCI

Special thanks to the students and staff of
- **Collège Eugène Delacroix,** *Paris*
- **Lycée Jean-Baptiste Corot,** *Savigny-sur-Orge*
for their cooperation and assistance.

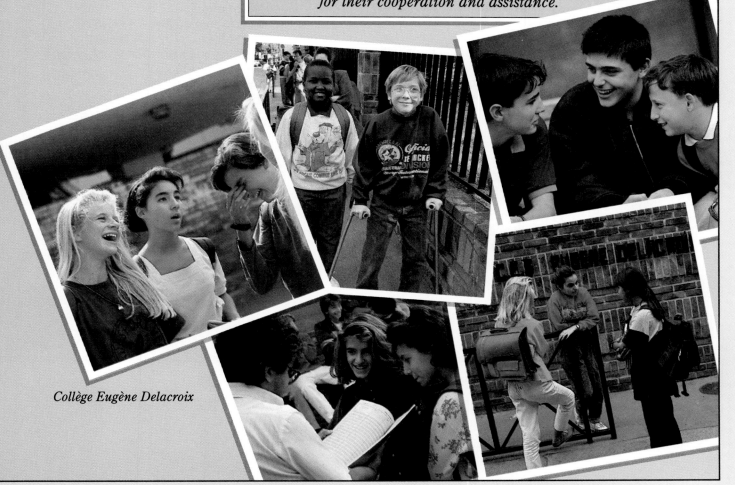

Collège Eugène Delacroix

Contents

UNITÉ 1 Bonjour! 12

Introduction culturelle: Salutations
Thème: Getting acquainted

vii

T vii

UNITÉ

5 Le monde personnel et familier 134

Thème: People and possessions

viii

ix

T x

xi

T xi

xii

Parlons français!

Chers amis,

Welcome to DISCOVERING FRENCH and congratulations on your choice of French as a foreign language!

There are many reasons why people decide to learn French. Some people choose French because they plan to visit Canada or Europe or French-speaking Africa. Others want to learn to read articles or books written in French. Still others study French because in their work, they will come into contact with French speakers or because their own family is of French or French-American heritage. And there are many people who learn French for pleasure: They want to enjoy French films and French music, and they like French poetry and French art.

There is another reason for studying French that you have perhaps not thought about. As you learn another language, you develop a better understanding of your own language and how it works. You also develop a better appreciation of your own country and culture as you expand your world view and discover the various French-speaking areas of the globe. You will discover cultural similarities and differences, and you will realize how much French civilization has contributed to our life in the United States.

And, of course, everyone will agree that studying a foreign language also helps us get to know and communicate with people from other cultures. By speaking French, you will be in touch with the many millions of people who use that language in their daily lives. These French speakers **(les francophones)** represent a wide variety of ethnic and cultural backgrounds. As you will see, they live not only in France and other parts of Europe but also in Africa, in North and South America, in Asia . . . in fact, on all continents!

On the pages of this book and in the accompanying video, you will meet many young people who speak French. Listen carefully to what they say and how they express themselves. They will help you understand not only their language but also the way they live.

Bonne chance!

Jean-Paul Valette   *Rebecca M. Valette*

Bienvenue!

Je m'appelle Jean-Paul.

Je m'appelle Nathalie.

Je m'appelle François.

■ **Photo note**
The photo in the center shows the authors with a group of French **lycéens.** This picture was taken at the **Place Igor Stravinski** near the **Centre Pompidou** in Paris. The church in the background is the **église Saint Merry.**

Bonjour!

Je m'appelle David.

Salut!

Je m'appelle Dominique.

Je m'appelle Marc.

1

TPR 🏃 **Total Physical Response**

Some teachers like to develop initial listening comprehension skills using Total Physical Response techniques.

For a brief description of this approach and instructions for three beginning activities, see the general discussion in the Front Matter.

Bonjour, les francophones!

Bonjour, les
francophones!

A.4 Des francophones aux États-Unis
(5:48–7:38 min.)
■ This video segment has brief interviews with several French speakers in the U.S., including Dr. Phan (#11).

*T*he people portrayed on these pages represent many different backgrounds. Some live in France, some in the United States. They are from Europe, Africa, Asia, and North America. They do, however, have one thing in common. They all speak French. Let's meet them.

1
Sophie Lafont, 14, is from Toulouse, a city in southern France. She is a student at the Lycée Saint-Exupéry. (A **lycée** is the equivalent of an American high school.)

2
Philippe Martin, 15, lives in Paris and goes to the Collège Eugène Delacroix.

3
Stéphanie Malle, 14, also lives in Paris and attends the Collège Eugène Delacroix. Her family is from Martinique, a French island in the Caribbean.

4
Ahmed Belkacem, 14, lives in Lyon, France, and goes to the Lycée Jean Moulin. His parents are from Algeria and speak French and Arabic. Ahmed, who was born in France, speaks only French.

■ **If students ask**
Prak Maph (#6): In Cambodia, the family name is always given first, and is then followed by the individual's name.

5
Fredy Vansattel, 20, lives near Lausanne, a city in French-speaking Switzerland. He is a student at the well-known École Hôtelière. In addition to French, Fredy also speaks English and German.

6
Prak Maph, 15, left Cambodia with his family when he was four. He lives in Paris and goes to the Lycée Claude Monet. Maph speaks French as well as Khmer, the national language of Cambodia.

2

Pre-reading
Have students look at the pictures of the various French-speakers.
Without reading the text, have them try to guess which countries these people are from.

Post-reading
Ask students to pick a person from the the text whom they would like to meet. Why would they like to talk to that person? What questions might they want to ask?

7

Amélan Konan, 13, lives in Abidjan, the capital of the Ivory Coast, a country of West Africa. Amélan goes to the Collège Moderne Voltaire, where many of the teachers are from France. Amélan is fluent in both French and Baoulé, the tribal language that she speaks with her relatives.

8

Pauline Lévêque, 14, is from Quebec City in the province of Quebec, in Canada. Pauline goes to the École Louis-Jolliet. She speaks both French and English, but she prefers to speak French with her friends and family.

9

Moustapha Badid is a French athlete of North African origin who lives in Paris. At age 23, he won the wheelchair title at the Boston Marathon and established a world record in the event. In that same year, he also won an Olympic gold medal. He speaks French, Arabic, and some English.

10

Dr. Michèle Klopner, a clinical psychologist, grew up in Haiti, where her family resides. She came to the United States to study at the University of Michigan and Rutgers University. Dr. Klopner speaks French, Haitian Creole, and English. She uses all these languages in her work at the Cambridge Hospital in Cambridge, Massachusetts.

11

Marie-Christine Mouis was born in Canada of a French father and a Canadian mother. At the age of 16, Marie-Christine joined the Paris Opera Ballet, becoming the youngest dancer in the world's oldest ballet company. She was the principal ballerina of the Boston Ballet for ten years.

12

Dr. Larry Phan was born in Vietnam. At the age of ten, he went to France, where he received his high school education. In 1976, he came to the United States to pursue a medical career. He attended the University of California and Tufts School of Dental Medicine. Dr. Phan is on the staff of the Children's Hospital in Boston.

ACTIVITÉS CULTURELLES

1. On a world map or globe, locate the cities and countries of origin for each of the people pictured.
2. Do you know any people in your community who have French names or people who speak French? Where are their families originally from?

3

Multi-cultural enrichment

Perhaps you would like to invite French speakers from your community to come visit your class. They could talk to students about why they think it is valuable to know how to speak French.

■ **Cultural note:** There are also two small French islands in the Atlantic, off the Canadian coast: Saint Pierre et Miquelon.

Bonjour, le monde français!

*I*n today's world, French is an international language spoken daily by more than 100 million people. French is understood by another 100 million in many countries and regions of the globe.

IN NORTH AMERICA

■ In Canada, about one third of the population speaks French. These French speakers live mainly in the province of Quebec **(le Québec)**. They are descendants of French settlers who came to Canada in the 17th and 18th centuries.

■ In the United States, French is understood and spoken in many families whose French and French-Canadian ancestors came to Louisiana **(la Louisiane)** and New England **(la Nouvelle-Angleterre)** at various times in our history.

■ In the Caribbean, French and Creole are spoken in the Republic of Haiti **(Haïti)**. French is also spoken on the islands of Martinique **(la Martinique)** and Guadeloupe **(la Guadeloupe)**; the inhabitants of these two islands are French citizens.

IN OTHER PARTS OF THE WORLD

■ French is spoken as far away as Tahiti **(Tahiti)** and New Caledonia **(la Nouvelle-Calédonie)**, two French territories in the South Pacific.

■ In the Middle East, French is still taught and spoken in Lebanon **(le Liban)**.

■ French is also used and understood by many Vietnamese and Cambodian families who have left their countries **(le Viêt-nam, le Cambodge)** to settle in other parts of the world.

LE CANADA

LE QUÉBEC

SAINT-PIERRE ET-MIQUELON

LA NOUVELLE-ANGLETERRE

LA LOUISIANE

HAÏTI

LA GUADELOUPE

LA MARTINIQUE

OCÉAN PACIFIQUE

TAHITI

France (including its overseas departments and territories)

Other French-speaking areas

4

IN EUROPE

French is not only spoken in France **(la France)** but also in parts of Belgium **(la Belgique)**, Switzerland **(la Suisse)**, and Luxembourg **(le Luxembourg)**.

IN AFRICA

French is an important language in countries which have strong commercial and cultural ties to France.

■ In Western and Central Africa, about 20 countries have adopted French as their official language.

These countries include Senegal **(le Sénégal)**, the Ivory Coast **(la Côte d'Ivoire)**, and Zaire **(le Zaïre)**. French is also spoken on the large island of Madagascar **(Madagascar)**.

■ In North Africa, French is understood and spoken by many people of Algeria **(l'Algérie)**, Morocco **(le Maroc)**, and Tunisia **(la Tunisie)**. More than two million people from these countries have emigrated to France and have become French citizens.

FRANCE
LA BELGIQUE
LE LUXEMBOURG
LA SUISSE
MAROC
L'ALGÉRIE
LA TUNISIE
LE LIBAN
NÉGAL
CÔTE D'IVOIRE
LE ZAÏRE
MADAGASCAR
LE VIÊT-NAM
LE CAMBODGE
LA NOUVELLE CALÉDONIE
OCÉAN PACIFIQUE
OCÉAN INDIEN
OCÉAN ATLANTIQUE

Cultural expansion
Names of African countries where French is an important language (capitals are given in parentheses):
Algérie (Alger)
Bénin (Porto-Novo)
Burkina Faso (Ougadougou)
Burundi (Bujumbura)
Cameroun (Yaoundé)
Congo (Brazzaville)
Côte-d'Ivoire (Yamoussoukro)
Djibouti (Djibouti)
Gabon (Libreville)
Guinée (Conakry)
Madagascar (Antananarivo)
Mali (Bamako)
Maroc (Rabat)
Mauritanie (Nouakchott)
Niger (Niamey)
République Centrafricaine (Bangui)
Ruanda [Rwanda] (Kigali)
Sénégal (Dakar)
Tchad (N'Djamena)
Togo (Lomé)
Tunisie (Tunis)
Zaire (Kinshasa)

ACTIVITÉS CULTURELLES

1. Name at least six African countries where French is spoken. Find out the capital of each country. (Source: atlas, encyclopedia)
2. Collect clippings from newspapers and magazines in which a French-speaking country is mentioned. Try to find one clipping for each of the areas on the map.

NOTE: You may also wish to refer to the reference map of the French-speaking world on pages R2–R3.

Bonjour, la France!

■ **Photo culture notes**
Pictures described clockwise:
Eghisheim, Alsace
The small village of Eghisheim is located on the **Route des vins** near **Colmar.**
Note the fountain and the typical half-timbered Alsatian houses with their sloped roofs.

Les Alpes et Chamonix
Chamonix is located in a valley in the Alps at the foot of the **Massif du Mont Blanc. (Mont Blanc** is the highest mountain in Europe.) Chamonix is a famous ski resort. The first Winter Olympics were held there in 1924.

Menton et la Côte d'Azur
Menton is located on the French Riviera, or **la Côte d'Azur,** just east of Monaco. The Côte d'Azur stretches about 100 miles along the Mediterranean, from the Toulon area to the Italian border. For the French, the Côte d'Azur is their favorite summer vacation place.

Les Pyrénées
The **Pyrénées** are a high mountain chain which separates France from Spain (**l'Espagne**).

Le Château d'Azay-le-Rideau
This castle, located in **la Touraine,** is one of the many **Châteaux de la Loire** which were built by the French kings nearly 500 years ago.

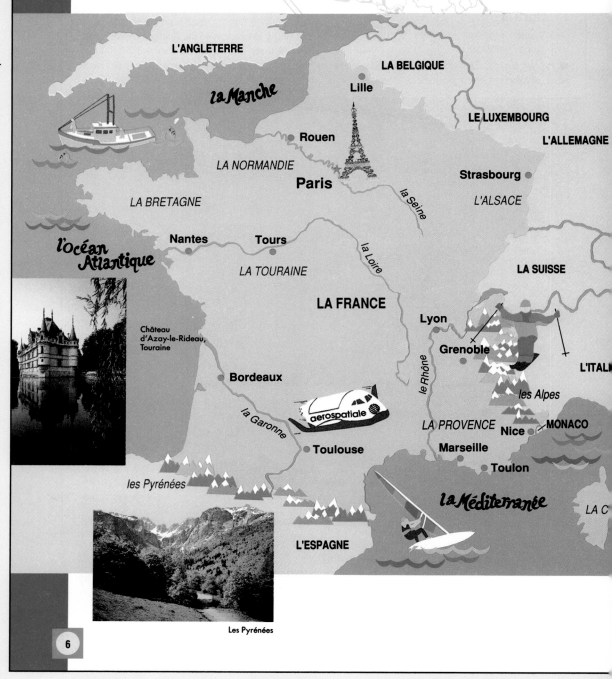

Château d'Azay-le-Rideau, Touraine

Les Pyrénées

6

Classroom project
You might have students prepare a bulletin board display about France using maps, postcards, travel brochures, etc.

Eguisheim, Alsace

Les Alpes, Chamonix

Menton, Côte d'Azur

CULTURE

*B*efore starting your study of French, you may be interested in learning a few facts about France.

■ In area, France is the largest country in Western Europe.

■ Economically, France is one of the most developed countries of the world with a sophisticated high-tech industry.

■ France is the only European country with a space exploration program. French communication satellites provide 400 million Europeans with direct TV transmission.

■ France is a country with a strong cultural tradition. French philosophers, writers, and artists have influenced our ways of thinking and looking at the world.

■ France has a long history reaching back through Roman times into distant prehistory.

■ Geographically, France is a very diversified country with the highest mountains in Europe (**les Alpes et les Pyrénées**) and an extensive coastline along the Atlantic (**l'océan Atlantique**) and the Mediterranean (**la Méditerranée**).

■ France consists of many different regions which have maintained their traditions, their culture, and—in some cases—their own language. Some of the traditional provinces are Normandy and Brittany (**la Normandie et la Bretagne**) in the west, Alsace (**l'Alsace**) in the east, Touraine (**la Touraine**) in the center, and Provence (**la Provence**) in the south.

ACTIVITÉS CULTURELLES

1. Find the countries which have a common border with France. What are their capitals? (Source: atlas, encyclopedia)
2. Imagine that you are spending a year in France. Where would you go if you wanted to ski in the winter? Which provinces would you want to visit in the summer if you wanted to swim in the Atlantic? in the Mediterranean? Are there any particular parts of France you would like to explore?

NOTE: You may also wish to refer to the reference map of France on page R4.

7

■ **Cultural notes**
• **Size:** In area, one can compare France to:
  (a) 4/5 of Texas, or
  (b) Wyoming plus Oregon, or
  (c) New England plus New York, Pennsylvania and Ohio.
• **Technology:** The French Ariane rockets are launched from French Guiana (**la Guyane française**) in South America.
• **French cultural tradition:**
  Philosophers: Voltaire, Montesquieu, Rousseau, Jean-Paul Sartre
  Writers: Victor Hugo, Albert Camus, Colette, Baudelaire
  Musicians: composers Debussy and Ravel, flutist Jean-Pierre Rampal
  Artists: Gauguin, Renoir, Matisse
• **Pre-history:** the Cro-Magnon caveman and the caves of Lascaux
• **Roman times:** Julius Caesar conquered France (Gaul) in 43 B.C.; one can still visit the Roman ruins in Provence: Nîmes, Orange, Pont du Gard.

■ **Activités culturelles**
Answers:
1. Belgium (Brussels)
   Luxembourg (Luxembourg)
   Germany (Berlin)
   Switzerland (Bern)
   Italy (Rome)
   Spain (Madrid)
2. Skiing: les Alpes, les Pyrénées
   Swimming in the Atlantic: La Bretagne, La Normandie
   Swimming in the Mediterranean: La Provence

T7

Bonjour, Je m'appelle...

■ **English equivalents of French boys' names:**

Alain (Alan)
André (Andrew)
Antoine (Anthony)
Christophe (Christopher)
Édouard (Edward)
Étienne (Steven)
François (Francis, Frank)
Frédéric (Frederick)
Geoffroy (Jeffrey)
Guillaume (William)
Henri (Henry)
Jacques (James)
Jean (John)
Julien (Julian)
Laurent (Lawrence)
Marc (Mark)
Matthieu (Matthew)
Michel (Michael)
Olivier (Oliver)
Philippe (Phillip)
Pierre (Peter)
Raoul (Ralph)

■ **Cultural note:** The notebooks that French students use often have graph paper rather than lined paper.

Here is a list of some traditional French names. As you begin your study of the French language, you may want to "adopt" a French name from the list.

Alain	Geoffroy	Mathieu
Albert	Georges	Michel
André	Grégoire	Nicolas
Antoine	Guillaume	Olivier
Bernard	Henri	Patrick
Bertrand	Jacques	Paul
Charles	Jean	Philippe
Christophe	Jean-Claude	Pierre
Daniel	Jean-François	Raoul
David	Jean-Louis	Raymond
Denis	Jean-Paul	Richard
Dominique	Jérôme	Robert
Édouard	Joseph	Roger
Éric	Julien	Samuel
Étienne	Laurent	Simon
François	Marc	Thomas
Frédéric		

Sylvie
Alice
Alain
Jean-Paul
Éric
Laure
Olivier

8

Teaching note: Choosing French names

Let students adopt a new French identity. Some may want to find a French version of their English name.

Others may want to pick a completely original name.

If some students do not want to choose a French name, teach them how to pronounce their own name with a French accent.

■ **English equivalents of French girls' names:**
Andrée (Andrea)
Cécile (Cecilia)
Diane (Diana)
Éléonore (Eleanor)
Émilie (Emily)
Françoise (Frances)
Hélène (Helen)
Jeanne (Jean)
Laure (Laura)
Lise (Lisa)
Lucie (Lucy)
Marguerite (Margaret)
Marie (Mary)
Marthe (Martha)
Michèle (Michelle)
Monique (Monica)
Nathalie (Natalie)
Suzanne (Susan)
Sylvie (Sylvia)
Thérèse (Teresa)
Virginie (Virginia)

Alice	Éléonore	Marthe
Andrée	Élisabeth	Michèle
Anne	Émilie	Monique
Anne-Marie	Florence	Nathalie
Barbara	Françoise	Nicole
Béatrice	Hélène	Patricia
Brigitte	Isabelle	Pauline
Caroline	Jeanne	Rachel
Catherine	Judith	Renée
Cécile	Juliette	Rose
Charlotte	Karine	Sophie
Christine	Laure	Stéphanie
Claire	Lise	Suzanne
Corinne	Louise	Sylvie
Delphine	Lucie	Thérèse
Denise	Marguerite	Véronique
Diane	Marie	Virginie
Dominique	Marie-Christine	

Nathalie

9

Teaching note: Pronunciation

Read the above lists aloud and have students repeat the names after you.

Be sure they always let the accent fall on the last syllable of each name.

T9

NIVEAU A

Faisons

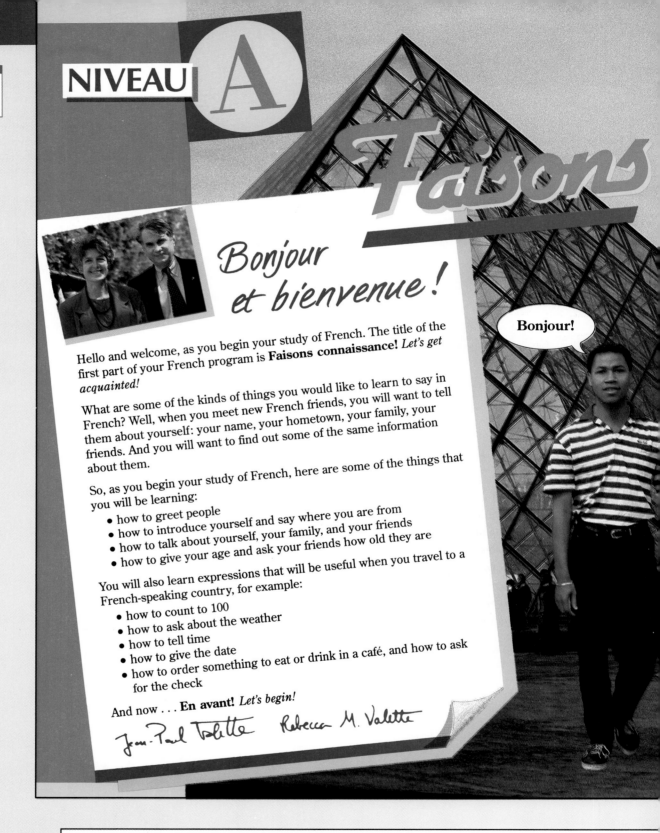

Bonjour et bienvenue!

Bonjour!

Hello and welcome, as you begin your study of French. The title of the first part of your French program is **Faisons connaissance!** *Let's get acquainted!*

What are some of the kinds of things you would like to learn to say in French? Well, when you meet new French friends, you will want to tell them about yourself: your name, your hometown, your family, your friends. And you will want to find out some of the same information about them.

So, as you begin your study of French, here are some of the things that you will be learning:

- how to greet people
- how to introduce yourself and say where you are from
- how to talk about yourself, your family, and your friends
- how to give your age and ask your friends how old they are

You will also learn expressions that will be useful when you travel to a French-speaking country, for example:

- how to count to 100
- how to ask about the weather
- how to tell time
- how to give the date
- how to order something to eat or drink in a café, and how to ask for the check

And now . . . **En avant!** *Let's begin!*

Jean-Paul Valette   Rebecca M. Valette

Overview of Niveau A

Niveau A begins **Discovering French — Bleu** with a focus on oral communication, both listening comprehension and speaking. Basic conversational skills are introduced without a formal presentation of structure.

New conversational patterns are grouped by function in the **Pour communiquer** sections.

Students will learn how to greet people, introduce themselves, talk about their friends and family, and even order in a café.

Telling time, talking about the days of the week, months and dates, the weather and seasons, and the numbers from 0-100 are introduced.

The first three lessons of each Niveau A unit develop simple conersational exchanges. The fourth lesson, subtitled **Le français pratique,** focuses on a specific communication topic.

Unité 1

MAIN THEME:

Getting acquainted

UNITÉ 1
Modules 1–4

1. La rentrée
2. Tu es français?
3. Salut! Ça va?
4. Le français pratique:
   L'heure

UNITÉ

1 Bonjour!

INTRODUCTION

culturelle

Salutations *(Greetings)*

How do you greet people in the United States? You may nod or smile. With adults, you may shake hands when you are introduced for the first time.

In France, people shake hands with friends and acquaintances each time they see one another, and not only to say hello but also when they say good-bye. Among teenagers, boys shake hands with boys. Girls kiss each other on the cheeks two or three times. (This is called **une bise**). Boys and girls who are close friends also greet each other with **une bise.**

LEÇON	**1**	**La rentrée**
LEÇON	**2**	**Tu es français?**
LEÇON	**3**	**Salut! Ça va?**
LEÇON	**4**	**Le français pratique: L'heure**

12

Unit overview

COMMUNICATION GOALS: Students will learn greetings and basic phrases. They will also learn how to count and tell time.
LINGUISTIC GOALS: Students will begin to recognize what French sounds like and learn how French words are pronounced.

CRITICAL THINKING GOALS: Students will encounter the concept of linguistic differences. They will discover that often there is no word-for-word correspondence between French and English.
CULTURAL GOALS: Students will discover that in France people greet one another and interact differently than in the U.S.

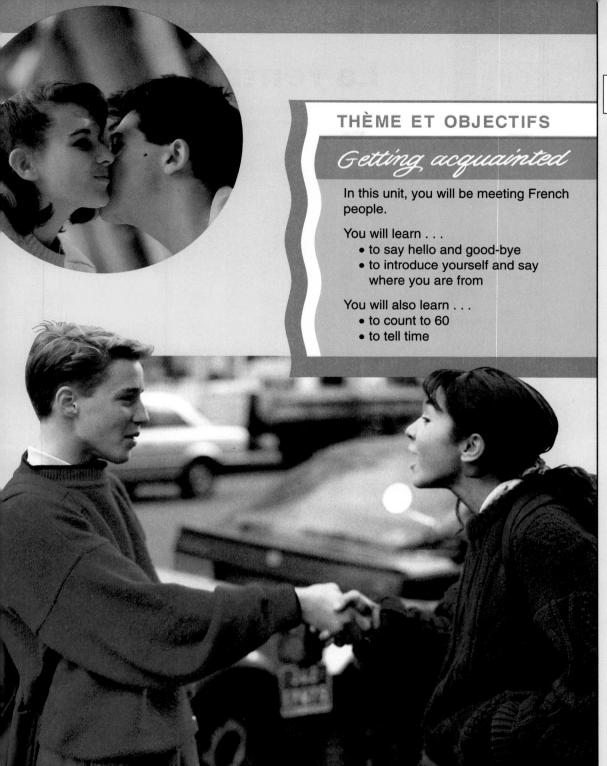

THÈME ET OBJECTIFS

Getting acquainted

In this unit, you will be meeting French people.

You will learn . . .
- to say hello and good-bye
- to introduce yourself and say where you are from

You will also learn . . .
- to count to 60
- to tell time

■ **Teaching notes:**
- **TPR (or Total Physical Response)** activities provide an excellent channel for introducing spoken French into the classroom. For many students, the demonstration of comprehension via physical movement enhances the ability to remember the new language.
- The Teacher Front Matter explains what TPR is and presents several initial TPR activities designed to introduce basic classroom commands and familiarize students with this type of activity. Throughout the book, suggestions for specific TPR activities will be given at the bottom of the page of this Teacher Edition.

Cross-cultural observation
Have students study each picture carefully, looking at the young people, their dress, and their way of greeting one another.
- Which elements in the pictures seem to be definitely French?
- Which elements could also be American?

Pacing
Try to move through this unit rather quickly, concentrating on listening and speaking.
In Niveau B, the students will encounter the same vocabulary again. At that time they will be expected to master the material in writing.

MAIN TOPIC:

Greeting and meeting friends

MODULE 1:
La rentrée
Total time: 3:42 min.
(Counter: 7:50 min.)

1.1 **La rentrée**
(7:58–8:50 min.)
1.2 **Mini-scenes: Meeting people**
(8:51–10:09 min.)
1.3 **Vignette culturelle: Bonjour!**
(10:10–11:28 min.)

■ **Comprehension practice:** Play the entire module through as an introduction to the lesson.

 1.1 La rentrée
(7:58–8:50 min)

 Leçon 1, Section 1

LEÇON 1

La rentrée

This is the first day of school. Students are greeting their friends and meeting new classmates.

Bonjour! Je m'appelle Philippe.

Et moi, je m'appelle Stéphanie.

«
—Bonjour! Je m'appelle Philippe.
—Et moi, je m'appelle Stéphanie.
»

Je m'appelle Marc. Et toi?

Moi, je m'appelle Isabelle.

Comment t'appelles-tu?

Je m'appelle Nathalie

«
—Je m'appelle Marc. Et toi?
—Moi, je m'appelle Isabelle.
»

«
—Comment t'appelles-tu?
—Je m'appelle Nathalie.
—Bonjour.
—Bonjour.
»

14 **Unité 1**

⌨ Using the video and the cassettes

For each lesson of Niveau A, the opening text corresponds to part 1 of the video. Similarly, the first section of the cassette program contains the video sound track of the scene with its varied and authentic voices. (See Front Matter for complete description.)

First play the entire video module through as an introduction to the lesson. Have students observe how young people greet one another in France.

Then play the opening scene several more times and have students practice repeating the new phrases.

POUR COMMUNIQUER

Bonjour!

How to say hello:

Bonjour!   *Hello!*   —**Bonjour**, Nathalie!
                                                   —**Bonjour**, Jean-Paul!

How to ask a classmate's name:

Comment t'appelles-tu?   *What's your name?*   —**Comment t'appelles-tu?**
Je m'appelle . . .   *My name is . . .*   —**Je m'appelle** Stéphanie.

OTHER EXPRESSIONS		
moi	*me*	**Moi,** je m'appelle Marc.
et toi?	*and you?*	**Et toi,** comment t'appelles-tu?

■ NOTES ■ CULTURELLES

Rentrée des classes
6^{em} → Lundi 10 Septembre à 9^H
  (pas de cours l'après.midi)

5e-4e-3e → Lundi 10 Septembre
       à 14^H

1 La rentrée *(Back to school)*

French and American students have about the same number of days of summer vacation. In France, summer vacation usually begins at the end of June and classes resume in early September. The first day back to school in fall is called **la rentrée.**

2 Les prénoms français
(French first names)

Many traditional French names have corresponding equivalents in English.

For boys:
Jean *(John)*
Pierre *(Peter)*
Marc *(Mark)*
Philippe *(Philip)*
Nicolas *(Nicholas)*

For girls:
Marie *(Mary)*
Monique *(Monica)*
Cécile *(Cecilia)*
Alice
Caroline

Often the names **Jean** and **Marie** are combined in double names such as **Jean-Paul** and **Marie-Christine.** In recent years, names of foreign origin, like **Dimitri** and **Karine,** have become quite popular.

Leçon 1 **15**

Pour communiquer

■ **Language note:** Literally, **bonjour** means *good day* and corresponds to *good morning* or *good afternoon.*
In the evening, **bonjour** may be replaced by **bonsoir** *(good evening).*
Bonne nuit *(good night)* is used when someone is going to bed.
Also: **Comment est-ce que tu t'appelles?**

■ **Language note:** When speaking among themselves, French people often use CASUAL SPEECH. Since these forms are spoken (and not written), they are not formally presented in the students' textbook. If you wish, you may introduce them orally in class for recognition. For example, to ask someone's name in casual French one may say: **Tu t'appelles comment?** or **Comment tu t'appelles?**

Notes culturelles

There are four grades in a French **collège:**
• **sixième** (sixth grade),
• **cinquième** (seventh grade),
• **quatrième** (eighth grade) and
• **troisième** (ninth grade).

🌐 **Cross-cultural observation:** Have students look at the photograph of the sign.
What is the date of **la rentrée?** [Monday, September 10]
At what time do the students in **sixième** report? [9:00 AM]
And the students in **cinquième, quatrième,** and **troisième?** [2:00 PM]
Which group does not have class in the afternoon? [students in sixième]
(At this point, you may wish to review the 24-hour system of telling time.)

Choosing names

Assign students French names or let them choose names for themselves from the list on pp. 8-9.
   Have students introduce themselves to the class. First practice the pronunciation of **je m'appelle** and then model the correct pronunciation of their French names.

If you do not wish to use French names, help students pronounce their own names with a French accent.

Petit commentaire
• Julius Caesar invaded Gaul around 50 B.C.
• The title of the book *Le tour de Gaule d'Astérix* is a take-off on the Tour de France bicycle race (see p. 38).

 1.2 Mini-scenes: Meeting people (8:51–10:09 min.)

 Leçon 1, Section 2

1 EXCHANGES: greetings

2 COMMUNICATION: identifying oneself

■ Chain activity in small groups: Student 1 asks Student 2 his/her name. Then Student 2 asks the name of Student 3, and so on. **Je m'appelle [Stéphanie]. Et toi? Moi, je m'appelle [David]. Et toi?** etc.

3 COMMUNICATION: asking someone's name

4 PRACTICE: greetings

■ **Teaching suggestion:** Model the correct pronunciation of the names so that students can pronounce them with a French accent.

▷ **L'alphabet**

 Leçon 1, Section 3

Bonjour! Je m'appelle Astérix.

Petit commentaire
Astérix le Gaulois *is one of the best-loved cartoon characters in France. Small in size but extremely clever and courageous, he represents the "little man" defending his country Gaul (the ancient name of France) against the invading Roman legions led by Julius Caesar.*

1 **Bonjour!**
Say hello to the student nearest to you.

▶
Bonjour! *Bonjour!*

2 **Je m'appelle . . .**
Introduce yourself to your classmates.

▶ Je m'appelle (Paul).
▶ Je m'appelle (Denise).

3 **Et toi?**
Ask a classmate his or her name.

▶ —Comment t'appelles-tu?
—Je m'appelle (Christine).

4 **Bonjour, les amis!** *(Hello everyone!)*
Say hello to the following students.

▶ **Bonjour, Marc!**

Marc

Juliette

Jean-Paul

Isabelle

Philippe

Stéphanie

François

Nathalie

L'alphabet

A	B	C	D	E	F	G	H	I	J	K	L
a	bé	cé	dé	e	effe	gé	hache	i	ji	ka	elle

Teaching the alphabet
Say each letter of the alphabet and have students repeat as you write it on the board. Then, have a volunteer come and point to the letters as you say them in random order. The others can point to the corresponding letters in their textbook.

Game: "Le pendu"
Play hangman in French using the names of famous people or well-known places, or French products available in the United States.

Les signes orthographiques *(Spelling marks)*

French uses accents and spelling marks that do not exist in English. These marks are part of the spelling and cannot be left out.

In French, there are four accents that may appear on vowels.

´	**l'accent aigu** *(acute accent)*	Cécile, Stéphanie
`	**l'accent grave** *(grave accent)*	Michèle, Hélène
^	**l'accent circonflexe** *(circumflex)*	Jérôme
¨	**le tréma** *(diaeresis)*	Noël, Joëlle

There is only one spelling mark used with a consonant. It occurs under the letter "c".

¸	**la cédille** *(cedilla)*	François

5 La rentrée

It is the first day of class. The following students are introducing themselves. Act out the dialogues with your classmates.

▶ Hélène et Philippe

Moi, je m'appelle Philippe.

Je m'appelle Hélène. Et toi?

1. Stéphanie et Marc
2. Cécile et Frédéric
3. Michèle et François
4. Béatrice et Joël
5. Céline et Jérôme

Les nombres de 0 à 10

0 zéro	**1** un	**2** deux	**3** trois
4 quatre	**5** cinq	**6** six	**7** sept
8 huit	**9** neuf	**10** dix	

6 Numéros de téléphone

Imagine you are visiting a family in Quebec. Give them your American phone number in French.

▶ 617-963-4028   six, un, sept — neuf, six, trois — quatre, zéro, deux, huit

M	N	O	P	Q	R	S	T	U	V	W	X	Y	Z
emme	enne	o	pé	ku	erre	esse	té	u	vé	double vé	ixe	i grec	zède

Leçon 1   **17**

▶ Les signes orthographes

■ Language notes:
- The acute accent ´ occurs only on **e** to show it is pronounced /e/.
- The grave accent ` occurs mainly on **e** to show it is pronounced /ɛ/, and in the words **à, là,** and **où.**
- The circumflex ^ can occur on all vowels; often the corresponding English word has an "s": **forêt, hôpital, mât.**
- The diaeresis ¨ is placed on the second of two vowels to show that they are pronounced separately: **naïf.**
- The c-cedilla ç is used before **a, o, u** to show it is pronounced /s/: **ça, garçon, reçu.** Otherwise, **c** before **a, o, u** is pronounced /k/: **café, collège, culturel.**
- **Note:** Accent marks are often not placed on capital letters. In this book, however, we will show accents on capital letters to make it easier for students.

5 EXCHANGES: making introductions

▷ Les nombres de 0 à 10

⊡ Leçon 1, Section 4

■ **Speaking activity:** To practice the numbers 0-10, knock loudly on your desk. Have the students identify the number of knocks in French. For example: (toc! toc!) **Deux!**, etc.

■ **If students ask:**
un nombre = number or numeral, in the mathematical sense
un numéro = number, in a series; e.g., phone number, house number

6 COMMUNICATION; giving one's telephone number

■ **Cultural note:** In Quebec, as in the United States, phone numbers are given digit by digit.

TPR 🏃 Numbers 0 to 10

With your right hand, demonstrate the numbers 0 to 5 as you say them:
Voici 0. [closed fist]
Voici 1. [thumb extended]
Voici 2. [thumb and index finger] …

Have students respond to commands with the same gestures:
Montrez-moi 0, 1, 2 …
Practice the numbers in random order:
Montrez-moi 3, 5, 2, …
Continue with numbers 6 through 10, using both hands.

MODULE 2:
Tu es français?
Total time: 7:28 min.
(Counter: 11:40 min.)

2.1 **Tu es français?**
(11:45–12:37 min.)
2.2 **Mini-scenes: Finding out where people are from**
(13:02–14:35 min.)
2.3 **Vignette culturelle: Qui est français?**
(14:36–18:48 min.)

■ **Comprehension practice:** Play the entire module through as an introduction to the lesson.

2.1 Tu es français?
(11:45–12:37 min.)

 Leçon 2, Section 1

■ **Cultural note:** Marc tells Stéphanie **Tu as de la chance!** because he thinks she is lucky to live in Martinique, a tropical island with beautiful beaches and exotic flowers. For French people, Martinique evokes the kinds of images that "Hawaii" evokes for Americans.

LEÇON 2

Tu es français?

It is the opening day of school and several of the students meet in the cafeteria (**la cantine**) at lunchtime. Marc discovers that not everyone is French.

Tu es français?

Oui, je suis français.

MARC: Tu es français?
JEAN-PAUL: Oui, je suis français.

MARC: Et toi, Patrick, tu es français aussi?
PATRICK: Non! Je suis américain. Je suis de Boston.

Non! Je suis américain.

MARC: Et toi, Stéphanie, tu es française ou américaine?
STÉPHANIE: Je suis française.
MARC: Tu es de Paris?
STÉPHANIE: Non, je suis de Fort-de-France.
MARC: Tu as de la chance!

Je suis française.

MARC: Are you French?
JEAN-PAUL: Yes, I'm French.

MARC: And you, Patrick, are you French too?
PATRICK: No! I'm American. I'm from Boston.

MARC: And you, Stéphanie, are you French or American?
STÉPHANIE: I'm French.
MARC: Are you from Paris?
STÉPHANIE: No, I'm from Fort-de-France.
MARC: You're lucky!

 Unité 1 18

Cooperative learning

Play the entire video module as an introduction to the lesson.

Divide the class into groups and name one person in each group as **secrétaire** (recorder). Play Part 1 of the video again.

Have the groups list things they observed in the French school that are similar to their own school, as well as things that are different.

Have the recorders come forward to read their lists. The team with the most complete list is the winner.
For confirmation, play the video once more.

POUR COMMUNIQUER

Tu es de Denver?

How to talk about where people are from:

Tu es de ...?	*Are you from . . . ?*	—**Tu es de** Denver?
Je suis de ...	*I'm from . . .*	—Non, **je suis de** Dallas.

How to talk about one's nationality:

Tu es ...?	*Are you . . . ?*	—Pierre, **tu es** français?
Je suis ...	*I am . . .*	—Oui, **je suis** français.

Les nationalités

🇫🇷	**français**	**française**
🇬🇧	**anglais**	**anglaise**
🇺🇸	**américain**	**américaine**
🇨🇦	**canadien**	**canadienne**

OTHER EXPRESSIONS

oui	*yes*	Tu es français? **Oui,** je suis français.
non	*no*	Tu es canadien? **Non,** je suis américain.
et	*and*	Je suis de Paris. **Et** toi?
ou	*or*	Tu es français **ou** canadien?
aussi	*also, too*	Moi **aussi,** je suis française.

■ NOTE ■ CULTURELLE

Fort-de-France et la Martinique

Fort-de-France is the capital of Martinique, a small French island in the Caribbean. Because Martinique is part of the French national territory, its inhabitants are French citizens. Most of them are of African origin. They speak French as well as a dialect called **créole.**

Martinique is also known as the Island of the Flowers (**l'Île aux Fleurs**) because of its warm tropical climate and magnificent vegetation. In the winter months, it attracts thousands of European and American tourists.

LA MARTINIQUE

B A L A T A
🌱 jardin botanique

Leçon 2 **19**

Pour communiquer

🖥 **Transparency 4**
US, Canada, England, France

▨ This is the students' first introduction to adjective agreement, and should be kept as simple as possible. The key objective is that students hear the sound differences and pronounce the masculine and feminine forms correctly.

▨ **Pronunciation:** Be sure students notice that the final consonant sound (/z/, /n/) is pronounced in the feminine forms but is silent in the masculine forms.

Note culturelle

🖥 **2.3 Vignette culturelle: Qui est français?** (14:36–18:48 min.)

🌐 **Cultural note:** As students have learned in the first photo essay (pp. 1–9), the French national territory extends beyond continental France (**la France métropolitaine**). Martinique is one of the five French overseas departments (**Départements d'Outre-Mer**).

Listening comprehension activity

Read the following eight sentences.
Have students raise their hands (or stand) if the sentence refers to a girl.

Tu es français?	**Tu es américaine?**
Tu es canadienne?	**Tu es anglaise?**
Tu es anglais?	**Tu es américain?**
Tu es française?	**Tu es canadien?**

Petit commentaire
The Statue of Liberty was sculpted by Auguste Bartholdi, who called upon Gustave Eiffel to design the interior metal framework. Although the arm and torch were exhibited at the World's Fair in Philadelphia in 1876, the statue itself was not inaugurated until ten years later.

▷ **français, française**

📼 Leçon 2, Section 2

① **COMMUNICATION:** identifying oneself

■ **Pronunciation:** If your students are from a city that begins with a vowel sound, have them use **d'**: **Je suis d'(Atlanta).**
(The concept of elision is presented formally in Niveau B, Lesson 13.)

② **ROLE PLAY:** discussing where people are from

💻 **2.2 Mini-scenes: Finding out where people are from**
(13:02–14:35 min.)

■ **Extra speaking activity:** Ask students to pretend they are a famous person. Have them introduce themselves to the class, say where they are from, and give their nationalities. For example: **Je m'appelle Margeret Thatcher. Je suis de Londres et je suis anglaise.**
(Be sure the students only use English, French, American, or Canadian personalities.)

Petit commentaire
The Statue of Liberty (la statue de la Liberté) was a gift to the United States from the French people on the occasion of the 100th anniversary of the American Revolution. The Eiffel Tower (la tour Eiffel) was built to celebrate the 100th anniversary of the French Revolution.

français, française

Names of nationalities may have two different forms, depending on whom they refer to:

MASCULINE	FEMININE
Je suis ... Tu es ...? français américain	française américaine

➡ Note that in written French the feminine forms always end in **-e.**

① **Et toi?**
Give your name, your nationality, and your city of origin.

> Bonjour!
> Je m'appelle Bob Jones.
> Je suis américain.
> Je suis de Providence.

> Bonjour!
> Je m'appelle Linda Carlson.
> Je suis américaine.
> Je suis de Boston.

⑳ Unité 1

② **Français ou française?**
You meet the following young people. Ask them if they are French. A classmate will answer you, as in the model. (Be sure to use **français** with boys and **française** with girls.)

▶ — Sophie, tu es française?
— Oui, je suis française. Je suis de Strasbourg.

Paris
Sophie
Strasbou[rg]
1. Jean-Pierre
2. Paul
3. Éric
Lyon
5. Nicole
Bordeaux
4. Michèle
Ni[ce]
Marseille

👥 **Cooperative pair practice**

In cooperative pair practice, students do activities together with a partner. (See Front Matter for a complete description.)
Introduce the class to Cooperative Pair Practice with Act. 2 and 3. Be sure each student has a partner.

First do the exercise with the entire class, having half the group give the first cue, and the other half the response.
Then let the students do the same activity again in pairs. For the odd numbered cues, Student A asks the question and Student B responds. For the even-numbered cues, the roles are reversed.

3 **Quelle nationalité?** *(Which nationality?)*

Greet the following young people and find out each one's nationality. A classmate will answer you, according to the model.

▶ —Bonjour, Marc. Tu es canadien?
—Oui, je suis canadien. Je suis de Montréal.

| Marc |
| Montréal |

| 1. Claire | 2. Patrick |
| Québec | Boston |

| 3. Denise | 4. Donna | 5. Paul |
| Liverpool | Memphis | Cambridge |

Les nombres de 10 à 20

10	11	12
dix	onze	douze
13	14	15
treize	quatorze	quinze
16	17	18
seize	dix-sept	dix-huit
19	20	
dix-neuf	vingt	

4 **La fusée Ariane**
(The Ariane rocket)

Give the countdown for the lift-off of the French rocket Ariane, from 20 to 0.

Prononciation

Les lettres muettes *(Silent letters)*

In French, the last letter of a word is often not pronounced.

Paris

- Final "e" is always silent.
  Répétez: **Sophie   Philippe   Stéphanie   anglaise   française
  onze   douze   treize   quatorze   quinze   seize**

- Final "s" is almost always silent.
  Répétez: **Paris   Nicolas   Jacques   anglais   français   trois**

- The letter "h" is always silent.
  Répétez: **Hélène   Henri   Thomas   Nathalie   Catherine**

Leçon 2   **21**

---

3 ROLE PLAY: discussing one's nationality

■ **Language note:** People from the province of Quebec will often say:
Je suis québécois(e).

▷ **Les nombres de 10 à 20**

🔲 Leçon 2, Section 3

■ **Pronunciation:** Note the pronunciation of **vingt** /vɛ̃/.

4 PRACTICE: numbers 0 to 20

■ **Language note:** In French, a *countdown* is **un compte à rebours.**

■ **Cultural note:** All the French Ariane rockets are launched from Kourou in French Guiana (South America). France is the only country in Europe with an ongoing space program.

Prononciation

🔲 Leçon 2, Section 4

- Have students pronounce the French /r/ in Paris as if they were clearing their throats.
- In later lessons, students will encounter a few common words where the final "s" is pronounced: **un fils, mars, tennis**
- The letters "ph" represent the sound /f/, as in English: **Philippe, Stéphanie.**
- The letters "ch" usually represent the sound /ʃ/, as in: **Chicago, Michèle.**
- The letters "chr" represent the sound /kr/ as in: **Christophe, Christine.**

TPR 🏃 **Numbers 11 to 20**

PROPS: index cards with numbers 11 to 20
Place the first five index cards on the chalkboard tray. Point to the numbers as you name them: **11, 12, 13, 14, 15.**
   Have students come forward to point out and touch the numbers as you name them.
   X, montre le 12. Touche le 15.

Present the second five cards.
   Place all cards randomly on the tray. Ask students to pass numbers to their classmates.
   Y, prends le 20 et donne-le à Z.

MODULE 3:
Salut! Ça va?
Total time: 4:35 min.
(Counter: 19:05 min.)

3.1 Salut! Ça va?
(19:10–19:45 min.)
3.2 Mini-scenes: Greeting people
(19:46–22:19 min.)
3.3 Vignette culturelle: Bonjour ou Salut?
(22:20–23:26 min.)

■ **Comprehension practice:** Play the entire module through as an introduction to the lesson.

  3.1 Salut! Ça va?
(19:10–19:45 min.)

Leçon 3, Section 1

Salut! Ça va?

On the way to school, François meets his friends.

Salut, Isabelle!

Salut! Ça va?

Ça va! Merci!

Salut, Nathalie! Ça va?

Ça va bien! Et toi?

Moi aussi!

Ça va, Philippe?

Ah non! Zut! Ça va mal.

François also meets his teachers.

Bonjour, monsieur.

Bonjour, François.

Monsieur Masson

Bonjour, madame.

Bonjour, François.

Madame Chollet

Bonjour, mademoiselle.

Bonjou[r] Françoi[s]

Mademoiselle Lacou[...]

After class, François says good-bye to his teacher and his friends.

Au revoir, mademoiselle.

Au revoir, François.

Au revoir, Nathalie.

Au revoir, François.

22 Unité 1

Setting the scene

Ask students how they greet their teachers when they meet them before school or in the hall.

Have them watch the video to see if French students greet their teachers with the same formality or informality.

POUR COMMUNIQUER

Salut!

How to greet a friend or classmate:

Salut!   *Hi!*

How to greet a teacher or another adult:

Bonjour!   *Hello!*

Bonjour, monsieur.
Bonjour, madame.
Bonjour, mademoiselle.

How to say good-bye:

Au revoir!   *Good-bye!*

Au revoir, Philippe.
Au revoir, monsieur.

➡ In written French, the following abbreviations are commonly used:

   M. Masson   Monsieur Masson
   Mme Chollet   Madame Chollet
   Mlle Lacour   Mademoiselle Lacour

➡ Young people often use **Salut!** to say good-bye to each other.

■ NOTE ■ CULTURELLE

Bonjour ou Salut?

French young people may greet one another with **Bonjour,** but they often prefer the less formal **Salut.** When they meet their teachers, however, they always use **Bonjour.** French young people are generally much more formal with adults than with their friends. This is especially true in their relationships with teachers, whom they treat with great respect.

Have you noticed that in France adults are addressed as **monsieur, madame,** or **mademoiselle?** The last name is almost never used in greeting people.

Leçon 3   23

Pour communiquer

■ **Language note:** When used alone, the titles **monsieur, madame,** and **mademoiselle** are not capitalized.

■ **Casual speech:** Young people often use **salut** or the Italian **ciao** / tʃau / to say good-bye.

■ **If students ask:** the French have no equivalent for "Ms." Instead they usually use **Madame.**

Abbreviations
- When an abbreviation includes only of the first letter of a word, a period is used:
  Monsieur = M.
- When an abbreviation consists of the first and last letters of a word, no period is needed:
  Madame = Mme,
  Mademoiselle = Mlle

Note culturelle

In France, young people almost never call adults by their first names.

🖥 **3.3 Vignette culturelle: Bonjour ou Salut?** (22:20–23:36 min.)

Teaching strategy: Greeting adults

To activate **Monsieur, Madame,** and **Mademoiselle,** give names of other teachers in your school. Ask students to imagine they see these people in the hall. Have them greet the teachers in French.

Mrs. Mills – **Bonjour, Madame!**
Mr. Tower – **Bonjour, Monsieur!**
Miss Swenson – **Bonjour, Mademoiselle!**

■ **Variation:** Say good-bye.
– Au revoir, Sophie.
– Au revoir, mademoiselle.

💻 **3.2 Mini-scenes: Greeting people**
(19:46–22:19 min.)
Listening and speaking practice

Pour communiquer

🖨 **Transparency 5**
Expressions with ça va

📼 **Leçon 3, Section 2**

2 EXCHANGES: greetings

■ **Teaching suggestion:**
Encourage students to use variety:
bien, très bien, mal, très mal,
comme ci, comme ça...

---

1 Bonjour ou salut?

You are enrolled in a French school.
Greet your friends and teachers.

▶ **Salut, Sophie!**

▶ **Bonjour, mademoiselle!**

 Sophie

 Mademoiselle Pinot

 1. Anne

 2. Monsieur Masson

 3. Nathalie

 4. Marc

 5. Madame Albert

6. Mademoiselle Boucher

POUR *COMMUNIQUER*

How to ask people how they feel:

—**Ça va?**   How are you? How are things going? How's everything?
—**Ça va!**   (I'm) fine. (I'm) okay. Everything's all right.

Ça va . . .   **très bien**   **bien**   **comme ci, comme ça**   **mal**   **très mal**

How to express one's feelings of frustration and appreciation:

Zut! *Darn!*   **Zut!** Ça va mal!   **Merci!** *Thanks!*   Ça va, **merci.**

➡ **Ça va?** *(How are you?)* is an informal greeting that corresponds to the following expressions:

   Comment vas-tu? (when addressing a friend)
      Bonjour, Paul. Comment vas-tu?
   Comment allez-vous? (when addressing an adult)
      Bonjour, madame. Comment allez-vous?

2 Dialogue

Exchange greetings with your class-mates and ask how they are doing.

▶ —Salut, (Thomas)! Ça va?
   —Ça va! Et toi?
   —Ça va bien. Merci.

ÇA VA?
OUI, ÇA VA TRÈS BIEN!
ÇA VA?
AH NON! ÇA VA MAL!

 Unité 1

Teaching note: Spoken and written numbers

The emphasis in Niveau A is on functional language use. In order to get around in a French-speaking country, it is very important to be able to understand and use numbers incommunicative situations.

At the basic level, students need a great deal of practice in order to understand and use numbers easily.

As a challenge activity, some students may want to learn to spell the numbers, but spelling is not necessary at this level. Most French people use digits to write numbers, especially numbers over 20.

3 Situations

Sometimes we feel good and sometimes we don't. How would you respond in the following situations?

▶ You have the flu.
—Ça va?
—Ça va mal!

1. You just received an "A" in French.
2. You lost your wallet.
3. Your uncle gave you five dollars.
4. Your grandparents sent you a check for 100 dollars.
5. You bent the front wheel of your bicycle.
6. Your parents bought you a new bicycle.
7. Your little brother broke your walkman.
8. It's your birthday.
9. You have a headache.
10. You just had an argument with your best friend.
11. Your favorite baseball team has just lost a game.
12. Your French teacher has just canceled a quiz.

4 Ça va?

How would the following people answer the question **Ça va?**

▶▶▶▶▶▶▶▶▶▶▶▶▶▶▶▶▶▶▶▶▶

Les nombres de 20 à 60

20 vingt	**30** trente	**40** quarante
vingt et un	trente et un	quarante et un
vingt-deux	trente-deux	quarante-deux
vingt-trois	trente-trois	quarante-trois
...	...	...
vingt-neuf	trente-neuf	quarante-neuf

50 cinquante	**60** soixante
cinquante et un	
cinquante-deux	
cinquante-trois	
...	
cinquante-neuf	

➡ Note the use of **et** in numbers with **un**:
vingt et un.

5 Loto

Read out loud the numbers on the French Loto tickets.

Prononciation

Les consonnes finales
(Final consonants)

$$1 \quad 2 \quad 3$$
uń   deuẋ   troiṣ

In French, the last consonant of a word is often not pronounced.

- Remember: Final "**s**" is usually silent.
  Répétez: **troiṣ   françaiṣ   anglaiṣ**

- Most other final consonants are usually silent.
  Répétez: **Richarḍ   Alberṭ   Roberṭ   saluṭ
  américaiń   canadień   bień   deuẋ**

EXCEPTION: The following final consonants are usually pronounced: "**c**," "**f**," "**l**," and sometimes "**r**."

Répétez: **Éric   Daniel   Lebeuf   Pascal   Victor**

However, the ending **-er** is usually pronounced /e/.

Répétez: **Rogeṛ   Olivieṛ**

---

3 ROLE PLAY: expressing one's feelings

4 PRACTICE: selecting an appropriate response

▷ **Les nombres de 20 à 60**

🔊 Leçon 3, Section 3

■ **Pronunciation:** Remind students that there is no liaison after **et**:/ 31 / trãteɛ̃ /, etc.

■ **Speaking activity:** Have the class say numbers in series.
- counting by 3s: 30 - 33 - 36 - 39 - 42 - 45 - 48 - 51...
- by 4s: 28 - 32 - 36 - 40 - 44...
- by 5s: 25 - 30 - 35 - 40 - 45...

5 PRACTICE: reading numbers up to 60

■ **Listening comprehension:** Read a number from one of the tickets and have students indicate whether the number appears on ticket A or B.

Prononciation

🔊 Leçon 3, Section 4

■ **Exceptions**
- The final consonant is pronounced in **zut!** and numbers used in counting like **six, sept, huit, dix.**
- The "r" in **monsieur** is silent.

■ **Memory aid:** These final consonants are found in the word: **CaReFuL.**

TPR 🏃 Numbers and prepositions

PROPS: Index for 10, 20, 30, 40, 50, 60
Spread out the index cards on a table. Place three cards in a row on the chalktray.

Je mets les nombres 10-20-30 en ligne droite.

Then have students perform similar actions.

X, mets les nombres 40-50-60 en ligne droite.

Introduce new numbers with **après** *(after)*.

**Maintenant, je mets le 30 après le 20.
Y, mets le 10 après le 30. ...**

Similarly introduce **avant** *(before)*, **derrière** *(behind)*, **devant** *(in front of)*.

**Je mets le 40 avant le 10. ...
Je mets le 50 derrière le 20. ...
Je mets le 60 devant le 40. ...**

MODULE 4:
Le français pratique:
L'heure
Total time: 8:56 min.
(Counter: 23:47 min.)

4.1 Un rendez-vous
(24:06–24:26 min.)

4.2 Mini-scenes:
Telling time
(24:36–28:44 min.)

4.3 À quelle heure
est le film?
(28:45–29:04 min.)

4.4 Mini-scenes:
Indicating at what
time an event occurs
(29:15–29:34 min.)

4.5 Vignette culturelle:
L'heure officielle
(29:35–32:01 min.)

■ **Comprehension practice:** Play the entire module through as an introduction to the lesson.

Pour communiquer

4.1 Un rendez-vous
4.2 Mini-scenes:
  Telling time
  (24:06–28:44 min.)

 Leçon 4, Section 1

T26

4

L'heure

A. Un rendez-vous

Jean-Paul and Stéphanie are sitting in a café. Stéphanie seems to be in a hurry to leave.

STÉPHANIE: Quelle heure est-il?
JEAN-PAUL: Il est trois heures.
STÉPHANIE: Trois heures?
JEAN-PAUL: Oui, trois heures.
STÉPHANIE: Oh là là. J'ai un rendez-vous avec David dans vingt minutes. Au revoir, Jean-Paul.
JEAN-PAUL: Au revoir, Stéphanie. À bientôt!

STÉPHANIE: What time is it?
JEAN-PAUL: It's three o'clock.
STÉPHANIE: Three o'clock?
JEAN-PAUL: Yes, three o'clock.
STÉPHANIE: Uh, oh! I have a date with David in twenty minutes. Good-bye, Jean-Paul.
JEAN-PAUL: Good-bye, Stéphanie. See you soon!

POUR COMMUNIQUER

How to talk about the time:

Quelle heure est-il?   *What time is it?*
Il est . . .   *It's . . .*

Il est huit heures!

une heure	deux heures	trois heures	quatre heures	cinq heures	six heures

sept heures	huit heures	neuf heures	dix heures	onze heures	midi	minuit

26 Unité 1

Have the students each write their phone numbers on a slip of paper and place them in a box.

Draw the first number and read it out loud (Quebec style: digit by digit).

The student whose number is read stands up and recites his/her phone number back. Then that student comes forward, draws a new number, and reads it aloud. The game continues until no numbers are left in the box.

1 Quelle heure est-il?

Ask your classmates what time it is.

2 L'heure d'été *(Daylight saving time)*

Philippe forgot to set his watch ahead for daylight saving time, so he is an hour off. Isabelle gives him the correct time.

▶ PHILIPPE: **Il est sept heures.**
ISABELLE: **Mais non, il est huit heures!**

→ Although *o'clock* may be left out in English, the expression **heure(s)** must be used in French when giving the time.

It's ten. (It's ten o'clock.) **Il est dix heures.**

→ To distinguish between A.M. and P.M., the French use the following expressions:

du matin	*in the morning*	Il est dix heures **du matin.**
de l'après-midi	*in the afternoon*	Il est deux heures **de l'après-midi.**
du soir	*in the evening*	Il est huit heures **du soir.**

NOTE DE PRONONCIATION: In telling time, the NUMBER and the word **heure(s)** are linked together. Remember, in French the letter "h" is always silent.

une heure   deux heures   trois heures   quatre heures   cinq heures   six heures
         z   z   k   z

sept heures   huit heures   neuf heures   dix heures   onze heures
     t   t   v   z

Leçon 4 **27**

▭ **Leçon 4, Section 2**

① PRACTICE: asking and telling the time

1. Il est trois heures.
2. Il est six heures.
3. Il est une heure.
4. Il est neuf heures.
5. Il est onze heures.
6. Il est midi.
7. Il est minuit.

② ROLE PLAY: talking about time

1. cinq heures / six heures
2. dix heures / onze heures
3. huit heures / neuf heures
4. deux heures / trois heures
5. midi / une heure

■ **If students ask:** French uses *mais* (*but*) for emphasis, much as English uses *why*.
Compare: **Mais non!** *Why no!*

🖥 **4.5 Vignette culturelle: L'heure officielle** (29:35–32:01 min.)

🌐 **Cross-cultural observation**
As is described in the video, the French use a 24-hour clock on timetables and TV schedules:
1 P.M. = 13h (treize heures)
8 P.M. = 20h (vingt heures)
• To go from P.M. to the 24-hour clock, add 12 hours:
  1 P.M. = 1 + 12 = 13 heures
• To go from the 24-hour clock to P.M., simply subtract 12 hours:
  20 heures = 20 – 12 = 8 P.M.

▭ **Leçon 4, Section 6** (optional)

TPR 🏃 **Telling time**

PROP: Clock with movable hands

Move the hands of the clock to show the hours and give the corresponding times.
  Quelle heure est-il? Il est une heure.
  Il est deux heures. etc.

Call on individual students to move the hands of the clock as you give the time.
  Il est cinq heures.
  X, viens ici. Montre-nous cinq heures.

T27

4.3 À quelle heure est le film?
4.4 Mini-scenes: Indicating at what time an event occurs
4.5 Vignette culturelle: L'heure officielle (28:45–32:01 min.)

 Leçon 4, Section 3

■ **If students ask:** To refer to *clock time*, the French use the word **heure:**
Quelle heure est-il?
To talk about *time* in the general sense, they use the word **temps:**
Nous avons le temps.

Pour communiquer

 Transparency 6
Clock face

 Leçon 4, Section 4

■ **Language notes:**
• Since people use digits when writing out times, students at the basic level do not need to spell these phrases out. (Therefore, the spelling **demi** as in **midi et demi**, is not presented here.)

• **Expansion:** You may want to introduce **moins** + *minutes*, as in **deux heures moins dix.** At the basic level, students can simply say **une heure cinquante.** This is becoming more and more common with the increased use of digital clocks in France.

B. À quelle heure est le film?

Stéphanie and David have decided to go to a movie.

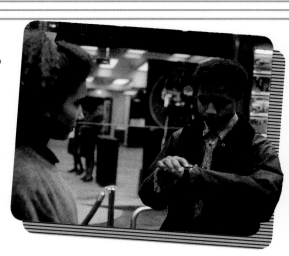

STÉPHANIE:	Quelle heure est-il?
DAVID:	Il est trois heures et demie.
STÉPHANIE:	Et à quelle heure est le film?
DAVID:	À quatre heures et quart.
STÉPHANIE:	Ça va. Nous avons le temps.

STÉPHANIE:	*What time is it?*
DAVID:	*It's three-thirty (half past three).*
STÉPHANIE:	*And at what time is the movie?*
DAVID:	*At four-fifteen (quarter past four).*
STÉPHANIE:	*That's okay. We have time.*

POUR COMMUNIQUER

À quelle heure est le dîner?

How to ask at what time something is scheduled:

À quelle heure est …?   *At what time is … ?*
—À quelle heure est le concert?   *At what time is the concert?*
—Le concert est à huit heures.   *The concert is at eight.*

How to say that you have an appointment or a date:

J'ai un rendez-vous à …   *I have an appointment (a date) at …*   **J'ai un rendez-vous à deux heures.**

How to indicate the minutes:

Il est …	dix heures dix	six heures vingt-cinq	sept heures trente-cinq	deux heures cinquante-deux

How to indicate the half hour and the quarter hours:

 et quart   **et demie**   **moins le quart**

 Il est une heure **et quart.**   Il est deux heures **et demie.**   Il est trois heures **moins le quart.**

28 Unité 1

TPR Quarter hours and minutes

PROP: clock with movable hands

Model the quarter hours and minutes, moving the hands on the clock.
    Il est trois heures et quart. etc.
Have students show the times on the clock.
    X, montre-nous cinq heures dix.

Send two students to the board to write the times as you say them.
    Y et Z, venez au tableau.
    Il est dix heures vingt. Écrivez l'heure. [Students write: "10h20".]
Students at their desks can also write down the times.

3 L'heure

Give the times according to the clocks.

▶ Il est une heure et quart.

▶   **1** **2** **3** **4** **5**

4 À quelle heure?

Ask your classmates at what time certain activities are scheduled. They will answer according to the information below.

▶ 8 h 50   le film
—À quelle heure est le film?
—Le film est à huit heures cinquante.

1. 7 h 15   le concert
2. 2 h 30   le match de football *(soccer)*
3. 3 h 45   le match de tennis
4. 5 h 10   le récital
5. 7 h 45   le dîner

Musée d'Orsay
Festival de cinéma
12h15   18F

5 Rendez-vous

Isabelle has appointments with various classmates and teachers. Look at her notebook and act out her dialogues with Philippe.

▶ ISABELLE: **J'ai un rendez-vous avec Marc.**
PHILIPPE: **À quelle heure?**
ISABELLE: **À onze heures trente.**

▶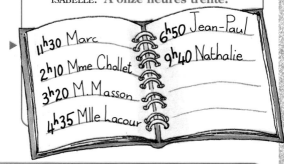

11h30 Marc
2h10 Mme Chollet
3h20 M. Masson
4h35 Mlle Lacour
6h50 Jean-Paul
9h40 Nathalie

6 À la gare *(At the train station)*

You are at the information desk of a French train station. Travelers ask you the departure times for the following trains. Answer them according to the posted schedule.

▶ le train de Nice

À quelle heure est le train de Nice?

Le train de Nice est à six heures dix.

▶

DÉPARTS			
NICE ◆ 6 h 10	TOULON	◆	9 h 35
LYON ◆ 7 h 15	COLMAR	◆	10 h 40
CANNES ◆ 7 h 30	TOULOUSE	◆	10 h 45
TOURS ◆ 8 h 12	MARSEILLE	◆	10 h 50
DIJON ◆ 8 h 25	BORDEAUX	◆	10 h 55

Leçon 4 **29**

---

3 PRACTICE: telling time

1. Il est deux heures trente (deux heures et demie).
2. Il est trois heures quarante cinq (quatre heures moins le quart).
3. Il est quatre heures quinze (quatre heures et quart).
4. Il est six heures trente (six heures et demie).
5. Il est dix heures quarante-cinq (onze heures moins le quart).

4 EXCHANGES: asking and answering questions about time of events

■ **If students ask**
• The "h" dividing the hours from the minutes in French stands for **heures** and corresponds to the colon used in English.
• U.S. football is **le football américain.**

▭ **Leçon 4, Section 5**

5 EXCHANGES: discussing appointment times

6 ROLE PLAY: asking and answering questions about train schedules

■ **Variation** (easier format):
— À quelle heure est le train de Nice?
— À six heures dix.

🌐 Geography skills

PROP: Transparency 1

As a warm-up, have individual students point to the cities in Act. 6 on the transparency.
X, viens ici et montre-nous Nice. [Voici Nice.]

Have the other students point to the same cities on the map of France in their book, p. R4.

À votre tour 1

MAIN TOPIC:

Recapitulation and review

1 COMPREHENSION

1-a   4-c
2-f   5-d
3-e   6-b

🔲 **AVT 1, Section 1**

2 GUIDED ORAL EXPRESSION

🔲 **AVT 1, Section 2**

■ **Speaking practice**
• Play the cassette, stopping after each question to elicit various student answers.
• Play the cassette activity straight through, having students whisper their answers quickly in the pauses.
• Play the cassette again, pointing to individual students to give their answers in the pauses.

3 GUIDED ORAL EXPRESSION

Sample dialogue:
JP: Bonjour
J: Bonjour. Ça va?
JP: Oui, ça va.
J: Comment t'appelles-tu?
JP: Je m'appelle Jean-Pierre. Et toi?
J: Je m'appelle Janet.
JP: Tu es anglaise?
J: Non, je suis américaine.
JP: Tu es de New York?
J: Non, je suis de San Francisco.

🔲 **AVT 1, Section 3**

T30

À votre tour!

1 Nathalie et Marc

It is the first day of school. Nathalie is talking to Marc and you hear parts of their conversation. For each of Nathalie's greetings or questions, select Marc's reply from the suggested responses on the right.

1 Salut!

2 Ça va?

3 Comment t'appelles-tu?

4 Tu es français?

5 Quelle heure est-il?

6 Au revoir!

• Bonjour!
• Au revoir!
• Non, je suis canadien.
• Il est deux heures moins le quart.
• Marc Boutin.
• Oui, ça va bien! Merci!

2 Et toi?

You and Nathalie meet at a sidewalk café. Respond to her greetings and questions.

1. Salut! Ça va?
2. Comment t'appelles-tu?
3. Tu es canadien (canadienne)?
4. Quelle heure est-il?
5. Oh là là. J'ai un rendez-vous dans (in) dix minutes. Au revoir.

3 Conversation dirigée

Two students, Jean-Pierre and Janet, meet on the Paris-Lyon train. With a partner, compose and act out their dialogue according to the suggested script.

Jean-Pierre				**Janet**
	says hello	→	responds and asks how things are	
	says things are fine	→	asks him what his name is	
	says his name is Jean-Pierre . . . asks her name	→	says her name is Janet	
	asks her if she is English	→	says no and responds that she is American	
	asks her if she is from New York	→	replies that she is from San Francisco	

30 Unité 1

À votre tour

The communicative activities in this section move from closely structured (Act. 1) to more open-ended (Act. 5).

Select those activities which are most appropriate for you students. You may or may not wish to do them all.

Cooperative practice

Pair work: Students do the activities in pairs. For Act. 1, 3, and 4, they can check their work by listening to the cassette tape.

Trios: Students work in groups of 3. Two students perform a dialogue. The third reads the Answer Key and acts as monitor.

4 Minidialogues

Create original dialogues on the basis of the pictures below.

1. David et Nicole

2. Monsieur Bertin et Mademoiselle Laval

3. Florence et Alain

4. Jean-Pierre et Sylvie

5. Thomas et Nicole

5 En scène

With a classmate, act out the following scene.

CHARACTERS:

You and a French exchange student

SITUATION:

You are at a party and meet a French exchange student who is happy to respond to your greetings and questions.

- Greet the student.
- Ask how things are going.
- Introduce yourself and ask his/her name.
- Ask if he/she is French.
- Ask if he/she is from Paris.
- Say good-bye.

6 Les nombres

1. Select any number between 0 and 15 and give the next five numbers in sequence.

2. Select a number between 1 and 9. Use that number as a starting point and count by tens to 60.

▶ deux

   douze, vingt-deux, trente-deux, etc.

À votre tour **31**

---

4 GUIDED ORAL EXPRESSION

Sample dialogues:
1. D: Salut, Nicole.
   N: Salut, David.
2. M. B: Bonjour, mademoiselle.
   Mlle L: Bonjour, monsieur.
3. F: Bonjour, Alain. Ça va?
   A: Non, ça va mal.
4. JP: Salut, Sylvie. Ça va?
   S: Ça va très bien.
5. T: Je suis français. Et toi? Tu es américaine?
   N: Oui, je suis américaine. Je suis de Chicago. Et toi?
   T: Moi, je suis de Lyon.

🔲 AVT 1, Section 4

■ **Listening practice:** Play the sample exchanges.

■ **Cooperative practice:** Have students in pairs prepare their own exchanges.

5 GUIDED ORAL EXPRESSION

6 GUIDED ORAL EXPRESSION

📁 Oral portfolios

For an introduction to oral portfolio assessment, see the Front Matter for a complete description.

Divide the class into pairs. Either assign all students the same activity, or let each pair select an activity at the appropriate level of challenge.

Have the pairs prepare their dialogues and make an audio (or video) recording. (Be sure they introduce themselves on the recording: **Je m'appelle X. Moi, je m'appelle Y.**)

If time allows, play all the recordings for the entire class. Store the cassettes as part of each student's oral portfolio.

Entracte 1

OBJECTIVES:

- Reading skills development
- Development of cultural awareness

Oui, vous parlez français!

OBJECTIVE:

- Reading simple signs

 Entracte 1, Section 1

■ **Teaching strategy:**
Read each sign aloud. Have students raise their hands if the French word is spelled exactly like its English cognate.

■ **Pronunciation practice**
- Have students repeat the words on the signs after you (or after the cassette). Be sure they use an even rhythm and that they accent the <u>last</u> syllable only.
  **parking munici<u>pal</u>
  office de tou<u>risme</u>**
- Ask which two of the English equivalent words are accented on the last syllable. (hotel, garage)

■ **Cultural note:** In France, toilets are often identified with the letters WC (water closet) plus the picture of a man or woman. Sometimes the following abbreviations are used:
- men: **H (hommes)** or **M (messieurs)**
- women: **F (femmes)** or **D (dames)**

Oui, vous parlez *français!*

Yes, you speak French! If you were visiting a French city, you would be able to understand many of the signs around you.

Look at the words on the following signs and compare them to their English equivalents. Which ones are spelled exactly the same? Which ones are spelled a little differently? What are the differences?

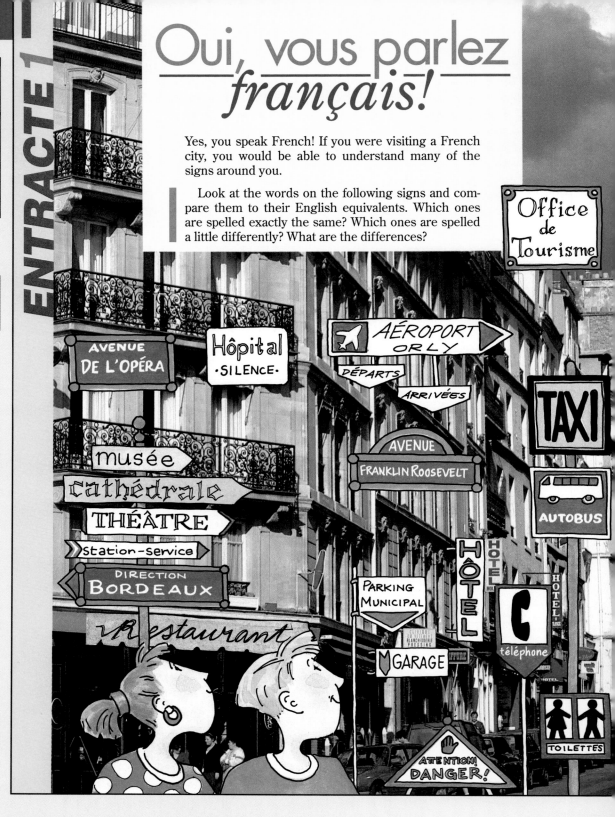

📖 Pre-reading

Play Section 1 of the cassette, with books closed. How many words can the class understand?

Then have students open their books and read the signs. They will probably understand them all. Play the cassette again as students read along.

Post-reading

Explain to students that words which look the same in both languages are called COGNATES. Stress that cognates in two languages are always <u>pronounced</u> <u>differently.</u>

La présence FRANÇAISE en Amérique

Between 1600 and 1750, the French explored large parts of Canada and the United States, which they called **La Nouvelle France** (New France). Today many American towns have French names, as you will see on the map below.

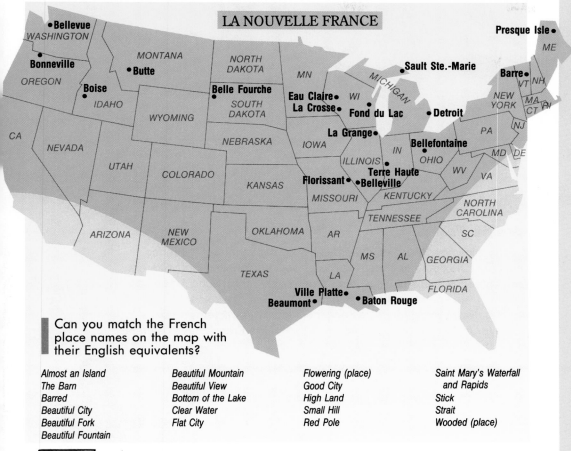

LA NOUVELLE FRANCE

Can you match the French place names on the map with their English equivalents?

Almost an Island	Beautiful Mountain	Flowering (place)	Saint Mary's Waterfall
The Barn	Beautiful View	Good City	and Rapids
Barred	Bottom of the Lake	High Land	Stick
Beautiful City	Clear Water	Small Hill	Strait
Beautiful Fork	Flat City	Red Pole	Wooded (place)
Beautiful Fountain			

Un jeu (game)

Many American cities were also named after:

• French people (such as King Louis XIV and his patron Saint Louis, General La Fayette, Napoleon, and of course, explorers like Champlain, Jolliet, Marquette, La Salle, Duluth, Dubuque)

• French cities (such as Paris, Montpellier, La Rochelle, Orléans)

In teams of three or four, see how many cities with French names you can locate on a map of the United States.

Entracte 1 ㉝

La présence française en Amérique

OBJECTIVE:
• Increasing student awareness of French place names in the United States

■ **Answers:**
Presque Isle (**presqu'île**), Maine
La Grange, Illinois
Barre (**barré**), Vermont
Belle Fourche, South Dakota
Bellefontaine, Ohio
Beaumont, Texas
Bellevue, Washington
Fond du Lac, Wisconsin
Eau Claire, Wisconsin
Ville Platte, Louisiana
Florissant, Missouri
Bonneville, Oregon
Terre Haute, Indiana
Butte, Montana
Baton Rouge, Louisiana
Sault Ste Marie, Michigan
La Crosse, Wisconsin
Detroit (**détroit**), Michigan
Boise (**boisé**), Idaho

■ **Cultural note:**
France lost the Eastern section of **Nouvelle France** to the British in 1763 at the end of the French-Indian War. Some of this land became part of the United States in 1776. In 1803, France sold the United States the territory which comprised the Mississippi basin (the Louisiana Purchase).

📖 Pre-reading activity

As an introduction to this selection, read the names of the cities aloud, first as they are said in America and then as they would be pronounced in France. Which ones sound most similar in the two languages?

Post-reading activity

Un jeu is a cooperative learning game.
VARIATION: Have students do their research as homework, and then have the teams pull together their answers in class the next day.

Un jeu can also be assigned for extra credit, or be developed into a wall map.

UNITÉ 2
Modules 5–8

5. Copain ou copine?
6. Une coïncidence
7. Les photos d'Isabelle
8. Le français pratique:
   Le jour et la date

UNITÉ 2 Les copains et la famille

INTRODUCTION

culturelle

L'amitié *(Friendship)*

Is friendship important to you? Friendship is very important to French teenagers. Of course, there are various levels of friendship and different types of friends: classmates whom we see every day in school, friends with whom we spend time outside of school, and the few special friends who are always there when we need them and who will remain our friends for the rest of our lives. As you will see, the French have different words to describe these various relationships.

LEÇON 5 Copain ou copine?

LEÇON 6 Une coïncidence

LEÇON 7 Les photos d'Isabelle

LEÇON 8 Le français pratique:
Le jour et la date

34

Unit overview

COMMUNICATION GOALS: Students will learn to introduce family and friends. They will also learn to identify dates and days of the week.

LINGUISTIC GOALS: The focus of this unit is on spoken French. Students learn about liaison and nasal vowels.

CRITICAL THINKING GOALS: Students begin to observe how gender influences form in French by contrasting masculine and feminine articles **un/une, le/la, mon/ma, ton/ta.**

CULTURAL GOALS: Students will become aware of the French concept of friendships and the importance of the French heritage in Québec, Canada.

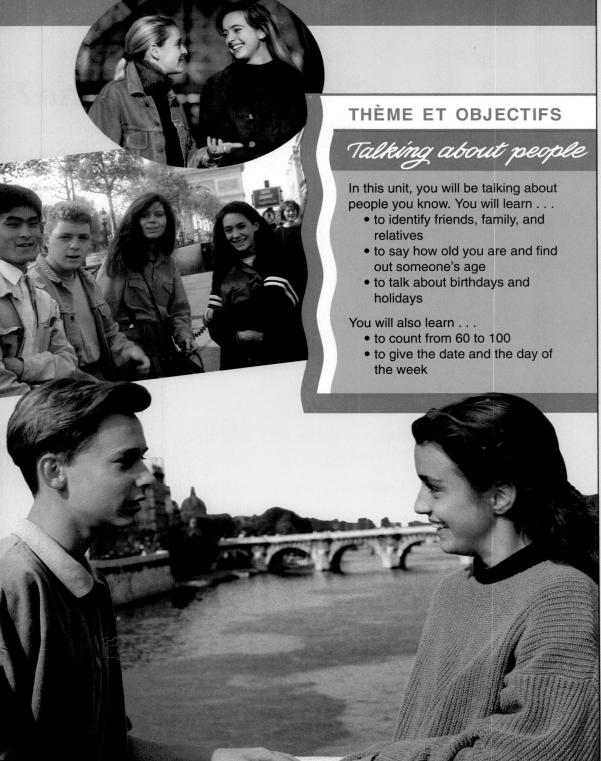

THÈME ET OBJECTIFS

Talking about people

In this unit, you will be talking about people you know. You will learn . . .
- to identify friends, family, and relatives
- to say how old you are and find out someone's age
- to talk about birthdays and holidays

You will also learn . . .
- to count from 60 to 100
- to give the date and the day of the week

🌐 **Cross-cultural observation**
Have students study the outdoor pictures carefully. These were taken in Paris.
- Can they find these well-known Parisian landmarks: the **Pont Neuf** ("new bridge") over the Seine and the **Arc de Triomphe**?
- Point out that French students often carry notebooks with graph paper rather than lined paper.

■ **Historical note:** Paris is over 2000 years old.
The **Pont Neuf** dates back to 1600.
The **Arc de Triomphe** was commissioned by Napoleon in 1806.

Pacing
Try to move through this unit rather quickly, concentrating on listening and speaking.

In Niveau B, students will encounter the same vocabulary again. At that time they will be expected to practice the material in writing.

MODULE 5:
Copain ou copine?
Total time: 3:23 min.
(Counter: 32:13 min.)

5.1 Dialogue: Copain ou copine?
(32:54–33:31 min.)
5.2 Mini-scenes: Listening — Pointing out people
(33:32–34:22 min.)
5.3 Vignette culturelle: La bande des copains
(34:23–35:31 min.)

■ **Comprehension practice:** Play the entire module through as an introduction to the lesson.

5.1 Dialogue: Copain ou copine?
(32:54–33:31 min.)

 Leçon 5, Section 1

Copain ou copine?

In French, there are certain girls' and boys' names that sound the same. Occasionally this can be confusing.

Dominique? Qui est-ce? Un copain ou une copine?

Scène 1. Philippe et Jean-Paul

Philippe is at home with his friend Jean-Paul. He seems to be expecting someone. Who could it be . . . ? The doorbell rings.

PHILIPPE: Tiens! Voilà Dominique!
JEAN-PAUL: Dominique? Qui est-ce? Un copain ou une copine?
PHILIPPE: C'est une copine.

Salut, Dominique! Ça va?

Scène 2. Philippe, Jean-Paul, Dominique

PHILIPPE: Salut, Dominique! Ça va?
DOMINIQUE: Oui, ça va! Et toi?
JEAN-PAUL: *(thinking)* C'est vrai! C'est une copine!

Scene 1. Philippe and Jean-Paul

PHILIPPE: *Hey! There's Dominique!*
JEAN-PAUL: *Dominique? Who's that? A boy(friend) or a girl(friend)?*
PHILIPPE: *A girl(friend).*

Scene 2. Philippe, Jean-Paul, Dominique

PHILIPPE: *Hi, Dominique! How's everything?*
DOMINIQUE: *Fine! And you?*
JEAN-PAUL: *(thinking) It's true! She is a girlfriend!*

36 Unité 2

Setting the stage

Ask students to think of names for boys and girls that sound the same.

For example: Kim, Lynn, Marty, Bobby/Bobbie, Gene/Jean.

In French, also, there are many boy's and girl's names that are pronounced alike.

Names spelled the same:
Dominique, Claude.
Names spelled differently:
René/Renée, André/Andrée, Joël/Joëlle, Noël/Noëlle, Michel/Michèle, Daniel/Danielle, Gabriel/Gabrielle, Frédéric/Frédérique.

POUR COMMUNIQUER

> Tiens! Voilà Caroline! C'est une copine!

How to introduce or point out someone:

Voici . . .　This is . . . , Here come(s) . . .

Voilà . . .　This (That) is . . . , There's . . .

Voici Jean-Paul.
Voici Nathalie et François.
Voilà Isabelle.
Voilà Philippe et Dominique.

How to find out who someone is:

Qui est-ce?　Who's that? Who is it?
C'est . . .　It's . . . , That's . . . , He's . . . , She's . . .

—**Qui est-ce?**
—**C'est** Patrick. **C'est** un copain.

How to get someone's attention or to express surprise:

Tiens!　Look! Hey!

Tiens, voilà Dominique!

Les personnes

un garçon	boy	**une fille**	girl
un ami	friend (male)	**une amie**	friend (female)
un copain	friend (male)	**une copine**	friend (female)
un monsieur	gentleman	**une dame**	lady
un prof	teacher	**une prof**	teacher

NOTE CULTURELLE

Amis et copains

French young people, like their American counterparts, enjoy spending time with their friends. They refer to their friends as **un ami** (for a boy) and **une amie** (for a girl) or — more commonly — as **un copain** or **une copine.** Note that the words **copain, copine** can also have special meanings. When a boy talks about **une copine,** he is referring to a friend who is a girl. However, when he says **ma** *(my)* **copine,** he may be referring to his girlfriend. Similarly, a girl would call her boyfriend **mon copain.**

Leçon 5　37

Pour communiquer

Language note: The expression **voilà** may also mean *That is, There is, There are.*
One can say: **C'est qui? Qui c'est?**

Transparency 7
Les personnes

5.2 Mini-scenes: Pointing out people (33:32–34:22 min.)

Note culturelle

5.3 Vignette culturelle: La bande des copains (34:23–35:31 min.)

Cultural note: There are several ways of referring to one's boyfriend or girlfriend:
- **mon petit ami, ma petite amie** (though these terms are not as commonly used as several years ago)
- **mon petit copain, ma petite copine**
- **mon ami, mon amie**
The possessive is used to signal a more personal relationship.

Language note:
Un prof/une prof. In casual speech, both teachers and students in France use the terms **un prof** and **une prof.** These expressions are easier for beginners and are therefore introduced here in Niveau A. The more formal term **un professeur,** which refers to both men and women, is introduced in Niveau B, Lesson 17.

TPR　**Nouns with un/une**

PROPS: Transparency 7
Red and blue index cards
Model new words on the transparency.
　Voici un garçon. Voici une fille. …
Have students come point out the words.
　X, viens ici. Montre-nous une fille.
Distribute two cards to each student.

Voici "un". [Hold up the blue card.]
Voici "une". [Hold up the red card.]
As you make statements using the new words, have students hold up their cards.
C'est un copain. Levez la carte bleue.
C'est une amie. Levez la carte rouge.
C'est un ami. [blue cards.]

Petit commentaire

• The **Tour de France,** which was created in 1904, is a month-long bicycle race that takes cyclists around France, with particularly grueling stages **(étapes)** in the Alps and the Pyrenees. Every year the route is somewhat different, but the finish line is always in Paris at the bottom of the Champs Elysées.

• The **Tour de France féminin** began in 1984. From 1987 to 1989, it was dominated by the French cyclist Jeannie Longo.

Petit commentaire

*Cycling is a popular competitive sport throughout France. The most popular races are the **Tour de France** and the **Tour de France féminin,** which take place every year in July. French women cyclists have won many world titles.*

---

un garçon, une fille

In French, all NOUNS are either MASCULINE or FEMININE.
Nouns referring to boys or men are almost always MASCULINE.
 They are introduced by **un** *(a, an).*
Nouns referring to girls or women are almost always FEMININE.
 They are introduced by **une** *(a, an).*

MASCULINE			FEMININE		
UN	**un** garçon	*a boy*	UNE	**une** fille	*a girl*
	un ami	*a friend (male)*		**une** amie	*a friend (female)*

---

① **PRACTICE:** identifying male and female friends

■ **Pronunciation:**
• Insist that students do not pronounce the "n" in **un** or **copain.**
• Note that liaison is common after **est:**
Christine est une copine.

② **ROLE PLAY:** meeting and identifying friends

■ **Pronunciation note:** Be sure students make the liaison in **un ami.**

③ **PRACTICE:** choosing genders

---

① **Copain ou copine?**

Say that the following people are your friends. Use **un copain** or **une copine,** as appropriate.

▶ **Christine est une copine.**

Christine

1. Alice

2. Marie-Jeanne

3. Éric

4. David

5. Sylvie

② **Les amis**

The same young people are visiting your school. Point them out to your classmates, using **un ami** or **une amie,** as appropriate.

▶ —**Tiens, voilà Christine!**
 —**Qui est-ce?**
 —**C'est une amie.**

③ **Un ou une?**

Identify the people below by completing the sentences with **un** or **une.**

1. Voici . . . fille.
2. Voilà . . . garçon.
3. Voici . . . dame.
4. C'est . . . amie.
5. Olivier est . . . ami.
6. Jean-Paul est . . . copain.
7. Cécile est . . . copine.
8. Voici Mlle Lacour. C'est . . . prof.
9. Voici M. Masson. C'est . . . prof.
10. Voici Mme Chollet. C'est . . . prof.

38 Unité 2

Teaching notes: un/une

The concept of gender is presented formally in Niveau B. The focus in this lesson is on sound discrimination between **un** and **une.**

 • Saying **un:** Be sure that students pronounce **un** <u>without</u> a final /n/ — except in liaison.

 • Saying **une:** Have students think of **une** as "een" (and not "oon"). Then ask them to round their lips as they say "een." (This way students will begin to acquire the French pronunciation.)

4 À la fenêtre *(At the window)*

You and a friend are walking down the street and you see the following people at their windows. Identify them in short dialogues.

—Tiens, voilà un monsieur!
—Qui est-ce?
—C'est Monsieur Mercier.

Monsieur Mercier

1. Nicole   2. Mademoiselle Lasalle   3. Éric   4. Madame Albert   5. Monsieur Lavie   6. Alain

Les nombres de 60 à 79

60 soixante

61 soixante et un   66 soixante-six
62 soixante-deux   67 soixante-sept
63 soixante-trois   68 soixante-huit
64 soixante-quatre   69 soixante-neuf
65 soixante-cinq

70 soixante-dix

71 soixante et onze   76 soixante-seize
72 soixante-douze   77 soixante-dix-sept
73 soixante-treize   78 soixante-dix-huit
74 soixante-quatorze   79 soixante-dix-neuf
75 soixante-quinze

➡ Note that in counting from 70 to 79, the French continue adding numbers to 60:
70 = 60 + 10   71 = 60 + 11   72 = 60 + 12, etc.

5 Numéros de téléphone

Read aloud the phone numbers of Jean-Paul's friends in Paris.

▶ Philippe   quarante-deux, soixante et un, dix-neuf, soixante-quinze

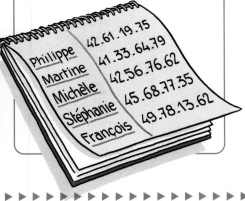

Philippe 42.61.19.75
Martine 41.33.64.79
Michèle 42.56.76.62
Stéphanie 45.68.77.35
François 49.78.13.62

Prononciation

La liaison

un ami

Pronounce the following words:

un ami   un Américain   un Anglais   un artiste

In general, the "n" of un is silent. However, in the above words, the "n" of un is pronounced as if it were the *first* letter of the next word. The two words are *linked* together in LIAISON.

Liaison occurs between two words when the second one begins with a VOWEL SOUND, that is, with "a", "e", "i", "o", "u", and sometimes "h" and "y".

➡ Although liaison is not marked in written French, it will be indicated in your book by the symbol ‿ where appropriate.

Contrastez et répétez:

LIAISON: un ami   un Américain   un Italien   un artiste
NO LIAISON: un copain   un Français   un Canadien   un prof

Leçon 5   39

▷ **Les nombres de 60 à 79**

4 ROLE PLAY: discussing the identity of people

■ Encourage varied responses.

▷ **Les nombres de 60 à 79**

🔲 Leçon 5, Section 3

■ If students ask: From 1 to 60, French uses the Roman system of counting by 10s. However, from 60 to 100, the French count by scores (or 20s). This system was brought to England and Normandy in the tenth century by the Vikings or Norsemen.

■ Pronunciation: Remind students that there is no liaison after et: soixante et un, soixante et onze.

5 PRACTICE: reading numbers up to 79

■ Cultural note: Paris phone numbers consist of 8 digits read in groups of two. The first digit for Paris is always 4.
■ Listening comprehension: Have students close their books. Slowly dictate the numbers from the phone list. Then have students open their books to correct their work as you read the numbers once more.

Prononciation

🔲 Leçon 5, Section 4

■ Pronunciation: You may want to point out that similar linking occurs in English after an: an apple, an uncle, an hour.

■ If students ask: Adjectives of nationality are capitalized when they are used as nouns referring to people.

✖ Game: Mini-loto (Numbers 60–79)

PREPARATION: Write the numbers from 60–79 on slips of paper (or use commercial bingo numbers).

Have students draw a tic-tac-toe grid and fill the nine squares with numbers of their choice between 60 and 79.

Call out the numbers as you draw the slips in random order. When a student has three numbers in a row in any direction, have him/her call out "Loto."

MODULE 6:
Une coïncidence
Total time: 4:42 min.
(Counter: 35:42 min.)

6.1 **Dialogue:**
Une coïncidence
(36:07–36:36 min.)
6.2 **Mini-scenes: Listening**
— Describing people
(36:37–38:16 min.)
6.3 **Vignette culturelle:**
Le Québec
(38:17–40:20 min.)

■ **Comprehension practice:** Play the entire module through as an introduction to the lesson.

6.1 Dialogue:
Une coïncidence
(36:07–36:36 min.)

Leçon 6, Section 1

LEÇON 6 — Une coïncidence

Isabelle is at a party with her new Canadian friend Marc. She wants him to meet some of the other guests.

Tu connais la fille là-bas?

Non. Qui est-ce?

C'est une copine. Elle s'appelle Juliette Savard.

Elle est française?

Non, elle est canadienne. Elle est de Montréal.

Moi aussi!

Quelle coïncidence!

ISABELLE: *Do you know the girl over there?*
MARC: *No. Who is she?*
ISABELLE: *She's a friend. Her name is Juliette Savard.*

MARC: *Is she French?*
ISABELLE: *No, she's Canadian. She is from Montreal.*
MARC: *Me too!*
ISABELLE: *What a coincidence!*

40 Unité 2

☀ **Warm-up and review: Nationalities**

PROP: Transparency 4

Ask students to give names to the 8 people, and write these names on the transparency next to each of the figures.

Pointing to the figures, have the students identify them.

Qui est-ce? [C'est Marie.]

Then, having the students take the role of the figure, ask their nationalities.

Marie, tu es française?
[Oui je suis française.]
Marie, tu es anglaise?
[Non, je suis française.]

POUR
COMMUNIQUER

> Tu connais la dame?

> Oui, elle s'appelle Madame Leblanc.

▸ How to inquire about people:

Tu connais . . . ?	*Do you know . . . ?*	**Tu connais** Jean-Paul?

▸ How to describe people and give their nationalities:

Il est . . .	*He is . . .*	**Il est** canadien.
Elle est . . .	*She is . . .*	**Elle est** canadienne.

▸ How to find out another person's name:

Comment s'appelle . . . ?	*What's the name of . . . ?*	**Comment s'appelle** le garçon?
		Comment s'appelle la fille?
Il s'appelle . . .	*His name is . . .*	**Il s'appelle** Marc.
Elle s'appelle . . .	*Her name is . . .*	**Elle s'appelle** Juliette.

■ NOTE ■
CULTURELLE

Montréal et la province de Québec

In population, metropolitan Montreal is the second-largest city in Canada. After Paris, it is also the second-largest French-speaking city in the world.

Montreal is located in the province of Quebec, where French is the official language. In fact, French speakers represent over 90% of the population. These people are the descendants of French settlers who came to Canada in the 17th and 18th centuries. If you visit Montreal, you will discover that the people of Quebec **(les Québécois)** are very proud of their heritage and dedicated to maintaining French as their language.

Leçon 6 41

Petit commentaire
Cross-cultural understanding
If students want to host a French student, they may contact Nacel (a non-profit organization that arranges student exchanges): 301 W. First St. #528, Duluth, MN 55802.

▷ **le garçon, la fille**

 Leçon 2, Section 2

■ **If students ask**
• The dropping of a final "e" (or "a," in the case of **la**) is called ELISION.
• A word that begins with **a, e, i, o,** or **u** is said to begin with a VOWEL SOUND.

① PRACTICE: asking about people, using definite article

② EXCHANGES: identifying people

■ **Expansion:** Have each student bring in a picture of a known personality:
– **Tu connais ce monsieur?** (holding up picture of a man)
– **Oui, c'est Bill Cosby. (Non, qui est-ce?)**

③ EXCHANGES: discussing people's names

■ **Teaching note:** Students should learn to understand the numbers and pronounce them correctly. They should not be expected to spell the numbers. (See notes and activities on page 25.)

Petit commentaire

French teenagers are very much interested in the United States. They love American music and American movies. Every year, more and more French high school students come to visit our country either through exchange programs or summer homestays.

le garçon, la fille

The French equivalent of *the* has two basic forms: **le** and **la.**

	MASCULINE			FEMININE	
LE	**le** garçon	*the boy*	**LA**	**la** fille	*the girl*
	le copain	*the friend*		**la** copine	*the friend*

NOTE: Both **le** and **la** become **l'** before a vowel sound.

un copain → le copain   une copine → la copine
un ami → **l'**ami   une amie → **l'**amie

① Qui est-ce?

Ask who the following people are, using **le, la,** or **l'.**

▶ une prof
   Qui est la prof?

1. un monsieur   3. une fille   5. un prof   7. une amie
2. une dame   4. un garçon   6. un ami

② Tu connais . . . ?

Ask your classmates if they know the following people. They will answer that they do.

▶ une dame / Madame Vallée

Tu connais la dame?
Oui, c'est Madame Vallée.

1. un prof / Monsieur Simon
2. un garçon / Christophe
3. une fille / Sophie
4. une dame / Mademoiselle Lenoir
5. une prof / Madame Boucher
6. un monsieur / Monsieur Duval

③ Comment s'appelle . . . ?

Ask the names of the following people, using the words **le garçon, la fille.** A classmate will respond.

▶ —**Comment s'appelle la fille?**
   —**Elle s'appelle Stéphanie.**

▶ **Stéphanie**   **1. Marc**   **2. Juliette**   **3. Franço**

4. Jean-Paul   **5. Nathalie**   **6. Philippe**   **7. Isabel**

42   **Unité 2**

TPR **Nouns with le/la**

PROPS: Cards with people of Transparency 7
Optional: red and blue index cards

Place the picture cards on the chalkboard tray. To review, have students point out people.
  X, viens ici. Montre-nous un garçon.
  Montre-nous une dame ....

Hand out the pictures to the class.
  Voici le prof. Je donne le prof à Y.
  Qui a le prof? [answer: Y]
Have students pass around the cards.
  Y, prends le garçon et donne-le à Z.
OPTIONAL: Describe classroom objects; have students raise blue (**le**) or red (**la**) cards:
  Voici le bureau. [blue]
  Voici la porte. [red]

4 Français, anglais ou américain?

Give the nationalities of the following people.

▶ Jane Fonda?
  Elle est américaine.

1. le prince Charles?
2. la princesse Diana?
3. Catherine Deneuve?

4. Vanna White?
5. Pierre Cardin?
6. Bill Cosby?

7. Oprah Winfrey?
8. Tom Cruise?
9. Paul McCartney?

Les nombres de 80 à 100

80 quatre-vingts

81 quatre-vingt-un	86 quatre-vingt-six
82 quatre-vingt-deux	87 quatre-vingt-sept
83 quatre-vingt-trois	88 quatre-vingt-huit
84 quatre-vingt-quatre	89 quatre-vingt-neuf
85 quatre-vingt-cinq	

90 quatre-vingt-dix

91 quatre-vingt-onze	96 quatre-vingt-seize
92 quatre-vingt-douze	97 quatre-vingt-dix-sept
93 quatre-vingt-treize	98 quatre-vingt-dix-huit
94 quatre-vingt-quatorze	99 quatre-vingt-dix-neuf
95 quatre-vingt-quinze	

100 cent

➡ Note that in counting from 80 to 99, the French add numbers to the base of **quatre-vingts** *(fourscore):*

$$80 = 4 \times 20 \qquad 90 = 4 \times 20 + 10$$
$$85 = 4 \times 20 + 5 \qquad 99 = 4 \times 20 + 19$$

---

5 Au téléphone

In France, the telephone area code (**l'indicatif**) is always a two-digit number. Your teacher will name a city (**une ville**) from the chart. Give the corresponding area code.

▶ Nice?
  C'est le quatre-vingt-treize.

VILLE	INDICATIF
Albi	63
Avignon	90
Cannes	93
Dijon	80
Marseille	91
Montpellier	67
Nancy	83
Nice	93
Nîmes	66
Rennes	99
Saint-Tropez	94
Strasbourg	88
Vichy	70

Prononciation /ɛ̃/

La voyelle nasale /ɛ̃/

In French, there are three nasal vowel sounds:

/ɛ̃/ **cinq** (5) /ɔ̃/ **onze** (11) /ɑ̃/ **trente** (30)

Practice the sound /ɛ̃/ in the following words. Note that this vowel sound can have several different spellings.

➡ Be sure not to pronounce an "**n**" or "**m**" after the nasal vowel.

Répétez:
"in" ci**n**q qui**n**ze vi**ngt** vi**ngt**-ci**n**q quatre-vi**ngt**-qui**n**ze
"ain" américai**n** Alai**n** copai**n**
"(i)en" bie**n** canadie**n** tie**n**s!
"un" u**n**

Tien**s! Voilà Alai**n**. Il est américai**n**. E**t** Julie**n**? Il est canadie**n**.

$$5$$
cinq

Game: Numbers 11 to 99

PROPS: Four sets of the numbers 0–9 on index cards

Divide the class into two teams. Have two students from each team come to the front, stand side by side, and face the class. Give each student a set of the numbers 0–9.

Say a number in French: e.g., **vingt-cinq**! The first pair to hold up the correct cards [2 and 5] wins a point for its team.

  You may wish to teach your students the expressions **Bravo!** (Great!), **Allez-y!** (Go for it!), and **C'est dommage!** (That's too bad!).

Right margin (teacher notes)

4 DESCRIPTION: discussing people's nationalities

1. anglais	6. américain
2. anglaise	7. américaine
3. française	8. américain
4. américaine	9. anglais
5. français	

▷ **Les nombres de 80 à 100**

🔊 Leçon 6, Section 3

■ **Language note:** Compare: **quatre-vingt-sept** = "Fourscore and seven years ago..." (opening words of the Gettysburg address)

■ **Pronunciation:** There is no liaison between **quatre-vingt** and the numbers **un, huit, onze.**

5 COMPREHENSION: identifying telephone area codes

■ **Variation: Quel est l'indicatif de Nice?**

■ **Map work:** You may want to have students locate these cities on a map of France (p. R4 in the student text or on Transparency 1).

■ **Cultural notes**
• Outside of Paris, the **indicatif** is now part of the local phone number. (All numbers have 8 digits.)
• For the Paris area, the indicatif is "1" and is used only for long distance calls.

Prononciation

🔊 Leçon 6, Section 4

■ **Pronunciation:** Some French people still distinguish between /ɛ̃/ (**in**) and /œ̃/ (**un**). However, most French speakers use only the nasal vowel /ɛ̃/. For simplicity, we are not introducing the nasal /œ̃/ at this level.

MODULE 7:
Les photos d'Isabelle
Total time: 5:32 min.
(Counter: 40:30 min.)

7.1 Dialogue: Les photos d'Isabelle
(40:45–41:16 min.)
7.2 Monologue: La famille d'Isabelle
(41:17–42:33 min.)
7.3 Mini-scenes: How old are you?
(42:34–44:13 min.)
7.4 Vignette culturelle: La famille française: un mariage
(44:14–45:57 min.)

■ **Comprehension practice:** Play the entire module through as an introduction to the lesson.

7.1 Dialogue: Les photos d'Isabelle
(40:45–41:16 min.)

Leçon 7, Section 1

LEÇON 7 Les photos d'Isabelle

Isabelle is showing her family photo album to her friend Jean-Paul.

ISABELLE: Voici ma mère.
JEAN-PAUL: Et le monsieur, c'est ton père?
ISABELLE: Non, c'est mon oncle Thomas.
JEAN-PAUL: Et la fille, c'est ta cousine?
ISABELLE: Oui, c'est ma cousine Béatrice. Elle a seize ans.
JEAN-PAUL: Et le garçon, c'est ton cousin?
ISABELLE: Non, c'est un copain.
JEAN-PAUL: Un copain ou ton copain?
ISABELLE: Dis donc, Jean-Paul, tu es vraiment trop curieux!

ma mère

mon oncle Thomas

ma cousine Béatrice

??

ISABELLE: This is my mother.
JEAN-PAUL: And the man, is he your father?
ISABELLE: No, that's my uncle Thomas.
JEAN-PAUL: And the girl, is she your cousin?
ISABELLE: Yes, that's my cousin Béatrice. She's sixteen.

JEAN-PAUL: And the boy, is he your cousin?
ISABELLE: No, that's a friend.
JEAN-PAUL: A friend or a boyfriend?
ISABELLE: Hey there, Jean-Paul, you are really too curious!

44 Unité 2

☀ Warm-up and review: Copains et copines

Ask questions about students in the class:
[Point to a girl] **Qui est-ce?** [C'est Anne.]
Est-ce que c'est un garçon ou une fille?
[C'est une fille.]
C'est un copain ou une copine?
[C'est une copine.]

Address a boy in the class:
Et toi, est-ce qu'Anne est une copine ou ta copine?
[C'est une copine. or: C'est ma copine.]
Ask similar questions about other students.

POUR COMMUNIQUER

Voici mon chien Malice.

How to introduce your family:

Voici mon père.   This is my father.
Et voici ma mère.   And this is my mother.

La famille *(Family)*

un frère	brother	**une soeur**	sister
un cousin	cousin	**une cousine**	cousin
un père	father	**une mère**	mother
un oncle	uncle	**une tante**	aunt
un grand-père	grandfather	**une grand-mère**	grandmother

Les animaux domestiques *(Pets)*

MIAOU

OUAF OUAF

un chat   **un chien**

■ NOTE ■ CULTURELLE

La famille française

When you and your friends talk about your families, you usually are referring to your brothers, sisters, and parents. In French, however, **la famille** refers not only to parents and children but also to grandparents, aunts, uncles, cousins, as well as a whole array of more distant relatives related by blood and marriage.

Since the various members of a family often live in the same region, French teenagers see their grandparents and cousins fairly frequently. Even when relatives do not live close by, the family finds many occasions to get together: for weekend visits, during school and summer vacations, on holidays, as well as on special occasions such as weddings and anniversaries.

Leçon 7 **45**

Pour communiquer

 7.2 Monologue: La famille d'Isabelle (41:17–42:33 min.)

 Leçon 7, Section 2

Transparency 8
Family tree

Supplementary vocabulary

FAMILY

un beau-père	stepfather
une belle-mère	stepmother
un beau-frère	stepbrother
une belle-soeur	stepsister
un demi-frère	halfbrother
une demi-soeur	halfsister

PETS

un hamster /ɛ̃amstɛr /, no liaison	
un cochon d'Inde	Guinea pig
un poisson rouge	goldfish
une souris blanche	white mouse
un oiseau	bird
une perruche	parakeet
un serpent	snake

Note culturelle

 7.3 Vignette culturelle: La famille française: un mariage (44:14–45:57 min.)

Cross-cultural observation
Ask students if they have ever attended a wedding. Discuss the similarities and differences between French and American weddings, pointing out especially the dual ceremony (church/**mairie**) in France.

TPR The family

PROP: Transparency 8
Describe the various family relationships, pointing to the transparency.

> **François Mallet est le père de Véronique.**
> **M. Mallet est aussi le père de Frédéric....**

Ask students to point out family members.

> **X, viens à l'écran. Montre-nous la cousine de Catherine. ...**

FOLLOW-UP: Ask the names of people.

> **Comment s'appelle le frère de Véronique?**
> [Il s'appelle Frédéric Mallet.]

Petit commentaire

The French people love pets, especially cats
and dogs. What is important is the animal's
personality and friendliness rather than its
pedigree. Some common names given to
animals are:

Minou, Pompon, Fifi *(cats)*
Titus, Milou, Médor *(dogs)*

mon cousin, ma cousine

The French equivalents of *my* and *your* have the following forms:

MASCULINE			FEMININE		
mon cousin	*my cousin (male)*		**ma** cousine	*my cousin (female)*
mon frère	*by brother*		**ma** soeur	*my sister*
ton cousin	*your cousin (male)*		**ta** cousine	*your cousin (female)*
ton frère	*your brother*		**ta** soeur	*your sister*

→ Note that the feminine **ma** becomes **mon** and the feminine **ta** becomes **ton** before a
vowel sound. Liaison is required.

une amie → **mon** amie **ton** amie

① **L'album de photos**

You are showing a friend your photo album. Identify the following people, using **mon** and **ma,**
as appropriate.

▶ cousine Jacqueline   **Voici ma cousine Jacqueline.**

1. frère
2. soeur
3. tante Monique
4. oncle Pierre
5. père
6. mère
7. copain Nicolas
8. ami Jérôme
9. copine Pauline
10. amie Florence
11. grand-mère Michèle
12. grand-père Robert
13. chien Toto
14. chat Minou
15. cousine Sophie

② **Comment s'appelle . . . ?**

Ask your classmates to name some of their friends,
relatives, and pets. They can invent names if they wish.

▶ le copain

1. l'oncle
2. la tante
3. le cousin
4. la cousine
5. la copine
6. le grand-père
7. la grand-mère
8. le chien
9. le chat

Comment s'appelle
ton copain?

Mon copain s'appelle
Bob.

 Warm-up and review: Numbers

Divide the class in half: side A and side B.
Point to side A and say a number. Then
point to side B and say another number.
Students on the side with the higher
number raise their hands.

A – 22. B – 35. [Students on Side B raise
their hands.]
A – 89. B – 64. [Students on Side A raise
their hands.]

POUR COMMUNIQUER

COMMUNICATION

Quel âge as-tu?

J'ai treize ans.

How to find out how old a friend is:

Quel âge as-tu?	*How old are you?*	—**Quel âge as-tu?**
J'ai . . . ans.	*I'm . . . (years old).*	—**J'ai treize ans.**

How to ask about how old others are:

—**Quel âge a ton père?**	*How old is your father?*
—**Il a quarante-deux ans.**	*He is 42 (years old).*
—**Quel âge a ta mère?**	*How old is your mother?*
—**Elle a trente-neuf ans.**	*She is 39 (years old).*

➡ Although *years old* may be left out in English, the word **ans** must be used in French when talking about someone's age.

Il a vingt ans.	*He's twenty. (He's twenty years old.)*

3 Quel âge as-tu?

Ask your classmates how old they are.

▶ —**Quel âge as-tu?**
　—**J'ai (treize) ans.**

4 Joyeux anniversaire!
(Happy birthday!)

Ask your classmates how old the following people are.

Stéphanie

▶ —**Quel âge a Stéphanie?**
　—**Elle a quatorze ans.**

1. Éric

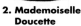
2. Mademoiselle Doucette

3. Monsieur Boucher

4. Madame Dupont

5. Monsieur Camus

6. Madame Simon

5 Curiosité

Find out the ages of your classmates' friends and relatives. If they are not sure, they can guess or invent an answer.

▶ la copine　—**Quel âge a ta copine?**
　　　　　　　—**Ma copine a (treize) ans.**

1. le père　　4. la tante　　7. le grand-père
2. la mère　　5. le cousin　　8. la grand-mère
3. l'oncle　　6. la cousine

Prononciation　　/ã/　　/ɔ̃/

Les voyelles nasales /ã/ et /ɔ̃/

tante　oncle

The letters "**an**" and "**en**" usually represent the nasal vowel /ã/. Be sure not to pronounce an "n" after the nasal vowel.

Répétez: **ans　tante　grand-père　français　anglais　quarante　cinquante　trente　comment　Henri　Laurent**

The letters "**on**" represent the nasal vowel /ɔ̃/. Be sure not to pronounce an "n" after the nasal vowel.

Répétez: **non　mon　ton　bonjour　oncle　garçon　onze**

Contrastez: **an—on　tante—ton　onze—ans**
Mon oncle François a trente ans.

Teaching strategy: Ages

PROP: Transparency 8

Ask students to determine the ages of the people on the transparency.

　–**Quel âge a Frédéric?**
　– [Student X]: **Il a quinze ans.**
　– **Vous êtes d'accord?** *Do you agree?*

Write "15" in the box next to Frédéric. Have students assign ages to the other members of the family.

Then ask questions about the transparency.

　Qui a quarante ans?
　Quel âge a la soeur de Frédéric?

Pour communiquer

■ **Photographs:** On the beach at Deauville

🖥 **7.3 Mini-scenes: How old are you?**
(42:34–44:13 min.)

📼 Leçon 7, Section 3

■ **If students ask:** Literally, these sentences mean:
What age do you have?
I have thirteen years.

3 COMMUNICATION: asking how old someone is

4 PRACTICE: discussing people's ages

■ **Listening comprehension:** Ask the ages of these people in random order. Students write down the number of the corresponding birthday cake.
Qui a soixante-quatre ans? (4)
Qui a trente-deux ans? (3)
Qui a dix-huit ans? (1)
Qui a quatre-vingt-trois ans? (6)
Qui a vingt-cinq ans? (2)
Qui a soixante-quinze ans? (5)

5 COMMUNICATION: discussing friends' and relatives' ages

Prononciation

📼 Leçon 7, Section 4

■ **Pronunciation:**
• The combination **ien** is pronounced /jɛ̃/: **bien**
• Remind students that they should not pronounce an "n" after the nasal vowel.

T47

Leçon 8

MAIN TOPICS:

Talking about days of the week and dates

MODULE 8:
Le français pratique:
Le jour et la date
Total time: 5:47 min.
(Counter: 46:08 min.)

8.1 Dialogues:
A. Quel jour est-ce?
(46:45–47:11 min.)
B. Anniversaire
(47:12–47:34 min.)
8.2 Mini-scenes:
Dates and birthdays
(47:35–50:04 min.)
8.3 Vignette culturelle:
Joyeux anniversaire!
(50:05–51:48 min.)

■ **Comprehension practice:** Play the entire module through as an introduction to the lesson.

8.1 Dialogue: A. Quel jour est-ce?
(46:45–47:11 min.)

▭▭ Leçon 8, Section 1

LE FRANÇAIS PRATIQUE

Le jour et la date

A. Quel jour est-ce?

For many people, the days of the week are not all alike.

Dialogue 1. Vendredi

PHILIPPE: Quel jour est-ce?
STÉPHANIE: C'est vendredi.
PHILIPPE: Super! Demain, c'est samedi!

Super! Demain, c'est samedi!

Dialogue 2. Mercredi

NATHALIE: Ça va?
MARC: Pas très bien.
NATHALIE: Pourquoi?
MARC: Aujourd'hui, c'est mercredi.
NATHALIE: Et alors?
MARC: Demain, c'est jeudi! Le jour de l'examen.
NATHALIE: Zut! C'est vrai! Au revoir, Marc.
MARC: Au revoir, Nathalie. À demain!

Demain, c'est jeudi! Le jour de l'examen.

Dialogue 1. *Friday*
PHILIPPE: *What day is it?*
STÉPHANIE: *It's Friday.*
PHILIPPE: *Great! Tomorrow is Saturday!*

Dialogue 2. *Wednesday*
NATHALIE: *How are things?*
MARC: *Not very good.*
NATHALIE: *Why?*
MARC: *Today is Wednesday.*

NATHALIE: *So?*
MARC: *Tomorrow is Thursday! The day of the exam.*
NATHALIE: *Darn! That's right! Good-bye, Marc.*
MARC: *Good-bye, Nathalie. See you tomorrow!*

48 Unité 2

☀ **Warm-up and review: Ça va?**

Ask students how they are feeling, reviewing the expressions from Lesson 3. For example:
Bonjour, X. ça va?
[Oui, ça va très bien.]
Et toi, Y, ça va bien ou ça va mal?
[Ça va mal.]

Z, demande à W si ça va.
[–Bonjour W, ça va?
–Ça va comme ci, comme ça.]

POUR
COMMUNIQUER

How to talk about days of the week:

Quel jour est-ce?   *What day is it?*
  Aujourd'hui, c'est mercredi.   *Today is Wednesday.*
  Demain, c'est jeudi.   *Tomorrow is Thursday.*

How to tell people when you will see them again:

À samedi!   *See you Saturday!*
À demain!   *See you tomorrow!*

À samedi!

Les jours de la semaine *(Days of the week)*					
lundi	*Monday*	**vendredi**	*Friday*	**aujourd'hui**	*today*
mardi	*Tuesday*	**samedi**	*Saturday*	**demain**	*tomorrow*
mercredi	*Wednesday*	**dimanche**	*Sunday*		
jeudi	*Thursday*				

1 **Questions**
1. Quel jour est-ce aujourd'hui?
2. Et demain, quel jour est-ce?

2 **Un jour de retard** *(One day behind)*
Georges has trouble keeping track of the date. He is always one day behind. Monique corrects him.

▶ samedi

Aujourd'hui, c'est samedi?

Non, aujourd'hui, c'est dimanche!

1. lundi	3. jeudi	5. dimanche
2. mardi	4. vendredi	6. mercredi

3 **Au revoir!**
You are on the phone with the following friends. Say good-bye and tell them when you will see them.

▶ Christine / lundi
  Au revoir, Christine. À lundi.

1. David / dimanche
2. Roger / samedi
3. Delphine / mercredi
4. Sophie / vendredi
5. Alain / mardi
6. Éric / jeudi

Leçon 8   **49**

Pour communiquer

■ **Language note:** Also:
Quel jour sommes-nous?
Quel jour est-on?

■ **Casual speech:** One can say:
C'est quel jour?
On est quel jour?

Supplementary vocabulary

À bientôt!   *See you soon!*

▷ **Les jours de la semaine**

⊡ Leçon 8, Section 2

■ **Cultural note:** On French calendars, the week traditionally begins with **lundi**. On Canadian calendars, however, the week begins with **dimanche**.

■ **If students ask:** The days of the week are usually not capitalized in French.

1 COMMUNICATION: stating today's and tomorrow's dates

2 EXCHANGES: getting the date right

■ **Variation:** Philippe is one day ahead.
– Aujourd'hui, c'est samedi?
– Non, aujourd'hui, c'est vendredi.

3 ROLE PLAY: telling people good-bye and when you will see them again

■ **Challenge** (dialogue format):
– Au revoir, Christine.
– Au revoir. à lundi.

Language note: Days of the week

You may wish to tell your students that the days are named for the Roman gods. The suffix **di** comes from the Latin **dies** (day).

lun-di	(moon-day)
mar-di	(Mars-day)
mercre-di	(Mercury-day)

jeu-di	(Jupiter-day)
vendre-di	(Venus-day)
same-di	(Saturn-day)

Dimanche comes from the Latin **Dominus** (the Lord).

8.1 Dialogue :
  B. Anniversaire
  (47:12–47:34 min.)

Leçon 8, Section 3

■ **If students ask:** Explain that *si* (yes) is used to respond to a negative statement or question.

Pour communiquer

8.2 Mini-scenes: Dates and birthdays
  (47:35–50:04 min.)

Leçon 8, Section 4

Transparency 9
Calendar

■ **Language note:** To ask for the date, one can also say:
Quel jour est-ce?
Quel jour est-on? or
Quel jour sommes-nous?

■ **If students ask:** The months are usually not capitalized in French.

B. Anniversaire

François and Isabelle are on their way to Nathalie's birthday party. As they are talking, François wants to know when Isabelle's birthday is.

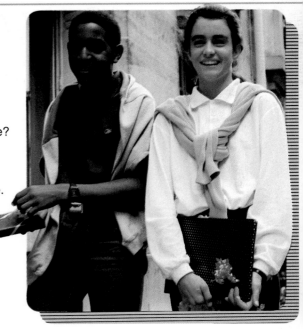

FRANÇOIS: C'est quand, ton anniversaire?
ISABELLE: C'est le 18 mars!
FRANÇOIS: Le 18 mars? Pas possible!
ISABELLE: Si! Pourquoi?
FRANÇOIS: C'est aussi mon anniversaire.
ISABELLE: Quelle coïncidence!

FRANÇOIS: When is your birthday?
ISABELLE: It's March 18!
FRANÇOIS: March 18? That's not possible!
ISABELLE: Yes, it is! Why?
FRANÇOIS: It's my birthday too.
ISABELLE: What a coincidence!

POUR *COMMUNIQUER*

Quelle est la date?

How to talk about the date:

Quelle est la date? — *What's the date?*
  C'est le 12 (douze) octobre. — *It's October 12.*
  C'est le premier juin. — *It's June first.*

How to talk about birthdays:

—**C'est quand, ton anniversaire?** — *When is your birthday?*
—**Mon anniversaire est le 2 (deux) mars.** — *My birthday is March 2.*

Les mois de l'année *(Months of the year)*			
janvier	avril	juillet	octobre
février	mai	août	novembre
mars	juin	septembre	décembre

 50 Unité 2

Casual speech

In French, casual speech is often heard, but rarely written. (This is like English, where people often say: *You coming?* and write: *Are you coming?*)

In this textbook, students are introduced to standard written French.

Some forms of casual speech are so common that they have been accepted into general usage. Two examples of this are **un prof** and **jouer au foot.**

In this lesson, students learn the casual **C'est quand, ton anniversaire?** which is simpler than **Quand est-ce, ton anniversaire?**

T50

La date

To express a date in French, the pattern is:

le	+	NUMBER	+	MONTH
le		11 (onze)		novembre
le		20 (vingt)		mai

EXCEPTION: The first of the month is **le premier**.

➡ In front of numbers, the French use **le** (and never **l'**): **le onze, le huit.**

➡ Note that when dates are abbreviated in French, the day always comes first.

2/8   **le deux** août   **1/11**   **le premier** novembre

Les Rolling Stones
à Paris
Au Parc des Princes
le 23 juin

4 **Anniversaires**

Ask your classmates when their birthdays are.

C'est quand, ton anniversaire?

Mon anniversaire est le 3 février.

5 **Quelle est la date?**

Ask what the date is.

12
SEPTEMBRE

▶ —Quelle est la date?
—C'est le douze septembre.

1	2	3	4	5	6
30 JUIN	**8** MAI	**4** MARS	**21** NOVEMBRE	**1** AVRIL	**25** AOÛT

6 **Dates importantes**

Give the following dates in French.

▶ Noël *(Christmas)*: 25/12   C'est le vingt-cinq décembre.

1. le Jour de l'An *(New Year's Day)*: 1/1
2. la fête *(holiday)* de Martin Luther King: 15/1
3. la Saint-Valentin: 14/2
4. la Saint-Patrick: 17/3
5. la fête nationale américaine: 4/7
6. la fête nationale française: 14/7
7. la fête de Christophe Colomb: 12/10

Leçon 8   **51**

▷ **La date**

📼 Leçon 8, Section 5

■ **Cultural Realia:** Ask your students:
• **Quel groupe donne un concert au Parc des Princes?** [Les Rolling Stones]
• **Quelle est la date du concert des Rolling Stones?** [C'est le 23 juin.]

■ **Language note:** Also: **le un** (when **un** is a number and not a pronoun).

■ **Language note:** Abbreviations of dates may also be punctuated with hyphens or periods.
• The months are sometimes expressed in roman numerals: **le 2.VIII.**
• Note: **le premier** may be abbreviated as **le 1ᵉʳ**.

4 COMMUNICATION: discussing birthdays

■ **Variation**
Have students walk around the room grouping themselves according to the month of their birth.
– C'est quand, ton anniversaire?
– Mon anniversaire est le 1ᵉʳ mai. Et toi?
As a follow-up, begin with January, and have students in each group give their birthdays before sitting back down.

5 EXCHANGES: asking today's date

6 PRACTICE: telling the date of certain events

Project: Calendars

You may wish to have your students prepare a calendar of the month of their next birthday. Have them label the month, the days of the week, and their birthday in French. Ask them to illustrate the top of the calendar with an original drawing.

This activity is particularly appropriate for younger learners.

1 COMPREHENSION

1-h	4-g	7-f
2-d	5-e	8-a
3-c	6-b	

🔲 **AVT 2, Section 1**

2 GUIDED ORAL EXPRESSION

🔲 **AVT 2, Section 2**

3 GUIDED ORAL EXPRESSION

Sample answers:
C: Nathalie, tu connais la fille?
N: Oui, c'est une amie (une copine).
C: Comment s'appelle ton amie (ta copine)?
N: Elle s'appelle Michèle Lafontaine.
C: Elle est canadienne?
N: Oui. Elle est de Québec.
C: Quelle coïncidence! Moi aussi, je suis de Québec.

🔲 **AVT 2, Section 3**

À votre tour!

1 Nathalie et Philippe

Nathalie is talking to Philippe and you hear parts of their conversation. For each of Nathalie's questions, select Philippe's response from the suggested answers.

1. Qui est-ce?
2. C'est ta soeur?
3. Quel âge as-tu?
4. C'est quand, ton anniversaire?
5. Quel âge a ton oncle?
6. Tu connais Stéphanie?
7. Comment s'appelle ta prof de français?
8. Quel jour est-ce aujourd'hui?

a. Vendredi.
b. Oui, c'est une copine.
c. Quinze ans.
d. Non, c'est ma cousine.
e. Quarante-cinq ans.
f. Elle s'appelle Madame Doucette.
g. Le dix-huit décembre.
h. C'est mon cousin Christophe.

2 Et toi?

You have just met Nathalie at a party. Answer her questions.

1. Quel âge as-tu?
2. Quel âge a ton copain (ta copine)?
3. C'est quand, ton anniversaire?
4. C'est quand, l'anniversaire de ton copain (ta copine)?
5. Comment s'appelle le (la) prof de français?

3 Conversation dirigée

Nathalie and Christophe are in a café. Christophe sees another girl that Nathalie seems to know. He wonders who she is.

Christophe			Nathalie
asks Nathalie if she knows the girl	→ ↙	says she does and that she is a friend	
asks Nathalie the name of her friend	→ ↙	says that her name is Michèle Lafontaine	
asks if she is Canadian	→ ↙	says yes and adds that she is from Quebec City **(de Québec)**	
says what a coincidence **(Quelle coïncidence!)** and adds that he is also from Quebec City			

52 Unité 2

À votre tour

This section is similar to the *À votre tour* of Unit 1 (see Teacher notes, page 30).

As before, you will want to select those activities which are most appropriate for your students. Encourage students to work cooperatively in pairs and trios.

🔲 Portfolio assessment

If you began Oral portfolio assessment in Unit 1 (see Teacher notes, page 31), you may have your students prepare a second audio (or video) recording to go with Unit 2. But you may prefer to wait until Unit 3, and only do portfolio recordings every other unit.

4 Ma famille *(My family)*

You are showing your friends a picture of your family. Introduce everyone, giving their ages.

▶ Voici ma soeur. Elle a douze ans.

5 En scène

With a classmate, act out the following scene.

CHARACTERS:

You and a French guest

SITUATION:

You are in France. Your French friends have invited you to a picnic. You meet one of the guests and have a conversation.

- Greet the guest.
- Introduce yourself and ask the guest's name.
- Tell the guest how old you are and ask his/her age.
- Tell the guest the date of your birthday and ask the date of his/her birthday.
- *(The guest waves to a friend.)* Ask the guest the name of his/her friend.
- *(It is the end of the picnic.)* Say good-bye.

6 Le loto

Loto is a French version of Bingo. Read out loud the numbers on your board.

13	24		42			75	89
8		25	31		53	68		
	16		36		57		79	90

Game: Loto

PREPARATION: Have your students make French Loto cards by drawing a grid with 27 squares and selecting fifteen numbers between 1 and 90. Place numbers between 1 and 10 in the first column, numbers between 11 to 20 in the second column, etc.

Each horizontal row must contain five numbers.

PLAY: Call out random numbers from 1 to 90, as in bingo. The first student to completely cover a horizontal row of five wins. This student then reads the numbers aloud so that they can be checked.

Entracte 2

OBJECTIVES:

- Development of cross-cultural awareness
- Vocabulary expansion

Les bruits français

OBJECTIVE:
- Learning that speakers of other languages may interpret sounds differently

Entracte 2, Section 1

■ Expansion
- **le coq** *(rooster):* **cocorico**
  le cheval *(horse):* **hî - hî - hî...**
  le mouton *(sheep):* **mè-è-è-è**
  le poisson *(fish):* **glou glou**
  l'oiseau *(bird):* **cui cui**
- **dog:** also **ouah ouah**

■ Photo culture notes
La campagne française
The scene is a rural landscape typical of southwestern France (**les Pyrénées**).
The farm (**la ferme**) is over 300 years old. Have students note:
- the main building (**le logis principal**)
- the square tower (**la tour carrée**)
- the barn (**la grange**)
- the wood shed (**la remise à bois**)
In the field there are rolled bales of hay (**les bottes de foin**) which will be stored in the barn for winter.

LES BRUITS FRANÇAIS *(French sounds)*

People in various countries can hear the same noises and interpret them differently. Notice how the French express certain common sounds.

What sounds do animals make in France? They make French sounds, of course!

54 Unité 2

📖 **Pre-reading activity**

- Have students look at the pictures and give the corresponding English equivalents for the sounds and animal noises.
- Model the sounds in French and have student repeat them. (Note that in **cot-cot-codèt**, the final "t's" are pronounced.)

Post-reading activities

- For each sound, have students vote whether they think the English version or the French version is closer to reality.
- If some students in the class are from other cultures, ask how these sounds are expressed in their languages.

ASTÉRIX
en action

Astérix and his friends lead an action-packed life. Can you match the sounds with the corresponding cartoon frames?

a 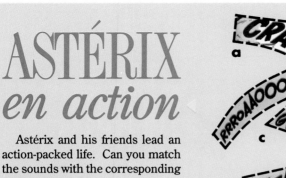 CRAAAC!

b POM POM! POM!

c RRROAÂOOO!

GRRRAOOR!

d GLOU! GLOU! GLOU! GLOU! GLOU!

e TATARARA TATA!

f PAFFF!

1 From ASTÉRIX LE GAULOIS

2 From ASTÉRIX GLADIATEUR

AU NOM DE CÉSAR, OUVREZ!

3 From ASTÉRIX CHEZ LES BRETONS

4 From ASTÉRIX CHEZ LES BRETONS

5 From ASTÉRIX GLADIATEUR

6 From ASTÉRIX LE GAULOIS

Entracte 2 55

Astérix en action

OBJECTIVES:
• Interpreting sounds
• Becoming familiar with a popular French cartoon character

■ **Teaching hint:**
• Model the sounds and have students repeat them.
• If necessary, clarify the pictures:
(1) Astérix is drinking the magic potion that gives him power.
(2) A Roman soldier leaves only his sandals and molars behind as a punch from Astérix sends him flying.
(3) Someone is pounding at the door and shouting: "Open up, in the name of Caesar!"
(4) Obélix has just kicked in the door.
(5) The lions are entering the ring to fight the gladiators.
(6) Roman soldiers are sounding reveille.

Pre-reading activity

• Ask students if they remember who Asterix is. (If not, turn back to page 16.)
• Point out that the Gauls **(les Gaulois)** get their strength from drinking a magic mistletoe potion (picture 1).
• Obélix (picture 4) is Astérix' strong and dependable companion.

Post-reading activity

Ask students how they would translate these frames into English.

UNITÉ 3
Modules 9–12

■ **Language note:** The expression **Bon appétit!** is used as people sit down to eat. It means *Enjoy the meal!*

UNITÉ

3 Bon appétit!

INTRODUCTION

culturelle

Bon appétit!

Where do you go when you want something to eat or drink? Maybe to a fast-food restaurant or an ice cream place?

French teenagers also have a large choice of places to go when they are hungry or thirsty. Some go to a bakery **(une boulangerie)** or a pastry shop **(une pâtisserie)** to buy croissants, éclairs, or other small pastries. Some may buy pizzas, crepes, hot dogs, or ice-cream cones from street vendors. Still others may go to a fast-food restaurant **(un fast-food).** But the favorite place to get something to eat or drink is the café. There are cafés practically everywhere in France. As you will see, the café plays an important role in the social life of all French people.

LEÇON	**9**	**Tu as faim?**
LEÇON	**10**	**Au café**
LEÇON	**11**	**Ça fait combien?**
LEÇON	**12**	**Le français pratique: Le temps**

56

Unit overview

COMMUNICATION GOALS: Students will learn to order something to eat or drink in a café or fast-food restaurant. They will also learn to talk about weather.

LINGUISTIC GOALS: Students will begin to acquire features of the French sound system, particularly rhythm, stress, intonation, and the French / r /.

CRITICAL THINKING GOALS: Students will discover that all nouns — even those referring to things — have gender. They will observe that in French *it* is expressed as either **il** or **elle.**

CULTURAL GOALS: Students will become aware of types of eating establishments and the French monetary system.

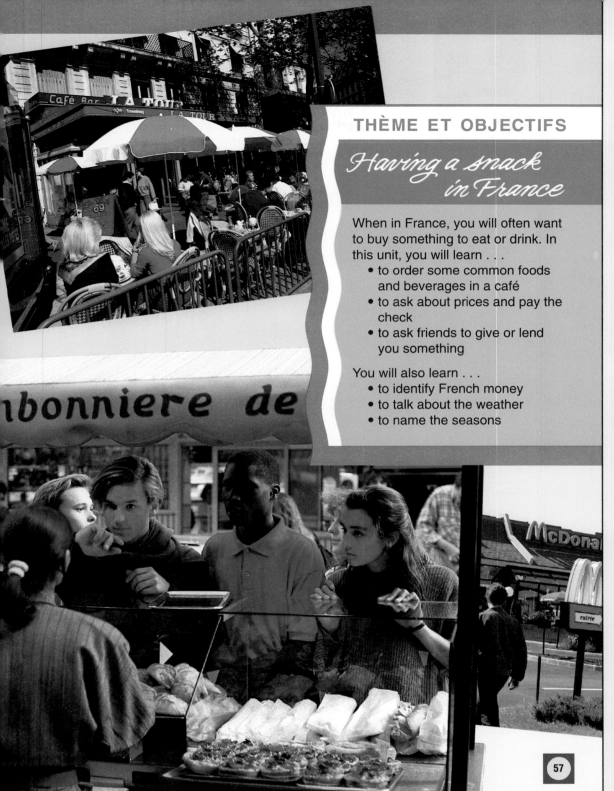

THÈME ET OBJECTIFS

Having a snack in France

When in France, you will often want to buy something to eat or drink. In this unit, you will learn . . .

- to order some common foods and beverages in a café
- to ask about prices and pay the check
- to ask friends to give or lend you something

You will also learn . . .

- to identify French money
- to talk about the weather
- to name the seasons

57

■ **Photo culture notes**

Le café
The café in the picture is very typical. Note that its sidewalk terrace (**la terrasse**) extends up to the pavement and is protected from the traffic by iron barriers. Note also:
- the wicker chairs (**les chaises d'osier**)
- the parasols (**les parasols**)
This particular café advertises light lunches at 69 francs (about $12).

La bonbonnière
This photo, taken in a Parisian department store, shows a stand that sells **croissants, sandwiches,** and **pâtisseries**. It is called **La bonbonnière** or "candy box."

Les fast-foods
Fast food restaurants (**les fast-foods,** or technically, **les restaurants de restauration rapide**) have multiplied in France in recent years and are now very popular with French teenagers. One can order:
- hamburgers (**des hamburgers**)
- hotdogs (**des saucisses, des hot dogs**)
- French fries (**des frites**)
- salads (**des salades**), and sometimes
- pastry (**des pâtisseries**)
A typical meal at a fast food restaurant costs about 23 francs (or about $4).
In addition to McDonald's and Burger King, there are also other chains, like Quick, Free Time, Le Duff, and La Croissanterie.

■ **Language Note:** The term for "drive-up" at fast-food restaurants like McDonald's is **service au volant** (service at the steering wheel).

Pacing
Try to move through this unit rather quickly, focusing on listening and speaking.

In later lessons, students will encounter the same vocabulary again. At that time they will be expected to master the material in writing.

MODULE 9:
Tu as faim?
Total time: 6:15 min.
(Counter: 52:02 min.)

9.1 Dialogue: Tu as faim?
(52:29–53:01 min.)
**9.2 Mini-scenes:
Ordering food**
(53:03–55:15 min.)
**9.3 Vignette culturelle:
Qu'est-ce qu'on mange?**
(55:16–58:13 min.)

■ **Comprehension practice:**
Play the entire module through as
an introduction to the lesson.

9.1 Dialogue: Tu as faim?
(52:29–53:01 min.)

 Leçon 9, Section 1

■ **Photo culture note**
Les pizzas
In France, pizzas are sold:
• at pizzerias (**une pizzéria**)
• at certain bakeries (**une
  boulangerie**)
• at deli shops (**une charcuterie**).
One can buy individual mini-
pizzas about 5 inches in diameter.
(These are sometimes served at
home as an hors-d'oeuvre.)
Pizzas may have the following
ingredients as toppings:
• cheese (**du fromage**)
• anchovies (**des anchois**)
• pepperoni (**du chorizo**)
• green peppers (**des poivrons**)
• mushrooms (**des champignons**)
Note the sign for take-out pizza
(**pizza à emporter**).

Tu as faim?

Pierre, Philippe, and Nathalie are on their way home from
school. They stop by a street vendor who sells sandwiches
and pizza. Today it is Pierre's turn to treat his friends.

Scène 1. Pierre et Nathalie

PIERRE: Tu as faim?
NATHALIE: Oui, j'ai faim.
PIERRE: Tu veux un sandwich
ou une pizza?
NATHALIE: Donne-moi une pizza,
s'il te plaît.
PIERRE: Voilà.
NATHALIE: Merci.

Scène 2. Pierre et Philippe

PIERRE: Et toi, Philippe, tu as faim?
PHILIPPE: Oh là là, oui, j'ai faim.
PIERRE: Qu'est-ce que tu veux? Un sandwich
ou une pizza?
PHILIPPE: Je voudrais un sandwich . . . euh . . .
et donne-moi aussi une pizza.
PIERRE: C'est vrai! Tu as vraiment faim!

Scene 1. Pierre and Nathalie

PIERRE: *Are you hungry?*
NATHALIE: *Yes, I'm hungry.*
PIERRE: *Do you want a sandwich
or a pizza?*
NATHALIE: *Give me a pizza, please.*
PIERRE: *Here you are.*
NATHALIE: *Thanks.*

Scene 2. Pierre and Philippe

PIERRE: *And you, Philippe, are you hungry?*
PHILIPPE: *Oh yes, I'm hungry.*
PIERRE: *What do you want? A sandwich or a pizza?*
PHILIPPE: *I would like a sandwich . . . er . . .
and give me a pizza too.*
PIERRE: *It's true! You are really hungry!*

58 Unité 3

🌐 Cross-cultural observation

Have students look at the foods pictured
in *Pour communiquer.*
    The only word that may be unfamiliar
to them is **frites** (French fries).
    Model the words and have students
repeat them with a French accent.

Observation questions:
• Which of the food names are originally
  American words?
• Which of the food names are French?
• Which food name is Italian?

POUR COMMUNIQUER

How to say that you are hungry:

J'ai faim. — I'm hungry.
Tu as faim? — Are you hungry?

> J'ai faim!
> Tu as faim?

How to offer a friend something:

Tu veux . . . ? — Do you want . . .?
Qu'est-ce que tu veux? — What do you want?

Tu veux un sandwich?
Qu'est-ce que tu veux? Un sandwich ou une pizza?

How to ask a friend for something:

Je voudrais . . . — I would like . . .
Donne-moi . . . — Give me . . .
S'il te plaît . . . — Please . . .

Je voudrais un sandwich.
Donne-moi une pizza.
S'il te plaît, François, donne-moi une pizza.

Les nourritures (Foods)

un croissant

un sandwich

un steak

un steak-frites

un hamburger

un hot dog

une salade

une pizza

une omelette

une crêpe

une glace

■ NOTE ■
CULTURELLE

Les jeunes et la nourriture

In general, French teenagers eat their main meals at home with their families. On weekends or after school, however, when they are with friends, they often stop at a fast-food restaurant or a café for something to eat.

At fast-food restaurants, French teenagers order pretty much the same types of foods as Americans: hamburgers, hot dogs, and pizza.

At a café, teenagers may order a croissant, a sandwich, or a dish of ice cream. Some favorite sandwiches are ham **(un sandwich au jambon),** Swiss cheese **(un sandwich au fromage),** or salami **(un sandwich au saucisson).** And, of course, they are made with French bread, which has a crunchy crust. Another traditional quick café meal is a small steak with French fries **(un steak-frites).**

Leçon 9 **59**

Pour communiquer

💻 **9.2 Mini-scenes: Ordering food** (53:03–55:15 min.)

📼 Leçon 9, Sections 2, 3

■ **Photo cultural note**
Le cornet de glace
Vendors usually sell ice cream in cones (**un cornet**).

■ **If students ask:** Literally, **j'ai faim** means *I have hunger.*

■ **Pronunciation:** Be sure the students say the American words with a French accent: nasal "a" and no "n" or "m" in **sandwich, hamburger;** no liaison and a silent "h" in **un hotdog.**

🖥 **Transparency 10** Foods

Supplementary vocabulary

FOODS
une salade verte
une salade de tomates
une tarte *pie*
un gâteau *cake*
un éclair
une glace à la vanille
une glace au chocolat

Note culturelle

💻 **9.3 Vignette culturelle: Qu'est-ce qu'on mange?** (55:16–58:13 min.)

🌐 **Cross-cultural observation** Have students note similarities and differences in where French young people stop for food and what they eat.

■ **Cultural note:** In France, **les fast-food** are not drive-ins, but are located in downtown areas and shopping malls. They often have only stand-up counters and are not designed for simply sitting and talking with friends.

TPR 🏃 Foods

PROPS: Pictures of the foods (above)
Present the French names of the foods.
   [Hold up "croissant."] **Voici un croissant.**
   [Hold up "sandwich."] **Voici un sandwich.**

Est-ce que c'est un croissant? [Non.]
Est-ce que c'est un sandwich? [Oui.]
Have students distribute the "foods."
   X, prends le croissant et donne-le à Y.
   Qui a le croissant? [Y.]
You may give more complex commands.
   X, prends une pizza et un steak.
   Donne la pizza à Y et le steak à Z.

T59

Petit commentaire

Two popular sandwiches sold in cafés are **le croque-monsieur** and **le croque-madame**.

The **croque-monsieur** is a grilled ham and cheese sandwich made with American-style bread.

The **croque-madame** is similar, but with a fried egg on top.

Petit commentaire

In France, sandwiches are traditionally very simple: a piece of French bread with a slice of ham or cheese. Usually sandwiches are not made with mayonnaise or lettuce.

un sandwich, une pizza

You may have noted that the names of some foods are masculine and others are feminine. In French, ALL NOUNS, whether they designate people or things, are either MASCULINE or FEMININE.

MASCULINE NOUNS		FEMININE NOUNS	
un sandwich	**le** sandwich	**une** pizza	**la** pizza
un croissant	**le** croissant	**une** salade	**la** salade

1 EXCHANGES: offering food and making a selection

■ **Variation:** To simplify this activity, have students choose one of the two foods in each item.
– **Donne-moi une pizza, s'il te plaît.**
– **Voilà.**
– **Merci.**

■ **Challenge** (dialogue format):
– **Tu as faim?**
– **Oui, j'ai faim.**
– **Tu veux un hamburger?**
– **Oui, donne-moi un hamburger, s'il te plaît.**

2 COMMUNICATION: ordering food

1. un sandwich
2. une salade
3. une pizza
4. une glace
5. une omelette
6. un steak-frites

1 **Au choix** *(Your choice)*

Offer your classmates a choice between the following items. They will decide which one they would like.

▶ une pizza ou un sandwich?

1. un hamburger ou un steak?
2. un hot dog ou un sandwich?
3. une salade ou une omelette?
4. un steak-frites ou une pizza?
5. une crêpe ou un croissant?
6. une glace à la vanille ou une glace au chocolat?

Qu'est-ce que tu veux? Une pizza ou un sandwich?

Donne-moi un sandwich s'il te plaît.

2 **Au café**

You are in a French café. Ask for the following dishes.

▶ **Je voudrais un croissant.**

 Cooperative pair practice Activities 1, 3

Listening practice: Gender identification

PROPS: Red and blue index cards for each student

Quickly read aloud sentences containing masculine and feminine nouns. Have the students hold up the blue card for masculine nouns and the red card for feminine nouns.

1. **Voici une salade.** [R]
2. **Voici le sandwich.** [B]
3. **Voici la glace.** [R]
4. **Voici une crêpe.** [R]
5. **Voici un steak.** [B]
6. **Voici le croissant.** [B]
7. **Voici la pizza.** [R]
8. **Voici un hot dog.** [B]

3 **Tu as faim?**

You have invited French friends to your home. Ask if they are hungry and offer them the following foods.

▶ — Tu as faim?
— Oui, j'ai faim.
— Tu veux un hamburger?
— Oui, merci.

1
2
3
4
5
6

4 **Qu'est-ce que tu veux?**

Say which foods you would like to have in the following circumstances.

▶ You are very hungry.

Je voudrais un steak-frites.

1. You are at an Italian restaurant.
2. You are on a diet.
3. You are a vegetarian.
4. You are having breakfast.
5. You would like a dessert.
6. You want to eat something light for supper.

3 ROLE PLAY: offering food and accepting it

1. une pizza
2. un steak
3. un sandwich
4. un hot dog
5. une glace
6. une crêpe

4 COMPREHENSION: selecting food according to specific circumstances

Prononciation

L'intonation

When you speak, your voice rises and falls. This is called INTONATION. In French, as in English, your voice goes down at the end of a statement.

Voici un steak . . . et une salade.

However, in French, your voice rises after each group of words in the middle of a sentence. (This is the opposite of English, where your voice drops a little when you pause in the middle of a sentence.)

Répétez: **Je voudrais une pizza.**

Je voudrais une pizza et un sandwich.

Je voudrais une pizza, un sandwich et un hamburger.

Voici un steak.

Voici un steak et une salade.

Voici un steak, une salade et une glace.

Prononciation

🔊 Leçon 9, Section 4

Sounding French

A key outcome of Niveau A is that students begin to "sound French" so that they can be easily understood by French speakers.

One of the most important parts of "sounding French" is to acquire the intonation patterns of the language.

An effective technique is to have students say English sentences using French intonation. Use English equivalents of the above sentences to practice. For example:
I would like a pizza.
I would like a pizza and a sandwich.
I would like a pizza, a sandwich, and a hamburger.

MODULE 10:
Au café
Total time: 5:25 min.
(Counter: 58:24 min.)

10.1 Dialogue: Au café
(58:40–59:24 min.)
10.2 Mini-scenes: Saying please
(59:25–1:01:25 min.)
10.3 Vignette culturelle: Qu'est-ce qu'on boit?
(1:01:26–1:03:45 min.)

■ **Comprehension practice:** Play the entire module through as an introduction to the lesson.

10.1 Dialogue: Au café
(58:40–59:24 min.)

 Leçon 10, Section 1

■ **Language notes**
• When calling a waiter, one may also say **"Garçon!"** It is becoming common, however, to use the more polite **"Monsieur!"**
• The traditional term **un garçon** is slowly being replaced by **un serveur.**
• A waitress is **une serveuse.**

■ **Photo culture note**
Le garçon de café
French waiters (**un garçon de café**) are usually dressed formally: black pants, white shirt and bow tie, vest or jacket.

T62

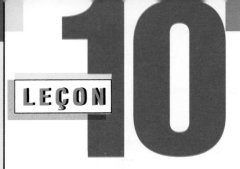

LEÇON 10   Au café

This afternoon Jean-Paul and Isabelle went shopping. They are now tired and thirsty. Jean-Paul invites Isabelle to a café.

Scène 1. Jean-Paul, Isabelle

JEAN-PAUL: Tu as soif?
ISABELLE: Oui, j'ai soif.
JEAN-PAUL: On va dans un café? Je t'invite.
ISABELLE: D'accord!

> Vous désirez, mademoiselle?

Scène 2. Le garçon, Isabelle, Jean-Paul

LE GARÇON: Vous désirez, mademoiselle?
ISABELLE: Un jus d'orange, s'il vous plaît.
LE GARÇON: Et pour vous, monsieur?
JEAN-PAUL: Donnez-moi une limonade,* s'il vous plaît.

> C'est pour vous, mademoiselle?

Scène 3. Le garçon, Isabelle, Jean-Paul

LE GARÇON: *(à Isabelle)* La limonade, c'est pour vous, mademoiselle?
JEAN-PAUL: Non, c'est pour moi.
LE GARÇON: Ah, excusez-moi. Voici le jus d'orange, mademoiselle.
ISABELLE: Merci.

Scene 2. *The waiter, Isabelle, Jean-Paul*

WAITER: *May I help you, Miss?*
ISABELLE: *An orange juice, please.*
WAITER: *And for you, Sir?*
JEAN-PAUL: *Give me a "limonade," please.*

Scene 3. *The waiter, Isabelle, Jean-Paul*

WAITER: *The "limonade" is for you, Miss?*
JEAN-PAUL: *No, it's for me.*
WAITER: *Oh, excuse me. Here is the orange juice, Miss.*
ISABELLE: *Thank you.*

Scene 1. *Jean-Paul, Isabelle*

JEAN-PAUL: *Are you thirsty?*
ISABELLE: *Yes, I'm thirsty.*
JEAN-PAUL: *Shall we go to a café? I'm treating (inviting) you.*
ISABELLE: *Okay!*

*Une limonade is a popular inexpensive soft drink with a slight lemon flavor.

 62   Unité 3

☀ Warm-up and review: Forms of address

PROPS: Magazine pictures of individual men, women, and teenagers.

Have students greet one another saying:
– **Salut, X! Comment vas-tu?**
– **Ça va très bien (comme ci, comme ça).**
Hold up the magazine pictures; point out that students do not know these people.

Ask them to greet each person in the picture formally:
Bonjour, madame (monsieur, mademoiselle). Comment allez-vous?
Then have them observe how people address one another in the café scene from the video.

POUR
COMMUNIQUER

Donnez-moi une limonade, s'il vous plaît!

How to say that you are thirsty:

J'ai soif.	*I'm thirsty.*
Tu as soif?	*Are you thirsty?*

How to order in a café:

Vous désirez?	*May I help you?*	—**Vous désirez?**
Je voudrais . . .	*I would like . . .*	—**Je voudrais** un Perrier.

How to request something . . .

from a friend:	*from an adult:*	
S'il te plaît, donne-moi . . .	**S'il vous plaît, donnez-moi . . .**	*Please, give me . . .*

➜ Note that French people have two ways of saying *please.* They use
  s'il te plaît with friends, and
  s'il vous plaît with adults.
As we will see later, young people address their friends as **tu** and adults that they do not know very well as **vous.**

Les boissons *(Beverages)*

un soda	**un jus d'orange**	**un jus de pomme**	**un jus de tomate**	**un jus de raisin***	**une limonade**	**un café**	**un thé**	**un chocolat**

■ NOTE ■
CULTURELLE

Le café

The café is a favorite gathering place for French young people. They go there not only when they are hungry or thirsty but also to meet their friends. They can sit at a table and talk for hours over a cup of coffee or a glass of juice. French young people also enjoy mineral water and soft drinks, which they order by brand name (**un Coca, un Orangina, un Pepsi, un Schweppes, un Perrier**). In a French café, a 15% service charge is included in the check. However, most people also leave some small change as an added tip.

*****Jus de raisin** is a golden-colored juice made from grapes. It is not at all like American grape juice.

 10.2 Mini-scenes: Using **s'il vous plaît** and **s'il te plaît** (59:25–1:01:25 min.)

 Leçon 10, Section 2

Language note: Literally, **tu as soif** means *you have thirst.*

Transparency 11 Beverages

Supplementary vocabulary

BEVERAGES
un café crème *coffee with cream*
un jus d'ananas *pineapple juice*
un jus de pamplemousse *grapefruit juice*
un citron pressé *freshly squeezed lemon juice, served with water and sugar on the side*
une orange pressée *freshly squeezed orange juice, served with water and sugar on the side*

Note culturelle

■ **Photo culture note**
On the table is a bottle of Badoit, a French mineral water.

10.3 Vignette culturelle: Qu'est-ce qu'on boit? (1:01:26–1:03:45 min.)

● **Cross-cultural observation**
Have students note similarities and differences in where French young people like to drink.

TPR 🏃 Beverages

PROPS: Transparency 11 red and blue transparency markers
Point out beverages on the transparency.
  Voici un café. Voici un soda. etc.
Have students point out beverages.
  X, viens ici. Montre-nous un café.
Hold up the blue and the red markers.

Voici un stylo bleu et un stylo rouge.
Si vous entendez <u>un</u>, prenez le stylo bleu. Si vous entendez <u>une</u>, prenez le rouge.
Dessinez un cercle autour de la boisson.
Écoutez. "Je voudrais un thé."
  [Draw a blue circle around the tea.]

T63

Petit commentaire

On the whole, French young people prefer natural beverages, such as flavored mineral water or juices, to carbonated soft drinks. In the larger cities, one can find inviting juice bars that offer a wide selection of freshly blended fruit drinks.

1 Tu as soif?

You have invited a French friend to your house. You offer a choice of beverages and your friend (played by a classmate) responds.

▶ un thé ou un chocolat?
—Tu veux un thé ou un chocolat?
—Donne-moi un chocolat, s'il te plaît.

1. un thé ou un café?
2. une limonade ou un soda?
3. un jus de pomme ou un jus d'orange?
4. un jus de raisin ou un jus de tomate?

2 Au café

You are in a French café. Get the attention of the waiter (**Monsieur**) or the waitress (**Mademoiselle**) and place your order. Act out the dialogue with a classmate.

Game: C'est logique?

PREPARATION: Prepare 2 bags of cards:
• (Bag A: 10 cards) On 5 cards, write **J'ai faim.** On the other 5, write **J'ai soif.**
• (Bag B: 21 cards) Begin each card with **Je voudrais, Donne-moi,** or **Donnez-moi** and add a food or beverage from pp. 59 and 63.

Divide the class into two teams: **logique** and **illogique.**

A player from each team comes up. One reads a card from Bag A, the other reads one from Bag B. If the sentences fit logically, the **logique** team earns a point. If not, a point goes to the **illogique** team. For example: **J'ai soif. Donne-moi une pizza. = illogique**

3 Que choisir? *(What to choose?)*

You are in a French café. Decide what beverage you are going to order in each of the following circumstances.

▶ You are very thirsty.
S'il vous plaît, une limonade (un jus de pomme) . . .

1. It is very cold outside.
2. You do not want to spend much money.
3. You like juice but are allergic to citrus fruits.
4. It is breakfast time.
5. You have a sore throat.

4 La faim et la soif *(Hungry and thirsty)*

You are having a meal in a French café. Order the food suggested in the picture. Then order something to drink with that dish. A classmate will play the part of the waiter.
Note: **Et avec ça?** means *And with that?*

Vous désirez?

Je voudrais un steak-frites.

Et avec ça?

Un Orangina, s'il vous plaît.

1 2 3 4

Prononciation

L'accent final

In French, the rhythm is very even and the accent always falls on the *last* syllable of a word or group of words.

Répétez: **Philippe Thomas Alice Sophie Dominique**

un café — **Je voudrais un café.**
une salade — **Donnez-moi un salade.**
un chocolat — **Donne-moi un chocolat.**

ŭn chŏcŏlāt

If you want French people to understand you, the most important thing is to speak with an even rhythm and to stress the last syllable in each group of words. (Try speaking English this way: people will think you have a French accent!)

Leçon 10 **65**

COMPREHENSION: selecting an appropriate beverage **3**

■ **Variation:**
Donnez-moi une limonade (un jus de pomme), s'il vous plaît.

ROLE PLAY: ordering food and a beverage **4**

1. une omelette
2. une glace
3. un hot dog
4. une salade

■ **Language note:** Since the French terms for *milk* and *water* are generally used with the partitive, they have not been included in this lesson.
OPTIONAL EXPANSION: You may want to teach:
du lait
de l'eau
de l'eau minérale

Prononciation

🎧 Leçon 10, Section 5

■ **Pronunciation:** For the sample sentences, you may want to tap out the syllables evenly making the last one somewhat longer than the rest.

Sounding French

Along with intonation, one of the most important parts of "sounding French" is to acquire the rhythm and stress patterns of the language.

An effective technique is to let students mimic a French accent in English. Have them speak in a staccato rhythm, ending each group of words with a longer syllable, and using rising intonation at the end of phrases in the middle of a sentence.

In-the-French-lan-GUAGE↗
all-syl-la-bles-are-e-VEN↗
ex-cept-the-last-ONE↗
which-gets-the-ac-CENT↘

MODULE 11:
Ça fait combien?
Total Time: 5:04 min.
(Counter: 1:03:56 min.)

11.1 Dialogue: Ça fait combien?
(1:04:12–1:04:45 min.)
11.2 Mini-scenes: Asking what one owes
(1:04:46–1:06:17 min.)
11.3 Vignette culturelle: L'argent français
(1:06:18–1:08:55 min.)

■ **Comprehension practice:** Play the entire module through as an introduction to the lesson.

11.1 Dialogue: Ça fait combien?
(1:04:12–1:04:45 min.)

▭▭▭ **Leçon 11, Section 1**

■ **If students ask**
French-speaking countries each have their own currency:
Quebec: **le dollar canadien**
Belgium: **le franc belge**
Switzerland: **le franc suisse**
Algeria and Tunisia: **le dinar**
Morocco: **le dirham**
Senegal, Ivory Coast, etc.: **le franc CFA (de la Communauté financière africaine)**

LEÇON 11 Ça fait combien?

At the café, Jean-Paul and Isabelle have talked about many things. It is now time to go. Jean-Paul calls the waiter so he can pay the check.

JEAN-PAUL:	S'il vous plaît?
LE GARÇON:	Oui, monsieur.
JEAN-PAUL:	Ça fait combien?
LE GARÇON:	Voyons, un jus d'orange, 12 francs, et une limonade, 10 francs. Ça fait 22 francs.
JEAN-PAUL:	22 francs . . . Très bien . . . Mais, euh . . . Zut! Où est mon porte-monnaie . . . ? Dis, Isabelle, prête-moi 30 francs, s'il te plaît.

Dis, Isabelle, prête-moi 30 francs, s'il te plaît.

JEAN-PAUL:	*Excuse me? (Please?)*
WAITER:	*Yes, Sir.*
JEAN-PAUL:	*What do I owe you? (How much does that make?)*
WAITER:	*Let's see, one orange juice, 12 francs, and one "limonade" 10 francs. That comes to (makes) 22 francs.*

JEAN-PAUL: *22 francs . . . Very well . . . But, uh . . . Darn! Where is my wallet . . . ? Hey, Isabelle, loan me 30 francs, please.*

■ NOTE ■ CULTURELLE

L'argent français *(French money)*

The monetary unit of France is the **franc,** which is divided into 100 **centimes.** French currency consists of bills and coins. French bills are of different sizes— the greater the value, the larger the bill: **500 francs, 200 francs, 100 francs, 50 francs,** and **20 francs.** The people represented on the bills are famous French writers, painters, and musicians.

66 Unité 3

☀ **Warm-up: Numbers**

Teach the students the following phrase: **Combien font deux plus deux?** (Note that the "s" on **plus** is pronounced /plys/.)

Have the class solve arithmetic problems.

Combien font quatorze plus seize? **[Trente]** or **[Quatorze plus seize font trente.]**

POUR COMMUNIQUER

C'est combien?

How to ask how much something costs:

C'est combien?	*How much is it?*	—**C'est combien?**
Ça fait combien?	*How much does that come to (make)?*	—**Ça fait combien?**
Ça fait . . .	*That's . . . , That comes to . . .*	—**Ça fait** 30 francs.
Combien coûte . . . ?	*How much does . . . cost?*	—**Combien coûte** le sandwich?
Il/Elle coûte . . .	*It costs . . .*	—**Il coûte** 14 francs.

How to ask a friend to lend you something:

Prête-moi . . .	*Lend me . . . , Loan me . . .*	**Prête-moi** 10 francs, s'il te plaît.

➡ Note that masculine nouns can be replaced by **il** and feminine nouns can be replaced by **elle.**

Voici **une glace.**	**Elle** coûte 8 francs.	*It costs 8 francs.*
Voici **un sandwich.**	**Il** coûte 15 francs.	*It costs 15 francs.*

Leçon 11 ⑥⑦

Pour communiquer

🖥 **11.2 Mini-scenes: Asking what one owes** (1:04:46–1:06:17 min.)

📼 Leçon 11, Sections 2, 3

◼ **Language note:** In asking for prices, the casual speech forms given are much more common than **Combien est-ce que c'est?** or **Combien est-ce que ça fait?**

Note culturelle

🖥 **11.3 Vignette culturelle: L'argent français** (1:06:18–1:08:55 min.)

◼ **Cultural note:** Depending upon exchange rates, one dollar usually equals about five or six francs.

◼ **Realia note**
Portraits found on French currency are:
20 francs: Claude Debussy (1862–1918), composer
50 francs: Quentin de la Tour (1704–1788), portrait artist
100 francs: Eugène Delacroix (1798–1863), painter
200 francs: Montesquieu (1689–1755), philosopher
500 francs: Blaise Pascal (1623–1662), philosopher and mathematician

🎲 Game

Divide the class into teams A and B. Two players come forward.

Player A asks a math question.

If player B answers correctly, both teams get a point.

If player B is wrong, and player A can answer his/her own question correctly, team A gets a point.

Then the next two players have their turn. This time player B asks the question. Etc.

Petit commentaire

The **Guide Michelin,** the classic guide to restaurants in France, annually grants "stars" for outstanding cuisine. About 575 restaurants are given one star, 85 restaurants receive two stars, and about 20 truly outstanding restaurants are awarded the coveted three stars.

1 PRACTICE: asking someone for a loan

2 EXCHANGES: asking how much things cost

🖥 **Transparency 12**
Menu from "Le Select"

■ **Teaching note:** You may wish to project Transparency 12 as students do the activities on this page.

■ **Realia note:**
Ask the students:
Comment s'appelle le café/restaurant? [Le Sélect]
Quel est le numéro de téléphone? [C'est le 45.22.46.29]

Petit commentaire

*French people of all ages love to eat out, and French restaurants have the reputation of offering the best cuisine in the world. Of course, there are all kinds of restaurants for all kinds of budgets, ranging from the simple country inn (**l'auberge de campagne**) with its hearty regional food to the elegant three-star restaurant (**restaurant trois étoiles**) with its exquisite—and expensive—menu.*

1 S'il te plaît . . .

You have been shopping in Paris and discover that you did not exchange enough money. Ask a friend to loan you the following sums.

▶ 10 francs
   S'il te plaît, prête-moi dix francs.

1. 20 francs	4. 60 francs	7. 85 francs
2. 30 francs	5. 75 francs	8. 90 francs
3. 45 francs	6. 80 francs	9. 95 francs

2 Décision

Before ordering at a café, Stéphanie and Émilie are checking the prices. Act out the dialogues.

▶ le chocolat

Combien coûte le chocolat?

Il coûte douze francs.

1. le thé
2. le jus d'orange
3. la salade de tomates
4. la glace à la vanille
5. le café
6. le steak-frites
7. le hot dog
8. l'omelette
9. la salade mixte
10. le jus de raisin

LE SELECT
P. SOULIE
CAFÉ RESTAURANT*
Tél. 45.22.46.29
30, boulevard des Batignolles 75017 Paris

LE SELECT

BOISSONS

café	8F
chocolat	12F
thé	8F
limonade	10F
jus d'orange	12F
jus de raisin	12F

GLACES

glace au chocolat	8F
glace à la vanille	8F

SANDWICHS

sandwich au jambon	15F
sandwich au fromage	15F

ET AUSSI . . .

steak-frites	35F
salade mixte	7F
salade de tomates	10F
omelette	15F
hot dog	15F
croissant	8F
pizza	12F

Project: Un menu

Using the "Le Sélect" menu as a model, have the students prepare menus in French. They should include the name, address, and telephone number of the café/restaurant and illustrate with original drawings or cut-out pictures.

Display the finished products on the bulletin board and/or around the room. If you choose to have your students do the Challenge activity on p. T73, they can use the menus in their café conversations.

3 Ça fait combien?

You have gone to Le Select with your friends and have ordered the following items. Now you are ready to leave the café, and each one wants to pay. Check the prices on the menu for Le Select, and act out the dialogue.

▶ —Ça fait combien, s'il vous plaît?
—Ça fait 12 francs.
—Voici 12 francs.
—Merci.

1 2

3

4 5

4 Au «Select»

You are at Le Select. Order something to eat and drink. Since you are in a hurry, ask for the check right away. Act out the dialogue with a classmate who will play the part of the waiter/waitress.

Monsieur, s'il vous plaît!

Vous désirez?

Je voudrais un sandwich au jambon et un café. Ça fait combien?

Ça fait 23 francs.

EXCHANGES: asking the price of something and paying for it

3

1. (un croissant) 8F
2. (une pizza) 12F
3. (un sandwich) 15F
4. (une limonade) 10F
5. (un thé) 8F

4 ROLE PLAY: ordering something to eat and drink

Prononciation

Leçon 11, Section 4

■ **Pronunciation:** If students have trouble producing the sound, it is better for them to identify the French "r" with an American "h" sound than with an American "r."

Classroom Notes

Prononciation

La consonne «r»   /r/

The French consonant "r" is not at all like the English "r". It is pronounced at the back of the throat. In fact, it is similar to the Spanish "jota" sound of José.

Répétez: Marie Paris orange Henri
franc très croissant fromage
bonjour pour Pierre quart
Robert Richard Renée Raoul

Marie, prête-moi trente francs.

Marie

MODULE 12:
**Le français pratique:
Le temps**
Total time: 5:38 min.
(Counter: 1:09:07 min.)

12.1 Dialogue: Le temps
(1:09:21–1:09:51 min.)
**12.2 Mini-scenes:
Talking about weather**
(1:09:52–1:11:45 min.)
**12.3 Vignette culturelle:
La géographie de la
France**
(1:11:46–1:14:42 min.)

■ **Comprehension practice:** Play the entire module through as an introduction to the lesson.

12.1 Dialogue: Le temps
(1:09:52–1:11:45 min.)

Leçon 12, Section 1

LE FRANÇAIS
PRATIQUE

LEÇON 12 Le temps

It is nine o'clock Sunday morning. Cécile and her brother Philippe have planned a picnic for the whole family. Cécile is asking about the weather.

Quel temps fait-il?

Il fait mauvais.

Zut, zut et zut!

Papa va nous inviter au restaurant.

CÉCILE:	Quel temps fait-il?
PHILIPPE:	Il fait mauvais!
CÉCILE:	Il fait mauvais?
PHILIPPE:	Oui, il fait mauvais! Regarde! Il pleut!
CÉCILE:	Zut, zut et zut!
PHILIPPE:	!!!???
CÉCILE:	Et le pique-nique?
PHILIPPE:	Le pique-nique? Ah oui, le pique-nique! . . . Écoute, ça n'a pas d'importance.
CÉCILE:	Pourquoi?
PHILIPPE:	Pourquoi? Parce que Papa va nous inviter au restaurant.
CÉCILE:	Super!

CÉCILE:	How's the weather?
PHILIPPE:	It's bad!
CÉCILE:	It's bad?
PHILIPPE:	Yes, it's bad! Look! It's raining!
CÉCILE:	Darn, darn, darn!
PHILIPPE:	!!!???
CÉCILE:	And the picnic?
PHILIPPE:	The picnic? Oh yes, the picnic! . . . Listen, it's not important (that has no importance).
CÉCILE:	Why?
PHILIPPE:	Why? Because Dad is going to take us out (invite us) to a restaurant.
CÉCILE:	Great!

70 **Unité 3**

☀ Warm-up and review: Months and dates

Have the class name the months of the year as you write their abbreviations across the top of the chalkboard.

Then go around the class asking all the students to give their birthdays.
Sue, c'est quand, ton anniversaire?
[Sue: C'est le 21 août.]

Write the student's name and abbreviated birthdate under the appropriate month.
[août] Sue: le 21/8.
Have students read the dates. Ask:
C'est quand, l'anniversaire de Sue?
NOTE: In a class of 25 the odds are 50/50 that two people will share the same birthday.

Quel temps fait-il?

POUR COMMUNIQUER

How to talk about the weather:

Quel temps fait-il? *How's the weather?*

Il fait beau.

Il fait bon.

Il fait chaud.

Il fait frais.

Il fait froid.

Il fait mauvais.

Il pleut.

Il neige.

Les saisons *(Seasons)*

le printemps	*spring*	**au printemps**	*in (the) spring*
l'été	*summer*	**en été**	*in (the) summer*
l'automne	*fall, autumn*	**en automne**	*in (the) fall*
l'hiver	*winter*	**en hiver**	*in (the)winter*

1 Ta région

Tell Cécile what the weather is like in your part of the country.

▶ en juillet

En juillet, il fait chaud.

1. en août
2. en septembre
3. en novembre
4. en janvier
5. en mars
6. en mai

2 Les quatre saisons

Describe what the weather is like in each of the four seasons in the following cities.

▶ à Miami

En été, il fait chaud. En automne, il fait chaud aussi. En hiver, il fait frais. Au printemps, il fait bon.

Miami

1. à Chicago
2. à San Francisco
3. à Denver
4. à Boston
5. à Seattle
6. à Dallas

Leçon 12 71

 12.2 Mini-scenes: Talking about the weather (1:09:52–1:11:45 min.)

 Leçon 12, Section 2

Transparency 13 Weather

■ **Language note:** Contrast:
Il fait beau. *It's beautiful weather, the sun is out.*
Il fait bon. *It's nice weather, comfortable, warm.*

■ **Expansion:**
Il fait <u>très</u> beau, <u>très</u> froid, etc.

■ **Pronunciation notes**
• Be sure students do not pronounce the silent letters in **temps** and **printemps.**
• Be sure students make the following liaisons:
en hiver, en été, en automne.

1 COMMUNICATION: talking about the weather

■ **Variation** (dialogue format):
– **Quel temps fait-il en juillet?**
– **Il fait chaud.**

2 DESCRIPTION: giving details about the weather

12.3 Vignette culturelle: La géographie de la France (1:11:46–1:14:42 min.)

Geography activity Pre-viewing activity
Have students turn to pages 6–7 and locate the following provinces on the map of France: Touraine, Alsace, Savoie, Provence.

TPR Weather

PROPS: Transparency 13
Teach the weather expressions by pointing to the pictures on the overhead.
Quel temps fait-il? Il fait beau. Et maintenant, quel temps fait-il? Il pleut. Est-ce qu'il fait beau? [Non.]

Have students point out the weather.
X, viens ici. Montre-nous le temps.
Il pleut. [points to rain]
Il neige. [points to snow] etc.

T71

MAIN FOCUS:

Recapitulation and review

1 COMPREHENSION

1-e   4-a
2-c   5-d
3-b

🖭 **AVT 3, Section 1**

2 ORAL EXPRESSION

🖭 **AVT 3, Section 2**

3 GUIDED ORAL EXPRESSION

Sample answer:
G: Bonjour, mademoiselle! Vous désirez?
S: (Donnez-moi, Je voudrais) un croissant, s'il vous plaît. Combien coûte un jus d'orange?
G: (Un jus d'orange coûte) 15 francs.
S: (Donnez-moi, Je voudrais) un jus d'orange, s'il vous plaît!... (Monsieur,) s'il vous plaît! Ça fait combien?
G: (Ça fait) 22 francs.
S: Voici 25 francs.
G: Merci, mademoiselle.

🖭 **AVT 3, Section 3**

À votre tour!

1 **Isabelle et Jean-Paul**

Isabelle is talking to Jean-Paul. You hear parts of their conversation. For each of Isabelle's questions, select Jean-Paul's response from the suggested answers.

1. Tu as faim?
2. Tu veux un jus de pommes?
3. Combien coûte le café au Café Français?
4. Quel temps fait-il?
5. Quelle est ta saison favorite?

a. Il fait chaud.
b. Huit francs.
c. Oui, merci, j'ai soif.
d. C'est le printemps.
e. Oui, je voudrais un sandwich.

2 **Et toi?**

Now Isabelle is phoning you. Answer her questions.

1. Quel temps fait-il aujourd'hui?
2. Quel temps fait-il en hiver?
3. Quelle est ta saison favorite?

3 **Conversation dirigée**

Stéphanie is in a café called Le Petit Bistrot. The waiter is taking her order. With a partner, compose and act out a dialogue according to the script suggested below.

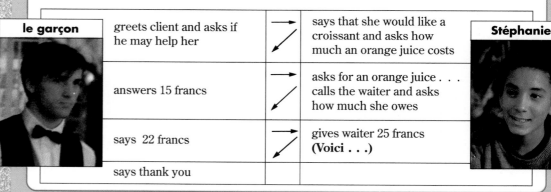

le garçon			Stéphanie
greets client and asks if he may help her	→ ↙	says that she would like a croissant and asks how much an orange juice costs	
answers 15 francs	→ ↙	asks for an orange juice . . . calls the waiter and asks how much she owes	
says 22 francs	→ ↙	gives waiter 25 francs **(Voici . . .)**	
says thank you			

À votre tour

For specific teaching suggestions, see the Teacher Notes in Unit 1, page 30.

You will want to select those activities which are most appropriate for your students. Encourage them to work in pairs and in trios (where one has the Answer Key).

The first 3 activities are on audiocassette.
Act. 1: Play Section 1 of the cassette so that students can check their answers.
Act. 2: Play Section 2 and have students answer the spoken questions orally.
Act. 3: Play Section 3 as a model. Then have students act out their own dialogues.

4 Au café

You are in a French café. Call the waiter/waitress and order the following items. A classmate will play the part of the waiter/waitress.

▶ —Monsieur (Mademoiselle), s'il vous plaît!
—Vous désirez?
—Un croissant, s'il vous plaît!
(Donnez-moi un croissant, s'il vous plaît!)
(Je voudrais un croissant, s'il vous plaît!).

1 2 3 4 5

5 En scène

With two classmates, act out the following scene.

CHARACTERS:

You, a French friend, and the waiter in the café

SITUATION:

A French friend has been showing you around Paris. You invite your friend to a café and discover too late that you have not changed enough money. Your friend will respond to your questions.

• Ask your friend if he/she is thirsty.
• Ask if he/she wants a soft drink.
• Ask if he/she is hungry.
• Ask if he/she wants a sandwich.
• When the waiter comes, your friend orders and you ask for a croissant and a cup of hot chocolate.
• Ask the waiter how much everything is.
• Ask your friend to please lend you 20 francs.

6 La date, la saison et le temps

Look at the calendar days. For each one, give the date, the season, and the weather.

▶ C'est le dix avril.
C'est le printemps.
Il pleut.

 1 JAN
 2 JUIL
 3 SEP
 4 MAI
 5 OCT

4 GUIDED ORAL EXPRESSION

1. une glace
2. une pizza
3. un chocolat
4. un jus de raisin
5. un steak-frites

■ **Challenge:** You are leaving the café and want to know what you owe. Your classmate will invent a reasonable price.
– Monsieur/Mademoiselle, s'il vous plaît! Ça fait combien?
– Ça fait huit francs.

5 GUIDED ORAL EXPRESSION

6 GUIDED ORAL EXPRESSION

1. Il neige.
2. Il fait chaud.
3. Il fait mauvais. (Il fait frais.)
4. Il fait beau.
5. Il fait frais.

■ Portfolio assessment

For more specific guidelines, see the Teacher Notes in Unit 1, page 31.

The café conversations of the **Challenge** activity on the right could be recorded for the oral portfolio.

Challenge activity

Students in groups of 3 or 4 prepare original café conversations. One person is the waiter, and the others are teenage customers who are talking to one another. Encourage them to use expressions they learned in Units 1 and 2: greetings, introductions, time, etc.

Entracte 3

Une chanson: Alouette

OBJECTIVES:
- Introducing a popular French-Canadian folksong
- Introducing parts of the body

 Entracte 3, Section 1

■ **Cultural note:** In Canada, the lark was formerly hunted as a game bird. In this song, the cook is plucking the bird's feathers before preparing to roast it.

■ **English equivalent**
Lark, sweet lark,
I will pluck you
I will pluck your head ...

I will pluck your beak ...
    your neck...
    your wing ...
    your back ...
    your legs ...
    your tail ...

Une chanson: Alouette

Alouette (The Lark) is a popular folksong of French-Canadian origin. As the song leader names the various parts of the bird's anatomy, he points to his own body. The chorus repeats the refrain with enthusiasm.

Alouette

le bec   la tête
le cou
le dos
les ailes
la queue
les pattes

1. Alouette, gentille, alouette,
   Alouette, je te plumerai.

   Je te plumerai la tête,
   Je te plumerai la tête.

   Et la tête—et la tête
   Alouette—Alouette
   Oh oh oh oh

2. Alouette, gentille alouette
   Alouette, je te plumerai.

   Je te plumerai le bec,
   Je te plumerai le bec.

   Et le bec—et le bec
   Et la tête—et la tête
   Alouette—Alouette
   Oh oh oh oh

3. Je te plumerai le cou . . .

4. Je te plumerai les ailes . . .

5. Je te plumerai le dos . . .

6. Je te plumerai les pattes . . .

7. Je te plumerai la queue . . .

74

Pre-reading activity

Ask how many students know the song "Alouette."
- What country is the song from?
- What kind of bird is an **alouette?**
- What is the song all about?

Post-reading activity

Ask students if they know other French songs. Perhaps they can sing "Frère Jacques."
Frère Jacques / Dormez-vous? / Sonnez les matines. / Din din don. /
(Are you sleeping / Brother John? / Morning bells are ringing / Ding dang dong)

Les parties du corps

(Parts of the body)

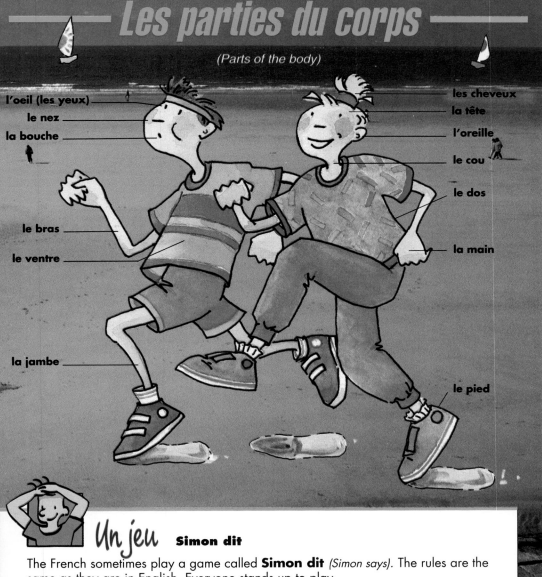

l'oeil (les yeux)
le nez
la bouche
le bras
le ventre
la jambe

les cheveux
la tête
l'oreille
le cou
le dos
la main
le pied

Un jeu   Simon dit

The French sometimes play a game called **Simon dit** *(Simon says)*. The rules are the same as they are in English. Everyone stands up to play.

The game leader says: **Simon dit: Les mains sur la tête!** placing her hands on her head. The other players also place their hands on their head.

Then the game leader may say: **Les mains sur le dos!** placing her hands on her back. This time, however, the other players should not move, because the game leader did not first say **Simon dit.** Any player that did move must sit down.

The game continues until only one player is left standing.

Entracte 3   **75**

OBJECTIVE:
• Learning parts of the body

 Entracte 3, Section 2a

■ **Game: Vrai ou faux?** When the teacher mentions a part of the body and points to it correctly, students respond by saying **vrai**. When the teacher points to the wrong part of the body, students respond by saying **faux**. E.g.,
Voici ma jambe (point to leg)
  vrai
Voici mon pied. (point to arm)
  faux

Entracte 3, Section 2b

■ **Expansion**
Les mains sur les épaules (shoulders).
Les mains sur la taille (waist).
Les mains sur les genoux (knees).

TPR **Parts of the body**

PROP: Halloween skeleton
Introduce the class to the skeleton, to whom you have given a name.
  Qui est-ce? C'est mon ami Victor.
Shake hands with the skeleton.
  Je donne la main à Victor.

Call on individual students to come up.
  X, viens ici et donne la main à Victor.
  Touche-lui l'épaule.
  Montre-nous sa bouche. ...
OPTIONAL: Have students contort Victor.
  Y, viens et mets-lui le pied sur la tête.
  Mets-lui la main gauche sur le cou.

T75

VIDEO ESSAY:
À l'école en France
Total time: 5:35 min.
(Counter: 00:40 min.)

B.1 Visite avec Nathalie Aubin
(00:53–1:37 min.)

B.2 Le lycée Jean-Baptiste Corot
(1:39–4:09 min.)

B.3 Mini-scenes: Quel est ton sujet favori?
(4:10–4:43 min.)

B.4 Conclusion de la visite
(4:44–6:11 min.)

À l'école en France

BONJOUR, Nathalie!

Bonjour!
Je m'appelle Nathalie Aubin.
J'ai 15 ans et j'habite° à Savigny-sur-Orge
avec ma famille. (Savigny est
une petite° ville° à 20 kilomètres
au sud° de Paris.)
J'ai un frère, Christophe, 17 ans,
et deux sœurs, Céline, 13 ans,
et Florence, 7 ans.
Mon père est programmeur.
(Il travaille° à Paris.)
Ma mère est dentiste.
(Elle travaille à Savigny.)
Je vais au lycée Jean-Baptiste
Corot.
Je suis élève° de seconde°.
Et vous?

Nathalie

j'habite *I live*   **petite** *small*   **ville** *city*   **sud** *south*
travaille *works*   **élève** *student*   **seconde** *tenth grade*

76

 🖥 **Using the video**
This Video Essay, **À l'école en France,**
was filmed at the Lycée Jean-Baptiste
Corot in Savigny-sur-Orge, near Paris.
Play the entire module as an introduction
to the photo essay.

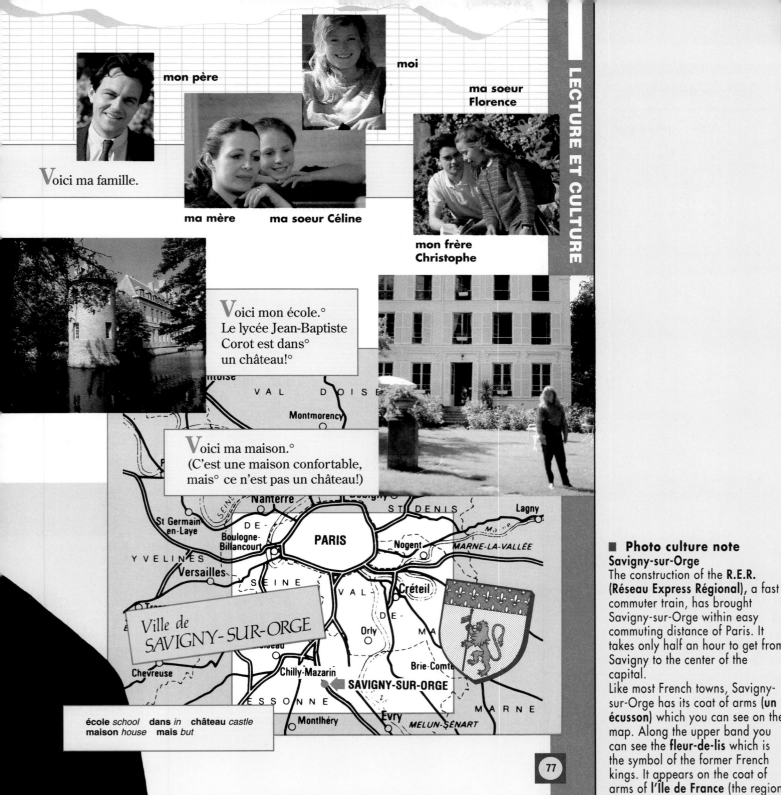

mon père

moi

ma soeur
Florence

Voici ma famille.

ma mère   ma soeur Céline

mon frère
Christophe

Voici mon école.°
Le lycée Jean-Baptiste
Corot est dans°
un château!°

Voici ma maison.°
(C'est une maison confortable,
mais° ce n'est pas un château!)

VAL   D'OISE

Montmorency

Nanterre   ST DENIS   Lagny

St Germain   DE-   Marne
en-Laye   Boulogne-   PARIS   Nogent   MARNE-LA-VALLÉE
             Billancourt

YVELINES
        Versailles   SEINE   VAL   Créteil

Ville de   DE-   MA
SAVIGNY-SUR-ORGE   Orly

Chevreuse   Brie-Comte-
        Chilly-Mazarin   SAVIGNY-SUR-ORGE
    ESSONNE   MARNE
              Montlhéry   Évry   MELUN-SÉNART

école *school*   dans *in*   château *castle*
maison *house*   mais *but*

77

■ **Photo culture note**
Savigny-sur-Orge
The construction of the **R.E.R.
(Réseau Express Régional),** a fast
commuter train, has brought
Savigny-sur-Orge within easy
commuting distance of Paris. It
takes only half an hour to get from
Savigny to the center of the
capital.
Like most French towns, Savigny-
sur-Orge has its coat of arms (**un
écusson**) which you can see on the
map. Along the upper band you
can see the **fleur-de-lis** which is
the symbol of the former French
kings. It appears on the coat of
arms of **l'Île de France** (the region
around Paris).

🧠👥 Cooperative learning

After showing the video, have students in
groups discuss the similarities and
differences between their school and the
Lycée Corot. Let each group name a
recorder (**secrétaire**) who will list their
findings.

As a full class activity, ask the
recorders to read their lists and compare
the findings. Which group was most
observant?

As a follow-up, you may want to play
the video a second time.

■ **Un jour de classe** is based on the above video segments.

Un jour de classe

Le matin

À la maison

Nathalie gets up every morning at seven. After a light breakfast (toasted bread with butter and jam, hot chocolate), she leaves for school.

Nathalie sur sa mobylette

Since she does not live too far from her lycée, she goes there on her moped **(sa mobylette).** Students who live farther away take the school bus.

La classe de sciences-éc

Nathalie arrives at school at about 8:25, five minutes before her first class. Today, Thursday, her first class is economics **(les sciences économiques),** which is her favorite subject.

L'après-midi

À la cantine

At 12:30, Nathalie goes to the school cafeteria **(la cantine)** for lunch. As in American schools, the food is served cafeteria-style. During lunch break, Nathalie meets with her friends from other classes.

La classe d'anglais

Classes start again at two o'clock. Today they finish at four.

Après les classes

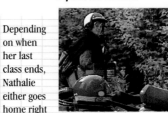

Depending on when her last class ends, Nathalie either goes home right after school or participates in one of the many school clubs.

Le soir

Dans la salle à manger

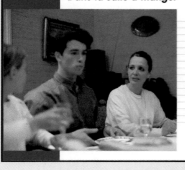

The Aubins have dinner around 7:30. Everyone helps with the kitchen chores. Today it is Christophe's turn.

Nathalie does her homework after dinner. She usually has about one or two hours of homework every night. When she is finished, she reads or listens to cassettes for a while, then goes to bed around 11 P.M.

Nathalie dans sa chambre

■ **Cultural note**

Le dîner

Note that the Aubin family has dinner at 7:30. French people eat later than Americans, usually not before 7:00 and often as late as 8:30. **Le dîner** is generally a lighter meal than the **le déjeuner** (which is served at noon.) In France, dinner is always a family meal, a time for children and parents to talk about how they spent the day.

L'emploi du temps

	LUNDI	MARDI	MERCREDI	JEUDI	VENDREDI	SAMEDI
LYCÉE JEAN-BAPTISTE COROT						
Étudiante: AUBIN, Nathalie						
8h30 à 9h30	Histoire	Allemand				
9h30 à 10h30	Anglais		Français Anglais	Sciences économiques		Français
10h30 à 11h30	Sport		Français	Sciences physiques	Allemand	Français
11h30 à 12h30	Français	Latin	Sciences économiques	(13h30) Maths	Latin	Latin
13h00 à 14h00			Maths	(13h30)	Sciences physiques	Histoire ou Civilisation
14h00 à 15h00	Sciences physiques	Maths				
15h00 à 16h00	Géographie	Maths		Allemand		
16h00 à 17h00	Civilisation	Anglais		Histoire		

NOTE CULTURELLE

Le programme scolaire

At the lycée, all students take a certain number of required subjects. These include French, math, one foreign language, history and geography, physical sciences, natural sciences, and physical education. Depending on their career plans, French students also have to choose among certain electives: a second foreign language, economics, computer science, biology, music.

Here are some of the subjects taught in French secondary schools. How many can you identify?

le français
l'anglais
l'espagnol
l'allemand
le latin

l'histoire
la géographie
les sciences
   économiques
l'éducation civique *(civics)*
la musique
le dessin
l'éducation physique

les maths
la biologie
la physique
la chimie
l'informatique *(computer science)*
les sciences naturelles

Supplementary vocabulary

la conduite *driver's ed*
la technologie
l'éducation manuelle et technique (EMT) *shop*

ACTIVITÉS CULTURELLES

1. Look carefully at Nathalie's class schedule. You may have noted certain differences between the French and the American school systems.
   - French students have more class hours than American students. How many hours of classes does Nathalie have each week?
   - French students learn more foreign languages than American students. In France, the study of foreign languages is compulsory. What languages is Nathalie learning?
   - French students usually have Wednesday afternoon free. Does Nathalie have school on Saturday morning? on Saturday afternoon?
2. Write out your own class schedule in French.

Activités culturelles
Answers:
- Nathalie has 30 hours of class each week. (Note that the **Sciences physiques** class on Thursdays is two hours long.)
- English, German, Latin
- Nathalie has classes Saturday morning, but not Saturday afternoon.

79

B.2 Le lycée Jean-Baptiste
Corot
B.3 Mini-scenes: Quel est
ton sujet favori?
(1:39–4:43 min.)

■ You may want to play these
two segments again, having
students focus on the school itself
rather than on Nathalie.

■ **If students ask:** On the
background map, the student
cafeteria (**la cantine**) is labeled
réfectoires élèves.
Another wing of the same building
houses the **réfectoire professeurs**
where the teachers take their
meals.

Le lycée Jean-Baptiste Corot

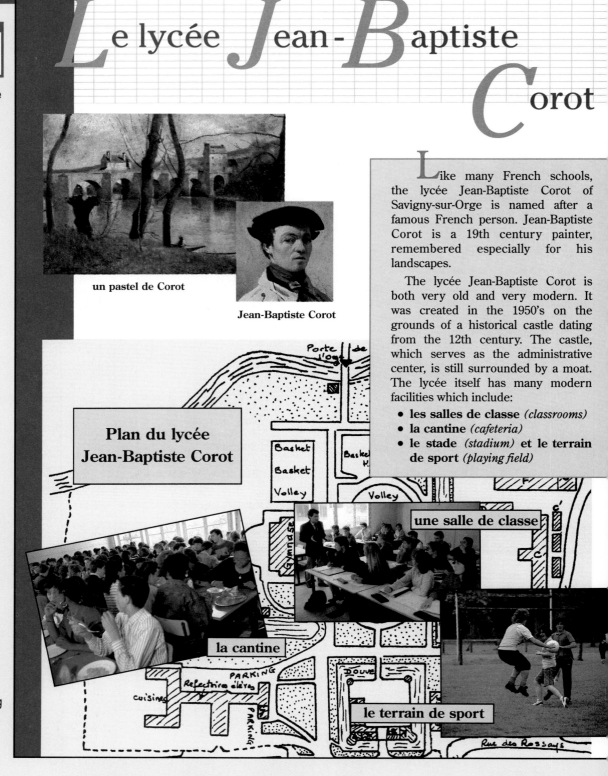

un pastel de Corot

Jean-Baptiste Corot

Like many French schools,
the lycée Jean-Baptiste Corot of
Savigny-sur-Orge is named after a
famous French person. Jean-Baptiste
Corot is a 19th century painter,
remembered especially for his
landscapes.

The lycée Jean-Baptiste Corot is
both very old and very modern. It
was created in the 1950's on the
grounds of a historical castle dating
from the 12th century. The castle,
which serves as the administrative
center, is still surrounded by a moat.
The lycée itself has many modern
facilities which include:

- **les salles de classe** *(classrooms)*
- **la cantine** *(cafeteria)*
- **le stade** *(stadium)* **et le terrain
  de sport** *(playing field)*

Plan du lycée
Jean-Baptiste Corot

une salle de classe

la cantine

le terrain de sport

Cultural background: Le baccalauréat

Students must pass a two-part
competitive national exam in order to
earn their **baccalauréat** (or **bac**) which
gives them entrance to the university.
- The first part, which focuses on French,
  is administered at the end of
  première.

- The second part, given at the end of
  terminale, focuses on the students'
  area of academic concentration.
  Students have the choice of over a
  dozen options. The most popular
  programs are:

NOTES CULTURELLES

1 L'école secondaire

There are two types of secondary schools in France:
- **le collège,** which corresponds to the U.S. middle school (grades 6 to 9)
- **le lycée,** which corresponds to the U.S. high school (grades 10 to 12)

On the following chart, you will notice that each grade (**une classe**) is designated by a number (as in the United States): **sixième (6e), cinquième (5e), quatrième (4e),** etc. However, the progression from grade to grade is the opposite in France. The secondary school begins in France with **sixième** and ends with **terminale.**

École	Classe	Âge des élèves	Équivalent américain
Le collège	sixième (6e)	11–12 ans	sixth grade
	cinquième (5e)	12–13 ans	seventh grade
	quatrième (4e)	13–14 ans	eighth grade
	troisième (3e)	14–15 ans	ninth grade
Le lycée	seconde (2e)	15–16 ans	tenth grade
	première (1e)	16–17 ans	eleventh grade
	terminale	17–18 ans	twelfth grade

2 Le bulletin de notes

At the end of each semester, French students receive a report card **(le bulletin de notes),** which must be signed by their parents. Most schools assign grades on a scale of 0 (low) to 20 (high). Most teachers also write a brief evaluation of the student's progress in each subject.

Here is a report card for the first semester.

LYCÉE J.-B. COROT   91605 SAVIGNY - SUR - ORGE   CLASSE 2e

PICARD Laurent

PREMIER TRIMESTRE

NIVEAU   A B C D E   Appréciations des Professeurs

Math.
M. Antoine   13,5   Élève sérieux.

Sc. Phys.
Mme. Durin.   +11,2   Un premier devoir médiocre. Depuis, c'est mieux. Il faut continuer.

Sc. Nat.
M. Lemaire.   +12,5   ASSEZ BON ENSEMBLE.

Hist. et Géogr.
M. Brunier   -13   Bien.

Français
M. Rivaud   11   Bon travail.

Anglais I
M. Nave   16   Très bien.

Allemand II
Mme. Dumet   15,2   Excellent élève.

ENSEMBLE DES RÉSULTATS : A Très satisfaisant   B Satisfaisant
C Tout juste suffisant   D Insuffisant   E Très insuffisant
Appréciations du Proviseur - du Proviseur Adjoint
du Conseiller Principal d'Éducation - du Professeur Principal
Bon trimestre

ACTIVITÉ CULTURELLE

1. What is the name of the student?
2. What is the name of his school?
3. What grade is he in?
4. What is his best subject? What grade did he get?
5. What is his weakest subject? What grade did he get?
6. How many foreign languages is he studying? Which ones?

81

■ **Le bulletin de notes**
Have students guess the meanings of the abbreviations on the report card:
Math. = Mathématiques
Sc. Phys. = Sciences physiques
Sc. Nat. = Sciences naturelles

■ **Vocabulary**
un appréciation comment
le proviseur principal
le proviseur adjoint vice principal
le conseiller principal d'education guidance counselor
le professeur principal homeroom teacher

■ **Activité culturelle**
Answers:
1. Picard
2. Lycée Jean-Baptiste Corot
3. seconde (tenth grade)
4. English; 16 (A)
5. French; 11 (C)
6. two; English and German

Baccalauréat A: French literature and Foreign Languages
Baccalauréat B: Economics and Social Studies
Baccalauréat C: Mathematics and Physical Sciences
Baccalauréat E: Mathematics and Natural Sciences

Expressions pour la classe

Le professeur dit . . .

à une élève | à un élève

Écoutez!

à la classe

Regarde! *(Look!)* **Regarde la vidéo.**	**Regardez!** **Regardez la vidéo.**
Écoute! *(Listen!)* **Écoute la bande** *(tape).*	**Écoutez!** **Écoutez la bande.**
Parle! *(Speak!)* **Parle plus fort** *(louder).*	**Parlez!** **Parlez plus fort.**
Réponds! *(Answer!)* **Réponds à la question.**	**Répondez!** **Répondez à la question.**
Répète! *(Repeat!)* **Répète la phrase** *(sentence).*	**Répétez!** **Répétez la phrase.**
Lis! *(Read!)* **Lis l'exercice.**	**Lisez!** **Lisez l'exercice.**
Écris! *(Write!)* **Écris dans ton cahier.**	**Écrivez!** **Écrivez dans vos cahiers.**

Prends *(Take)*	**une feuille de papier.** **un crayon**	**Prenez**	**une feuille de papier.** **un crayon**
Ouvre *(Open)*	**ton livre.** **la porte**	**Ouvrez**	**vos livres.** **la porte**
Ferme *(Close)*	**ton cahier.** **la fenêtre**	**Fermez**	**vos cahiers.** **la fenêtre**

Viens! *(Come!)* **Viens ici.**	**Venez!** **Venez ici.**
Va! *(Go!)* **Va au tableau.**	**Allez!** **Allez au tableau.**
Lève-toi! *(Stand up!)*	**Levez-vous!**
Assieds-toi! *(Sit down!)*	**Asseyez-vous!**

Apporte-moi *(Bring me)*		**Apportez-moi**	
Donne-moi *(Give me)*	**ton devoir.**	**Donnez-moi**	**vos devoirs.**
Montre-moi *(Show me)*		**Montrez-moi**	

82

Teaching note

Le professeur dit
These phrases are primarily for LISTENING
COMPREHENSION. Try to use these
regularly in class so that students can
internalize them and acquire a feeling for
French rhythm and intonation patterns.

Quelques objets; Tu dis
These words and phrases are ACTIVE.
Students will be using them to express
themselves in class and ask questions.

Quelques objets

un crayon

un livre

une feuille de papier

un stylo

un cahier

une cassette

un devoir

un morceau de craie

une vidéocassette

un bureau

un ordinateur

une télé

une carte

une porte

un tableau

un magnétoscope

une table

une chaise

une fenêtre

Tu dis …

Je sais. — *I know.*

Je ne sais pas. — *I don't know.*

Je ne comprends pas. — *I don't understand.*

Que veut dire … ? — *What does … mean?*

Comment dit-on … en français? — *How does one say … in French?*

83

TPR Classroom objects

You may want to introduce these words
with TPR activities (see Front Matter).
Montrez-moi une feuille de papier. etc.
Mettez un stylo sur la feuille de papier.
Mettez un livre sur le stylo.
**Mettez un morceau de craie sur le
    bureau.**

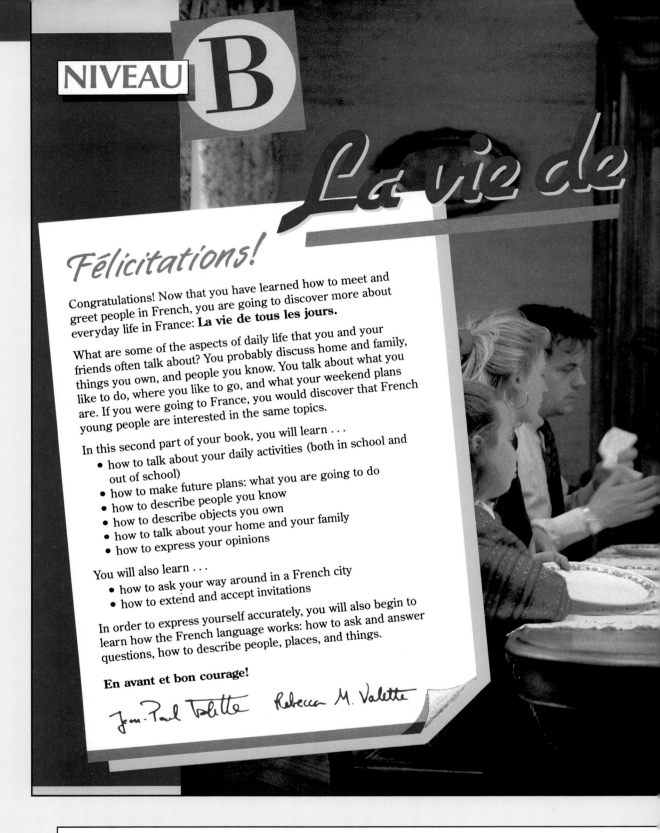

NIVEAU B

La vie de

Félicitations!

Congratulations! Now that you have learned how to meet and greet people in French, you are going to discover more about everyday life in France: **La vie de tous les jours.**

What are some of the aspects of daily life that you and your friends often talk about? You probably discuss home and family, things you own, and people you know. You talk about what you like to do, where you like to go, and what your weekend plans are. If you were going to France, you would discover that French young people are interested in the same topics.

In this second part of your book, you will learn . . .
- how to talk about your daily activities (both in school and out of school)
- how to make future plans: what you are going to do
- how to describe people you know
- how to describe objects you own
- how to talk about your home and your family
- how to express your opinions

You will also learn . . .
- how to ask your way around in a French city
- how to extend and accept invitations

In order to express yourself accurately, you will also begin to learn how the French language works: how to ask and answer questions, how to describe people, places, and things.

En avant et bon courage!

Overview of Niveau B

Niveau B contains the core of **Discovering French — Bleu.** Students will be acquiring the linguistic foundation needed for basic communication skills: the ability to ask and answer questions and the ability to use French creatively for self-expression.

In particular, in Niveau B there will be:
- a shift from primarily oral practice (which characterized Niveau A) to a four-skills approach including reading and writing,
- a focus on basic French sentence patterns and high frequency vocabulary,

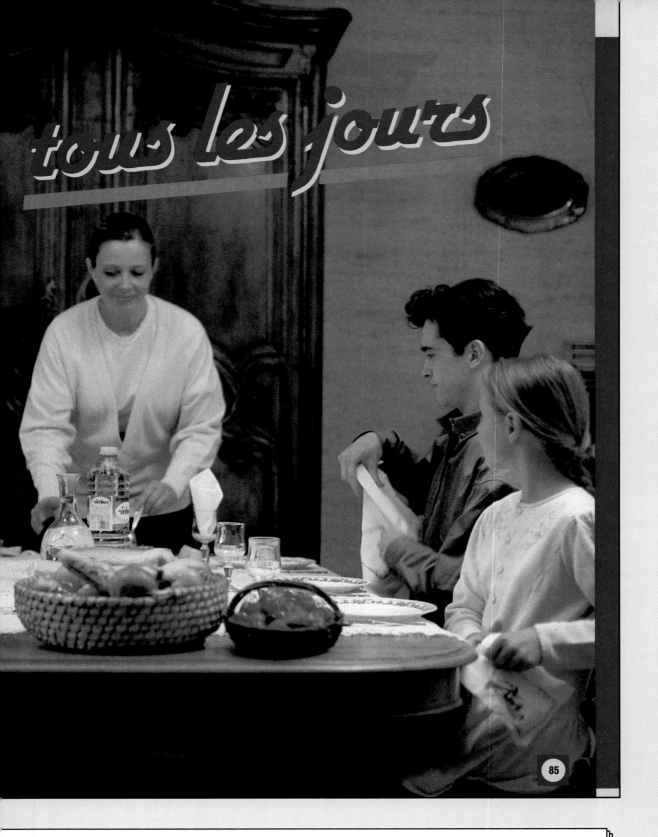

tous les jours

85

- an introduction to critical thinking about language and how the French language works,
- an emphasis on linguistic interaction, with numerous role play and dialogue activities.

Unité 4

MAIN THEME:

Daily activities

UNITÉ 4
Modules 13–16

13. Le français pratique:
    Mes activités
14. Où est Jean-Claude?
15. Une boum
16. Une interview

Classroom Notes

UNITÉ 4

Qu'est-ce qu'on fait?

LEÇON **13** Le français pratique: Mes activités

LEÇON **14** Qui est là?

LEÇON **15** Une boum

LEÇON **16** Une interview

Unit overview

COMMUNICATION GOALS: Students will learn to talk about their daily activities and how to extend and respond to invitations.
LINGUISTIC GOALS: The primary focus is on the present tense (affirmative, negative) and question formation.

CRITICAL THINKING GOALS: Students are introduced to the concept of subject-verb agreement and the importance of verb endings in French.
CULTURAL GOALS: This unit focuses on the daily activities of French young people: school and homework, as well as sports and leisure activities.

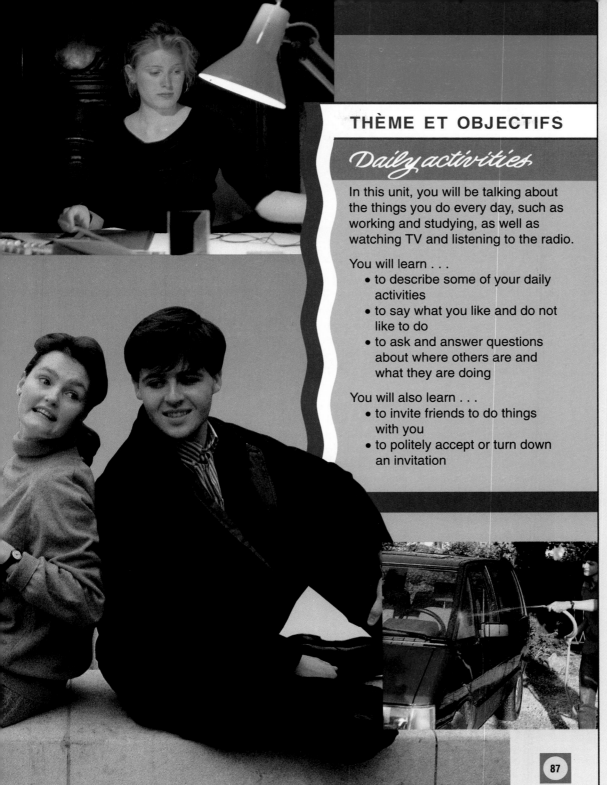

THÈME ET OBJECTIFS

Daily activities

In this unit, you will be talking about the things you do every day, such as working and studying, as well as watching TV and listening to the radio.

You will learn . . .
- to describe some of your daily activities
- to say what you like and do not like to do
- to ask and answer questions about where others are and what they are doing

You will also learn . . .
- to invite friends to do things with you
- to politely accept or turn down an invitation

87

 Cross-cultural observation
All of these pictures were taken in France.
As usual, have students look at the photos and answer the following questions:
- Could any of them have been taken in the United States?
- Why or why not?
- Which elements in the pictures seem to be definitely French?

■ **Photo culture note:**
L'armoire
Note the **armoire** *(wardrobe)* in the top picture. Traditionally French homes have few closets, so most rooms have free-standing **armoires** which are used to store clothes, linen, dishes, and so forth.

Pacing
Beginning with Unit 4, the lessons are longer and there is a dual emphasis on both oral and written skills.
    For specific suggestions on pacing, turn to the Front Matter.

Leçon 13

MAIN TOPICS:

**Describing daily
activities
Offering and
receiving invitations**

MODULE 13:
Le français pratique:
Mes activités
Total time: 5:56 min.
(Counter: 6:24 min.)

**13.1 Mini-scenes: Listening
— J'aime téléphoner**
(7:22–8:04 min.)

**13.2 Mini-scenes: Speaking
— Tu aimes écouter la
radio?** (8:05–9:07 min.)

**13.3 Mini-scenes: Listening
— Invitations**
(9:08–9:24 min.)

13.4 Dialogue: Tennis
(9:25–10:32 min.)

**13.5 Vignette culturelle:
Le téléphone**
(10:33–12:15 min.)

■ **Comprehension practice:** Play
the entire module through as an
introduction to the lesson.

LE FRANÇAIS
P R A T I Q U E

LEÇON 13 Mes activités

Accent sur ... Les activités de la semaine

French teenagers, as well as their
parents, put a lot of emphasis on
doing well in school. On the whole,
French students spend a great deal of
time on their studies. French schools
have a longer class day than American
schools, and teachers tend to assign quite a
lot of homework.

However, French teenagers do not study all
the time. They also watch TV and listen to
music. Many participate in various sports
activities, but to a lesser extent than young
Americans. On weekends, French teenagers
like to go out with their friends. Some go
shopping. Others go to the movies. Many
enjoy dancing and going to parties. Sunday
is usually a family day for visiting relatives or
going for a drive in the country.

■ **Au cinéma**
Des copains sont au cinéma.

■ **Au café**
Stéphanie est au café.

🖥 Using the video

Beginning with this lesson, there is more
variety in the sequencing of the video
modules.
    Play the entire module through as an
introduction to the cultural themes and
new linguistic material of the lesson.

The various parts of the video are closely
correlated to specific sections in the
lesson. Notes in the Teacher Edition
(prefaced with the video logo) indicate
points at which you may want to use
certain video segments.

Une boum
Dominique et Stéphanie
sont à une boum.

**Le terrain de foot
au lycée Corot**
Des jeunes jouent au foot.

En classe
Marc et Patrick sont en classe.

■ **Photo culture notes**

Au cinéma
The Danton movie theater in the
Latin Quarter of Paris is showing
"Cyrano" and "La Gloire de mon
père" (My Father's Glory). Note
the neon arrows that tell people
where to line up to buy tickets for
each movie.

Au café
French cafés traditionally have
wicker chairs.

Une boum
Note the moldings on the walls
and ceiling. These are traditional
design elements in older French
homes and apartments.

Lycée Corot
For more information about the
Lycée Corot, turn to pages 76–83.

En classe
Traditionally, French students are
required to have different bound
notebooks for each subject.

Teaching strategy: Le français pratique

Beginning with Niveau B, the first lesson
of each unit introduces the communication theme and the related vocabulary.
All of these new words and phrases are
then re-entered in a variety of situations
in the remainder of the unit.

Try to move rather quickly through *Le
français pratique* because students will
have ample opportunity to master the
new material as they do the many
activities in the next three lessons.

COMMUNICATIVE FUNCTION:
Expressing likes and
dislikes

 Transparencies 14A, 14B
Verbs

 Leçon 13, Section 1

■ **Pronunciation practice:** This casette activity models the new vocabulary in sentence context.

■ **Looking ahead:** In this lesson, students will become familiar with the meaning of these verbs in the infinitive form.
   In Lesson 15, they will learn how to use them in the present tense.

 COMMUNICATION:
indicating preferences

■ **Oral introduction**
• Model the options in each question for listening compre-hen-sion, asking for a show of hands.
   En classe, qui aime étudier?
   Qui aime écouter le pro-fesseur?
   Qui préfère parler avec un copain?
   Qui préfère parler avec une copine?
• Ask individual students who have raised their hands to respond orally:
   X, en classe, est-ce que tu aimes étudier?
   X: Oui, j'aime étudier.

A. Préférences

How to talk about what you like and don't like to do:

Est-ce que tu aimes . . .?	*Do you like . . .?*	**Est-ce que tu aimes** parler *(to speak)* français?
J'aime . . .	*I like . . .*	Oui, **j'aime** parler français.
Je n'aime pas . . .	*I don't like . . .*	Non, **je n'aime pas** parler français.
Je préfère . . .	*I prefer . . .*	**Je préfère** parler anglais.

 J'aime . . .

| **téléphoner** | **parler français** | **parler anglais** | **parler espagnol** |
| *to phone* | *to talk, speak French* | *to speak English* | *to speak Spanish* |

| **manger** | **chanter** | **danser** | **nager** |
| *to eat* | *to sing* | *to dance* | *to swim* |

1 **Et toi?**

Indicate what you like to do in the following situations by completing the sentences.

1. En classe,
   j'aime . . .
   mais je préfère . . .
   • étudier
   • écouter le professeur
   • parler avec *(with)* un copain
   • parler avec une copine

2. En été,
   j'aime . . .
   mais je préfère . . .
   • travailler
   • nager
   • voyager
   • jouer au volley

 TPR 🏃 **Everyday activities**

PROPS: Transparencies 14a and 14b
   Develop a gesture for each verb.
Model the sentences in the verb charts and have the class mimic the action with you.
   J'aime téléphoner. [Gesture "dialing"]
   J'aime manger. [Gesture "eating"]
   J'aime jouer au foot. [Gesture "kicking"]

Say sentences with students acting out verbs. Have students point out the actions on the transparency:
   X, montre-nous l'action: J'aime chanter. etc.
Have students repeat each sentence with you as they gesture the action. Do the action and have class say the sentence.

J'aime aussi *(also)* . . .

jouer au tennis
to play tennis

jouer au volley
to play volleyball

jouer au basket
to play basketball

jouer au foot
to play soccer

Mais *(but)* **je préfère** . . .

regarder la télé
to watch TV

écouter la radio
to listen to the radio

dîner au restaurant
to have dinner at the restaurant; to eat out

voyager
to travel

Je n'aime pas toujours *(always)* . . .

étudier
to study

travailler
to work

HAVE YOU NOTED?

1. French people like to shorten words. For example, the words **volleyball, basketball, football,** and **télévision** are often shortened to **volley, basket, foot,** and **télé.**
2. In French, **foot** (or **football**) refers to *soccer.*

13.1 Mini-scenes: J'aime téléphoner
13.2 Mini-scenes: Tu aimes écouter la radio?
(7:22–9:07 min.)

Leçon 13, Sections 2, 3

Classroom Notes

---

3. Avec mes *(my)* copains,
   j'aime . . .
   mais je préfère . . .

   - chanter
   - manger

   - écouter la radio
   - jouer au basket

4. Avec ma famille,
   j'aime . . .
   mais je préfère . . .

   - voyager
   - regarder la télé

   - jouer à «Trivial Pursuit»
   - dîner au restaurant

5. À la maison *(At home)*,
   j'aime . . .
   mais je préfère . . .

   - étudier
   - téléphoner

   - manger
   - écouter mon walkman

👥 Cooperative group practice

As a preparation for group work, first introduce Activity 1 orally. (See side note.)

Then divide the class into groups, each with a recorder (**un/une secrétaire**).

Individual group members take turns indicating their preferences (Act. 1).

En classe, je préfère étudier.

The **secrétaire** tallies the group's responses.

#1. La majorité préfère étudier. (La majorité préfère écouter le professeur.)

The results can be reported back to the class, or handed in to the teacher.

■ Photo culture note
Un café à Tours
The green drink on the table is **un diabolo-menthe**. This drink is made by adding green mint syrup (**du sirop de menthe**) to lemon-flavored soda (**une limonade**). It is very popular among teenagers.

3 EXCHANGES: asking friends what they like to do

1. jouer au tennis
2. écouter la radio
3. jouer au foot
4. voyager
5. étudier
6. nager
7. chanter
8. dîner au restaurant
9. travailler

4 ROLE PLAY: discussing preferred activities

1. jouer au basket / jouer au volley
2. parler anglais / parler espagnol
3. chanter / danser
4. écouter la radio / regarder la télé
5. étudier / [jouer au foot]

■ **Variation:** Have "Hélène" ask the question using the activity in the bottom row. Philippe answers, using the activity in the top row.
H: Est-ce que tu aimes jouer au tennis?
P: Oui, mais je préfère nager.

---

2 Tu aimes ou tu n'aimes pas?
Say whether or not you like to do the following things.

▶ parler français?

J'aime parler français.

Je n'aime pas parler français.

1. parler anglais?	7. regarder la télé?
2. étudier?	8. dîner au restaurant?
3. danser?	9. manger?
4. chanter?	10. travailler?
5. jouer au basket?	11. écouter la radio?
6. jouer au tennis?	12. téléphoner?

3 Préférences
Ask your classmates if they like to do the following things.

▶ —Est-ce que tu aimes téléphoner?
—Oui, j'aime téléphoner. (Non, je n'aime pas téléphoner.)

4 Dialogue
Philippe is asking Hélène if she likes to do certain things. She replies that she prefers to do other things. Play both roles. Note: "??" means you can invent an answer.

▶ PHILIPPE: Est-ce que tu aimes nager?
HÉLÈNE: Oui, mais je préfère jouer au tennis.

Cooperative pair practice
Activities 2, 3, 4

Teaching note: Writing activities
Beginning with Unit 4, students will be developing both their writing and speaking skills. Activities which lend themselves to written (as well as oral) practice will be signaled in the Teacher Edition with a paper and pencil symbol.

The Student Activity Book provides a wide variety of additional writing activities.

B. Souhaits *(Wishes)*

Je voudrais voyager en France.

How to talk about what you want, would like, and do not want to do:

Je veux . . .	*I want . . .*	**Je veux** parler français.
Je voudrais . . .	*I would like . . .*	**Je voudrais** voyager en France.
Je ne veux pas . . .	*I don't want . . .*	**Je ne veux pas** étudier aujourd'hui.

5 **Ce soir** *(Tonight)*

Say whether or not you want to do the following things tonight.

▶ étudier?
  Oui, je veux étudier.
  (Non, je ne veux pas étudier.)

1. parler français?
2. travailler?
3. jouer au ping-pong?
4. chanter?
5. danser?
6. regarder la télé?
7. écouter la radio?
8. dîner avec une copine?
9. parler à *(to)* mon frère?
10. téléphoner à mon cousin?

6 **Weekend**

Caroline and her friends are discussing their weekend plans. What do they say they would like to do?

▶ CAROLINE: Je voudrais jouer au tennis.

Caroline

1. Jérôme 2. Monique

3. Jean-Louis 4. Céline 5. Patrick

7 **Trois souhaits** *(Three wishes)*

Read the list of suggested activities and select the three that you would like to do most.

parler français   voyager avec ma cousine
parler espagnol   voyager en France
parler avec *(with)* Oprah Winfrey   chanter comme *(like)* Bruce Springsteen
dîner avec le Président   jouer au tennis avec Steffi Graf
dîner avec Tom Cruise   jouer au basket comme Michael Jordan

▶ Je voudrais parler espagnol.
  Je voudrais chanter comme Bruce Springsteen.
  Je voudrais voyager en France.

COMMUNICATIVE FUNCTION: expressing wishes

COMMUNICATION: indicating what you want/don't want to do

5

■ **Language note:** In French, one must say **téléphoner à,** *to phone "to" someone.*

DESCRIPTION: indicating what people would like to do

6

1. nager
2. dîner au restaurant
3. danser
4. jouer au basket
5. écouter la radio

■ **Challenge:** Add **Et toi?** The next student replies with an alternative activity.
Caroline: **Je voudrais jouer au tennis. Et toi?**
Élève A: **Je voudrais jouer au foot (chanter, etc.).**

COMMUNICATION: indicating what you would like to do

7

■ **Variation:** Have students substitute other names in their responses.
Je voudrais parler avec Arsenio Hall.

■ **Variation:** Have the students select the three activities they would like to do <u>least</u>. Then have them compare their responses with a partner.
Je ne voudrais pas voyager avec ma cousine., etc.

13.3 Mini-scenes:
Invitations
(9:08–9:24 min.)

Leçon 13, Sections 3, 4

ROLE PLAY: extending and
8 accepting invitations

■ **Challenge:** Students can use
other phrases as they accept the
invitations: e.g., **D'accord / Oui,**
merci / Oui, bien sûr.

EXCHANGES: extending
9 and refusing invitations

13.4 Dialogue: Tennis?
(9:25–10:32 min.)

Leçon 13, Section 5

C. Invitations

Est-ce que tu veux jouer au tennis?

▶ *How to invite a friend:*

Est-ce que tu veux ...?	*Do you want to . . . ?*	**Est-ce que tu veux** jouer au tennis?
Est-ce que tu peux ...?	*Can you . . . ?*	**Est-ce que tu peux** parler à mon copain?
avec moi/toi	*with me/you*	Est-ce que tu veux dîner **avec moi?**

▶ *How to accept an invitation:*

Oui, bien sûr ...	*Yes, of course . . .*	
Oui, merci ...	*Yes, thanks . . .*	
Oui, d'accord ...	*Yes, all right, okay . . .*	
je veux bien.	*I'd love to.*	**Oui, bien sûr, je veux bien.**
je veux bien ...	*I'd love to . . .*	**Oui, merci, je veux bien** dîner avec toi.

▶ *How to turn down an invitation:*

Je regrette, mais	*I'm sorry, but*	**Je regrette, mais je ne peux pas**
je ne peux pas ...	*I can't . . .*	dîner avec toi.
Je dois ...	*I have to, I must . . .*	**Je dois** étudier.

8 **Invitations**
Imagine a French exchange group is
visiting your school. Invite the following
French students to do things with you.
They will accept. (Your classmates will
play the parts of the students.)

▶ Monique / dîner

Monique, est-ce que
tu veux dîner
avec moi?

Oui, d'accord,
je veux bien dîner
avec toi.

1. Éric / parler français
2. Philippe / étudier
3. Céline / jouer au tennis
4. Anne / manger une pizza
5. Jean-Claude / chanter
6. Caroline / danser

9 **Conversation**
Ask your classmates if they want to do
the following things. They will answer
that they cannot and explain what they
have to do.

▶ jouer au tennis? (étudier)
  —Est-ce que tu veux jouer au
    basket?
  —Non, je ne peux pas. Je dois
    étudier.

1. jouer au volley? (travailler)
2. jouer au ping-pong? (téléphoner à ma
   cousine)
3. étudier avec moi? (étudier avec ma
   copine)
4. dîner avec moi? (dîner avec ma
   famille)
5. nager? (jouer au foot à deux
   heures)

Cooperative
pair practice
Activities 8, 9

📺 Teaching the video dialogue

For Lesson 13, the video (part 4) and the
cassette program (part 5) contain a series
of conversations.
Step 1: Set the scene. Tell students: In
this scene Jean-Claude is looking for a
tennis partner. **Regardez. (Écoutez.)**
Step 2: Play the video/cassette segment.

Step 3: Have students in small groups try
to recall the scenes.
    Écrivez l'invitation de Jean-Claude
    et les réponses de ses amis.
Step 4: Play the segment again to let
groups check their work.
Step 5: Compare the group answers.

À votre tour!

1 Créa-dialogue

Ask your classmates if they want to do the following things with you. They will answer that they cannot and will give one of the excuses in the box.

▶ jouer au tennis

1. jouer au basket
2. manger une pizza
3. regarder la télé
4. jouer au ping-pong
5. dîner au restaurant

Est-ce que tu veux <u>jouer au tennis</u> avec moi?

Non, je ne peux pas. Je dois <u>travailler</u>.

Excuses:
étudier
travailler
téléphoner à une copine
dîner avec ma cousine
parler avec ma mère
chanter avec la chorale *(choir)*

2 Conversation dirigée

Philippe is phoning Stéphanie. Write out their conversation according to the directions. You may want to act out the dialogue with a classmate.

Philippe				Stéphanie
asks Stéphanie how she is	⇄	answers that she is fine		
asks her if she wants to eat out	⇄	asks at what time		
says at 8 o'clock	→	says that she is sorry but that she has to study		
says it is too bad (**Dommage!**)				

3 Expression personnelle

What we like to do often depends on the circumstances. Complete the sentences below saying what you like and don't like to do in the following situations.

▶ En hiver . . .
  En hiver, j'aime regarder la télé. J'aime aussi jouer au basket. Je n'aime pas nager.

1. En été . . .
2. En automne . . .
3. Le samedi *(On Saturdays)* . . .
4. Le dimanche . . .
5. Le soir *(In the evening)* . . .
6. En classe . . .
7. Avec mes *(my)* amis . . .
8. Avec ma famille . . .

4 Composition

Write three things that you like to do and three things that you do not like to do.

J'aime jouer au volley. Je n'aime pas jouer au foot.

5 Correspondance

This summer, you are going to spend two weeks in France. Your pen pal Philippe has written, asking what you like and don't like to do on vacation (**en vacances**). Write a postcard answering his questions.

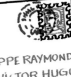

Cher Philippe,
En vacances,
j'aime . . .

PHILIPPE RAYMOND
12 AV. VICTOR HUGO
PARIS 75116
FRANCE

À votre tour

Beginning with this lesson, the **À votre tour** sections have both oral and written communication activities.

Depending on your goals and objectives, you may or may not wish to assign all of the activities in the **À votre tour** section.

📁 Portfolio assessment

Beginning with Unit 4, students may start a Written Portfolio (see Front Matter for a complete description).

You will perhaps want to do only one oral portfolio recording and one written composition per unit. In this lesson, a good written portfolio topic is Act. 5.

---

1 GUIDED ORAL EXPRESSION

Leçon 13, Section 6

2 GUIDED ORAL EXPRESSION

P: (Salut, Stéphanie.) Ça va?
S: Oui, ça va (merci).
P: Tu veux dîner au restaurant?
S: À quelle heure?
P: À 8 heures.
S: Je regrette, mais je dois étudier.
P: Dommage!

Leçon 13, Section 7

💻 **13.5 Vignette culturelle: Le téléphone** (10:33–12:15 min.)

3 ORAL EXPRESSION

4 WRITTEN SELF-EXPRESSION

5 WRITTEN SELF-EXPRESSION

■ **Cooperative reading practice:** Have students prepare a writing activity for homework. Then, in class, divide students into small groups and let them read one another's compositions.

Leçon 14

MAIN TOPIC:

Finding out where people are

MODULE 14:
Où est Jean-Claude?
Total time: 5:02 min.
(Counter: 12:28 min.)

14.1 Mini-scenes: Listening
— Je suis en classe
(13:02–13:30 min.)

14.2 Mini-scenes: Speaking
— Où sont-ils?
(13:31–14:44 min.)

14.3 Dialogue: Où est Jean-Claude?
(14:45–15:52 min.)

14.4 Vignette culturelle: Au café (15:53–17:26 min.)

■ **Comprehension practice:** Play the entire module through as an introduction to the lesson.

 Leçon 14, Section 1

 COMPREHENSION

1. (b) à la maison
2. (c) en ville
3. (d) au restaurant
4. (a) au café

■ **Oral comprehension:** Read each statement and have students indicate whether it is true (**vrai**) or false (**faux**).
1. Jacqueline est à la maison. (vrai)
2. Jean-Claude est à la maison. (faux)
3. Nicole est au restaurant. (vrai)
4. Sandrine est au cinéma. (faux)
5. Hélène est au café. (vrai)

T96

LEÇON 14 Qui est là?

It is Wednesday afternoon. Pierre is looking for his friends but cannot find anyone. Finally he sees Hélène at the Café Bellevue and asks her where everyone is.

PIERRE:	<u>Où</u> est Jacqueline?	*Where*
HÉLÈNE:	Elle est <u>à la maison</u>.	*at home*
PIERRE:	Et Jean-Claude? Il est <u>là</u>?	*here*
HÉLÈNE:	Non, il n'est pas là.	
PIERRE:	Où est-il?	
HÉLÈNE:	Il est <u>en ville</u> avec une copine.	*in town*
PIERRE:	Et Nicole et Sandrine? Est-ce qu'elles sont <u>ici</u>?	*here*
HÉLÈNE:	Non, elles sont au restaurant.	
PIERRE:	<u>Alors</u>, qui est là?	*So*
HÉLÈNE:	Moi, je suis ici.	
PIERRE:	C'est <u>vrai</u>, tu es ici! Eh bien, <u>puisque</u> tu es là, je <u>t'invite au cinéma</u>. D'accord?	*true / since* *I'll invite you to the movies*
HÉLÈNE:	Super! Pierre, tu es un <u>vrai</u> copain!	*real*

● **Compréhension**

Indicate where the following people are by selecting the appropriate completions.

1. Jacqueline est . . .	a) au café
2. Jean-Claude est . . .	b) à la maison
3. Nicole et Sandrine sont . . .	c) en ville
4. Hélène et Pierre sont . . .	d) au restaurant

 Setting the stage

You may want to introduce the opening text by having students listen to the cassette recording with their books closed. They will hear a conversation between Pierre and Hélène. Pierre is looking for **Jacqueline, Jean-Claude,** and **Nicole et Sandrine.**

Draw three sets of stick figures (a girl, a boy, two girls) and identify them, as above.

Then label line drawings of three places: **en ville, au restaurant, à la maison.**

Tell students they are to listen to the conversation carefully and determine who is where.

■ NOTE ■
CULTURELLE

Le mercredi après-midi

French high school students do not have classes on Wednesday afternoons. They use this free time to go out with their friends or to catch up on their homework. For some students, Wednesday afternoon is also the time for music and dance lessons as well as sports club activities. However, in contrast to the United States, many French schools have classes on Saturday mornings.

Note culturelle

For more information about the French school system, turn to the photo essay on pp. 76–81, À l'école en France.

■ Photo culture note
Le cartable
In France, students often carry their books and school supplies in a **cartable** (a large briefcase).

 14.4 Vignette culturelle: Au café
(15:53–17:26 min.)

● **Cross-cultural observation:** After showing the video segment, have students in pairs make a list of similarities and differences between the French **café** and similar places where teens go in the United States.

▢ Using the video

In many lessons of Niveau B, like this one, the video dialogue is different from the one in the opening text. (This is visually indicated by the presence of cartoon characters in the opening photograph.)

You may still want to play the entire video as an introduction to the lesson,

because it develops the communication themes and highlights the new structures.

The video logos in the Teacher Edition will let you know where to use specific video segments.

T97

COMMUNICATIVE FUNCTION:
Identifying people and
where they are

🔁 **Re-entry and review:**
Remind students that they have
already been using the singular
forms of **être**:
Je suis américain.
Tu es français.
Il est canadien.

■ **Pronunciation note:** There is
usually liaison after **est**:
Elle est‿ici.
Liaison is optional after other
forms of **être**:
Ils sont‿ici. or
Ils sont ici.

■ **If students ask:** The pronouns
il and **elle** may also mean *it*.
Remind them that in Niveau A
they used sentences like:
[le sandwich] Il coûte 15 francs.

■ **Learning aid:** Always use
vous with people you address as
Monsieur, Madame, or
Mademoiselle.

■ **Teaching tip:** Use Transparency 16 (subject pronouns) as
a visual aid to present and
practice verb forms throughout
this program.

A. Le verbe *être* et les pronoms sujets

Être *(to be)* is the most frequently used verb in French. Note the forms of **être** in the
chart below.

	être	to be	
SINGULAR	je **suis** tu **es** il/elle **est**	*I am* *you are* *he/she is*	Je **suis** américain. Tu **es** canadienne. Il **est** anglais.
PLURAL	nous **sommes** vous **êtes** ils/elles **sont**	*we are* *you are* *they are*	Nous **sommes** à Paris. Vous **êtes** à San Francisco. Ils **sont** à Genève.

➡ Note the liaison in the **vous**-form:
   Vous‿êtes français?

➡ Note the expression **être d'accord** *(to agree)*:
   —Tu **es** d'accord   *Do you agree*
      avec moi?   *with me?*
   —Oui, je **suis d'accord!** *Yes, I agree.*

TU or *VOUS?*

When talking to ONE person, the French have two
ways of saying *you*:

- **tu** ("familiar *you*") is used to talk to someone
  your own age (or younger) or to a member of
  your family
- **vous** ("formal *you*") is used when talking to
  anyone else

When talking to TWO or more people, the French
use **vous.**

Learning about language
The words **je** *(I)*, **tu** *(you)*, **il** *(he)*, **elle**
(she), etc. are called SUBJECT PRONOUNS.

- SINGULAR pronouns refer to one
  person (or object).
- PLURAL pronouns refer to two or
  more people (or objects).

The VERB **être** *(to be)* is IRREGULAR because
its forms do not follow a predictable
pattern.
A chart showing the subject pronouns
and their corresponding verb forms is
called a CONJUGATION.

REMINDER: You should use . . .
- **vous** to address your teacher
- **tu** to address a classmate

Tu es français?

Vous êtes français?

Vous êtes français?

Teaching note: Learning styles

Since different students have different
learning styles, **Discovering French**
presents French structures in several
ways:
- STRUCTURES IN CONTEXT (in dialogues)
— for those who learn best by hearing
and repeating.

- CHARTS AND BRIEF EXPLANATIONS
— for those who need to understand a
pattern before practicing it.
- CARTOON DRAWINGS (where appropriate)
— for those who find it helpful to visual-
ize a concept in picture form.

ILS or ELLES?

The French have two ways of saying *they:*

- **ils** refers to two or more males or to a mixed group of males and females
- **elles** refers to two or more females

Ils sont à Paris.   Ils sont à Bordeaux.

Ils sont à Lyon.   Elles sont à Nice.

PRACTICE: saying where people are

1 En France

The following students are on vacation in France.
Which cities are they in?

▶ Alice . . . à Nice.   **Alice est à Nice.**

1. Philippe . . . à Toulon.
2. Nous . . . à Paris.
3. Vous . . . à Marseille.
4. Je . . . à Lyon.
5. Tu . . . à Tours.
6. Michèle et Francine . . . à Lille.
7. Éric et Vincent . . . à Strasbourg.
8. Ma cousine . . . à Toulouse.
9. Mon copain . . . à Bordeaux.

(map of France with cities: Lille, Paris, Strasbourg, Tours, Lyon, Bordeaux, Nice, Marseille, Toulouse, Toulon)

Vocabulaire: *Où?*

Où est Cécile?   *Where is Cécile?*

Elle est . . .

ici *(here)*	**là** *(here, there)*	**là-bas** *(over there)*
à Paris *(in Paris)*	**à Boston**	**à Québec**
en classe *(in class)*	**en ville** *(downtown, in town, in the city)*	
en vacances *(on vacation)*	**en France** *(in France)*	
au café *(at the café)*	**au restaurant**	**au cinéma** *(at the movies)*
à la maison *(at home)*		

▷ **Vocabulaire**

 Transparency 15
Où sont-ils?

 14.1 Mini-scenes: Je suis en classe
14.2 Mini-scenes: Où sont-ils?
(13:02–14:44 min.)

 Leçon 14, Sections 2, 3

COMPREHENSION: using **tu** and **vous**

2 À Nice

Catherine is spending her summer vacation in Nice at the home of her pen pal Stéphanie Lambert. Catherine has met many different people and is asking them various questions. Complete her questions with **Tu es** or **Vous êtes,** as appropriate.

▶ *(Stéphanie's brother)* . . . en vacances?
<u>Tu es</u> en vacances?

▶ *(Monsieur Lambert)* . . . de *(from)* Tours?
<u>Vous êtes</u> de Tours?

1. *(Mélanie, a friend of Stéphanie's)* . . . canadienne?
2. *(Olivier, Stéphanie's boyfriend)* . . . souvent *(often)* avec Stéphanie?
3. *(Monsieur Tardif, the neighbor)* . . . en vacances?
4. *(the mailman)* . . . de Nice?
5. *(Frédéric, Stéphanie's young cousin)* . . . souvent à Nice?
6. *(a woman in the park)* . . . française?
7. *(a little girl at the beach)* . . . en vacances?
8. *(a man reading Time magazine)* . . . américain?

■ **If students ask:** In French, the word for vacation (**les vacances**) is always plural.

Leçon 14   **99**

TPR In France

PROPS: signs: Paris, Bordeaux, Lyon, Nice
Place signs dividing class into 4 "cities."
   Voici Paris. Voici Bordeaux. etc.
Ask in which city students are.
   Où est X? [À Bordeaux.]
   Où sont Y et Z? [À Paris.]

Then have students move around.
   X, où es-tu? [À Bordeaux.]
   Lève-toi et va à Nice.
   Où es-tu maintenant? [À Nice.] . . .
   Y et Z, levez-vous et allez à Lyon.
   Où êtes-vous? [À Lyon.] . . .
Optional, with full answers:
   [Je suis à Nice.]

■ **TPR Variation:**
Use places from the **Vocabulaire** section: **en classe, au café, au cinéma, à la maison**...

T99

3 Où sont-ils?

Corinne is wondering if some of the people she knows are in certain places. Tell her she is right, using **il, elle, ils,** or **elles** in your answers.

▶ —Ta cousine est à Chicago?
—Oui, elle est à Chicago.

▶ —Pierre et Vincent sont au café?
—Oui, ils sont au café.

1. Stéphanie est à Lyon?
2. Monsieur Thomas est à San Francisco?
3. Suzanne et Monique sont à Genève?
4. Cécile et Charlotte sont au café?

5. Ta soeur est en ville?
6. Ton cousin est en vacances?
7. Claire, Alice et Éric sont au cinéma?
8. Monsieur et Madame Joli sont à Montréal?

4 Où?

You want to know where certain people are. A classmate will answer you on the basis of the illustrations.

▶ —Où est Céline?
—Elle est à New York.

Céline

1. Daniel

2. Caroline

3. Jean-Louis

4. Robert

5. Florence

6. Hélène

7. Julien

B. Les questions à réponse affirmative ou négative

The sentences on the left are statements. The sentences on the right are questions. These questions are called YES/NO QUESTIONS because they can be answered by *yes* or *no*. Note how the French questions begin with **est-ce que.**

STATEMENTS	YES/NO QUESTIONS	
Stéphanie est ici.	**Est-ce que** Stéphanie est ici?	*Is Stéphanie here?*
Tu es français.	**Est-ce que** tu es français?	*Are you French?*
Paul et Marc sont au café.	**Est-ce que** Paul et Marc sont au café?	*Are Paul and Marc at the café?*
Tu veux dîner avec moi.	**Est-ce que** tu veux dîner avec moi?	*Do you want to have dinner with me?*

Yes/no questions can be formed according to the pattern:

est-ce que + STATEMENT?	**Est-ce que** Pierre est ici?
↓	
est-ce qu' (+ VOWEL SOUND)	**Est-ce qu'**il est en ville?

Teaching note: Elision

The dropping of the final letter (usually "e") of a one-syllable word, as in **que → qu'**, is called ELISION.

Students have seen examples of elision already with **le, la → l'**. In this lesson they will also encounter **ne → n'** and **de → d'**.

The term "elision" is not used in the student text. Note, however, that words which have an elision form will be pointed out in the appropriate grammar sections.

➡ In yes/no questions, the voice goes up at the end of the sentence.

Est-ce que Paul et Florence sont au café?

➡ In casual conversation, yes/no questions can be formed without **est-ce que** simply by letting your voice rise at the end of the sentence.

Tu es français?   Cécile est en ville?

OBSERVATION: When you expect someone to agree with you, another way to form a yes/no question is to add the tag **n'est-ce pas** at the end of the sentence.

Tu es américain, **n'est-ce pas?**   *You are American, **aren't you?***
Tu aimes parler français, **n'est-ce pas?**   *You like to speak French, **don't you?***
Vous êtes d'accord, **n'est-ce pas?**   *You agree, **don't you?***

5 **Nationalités**

You are attending an international music camp. Ask about the nationalities of the other participants.

▶ Marc/canadien?   **Est-ce que Marc est canadien?**

1. Jim/américain?   3. Paul et Philippe/français?   5. vous/anglais?   7. Ellen et Carol/
2. Luisa/mexicaine?   4. tu/canadien?   6. Anne/française?   américaines?

Expressions pour la conversation

How to answer a yes/no question:

Oui!	*Yes!*	**Non!**	*No!*
Mais oui!	*Sure!*	**Mais non!**	*Of course not!*
Bien sûr!	*Of course!*		
Peut-être ...	*Maybe ...*		

6 **Conversation**

Ask your classmates the following questions. They will answer, using an expression from **Expressions pour la conversation**.

▶ Ton cousin est français?

1. Ta mère est à la maison?
2. Ta cousine est en France?
3. Ton copain est en classe?
4. Tu veux dîner avec moi?
5. Tu veux jouer au tennis avec moi?

Mais oui!   (Mais non!)

Alice, est-ce que ton cousin est français?

Leçon 14 **101**

Teaching note: Tag questions
You may want to point out to students that it is very easy to ask tag questions in French because there is only one tag:
n'est-ce pas?
This expression literally means
is it not so?

In English, on the other hand, tags are many and complex:
You will come, *won't you?*
You didn't refuse, *did you?* etc.
The multiplicity of tags makes French students feel that English is at times a difficult language to learn.

■ **Pronunciation:** As in English, your voice goes up at the end of the tag.

5 PRACTICE: asking questions about nationality

🔄 **Re-entry and Review:** Nationalities from Lesson 2.

■ **Challenge:** Answer each question affirmatively.
– Est-ce que Marc est canadien?
– Oui, il est canadien.
Note: Help students differentiate between singular and plural in items 4 and 5:
4. Oui, je suis...
5. Oui, nous sommes...

■ **Variation:** Formulate tag questions with n'est-ce pas.
Marc est canadian, n'est-ce pas?

Supplementary vocabulary

Bien sûr que oui!
Why of course!
Bien sûr que non!
Why of course not!

6 COMMUNICATION: asking personal questions

■ **Photo culture note**
Un café à Paris
The two girls are having ice cream which in France is usually served with a wafer (**une gaufrette**). In the background you can see cone-shaped folded parasols.

T101

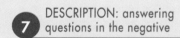
■ **Language note:** Ne → n' is another example of elision.

7 DESCRIPTION: answering questions in the negative

■ **Expansion:** Continue your answer with a positive statement.
– Est-ce que tu es français?
– Non, je ne suis pas français(e). Je suis américain(e).

8 PRACTICE: saying who does/doesn't agree

C. La négation

Compare the affirmative and negative sentences below:

AFFIRMATIVE	NEGATIVE	
Je **suis** américain.	Je **ne suis pas** français.	*I'm not French.*
Nous **sommes** en classe.	Nous **ne sommes pas** en vacances.	*We are not on vacation.*
Claire **est** là-bas.	Elle **n'est pas** ici.	*She is not here.*
Vous **êtes** à Paris.	Vous **n'êtes pas** à Lyon.	*You are not in Lyon.*
Tu **es** d'accord avec moi.	Tu **n'es pas** d'accord avec Marc.	*You do not agree with Marc.*

Negative sentences are formed as follows:

SUBJECT + **ne** + VERB + **pas** . . .
↓
n' (+ VOWEL SOUND)

Éric et Anne **ne** sont **pas** là.

Michèle **n'est pas** avec moi.

Je suis en classe.
Je [**ne**] suis [**pas**] à la maison.

7 Non!

Answer the following questions negatively.

▶ —Est-ce que tu es français (française)?
—**Non, je ne suis pas français (française).**

1. Est-ce que tu es canadien (canadienne)?
2. Est-ce que tu es à Québec?
3. Est-ce que tu es à la maison?
4. Est-ce que tu es au café?
5. Est-ce que tu es en vacances?
6. Est-ce que tu es au cinéma?

8 D'accord

It is raining. François suggests to his friends that they go to the movies. Say who agrees and who does not, using the expression **être d'accord.**

▶ ☹ Philippe Philippe n'est pas d'accord.
▶ ☺ Hélène Hélène est d'accord.

1. ☺ nous
2. ☺ je
3. ☹ tu
4. ☺ Patrick et Marc
5. ☹ Claire et Stéphanie
6. ☹ vous
7. ☺ ma copine
8. ☹ mon frère

Cooperative pair practice
Activity 8

Speaking practice

PROP: Transparency 15 with names written in the boxes below each picture.
Point to the picture of the café.
Qui est-ce? [C'est Sophie.]
Est-ce que Sophie est au café?
[Mais oui, elle est au café.]
Similarly introduce each picture.

Then practice negatives. Point to Sophie.
Qui est-ce? C'est Marc?
[Non, ce n'est pas Marc. C'est Sophie.]
Est-ce que Sophie est en classe?
[Non, elle n'est pas en classe.]
Est-ce que Sophie est à la maison?
[Mais non, elle n'est pas à la maison.]
Où est Sophie? [Elle est au café.]

Vocabulaire: Mots utiles *(Useful words)*

à	at	Je suis **à** la maison **à** dix heures.
	in	Nous sommes **à** Paris.
de	from	Vous êtes **de** San Francisco.
	of	Voici une photo **de** Paris.
et	and	Anne **et** Sophie sont en vacances.
ou	or	Qui est-ce? Juliette **ou** Sophie?
avec	with	Philippe est **avec** Pauline.
pour	for	Je veux travailler **pour** Monsieur Martin.
mais	but	Je ne suis pas français, **mais** j'aime parler français.

➡ **De** becomes **d'** before a vowel sound:
    Patrick est **de** Lyon.   François est **d'**Annecy.

Fête Nationale
mardi 14 juillet
à 22h

P A R I S

■ **Language note:** You may wish to point out the spelling difference between *ou* (or) and *où* (where):
Où est Juliette?
Au café ou au cinéma?

■ **Cultural realia:**
Ask your students:
– What event is taking place in Paris? [the national holiday]
– What is the date of this event? [Tuesday, July 14]
– **Quelle est la date de la Fête Nationale? [le mardi 14 juillet]**
– **À quelle heure est la fête? [À 22h.]**

⑨ Le mot juste *(The right word)* —
Complete the sentences below with the word in parentheses that fits logically.

1. Monsieur Moreau est en France. Aujourd'hui, il est . . . Lyon. (à/de)
2. Martine est canadienne. Elle est . . . Montréal. (de/et)
3. Florence n'est pas ici. Elle est . . . Jean-Claude. (et/avec)
4. Alice . . . Paul sont au restaurant. (avec/et)
5. Jean-Pierre n'est pas à la maison. Il est au café . . . au cinéma. (ou/et)
6. J'aime jouer au tennis . . . je ne veux pas jouer avec toi. (ou/mais)
7. Je dois travailler . . . mon père. (pour/à)

⑩ Être ou ne pas être *(To be or not to be)*
We cannot be in different places at the same time. Express this according to the model.

▶ Aline est en ville. (ici)
  Aline n'est pas ici.

1. Frédéric est là-bas. (à la maison)
2. Nous sommes en classe. (au restaurant)
3. Tu es à Nice. (à Toulon)
4. Vous êtes au café. (au cinéma)
5. Jérôme est avec Sylvie. (avec Catherine)
6. Juliette et Sophie sont avec Éric. (avec Marc)

COMPREHENSION: choosing prepositions and conjunctions

DESCRIPTION: saying where people are not

14.3 Dialogue: Où est Jean-Claude? (14:45–15:52 min.)

Leçon 14, Section 5

Prononciation

/a/

La voyelle /a/

The letter "**a**" alone always represents the sound /a/ as in the English word *ah*. It never has the sound of "*a*" as in English words like *class, date,* or *cinema*.

chat

Répétez: ch**a**t **ç**a v**a** **à** l**a** l**à**-b**a**s **a**vec **a**mi voil**à**
classe c**a**fé s**a**l**a**de d**a**me d**a**te M**a**d**a**me C**a**n**a**d**a**

Anne est au Ca**n**a**d**a** **a**vec M**a**d**a**me L**a**v**a**l.**

Prononciation

Leçon 14, Section 6

⌨ Listening game: Où est Jean-Claude?

Prepare a cloze version of the video/cassette script of *Où est Jean-Claude?* with selected words deleted.
    Play the video or the cassette dialogue.
    Divide the class into teams of three and distribute one script to each team. The teams all try to fill in as many missing words as they can remember. Replay the video/cassette, pausing after each sentence so that the teams can try to complete their texts.
    Have teams exchange and correct their scripts. The team with the most correct completions is the winner.

Leçon 14, Section 7

2 COMPREHENSION

1. au cinéma
2. en vacances
3. au restaurant (au café)
4. à la maison
5. en vacances

Classroom Notes

À votre tour!

1 Allô!

Jacques is phoning some friends. Match his questions on the left with his friends' answers on the right.

1. Où es-tu?
2. Où est ta soeur?
3. Est-ce que ton frère est à la maison?
4. Tes parents sont en vacances, n'est-ce pas?
5. Ta soeur est avec une copine?

a. Non, il est au cinéma.
b. Oui, elles sont au restaurant.
c. Je suis à la maison.
d. Elle est en classe.
e. Oui! Ils sont à Paris.

2 Où sont-ils?

Read what the following people are saying and decide where they are.

▶ Anne et Éric sont au café.

Une limonade, s'il vous plaît.

Le film est excellent.

Où est le musée *(museum)*?

▶ **Anne et Éric**   **1. nous**   **2. les touristes**

Une pizza, s'il vous plaît.

Bonjour, Maman.

Stéphanie, est-ce que tu veux nager?

3. vous   **4. tu**   **5. Paul**

À votre tour

Depending on your goals and objectives, you may or may not wish to assign all of the activities in the **À votre tour** section.

Cooperative practice

Act. 1 and 3 lend themselves to cooperative pair practice.

For Act. 3, you may prefer to have students work in trios, with two performing while the other holds the Answer Key and acts as a monitor.

3 Créa-dialogue

You are working for a student magazine in France. Your assignment is to interview tourists who are visiting Paris. Ask them where they are from. (Make sure to address the people appropriately as **tu** or **vous**.) Remember: The symbol "??" means you may invent your own responses.

Nationalité	Villes (Cities)	
▸ anglaise	Londres? *(London)* Liverpool	

▸ — Bonjour. Vous êtes anglaise?
— Oui, je suis anglaise.
— Est-ce que vous êtes de Londres?
— Mais non, je ne suis pas de Londres. Je suis de Liverpool.

Nationalité	Villes	
1 américaine	New York? Washington	
2 canadien	Québec? Montréal	
3 française	Paris? Nice	
4 mexicain	Mexico? Puebla	
5 ??	?? ??	
6 ??	?? ??	

4 Composition: Et toi?

Write a short paragraph about yourself and your friends.

1. Say what city you are from. **(Je suis de ...)**
2. Say what city your father or your mother is from. **(Mon père / ma mère est de ...)**
3. Say where one of your friends is from. **(Mon copain / ma copine ...)**
4. Name an activity you like to do with a friend. **(J'aime ... avec ...)**
5. Name an activity you want to do with two friends. **(Je veux ...)**
6. Name an activity you would like to do with one of your relatives. **(Je voudrais ...)**

5 Composition: Personnellement

On a separate piece of paper, write where you are and where you are not at each of the following times.

▸ à 9 heures du matin
  • à 4 heures
  • à 7 heures du soir
  • samedi
  • dimanche
  • en juillet

À neuf heures du matin, je suis en classe. Je ne suis pas à la maison.

Leçon 14 **105**

3 GUIDED ORAL EXPRESSION
Leçon 14, Section 8

4 WRITTEN SELF-EXPRESSION

5 WRITTEN SELF-EXPRESSION

Classroom Notes

Portfolio assessment

You will probably select only one speaking activity and one writing activity to go into the students' portfolios for Unit 4.

In this lesson, Act. 3 lends itself well to an oral portfolio recording. Act. 4 and 5 are both good writing portfolio topics.

(Encourage your students to invent their own responses as in items 5 and 6 in Act. 3.)

T105

Leçon 15

MAIN TOPIC:

Talking about one's activities

MODULE 15:
Une boum
Total time: 4:50 min.
(Counter: 17:36 min.)

15.1 Mini-scenes: Listening — J'étudie
(17:51–18:51 min.)

15.2 Mini-scenes: Listening — Tu téléphones?
(18:52–19:25 min.)

15.3 Mini-scenes: Speaking — Est-ce qu'il travaille?
(19:26–20:27 min.)

15.4 Dialogue: Jean-Paul à la boum
(20:28–21:21 min.)

15.5 Vignette culturelle: Une boum
(21:22–22:16 min.)

■ **Comprehension practice:** Play the entire module through as an introduction to the lesson.

[▭] **Leçon 15, Section 1**

■ **Photo culture note**
La Défense
The new high-rise business center of Paris is located at La Défense, in the suburb of Nanterre just west of the city. **L'Arche de la Défense,** which is an actual building housing many offices, was inaugurated in 1989 as part of the celebrations of the bicentenary of the French Revolution.

 COMPREHENSION

1. C'est vrai!
2. C'est vrai!
3. C'est faux! (Elle ne danse pas très bien.)
4. C'est faux! (Il invite Valérie.)
5. C'est vrai!

LEÇON 15

Une boum

Jean-Marc has been invited to a party. He is trying to decide whether to bring Béatrice or Valérie. First he talks to Béatrice.

JEAN-MARC:	<u>Dis</u>, Béatrice, tu aimes danser?	*Hey*
BÉATRICE:	Bien sûr, j'aime danser!	
JEAN-MARC:	Est-ce que tu danses bien?	
BÉATRICE:	Oui, je danse très, <u>très bien</u>.	*very well*
JEAN-MARC:	Et ta cousine Valérie? Est-ce qu'elle danse bien?	
BÉATRICE:	Non, elle ne danse pas très bien.	
JEAN-MARC:	<u>Alors</u>, c'est Valérie <u>que</u> j'invite à la <u>boum</u>.	*So / that / party*
BÉATRICE:	Mais <u>pourquoi</u> elle? Pourquoi pas moi?	*why*
JEAN-MARC:	Écoute, Béatrice, <u>je ne sais pas</u> danser! <u>Alors</u>, je préfère inviter une fille qui ne danse pas très bien. C'est normal, non?	*don't know how / So*

● **Compréhension: Vrai ou faux?**

Read the following statements and say whether they are true (**C'est vrai!**) or false (**C'est faux!**).

1. Béatrice aime danser.
2. Elle danse bien.
3. Valérie danse très bien.
4. Jean-Marc invite Béatrice.
5. Il invite Valérie.

106 Unité 4

Setting the stage
Ask students if they organize informal parties at home for their friends.
    What do they serve to eat and drink?
    What do they do? Talk? Dance? Sing?
Tell them that in this lesson they will learn about French parties.

■ NOTE ■
CULTURELLE

Une boum

On weekends, French teenagers like to go to parties that are organized at a friend's home. Often the guests contribute something to the buffet: sandwiches or soft drinks. There is also a lot of music and dancing. (French teenagers love to dance!)

These informal parties have different names according to the age group of the participants. For students at a **collège** (or junior high), a party is known as **une boum.** For older students at a **lycée** (or high school), it is called **une soirée.**

Note culturelle

■ **Photo culture notes**
The top buffet spread shows:
* potato chips (**des chips**)
* crackers (**des biscuits**)
* peanuts (**des cacahuètes**)
* little sandwiches with caviar or pâté (**des sandwiches au caviar et au pâté**)
* paper cups (**des timbales en papier**)

The bottom table contains:
* soft drinks (**des sodas**)
* apples (**des pommes**)
* bananas (**des bananes**)
* cheeses (**des fromages**)
* slices of cake (**des portions de gâteau**)

 15.5 Vignette culturelle: Une boum (21:22–22:16 min.)

 ## 🌐 Cross-cultural understanding

Have students watch the video (or look at the above photographs taken from the video scenes).

What kinds of similarities and differences do they notice between parties in France and parties that they go to?

Transparency 16
Subject pronouns

15.1 Mini-scenes: J'étudie
15.2 Mini-scenes: Tu
téléphones?
(17:51–19:25 min.)

Leçon 15, Sections 2, 3

■ **Pronunciation:** You may want to point out that the singular forms of **-er** verbs all sound the same. There is a difference in spelling in the **tu**-form.

1 ROLE PLAY: getting acquainted

Cooperative pair practice Activities 1, 2

T108

A. Les verbes en *-er:* le singulier

Many French verbs end in **-er** in the infinitive. Most of these verbs are conjugated like **parler** *(to speak)* and **habiter** *(to live)*. Note the forms of the present tense of these verbs in the singular. Pay attention to their endings.

> **Learning about language**
> The basic form of the VERB is the INFINITIVE:
> **jouer** *(to play)*   **travailler** *(to work)*
> In French dictionaries, verbs are listed by their infinitives.

INFINITIVE	**parler**	**habiter**	ENDINGS
STEM	**parl-**	**habit-**	
PRESENT TENSE (SINGULAR)	Je **parle** français. Tu **parles** anglais. Il / Elle **parle** espagnol.	J' **habite** à Paris. Tu **habites** à Boston. Il / Elle **habite** à Madrid.	-e -es -e

The present tense forms of -er verbs consist of two parts:

STEM + ENDING

- The STEM does not change. It is the infinitive minus **-er**:
  parler   **parl-**   habiter   **habit-**
- The ENDINGS change with the subject:
  je → **-e**   **tu** → **-es**   **il / elle** → **-e**

➡ The above endings are silent.
➡ **Je** becomes **j'** before a vowel sound.
    je parle   **j'**habite

> **Learning about language**
> Verbs conjugated like **parler** and **habiter** follow a *predictable pattern*.
> They are called REGULAR VERBS.

1 **Curiosité**

At the party, Olivier wants to learn more about Isabelle. She answers his questions affirmatively. Play both roles.

Tu parles anglais?   Oui, je parle anglais.

▶ parler anglais?

1. parler espagnol?
2. habiter à Paris?
3. étudier ici?
4. jouer au volley?
5. jouer au basket?
6. chanter?

108 Unité 4

Critical thinking about language

In this lesson, students are encouraged to think about how verbs work in French.

In Section A, they will learn the singular forms, which sound the same, but which are not all spelled the same.

In Section B, they will learn the plural forms with their endings, and notice how

liaison helps link subject and verb together.

Finally in Section C, they will see the complete verb charts with both affirmative and negative forms. They will learn what a paradigm for regular verbs looks like, and how it can serve as a model.

Vocabulaire: Les verbes en -er

Verbs you already know:

chanter	*to sing*	**nager**	*to swim*
danser	*to dance*	**parler**	*to speak, talk*
dîner	*to have dinner*	**regarder**	*to watch, look at*
écouter	*to listen (to)*	**téléphoner**	*to phone, call*
étudier	*to study*	**travailler**	*to work*
jouer	*to play*	**voyager**	*to travel*
manger	*to eat*		

New verbs:

aimer	*to like*	Tu **aimes** Paris?
habiter	*to live*	Philippe **habite** à Toulouse?
inviter	*to invite*	J'**invite** un copain.
organiser	*to organize*	Sophie **organise** une **boum** *(party)*.
visiter	*to visit (places)*	Hélène **visite** Québec.

➡ **Regarder** has two meanings:
- *to look (at)* — Paul **regarde** Cécile.
- *to watch* — Cécile **regarde** la télé.

➡ Note the construction **téléphoner à:**

Hélène **téléphone**	à	Marc.
Hélène calls	. . .	*Marc.*

➡ Note the constructions with **regarder** and **écouter:**

Philippe **regarde**	. . .	Alice.
Philippe looks	*at*	*Alice.*

Alice **écoute**	. . .	le professeur.
Alice listens	*to*	*the teacher.*

2 Quelle activité?

Describe what the following people are doing by completing the sentences with one of the verbs below. Be logical in your choice of activity.

      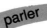

chanter écouter parler travailler manger voyager regarder inviter

1. Je . . . un sandwich. Tu . . . une pizza.
2. Tu . . . anglais. Je . . . français.
3. Éric . . . la radio. Claire . . . un compact (un CD).
4. Jean-Paul . . . la télé. Tu . . . un match de tennis.
5. M. Simon . . . en *(by)* bus. Mme Dupont . . . en train.
6. Nicolas . . . Marie à la boum. Tu . . . Alain.
7. Mlle Thomas . . . dans *(in)* un hôpital. Je . . . dans un supermarché *(supermarket)*.
8. Mick Jagger . . . bien. Est-ce que tu . . . bien?

▷ **Vocabulaire**

 Transparency 17
Verbs

 2 COMPREHENSION: saying what people are doing

1. mange / manges
2. parles / parle
3. écoute / écoute
4. regarde / regardes
5. voyage / voyage
6. invite / invites
7. travaille / travaille
8. chante / chantes

TPR **Activities**

Together with the class, develop gestures for the new verbs in the chart. E.g.:
aimer: hands across one's heart
habiter: arms over head in a "roof" shape

Review gestures you created for the other verbs (page T90).

J'habite à Paris. ["roof"gesture] …
Then address individual students directly.
X, tu danses bien. [X shows "dancing"]
Ask students what they are doing.
Y, qu'est-ce que tu fais?
[Y gestures "tennis"]
Est-ce que Y chante? [non]
Est-ce qu'il joue au tennis? [oui]

T109

DESCRIPTION: describing what people are doing

1. Madame Dumas téléphone.
2. Monsieur Dupin regarde la télé.
3. Madame Ménard écoute la radio.
4. Patrick étudie.
5. Florence chante.
6. Coco parle.

EXCHANGES: discussing where people are

■ **Variation:** Divide the class into three sections: A, B, C. Elicit part-choral or individual responses from the students in each section.
A: **Où est Jacques?**
B: **Il est en classe.**
C: **Il étudie.**

Section B

COMMUNICATIVE FUNCTION: Describing what several people are doing

■ **Pronunciation:** Note that **il parle** and **ils parlent** sound the same.

■ **Language notes**
• The "e" is inserted to keep the soft "g" sound.
• This spelling change is presented mainly for recognition.

---

3 Le télescope

Curious Georges has set up a telescope to observe what his neighbors are doing. Describe each person's activity.

▶ Monsieur Thomas dîne.

4 Où sont-ils?

You want to know where the following people are. A classmate will answer, telling you where the people are and what they are doing.

▶ Jacques? (en classe/étudier)

Où est Jacques?

Il est en classe. Il étudie.

1. Pauline? (au restaurant/dîner)
2. Véronique? (à la maison/téléphoner)
3. Mme Dupont? (en ville/travailler)
4. M. Lemaire? (en France/voyager)
5. Jean-Claude? (à Paris/visiter la tour Eiffel)
6. André? (au Tennis Club/jouer au tennis)
7. Alice? (à l'Olympic Club/nager)

B. Les verbes en -er: le pluriel

Note the plural forms of **parler** and **habiter,** paying attention to the endings.

INFINITIVE	parler	habiter	ENDINGS
STEM	parl-	habit-	
PRESENT TENSE (PLURAL)	Nous **parlons** français. / Vous **parlez** anglais. / Ils/Elles **parlent** espagnol.	Nous **habitons** à Québec. / Vous **habitez** à Chicago. / Ils/Elles **habitent** à Caracas.	-ons / -ez / -ent

➡ In the present tense, the plural endings of **-er** verbs are:

nous → **-ons**   vous → **-ez**   ils/elles → **-ent**

➡ The **-ent** ending is silent.

➡ Note the liaison when the verb begins with a vowel sound:

Nous étudions.   Vous invitez Thomas.   Ils habitent en France.   Elles aiment Paris.

OBSERVATION: When the infinitive of the verb ends in **-ger,** the **nous**-form ends in **-geons.**

nager: nous na**geons**   manger: nous man**geons**   voyager: nous voya**geons**

Cooperative pair practice
Activities 4, 6, 8

TPR 🕺 Subject pronouns

Teach students gestures for each pronoun.

Montrez-moi "je". [point to self]
  Montrez-moi "tu". [point straight ahead, somewhat down, as if to a child]
  Montrez-moi "il" ou "elle" [stretch one arm out to the side, hand open]

Add: **"nous"** [both hands point to self]
  "vous" [both hands point straight ahead]
  "ils/elles" [both arms stretched to side]
Have students identify subjects.
  Nous organisons une boum. ["nous"]
The subjects **il(s)/elle(s)** may be ambiguous.
  Il(s) joue(nt) au tennis. ["il" or "ils"]
Clarify: **Pierre joue au tennis.** ["il"]

5 Qui?

Stéphanie is speaking to or about her friends. Complete her sentences with **tu, elle, vous,** or **ils.**

▶ . . . étudient à Toulouse.
   Ils étudient à Toulouse.

1. . . . habitez à Tours.
2. . . . aime Paris.
3. . . . étudiez à Tours.
4. . . . aiment danser.
5. . . . organisent une boum.
6. . . . parlez espagnol.
7. . . . téléphone à Jean-Pierre.
8. . . . invites un copain.
9. . . . dîne avec Cécile.
10. . . . invitent Monique.

6 À la boum

At a party, Olivier is talking to two Canadian students, Monique and her friend. Monique answers yes to his questions.

▶ parler français?

Vous parlez français, n'est-ce pas?

Oui, nous parlons français.

1. parler anglais?
2. habiter à Québec?
3. étudier à Montréal?
4. voyager en France?
5. voyager en train?
6. visiter Paris?
7. aimer Paris?
8. aimer la France?

7 Le camp français

At summer camp, everything is organized according to a schedule. Describe the activities of the following campers by completing the sentences according to the illustrations.

▶ À cinq heures, Alice et Marc . . .   À cinq heures, Alice et Marc jouent au volley.

▶

1. À neuf heures, nous . . .
2. À quatre heures, vous . . .
3. À huit heures, Véronique et Pierre . . .
4. À sept heures, nous . . .
5. À trois heures, Thomas et François . . .
6. À six heures, vous . . .

8 Un voyage à Paris

A group of American students are visiting Paris. During their stay, they do all of the following things:

voyager en bus

téléphoner à un copain

visiter la tour Eiffel

dîner au restaurant

inviter une copine

écouter un opéra

Describe the trips of the following people.

▶ Jim   **Il voyage en bus, il visite la tour Eiffel . . .**

1. Linda   2. Paul et Louise   3. nous   4. vous

Leçon 15 111

 PRACTICE: selecting subject pronouns

1. Vous   5. Ils   8. Tu
2. Elle   6. Vous   9. Elle
3. Vous   7. Elle   10. Ils
4. Ils

■ Be sure students make the liaison in 1, 3, 4, 5, and 10.

 ROLE PLAY: getting to know people

■ **Variation:** Ask questions with **est-ce que**; respond with **bien sûr.**
– Est-ce que vous parlez français?
– Bien sûr, nous parlons français.

 COMPREHENSION: describing what people do at various times of day

1. téléphonons
2. jouez au tennis
3. regardent la télé
4. dînons
5. jouent au basket
6. nagez

↺ **Re-entry and review:** Before doing this exercise you may want to review telling time (Lesson 4).

 PRACTICE: describing activities on a trip

■ **Pronunciation: bus /bys/**

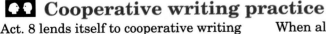

👥 Cooperative writing practice

Act. 8 lends itself to cooperative writing practice. First go through the entire model paragraph with the whole class.

Then group students in pairs and as-sign each pair a number (1, 2, 3, or 4). Each pair then writes out the paragraph corresponding to their number.

When all are done, have each pair pass their paper to the next pair. The pairs then read and check the new paragraph they have received. (For example, pair 2 passes their paper to pair 3 and reads the paper they receive from pair 1.)

Section C

COMMUNICATIVE FUNCTION:
Describing what people do
and don't do

 15.3 Mini-scenes:
Est-ce qu'il travaille?
(19:26–20:27 min.)

 Leçon 15, Section 4

Transparency 16
Subject pronouns

■ **Teaching tip:** You can make large subject pronoun flash cards by projecting the drawings from the transparency onto heavy paper and tracing the outlines with markers. If desired, you can label each drawing with the corresponding pronoun. Use these cards throughout the program to practice verb forms.

■ **Language note:** Be sure students notice that the one word **parle** in French may correspond to two words in English:
is speaking, does speak.
Point out that *is* corresponds to **est** only when it represents the main verb.

C. Le présent des verbes en *-er:* forme affirmative et forme négative

FORMS

Compare the affirmative and negative forms of **parler.**

AFFIRMATIVE	NEGATIVE
je **parle** tu **parles** il/elle **parle**	je **ne parle pas** tu **ne parles pas** il/elle **ne parle pas**
nous **parlons** vous **parlez** ils/elles **parlent**	nous **ne parlons pas** vous **ne parlez pas** ils/elles **ne parlent pas**

REMEMBER: The negative form of the verb follows the pattern:

SUBJECT + **ne** + VERB + **pas**	Il **ne** travaille **pas** ici.
n' (+ VOWEL SOUND)	Je **n'**invite **pas** Pierre.

Il ne travaille pas.   Ils n'écoutent pas.   Elle ne chante pas bien.

USES

In the present tense, French verbs have several English equivalents:

Je **joue** au tennis.
{ *I play tennis.*
{ *I do play tennis.*
{ *I am playing tennis.*

Je **ne joue pas** au tennis.
{ *I do not play tennis. (I don't play tennis.)*
{ *I am not playing tennis. (I'm not playing tennis.)*

> Studying French helps you better appreciate how the English language works.

Teaching note: Verb endings

Use Transparency 16 to help students learn to spell the verb endings and say the forms. First have the students identify the pronoun cartoons (**je, tu,...**).

With a washable transparency marker, write the forms of **dîner** below each picture.

With a second color, box the endings.

Have students read the verbs aloud, first in sequence (**je dîne, tu dînes, ...**) and then randomly as you point to them (**nous dînons, elle dîne, ...**).

Erase the forms of **dîner.** Have volunteers come write the forms of other verbs.

9 Non!

One cannot do everything. From the following list of activities, select at least three that you do *not* do.

▶ Je ne joue pas au bridge.

parler espagnol	étudier à Paris
parler italien	habiter à Québec
danser le tango	étudier le japonais
jouer au hockey	nager en hiver
jouer au water-polo	dîner avec le prof
jouer au bridge	travailler dans un restaurant

10 Pas aujourd'hui

Today the following people are tired and are not doing what they usually do. Express this according to the model.

▶ Pierre joue au tennis.
Aujourd'hui, il ne joue pas au tennis.

1. Je joue au foot.
2. Tu étudies.
3. Madame Simonet travaille.
4. Vous dînez à la maison.
5. Marc téléphone à Martine.
6. Nous nageons.
7. Jacques et Florence étudient.

11 Un jeu: Weekend!

On weekends, people like to do different things. For each person, pick an activity and say what that person does. Select another activity and say what that person does not do.

▶ **Antoine et Isabelle dansent.
Ils ne regardent pas la télé.**

je
tu
ma cousine
nous
Antoine et Isabelle
Monsieur Leblanc
Madame Jolivet
vous
le professeur

COMMUNICATION: stating activities that one does not do

9

Cooperative pair practice
• Use the cues as the basis of a poll.
• Divide the class into pairs, and have students interview one another to discover what their partners do and do not do.
  – **Tu joues au bridge?**
  – **Oui, je joue au bridge. (Non, je ne joue pas au bridge.)**

■ **Variation:** Use other subjects: **nous, tu, mon copain, ma copine.**

PRACTICE: saying what people are not doing today
10

COMPREHENSION: stating what people do and don't do
11

jouer au tennis
jouer au basket
regarder la télé
écouter la radio
travailler
étudier
danser
dîner au restaurant
nager

Classroom Notes

❖ Game: Weekend!

You can treat Act. 11 as a game. Divide the class into teams of three. Each team picks a person from the list and decides what that subject is doing and not doing. All three team members must write the same two sentences correctly.

Then the team chooses another subject plus two other activities. All three write down the next two sentences.

The game is played against the clock. For example, you may set a 5-minute time limit. The team whose three members have written the greatest number of correct sentences in that time is the winner.

■ **Teaching tip:** Have students notice the two-column (French-English) format in the **Vocabulaire** sections. Encourage them to practice the vocabulary by covering one of the two columns with a slip of paper and then saying or writing the corresponding expression in the other language. They can verify their responses by sliding the paper down the page as they go through the list.

COMMUNICATION:
describing how well or often one does things

⓬

COMMUNICATION:
expressing approval or regret

⓭

■ **Variation:** Address two or more students.
– **Est-ce que vous chantez?**
– **Oui, nous aimons chanter. (Non, nous n'aimons pas chanter.)**

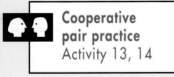

Cooperative pair practice
Activity 13, 14

T114

Vocabulaire: Mots utiles

bien	*well*	Je joue **bien** au tennis.
très bien	*very well*	Je ne chante pas **très bien.**
mal	*badly, poorly*	Tu joues **mal** au volley.
beaucoup	*a lot, much, very much*	Paul aime **beaucoup** voyager.
un peu	*a little, a little bit*	Nous parlons **un peu** français.
souvent	*often*	Charles invite **souvent** Nathalie.
toujours	*always*	Je travaille **toujours** en été.
aussi	*also, too*	Je téléphone à Marc. Je téléphone **aussi** à Véronique.
maintenant	*now*	J'étudie **maintenant.**
rarement	*rarely, seldom*	Vous voyagez **rarement.**

➡ In French, the above expressions *never* come *between* the subject and the verb. They usually come *after* the verb. Compare their positions in French and English.

Nous parlons **toujours** français.	We *always* speak French.
Tu joues **bien** au tennis.	You play tennis *well*.

⓬ **Expression personnelle**

Complete the following sentences with an expression from the list below.

bien	mal	très bien	toujours	souvent	rarement	un peu	beaucoup

1. Je chante . . .
2. Je nage . . .
3. Je regarde . . . la télé.
4. Je mange . . .
5. Je voyage . . . en bus.
6. Le prof parle . . . français.
7. Nous parlons . . . français en classe.
8. Les Rolling Stones chantent . . .
9. Michael Jordan joue . . . au basket.
10. Les Yankees jouent . . . au baseball.

Expressions pour la conversation

How to express approval or regret:

Super!	*Terrific!*	Tu parles français? **Super!**
Dommage!	*Too bad!*	Tu ne joues pas au tennis? **Dommage!**

Tu parles français?

Oui, je parle français.

Super!

⓭ **Conversation**

Ask your classmates if they do the following things. Then express approval or regret, according to their answers.

▶ parler français?   —**Est-ce que tu parles français?**
                     —**Oui, je parle français. (Non, je ne parle pas français.)**
                     —**Super! (Dommage!)**

1. parler espagnol?
2. jouer au tennis?
3. danser bien?
4. voyager beaucoup?
5. dîner souvent au restaurant?
6. inviter souvent ton copain?

D. La construction: verbe + infinitif

Note the use of the infinitive in the following sentences.

J'aime **parler** français.	I like **to speak** French. I like **speaking** French.
Nous aimons **voyager**.	We like **to travel**. We like **traveling**.
Tu n'aimes pas **étudier**.	You don't like **to study**. You don't like **studying**.
Ils n'aiment pas **danser**.	They don't like **to dance**. They don't like **dancing**.

To express what they like and don't like to do, the French use these constructions:

SUBJECT + PRESENT TENSE + INFINITIVE . . . of **aimer**		SUBJECT + **n'** + PRESENT TENSE + **pas** + INFINITIVE . . . of **aimer**		
Nous	**aimons**	**voyager**.	Nous	**n'aimons pas**	**voyager**.

➡ Note that in this construction, the verb **aimer** may be affirmative or negative:

AFFIRMATIVE: Jacques **aime** voyager. NEGATIVE: Philippe **n'aime pas** voyager.

➡ The above construction is used in questions: Est-ce que Paul **aime voyager?**

OBSERVATION: The infinitive is also used after the following expressions:

Je préfère . . .	I prefer . . .	Je préfère travailler.
Je voudrais . . .	I would like . . .	Je voudrais voyager.
Je (ne) veux (pas) . . .	I (don't) want . . .	Je veux jouer au foot.
Est-ce que tu veux . . .	Do you want . . .	Est-ce que tu veux danser?
Je (ne) peux (pas) . . .	I can (I can't) . . .	Je ne peux pas dîner avec toi.
Je dois . . .	I have to . . .	Je dois étudier.

14 Dialogue

Ask your classmates if they like to do the following things.

▶ chanter?
—Est-ce que tu aimes chanter?
—Oui, j'aime chanter.   (Non, je n'aime pas chanter.)

1. étudier?
2. voyager?
3. téléphoner?
4. danser?
5. parler français en classe?
6. nager en été?
7. nager en hiver?
8. travailler le week-end (on weekends)?

15 Une excellente raison (An excellent reason)

The following people are doing certain things. Say that they like these activities.

▶ Thomas voyage.   **Il aime voyager.**

1. Monique chante.
2. Charles étudie la musique.
3. Henri téléphone.
4. Isabelle organise une boum.
5. Marc et Sophie nagent.
6. Annie et Vincent dansent.
7. Lise et Rose jouent au frisbee.
8. Éric et Denis écoutent la radio.
9. Nous travaillons.
10. Nous parlons espagnol.
11. Vous regardez la télé.
12. Vous mangez.

Prononciation

Les voyelles /i/ et /u/

/u/ **où?**   /i/ **ici!**

The vowel sounds /i/ and /u/ are easy to say. Remember to pronounce the French "**i**" as in **Mimi** and not as in the English *him*.

Répétez:
/i/ **ici Philippe il
Mimi Sylvie visite**
Philippe visite Paris avec Sylvie.

/u/ **où nous vous
écoute joue toujours**

Vous jouez au foot avec nous?

Section D

COMMUNICATIVE FUNCTION: Talking about what people like and don't like to do

 15.4 Dialogue: Jean-Paul à la boum (20:28–21:21 min.)

Leçon 15, Section 5

14 COMMUNICATION: discussing likes and dislikes

■ **Expansion:** In the event of an affirmative answer, a follow-up question could be asked with **bien** or **souvent.**
Est-ce que tu chantes bien?

15 PRACTICE: saying what people like to do

■ **Challenge:** Continue the response by inventing an activity that the person does not like to do.
Il aime voyager mais il n'aime pas parler anglais.

Prononciation

■ /i/ Spelled **i, y.**
Be sure students pronounce /i/ like "ee" of *beet* and not the "i" of *bit*.
■ /y/ Spelled **ou, où.**

 ## 🖥 Jean-Paul à la boum

• Divide the class into teams of four.
• Play the video or the cassette segment *Jean-Paul à la boum.*
• Replay the first scene and pause so that each team can write as many phrases from the conversation as they can remember. Do the same for the second scene.

• Then play both scenes once more so the teams can try to complete their texts.
• Distribute a copy of the video/cassette script to each team so that they can circle all the phrases they listed correctly. Play the scenes a final time for confirmation.

1 COMPREHENSION

1-d	3-e	5-c
2-b	4-a	

🔊 Leçon 15, Section 7

2 GUIDED ORAL EXPRESSION

jouer au tennis
écouter la radio
nager
voyager
chanter
regarder la télé
étudier
travailler

🔊 Leçon 15, Section 7

Classroom Notes

À votre tour!

1 Allô!

Sophie is phoning some friends. Match her questions on the left with her friends' answers on the right.

1. Est-ce que Marc est canadien?
2. Est-ce que tu joues au tennis?
3. Ton frère est à la maison?
4. Ta mère est en vacances?
5. Tu invites Christine et Juliette à la boum?

a. Non, elle travaille.
b. Oui, mais pas très bien.
c. Bien sûr! Elles aiment beaucoup danser.
d. Oui, il habite à Montréal.
e. Non, il dîne au restaurant avec un copain.

2 Créa-dialogue

Find out how frequently your classmates do the following activities. They will respond using one of the expressions on the scale.

NON	OUI		
	un peu →	souvent →	beaucoup

▶ — **Robert**, est-ce que tu **joues au tennis**?
— Non, je **ne joue pas au tennis**.
— Est-ce que tu **écoutes la radio**?
— Oui, j'**écoute souvent la radio**.

116 **Unité 4**

À votre tour

Depending on your goals and objectives, you may or may not wish to assign all of the activities in the **À votre tour** section.

🗣🗣 Cooperative practice

In Act. 2, 3, and 4, you may want to have students work together in trios, with two performing and one consulting the Answer Key and acting as monitor.

T116

3 Qu'est-ce qu'ils font?
(What do they do?)

Look at what the following students have put in their lockers and say what they like to do.

Éric aime jouer au tennis.
Il aime aussi . . .

4 Message illustré

Marc wrote about certain activities, using pictures. On a separate sheet, write out his description replacing these pictures with the missing words.

À la maison, ma soeur Catherine ☎ à une copine. Mon frère Éric 📻♪♫. En général, nous 👨‍👩‍👧‍👦 à sept heures et demie. Après° le dîner, mes° parents 📺. Moi, j'📖 pour la classe de français. En vacances, nous ❌📖. Je 🏊. Éric et Catherine 🎾. Parfois° mes parents 🍷 au restaurant.

Après *After*   **mes** *my*   **Parfois** *Sometimes*

5 Point de vue personnel

Select one of the following situations. On a separate sheet of paper, write two things you do and one thing you do not do in that situation. Use complete sentences.

En classe, je...

À la maison,....

En vacances,....

Avec mes (my) copains,....

Avec mes parents,....

Leçon 15   117

📁 Portfolio assessment

You will probably only select one speaking activity and one writing activity to go into the students' portfolios for Unit 4.

In this lesson, Act. 2 can be the basis of an oral portfolio recording.

(You may want to use the **Challenge** version of Act. 4 for the written portfolio.)

MODULE 16:
Une interview
Total time: 6:12 min.
(Counter: 22:27 min.)

16.1 Mini-scenes: Listening — Où est-ce qu'il va?
(23:17–24:44 min.)

16.2 Mini-scenes: Listening — Qu'est-ce que tu fais?
(24:45–25:29 min.)

16.3 Mini-scenes: Speaking — Questions
(25:30–26:13 min.)

16.4 Dialogue: Une interview
(26:14–27:02 min.)

16.5 Vignette culturelle: Le Sénégal
(27:03–28:33 min.)

■ **Comprehension practice:** Play the entire module through as an introduction to the lesson.

 16.5 Vignette culturelle: Le Sénégal
(27:03–28:33 min.)

🌐 **Cross-cultural observation:** Have students in pairs make a list of similarities and differences between Sénégal and the United States.

 Leçon 16, Section 5 (optional)

■ **Photo culture note**
À Dakar au Sénégal
On her head, in typical Senegalese fashion, the young woman is wearing a cotton scarf (**un foulard**).

LEÇON 16

Une interview

Nicolas is a reporter for *La Gazette des Étudiants,* the student newspaper. He has decided to write an article on the foreign students who attend his school. Today he is interviewing Fatou, a student from Senegal.

NICOLAS:	Bonjour, Fatou. Est-ce que je peux <u>te poser quelques questions</u>?	*ask you some questions*
FATOU:	Oui, bien sûr.	
NICOLAS:	Tu es <u>sénégalaise</u>, n'est-ce pas?	*Senegalese*
FATOU:	Oui, je suis sénégalaise.	
NICOLAS:	Où est-ce que tu habites?	
FATOU:	Je suis de Dakar, mais maintenant j'habite à Paris avec ma famille.	
NICOLAS:	<u>Pourquoi</u> est-ce que vous habitez à Paris?	*Why*
FATOU:	<u>Parce que</u> ma mère travaille pour l'Unesco.	*Because*
NICOLAS:	Est-ce que tu aimes Paris?	
FATOU:	J'adore Paris.	
NICOLAS:	<u>Qu'est-ce que tu fais le weekend</u>?	*What do you do on weekends?*
FATOU:	<u>Ça</u> dépend! Je regarde la télé ou je joue au tennis avec <u>mes</u> copains.	*That* *my*
NICOLAS:	Merci beaucoup, Fatou.	
FATOU:	C'est <u>tout</u>?	*all*
NICOLAS:	Oui, c'est tout!	

■ NOTES ■ CULTURELLES

1 Le Sénégal

Senegal is a country in western Africa, whose capital is Dakar. Its population includes seventeen different tribes, all speaking their own dialects. Because of the historical and cultural ties between Senegal and France, French has been adopted as the official language.

Most of the people of Senegal are Muslims. Some common names are **Awa** and **Fatou** (for girls), **Babacar** and **Mamadou** (for boys).

Setting the scene

Ask students how many African countries they can name. Write these on the board. Do they remember which of these countries use French as an official language? Circle these countries. (If necessary, have them turn back to the photo essay on pages 1–9.)

Locate these French-speaking countries on the map.

In particular, have students locate Senegal and its capital city Dakar. Tell them that in this chapter they will meet a student from Dakar.

Note culturelle

 16.4 Dialogue: Une interview (26:14–27:02 min.)

Leçon 16, Section 1

■ Photo culture note
Un café à Paris
On the table you can see:
- a ham and cheese sandwich (**un sandwich au jambon et au fromage**) made from half a loaf of French bread (**une baguette**).
- a plate of mixed vegetable salades (**des crudités**) including grated carrots (**des carottes râpées**) and beets (**des betteraves**).

In the background is a hotel (**un hôtel**). To the right is a confectionary (**une confiserie**) or shop specializing in home-made candies. The awning says **glacier**, indicating that the store makes its own ice cream.

FATOU:	Bon. <u>Alors</u>, maintenant c'est mon <u>tour</u>! Est-ce que je peux te poser une question?	*So / turn*
NICOLAS:	Bien sûr!	
FATOU:	Qu'est-ce que tu fais samedi?	
NICOLAS:	Euh . . . <u>je ne sais pas</u>.	*I don't know*
FATOU:	Alors, est-ce que tu veux <u>aller</u> à un concert de musique africaine?	*to go*
NICOLAS:	Avec qui?	
FATOU:	Avec moi, bien sûr!	
NICOLAS:	D'accord! Où? <u>Quand</u>? Et à quelle heure?	*When*

2 L'Unesco

UNESCO (United Nations Educational Scientific and Cultural Organization) was founded in 1946 to promote international cooperation in education, science, and the arts. The organization has its headquarters in Paris and is staffed by people from all member countries.

● **Compréhension: Vrai ou faux?**

Read the following statements and say whether they are true (**C'est vrai!**) or false (**C'est faux!**).

1. Fatou est française.
2. Elle habite à Paris.
3. Le père de Fatou travaille pour l'Unesco.
4. Le weekend, Fatou aime jouer au tennis.
5. Nicolas invite Fatou à un concert.
6. Fatou accepte l'invitation.

 COMPREHENSION

1. C'est faux! Elle est sénégalaise.
2. C'est vrai!
3. C'est faux! La mère de Fatou travaille pour l'Unesco.
4. C'est vrai!
5. C'est faux! Fatou invite Nicolas (à un concert).
6. C'est faux! C'est Nicolas qui accepte l'invitation de Fatou.

Leçon 16 (119)

🖥 **Using the video**

In this lesson, the opening text corresponds to the video interview. (This is why the student text has a photograph from the video rather than a cartoon montage.) However, the printed text is somewhat longer than the edited video/cassette version.

- First, have students follow in their books as you read the text aloud.
- Tell the class that the recorded version will not be exactly the same, and play it for them.
- Then play the video/cassette a second time. Have students find those sentences which are not in the recorded interview, and note those which have been modified.

16.1 Mini-scenes:
Où est-ce qu'il va?
(23:17–24:44 min.)

Leçon 16, Section 2
The video/cassette sequence
includes questions with **qui**.

Classroom Notes

A. Les questions d'information

The questions below ask for specific information and are called INFORMATION QUESTIONS. The INTERROGATIVE EXPRESSIONS in heavy print indicate what kind of information is requested.

—**Où** est-ce que tu habites?	*Where do you live?*
—J'habite **à** Nice.	*I live in Nice.*
—**À quelle heure** est-ce que vous dînez?	*At what time do you eat dinner?*
—Nous dînons à **sept heures.**	*We eat at seven.*

In French, information questions may be formed according to the pattern:

INTERROGATIVE EXPRESSION	+ **est-ce que**	+SUBJECT	+ VERB . . . ?
À quelle heure	**est-ce que**	vous	travaillez?

➡ **Est-ce que** becomes **est-ce qu'** before a vowel sound.
   Quand **est-ce qu'**Alice et Roger dînent?

➡ In information questions, your voice rises on the interrogative expression and then falls until the last syllable.

Quand est-ce que tu travailles?   **À quelle heure** est-ce que vous dînez?

OBSERVATION: In casual conversation, French speakers frequently form information questions by placing the interrogative expression at the end of the sentence. The voice rises on the interrogative expression.

Vous habitez **où?**   Vous dînez **à quelle heure?**

Vocabulaire: Expressions interrogatives

où	*where?*	**Où** est-ce que vous travaillez?
quand?	*when?*	**Quand** est-ce que ton copain organise une boum?
à quelle heure?	*at what time?*	**À quelle heure** est-ce que tu regardes la télé?
comment?	*how?*	**Comment** est-ce que tu chantes? Bien ou mal?
pourquoi?	*why?*	—**Pourquoi** est-ce que tu étudies le français?
parce que	*because*	—**Parce que** je veux voyager en France.

➡ **Parce que** becomes **parce qu'** before a vowel sound.
   Juliette invite Olivier **parce qu'**il danse bien.

---

120 Unité 4

☀ Warm-up and review

PROP: Transparency 6 or clock with hands
  Review times by asking students at what time they do certain things. Then ask a classmate to show the corresponding time on the clock face.
Dis-moi, W, à quelle heure est-ce que tu dînes?

[Je dîne à six heures et quart.]
X, viens ici et montre-nous six heures et quart.
Y, à quelle heure est-ce que tu étudies? ...
Z, à quelle heure est-ce que tu écoutes la radio? ...

1 Le Club International

The president of the International Club wants to know where some of the members are from. The secretary tells her where each one lives.

▶ Sylvie (à Québec)

LA PRÉSIDENTE: **Où est-ce que Sylvie habite?**

LE SECRÉTAIRE: **Elle habite à Québec.**

1. Jacques (à Montréal)
2. Awa (à Dakar)
3. Marc et Frédéric (à Toulouse)
4. Jean-Pierre (à Genève)
5. Sophie et Michèle (à Nice)
6. Isabelle (à Paris)

2 Curiosité

At a party in Paris, Nicolas meets Béatrice, a Canadian student. He wants to know more about her. Play both roles.

▶ où / habiter? (à Québec)

NICOLAS: **Où est-ce que tu habites?**

BÉATRICE: **J'habite à Québec.**

1. où / étudier? (à Montréal)
2. où / travailler? (dans [in] une pharmacie)
3. quand / parler français? (toujours)
4. quand / parler anglais? (souvent)
5. comment / jouer au tennis? (bien)
6. comment / danser? (très bien)
7. pourquoi / être en France? (parce que j'aime voyager)
8. pourquoi / être à Paris? (parce que j'ai [I have] un copain ici)

Expression pour la conversation

How to express surprise or mild doubt:

Ah bon?   *Oh? Really?*   —Stéphanie organise une boum.
—**Ah bon?** Quand?

3 Au téléphone

When Philippe phones his cousin Michèle, he likes to tell her what his plans are. She asks him a few questions. Play both roles.

J'organise une boum.

Samedi.

Ah bon? Quand est-ce que tu organises une boum?

▶ organiser une boum (quand? samedi)

1. organiser un pique-nique (quand? dimanche)
2. dîner avec Pauline (quand? lundi)
3. dîner avec Caroline (où? au restaurant Belcour)
4. regarder «Batman» (à quelle heure? à 9 heures)
5. jouer au tennis (quand ? demain)
6. inviter Brigitte (où? à un concert)
7. parler espagnol (comment? assez bien)
8. étudier l'italien (pourquoi? je veux voyager en Italie)

4 Questions personnelles

1. Où est-ce que tu habites? *(name of your city)*
2. Où est-ce que tu étudies? *(name of your school)*
3. À quelle heure est-ce que tu dînes?
4. À quelle heure est-ce que tu regardes la télé?
5. Quand est-ce que tu nages?
6. Quand est-ce que tu joues au tennis? (en mai? en juillet?)
7. Comment est-ce que tu chantes? (bien? très bien? mal?)
8. Comment est-ce que tu nages?

Leçon 16 121

---

1 ROLE PLAY: discussing where people live

■ **Pronunciation:** Note that the "t" is not pronounced in **Montréal** since it is considered as the final consonant of a word: **Mont Réal** *(Mount Royal).*

2 ROLE PLAY: finding out information about someone

3 ROLE PLAY: asking for information

4 COMMUNICATION: answering personal questions

■ **Variation** (written self-expression):
Have students describe themselves by answering the questions in writing. They may vary the sequence of their answers and add additional information for extra credit.

Cooperative pair practice
Activities 1, 2, 3

■ **Language note:** Unlike their English equivalents, the two words in expressions like **à qui** and **avec qui** cannot be separated.
<u>Avec qui</u> est-ce que tu travailles?
Who(m) do you work <u>with</u>?

■ **Casual speech:** In casual conversation, the entire interrogative expression may go to the end of the sentence:
Tu travailles <u>avec qui?</u>

■ **Language note:** In French as in English, the verb in **qui** questions is singular even if the expected answer is plural.
– **Qui joue au tennis?**
  (Who is playing tennis?)
– **Paul et Monique.**

ROLE PLAY: finding out information about others

■ **Variation:** Use casual speech.
– **Alice dîne.**
– **Ah bon? Elle dîne avec qui?**
– **Avec une copine.**

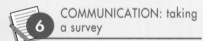
COMMUNICATION: taking a survey

■ **Pronunciation: clips** /klips/

Note: **un clip** is a music video.

B. Les expressions interrogatives avec *qui*

To ask about PEOPLE, French speakers use the following interrogative expressions:

qui?	who(m)?	Qui est-ce que tu invites au concert?
à qui? de qui?	to who(m)? about who(m)?	À qui est-ce que tu téléphones? De qui est-ce que vous parlez?
avec qui? pour qui?	with who(m)? for who(m)?	Avec qui est-ce que Pierre étudie? Pour qui est-ce que Laure organise la boum?

To ask <u>who is doing something</u>, French speakers use the construction:

qui + VERB . . . ?	
Qui habite ici?	*Who lives here?*
Qui organise la boum?	*Who is organizing the party?*

5 **Précisions** *(Details)*

Anne is telling Hélène what certain people are doing. She asks for more details. Play both roles.

Alice dîne.
Elle dîne avec une copine.
Ah bon? Avec qui est-ce qu'elle dîne?

▶ Alice dîne. (avec qui? avec une copine)

1. Jean-Pierre téléphone. (à qui? à Sylvie)
2. Frédéric étudie. (avec qui? avec un copain)
3. Madame Masson parle. (à qui? à Madame Bonnot)
4. Monsieur Lambert travaille. (avec qui? avec Monsieur Dumont)
5. Juliette danse. (avec qui? avec Georges)
6. François parle à Michèle. (de qui? de toi)

6 **Un sondage** *(A poll)*

Take a survey to find out how your classmates spend their free time. Ask who does the following things.

▶ écouter la radio
  Qui écoute la radio?

1. voyager souvent
2. aimer chanter
3. nager
4. aimer danser
5. regarder la télé
6. jouer au tennis
7. jouer au foot
8. travailler
9. regarder les clips *(MTV)*
10. parler italien
11. étudier beaucoup
12. visiter souvent New York

Cooperative pair practice
Activities 5, 7, 8

 Game: Getting acquainted

On a separate sheet of paper, have each student copy the model and 12 cues of Act. 6.

Students then move around asking classmates one by one if they do an activity on the list.

Annie: **Marc, est-ce que tu nages?**
Marc: **Oui, je nage.**
Annie writes Marc's name next to **nager.**
If Marc says no, Annie asks someone else.

The first person to complete his/her sheet with 13 different names is the winner.

7 Questions

Prepare short dialogues with your classmates, using the information in the illustrations.

où?

à la maison

▶ —Où est-ce que tu dînes?
—Je dîne à la maison.

1. à quelle heure?

à 8 heures

2. quand?

en septembre

3. comment?

BONJOUR!

très bien

4. avec qui?

avec Denise

5. à qui?

à mon cousin

6. de qui?

BLA BLA BLA...

de toi

7. pour qui?

pour M. Lambert

C. Qu'est-ce que?

Note the use of the interrogative expression **qu'est-ce que** *(what)* in the questions below.

Qu'est-ce que tu regardes? Je regarde un match de tennis.
Qu'est-ce qu'Alice mange? Elle mange une pizza.

To ask *what people are doing,* the French use the following construction:

qu'est-ce que + SUBJECT + VERB + . . . ?	**Qu'est-ce que** tu fais?
↓	
qu'est-ce qu' (+ VOWEL SOUND)	**Qu'est-ce qu'**elle fait?

8 La Boutique-Musique

People in Column A are at the Boutique-Musique, a local music shop. Use a verb from Column B to ask what they are listening to or looking at. A classmate will answer you, using an item from Column C.

A	B	C
tu	écouter?	une guitare
vous	regarder?	un poster
Alice		un compact (CD) de jazz
Éric		une cassette de rock
Antoine et Claire		un album de Paul Simon

Qu'est-ce qu'Éric écoute?

Il écoute un album de Paul Simon.

---

1. ... regardes la télé?
2. ... visites Paris?
3. ... parles français?
4. ... joues au tennis?
5. ... téléphones?
6. ... parles?
7. ... travailles?

■ **Expansion:** Have students make up their own answers to the questions.
– Où est-ce que tu dînes?
– Je dîne **au restaurant.** (etc.)

Section C

COMMUNICATIVE FUNCTION: Asking what people are doing

■ **Casual speech:** Note how **quoi** is used instead of **qu'est-ce que** in casual questions.
Tu regardes quoi?
Alice mange quoi?

16.2 Mini-scenes: Qu'est-ce que tu fais?
16.2 Mini-scenes: Questions (24:45–26:13 min.)

Leçon 16, Sections 3, 4

8 EXCHANGES: asking and answering questions

■ **Variation: Un jeu.** Have teams of students see how many correct dialogues they can write in five minutes.

T123

Section D

■ **Teaching strategy:** Ask students what other irregular verb they have learned (**être**). Have them point out the similarities between **être** and **faire**: singular forms end in **-s, -s, -t**; **vous**-form ends in **-tes**; **ils**-form ends in **-ont**.

■ **Practice drill:** Have students practice sentences with **faire**.
Je fais une pizza.
(Tu) Tu fais une pizza. etc.
Qu'est-ce que je fais?
(Vous) Qu'est-ce que vous faites? etc.

 Transparency18
Expressions with **faire**

Supplementary vocabulary

faire un pique-nique
to have a picnic
faire un tour
to go for a short walk or ride
Note: **faire une promenade** may also mean *to go for a ride*: **faire une promenade à vélo, en voiture.** (This is re-entered in Lesson 22.)

↩ **Review:** Remind students that **faire** is used in many weather expressions.
Il fait beau. Il fait mauvais.

 9 PRACTICE: describing what people are making

1. faisons   4. font   7. font
2. fais   5. fait   8. font
3. faites   6. fais

 10 COMPREHENSION: describing what people are doing

D. Le verbe *faire*

Faire *(to do, make)* is one of the most useful French verbs. It is an IRREGULAR verb since it does not follow a predictable pattern. Note the forms of **faire** in the present tense.

faire *(to do, make)*	
je **fais**	Je **fais** un sandwich.
tu **fais**	Qu'est-ce que tu **fais** maintenant?
il/elle **fait**	Qu'est-ce que ton copain **fait** samedi?
nous **faisons**	Nous **faisons** une pizza.
vous **faites**	Qu'est-ce que vous **faites** ici?
ils/elles **font**	Qu'est-ce qu'elles **font** pour la boum?

Vocabulaire: Expressions avec *faire*

faire un match	*to play a game (match)*	Mes cousins **font un match** de tennis.
faire une promenade	*to go for a walk*	Caroline **fait une promenade** avec Olivier.
faire un voyage	*to take a trip*	Ma copine **fait un voyage** en France.
faire attention	*to pay attention*	Est-ce que tu **fais attention** quand le professeur parle?

9 **La boum de Juliette**

Juliette's friends are helping her prepare food for a party. Use the verb **faire** to say what everyone is doing.

▶ Je . . . une crêpe.

Je fais une crêpe.

1. Nous . . . une salade.
2. Tu . . . une salade de fruits.
3. Vous . . . une tarte *(pie)*.
4. Cécile et Marina . . . un gâteau *(cake)*.
5. Christine . . . une pizza.
6. Marc . . . un sandwich.
7. Patrick et Thomas . . . une omelette.
8. Pierre et Karine . . . une quiche.

10 **Qu'est-ce qu'ils font?**

Read the descriptions below and say what the people are doing. Use the verb **faire** and an expression from the list below. Be logical.

un voyage   une promenade   une pizza   un match   attention

▶ Madame Dumont est en Chine.
   Elle fait un voyage.

1. Nicolas travaille dans *(in)* un restaurant.
2. Nous sommes en ville.
3. Hélène et Jean-Paul jouent au tennis.
4. Je suis dans la cuisine *(kitchen)*.
5. Marc est dans le train Paris–Nice.
6. Vous jouez au volley.
7. Je suis dans le parc.
8. Monsieur Lambert visite Tokyo.
9. Nous écoutons le prof.

E. L'interrogation avec inversion

Learning about language

In conversational French, questions are usually formed with **est-ce que.** However, when the subject of the sentence is a pronoun, French speakers often use INVERSION, that is, they invert or reverse the order of the subject pronoun and the verb.

REGULAR ORDER: **Vous parlez** français.
         SUBJECT VERB

INVERSION: **Parlez-vous** anglais?
        VERB   SUBJECT

Look at the two sets of questions below. They both ask the same thing. Compare the position of the subject pronouns in heavy print.

Est-ce que **tu** parles anglais?   Parles-**tu** anglais?   *Do you speak English?*
Est-ce que **vous** habitez ici?   Habitez-**vous** ici?   *Do you live here?*

Où est-ce que **nous** dînons?   Où dînons-**nous?**   *Where are we having dinner?*
Où est-ce qu'**il** est?   Où est-**il?**   *Where is he?*

Inverted questions are formed according to the patterns:

YES / NO QUESTION	VERB / SUBJECT PRONOUN . . . ?
	Voyagez-vous souvent?

INFORMATION QUESTION	INTERROGATIVE EXPRESSION + VERB / SUBJECT PRONOUN . . . ?
	Avec qui **travaillez-vous** demain?

➡ In inversion, the verb and the subject pronoun are connected by a hyphen.

OBSERVATION: In inversion, liaison is required before **il/elle** and **ils/elles.** If a verb in the singular ends on a vowel, the letter "**t**" is inserted between the verb and the subject pronoun so that liaison can occur:

Où travaille-**t**-il?   Où travaille-**t**-elle?
Avec qui dîne-**t**-il?   Avec qui dîne-**t**-elle?

11 Conversation

Get better acquainted with your classmates by asking them a few questions. Use inversion.

▶ où / habiter? —Où habites-tu?
                —J'habite à (Boston).

1. à quelle heure / dîner?
2. à quelle heure / regarder la télé?
3. avec qui / parler français?
4. à qui / téléphoner souvent?
5. comment / nager?
6. avec qui / étudier?

Prononciation   /y/

La voyelle /y/

Super!

The vowel sound /y/ – represented by the letter "**u**" – does not exist in English. Here is a helpful trick for producing this new sound.

First say the French word **si.** Then round your lips as if to whistle and say **si** with rounded lips: /sy/. Now say **si-per.** Then round your lips as you say the first syllable: **super!**

Répétez: /y/   s**u**per   t**u**   ét**u**die   bien s**û**r
                L**u**cie   L**u**c
                T**u** ét**u**dies avec L**u**cie.

▶ ▶

Section E

COMMUNICATIVE FUNCTION:
Asking questions

■ **Teaching note:** Inversion is taught mainly for recognition here. It is not emphasized in Book One.

11 COMMUNICATION:
getting acquainted

■ **Additional practice:** To practice inversion with **il/elle,** have the students redo Act. 5, p. 122 using inversion instead of **est-ce que.**
– Alice dîne.
– Ah bon? Avec qui dîne-t-elle?
– Elle dîne avec une copine.

Prononciation

🔘 Leçon 16, Section 6

■ **Teaching strategy:** If students have trouble producing /y/, have them pronounce the sound as /i/. They should not pronounce it as /u/.

Classroom Notes

À votre tour!

① Allô!

Awa is phoning some friends. Match her questions on the left with her friends' answers on the right.

1. Qu'est-ce que tu fais?
2. Qu'est-ce que vous faites samedi?
3. Où est ton père?
4. Quand est-ce que tu veux jouer au tennis avec moi?
5. Qui est-ce que tu invites au cinéma?
6. Pourquoi est-ce que tu étudies l'anglais?

a. Il fait une promenade.
b. Ma cousine Alice.
c. Dimanche. D'accord?
d. J'étudie.
e. Nous faisons un match de tennis.
f. Parce que je voudrais habiter à New York.

② Les questions

The following people are answering questions. Read what they say and figure out what questions they were asked.

Je chante très mal.

► Comment est-ce que tu chantes?

1. J'habite à Québec.
2. Je dîne à sept heures.
3. Nous dînons à l'Hippopotame.
4. Je mange une pizza.
5. Je regarde un film.
6. J'invite Catherine.

126 Unité 4

À votre tour

Depending on your goals and objectives, you may or may not wish to assign all of the activities in the **À votre tour** section.

👤👤 **Cooperative practice**

Act. 1–4 lend themselves to cooperative pair practice.

T126

3 Créa-dialogue

Ask your classmates what they do on different days of the week. Carry out conversations similar to the model. Note: "??" means you can invent your own answers.

▶ —Qu'est-ce que tu fais <u>lundi</u>?
—Je <u>joue au tennis</u>.
—Ah bon? À quelle heure est-ce que tu <u>joues</u>?
—<u>À deux heures</u>.
—Et avec qui?
—Avec <u>Anne-Marie</u>.

3 GUIDED ORAL EXPRESSION

📼 Leçon 16, Section 8

	lundi	mardi	mercredi	jeudi	vendredi	samedi	dimanche
ACTIVITÉ						??	??
À QUELLE HEURE?	2 heures	6 heures	??	??	??	??	??
AVEC QUI?	avec Anne-Marie	avec un copain	??	??	??	??	??

4 Faisons connaissance!
(Let's get acquainted!)

Get better acquainted with a classmate that you don't know very well. Ask questions in French. For instance:

- Where does he/she live?
- Does he/she study much at home?
- Does he/she speak French at home? (with whom?)
- Does he/she watch TV? (at what time?)
- Does he/she like to phone? (whom? [**à qui?**])

5 Interview

A famous rock star is visiting the United States. You are going to interview her for your school paper. Write out five questions you would want to ask the singer, addressing her as **vous.** For example, you may want to know . . .
- where she lives in France
- where she is singing
- why she is visiting your city
- how she is traveling
- how (well) she speaks English

4 GUIDED CONVERSATION

- Où est-ce que tu habites? (Où habites-tu?)
- Est-ce que tu étudies beaucoup à la maison? (Études-tu beaucoup à la maison?)
- Est-ce que tu parles français à la maison? (Parles-tu français à la maison?) (Avec qui?)
- Est-ce que tu regardes la télé? (Regardes-tu la télé?)
- Est-ce que tu aimes téléphoner? (Aimes-tu téléphoner?) (À qui?)

6 Curiosité

Imagine that a French friend has just made the following statements. For each one, write down three or four related questions you could ask him or her.

Je joue au foot demain.

Je joue au tennis. **1**

2 Je dîne avec un copain.

3 Je fais une promenade.

4

J'organise une boum.

- Avec qui est-ce que tu joues?
- Où est-ce que vous jouez?
- À quelle heure est-ce que vous jouez?
- Pourquoi est-ce que vous jouez au foot?

5 WRITTEN SELF-EXPRESSION

6 WRITTEN SELF-EXPRESSION

Leçon 16 127

📁 Portfolio assessment

You will probably only select one speaking activity and one writing activity to go into the students' portfolios for Unit 4.

In this lesson, Act. 3 and 4 are good oral portfolio conversation topics.

Entracte 4

OBJECTIVES:

- Reading skill development
- Re-entry of materials in the unit
- Development of cultural awareness
- Vocabulary expansion

Les activités quotidiens

OBJECTIVES:
- Rapid reading at the sentence level
- Reading for information about French daily life

■ **Teaching strategy:** Do not have students read aloud since they will have difficulty pronouncing the new words and cognates. Have them follow along silently as you read the text. If you wish, you may call on students to read the **Et les Français?** answers.

Vive la différence!

Les activités quotidiennes

Nous sommes américains, français, anglais, canadiens . . . Nos° cultures ont° beaucoup de points communs, mais elles ne sont pas identiques.

Parlons° de la vie quotidienne.° Nous faisons les mêmes choses,° mais souvent nous faisons ces° choses un peu différemment.° Voici plusieurs° questions. Répondez° à ces questions. À votre avis,° quelles° sont les réponses des jeunes Français?°

1 Quel jour de la semaine est-ce que vous préférez?
- le lundi
- le vendredi
- le samedi
- le dimanche

Et les Français, quel jour est-ce qu'ils préfèrent?

3 Voici quatre sports. Quel sport est-ce que vous pratiquez le plus?°
- Je nage.
- Je joue au basket.
- Je fais du jogging.
- Je joue au football.

Et les jeunes Français, quel sport est-ce qu'ils pratiquent le plus?

5 En moyenne,° combien d'heures° par jour° est-ce que vous regardez la télé?
- une heure
- deux heures
- trois heures
- quatre heures ou plus°

Et les jeunes Français? Combien d'heures par jour est-ce qu'ils regardent la télé?

2 Pendant° la semaine, qu'est-ce que vous préférez faire quand vous n'étudiez pas?
- Je préfère regarder la télé.
- Je préfère lire.°
- Je préfère jouer au basket.
- Je préfère téléphoner à mes° copains.

Et les jeunes Français, qu'est-ce qu'ils préfèrent faire?

4 À quelle heure est-ce que vous dînez en général?
- entre° cinq heures et demie et six heures
- entre six heures et sept heures
- entre sept heures et huit heures
- après huit heures

Et les Français, à quelle heure est-ce qu'ils dînent?

6 Qu'est-ce que vous préférez regarder à la télé?
- les sports
- les films
- la publicité°
- les feuilletons°

Et les jeunes Français, qu'est-ce qu'ils préfèrent regarder?

Et les Français?
1. Ils préfèrent le samedi.   2. Ils préfèrent regarder la télé.   3. Ils jouent au football.   4. Ils dînent entre sept heures et huit heures.   5. Ils regardent la télé deux heures par jour.   6. Ils préfèrent regarder les films.

Nos *Our*   **ont** *have*   **Parlons** *Let's talk*   **vie quotidienne** *daily life*   **mêmes choses** *same things*   **ces** *these* **différemment** *differently*   **plusieurs** *several*   **Répondez** *Answer*   **À votre avis** *In your opinion*   **quelles** *what* **jeunes Français** *young French people*   **Pendant** *During*   **lire** *to read*   **mes** *my*   **le plus** *the most*   **entre** *between* **En moyenne** *On the average*   **combien d'heures** *how many hours*   **par jour** *per day*   **plus** *more*   **publicité** *commercials*   **feuilletons** *series*

 Cooperative reading practice

Divide the class into groups of 4 or 5, each with a recorder (**un/une secrétaire**).

For each question, have the groups first vote on their own preferences and then on what they imagine the preferences of French young people to be. (Keep answers covered.)

Then have the recorders announce their results to the entire class. For example:
1. Nous préférons le samedi.
Selon nous, les Français préfèrent le samedi aussi.

EN FRANCE

À la télé, ce weekend

In France, TV viewers have a choice of six main channels: **TF1, Antenne 2, FR3, La 5, M6,** and **Canal Plus.** (People who want to watch **Canal Plus** need to have a special decoding machine for which they pay a monthly fee.)

Note that in TV listings, times are expressed using a 24-hour clock. In this system, 8 P.M. is **20.00 (vingt heures);** 10 P.M. is **22.00 (vingt-deux heures).**

Imagine that you are spending a month in Paris with a French family. This Friday and Saturday you have decided to stay home and watch TV. Look at the program listings at the right.

📺 Which programs would you like to watch on Friday? When do they start?

📺 Which programs would you choose on Saturday evening? When do they start?

📺 Your French hosts are soccer fans. What program would they want to watch and when? Which teams are playing? (Locate these cities on the map of France.)

📺 What program is featured on **Antenne 2** on Saturday evening? Who are the guests on this program? Do you know any of them?

📺 How many different movies are being shown over the weekend? How many of these movies are American? Which movie would you choose to see? At what time and on which channel?

📺 You are interested in watching a French TV series. Which program would you select? On which channel? According to its title, what kind of a series do you think it is?

SÉLECTION DE LA SEMAINE	VEN	SAM
TF1	**20.30** VARIÉTÉS **SALUT L'ARTISTE** — Sketches de **Thierry Le Luron** — **22.05** DOCUMENT **HISTOIRES NATURELLES**	**20.35** SPECTACLE **HOLIDAY ON ICE** — Mis en scène par **Jérôme Savary** — **22.10** SÉRIE **DANS LA CHALEUR DE LA NUIT**
a2	**20.35** SÉRIE **HÔTEL DE POLICE** — LE GENTIL MONSIEUR de Claude Barrois avec Cécile Magnet — **23.20** FILM **ALICE DANS LES VILLES** de Wim Wenders	**20.40** VARIÉTÉS **CHAMPS-ÉLYSÉES** — Invités: Elton John, Isabelle Adjani, Tom Cruise — **22.25** SÉRIE **MÉDECINS DE NUIT**
FR3	**21.30** SÉRIE **LE MASQUE** — MADEMOISELLE EVELYNE de Jean-Louis Fournier — **23.45** CONCERT **MUSIQUES, MUSIQUE**	**20.35** JEUNESSE **SAMDYNAMITE** — DESSINS ANIMÉS Série: **BATMAN** — **22.25** ENTRETIEN **LE DIVAN** Pierre Dumayet
LA CINQ 5	**20.30** FILM **MON PROF EST UN EXTRA-TERRESTRE** de Dave De Coteau — **22.15** SÉRIE **DEUX FLICS À MIAMI**	**20.30** FILM TV **OPÉRATION COMMANDO** de Ted Kaplan avec D. Stephen, R. Kristoff — **22.25** SÉRIE **DEUX FLICS À MIAMI**
M6	**20.30** FILM TV **COPACABANA** de Warris Hussein avec Barry Manilow, Annette O'Toole — **22.05** THÉÂTRE **LE SEXE FAIBLE**	**20.35** FILM TV **L'ÉCLOSION DES MONSTRES** de J. Piquer Simon avec Yan Sera — **22.20** SÉRIE **LE COMTE DE MONTE-CRISTO**
CANAL+	**20.30** FOOTBALL **CAEN - TOULOUSE** — Championnat de France 28ᵉ journée — **22.40** FILM **AFTER HOURS** de Martin Scorsese	**20.30** FILM **ALIENS, LE RETOUR** de James Cameron avec Sigourney Weaver — **22.45** FILM **UNE NUIT À L'ASSEMBLÉE NATIONALE** de Jean-Pierre Mocky

Entracte 4 129

À la télé

OBJECTIVES:
- Reading for information
- Selecting programs from a French TV guide

◼ **Sélection de la semaine**
chaleur *heat ("In the Heat of the Night")*
nuit *night*
hôtel de police *police department*
médecins de nuit *doctors on night duty*
dessins animés *cartoons*
entretien *discussion*
flic *cop ("Miami Vice")*
éclosion *hatching*
comte *count*

◼ **Cultural notes**
- *Le Masque* is a detective series.
- *Le comte de Monte Cristo* is a historical adventure story, based on the novel by Alexandre Dumas.

📖 Pre-reading

Ask pairs of students to name their favorite TV programs.

Quel est votre émission favorite?
Nous aimons [Jeopardy].

Group reading activity

Divide the class into groups of 4 or 5. Each group must decide on which early and which late show they will watch each night. Then they report their decision to the class.

Vendredi nous allons regarder ... et ...
Samedi nous allons regarder ... et ...

Entre amis: Bonjour, Patrick!

Qu'est-ce que vous aimez faire? Dans° une lettre, Patrick répond° à cette question. Voici la lettre de Patrick.

Bonjour!

Je m'appelle Patrick Lacaze. J'ai 14 ans. J'habite à Tours avec ma famille. Je suis élève° de troisième.° J'étudie beaucoup, mais je n'étudie pas tout le temps.° Voici ce que° j'aime faire.

J'aime les boums parce que j'adore danser.

J'aime la musique. J'aime surtout° le rock. J'aimerais° jouer de la guitare, mais je ne sais pas.°

J'aime les sports. En hiver je skie et en été je nage et je joue au tennis. (Je ne suis pas un champion, mais je joue assez° bien.) J'aime jouer au basket, mais je préfère jouer au foot. (J'aime jouer au babyfoot, mais ce n'est pas un sport.) J'aime faire des promenades à vélo° le weekend avec mes copains.

J'aime mon école.° J'aime surtout l'anglais parce que le prof est sympa.° (Il s'appelle Mr. Ross, mais il est très gentil.°) Je n'aime pas trop° les maths.

À la maison, j'aime regarder la télé. J'adore les séries américaines! J'aime aussi écouter mes cassettes.

J'aime téléphoner à ma copine, mais je ne téléphone pas souvent. (Mon père n'aime pas ça.°)

J'aime jouer aux jeux° sur le Minitel!

Et vous, qu'est-ce que vous aimez faire? Répondez-moi° vite.°

Amicalement,°
Patrick Lacaze

Dans *In*   **répond** *answers*   **élève** *student*   **troisième** *ninth grade*   **tout le temps** *all the time*   **ce que** *what*   **surtout** *especially*   **aimerais** *would like*   **je ne sais pas** *I don't know how*   **assez** *rather*   **promenades à vélo** *bike rides*   **école** *school*   **sympa** *nice*   **gentil** *nice*   **trop** *too much*   **ça** *that*   **jeux** *games*   **Répondez-moi** *Answer me*   **vite** *quickly*   **Amicalement** *Cordially (In friendship)*

■ NOTES ■
CULTURELLES

1 Tours

Tours is an attractive city located about 150 miles southwest of Paris. It is the capital of Touraine, an area of France known for its beautiful castles.

2 Le babyfoot

Babyfoot is a tabletop soccer game in which two teams of two people each try to score goals by manipulating rows of toy players. **Babyfoot** is very popular among French teenagers, who play it in cafés or in youth clubs.

130   Unité 4

Bonjour, Patrick!

OBJECTIVE:
• Reading a longer text

■ **Language notes**
• Patrick writes in a casual style. Point out the shortened words:
  un prof (professeur)
  sympa (sympathique)
• When pronounced the French way, "Ross" sounds like **rosse** which is slang for *nasty*.

■ **Questions sur le texte**
1. Pourquoi est-ce que Patrick aime les boums?
2. Quelle sorte de musique est-ce qu'il aime?
3. Quels sports est-ce qu'il pratique en hiver? Et en été?
4. Comment est-ce qu'il joue au tennis?
5. Pourquoi est-ce qu'il aime l'anglais?
6. Qu'est-ce qu'il aime regarder à la télé?
7. À qui est-ce qu'il téléphone?
8. Pourquoi est-ce qu'il ne téléphone pas souvent?

■ **Questions personnelles**
1. Est-ce que tu aimes la musique? Quelle sorte de musique est-ce que tu aimes écouter?
2. Est-ce que tu joues d'un instrument?
3. Quels sports est-ce que tu pratiques en hiver? en été?
4. Est-ce que tu aimes ton école? Quels sujets est-ce que tu aimes? Quels sujets est-ce que tu n'aimes pas?
5. Est-ce que tu aimes étudier le français? (Pourquoi ou pourquoi pas?)
6. Est-ce que tu téléphones souvent? À qui? Est-ce que tu aimes téléphoner?

📖 Pre-reading

Ask if any of the students in the class have penpals.

Est-ce que vous avez un correspondant ou une correspondante?
Où habite votre correspondant(e)?

Tell them this is a letter from a French penpal.

Comment lire *(Reading hints)*

GETTING THE MEANING

When you read French, try to understand the meaning. Don't look for a word-for-word English translation for each sentence.

- Sometimes the two languages use different constructions.

  Je m'appelle . . .   *(I call myself . . .)*   *My name is . . .*

- Sometimes French uses some words that English leaves out.

  J'aime <u>le</u> rock.   *I love rock.*
  J'aime jouer <u>de</u> la guitare.   *I like to play the guitar.*

- And sometimes French leaves out words that English uses.

  Je suis élève de troisième.   *I am <u>a</u> student in ninth <u>grade</u>.*

- Word order may also be different.

  des promenades à vélo   *bike rides*

Enrichissez votre vocabulaire

COGNATES

You have already discovered that there are many words in French that look like English words and have similar meanings. These are called COGNATES. Cognates let you increase your vocabulary effortlessly. But be sure to pronounce them the French way!

- Sometimes the spelling is the same, or almost the same.

  la radio   *radio*
  un champion   *champion*

- Sometimes the spelling is a little different.

  américain   *American*

Activité

Read the letter from Patrick again and find five more French-English cognates.

Activité: Une lettre à Patrick

You are writing a letter to Patrick in which you introduce yourself and explain what you like to do. You may tell him:

- if you like music (and what kind)
- what sports you like to do in fall or winter
- what sports you like to do in spring or summer
- what you like to do at home
- whether or not you like French and math
- what you like to do on weekends
- what programs you like to watch on TV

You may start your letter with the words:
Mon cher Patrick,
(My dear Patrick)
and end it with:
Amicalement,

Mon cher Patrick,

Amicalement,

■ **Additional cognates:**
adore
la musique
le rock
la guitare
les sports
le tennis
le weekend
les séries
mes cassettes
les maths...

Entracte 4 131

■ **Teaching note:**
If your school has computer capabilities, you may want to explore the possibility of linking your class with an English class in France using the Minitel network.
For more information on educational Minitel networks, write:
Minitel Commission
American Association of Teachers of French (AATF)
57 E. Armory Avenue
Champaign, IL 61820

Classroom Notes

■ NOTE ■
CULTURELLE

Le Minitel

If you lived in Paris and wanted to find the phone number or address of a friend, you wouldn't call information. You would turn to your **Minitel.** The **Minitel** is a small computer terminal connected to the telephone. By entering certain codes, you can gain access to a large variety of services. The most popular is the **annuaire électronique** (*computerized phone directory*).

However, the **Minitel** has much more to offer. You can check plane and train schedules, reserve theater tickets, and send electronic messages. For recreation, there are all sorts of games sponsored by various companies. If you answer a certain number of questions correctly, for example, you can win prizes like a pair of movie tickets or even a trip abroad.

But there is a catch! Although the **Minitel** terminals are distributed free of charge, users are billed each month according to the types of services used and time spent on the line. Because the **Minitel** may become expensive, French parents insist on limiting its use.

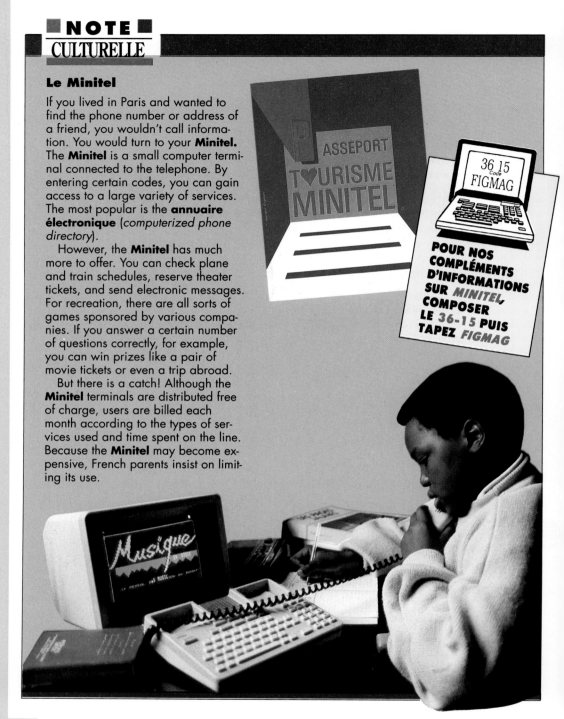

PASSEPORT TOURISME MINITEL

36.15 Code FIGMAG

POUR NOS COMPLÉMENTS D'INFORMATIONS SUR *MINITEL,* COMPOSER LE 36-15 PUIS TAPEZ *FIGMAG*

Musique

Variétés

Cinq portraits

Cinq jeunes parlent de ce qu'ils font,° mais ils ne révèlent pas leur° identité. Est-ce que vous pouvez° identifier chacun?° Lisez° les paragraphes suivants° et faites correspondre° chaque° paragraphe à une photo.

1 Je ne suis pas français, mais je parle français. Je parle anglais aussi, mais je préfère parler français. J'aime les sports. Je joue au volley et au basket, mais mon sport préféré° est le hockey. Je m'appelle . . .

2 Je suis française, mais je n'habite pas à Paris. J'habite dans une île tropicale. Au lycée, j'étudie beaucoup. Mon sujet préféré est la biologie. (Je voudrais être médecin.°) J'aime la musique. J'aime beaucoup le reggae et j'adore chanter. J'aime les sports. Je nage souvent. Là où j'habite je peux nager en toute saison.° Je m'appelle . . .

3 Je n'habite pas à Paris. J'habite dans° une grande° ville° à 600 kilomètres de Paris. Je suis élève° dans un lycée. J'étudie beaucoup. Mes sujets préférés sont l'espagnol, la gymnastique, le français et la musique. J'aime beaucoup le jazz et le rock. J'adore danser. Je m'appelle . . .

4 Je n'habite pas en France, mais un jour je voudrais étudier à Paris. J'habite en Afrique. Je suis élève au Collège Moderne du Plateau. J'étudie l'anglais, les maths et la physique. Mon ambition est d'être architecte. Je m'appelle . . .

5 J'habite dans un petit° pays° européen. Dans mon pays les gens° parlent des langues différentes. Moi, je parle français. En classe j'étudie l'anglais et l'allemand.° J'aime voyager. Je voudrais visiter le Canada. Ma cousine Christine habite là-bas. Je m'appelle . . .

Moussa Dembila
Abidjan, Côte d'Ivoire

Catherine Miguel
Bordeaux, France

Laurent Arnold
Genève, Suisse

Isabelle Lamy
Trois Îlets, Martinique

Denis Lévêque
Montréal, Québec

ce qu'ils font *what they do* **leur** *their* **pouvez** *can* **chacun** *each one* **Lisez** *Read*
suivants *following* **faites correspondre** *match* **chaque** *each* **préféré** *favorite*
médecin *doctor* **en toute saison** *all year round (in any season)* **dans** *in*
grande *large* **ville** *city* **élève** *student* **petit** *small* **pays** *country* **gens** *people*
allemand *German*

Entracte 4 133

OBJECTIVES:
- Reading at the paragraph level
- Developing logical thinking

Game: Cooperative pair reading

Be sure all students have their books closed. Divide the class into pairs. Each pair prepares a sheet of paper with the numbers 1 to 5.
  Prenez une feuille de papier et écrivez les numéros 1, 2, 3, 4, 5.
When you give the signal, they are to turn to page 133 and do the reading activity, writing the five names next to the corresponding numbers.
  The first pair to complete the list correctly is the winner.
  Maintenant, tournez à la page cent trente-trois et commencez.

■ **Photo culture note**
Le vélo
The student on the left is riding a mountain bike (**un vélo tout terrain: un VTT**). These bikes are becoming very popular with French teenagers. In the school parking lot, one can also see many mopeds (**un velomoteur**) and scooters (**un scooter**).

UNITÉ

5

Le monde personnel et familier

Unit overview
COMMUNICATION GOALS: Students will learn to describe themselves and their family, friends, and personal possessions.
LINGUISTIC GOALS: The focus is on the noun group: articles, nouns, and adjectives. The passé composé is introduced informally.

CRITICAL THINKING GOALS: Students are introduced to the concepts of gender and noun-adjective agreement. They learn to observe and apply these patterns in French.
CULTURAL GOALS: This unit presents the multi-cultural reality of contemporary France, while highlighting the common interests of French and American youth.

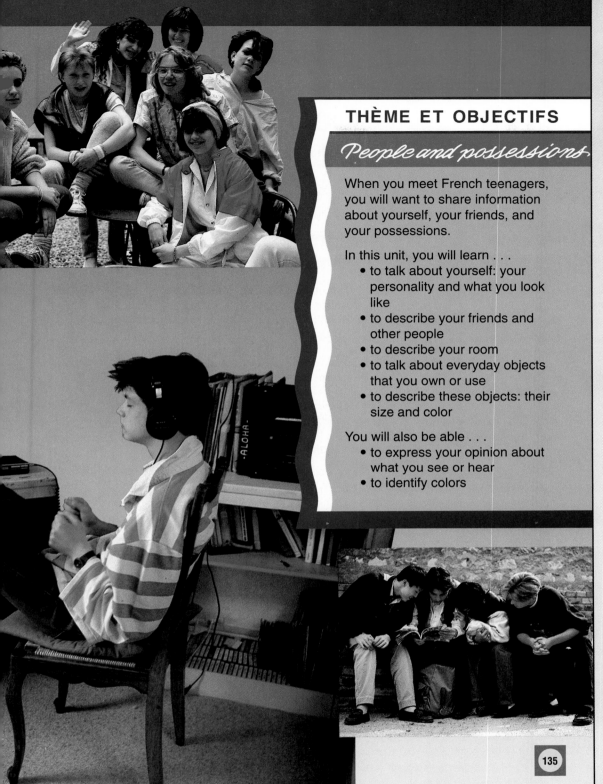

THÈME ET OBJECTIFS

People and possessions

When you meet French teenagers, you will want to share information about yourself, your friends, and your possessions.

In this unit, you will learn . . .
- to talk about yourself: your personality and what you look like
- to describe your friends and other people
- to describe your room
- to talk about everyday objects that you own or use
- to describe these objects: their size and color

You will also be able . . .
- to express your opinion about what you see or hear
- to identify colors

135

■ **Photo culture note**
Le walkman
Like their American counterparts, French teenagers love to listen to music through headphones (**des écouteurs**) on their personal stereos (**un walkman**, or technically **un baladeur**).

Les bandes dessinées
On the bottom right, the students are looking at the latest comic book (**des bandes dessinées: des B.D.**). In France, there is a wide variety of **bandes dessinées** created for teens and young adults.

Classroom Notes

Pacing

Unit 5 reviews and expands considerably on Unit 2 of Niveau A. As in Unit 4, there is a dual emphasis on both oral and written skills.

For specific suggestions on pacing, turn to Section 7 in the Front Matter.

MODULE 17:
Le français pratique:
Les personnes et les objets
Total time: 6:58 min.
(Counter: 28:45 min.)

17.1 Mini-scenes: Listening — J'ai un walkman
(29:53–30:56 min.)

17.2 Mini-scenes: Speaking — Qu'est-ce que c'est?
(30:57–32:02 min.)

17.3 Dialogue: Tu as un walkman?
(32:03–33:01 min.)

17.4 Mini-scenes: Speaking — Où est-il?
(33:02–34:19 min.)

17.5 Vignette culturelle: La chambre de Catherine
(34:20–35:41 min.)

■ **Comprehension practice:** Play the entire module through as an introduction to the lesson.

■ **Cultural notes**
• The U.S. population is about 250 million.
• North Africa, French-speaking West Africa, Vietnam, Laos, and Cambodia were all former French colonies.
• Less than 20% percent of the U.S. population is under 20.

T136

LE FRANÇAIS PRATIQUE

Les personnes et les objets

Accent sur . . . Les Français

France has a population of 55 million people. France is a European country, but its population includes people of many different ethnic backgrounds and cultural origins. There are many French citizens whose families have come from North Africa and French-speaking West Africa, as well as from Vietnam, Laos, and Cambodia.

• France is a country of Catholic tradition, but it also has:
— the largest Jewish population of Western Europe (about 600,000 people).
— the largest Muslim population of Western Europe (about five million people).

• France is a young country. Thirty percent of its population is under the age of 20.

• French young people tend to be idealists. They believe in freedom and democracy. They also believe in friendship and family. In fact, they rank these values far above money and material success.

• French young people in general have a positive attitude toward Americans. They like American music and would enjoy visiting the United States.

• Because language study is required in French secondary schools, many French teenagers can communicate in a second language, such as English or German.

136 Unité 5

Setting the scene

Ask students what kinds of things they buy, other than food and clothes: school supplies, books, posters, cassettes, CDs, audio equipment, etc.

Ask what other possessions they have: a watch, a camera, a bicycle, etc.

As they watch Video Module 17, they will meet many French young people who will talk about their own possessions.

In the last segment, Catherine invites them to her room and points out some of her favorite things.

Au Café Montparnasse
Stéphanie parle avec ses amis.

Chez le marchand de glaces
Philippe est chez le marchand de glaces avec une copine.

À Paris
Des jeunes font une promenade sur les Champs-Élysées.

Chez des amis
Stéphanie écoute des disques avec un copain.

■ **Photo culture notes**
Montparnasse
At the turn of the century, the Montparnasse neighborhood on the Left Bank (**la rive gauche**) of Paris was the home to many artists, including Picasso, Modigliani, and Chagall. Renovated in the 1960s, the area is now dominated by the 52-floor Tour Maine-Montparnasse. Students and other visitors come to Montparnasse to explore its numerous cafés, restaurants, and movie theaters.

Les glaces
In France, one can buy ice cream (**une glace**) and sherbets (**un sorbet**) from street vendors or in specialized shops. Some pastry shops (**une pâtisserie**) also sell ice cream.
Favorite flavors of ice cream include:
coffee (**une glace au café**)
strawberry (**une glace aux fraises**)
raspberry (**un sorbet aux framboises**)
black currant (**un sorbet aux cassis**)

Les Champs-Élysées
Les Champs-Élysées is the most famous avenue of Paris and a favorite place for strolling with friends. The avenue runs from the **Arc de Triomphe** (in the picture) to the **Place de la Concorde**.

 ## 🌐 Multi-culturalism in France

PROP: Transparency 2 (world map)

French society is becoming increasingly multi-cultural as the country attracts immigrants representing many different traditions and backgrounds.

On the world map on p. R2, have students find the main countries of origin of these French immigrant groups:

Les Arabes et les Musulmans:
  l'Algérie, la Tunisie, le Maroc
Les Noirs: l'Afrique occidentale — la
  Côte d'Ivoire, le Sénégal, le Mali ...
Les Orientaux: le Viêt-nam, le
  Cambodge

Section A

↺ **Review and expansion:**
Phrases from Niveau A.

▢ **Casual speech:** Questions can be formed using a rising intonation:
C'est qui?
Il/Elle s'appelle comment?
Il/Elle a quel âge?

▷ **Les personnes**

▢ **Language note:** The term **un étudiant (une étudiante)** refers to college students, although it is now sometimes used in talking about high school students, especially older ones. The traditional term for high school students is **un lycéen (une lycéenne).**

▢ **Teaching strategy:** To help students differentiate between the sound of **un** and **une**, point to various students and ask:
Est-ce que c'est un élève ou une élève?
Est-ce que c'est un camarade ou une camarade?

A. La description des personnes

▶ *How to describe someone:*

Qui est-ce?
C'est un copain.

Comment s'appelle-t-il?
Il s'appelle Marc.

Quel âge a-t-il?
Il a seize ans.

Comment est-il?
Il est petit.
Il est blond.

Qui est-ce?
C'est une copine.

Comment s'appelle-t-elle?
Elle s'appelle Sophie.

Quel âge a-t-elle?
Elle a quinze ans.

Comment est-elle?
Elle est grande.
Elle est brune.

Les personnes

une **personne**		une **personne**	
un **étudiant**	*(student)*	une **étudiante**	
un **élève**	*(pupil)*	une **élève**	
un **camarade**	*(classmate)*	une **camarade**	
un **homme**	*(man)*	une **femme**	*(woman)*
un **professeur**, un **prof**	*(teacher)*	un **professeur**, une **prof**	
un **voisin**	*(neighbor)*	une **voisine**	

➡ **Une personne** is always feminine whether it refers to a male or female person.

➡ **Un professeur** is always masculine whether it refers to a male or female teacher. However, in casual French, one distinguishes between **un prof** (male) and **une prof** (female).

TPR 🏃 **Descriptive adjectives**

PROPS: Blue and red index cards

Give each student a blue and a red card. On the board, draw a stick figure of a boy (labeled Michel) and a girl (labeled Michelle).
Voici Michel. C'est un copain.
Et voilà Michelle. C'est une copine.

Hold a blue card next to Michel, and a red card next to Michelle.
La carte bleue est pour Michel.
La carte rouge est pour Michelle.
Read descriptions using new vocabulary and have students hold up the right card.
Michel est grand. [blue card]
Michelle est belle. [red card]
Michel(le) est jeune. [either: both cards]

La description physique

Il est ...

grand   petit   brun   blond   **beau**
handsome,
good-looking   **jeune**
young

Elle est ...

grande   petite   brune   blonde   **belle**
beautiful   **jolie**
pretty   jeune

---

1 **Oui ou non?**

Describe the people below in affirmative or negative sentences.

▶ Michael Jordan / petit?
  Michael Jordan n'est pas petit.

▶ Cher / grande?
  Cher est grande.

1. Larry Bird / grand?
2. Tom Cruise / blond?
3. Dracula / beau?
4. mon copain / brun?
5. mon père / petit?
6. mon voisin / jeune?
7. la princesse Diana / belle?
8. Jane Fonda / jeune?
9. Oprah Winfrey / grande?
10. ma copine / petite?
11. ma mère / brune?
12. ma voisine / jolie?

---

2 **Vacances à Québec**

You spent last summer in Quebec and have just had your photographs developed. Describe each of the people, giving name, approximate age, and two or three characteristics.

blond(e) petit(e)
brun(e) beau (belle)
grand(e) jeune

▶ Il s'appelle Alain.
  Il est brun.
  Il a seize ans.
  Il n'est pas grand.
  Il est petit.

▶ **Alain**

1. Anne-Marie   2. Jean-Pierre   3. Claire

4. Mademoiselle Lévêque   5. Madame Paquette   6. Monsieur Beliveau

Leçon 17   **139**

▷ La description physique

🖥 Transparency 19
La description physique

📼 Leçon 17, Section 1

■ **Looking ahead**
• Noun-adjective agreement is formally presented in Lesson 19.
• The masculine form **joli** is introduced in Lesson 20. Note that **joli** is not used to describe men and boys.

■ **Extra practice:** Have students describe similar-looking twins:
▶ **Marc et Sophie.**
  Marc est grand. Sophie est grande.
  Sophie est belle. Marc est beau. etc.

Supplementary vocabulary

roux (rousse) *red-head*
fort (forte) *strong*
faible *weak*
laid (laide) *ugly*
moche *plain*
âgé (âgée) *old*
vieux (vieille) *old*

1 DESCRIPTION: describing people

2 COMMUNICATION: describing appearance and age

■ **Teaching strategy:** If you do not introduce **âgé** (old) at this point, students can describe an older person by saying:
  Il/Elle n'est pas jeune.

🎲 Game: Qui est-ce?

PROPS: Magazine pictures showing a variety of individuals with different looks

Tape the pictures across the chalkboard. Have the class identify each one. Write the names.
Voici une femme. Comment s'appelle-t-elle? [Elle s'appelle Mme Duroc.] ...

Each student stands and describes one of the people without mentioning his/her name. The others try to guess who it is.
C'est une femme. Elle est blonde. Elle est grande. Elle n'est pas jeune. Qui est-ce? [C'est Madame Duroc.]
VARIATION: Use well-known personalities.

B. Les objets

Qu'est-ce que c'est?

▶ *How to identify something:*

Qu'est-ce que c'est?	*What is it? What's that?*	—**Qu'est-ce que c'est?**
C'est . . .	*It's . . . , That's . . .*	—**C'est** une radio.

▶ *How to say that you know or do not know:*

Je sais.	*I know.*
Je ne sais pas.	*I don't know.*

▶ *How to point out something:*

—**Regarde ça.**	*Look at that.*
—**Quoi?**	*What?*
—**Ça,** là-bas.	*That, over there.*

Quelques objets (*A few objects*)

un objet   un stylo   un crayon   un livre

un disque   un compact (un CD)   un sac

une chose (*thing*)   une raquette   une guitare

une affiche   une cassette

DO YOU REMEMBER?

In French, the names of objects are MASCULINE or FEMININE.

Masculine objects can be introduced by **un** or **le (l')**: **un disque, le disque, l'objet.**

Feminine objects can be introduced by **une** or **la (l')**: **une cassette, la cassette, l'affiche.**

140   Unité 5

Classroom Notes

TPR 🏃 Everyday objects

PROPS: Objects from the above vocabulary

Hold up the objects (or corresponding pictures), identifying them one by one.
   Voici un stylo.
   Voici une cassette. ...
Go over the objects, misidentifying some.

Voici un stylo. [holding a pencil]
Ah non, ce n'est pas un stylo.
Est-ce que c'est un livre? [non]
Est-ce que c'est un crayon? [oui]
Have students manipulate the objects.
   X, viens ici. Montre-nous le sac.
   Y, prends la raquette et donne-la à Z.

— QU'EST-CE QUE
C'EST QUE ÇA?
— QUOI?
— ÇA, LÀ-BAS!
— C'EST UNE TÉLÉ.

—OH LÀ LÀ, NON!
REGARDE! C'EST
UN EXTRA-
TERRESTRE!

■ **Teaching strategy:** Have students note the use of **ça** and **quoi** in the cartoon at left.

3 Qu'est-ce que c'est?

Ask a classmate to identify the following objects.

u'est-ce que
c'est?

C'est un stylo.

4 S'il te plaît

Ask a classmate to give you the following objects.

► —S'il te plaît, donne-moi
   la cassette.
  —Voilà la cassette.
  —Merci.

C'EST VUARNET!

VUARNET.
FRANCE

3 DESCRIPTION: identifying objects

1. un livre
2. une affiche
3. une guitare
4. une raquette
5. un sac

■ **Variation:** Go around the classroom holding up or pointing to objects students can identify.
– **Regardez ça. Qu'est-ce que c'est?**
– **C'est [un crayon].**
– **Et ça? Qu'est-ce que c'est?**
– **C'est [un stylo].**

4 EXCHANGES: asking for things

1. le crayon
2. l'affiche
3. le livre
4. le disque
5. le compact (le CD)

■ **Realia note**
Jean Vuarnet, one of the best-known French skiers, was a gold medalist at the 1960 Winter Olympic Games. The company which bears his name manufactures sunglasses (**des lunettes de soleil**) and other sports accessories.

Cooperative
pair practice
Activities 3, 4

141

17.1 Mini-scenes: J'ai un walkman
(29:53–30:56 min.)

17.2 Mini-scenes: Qu'est-ce que c'est?
(30:57–32:02 min.)

 Leçon 17, Sections 2, 3

Looking ahead: The negative **pas de** (je n'ai pas de guitare) is taught in Lesson 19.

Transparency 21
Quelques objets (b)

Supplementary vocabulary

un magnétoscope *VCR*
un caméscope *video camcorder*
une vidéocassette *video cassette*
une platine laser *CD player*
   also: **un lecteur de CD, un lecteur de compact disques**
une machine à écrire *typewriter*
une caméra *movie camera*
une planche à roulettes *skateboard*
   also: **un skateboard, un skate**
un ballon (de foot, de volley, de basket) *soccer ball, basketball volleyball*
une balle de baseball *baseball*
une batte de baseball *baseball bat*

Language note: Remind students that *to work* in the sense of *doing work* is **travailler.**
You may want to point out that in English something "runs" well, whereas in French it "walks."

 Leçon 17, Section 5

Casual speech: Common shortened forms:
un appareil
un magnéto
une mob
une chaîne

C. Les possessions personnelles

Est-ce que tu as une moto?

Oui, j'ai une mot[o]

▶ How to talk about things you have:

Est-ce que tu as . . . ?   *Do you have . . . ?*   —**Est-ce que tu as** un sac?
Oui, j'ai . . .   *Yes, I have . . .*   —**Oui, j'ai** un sac.

Quelques objets

un vélo (une bicyclette)   un scooter   un téléphone   un walkman

un appareil-photo   un magnétophone   un ordinateur

une voiture (une auto)   une moto   une mobylette   une montre   une calculatrice

une radio   une radiocassette   une télé   une chaîne stéréo

▶ How to ask if an object works:

—Est-ce que la radio **marche?**   *Does the radio* **work?**
—Oui, elle **marche.**   *Yes, it works.*

➡ The verb **marcher** has two meanings:

for people:
to walk   Nous **marchons.**

for things:
to work, to run   Le scooter ne **marche** pas bien.

DO YOU REMEMBER?
Masculine nouns can be replaced by **il.**
   Le vélo marche.
   Il marche.

Feminine nouns can be replaced by **elle.**
   La voiture marche.
   Elle marche.

142 Unité 5

Speaking practice

Have students bring in a picture of one of the above vocabulary items. Ask each one to describe his/her object and say if it works.
   Voici une montre. Elle est belle.
   Elle marche bien.

5 Et toi?

1. J'ai . . .
   (Name 3 objects you own.)
2. Je voudrais . . .
   (Name 3 things you would like to have.)
3. Pour Noël / Hanoukka, je voudrais . . .
   (Name 2 gifts you would like to receive.)

6 Joyeux anniversaire
(Happy birthday)

For your birthday, a rich aunt is giving you the choice between different possible gifts. Indicate your preferences.

▶ vélo ou scooter?

1. mobylette ou moto?
2. montre ou radio?
3. appareil-photo ou walkman?
4. radiocassette ou chaîne stéréo?
5. télé ou ordinateur?
6. magnétophone ou calculatrice?

Je préfère le vélo.

Je préfère le scooter.

7 Qu'est-ce que tu as?

Philippe asks Christine if she has the following objects. She says that she does. Play both roles.

▶ PHILIPPE: **Est-ce que tu as une guitare?**
CHRISTINE: **Oui, j'ai une guitare.**

▶

8 Est-ce qu'il marche bien?

Tell your classmates that you own the following objects. They will ask you if the objects are working. Answer according to the illustrations.

▶ —J'ai un vélo.
—Est-ce qu'il marche bien?
—Non, il ne marche pas.

▶ —J'ai une télé.
—Est-ce qu'elle marche bien?
—Oui, elle marche très bien.

■ **Expansion:** Ask students if the objects they mentioned in number 1 of Act. 5 work well.
– **J'ai une chaîne-stéréo.**
– **Est-ce qu'elle marche bien?**
– **Non, elle ne marche pas bien.**

COMMUNICATION:
indicating preferences

6

■ **Photo culture note**
Scooters are an increasingly popular mode of transportation among French young people. To drive a scooter you must be 14 years old, carry a license (**un permis**), and wear a helmet (**un casque**).

ROLE PLAY: discussing
what one has

7

1. un téléphone
2. une télé
3. un vélo (une bicyclette)
4. un ordinateur
5. un appareil-photo
6. une chaîne stéréo

EXCHANGES: talking about
whether things work

8

1. un appareil-photo; non
2. une voiture (une auto); oui
3. une chaîne stéréo; oui
4. un vélo (une bicyclette); non
5. un magnétophone; oui
6. une montre; non

Language note

The word **mobylette** was originally a brand name. The word has become the generic term for *motorbike* in French, replacing **vélomoteur.** Other common examples of brand names that have become generic terms are:

un frigidaire or **un frigo** (replacing **un réfrigérateur**)
un walkman (replacing **un baladeur**)
un bic (replacing **un stylo à bille**)

Cooperative pair practice
Activities 7, 8

T143

COMMUNICATIVE FUNCTION:
Describing one's room

17.3 Dialogue: Tu as un walkman?
(32:03–33:01 min.)

Leçon 17, Section 4

■ **Looking ahead:** Plural nouns are presented in Lesson 18.

Transparency 22
Dans ma chambre

■ **Language note: Une chambre** is a *bedroom*. The general word for *room* is **une pièce.**

Supplementary vocabulary

un meuble *piece of furniture*
un fauteuil *armchair*
un placard *closet*
un tapis *rug, carpet*
une bibliothèque *bookcase*
une étagère *shelf*
une commode *dresser*

D. Ma chambre *(My room)*

How to talk about what there is in a place:

il y a	there is there are	Dans *(In)* ma chambre, **il y a** une télé. Dans le garage, **il y a** deux voitures.
est-ce qu'il y a . . . ?	is/are there . . . ?	**Est-ce qu'il y a** un ordinateur dans la classe?
qu'est-ce qu'il y a . . . ?	what is there . . . ?	**Qu'est-ce qu'il y a** dans le garage?

Dans ma chambre il y a une télé.

How to say where something or someone is:

144 Unité 5

TPR Location

PROPS: Objects from the lesson

Demonstrate prepositions of place:
 Je mets le CD dans le sac.
 Je mets la raquette sur la chaise.
 Je mets la guitare sous la table.
 Je mets le stylo derrière le livre. ...

Have students move the objects around.
 X, viens ici. Mets la cassette dans le sac.
 Y, viens et mets le crayon devant le sac.
 Z, prends le livre et mets-le derrière le sac.

9 **Qu'est-ce qu'il y a?**

Describe the various objects that are in the pictures.

1. Sur la table, il y a . . .   2. Sous le lit, il y a . . .   3. Dans le garage, il y a . . .

10 **Ma chambre**

Describe the various objects (pieces of furniture and personal belongings) that are in your room.

▶ Il y a une radio, . . .
  Il y a aussi . . .

11 **Où est le téléphone?**

Michèle is looking for the telephone. Jean-Claude tells her where it is.

▶ MICHÈLE: **Où est le téléphone?**
  JEAN-CLAUDE: **Il est sur la table.**

12 **C'est étrange!** *(It's strange!)*

Funny things sometimes happen. Describe these curious happenings by selecting an item from Column A and putting it in one of the places listed in Column B.

▶ Il y a un éléphant sous le lit!

▶ Il y a . . .

A	B
un rhinocéros	dans la classe
un éléphant	sur le bureau
une girafe	sous la table
un crabe	sous le lit
une souris *(mouse)*	derrière la porte
un ami de King Kong	sur la tour Eiffel
un extra-terrestre	dans le jardin *(garden)*
	devant le restaurant

Leçon 17 **145**

---

9 DESCRIPTION: saying where things are

1. une radio, un stylo et un livre
2. une raquette, un disque et un téléphone
3. un scooter, une voiture (une auto) et un vélo (une bicyclette)

 10 COMMUNICATION: describing one's room

11 ROLE PLAY: saying where something is

1. sur le bureau
2. sur la chaise
3. sous le lit
4. devant la fenêtre
5. derrière la porte

 12 COMMUNICATION: describing improbable locations

■ **Expansion:** Have students invent other improbable statements using known vocabulary.

🖥 **17.4 Mini-scenes: Où est-il?** (33:02–34:19 min.)

▭▭ **Leçon 17, Section 5**

OPTIONAL: give more complex commands.
  X, mets le crayon dans le sac.
  Et puis mets le sac sous la chaise de Y.

Cooperative pair practice
Activity 11

17.5 Vignette culturelle:
La chambre de
Catherine
(34:20–35:41 min.)

 Leçon 17, Section 6

ROLE PLAY: asking where
13 things are

1. sur la table
2. derrière la chaise
3. dans le sac
4. devant la fenêtre
5. sur le bureau
6. devant la télé (sur la table)
7. sur le bureau
8. sur la table
9. sur la chaise

 COMPREHENSION:
14 describing where someone is

1. dans
2. sous
3. derrière
4. devant

■ **Cultural note**
La contractuelle is an auxiliary
police officer who is authorized to
write tickets (**une contravention**)
for illegally parked vehicles.
The traffic sign in the cartoon sig-
nals a no parking zone (**stationne-
ment interdit**).

 **Cooperative
pair practice**
Activity 13

T146

---

13 **La chambre de Nicole**
Florence wants to borrow a few things
from Nicole's room. Nicole tells her
where each object is.

▶ la raquette

1. la télé   6. le sac
2. la guitare   7. la radio
3. le livre   8. le compact
4. le vélo   9. la cassette
5. l'ordinateur

Où est la raquette?

Elle est
sous le lit.

14 **Pauvre Monsieur Vénard** (*Poor Mr. Vénard*)
Today Monsieur Vénard left on vacation, but he soon ran out of luck. Describe the four
cartoons by completing the sentences below.

Le voyage de Monsieur Vénard

1. M. Vénard est
___ la voiture.

2. M. Vénard est
___ la voiture.

3. M. Vénard est
___ la voiture.

4. La contractuelle°
est ___ la voiture.

la contractuelle *meter maid*

146 **Unité 5**

À votre tour!

1 Créa-dialogue

Daniel is showing Nathalie his recent photographs, and she is asking questions about the various people. Create similar dialogues and act them out in class.

un copain

Éric/14

▶
—Qui est-ce?
—C'est <u>un copain</u>.
—Comment s'appelle-t-<u>il</u>?
—<u>Il</u> s'appelle <u>Eric</u>.
—Quel âge a-t-<u>il</u>?
—<u>Il</u> a <u>quatorze</u> ans.

1. une cousine	2. un camarade	3. une camarade	4. un voisin	5. une voisine	6. un professeur
Valérie/20	Philippe Boucher/13	Nathalie Masson/15	Monsieur Dumas/70	Madame Smith/51	Monsieur Laval/35

2 Conversation dirigée

Olivier is visiting his new friend Valérie. Act out the dialogue according to the instructions.

Olivier

asks Valérie if she has a boom box	⇄	answers affirmatively
asks her if it works well	⇄	says that it works very well and asks why
says he would like to listen to his new **(sa nouvelle)** cassette	→	says that the boom box is on the table in the living room **(le salon)**

Valérie

3 Mes possessions

Imagine that your family is going to move to another city. Prepare for the move by making a list of the objects you own. Use a separate sheet of paper.

4 Composition: Un objet

Write a short paragraph describing a real or an imaginary object. You may want to include a picture. (Use only vocabulary that you know.) You may begin your sentences with the following phrases:

▶
Voici mon/ma ...
Il/Elle est ...
Il/Elle marche (ne marche pas) ...

1 GUIDED ORAL EXPRESSION

Leçon 17, Section 7

2 GUIDED ORAL EXPRESSION

O: Est-ce que tu as une radio-cassette?
V: Oui.
O: Est-ce qu'elle marche bien?
V: Oui, elle marche très bien. Pourquoi?
O: Je voudrais écouter ma nouvelle cassette.
V: La radiocassette est sur la table dans le salon.

Leçon 17, Section 8

3 WRITTEN SELF-EXPRESSION

4 WRITTEN SELF-EXPRESSION

À votre tour

Select those activities which are most appropriate for your students.

Cooperative practice

In Act. 1 and 2, you may want to have students work cooperatively in trios, with two performing and one consulting the Answer Key and acting as monitor.

Portfolio assessment

You will probably select only one speaking activity and one writing activity to go into the students' portfolios for Unit 5.

In this lesson, Act. 4 is an appropriate writing portfolio topic.

Leçon 18, Section 1

■ **Language note:** In French, **pas de** is often followed by a singular noun.
Il n'a pas de frère. =
He doesn't have a brother.
(He has no brothers.)

COMPREHENSION

■ **Teaching strategy:** Have students give short answers since they do not know the plural forms of **avoir.**
1. Caroline et Jean-Pierre
2. Jean-Pierre
3. Jean-Pierre
4. Caroline et Jean-Pierre
5. Caroline
6. Jean-Pierre
7. Caroline et Jean-Pierre

T148

Vive la différence!

We are not necessarily like our friends. Caroline, a French girl from Montpellier, describes herself. She also talks about her friend Jean-Pierre.

Caroline

Jean-Pierre

Je m'appelle Caroline.
J'habite à Montpellier.
J'ai des frères.

J'ai un chien.

J'ai un scooter.

J'aime le cinéma.
J'aime les films de science-fiction.
J'aime les sports.
J'étudie l'anglais.

Il s'appelle Jean-Pierre.
Il habite à Strasbourg.
Il n'a pas de frère,
   mais il a des soeurs.

Il n'a pas de chien,
   mais il a deux horribles chats.

Il a une moto.

Il préfère le théâtre.
Il préfère les westerns.
Il préfère la musique.
Il étudie l'espagnol.

Jean-Pierre et moi, nous sommes très différents . . . mais nous sommes copains.

C'est l'essentiel, non?

● **Compréhension**

Answer the questions below with the appropriate names: **Caroline, Jean-Pierre,** or **Caroline et Jean-Pierre.**

1. Qui habite en France?
2. Qui a des soeurs?
3. Qui n'a pas de frère?
4. Qui a un animal domestique?
5. Qui aime jouer au volley?
6. Qui préfère écouter un concert?
7. Qui étudie une langue *(language)*?

Setting the scene

The theme of thi ays have identical tastes and backgrounds. **Et toi?** encourages students to talk about their own similarities and differences.

Using the video

Video Module 18 prepares students to talk about various things they own. They will meet a wide variety of French people who will describe their possessions. The *Vignette culturelle* is about the moped.

Et toi?

Describe yourself and your best friend by completing the sentences below with a phrase of your choice.

1. J'ai . . .
   Mon copain (ma copine) a . . .
   - un frère
   - une soeur
   - des frères
   - des soeurs

2. J'ai . . .
   Mon copain (ma copine) a . . .
   - un chien
   - un chat
   - un perroquet *(parrot)*
   - un poisson rouge *(goldfish)*

3. J'ai . . .
   Mon copain (ma copine) a . . .
   - un vélo
   - une moto
   - un scooter
   - une mobylette

4. J'aime . . .
   Mon copain (ma copine) aime . . .
   - le cinéma
   - le théâtre
   - la musique
   - les sports

5. Je préfère . . .
   Mon copain (ma copine) préfère . . .
   - les westerns
   - les comédies
   - les films d'aventures
   - les films de science-fiction

6. J'étudie . . .
   Mon copain (ma copine) étudie . . .
   - l'espagnol
   - le français
   - l'italien
   - l'allemand *(German)*

7. Mon ami(e) et moi,
   nous sommes . . .
   - assez *(rather)* différent(e)s
   - très différent(e)s
   - assez semblables *(similar)*
   - très semblables

COMMUNICATION: describing oneself and one's friend

■ **Teaching note:** If certain students need to answer items 1, 2, and 3 negatively, quickly introduce the construction **Je n'ai pas de** (frère, chien, vélo...).

NOTE CULTURELLE

Montpellier et Strasbourg

Montpellier and Strasbourg are two very different cities.

- Montpellier is a city of about 200,000 inhabitants located in southern France near the Mediterranean. It is an important university center with a School of Medicine founded in 1221.

- Strasbourg, a city of 250,000 inhabitants, is the capital of the French province of Alsace. Because of its location near Germany and Switzerland, it has always been an international city. Strasbourg is now the seat of important European institutions.

Note culturelle

■ **Photo culture notes**
Strasbourg
Since Strasbourg is the seat of the European Parliament (**le Parlement européen**), it is sometimes called "**la capitale de l'Europe**". The photo shows the medieval section of the city, with its famous cathedral of pink sandstone and its picturesque half-timbered Alsatian buildings.

Montpellier
The photo of Montpellier shows **la Place de la Comédie** with its sidewalk cafés and **la Fontaine des Trois Grâces**, a fountain dating back to the 18th century.

Composition

Have students use the cues in **Et toi?** as a point of departure for writing a composition about themselves and one of their friends.

Suggest that they write their descriptions in two columns, using as a model Caroline's text on p. 148.

🔄 **Review and expansion:**
Students learned the singular forms of **avoir** in Niveau A. Point out that the plural form **ont** is similar to **sont** and **font**.

■ **Teaching note:** Use flash cards for subject pronouns and known objects to practice the forms of **avoir**.
On the chalkledge place 2 cards, e.g., card [**nous**] + card [*tennis racket*]
Response: **Nous avons une raquette.**

1 PRACTICE: saying what type of car people have

1. une Chevrolet
2. une Mercedes /mɛrsedɛs/
3. une Volvo
4. une Renault
5. une Jaguar
6. une Alfa Roméo

■ **Language note:** Makes of cars are always feminine.

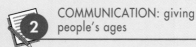

2 COMMUNICATION: giving people's ages

■ **Expansion:** Have students guess the ages of well-known sports and TV figures.

■ **Language note:** The French always use **ans** after the number when giving someone's age.

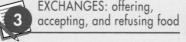

3 EXCHANGES: offering, accepting, and refusing food

🔄 **Re-entry and review:** Foods and **avoir faim/soif** from Lessons 9 and 10.

■ **Language note:** French people say **merci** both to accept and refuse something.

T150

A. Le verbe *avoir*

The verb **avoir** *(to have, to own)* is irregular. Note the forms of this verb in the present tense.

avoir	to have	
j' **ai**	*I have*	J'**ai** une copine à Québec.
tu **as**	*you have*	Est-ce que tu **as** un frère?
il/elle **a**	*he/she has*	Philippe **a** une cousine à Paris.
nous **avons**	*we have*	Nous **avons** un ordinateur.
vous **avez**	*you have*	Est-ce que vous **avez** une moto?
ils/elles **ont**	*they have*	Ils n'**ont** pas ton appareil-photo.

➡ There is liaison in the forms: **nous avons, vous avez, ils ont, elles ont.**

Vocabulaire: Expressions avec *avoir*

avoir faim	*to be hungry*	J'**ai faim.** Et toi, est-ce que tu **as faim?**
avoir soif	*to be thirsty*	Paul **a soif.** Sylvie n'**a** pas **soif.**
avoir . . . ans	*to be . . . (years old)*	J'**ai** 14 **ans.** Le prof **a** 35 **ans.**

---

1 **Les voitures**

The people below own cars made in the countries where they live. Match each car with its owner.

▶ Monsieur Sato habite à Tokyo.

Il a une Toyota.

1. Tu habites à Boston.
2. Vous habitez à Munich.
3. Madame Ericson habite à Stockholm.
4. J'habite à Paris.
5. Nous habitons à Oxford.
6. Mes cousines habitent à Rome.

une Alfa Roméo
une Jaguar
une Renault
une Chevrolet
une Volvo
une Mercedes
une Toyota

2 **Expression personnelle**

How old are the following people? Complete the sentences below. If you don't know the exact age, make a guess.

1. J'ai . . .
2. *(The student on your right)* Tu as . . .
3. *(The teacher)* Vous . . .
4. Mon copain . . .
5. Ma copine . . .
6. La voisine . . .

3 **Faim ou soif?**

You are at a party with your classmates. Offer them the following foods and beverages. They will accept or refuse by saying whether they are hungry or thirsty.

1. une crêpe
2. un soda
3. un hamburger
4. un jus d'orange
5. un croissant
6. un jus de raisin
7. une pizza
8. un Perrier

▶ un sandwich
▶ une limonade

Tu veux un sandwich?

Oui, merci! J'ai faim.

(Non, mer... Je n'ai pa... faim.)

Tu veux une limonade?

Oui, merci! J'ai soif.

(Non, merci! Je n'ai pas soif.)

Teaching note: Introducing the past tense

Once students learn the present tense forms of **avoir,** you may want to introduce the PASSÉ COMPOSÉ for conversation practice. (The tense is presented formally in Unit 8.)

Beginning with this lesson, you will find optional oral questions about past events.

To talk about what happened yesterday (**hier**), the French use the PASSÉ COMPOSÉ:

> present of **avoir** + past participle

For **-er** verbs, the past participle ends in **-é.** (You may want to use the chart on p. 309.)

B. Les noms et les articles: masculin et féminin

NOUNS

• Nouns designating PEOPLE
Nouns that designate male persons
are almost always *masculine:*
   un garçon   un ami
Nouns that designate female persons
are almost always *feminine:*
   une fille   une amie

> **Learning about language**
> NOUNS are words that designate people,
> animals, objects, and things.
>
> In French, all nouns have GENDER: they are
> either MASCULINE or FEMININE.

➡ EXCEPTIONS:
   une personne is always feminine (even when it refers to a male)
   un professeur is always masculine (even when it refers to a woman)

• Nouns designating ANIMALS, OBJECTS, and THINGS
   There is no systematic way to determine whether these nouns are
   masculine or feminine. Therefore, it is very important to learn these
   nouns with their articles.

   MASCULINE: **un** disque   **un** vélo   **un** ordinateur
   FEMININE: **une** cassette   **une** moto   **une** affiche

ARTICLES

Note the forms of the articles in the chart below.

	MASCULINE	FEMININE		
INDEFINITE ARTICLE	**un** *a, an*	**une** *a, an*	**un** garçon	**une** fille
DEFINITE ARTICLE	**le** *the*	**la** *the*	**le** garçon	**la** fille

> **Learning about language**
> Nouns are often introduced by
> ARTICLES. In French, ARTICLES have
> the *same* gender as the nouns
> they introduce.

➡ Both **le** and **la** become **l'** before a vowel sound:
   le garçon   l'ami
   la fille   l'amie

> **Learning about language**
> Nouns may be replaced by PRONOUNS.
> In French, PRONOUNS have the *same*
> gender as the nouns they replace.

PRONOUNS

Note the forms of the pronouns in the chart below.

MASCULINE	**il**	*he* *it*	Où est **le** garçon? / Où est **le** disque?	**Il** est en classe. / **Il** est sur la table.
FEMININE	**elle**	*she* *it*	Où est **la** fille? / Où est **la** voiture?	**Elle** est en ville. / **Elle** est là-bas.

Leçon 18   151

Talking about past events
Let's talk about what you did yesterday.
▶ **Est-ce que tu as étudié hier?**
   Oui, j'ai étudié hier.
   (Non, je n'ai pas étudié hier.)
• **Est-ce que tu as étudié hier?**
• **Est-ce que tu as travaillé hier?**
• **Est-ce que tu as regardé la télé hier?**

• **Est-ce que tu as écouté la radio?**
• **Est-ce que tu as parlé français?**
• **Est-ce que tu as joué au tennis?**
• **Est-ce que tu as dîné au restaurant?**
• **Est-ce que tu as mangé un steak?**
   (Reminder: use pas de in the negative.)
• **Est-ce que tu as mangé une omelette?**

T151

■ **Expansion:** Have students suggest other names for each of the categories in Act. 4: e.g., **Leslie Stahl est une journaliste.**

1. Il est sur la table.
2. Il est sur la table.
3. Elle est sur la table.
4. Elle est sous la table.
5. Elle est sous la table.
6. Il est sous la table.
7. Elle est sous la table.
8. Elle est sous la table.

■ **Expansion:** Use classroom objects.
– **Où est le livre?**
– **Il est sur le bureau.**

Section C

COMMUNICATIVE FUNCTION: Identifying people and things

■ **Language note:** Note the following plurals:
des appareils-photo
des chaînes stéréo
There is no "s" on **photo** or **stéréo** since these are shortened forms of **photographique(s)** and **stéréophonique(s).**

■ **Vocabulary note: gens** is masculine.

■ **Realia note**
The **Galeries Lafayette** is a well-known Parisian department store.

---

4 Les célébrités

You and Jean-Pierre have been invited to a gala dinner attended by many American celebrities. Jean-Pierre asks you who each person is. Answer him using **un** or **une,** as appropriate.

Tiens, voilà Connie Chung!

Une journaliste.

Qui est-ce?

▶ Connie Chung / journaliste

1. Peter Jennings / journaliste
2. Michelle Pfeiffer / actrice
3. Tom Cruise / acteur
4. Lily Tomlin / comédienne
5. Cher / chanteuse *(singer)*
6. Michael Jordan / athlète
7. Eddie Murphy / comédien
8. Michael Jackson / chanteur

5 **Sur la table ou sous la table?**

Caroline is looking for the following objects. Cécile tells her where each one is: on or under the table.

▶ walkman
CAROLINE: **Où est le walkman?**
CÉCILE: **Le walkman? Il est sur la table.**

1. ordinateur 3. affiche 5. raquette 7. radiocassette
2. sac 4. calculatrice 6. disque 8. télé

C. Les noms et les articles: le pluriel

Compare the singular and plural forms of the articles and nouns in the sentences below.

SINGULAR	PLURAL
Tu as **le disque?**	Tu as **les disques?**
Qui est **la fille** là-bas?	Qui sont **les filles** là-bas?
Voici **un livre.**	Voici **des livres.**
J'invite **une copine.**	J'invite **des copines.**

PLURAL NOUNS

In written French, the plural of most nouns is formed as follows:

SINGULAR NOUN + **s** = PLURAL NOUN

➡ If the noun ends in **-s** in the singular, the singular and plural forms are the same.
Voici **un Français.** Voici **des Français.**
➡ In spoken French, the final **-s** of the plural is always silent.
➡ NOTE: **des gens** *(people)* is always plural. Compare:

| **une personne** | *person* | Qui est **la personne** là-bas? |
| **des gens** | *people* | Qui sont **les gens** là-bas? |

Cooperative pair practice
Activities 4, 5, 7

TPR **Singular and plural forms**

PROPS: Classroom objects

Point out either one or two common objects.
Voici un crayon.
Voici des crayons.
Voilà une fenêtre.
Voilà des fenêtres.
Où sont les livres? Où est le livre?

Then have individual students point out one or several objects.
X, montre-nous un stylo.
Maintenant, montre-nous des stylos.
Y, montre-nous le livre de français.
Où sont les livres de français?
Z, montre-nous des élèves.
Maintenant, montre-nous une élève.

SINGULAR AND PLURAL ARTICLES

The forms of the articles are summarized in the chart below.

	SINGULAR	PLURAL		
DEFINITE ARTICLE	**le (l′)** *the* **la (l′)**	**les** *the*	**les** garçons **les** filles	**les** ordinateurs **les** affiches
INDEFINITE ARTICLE	**un** *a, an* **une**	**des** *some*	**des** garçons **des** filles	**des** ordinateurs **des** affiches

➡ There is liaison after **les** and **des** when the next word begins with a vowel sound.

➡ **Des** corresponds to the English article *some*. While *some* is often omitted in English, **des** MUST be expressed in French. Contrast:

Il y a *There are*	**des** *some*	**livres sur la table.** *books on the table.*

Je dîne avec *I'm having dinner with*	**des** *. . .*	**amis.** *friends.*

6 Pluriel, s'il vous plaît

Give the plurals of the following nouns.

▶ un copine <br> des copines

▶ l'ami <br> les amis

1. un copain
2. une amie
3. un homme
4. une femme
5. un vélo
6. une affiche
7. le voisin
8. l'élève
9. la cousine
10. le livre
11. l'ordinateur
12. la voiture

8 Qu'est-ce qu'il y a?

Explain what there is in the following places. Complete the sentences with **il y a** and a noun from the box. Be sure to use the appropriate articles: **un, une, des.** Be logical. Often several choices are possible.

▶ Dans le garage, . . .

> Dans le garage, il y a une moto (des voitures . . .).

1. Sur le bureau, . . .
2. À la boum, . . .
3. Dans la classe, . . .
4. Au café, sur la table, . . .
5. Dans ma chambre, . . .
6. Dans le laboratoire de maths, . . .

limonade	stylo	livres	affiches	moto
professeur	lit	croissants	voitures	filles
ordinateur	garçons	élèves	table	

7 Shopping

You are in a department store in Montpellier looking for the following items. Ask the salesperson if he or she has these items. The salesperson will answer affirmatively.

▶ —Pardon, monsieur (madame). Est-ce que vous avez des sacs?
 —Bien sûr, nous avons des sacs.

Leçon 18 153

6 PRACTICE: plural articles and nouns

7 ROLE PLAY: asking for items in a store

1. des télés
2. des radios
3. des ordinateurs
4. des cassettes
5. des raquettes
6. des magnétophones
7. des montres
8. des affiches
9. des calculatrices

■ Be sure students make the required liaisons in items 3 and 8.

■ **Listening activity:** Read the following sentences aloud and have students mark whether the nouns are singular or plural.
 Voici le professeur. [singular]
 Voici les élèves. [plural], etc.

8 COMPREHENSION: saying where things are

Listening activity

Quickly read off sentences containing singular or plural articles. Have students raise one finger if they hear a singular article. Have them extend all fingers if they hear a plural article.

1. **Voici des copines.** [P]
2. **Voici le vélo.** [S]
3. **Voici une affiche.** [S]
4. **Voici les professeurs.** [P]
5. **Voici des ordinateurs.** [P]
6. **Voici un camarade.** [S]
7. **Voici les amis.** [P]
8. **Voici l'appareil-photo.** [S]

18.1 **Mini-scenes:** Tu as un vélo?

18.2 **Mini-scenes:** Qu'est-ce que tu as?

18.3 **Mini-scenes:** Est-ce que tu as un vélo? (36:23–39:11 min.)

 Leçon 18, Sections 2, 3

---

9 EXCHANGES: discussing possessions

■ **Expansion:** Ask a third person to report the answer.
X a un ordinateur.
(**X n'a pas d'ordinateur.**)

■ **Variation** (with people):
1. un copain à Paris
2. une copine à Québec
3. un oncle très riche
4. des cousins à Strasbourg
5. des cousines à Montpellier

---

10 PRACTICE: saying what people don't have

■ **Language note:** Remind students that in French, the noun after **pas de** may be in the singular.
Je n'ai pas de copain à Lyon.
or: **Je n'ai pas de copains à Lyon.**

D. L'article indéfini dans les phrases négatives

Compare the forms of the indefinite article in affirmative and negative sentences.

AFFIRMATIVE	NEGATIVE	
Tu as **un** vélo?	Non, je n'ai **pas de** vélo.	*No, I don't have a bike.*
Est-ce que Paul a **une** radio?	Non, il n'a **pas de** radio.	*No, he doesn't have a radio.*
Vous invitez **des** copains demain?	Non, nous n'invitons **pas de** copains.	*No, we are not inviting any friends.*

After a NEGATIVE verb:

> **pas + un, une, des   becomes   pas de**

➡ Note that **pas de** becomes **pas d'** before a vowel sound.
  Alice a un ordinateur.   Paul n'a **pas d'**ordinateur.
  J'ai des amis à Québec.   Je n'ai **pas d'**amis à Montréal.

➡ The negative form of **il y a** is **il n'y a pas:**
  Dans ma chambre,
    il y a une radio.   **Il n'y a pas de** télé.   *There is no TV.*
    il y a des affiches.   **Il n'y a pas de** photos.   *There are no photographs.*

➡ After **être,** the articles **un, une,** and **des** do NOT change.
  Philippe est un voisin.   Éric n'est **pas un** voisin.
  Ce sont des vélos.   Ce ne sont **pas des** mobylettes.

---

9 **Possessions**

Ask your classmates if they own the following.

▶ un ordinateur

Est-ce que tu as un ordinateur?   **Oui, j'ai un ordinateur.**

(Non, je n'ai pas d'ordinateur.)

1. un appareil-photo
2. une moto
3. une mobylette
4. une clarinette
5. des disques de jazz
6. des affiches
7. un boa
8. un alligator
9. des hamsters

---

10 **Oui et non**

One cannot have everything. Say that the following people do not have what is indicated in parentheses.

▶ Paul a un vélo. (un scooter)
  Il n'a pas de scooter.

1. Julien a un scooter. (une voiture).
2. J'ai une radio. (une télé)
3. Vous avez des cassettes. (des compacts)
4. Vous avez des frères. (une soeur)
5. Nous avons un chien. (des chats)
6. Tu as des copains à Bordeaux. (des copains à Lyon)
7. Marc a un oncle à Québec. (un oncle à Montréal)
8. Nathalie a des cousins à San Francisco. (des cousins à Los Angeíes)

Teaching strategy: Il y a with objects

PROP: Transparency 21

Using a transparency marker, draw an "X" through eight of the objects shown. Describe what is and is not in the picture. Point to the bicycle, saying: **Il y a un vélo.** Cross out the scooter: **Il n'y a pas de scooter.**

Continue, having students repeat after you.
When eight items have been crossed out, ask questions about the transparency.
Est-ce qu'il y a une voiture?
  [Oui, il y a une voiture.]
Est-ce qu'il y a un ordinateur?
  [Non, il n'y a pas d'ordinateur.]

11 **Le grenier** *(The attic)*

Your friend is cleaning the attic. Ask if the following items are up there. Your friend (a classmate) will answer according to the illustration.

▶ une raquette?

—Est-ce qu'il y a une raquette?

—Non, il n'y a pas de raquette.

1. des vélos?
2. une guitare?
3. des livres?
4. un magnétophone?
5. des disques?

6. des cassettes?
7. une télé?
8. une radiocassette?
9. un bureau?
10. une table?

Expression pour la conversation

How to contradict a negative statement or question:

Si! *Yes!* —Tu n'as pas de chaîne stéréo?

—**Si!** J'ai une chaîne stéréo.

> Tu n'as pas de chaîne stéréo?

> Si! J'ai une chaîne stéréo.

12 **Contradictions!**

Contradict all of the following negative statements.

▶ Tu ne parles pas anglais!   **Si, je parle anglais!**

1. Tu ne parles pas français!
2. Tu n'étudies pas!
3. Tu ne joues pas au basket!
4. Tu n'aimes pas les sports!
5. Tu n'aimes pas la musique!
6. Tu n'écoutes pas le professeur!

Leçon 18 **155**

---

11 EXCHANGES: locating objects

1. oui	6. non
2. non	7. oui
3. oui	8. oui
4. non	9. oui
5. non	10. oui

Transparency 24
Le grenier

12 PRACTICE: contradicting negative statements

↩ **Re-entry and review:** Verbs from Unit 4.

■ **Teaching strategy:** Have students contrast the negative question and response in the example with the following affirmative question and response:
– Tu as une chaîne stéréo?
– <u>Oui</u>, j'ai une chaîne stéréo.

💻 18.4 Dialogue: J'organise une boum
18.5 Vignette culturelle: La mobylette
(39:12–41:03 min.)

Cooperative pair practice
Activities 9, 11

■ **Language note:** Usually, English does not use articles to introduce abstract nouns or nouns used in a general sense.

■ **Realia note**
Have students read the sign: **J'aime le français.** (They may want to make similar signs of their own.)

COMMUNICATION:
expressing likes and dislikes

■ **Teaching hint:** Model the new words and cognates, being sure that students pronounce them the French way.

COMPREHENSION:
describing what people like

■ **Teaching hint:** Have students memorize the **comptine** that accompanies the daisy petals. (It begins: **Elle m'aime un peu...** and continues clockwise.) Point out that the odds of being "loved" are much greater in the French than in the English version (*he/she loves me, he/she loves me not...*).

E. L'usage de l'article défini dans le sens général

In French, the definite article (**le, la, les**) is used more often than in English. Note its use in the following sentences.

J'aime **la musique.**	*(In general) I like* **music.**
Tu préfères **le tennis** ou **le golf?**	*(Generally) do you prefer* **tennis or golf?**
Pauline aime **les westerns.**	*(In general) Pauline likes* **westerns.**
Nous aimons **la liberté.**	*(In general) we love* **liberty.**

The definite article (**le, la, les**) is used to introduce ABSTRACT nouns, or nouns used in a GENERAL or COLLECTIVE sense.

13 Expression personnelle

Say how you feel about the following things, using one of the suggested expressions.

Je n'aime pas . . .
J'aime un peu . . .
J'aime beaucoup . . .

▶ **Je n'aime pas la violence.**

la musique	le français	la violence	le théâtre
la nature	les maths	l'injustice	le cinéma
les sports	les sciences	la liberté	la danse
le camping			la photo
			(photography)

14 C'est évident! *(It's obvious!)*

Read about the following people and say what they like. Choose the appropriate item from the list. (Masculine nouns are in blue. Feminine nouns are in red.)

▶ Cécile écoute des cassettes.
  Cécile aime la musique.

art   cinéma   danse   français   musique   nature   tennis

1. Jean-Claude a une raquette.
2. Vous faites une promenade dans la forêt.
3. Les touristes visitent un musée *(museum)*.
4. Tu regardes un film.
5. Nous étudions en classe de français.
6. Véronique et Roger sont dans une discothèque.

F. L'usage de l'article défini avec les jours de la semaine

Compare the following sentences.

REPEATED EVENTS	SINGLE EVENT
Le samedi, je dîne avec des copains.	**Samedi,** je dîne avec mon cousin.
(On) Saturdays (in general), I have dinner with friends.	*(On) Saturday (that is, this Saturday), I am having dinner with my cousin.*

To indicate a repeated or habitual event, French uses the construction:

> **le** + DAY OF THE WEEK

➡ When an event happens only once, no article is used.

15 Questions personnelles

1. Est-ce que tu étudies le samedi?
2. Est-ce que tu dînes au restaurant le dimanche? Si *(If)* oui, avec qui?
3. Est-ce que tu as une classe de français le lundi? le mercredi?
4. Est-ce que tu regardes les matchs de football américain le samedi? le dimanche?
5. Quel programme de télé est-ce que tu regardes le vendredi? le jeudi?
6. Est-ce que tu travailles? Où? *(Name of place or store)* Quand?

16 L'emploi du temps

	LUNDI	MARDI	MERCREDI	JEUDI	VENDREDI
9 h	français	physique	sciences	biologie	
10 h		histoire		maths	anglais
11 h	maths	sciences	anglais		français

The following students all have the same morning schedule. Complete the sentences accordingly.

▶ **Nous avons une classe de français le lundi . . .**

1. J'ai une classe de maths _____ .
2. Tu as une classe de sciences _____ .
3. Jacques a une classe de physique _____ .
4. Thérèse a une classe d'histoire _____ .
5. Vous avez une classe de biologie _____ .
6. Les élèves ont une classe d'anglais _____ .

Prononciation   le /lə/   les /le/

Les articles *le* et *les*

Be sure to distinguish between the pronunciation of **le** and **les.** In spoken French, that is often the only way to tell the difference between a singular and a plural noun.

le sac   les sacs

Répétez:	/lə/	**le**	**le sac**	**le vélo**	**le disque**	**le copain**	**le voisin**
	/le/	**les**	**les sacs**	**les vélos**	**les disques**	**les copains**	**les voisins**

Leçon 18 **157**

Talking about past events

Let's talk about what you did last Saturday.

▶ **Est-ce que tu as étudié samedi dernier?**
  Oui, j'ai étudié samedi dernier.
  (Non, je n'ai pas étudié samedi dernier.)
• **Est-ce que tu as travaillé?**
• **Est-ce que tu as regardé la télé?**

• **Est-ce que tu as joué au basket?**
• **Est-ce que tu as organisé une boum?**
• **Est-ce que tu as dansé?**
• **Est-ce que tu as dîné au restaurant?**
• **Est-ce que tu as mangé un hot dog?**
  (Reminder: use **pas de** in the negative.)
• **Est-ce que tu as mangé une pizza?**

Section F

COMMUNICATIVE FUNCTION: Discussing repeated events

↻ **Re-entry and review:** Days of the week from Lesson 8.

■ **Language note:** In French, the word **sur** (*on*) is never used with days of the week.

COMMUNICATION: answering personal questions **15**

■ **Language note:** Point out that in French, **si** has two meanings:
• *if* (as in **s'il vous plaît**: literally, *if it pleases you*)
• *yes* (to contradict a negative statement)

 COMPREHENSION: describing school schedules **16**

Transparency 25 Class schedule

■ **Additional practice:** Show Transparency 25 or have students turn to the **emploi du temps** on p. 79. Let them imagine that they have the same schedule and ask them questions:
Quel jour avez-vous une classe de français?
Nous avons une classe de français le lundi, le mardi, etc.

Prononciation

🔊 Leçon 18, Section 6

1 **Allô!**

Jean-Marc is phoning some friends. Match his questions on the left with his friends' answers on the right.

1. Quel âge a ton copain?
2. Est-ce qu'Éric a un scooter?
3. Où est l'appareil-photo?
4. Tu as des cassettes?
5. Est-ce que tu aimes étudier l'anglais?
6. Tu as soif?

a. Oui, mais je n'ai pas de magnétophone.
b. Il est sur la table.
c. Quatorze ans.
d. Oui, je voudrais une limonade.
e. Oui, mais je préfère l'espagnol.
f. Non, mais il a une moto.

2 **Un sondage**

A French consumer research group wants to know what things American teenagers own. Conduct a survey in your class asking who has the objects on the list. Count the number of students who raise their hands for each object, and report your findings on a separate piece of paper.

Qui a des cassettes?... Quinze élèves ont des cassettes.

UN SONDAGE

15

3 Créa-dialogue

Ask your classmates if they like the following things. Then ask if they own the corresponding object.

 Leçon 18, Section 8

| le tennis | 1. la musique | 2. le jogging | 3. les maths | 4. la photo | 5. les matchs de baseball | 6. l'exercice |

▶ —Tu aimes le tennis?
—Oui, j'aime le tennis.
(Non, je n'aime pas le tennis.)

—Tu as une raquette?
—Oui, j'ai une raquette.
(Non, je n'ai pas de raquette.)

4 Quelle est la différence?

Sophie went away with her family for the weekend and she took some of her belongings with her. Describe what is in her room on Friday and what is missing on Saturday.

VENDREDI

SAMEDI

▶ Il y a . . .   ▶ Il n'y a pas de . . .

 4 COMPREHENSION

Vendredi: Il y a...

un bureau	un lit
une chaise	un sac
un appareil-	un chat
photo	une radio
des crayons	une télé
des stylos	des disques
une chaîne	des cassettes
stéréo	une guitare
des compacts	une raquette
des livres	une affiche
un téléphone	

Samedi: Il n'y a pas...

d'appareil-	de compacts
photo	de radio
de sac	de cassettes
de chat	de raquette

5 Inventaire *(Inventory)*

Write a short paragraph naming two things that may be found in each of the following places. Also indicate one thing that is usually not found in that place.

▶ Dans le salon, il y a une télé et des chaises. Il n'y a pas de lit.

- dans ma chambre
- dans mon sac
- dans le garage
- dans la rue *(street)*
- sur la table

6 Composition: Ma semaine

In a short paragraph, describe what you do (or do not do) regularly on various days of the week. Select three days and two different activities for each day. Use only vocabulary that you know.

▶

Le lundi, j'ai une classe de français.
Je regarde « La roue de la fortune »
(Wheel of Fortune) à la télé.

Le samedi, je n'étudie pas. Je dîne
au restaurant avec mon copain.

Portfolio assessment

You will probably select only one speaking activity and one writing activity to go into the students' portfolios for Unit 5.

In this lesson, Act. 6 is a good written portfolio topic. You might also wish to use the composition suggested at the bottom of page T149.

MODULE 19:
Le copain de Mireille
Total time: 5:03 min.
(Counter: 41:11 min.)

**19.1 Mini-scenes: Listening
— Je suis américain**
(41:43–42:00 min.)

**19.2 Mini-scenes: Listening
— Qui est-ce?**
(42:01–42:55 min.)

**19.3 Mini-scenes: Speaking
— Comment sont-ils?**
(42:56–43:55 min.)

**19.4 Dialogue: Le copain
de Mireille**
(43:56–44:43 min.)

**19.5 Vignette culturelle:
La France et ses
voisins**
(44:44–46:13 min.)

 **19.4 Dialogue: Le copain
de Mireille**
(43:56–44:43 min.)

 Leçon 19, Section 1

 COMPREHENSION

1. une fille
2. Mireille Labé
3. oui
4. Oui! Elle est amusante,
intelligente et sympathique.
5. oui
6. C'est Jean-Claude.
7. Caroline et Jean-Pierre

LEÇON 19 Le copain de Mireille

Nicolas and Jean-Claude are having lunch at the school cafeteria. Nicolas is looking at the students seated at the other end of their table.

NICOLAS:	Regarde la fille là-bas!	
JEAN-CLAUDE:	La fille blonde?	
NICOLAS:	Oui! Qui est-ce?	
JEAN-CLAUDE:	C'est Mireille Labé.	
NICOLAS:	Elle est <u>mignonne</u>!	*cute*
JEAN-CLAUDE:	Elle est aussi <u>amusante</u>, intelligente et <u>sympathique</u>.	*fun / nice*
NICOLAS:	Est-ce qu'elle a un copain?	
JEAN-CLAUDE:	Oui, elle a un copain.	
NICOLAS:	Il est sympathique?	
JEAN-CLAUDE:	Oui . . . Très sympathique!	
NICOLAS:	Et intelligent?	
JEAN-CLAUDE:	Aussi!	
NICOLAS:	Dommage! . . . Qui est-ce?	
JEAN-CLAUDE:	C'est moi!	
NICOLAS:	Euh . . . oh . . . Excuse-moi et <u>félicitations</u>!	*congratulations*

● **Compréhension**

1. Qui est-ce que Nicolas regarde?
2. Comment s'appelle la fille?
3. Est-ce qu'elle est jolie?
4. Est-ce qu'elle a d'autres *(other)* qualités?
5. Est-ce qu'elle a un copain?
6. Qui est le copain de Mireille *(Mireille's boyfriend)*?

160 Unité 5

 Setting the scene

The opening text introduces several students having lunch at the Lycée Corot. Not untypically, they are engaged in people-watching.

(For more background on this **lycée**, have students turn to pp. 76–81.)

To help students develop listening comprehension skills, have them keep their books closed as they watch the video (Section 4) or listen to the audiocassette version of the video soundtrack.

Then have them open their books and read the text.

■ NOTE ■
CULTURELLE

L'amitié *(Friendship)*

For the French, friendship is very important. On the scale of personal values, it ranks first — before family, freedom, justice, love, and money.

What qualities do French young people expect in their friends? As in the United States, friends must be fun to be with, since French teenagers like to do things as a group with their **bande de copains.** Friends should be helpful and understanding because when French teenagers have a problem, they tend to talk to their friends before talking to their parents. And, of course, friends must be loyal, because the French tend to remain close to their high school friends for the rest of their lives.

Leçon 19 161

Note culturelle

■ **Photo culture note**
Les posters
In the bottom photo, French teenagers are looking at posters (**une affiche, un poster**) which are displayed in plastic cases outside a bookstore. The stand in the back has greeting cards (**une carte de voeux**).

Classroom Notes

 Multi-culturalism in France

The opening segments of Video Module 19 focus on the diversity of the French population. The final *Vignette culturelle* presents the various national origins of the people of contemporary France.

T161

COMMUNICATIVE FUNCTION:
Describing people and
objects

📖 **Transparency 26**
La description

■ **Teaching hint:** Use Transparency 26 and the overlay to present the descriptive adjectives.

A. Les adjectifs: masculin et féminin

Compare the forms of the adjectives in heavy print as they describe masculine and feminine nouns.

<table>
<tr><td>MASCULINE</td><td>FEMININE</td></tr>
<tr><td>Le scooter est petit.</td><td>La voiture est petite.</td></tr>
<tr><td>Patrick est intelligent.</td><td>Caroline est intelligente.</td></tr>
<tr><td>L'ordinateur est moderne.</td><td>La télé est moderne.</td></tr>
</table>

In written French, feminine adjectives are usually formed as follows:

> MASCULINE ADJECTIVE + **-e** = FEMININE ADJECTIVE

➜ If the masculine adjective ends in **-e,** there is no change in the feminine form.
> Jérôme est **timide**.   Juliette est **timide**.

➜ Adjectives that follow the above patterns are called REGULAR adjectives. Those that do not are called IRREGULAR adjectives. For example:
> Marc est **beau**.   Sylvie est **belle**.
> Paul est **canadien**.   Marie est **canadienne**.

NOTE: French dictionaries list adjectives by their masculine forms. For irregular adjectives, the feminine form is indicated in parentheses.

NOTES DE PRONONCIATION:
- If the masculine form of an adjective ends in a silent consonant, that consonant is pronounced in the feminine form.
- If the masculine form of an adjective ends in a vowel or a pronounced consonant, the masculine and feminine forms sound the same.

<table>
<tr><td colspan="2">DIFFERENT PRONUNCIATION</td><td colspan="2">SAME PRONUNCIATION</td></tr>
<tr><td>peti<s>t</s></td><td>petite</td><td>timide</td><td>timide</td></tr>
<tr><td>blon<s>d</s></td><td>blonde</td><td>joli</td><td>jolie</td></tr>
<tr><td>françai<s>s</s></td><td>française</td><td>espagnol</td><td>espagnole</td></tr>
</table>

Learning about language

ADJECTIVES are words that describe people, places, and things.
In French, MASCULINE adjectives are used with masculine nouns, and FEMININE adjectives are used with feminine nouns. This is called NOUN-ADJECTIVE AGREEMENT.

---

1 PRACTICE: adjective forms

■ **Language note:** Point out that nationalities are adjectives.

■ **Expansion** (dialogue format):
▶ **Jean-Claude est brun.
(Nathalie)**
 – Jean-Claude est brun.
 – Et Nathalie? Elle est brune?
 – Mais non, elle n'est pas brune.

1 Vive la différence!

People can be friends and yet be quite different.
Describe the girls named in parentheses,
indicating that they are not like their friends.

> ▶ Jean-Claude est brun. (Nathalie)
> Nathalie n'est pas brune.

1. Jean-Louis est blond. (Carole)
2. Paul est petit. (Mireille)
3. Éric est beau. (Marthe)
4. Jérôme est grand. (Louise)
5. Michel est riche. (Émilie)
6. André est français. (Lisa)
7. Antonio est espagnol. (Céline)
8. Bill est américain. (Julie)

TPR 🏃 **Descriptions**

This is similar to the activity on p. 138.
PROPS: Blue and red index cards

On the board, draw a stick figure of a boy
(labeled René) and a girl (labeled Renée).
 Voici René. C'est un voisin. [blue]
 Et ici Renée. C'est une voisine. [red]
Give each student a blue and a red card.

As you read descriptions using the new
vocabulary, they raise the appropriate card.
 René est amusant. [blue card]
 Renée est mignonne. [red card]
 René(e) est timide. [either: both cards]
 Renée est assez sportive. [red card]
 René est très intelligent. [blue card] …

Vocabulaire: La description

▷ Vocabulaire

🔊 Leçon 19, Section 2

ADJECTIFS		Voici Jean-Claude.	Voici Mireille.
amusant	amusing, fun	Il est **amusant**.	Elle est **amusante**.
intelligent	intelligent	Il est **intelligent**.	Elle est **intelligente**.
intéressant	interesting	Il est **intéressant**.	Elle est **intéressante**.
méchant	mean, nasty	Il n'est pas **méchant**.	Elle n'est pas **méchante**.
bête	silly, dumb	Il n'est pas **bête**.	Elle n'est pas **bête**.
sympathique	nice, pleasant	Il est **sympathique**.	Elle est **sympathique**.
timide	timid	Il est **timide**.	Elle n'est pas **timide**.
gentil (gentille)	nice, kind	Il est **gentil**.	Elle est **gentille**.
mignon (mignonne)	cute	Il est **mignon**.	Elle est **mignonne**.
sportif (sportive)	athletic	Il est **sportif**.	Elle est **sportive**.

ADVERBES		
assez	rather	Nous sommes **assez** intelligents.
très	very	Vous n'êtes pas **très** sportifs!

■ **Pronunciation**
gentil /ʒãti/
gentille /ʒãtij/

■ **Language note:** Adverbs like **assez** and **très** often modify adjectives. Note that liaison is required after **très**. In conversation, there is usually no liaison after **assez**.

Supplementary vocabulary

content ≠ triste *happy ≠ sad*
fort ≠ faible *strong ≠ weak*
riche ≠ pauvre *rich ≠ poor*
fatigué ≠ énergique *tired ≠ energetic*
génial ≠ stupide *brilliant ≠ dumb*
poli ≠ impoli *polite ≠ impolite*
drôle ≠ pénible *funny ≠ "a pain"*

optimiste ≠ pessimiste
sincère
indépendant
athlétique
dynamique

2 Oui ou non?

In your opinion, do the following people have the suggested traits? (Note: These traits are given in the masculine form only.)

Il est intéressant.

Il n'est pas intéressant.

▶ le prince Charles / intéressant. ▶

1. le Président / sympathique?
2. Steffi Graf / sportif?
3. ma copine / gentil?
4. Vanna White / mignon?
5. Oprah Winfrey / intelligent?
6. Einstein / bête?
7. Eddie Murphy / amusant?
8. le prof / méchant?

2 COMMUNICATION:
describing people

■ **Variation** (dialogue format):
– Est-ce que le prince Charles est intéressant?
– Oui, il est intéressant.
  (Non, il n'est pas intéressant.)

3 Descriptions

Select one of the following characters. Using words from the **Vocabulaire,** describe this character in two affirmative or negative sentences.

▶ Frankenstein
  Il est très méchant.
  Il n'est pas très mignon.

1. Tarzan
2. King Kong
3. Big Bird
4. Batman
5. Miss Piggy
6. Wonder Woman
7. Charlie Brown
8. Blanche-Neige *(Snow White)*
9. Garfield
10. Snoopy

4 L'idéal

Now you have the chance to describe your ideal people. Use two adjectives for each one.

1. Le copain idéal est . . . et . . .
2. La copine idéale est . . . et . . .
3. Le professeur idéal est . . . et . . .
4. L'étudiant idéal est . . . et . . .
5. L'étudiante idéale est . . . et . . .

3 COMMUNICATION:
describing people

4 COMMUNICATION:
describing ideal people

■ **Variation** (in the negative):
Le copain idéal n'est pas (méchant)...

■ **Expansion:** le père idéal, la mère idéale, le frère idéal, la soeur idéale

Game: Descriptions

Have students in pairs pick one of the characters in Act. 3 and write a description in two identical copies.

Then ask each pair to give one copy of the description to the pair on their left, and the other to the pair on their right.

Each pair now has two new descriptions to read. They read the two descrip-

tions and at the bottom of each they write down the name of the person they think is being described.

The descriptions are then returned to the "original authors." The winners are those pairs who had both copies of their descriptions identified correctly.

Section B

COMMUNICATIVE FUNCTION:
Describing people and objects

■ **Language note:** When a plural adjective describes two or more nouns, one of which is masculine, the masculine plural is used. **Patrick et Anne sont français. Ils ne sont pas américains.**

■ **Looking ahead:** Irregular plural forms like **beau–beaux** are taught in Lesson 27.

COMPREHENSION:
describing more than one person

⑤

Classroom Notes

B. Les adjectifs: le pluriel

Compare the forms of the adjectives in heavy print as they describe singular and plural nouns.

SINGULAR | PLURAL
Paul est **intelligent** et **timide**. | Paul et Éric sont **intelligents** et **timides**.
Alice est **intelligente** et **timide**. | Alice et Claire sont **intelligentes** et **timides**.

In written French, plural adjectives are usually formed as follows:

> SINGULAR ADJECTIVE + **-s** = PLURAL ADJECTIVE

➡ If the masculine singular adjective already ends in **-s,** there is no change in the plural form.

Patrick est **français.**   Patrick et Daniel sont **français.**
BUT: Anne est **française.**   Anne et Alice sont **françaises.**

NOTE DE PRONONCIATION: Because the final **-s** of plural adjectives is silent, singular and plural adjectives sound the same.

SUMMARY: Forms of regular adjectives

	MASCULINE	FEMININE	*also:*
SINGULAR	**–** **grand**	**-e** **grande**	timide timide
PLURAL	**-s** **grands**	**-es** **grandes**	français françaises

⑤ **Une question de personnalité**

Indicate whether or not the following people exhibit the personality traits in parentheses. (These traits are given in the masculine singular form only. Make the necessary agreements.)

> *Elles ne sont pas timides.*

▶ Alice et Thérèse aiment parler en public. (timide?)

1. Claire et Valérie sont très populaires. (amusant?)
2. Robert et Jean-Luc n'aiment pas danser. (timide?)
3. Catherine et Martine aiment jouer au foot. (sportif?)
4. Laure et Gisèle ont un «A» en français. (intelligent?)
5. Thomas et Vincent n'aiment pas le jogging. (sportif?)
6. Les voisins n'aiment pas parler avec nous. (sympathique?)

Cooperative pair practice
Activity 6

Talking about past events

Let's talk about what you did last summer.
▶ **Est-ce que tu as voyagé l'été dernier?**
Oui, j'ai voyagé l'été dernier.
(Non, je n'ai pas voyagé l'été dernier.)
• **Est-ce que tu as voyagé l'été dernier?**
• **Est-ce que tu as visité Paris l'été dernier?**

• **Est-ce que tu as visité Québec?**
• **Est-ce que tu as étudié?**
• **Est-ce que tu as travaillé?**
• **Est-ce que tu as joué au volley?**
• **Est-ce que tu as joué au tennis?**
• **Est-ce que tu as nagé?**
• **Est-ce que tu as dîné au restaurant?**

Vocabulaire: Les adjectifs de nationalité

américain	American	**italien (italienne)**	Italian
mexicain	Mexican	**canadien (canadienne)**	Canadian
français	French	**japonais**	Japanese
anglais	English	**chinois**	Chinese
espagnol	Spanish		
suisse	Swiss		

➡ Words that describe nationality are adjectives and take adjective endings.

Monsieur Katagiri est **japonais.**

Kumi et Michiko sont **japonaises.**

Expression pour la conversation

How to introduce a conclusion:

alors   *so, then*   —J'habite à Québec.

                      —**Alors,** tu es canadien!

J'habite à Québec. / Alors, tu es canadien.

6 **Quelle nationalité?**

Your classmate wants to know more about the following people: where they live and what their nationality is. Act out the dialogues.

▶ —Où habitent Janet et Barbara?
—Elles habitent à San Francisco.
—Alors, elles sont américaines?
—Mais oui, elles sont américaines.

Janet et Barbara	1. Jim et Bob	2. Laure et Céline
San Francisco	Liverpool	Toulouse
américain	anglais	français

3. Luisa et Teresa	4. Éric et Vincent	5. ??
Madrid	Montréal	??
espagnol	??	??

7 **Les nationalités**

Read the descriptions of the following people and give their nationalities.

▶ Silvia et Maria sont étudiantes à Rome.
Elles sont italiennes.

1. Lise et Nathalie étudient à Québec.
2. Michael et Dennis sont de Liverpool.
3. Luis et Paco étudient à Madrid.
4. Isabel et Carmen travaillent à Acapulco.
5. Yoko et Liliko sont étudiantes à l'université de Tokyo.
6. Monsieur et Madame Chen habitent à Beijing.
7. Jean-Pierre et Claude sont de Genève.
8. Françoise et Sylvie travaillent à Paris.

Leçon 19   **165**

▷ Vocabulaire

Transparency 27
Les adjectifs de nationalité

Review and expansion:
Adjectives of nationality from Lesson 2.

▪ **Language note:** Remind students that adjectives of nationality are not capitalized in French.

Supplementary vocabulary

allemand *German*
hollandais *Dutch*
portugais *Portuguese*
libanais *Lebanese*
russe *Russian*
grec (grecque) *Greek*
égyptien(ne) *Egyptian*
israélien(ne) *Israeli*
brésilien(ne) *Brazilian*
péruvien(ne) *Peruvian*
coréen(ne) *Korean*
vietnamien(ne) *Vietnamese*

💻   19.1 Mini-scenes: Je suis americain
     19.2 Mini-scenes: Qui est-ce?
     19.3 Mini-scenes: Comment sont-ils? (41:43–44:43 min.)

▭   Leçon 19, Sections 3, 4, 5

6 EXCHANGES: discussing nationalities

7 COMPREHENSION: identifying nationality

1. canadiennes	5. japonaises
2. anglais	6. chinois
3. espagnols	7. suisses
4. mexicaines	8. françaises

Now you will learn to talk about what others did last summer.
(First ask one student what he/she did. Then ask the class to reaffirm.)

▶ **X, est-ce que tu as voyagé l'été dernier?**
Oui, j'ai voyagé.
(to the class) **Est-ce que X a voyagé?**
Oui, il a voyagé.

▶ **Z, est-ce que tu as visité Paris?**
Non, je n'ai pas visité Paris.
(to the class) **Est-ce que Z a visité Paris?**
Non, elle n'a pas visité Paris.

(Use the questions on the facing page.)

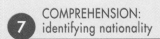

COMMUNICATIVE FUNCTION:
Using adjectives to describe
people and things

■ **Looking ahead:** Adjectives which precede the noun will be presented in Lesson 20.

■ **Realia note**
Ask students to read the penpal ad.
• Was it written by a boy or a girl? [a boy]
• How do you know? [from the word **étudiant** and the masculine adjectives]
• Is the person looking for a male or female penpal? [a female penpal]
• How do you know? [from the word **étudiante** and the feminine adjectives]

OPTIONAL: Have students write their own penpal ads.

NOTE: Please do <u>not</u> allow students to use the address that appears in the realia.

8 COMMUNICATION: expressing preferences

9 PRACTICE: pointing out similarities

C. La place des adjectifs

Note the position of the adjectives in the sentences on the right.

Philippe a une voiture.	Il a une voiture **anglaise.**
Denise invite des copains.	Elle invite des copains **américains.**
Voici un livre.	Voici un livre **intéressant.**
J'ai des amies.	J'ai des amies **sympathiques.**

In French, adjectives usually come AFTER the noun they modify, according to the pattern:

ARTICLE	+	NOUN	+	ADJECTIVE
une		voiture		**française**
des		copains		**intéressants**

R.S.V.P.
Le Club de Correspondance

Étudiant français, 16 ans, brun, grand, sportif, assez intelligent, un peu timide, voudrait correspondre avec étudiante américaine sportive et sympathique.

Envoyez votre message à :
Correspondants
13 rue de la Cerisaie
75004 Paris

8 **Préférences personnelles**

For each person or object below, choose among the characteristics in parentheses. Indicate your preference.

▶ avoir un copain (sympathique, intelligent, sportif)
Je préfère avoir un copain intelligent.

1. avoir une copine (amusante, mignonne, intelligente)
2. avoir un professeur (gentil, intelligent, amusant)
3. avoir des voisins (sympathiques, intéressants, riches)
4. avoir une voiture (moderne, confortable, rapide)
5. avoir une calculatrice (japonaise, américaine, française)
6. avoir une montre (suisse, japonaise, française)
7. dîner dans un restaurant (italien, chinois, français)
8. regarder un film (intéressant, amusant, intelligent)
9. travailler avec des personnes (gentilles, amusantes, sérieuses)
10. faire un voyage avec des gens (amusants, riches, sympathiques)

9 **Qui se ressemble . . .**
(Birds of a feather . . .)
Say that the following people have friends, relatives, or acquaintances with the same personality or nationality.

▶ Claire est anglaise. (un copain)
Elle a un copain anglais.

1. Jean-Pierre est sympathique. (des cousines)
2. La prof est intelligente. (des étudiants)
3. Madame Simon est intéressante. (des voisines)
4. Alice est américaine. (des copines)
5. Véronique est amusante. (un frère)
6. Michel est sportif. (une soeur)
7. Pedro est espagnol. (des camarades)
8. Antonio est mexicain. (une copine)
9. Bernard est sportif. (un voisin)

Birds of a feather flock together.

Talking about past events

Let's talk about what you and your friends did last weekend.
▶ **W et X, est-ce que vous avez étudié le weekend dernier?**
Oui, nous avons étudié.
(Non, nous n'avons pas étudié.)
• **Est-ce que vous avez regardé la télé?**

• **Est-ce que vous avez joué au foot?**
• **Est-ce que vous avez joué au tennis?**
• **Est-ce que vous avez nagé?**
• **Est-ce que vous avez organisé une boum?**
• **Est-ce que vous avez invité des copains?**
• **Est-ce que vous avez dansé?**
• **Est-ce que vous avez chanté?**

10 Préférences internationales

Choose an item from Column A and indicate your preference as to country of origin by choosing an adjective from Column B. Be sure to make the necessary agreement.

> Je préfère
> les voitures italiennes.

A	B
la musique	anglais
la cuisine	américain
les voitures	français
les ordinateurs	mexicain
les appareils-photo	chinois
les compacts	japonais
les restaurants	italien

Je préfère . . .

COMPREHENSION: expressing preferences

10

■ **Language note:** Remind students that the plural of **l'appareil-photo** is **les appareils-photo.**

■ **Expansion** (dialogue format):
– Je préfère les voitures anglaises. Et toi?
– Moi, je préfère les voitures américaines.

 19.5 Vignette culturelle: La France et ses voisins (44:44–46:13 min.)

Prononciation

Les consonnes finales

As you know, when the last letter of a word is a consonant, that consonant is often silent. But when a word ends in "**e**," the consonant before it is pronounced. As you practice the following adjectives, be sure to distinguish between the masculine and the feminine forms.

/-/ blon**d**   /d/ blon**de**

MASCULINE ADJECTIVE *(no final consonant sound)*		FEMININE ADJECTIVE *(final consonant sound)*
Répétez:	blon**d**	/d/ blon**de**
	gran**d**	gran**de**
	peti**t**	/t/ peti**te**
	amusan**t**	amusan**te**
	françai**s**	/z/ françai**se**
	anglai**s**	anglai**se**
	américai**n**	/n/ américai**ne**
	canadie**n**	canadie**nne**

Prononciation

🔊 Leçon 19, Section 6

■ **Teaching strategy:** Be sure students end the masculine adjectives on a vowel sound. In contrast, have them exaggerate the final consonants on the feminine adjectives.

Joli, petit et bon!

Bureau **195**F

Table **325**F

Jolie, petite et bonne!

IKEA *Miracle économique!*

Leçon 19 | **167**

Now you will learn to talk about what others did last weekend. (First ask one pair what they did. Then ask the class to reaffirm.)

▶ **W et X, est-ce que vous avez étudié le weekend dernier?**
Oui, nous avons étudié. (Turn to class:)
Est-ce que W et X ont étudié?
Oui, ils/elles ont étudié.

▶ **Y et Z, est-ce que vous avez étudié?**
Non, nous n'avons pas étudié.
(Then ask the class:)
Est-ce que Y et Z ont étudié?
Non, ils/elles n'ont pas étudié.

(Use the questions on the facing page.)

1 COMPREHENSION

1-d   4-c
2-a   5-e
3-b

🔊 **Leçon 19, Section 7**

2 GUIDED ORAL EXPRESSION

1. une voisine anglaise
2. un prof canadien
3. des cousins mexicains
4. un livre français
5. une voiture japonaise

🔊 **Leçon 19, Section 8**

■ **Teaching tip:** As a preliminary activity, have students identify the flags.
1. C'est un drapeau anglais.
2. C'est un drapeau canadien.
3. C'est un drapeau suisse.
4. C'est un drapeau français.
5. C'est un drapeau japonaise.

À votre tour!

1 Allô!

Valérie is phoning some friends. Match her questions on the left with her friends' answers on the right.

1. Ton frère aime jouer au foot?
2. Cécile et Sophie sont mignonnes, n'est-ce pas?
3. Pourquoi est-ce que tu invites Olivier?
4. Tu aimes la classe?
5. Tu as des cousins?

a. Oui, et intelligentes aussi!
b. Parce qu'il est amusant et sympathique.
c. Oui, j'ai un professeur très intéressant.
d. Oui, il est très sportif.
e. Oui, mais ils ne sont pas très sympathiques.

2 Créa-dialogue

With your classmates, talk about the people of different nationalities you may know or objects you may own.

des cousins

sportif?

▶ —J'ai des <u>cousins mexicains</u>.
  —<u>Ils sont mignons?</u>
  —<u>Oui, ils sont très mignons.</u>

1. une voisine	2. un prof	3. des copines	4. un livre	5. une voiture
blond?	sympathique?	mignon?	intéressant?	grand?

168 Unité 5

À votre tour

Depending on your goals and objectives, you may or may not wish to assign all of the activities in the **À votre tour** section.

👥👥 Cooperative practice

Act. 1 and 2 lend themselves to cooperative pair practice. They can also be done in trios, with two students performing and the third acting as monitor and following along in the Answer Key.

3 Une invitation

A French friend has invited you to go to a party with his/her cousin. You want to know as much as you can about this cousin. You may first ask your friend the cousin's name and age.

> Comment s'appelle ta cousine?
> Quel âge a-t-elle?

Then ask as many questions as you can about the cousin's physical appearance and personality traits. Act out your conversation with a classmate.

4 Avis de recherche
(Missing person's bulletin)

The two people in the pictures below have been reported missing. Describe each one as well as you can, using your imagination. Mention:

- the (approximate) age of the person
- the way he/she looks
- personality traits
- other features or characteristics

5 Composition: Descriptions

Describe one of the following well-known French people in a short paragraph, giving the person's name, profession, and approximate age. Also briefly describe the person's physical appearance.

Isabelle Adjani (actrice)

Yannick Noah (athlète)

Jean-Jacques Goldman (chanteur)

François Mitterrand (président)

6 Composition: Rencontres

Select two people whom you would like to meet (a man and a woman). These people may be famous singers, actors or actresses, sports figures, politicians, professional people, community leaders, etc. Describe each person (physical traits and personality), using either affirmative or negative sentences.

Je voudrais
rencontrer X.
Il (Elle) est...

169

---

3 CONVERSATION

■ **Teaching strategy:** Have each student bring in a magazine picture of an imaginary "cousin" who will form the basis of the dialogue.

4 ORAL EXPRESSION

5 WRITTEN SELF-EXPRESSION

6 WRITTEN SELF-EXPRESSION

Classroom Notes

 ■ **Portfolio assessment**

You will probably select only one speaking activity and one writing activity to go into the students' portfolios for Unit 5.

In this lesson, Act. 3 is good oral portfolio topic.

Act. 5 and 6 lend themselves well to written portfolio compositions.

MODULE 20:
La voiture de Roger
Total time: 6:33 min.
(Counter: 46:25 min.)

20.4 Dialogue: La
voiture de Roger
(50:24–51:27 min.)

Leçon 20, Section 1

■ **Photo culture note**
Saint Germain des Prés
The neighborhood around Saint Germain des Prés (**le quartier Saint Germain**) is one of the oldest areas of Paris.
Because of its numerous shops and movie theaters, **le boulevard Saint Germain** is a favorite strolling place for Parisians. There are also many cafés, including the famous **Café des Deux Magots**.

LEÇON 20 La voiture de Roger

Dans la <u>rue</u>, il y a une voiture <u>rouge</u>. *street / red*
C'est une petite voiture. C'est une voiture de sport.
Dans la rue, il y a aussi un café. Au café, il y a un jeune homme.
Il s'appelle Roger.
C'est le <u>propriétaire</u> de la voiture rouge. *owner*

Une jeune fille <u>entre dans</u> le café. *enters*
Elle s'appelle Véronique.
C'est <u>l'amie de Roger</u>. *Roger's*
Véronique parle à Roger. *friend*

VÉRONIQUE: Tu as une <u>nouvelle</u> voiture, *new*
n'est-ce pas?
ROGER: Oui, j'ai une nouvelle voiture.
VÉRONIQUE: Est-ce qu'elle est grande ou petite?
ROGER: C'est une petite voiture.
VÉRONIQUE: De quelle couleur est-elle?
ROGER: C'est une voiture rouge.
VÉRONIQUE: Est-ce que c'est une voiture italienne?
ROGER: Oui, c'est une voiture italienne. Mais <u>dis donc</u>, *hey there*
Véronique, tu es <u>vraiment</u> *really*
très curieuse!
VÉRONIQUE: Et toi, tu n'es pas <u>assez</u> *curious*
<u>curieux</u>! *enough*
ROGER: Ah bon? Pourquoi?
VÉRONIQUE: Pourquoi?! . . . Regarde
la <u>contractuelle</u> là-bas! *meter maid*
ROGER: Ah, zut alors!

Setting the scene
Video Module 20 prepares students for the introductory dialogue by first teaching the colors.

The scene with Roger and his car constitutes Segment 4 of the video. (Section 1 of the audiocassette contains the video soundtrack.)

The *Vignette culturelle* develops the *Note culturelle* on the facing page about the French and their cars.

Compréhension

1. Qu'est-ce qu'il y a dans la rue?
2. Est-ce que la voiture est grande?
3. Comment s'appelle le jeune homme?
4. Où est-il?
5. Comment s'appelle la jeune fille?
6. De quelle couleur est la voiture?

COMPREHENSION

1. une voiture rouge
2. Non, elle est petite.
3. Roger
4. dans un café
5. Véronique
6. rouge

NOTE CULTURELLE

Les Français et l'auto

France is one of the leading producers of automobiles in the world. The two major automakers are **Renault** and **Peugeot.** They manufacture a variety of models ranging from sports cars to mini-vans and buses.

To obtain a driver's license in France, you must be eighteen years old and pass a very difficult driving test. French teenagers can, however, begin to drive at the age of sixteen, as long as they take lessons at an accredited driving school **(auto-école)** and are accompanied by an adult.

On the whole, because cars (even used cars) are expensive to buy and maintain, few French teenagers have cars. Instead, many get around on two-wheelers: motorcycles, scooters, and mopeds.

Note culturelle

 20.5 Vignette culturelle: Les Français et l'auto (51:28–52:55 min.)

■ Cultural background
• The third French automaker is Citroën.
• Gasoline costs about 5 francs a liter, which comes to over 3 dollars a gallon.

■ Photo culture note
Renault
With a production of nearly 2 million vehicles per year, Renault is one of the leading European automobile manufacturers. It is owned by the French government (**régie nationale** = government enterprise).

■ Language note: In Québec, a driving school is **une école de conduite.**

Leçon 20 **171**

Talking about past events

Let's talk about what you did last weekend. Note that the past participle of **faire** is **fait.**
▶ **Est-ce que tu as fait une promenade le weekend dernier?**
Oui, j'ai fait une promenade.
(Non, je n'ai pas fait de promenade.)

• **Est-ce que tu as fait une promenade?**
• **Est-ce que tu as fait un match de tennis?**
• **Est-ce que tu as fait un match de basket?**
• **Est-ce que tu as fait un match de foot?**
• **Est-ce que tu as fait un pique-nique?**
(Remember to use **pas de** in the negative.)

COMMUNICATIVE FUNCTION:
Describing colors

20.1 Introduction: Les couleurs
20.2 Mini-scenes: De quelle couleur?
20.3 Mini-scenes: Qu'est-ce que tu préfères? (46:36–50:23 min.)

Leçon 20, Sections 2, 3, 4

Transparency 28
Les couleurs

■ **Language notes**
• When colors are used as nouns they are always masculine. J'aime **le noir.** Je déteste **le rose.**
• Another word for *brown* is **brun(e),** which is used to describe hair and eyes.

■ **Teaching strategy:** To activate colors, use names of articles of clothing, especially **tee-shirt** which is a cognate. **De quelle couleur est le tee-shirt de Jim? Il est bleu et jaune.**

■ **Looking ahead:** In conjunction with colors, you may want to pre-teach selected items of clothing:
un pantalon   une chemise
un tee-shirt   une robe
un sweater   une jupe
un polo   des chaussures
(Clothes are taught in Lesson 25.)

① COMMUNICATION: asking about colors

② EXCHANGES: describing colors

1. une voiture rouge
2. un scooter jaune
3. un vélo noir
4. une guitare orange
5. un chien blanc
6. un chat jaune

T172

A. Les couleurs

Note the form and position of the color words in the following sentences:

Alice a un vélo **bleu.**   *Alice has a **blue** bicycle.*
Nous avons des chemises **bleues.**   *We have **blue** shirts.*

Names of colors are ADJECTIVES and take adjective ENDINGS. Like most descriptive adjectives, they come *after* the noun.

Vocabulaire: Les couleurs

De quelle couleur . . . ?   *What color . . . ?*   —**De quelle couleur** est la moto?
—Elle est rouge.

| blanc (blanche) | noir (noire) | bleu (bleue) | rouge (rouge) | jaune (jaune) | vert (verte) | gris (grise) | marron (marron) | orange (orange) | rose (rose) |

➡ The colors **orange** and **marron** are INVARIABLE. They do not take any endings.
un sac **orange**   des sacs **orange**
un tee-shirt **marron**   une chemise **marron**

1 **De quelle couleur?**
Ask your classmates to name the colors of things they own. (They may invent answers.)

▶ ta chambre?

De quelle couleur est ta chambre?

Elle est blanche et bleue.

1. ta bicyclette?
2. ton tee-shirt?
3. ton appareil-photo?
4. ta montre?
5. ta raquette de tennis?
6. ton livre de français?
7. ton livre d'anglais?
8. ton chien (chat)?

172 Unité 5

2 **Possessions**
Ask what objects or pets the following people own. A classmate will answer, giving the color.

▶ —Est-ce que Monsieur Thomas a une voiture?
—Oui, il a une voiture bleue.

M. Thomas

1. Mme Mercier

2. Marc

3. Delphine

4. Sophie

5. Éric

6. Stéphanie

TPR **Colors**

PROPS: For each student: scissors and colored paper (red, yellow, blue, green, orange, pink, brown, white, black, gray)

Have students cut out shapes. **Découpez un cercle, un carré** (square), **un triangle.**
(Or distribute precut colored paper shapes.)

Have students hold up a shape.
Montrez-moi un cercle.
Take one student's circle and name its color.
Voici un cercle vert.
Si vous avez un cercle vert, levez la main.
Continue, teaching other colors and shapes.
X a un carré noir. Qui a un carré blanc?
Y a un triangle gris. Qui a un cercle gris?

3 L'arche de Noé

Noah's ark has just landed. Give the colors of the animals as they get off the ship.

▶ le chien   **Le chien est blanc.**

1. le chat
2. l'éléphant *(m.)*
3. la panthère
4. le zèbre
5. le flamant
6. le cardinal
7. le lion
8. le perroquet

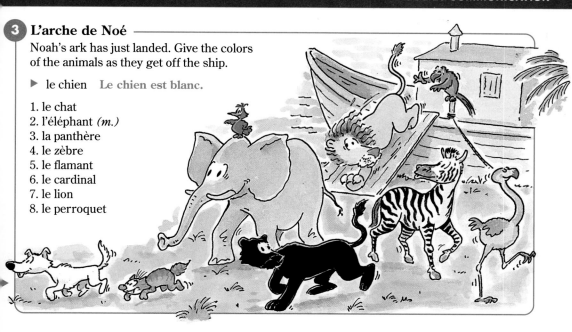

B. La place des adjectifs avant le nom

Compare the position of the adjectives in the following sentences.

Voici une voiture **française**.   Voici une **petite** voiture.
Paul est un garçon **intelligent**.   Pierre est un **beau** garçon.

❚ A few adjectives like **petit** and **beau** come BEFORE the noun they modify.

➡ The article **des** often becomes **de** before an adjective. Compare:
    des voitures → **de** petites voitures

Vocabulaire: Les adjectifs qui précèdent le nom

beau (belle)	beautiful, handsome	Regarde la **belle** voiture!
joli	pretty	Qui est la **jolie** fille avec André?
grand	big, large, tall	Nous habitons dans un **grand** appartement.
petit	little, small, short	Ma soeur a un **petit** ordinateur.
bon (bonne)	good	Tu es un **bon** copain.
mauvais	bad	Patrick est un **mauvais** élève.

➡ There is a LIAISON after the above adjectives when the noun which follows begins with a vowel sound. Note that in liaison:
   • the "**d**" of **grand** is pronounced /t/: **un grand appartement**
   • **bon** is pronounced like **bonne: un bon élève**

---

3 DESCRIPTION: describing colors of animals

1. Le chat est orange.
2. La panthère est noire.
3. L'éléphant est gris.
4. Le lion est jaune.
5. Le perroquet est rouge.
6. Le flamant est rose.
7. Le zèbre est [noir et blanc].
8. Le cardinal est rouge.

■ **Teaching strategy:** Model the pronunciation of the animal names for students.

Section B

COMMUNICATIVE FUNCTION:
Describing objects

■ **Language notes**
• In current French, it is becoming more and more common to use **des** before the adjective. Therefore, students should be able to recognize the **de** construction when they encounter it, but should not be penalized for failing to produce it.
• **Jeune** comes before the noun in expressions like **un jeune homme** and **une jeune fille**.

 Leçon 20, Section 5

Cooperative pair practice
Activities 1, 2

T173

4 Opinions personnelles

Give your opinion about the following people and things, using the adjectives **bon** or **mauvais**.

▶ Meryl Streep est (une) actrice *(actress)*.
   Meryl Streep est une bonne actrice (une mauvaise actrice).

1. *Rambo* est un film.
2. Le «Bill Cosby Show» est un programme de télé.
3. Whitney Houston est (une) chanteuse *(singer)*.
4. Steve Martin est (un) acteur.
5. Cybil Shepherd est (une) actrice.
6. Dracula est une personne.
7. McDonald's est un restaurant.
8. Les Yankees sont une équipe *(team)* de baseball.
9. Les Lakers sont une équipe de basket.
10. Je suis [un(e)] élève.

Expressions pour la conversation

How to get someone's attention:

Dis!	*Say! Hey!*	**Dis,** Éric, est-ce que tu as une voiture?
Dis donc!	*Hey there!*	**Dis donc,** est-ce que tu veux faire une promenade avec moi?

5 Dialogue

Christine asks her cousin Thomas if he has certain things. He responds affirmatively, describing each one. Play both roles.

▶ un ordinateur (petit)   ▶ une voiture (anglaise)

Dis, Thomas, tu as un ordinateur?
Oui, j'ai un petit ordinateur.

Dis, Thomas, tu as une voiture?
Oui, j'ai une voiture anglaise.

1. une télé (petite)
2. une guitare (espagnole)
3. un vélo (rouge)
4. une calculatrice (petite)
5. un sac (grand)
6. des livres (intéressants)
7. une copine (amusante)
8. une mobylette (bleue)
9. une montre (belle)
10. un copain (bon)
11. une cousine (jolie)
12. une radio (japonaise)

Teaching strategy: Using chants

Certain grammatical constructions, such as the use of **c'est** vs. **il est,** can be internalized through the use of chants.

For example, the phrase **c'est un** can be chanted to the Mexican Hat Dance tune.

C'est un, c'est un, c'est un...
C'est un ami mexicain.
C'est une, c'est une, c'est une...
C'est une amie mexicaine.
C'est un, c'est un, c'est un...
C'est un vélo italien.
C'est une, c'est une, c'est une...
C'est une voiture italienne.

C. *Il est* ou *c'est?*

When describing a person or thing, French speakers use two different constructions, **il est (elle est)** and **c'est.**

		Il est + ADJECTIVE **Elle est** + ADJECTIVE	**C'est** + ARTICLE + NOUN (+ ADJECTIVE)
Roger	*He is . . .*	**Il est** amusant.	**C'est** un copain. **C'est** un copain amusant.
Véronique	*She is . . .*	**Elle est** sportive.	**C'est** une amie. **C'est** une bonne amie.
un scooter	*It is . . .*	**Il est** joli.	**C'est** un scooter français. **C'est** un bon scooter.
une voiture	*It is . . .*	**Elle est** petite.	**C'est** une voiture anglaise. **C'est** une petite voiture.

➡ Note the corresponding plural forms:

(Pierre et Marc) *They are . . .* **Ils sont** amusants. **Ce sont** des copains.
(Claire et Anne) *They are . . .* **Elles sont** timides. **Ce sont** des copines.

➡ In negative sentences, **c'est** becomes **ce n'est pas.**

Ce n'est pas un mauvais élève. *He's not a bad student.*
Ce n'est pas une Peugeot. *It's not a Peugeot.*

➡ **C'est** is also used with names of people

C'est Véronique. **C'est** Madame Lamblet.

SCOOTERS PEUGEOT

6 Descriptions

Complete the following descriptions with **Il est, Elle est,** or **C'est,** as appropriate.

A. Roger
1. _____ grand.
2. _____ brun.
3. _____ un garçon sympathique.
4. _____ un mauvais élève.

B. Véronique
5. _____ une fille brune.
6. _____ une amie sympathique.
7. _____ très amusante.
8. _____ assez grande.

C. La voiture de Roger
9. _____ une voiture moderne.
10. _____ une petite voiture.
11. _____ rouge.
12. _____ très rapide.

D. Le scooter de Véronique
13. _____ bleu et blanc.
14. _____ très économique.
15. _____ un joli scooter.
16. _____ assez confortable.

Leçon 20 **175**

Section C

COMMUNICATIVE FUNCTION:
Describing people and things

■ **Language notes**
• The adjective may either follow or precede the noun.
• **C'est** is also used when a possessive adjective introduces the noun:
C'est mon frère.
He's my brother.
• In *negative* sentences with **être,** the articles **un, une,** and **des** remain unchanged. Compare:
Ce **n'est pas un** copain.
Je **n'ai pas de** copain.
Ce **ne sont pas des** motos japonaises.
Nous **n'avons pas de** motos japonaises.

Leçon 20, Section 6

DESCRIPTION: pointing out people and things

6

1. Il est	9. C'est
2. Il est	10. C'est
3. C'est	11. Elle est
4. C'est	12. Elle est
5. C'est	13. Il est
6. C'est	14. Il est
7. Elle est	15. C'est
8. Elle est	16. Elle est

Speaking activity: Show and tell

Have students bring an object to class and describe it using **il/elle est...**, **c'est...** and appropriate adjectives.
J'ai une montre.
Ce n'est pas une Timex. C'est une Swatch.
C'est une montre suisse.
Elle est rouge et noire.

C'est une jolie montre; elle marche très bien. J'aime beaucoup ma montre!
VARIATION: This can also be done as a written activity with students illustrating their objects.
NOTE: This works particularly well after the holiday season when students have gifts to talk about.

■ **Language note:** This construction is not used to describe specific people and things.
Paul? Il est amusant.
Les livres? Ils sont intéressants.

■ **Casual speech:** It is very common to drop the **ne** in negative expressions:
C'est pas amusant.
C'est pas vrai.

■ **Language notes**
• The French often tend to use negative constructions in a positive sense:
Ce (n')est pas mal. *That's not bad. = That's very good.*
Ce (n')est pas bête. *That's not stupid = That's a smart idea.*
• A current popular anglicism is:
C'est cool.
• **Super** may be used in combination with other expressions:
C'est super-chouette.
C'est super-difficile.
• **Extra** is the short form of **extraordinaire.**

COMPREHENSION:
geographic locations

7

1. vrai
2. vrai
3. faux (en Suisse)
4. vrai
5. faux (à la Martinique)
6. faux (au Canada)

■ **Additional cues**
Montréal est au Canada. (vrai)
Casablanca est en Afrique. (vrai)
Rome est en France (faux: en Italie)
Vancouver est en France. (faux: au Canada)
Strasbourg est en France. (vrai)
Bordeaux est en Italie. (faux: en France)

T176

D. Les expressions impersonnelles avec *c'est*

Note the use of **c'est** in the following sentences.

J'aime parler français.   **C'est** intéressant.   *It's interesting.*
Je n'aime pas travailler le weekend.   **Ce n'est pas** amusant.   *It's no(t) fun.*

To express an opinion on a general topic, the French use the construction:

C'est
Ce n'est pas } + MASCULINE ADJECTIVE

Vocabulaire: Opinions

C'est . . .		It's . . . , That's . . .	
Ce n'est pas . . .		It's not . . . , That's not . . .	
vrai	*true*	**chouette**	*neat*
faux	*false*	**super**	*great*
		extra	*terrific*
facile	*easy*	**pénible**	*a pain, annoying*
difficile	*hard, difficult*	**drôle**	*funny*

➡ To express an opinion, the French also use adverbs like **bien** and **mal**.

C'est bien. *That's good.*   Tu étudies? **C'est bien.**
C'est mal. *That's bad.*   Alain n'étudie pas. **C'est mal.**

7 **Vrai ou faux?**

Imagine that your little sister is talking about where certain cities are located. Tell her whether her statements are right or wrong.

1. Paris est en Italie.
2. Los Angeles est en Californie.
3. Genève est en Italie.
4. Dakar est en Afrique.
5. Fort-de-France est au Canada.
6. Québec est en France.

Talking about past events

▶ **V, qu'est-ce que tu as fait hier soir?**
J'ai étudié (regardé la télé, travaillé...).

▶ **W et X, qu'est-ce que vous avez fait?**
Nous avons joué au Nintendo (...).

Ask individuals what they did. Have others report back. Ask if they did the same thing.

• **V, qu'est-ce que tu as fait hier soir?**
• **Y, qu'est-ce que V a fait hier soir?**
  Est-ce que tu as fait la même chose?
• **W et X, qu'est-ce que vous avez fait?**
• **Z, qu'est-ce que W et X ont fait hier soir?**
  Est-ce que tu as fait la même chose?

8 **Opinion personelle**

Ask your classmates if they like to do the following things. They will answer, using an expression from the **Vocabulaire.**

▶ parler français

Tu aimes parler français?

Oui, c'est extra!

(Non, c'est difficile!)

1. téléphoner
2. parler en public
3. nager
4. danser
5. voyager
6. dîner en ville
7. regarder le «Bill Cosby Show»
8. étudier le weekend
9. écouter la musique classique

Prononciation   ch /ʃ/

Les lettres «ch»

The letters "**ch**" are usually pronounced like the English "*sh.*"

Répétez: **chien   chat   chose   marche chouette   chocolat   affiche Michèle a un chat et deux chiens.**

chien

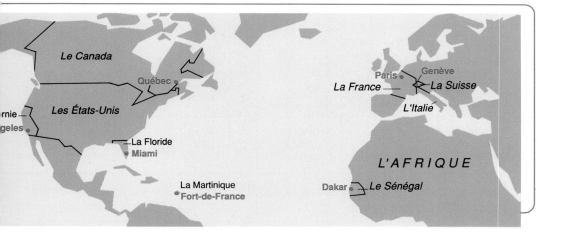

Le Canada

Québec

Les États-Unis

rnie
geles

La Floride
Miami

La Martinique
Fort-de-France

Paris   Genève

La France   La Suisse

L'Italie

L'AFRIQUE

Dakar   Le Sénégal

Leçon 20   **177**

---

8 COMMUNICATION: talking about what one likes to do

↩ **Re-entry and review:** Verbs from Unit 4.

■ **Challenge:** The second student asks the same question of the first student, who must respond using another adjective.
– **Tu aimes parler français?**
– **Oui, c'est extra! Et toi, tu aimes parler français?**
– **Non, c'est difficile.**

Prononciation

 Leçon 20, Section 7

■ **Pronunciation notes**
• Although "ch" is usually pronounced /tʃ/ in English, as in *march* and *chocolate*, the letters do represent the sound /ʃ/ in words and names that came directly from French: **Chevrolet, chef, chauffeur, chic, touché,** etc.
• Sometimes the letters "ch" are pronounced /k/ in French, just as they are in the corresponding English cognates: **orchestre, Christine, écho.**

Cooperative pair practice Activity 8

T177

2 GUIDED ORAL EXPRESSION

1. devant le café / une petite voiture
2. devant la pharmacie / une moto rouge
3. devant la librairie / une petite fille
4. devant le restaurant / un homme blond
5. devant le cinéma / un garçon anglais
6. devant la fontaine / un chien jaune

[cassette] Leçon 20, Section 9

À votre tour!

1 Allô!

Christophe is phoning some friends. Match his questions on the left with his friends' answers on the right.

1 De quelle couleur est ton vélo?

2 Ta raquette est bleue?

3 Tu aimes regarder la télé?

4 C'est un magazine français?

5 Philippe n'aime pas parler en public?

a Non, il est canadien.

b C'est vrai! Il est très timide.

c Non, elle est blanche.

d Oui, c'est amusant.

e Il est vert.

2 Créa-dialogue

There has been a burglary in the rue Saint-Pierre. By walkie-talkie, two detectives are describing what they see. Play both roles.

(le)	1. (la)	2. (la)	3. (le)	4. (le)	5. (la)
CAFÉ	PHARMACIE+	LIBRAIRIE	Restaurant	CINÉMA	fontaine
grande ou petite?	rouge ou bleue?	grande ou petite?	brun ou blond?	anglais ou français?	noir ou jaune?

▶ DÉTECTIVE 1: **Qu'est-ce qu'il y a devant _le café_?**
DÉTECTIVE 2: **Il y a _une voiture_.**

DÉTECTIVE 1: **_Elle_ est _grande_ ou _petite_?**
DÉTECTIVE 2: **C'est _une petite voiture_.**

À votre tour

Depending on your goals and objectives, you may or may not wish to assign all of the activities in the **À votre tour** section.

🗣🗣 Cooperative practice

Act. 1 and 4 lend themselves to cooperative pair practice.

3 Faisons connaissance!

Try to find out which students have the same interests you do. Select two activities you enjoy from Column A and ask a classmate if he/she likes to do them. Your classmate will answer yes or no, using an appropriate expression from Column B.

A	B
chanter	chouette
danser	super
nager	extra
téléphoner	amusant
voyager	intéressant
jouer au foot	pénible
jouer au volley	drôle
organiser des boums	difficile
parler avec les voisins	facile
parler français en classe	
dîner au restaurant	

Tu aimes voyager?

Oui, c'est amusant.

Tu aimes parler français en classe?

Non, c'est difficile.

4 Composition: La chambre de Véronique

Look at the picture of Véronique's room. Write a short paragraph in which you describe five of the following items. You may want to mention color or size **(grand? petit?)**, and perhaps give your opinion **(joli? beau? drôle? bon?,** etc.)

la chambre
la porte
le lit
la table
la chaise
la radiocassette
la guitare
l'affiche

▶ La chambre de Véronique est bleue et blanche. Elle a un grand lit. . . .

5 Composition: Ma chambre

Write a short description of your own room: real or imaginary. Use only vocabulary that you know. You may use the suggestions about Véronique's room as a guide.

3 CONVERSATION

4 GUIDED WRITTEN EXPRESSION

5 WRITTEN SELF-EXPRESSION

■ **Teaching strategy:** You may wish to have your students include a drawing of their room with their composition. They should label all furniture and items in French.

Classroom Notes

 Portfolio assessment

You will probably select only one speaking activity and one writing activity to go into the students' portfolios for Unit 5.

In this lesson, Act. 5 is a good written portfolio topic.

OBJECTIVES:

- Reading skills development
- Re-entry of materials in the unit
- Development of cultural awareness

Le monde personnel

OBJECTIVES:

- Rapid reading at the sentence level
- Reading for cultural information about personal possessions and attitudes of French people

Vive la différence!
Le monde personnel

Parlons° de votre monde° personnel. Répondez aux questions suivantes.° D'après° vous, quelles sont les réponses des jeunes Français en général à ces° questions?

1 **Combien de télés est-ce qu'il y a chez vous?°**

- zéro
- une
- deux
- trois ou plus°

Et dans une maison française typique, combien est-ce qu'il y a de télés?

2 **Combien de livres est-ce qu'il y a chez vous?**

- dix
- cinquante
- cent
- plus de° cent
- cinquante

Et dans une maison française typique, combien de livres est-ce qu'il y a?

3 **Dans la classe de français, quel est le pourcentage d'élèves qui ont un walkman?**

- moins de° 25% (vingt-cinq pour cent)
- entre° 26% et 50%
- entre 51% et 75%
- entre 76% et 100% (cent pour cent)

Selon° vous, quel est le pourcentage de jeunes Français qui ont un walkman?

4 **En général, comment sont vos relations avec vos parents?**

- très bonnes
- bonnes
- assez bonnes
- mauvaises

Et en France, comment sont les relations entre parents et enfants?°

5 **Quand vous avez une chos importante à discuter° (par exemple, un problème personnel), à qui est-ce que vous préférez parler?**

- à votre frère ou à votre soe
- à votre père ou à votre mèr
- à un copain ou à une copin
- à un professeur

Et les jeunes Français, à qu est-ce qu'ils préfèrent parle de leurs° problèmes?

6 **En général, qu'est-ce que vous pensez° de vos professeurs?**

- Ils sont «cool».
- Ils sont compréhensifs.°
- Ils sont sévères.°
- Ils sont sympathiques.

Et les élèves français, qu'est-ce qu'ils pensent de leurs professeurs?

7 **Quelle est la chose la plus° importante dans votre vie?**

- l'argent°
- l'amitié°
- l'indépendar
- les études°

Et pour les jeunes Français quelle est la chose la plus importante?

Et les Français?

1. La majorité des familles françaises ont seulement *(only)* une télé. 2. Les Français aiment lire *(to read)*. Ils ont en moyenne *(on the average)* plus de cent livres par famille. 3. 41% (quarante et un pour cent) 4. La majorité très des jeunes Français ont de très bonnes relations avec leurs parents. 5. En général, ils préfèrent parler avec un copain ou une copine. 6. En général, ils pensent que leurs professeurs sont sympathiques. 7. C'est l'amitié.

Parlons *Let's talk* **monde** *world* **suivantes** *following* **D'après** *According to* **ces** *these* **chez vous** *in your home* **plus** *more* **plus de** *more than* **moins de** *less than* **entre** *between* **Selon** *According to* **enfants** *children* **discuter** *to discuss* **leurs** *their* **pensez** *think* **compréhensifs** *understanding* **sévères** *strict* **la plus** *the most* **vie** *life* **argent** *money* **amitié** *friendship* **études** *studies*

👀 Cooperative reading practice

Divide the class into groups of 4 or 5, each with a **secrétaire.**

For each question, have the students give their own opinions and then vote on what they imagine French responses to be. (Keep answers covered.)

Then have the recorders announce their results to the entire class. For example:

1. Nous avons deux télés chez nous. Selon nous, dans une maison française typique il y a deux télés.

When all results have been announced, let the students look at the answers.

La mobylette

Because mopeds or cyclomoteurs are easy and fun to drive, they are very popular with French teenagers. During the week, many students go to school on their mopeds. On weekends, they take their mopeds to go downtown or to go for a ride in the country with their friends.

Although the term mobylette is a trade name, students tend to use the term (or its shortened form mob) to refer to any type of moped. In France, you can drive a mobylette at age 14, and the only restrictions are that you must wear a helmet and cannot exceed 45 kilometers per hour.

Look at the ads on the right. Which moped would you like to have? Describe it using words that you know. (What color is it? What country is it from? Is it big or small?)

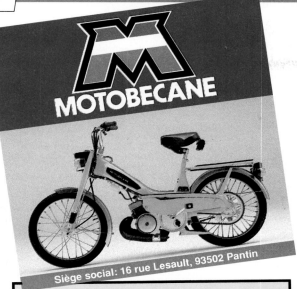

MOTOBECANE

Siège social: 16 rue Lesault, 93502 Pantin

PEUGEOT
concessionnaire
Ets SOUHART

scooters • cyclos • motos
métro Bir Hakeim   5, bd. de Grenelle   75015 PARIS
(1) 45 79 33 01

boulmich' MOTO
129, bd St-Michel Paris 5
(1) 43 29 53 10

LA MOTO VERTE
Concessionnaire Exclusif
Yamaha
85 r Chardon Lagache
75016 Paris .... (1) 42 24 56 56

Entracte 5 181

OBJECTIVES:
- Reading a complete text
- Building reading skills

■ Questions sur le texte
1. Quel âge a Brigitte?
2. Comment est-elle physique-ment?
3. Quels sports est-ce qu'elle aime?
4. Où est-ce qu'elle habite?
5. Où travaille son père? Qu'est-ce qu'il fait?
6. Où travaille sa mère? Qu'est-ce qu'elle fait?
7. Comment s'appelle la soeur de Brigitte? Quel âge a-t-elle? Comment est-elle?
8. Comment s'appelle le frère de Brigitte? Quel âge a-t-il? Comment est-il?
9. Est-ce que Brigitte a des ani-maux?
10. Quelles choses est-ce qu'elle a?
11. Est-ce qu'elle a un petit copain?

■ Questions personnelles
1. Quel âge as-tu?
2. Est-ce que tu es grand(e), petit(e) ou de taille moyenne?
3. Est-ce que tu as les yeux bleus ou marron (brown) ou noirs?
4. Est-ce que tu as des frères ou des soeurs?
5. (Pour chaque frère ou chaque soeur):
   Comment est-ce qu'il/elle s'appelle?
   Quel âge est-ce qu'il/elle a?
   Comment est-il/elle?
6. Est-ce que tu as un chien? un chat? un poisson rouge? Comment est-ce qu'il s'appelle?
7. Est-ce que tu as un vélo? Est-ce que tu aimes faire des promenades à vélo?
8. Quels autres (other) objets est-ce que tu as?

Entre amis: Bonjour, Brigitte!

Chers copains américains,

Je m'appelle Brigitte Lavie. J'ai quatorze ans. Voici ma photo. Je ne suis pas très grande, mais je ne suis pas petite. Je suis de taille° moyenne.° Je suis brune mais j'ai les yeux° verts. Je suis sportive. J'aime le ski, le jogging et la danse moderne.

J'habite à Toulouse avec ma famille. Mon père travaille dans l'industrie aéronautique. Il est ingénieur.° Ma mère travaille dans une banque. Elle est directrice° du personnel.

J'ai une soeur et un frère. Ma petite soeur s'appelle Ariane. Elle a cinq ans. Elle est très mignonne. Mon frère s'appelle Jérôme. Il a treize ans. Il est pénible. J'ai un chien. Il s'appelle Attila mais il est très gentil. (Il est plus gentil que° mon frère!) J'ai aussi deux poissons rouges.° Ils n'ont pas de nom.°

J'ai une chaîne stéréo et des quantités de compacts. J'ai aussi une moblyette. Le weekend, j'adore faire des promenades° à moblyette avec mes copains. J'ai beaucoup de copains, mais je n'ai pas de «petit copain».° Ça n'a pas d'importance!° Je suis heureuse° comme ça!°

Amitiés,
Brigitte

Chers *Dear* **taille** *size* **moyenne** *average* **yeux** *eyes* **ingénieur** *engineer* **directrice** *director* **plus gentil que** *nicer than* **poissons rouges** *goldfish* **nom** *name* **faire des promenades** *go for rides* **petit copain** *boyfriend* **Ça n'a pas d'importance!** *It doesn't matter!* **heureuse** *happy* **comme ça** *like that*

■ NOTE ■
CULTURELLE

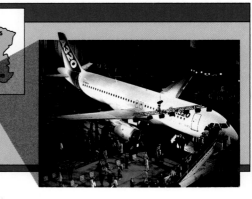

Toulouse
Toulouse, with a population of over half a million people, is the center of the French aeronautic and space industry. It is in Toulouse that the Airbus planes and the Ariane rockets are being built in cooperation with other European countries.

182 Unité 5

◆ Pre-reading
Ask if students know in which American city NASA (National Aeronautic and Space Agency) is headquartered. [Houston]

Then ask if they know where the French space center is located. [Toulouse]
Tell them they will be reading a letter from Toulouse.

Comment lire
GUESSING FROM CONTEXT

- As you read French, try to guess the meanings of unfamiliar words before you look at the English equivalents. Often the context provides good hints. For example, Brigitte writes:

  Je ne suis pas très grande, mais je ne suis pas petite.
  Je suis <u>de taille moyenne</u>.

  She is neither tall nor short. She must be about average:

  de taille moyenne = *of medium height or size*

- Sometimes you know what individual words in an expression mean, but the phrase does not seem to make sense. Then you have to guess at the real meaning. For example, Brigitte writes that she has:

  deux poissons rouges *??red fish??*

  If you guessed that these are most likely *goldfish*, you are right!

Enrichissez votre vocabulaire
MORE ON COGNATES

- Some words are PARTIAL COGNATES. The English word may help you remember the regular meaning. For example:

gentil	looks like	*gentle*	but means	*nice*
grand	looks like	*grand*	but means	*tall, big*
j'adore	looks like	*I adore*	but means	*I love*

- Some cognates are spelled differently in the two languages. Knowing cognate patterns makes it easier to identify new words. For example:

FRENCH	ENGLISH	FRENCH	ENGLISH
-ique	-ic	aéronautique	*aeronautic, aeronautical*
-ique	-ical	typique	*typical*
-té	-ty	quantité	*quantity*

Activité
Can you identify the English equivalents of the following French words?
la musique classique, une personne dynamique, un film comique,
une guitare électrique, une société, une activité, une possibilité,
la curiosité, la beauté

Activité: Une lettre à Brigitte
Write a letter to Brigitte in which you describe yourself and your family. You may tell her:

- your name and how old you are
- if you are tall or short
- if you like sports
- if you have brothers and sisters (If so, give their names and ages.)

Comment écrire *(to write)* **une lettre**

Begin with: (to a boy) **Cher** Cher Patrick,
(to a girl) **Chère** Chère Brigitte,

End with: **Amicalement,** *(In friendship,)*
Amitiés, *(Best regards,)*

- if you have pets (If so, say what type and give their names.)
- a few things you own
- a few things you like to do with your friends

Entracte 5 183

Classroom Notes

Post-reading activity

Maybe your class would like to exchange letters with a French class in another school in your area. (The advantage of cross-city exchanges is that letters can be exchanged easily.)

Have your students each write letters introducing themselves.

Place these in a large envelope and exchange packets with a French teacher in another school. The first set of correspondence will be distributed randomly. From then on, however, students will have a specific penpal to correspond with during the year.

Variétés

Petit catalogue des compliments et des insultes

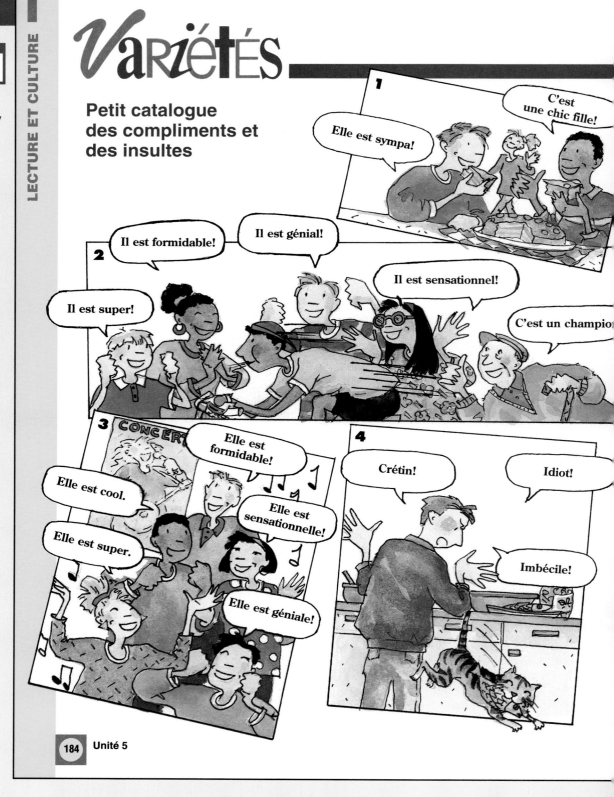

184 Unité 5

T184

LES ANIMAUX
ET
LE LANGAGE

Selon° toi, est-ce que les animaux ont une personnalité? Pour les Français, les animaux ont des qualités et des défauts,° comme° nous. Devine° comment on° complète les phrases suivantes° en français.

1 Philippe n'aime pas étudier. Il préfère dormir.° Il est paresseux° comme° . . .

un tigre

un chat

un lézard

2 Charlotte adore parler. Elle est bavarde° comme . . .

une poule

une pie

un lion

3 Isabelle est une excellente élève. Elle a une mémoire extraordinaire. Elle a la mémoire d' . . .

un éléphant

un hippopotame

un kangourou

4 Le petit frère de Christine est jeune, mais il est très intelligent. Il est malin° comme . . .

un cheval

un singe

une girafe

5 Où est Jacques? Il n'est pas prêt!° Oh là là! Il est lent° comme . . .

une tortue

un poisson

un rhinocéros

6 Nicole a très, très faim. Elle a une faim de (d') . . .

lion

ours

loup

Voici les réponses:

1. un lézard 2. une pie 3. un éléphant 4. un singe 5. une tortue 6. loup

Selon According to   **défauts** shortcomings   **comme** like   **Devine** Guess   **on** one   **phrases suivantes** following sentences   **dormir** to sleep   **paresseux** lazy   **comme** as   **bavarde** talkative   **malin** clever   **prêt** ready   **lent** slow

Entracte 5   185

Game: Cooperative pair reading

Be sure all students cover the answers at the bottom of the page. (If you prefer, you can make a transparency of the questions and project it on the overhead.)

Divide the class into pairs. How many groups can complete the six expressions correctly?

UNITÉ 6
Modules 21–24

21. Le français pratique:
    La ville at la maison
22. Une promenade en ville
23. Sports et musique
24. Où habitez-vous?

UNITÉ

6 En ville

186

Unit overview

COMMUNICATION GOALS: Students will be able to ask and give directions, and to describe their city and their home. They will also learn to talk about future plans.
LINGUISTIC GOALS: Students will learn to use the verbs **aller** and **venir**, and the possessive adjectives.

CRITICAL THINKING GOALS: Students will observe both linguistic similarities (use of **aller** to express future time) and differences (use of possessive adjectives) between French and English.
CULTURAL GOALS: This unit introduces students to two French cities: Paris (in the student text) and Tours (in the video).

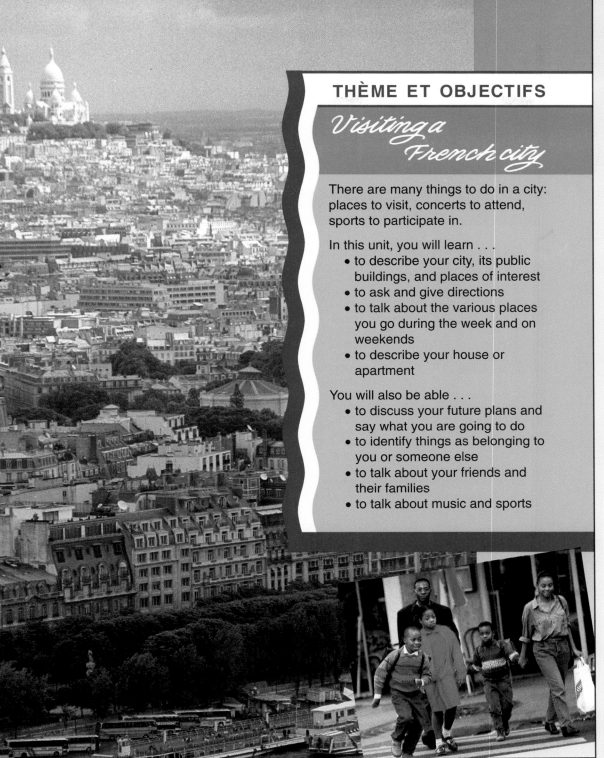

THÈME ET OBJECTIFS

Visiting a French city

There are many things to do in a city: places to visit, concerts to attend, sports to participate in.

In this unit, you will learn . . .
- to describe your city, its public buildings, and places of interest
- to ask and give directions
- to talk about the various places you go during the week and on weekends
- to describe your house or apartment

You will also be able . . .
- to discuss your future plans and say what you are going to do
- to identify things as belonging to you or someone else
- to talk about your friends and their families
- to talk about music and sports

Classroom Notes

Leçon 21

MAIN TOPIC:

Getting around in a French city

MODULE 21:
Le français pratique:
La ville et la maison
Total time: 7:17 min.
(Counter 00:40 min.)

21.1 Introduction: Listening — Les villes de France (00:50–1:57 min.)

21.2 Dialogue: La ville de Tours (1:58–5:02 min.)

21.3 Mini-scenes: Speaking — Qu'est-ce que c'est? (5:03–6:05 min.)

21.4 Mini-scenes: Listening — Pardon! Excusez-moi! (6:06–6:58 min.)

21.5 Vignette culturelle: La maison d'Olivier (6:59–7:55 min.)

■ **Comprehension practice:** Play the entire module through as an introduction to the lesson.

21.1 Introduction: Les villes de France
21.2 Dialogue: La ville de Tours (00:50–5:02 min.)

■ **Cultural note:** Marseille was founded by the Phoenicians in 600 B.C. Paris and Lyon were founded by the Romans at the time of Julius Caesar around 43 B.C.

LEÇON **21**

LE FRANÇAIS PRATIQUE

La ville et la maison

Accent sur ... Les villes françaises

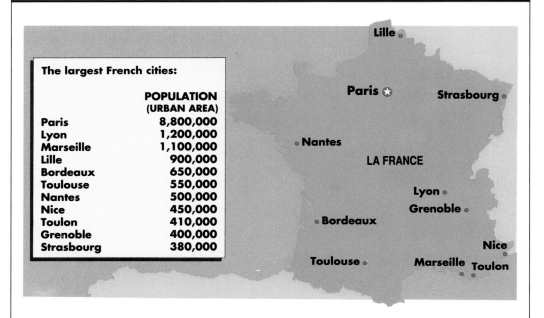

The largest French cities:

	POPULATION (URBAN AREA)
Paris	8,800,000
Lyon	1,200,000
Marseille	1,100,000
Lille	900,000
Bordeaux	650,000
Toulouse	550,000
Nantes	500,000
Nice	450,000
Toulon	410,000
Grenoble	400,000
Strasbourg	380,000

- Today 80% of the French population lives in cities and their surrounding suburbs.

- French cities have a long history. Paris, Lyon, and Marseille, the three largest French cities, were founded well over two thousand years ago! Many cities have a historical district with houses and monuments dating back several centuries. At the same time, French cities also appear very modern, with growing numbers of new houses and modern office buildings.

- French cities differ in architectural style from region to region because of their geographical location and their historical background. However, they also share many common features.

 188 Unité 6

Setting the scene

PROPS: Worksheets with a map of France and 11 dots representing the above cities + Tours. Names of the 11 cities are listed at bottom.

Have students keep their books closed. Divide the class into teams of 4 or 5. Have the teams try to locate the cities on the map.

Have the teams open their books to correct their maps.
- How many cities did they find correctly?
- Have they heard about any of these cities?

Tell students that in the video they will visit the city of Tours, in the Loire valley.

Here are some of the places you may see when you visit a French city:

● **La gare**
For French people, the train is a rapid and inexpensive means of travel. In general, the railroad station is located near the center of the city or town. The station **(la gare)** offers many useful services to travelers: an information desk, a bicycle rental agency, and a place to check luggage.

● **La poste**
There are many things you can do in a French post office **(la poste)** besides buying stamps. You can make long-distance phone calls. You can deposit and withdraw money with special postal checking accounts. In many post offices you can use the **Minitel.**

● **Les magasins**
Although supermarkets and grocery chain stores now exist all over France, most French people still love to shop at the local bakery **(la boulangerie),** the pastry shop **(la pâtisserie),** the butcher shop **(la boucherie),** the grocery store **(l'épicerie),** etc.

● **Le parc**
The city park **(le parc public)** or public garden **(le jardin public)** is the place where French young people come at noon or after class to walk around or to sit on chairs and talk. The colorful flower beds and shrubbery of the public parks reflect the French love of nature and beauty. This is the Jardin du Luxembourg in Paris.

● **Le château**
Many French cities were built around a medieval castle **(un château),** which offered protection against enemy attack. This is the castle of Angers built in the XIIIth century.

Leçon 21 189

■ **Photo culture note**
La gare
This picture shows the main hall in the **Gare de Lyon** in Paris. The train waiting on the track is a **TGV (un train à grande vitesse).**

La poste
Formerly known as the **PTT (Poste, Téléphone, Télégraphe)** and then as the **P et T (Poste et Télécommunications),** the French post office has now changed its official name to **La Poste.**
Note that French post offices often have mail drops **(une boîte à lettres)** on the outside wall so pedestrians can mail letters at any time of day.

Les magasins
This photograph shows a combined bakery and pastry shop **(une boulangerie-pâtisserie).** There one can buy French bread **(une baguette)** as well as croissants, eclairs **(un éclair),** cakes **(un gâteau),** and pies **(une tarte).**

Angers
The city of Angers is the capital of the province of **Anjou,** located in the western part of France. This province was the home of the Angevin kings of England, the most famous of whom was Richard the Lion-Hearted **(Richard Coeur de Lion: 1157–1199).**

↩ **Le Minitel**
To review information on the **Minitel,** see p. 132.

Talking about past events
Let's talk about what time you did certain things. (Review times, if needed.)

▶ **À quelle heure est-ce que tu as dîné hier?**
J'ai dîné à sept heures et quart.
• **X, à quelle heure est-ce que tu as étudié?**
• **À quelle heure est-ce que tu as téléphoné à des amis?**
• **Y et Z, à quelle heure est-ce que vous avez dîné samedi soir?**
• **À quelle heure est-ce que vous avez regardé la télé?**

Section A

■ **Vocabulary note:** Point out that **adresse** is feminine.

Supplementary vocabulary

au centre-ville *downtown*
dans la banlieue *in the suburbs*
à la campagne *in the country*
dans un immeuble *in an apart-ment house*

■ **Photo culture note**
Le "Vieux Tours"
In the background you see the **Place Plumereau** with its houses dating back to the 16th and 17th centuries. The exposed wooden beams and the steep slate roofs are typical of the period. Since its renovation in the 1960s, this area of Tours with its cafés and outdoor concerts has become very popular with young people.

1 COMMUNICATION:
describing where you live

■ **Language note:** In item 4, help students with numbers.
In France, *P.O. Box* = **B.P. (Boîte postale).**
In Canada, *P.O. Box* = **C.P. (Case postale).**

2 ROLE PLAY:
asking where people live

■ **Expansion:** Ask students questions about the person they were interviewing.
X, où est-ce que Y habite?

Cooperative pair practice
Activity 2

T190

A. Où habites-tu?

▶ *How to talk about where one lives:*

Où habites-tu?
J'habite | à Tours.
à Villeneuve
dans **une grande ville** *(city, town)*
dans **un petit village**
dans **un joli quartier** *(neighborhood)*
dans **une rue** *(street)* intéressante

Quelle est **ton adresse?**
J'habite | 32, **avenue** Victor Hugo.
14, **rue** La Fayette
50, **boulevard** Wilson

J'habite à Tours.

■ **NOTE** ■
CULTURELLE

Le nom des rues

In France, streets are often named after famous people, especially writers, artists, and politicians.

• Victor Hugo (1802–1885), novelist and poet, is best known for his monumental novel *Les Misérables*.
• La Fayette (1757–1834) played an important role in the American and French Revolutions.
• Woodrow Wilson (1856–1924) is remembered as the United States President who sent American troops to help French forces fight against Germany during World War I (1914–1918).

16ᵉ Arrᵗ
AVENUE VICTOR HUGO
(1802–1885)
ECRIVAIN, POÈTE
ET HOMME POLITIQUE

9ᵉ Arrᵗ
RUE LA FAYETTE
1757–1834
HÉROS DE LA GUERRE D'INDÉPENDANCE
AMÉRICAINE DE 1777 À 1782

---

1 Expression personnelle

Describe where you live by completing the following sentences.

1. J'habite à . . .
2. Ma ville est (n'est pas) . . . (grande? petite? moderne? jolie?)
   Mon village est (n'est pas) . . . (grand? petit? joli?)
3. Mon quartier est (n'est pas) . . . (intéressant? joli? moderne?)
4. Mon adresse est . . .
5. Ma ville favorite est . . .
6. Un jour, je voudrais visiter . . . *(name of city)*

2 Interview

You are a French journalist writing an article about living conditions in the United States. Interview a classmate and find out the following information.

1. Where does he/she live?
2. Is his/her city large or small?
3. Is his/her city pretty?
4. What is his/her address?

190 Unité 6

TPR **Places**

PROPS: Vocabulary cards of the places on p. 191: blue borders on masculine nouns, red borders on feminine nouns.

Model nouns as you place them on chalk-tray.
Voici un théâtre. Voici une église. ...

Hold up a picture. [museum card]
Est-ce un café? [non]
Est-ce un musée? [oui]
Ask students to pass cards to classmates.
X, prends le parc et donne-le à Y. ...
Qui a le parc? [Y] ...
Have all students with cards hold them up.
Montrez-nous vos cartes.

B. Ma ville

▶ *How to talk about one's hometown:*

Dans ma rue, il y a . . .

un hôtel   un café   un restaurant   un supermarché   un magasin

Dans mon quartier, il y a . . .

un cinéma   une école   une église   un centre commercial

Dans ma ville, il y a . . .

une bibliothèque   un théâtre   un musée   un hôpital

Il y a aussi . . .

une piscine   un parc   un stade   une plage

Leçon 21   **191**

Section B

COMMUNICATIVE FUNCTION: Identifying places in one's hometown

 21.3 Mini-scenes: Qu'est-ce que c'est? (5:03–6:05 min.)

 Leçon 21, Sections 1, 2, 3

 Transparency 30 Ma ville

▪ **Language note:** Compare:
une église *Catholic church*
un temple (protestant) *Protestant church*
une synagogue *Jewish temple or synagogue*

Supplementary vocabulary

un aéroport *airport*
un collège *junior high school*
un fast-food *fast-food restaurant*
un lycée *senior high school*
un terrain de sport *athletic fields*

une banque *bank*
une boutique *shop*
une gare *(train) station*
une mairie *city hall*
une Maison des jeunes *youth center*
une pharmacie *drugstore*
la poste *post office*
une station-service *gas station*
une université *university*

Note two cards on either side of the room.
Qui a l'hôtel? [X] **Qui a la piscine?** [Z]
Oh là là! L'hôtel est loin de la piscine! [gesture distance]
Note two cards that are close together.
Où est le stade? Où est le parc?
Est-ce que le stade est loin du parc? [non]
Non, le stade est près du parc. ...

If time allows, have students pass around the cards. For example, have X give the hotel card to a student who is near Z.
X, lève-toi et donne l'hôtel à Y.
Et maintenant, est-ce que l'hôtel est loin de la piscine? [non]
L'hôtel est près de la piscine.

3 Ton quartier

Say whether the following places are located in the area where you live. If so, you may want to give the name of the place.

▶ école **Il y a une école. Elle s'appelle «Washington School».**
(Il n'y a pas d'école.)

1. restaurant
2. cinéma
3. église
4. centre commercial
5. bibliothèque

6. café
7. plage
8. supermarché
9. hôpital
10. parc

11. stade
12. musée
13. hôtel
14. piscine
15. théâtre

■ **Teaching strategy:** Be sure students use expressions they have learned in the lesson.

▭▭ **Leçon 21, Section 3**

4 À Montréal

You are visiting your friend Pauline in Montreal. For each of the situations below, decide where you would like to go. Ask Pauline if there is such a place in her neighborhood.

▶ You are hungry.

> Pauline, est-ce qu'il y a un restaurant dans ton quartier?

1. You want to have a soft drink.
2. You want to see a movie.
3. You want to swim a few laps.
4. You want to run on a track.
5. You want to read a book about Canada.
6. You want to see a French play.

7. You want to buy some fruit and crackers.
8. You want to see an art exhibit.
9. You want to play frisbee on the grass.
10. You slipped and you're afraid you sprained your ankle.

■ **Realia note**
Aux Anciens Canadiens is a traditional restaurant in Quebec City. **Le Grill** is located in Montréal. Have students note that prices are given in Canadian dollars (**un dollar canadien**).

aux Anciens Canadiens RESTAURANT

LE GRILL 183 ST-PAUL EST 397-1044
LE BISTROT DU GRILL
LE RESTAURANT
CUISINE FRANÇAISE

• Steak frites
Salade
$5,95

• Poulet rôti
frites, salade
$5,95

CHANSON FRANÇAISE
jeu., ven. et sam.
dès 21h.
AMBIANCE GARANTIE

Atmosphère chaleureuse
Vieille maison du 17e siècle
LA PLUS BELLE TERRASSE DU VIEUX-MONTRÉAL

192 Unité 6

**Cooperative
pair practice**
Activities 4, 5

Teaching note: Sounding French

An aim of Act. 3 is to get students to sound French as they use the new words.

Warm-up: First, have students imagine that they live in a large city. Ask the class:
Est-ce qu'il y a une école?
Oui, il y a une école. ...
Be sure to correct pronunciation problems.

Then ask them to imagine they live in the desert, and have them answer negatively.
Est-ce qu'il y a une école?
Non, il n'y a pas d'école. ...
When they can handle the place names fluently, have students describe the area where they actually live.

C. Pour demander un renseignement (information)

▶ *How to ask for directions:*

Pardon,	monsieur.	Où est l'hôtel Normandie?
Excusez-moi,	madame	
	mademoiselle	

Il est dans la rue Jean Moulin.

Où est-ce qu'il y a un café?

Il y a un café	**rue** Saint Paul.	**une rue**
	boulevard Masséna	**un boulevard**
	avenue de Lyon	**une avenue**

Où est-ce? *(Where is it?)*
Est-ce que c'est **loin** *(far)?*

Non, ce n'est pas loin.
C'est **près** *(nearby).*

C'est	**à gauche** *(to the left).*	**Tournez**	à gauche.
	à droite *(to the right)*		à droite.
	tout droit *(straight ahead)*	**Continuez**	tout droit.

Merci beaucoup!

Pardon, monsieur.
Où est l'hôtel Normandie?

Il est dans
la rue Jean Moulin.

Où est-ce? Est-ce
que c'est loin?

Non, ce n'est pas loin.
C'est près.

5 En ville

A tourist who is visiting a French city asks a
local resident how to get to the following
places. Act out the dialogues.

▶ — Pardon, mademoiselle (monsieur).
  Où est le Café de la Poste?
— Le Café de la Poste? Il est dans la
  rue Pascal.
— Où est-ce?
— Continuez tout droit!
— Merci, mademoiselle
  (monsieur).

1 HÔTEL CONTINENTAL — AVENUE VICTOR HUGO
2 CAFÉ LE BISTRO — RUE SULLY
3 HÔTEL TERMINUS — RUE MOLIÈRE
4 RESTAURANT Chez Jean — AVENUE BELCOUR
5 CINÉMA LUX — RUE MASSÉNA

Leçon 21 193

Section C

COMMUNICATIVE FUNCTION:
Asking for directions

🖥 **21.4 Mini-scenes: Pardon!
Excusez-moi!**
(6:06–6:58 min.)

▶ Leçon 21, Section 4

■ **Cultural notes**
• Jean Moulin (1899–1943) was a
hero of the French resistance
against the Nazi occupation in
World War II.
• Masséna (1758–1817) was one
of Napoléon's marshals.

Supplementary vocabulary

C'est près d'ici.   C'est à côté.
C'est tout près.   C'est en face.
C'est loin d'ici.

5 ROLE PLAY:
asking and giving directions

1. l'hôtel Continental / dans
   l'avenue Victor Hugo / à droite
2. le café «Le Bistro» / dans la
   rue Sully / à gauche
3. l'hôtel Terminus / dans la rue
   Molière / à gauche
4. le restaurant «Chez Jean» /
   dans l'avenue Belcour / tout
   droit
5. le cinéma Lux / dans la rue
   Masséna / à droite

■ **Cultural notes**
• Blaise Pascal (1623–1662),
mathematician and philosopher.
• Duc de Sully (1559–1641),
finance minister of Henri IV.
• Molière (1622–1673), classical
author, writer of comedies.

👥 **Class project**
Have students prepare a map of their city
or neighborhood, marking the various
place names in French.
   Let them use this map for role-play
activities in which they show visitors how
to get around.

21.5 Vignette culturelle:
La maison d'Olivier
(6:59–7:55 min.)

 Leçon 21, Section 5

 Transparency 31
La maison

■ **Pronunciation:** Be sure students do NOT pronounce an "n" in **en haut:** /ã o/. The word **haut** begins with an *aspirate h*. There is never liaison or elision before an *aspirate h*.

■ **Language notes**
• **Les toilettes:** also **les WC** (called **double vécé** or simply **vécé**); or **les cabinets**.
• **Une chambre** is a *room*, in the sense of *bedroom*.
• **Une pièce** is the more general word for *room of a house*.

■ **Cultural notes**
• Traditionally in a French home the toilet is in a small room separate from the bathroom.
• **Un salon** is a traditional formal living room. In modern, less formal homes, one may find **un séjour (une salle de séjour),** also referred to as **un living (un living-room).**
• In French homes, the shutters (**les volets**) are usually closed every night.

Supplementary vocabulary

une entrée
un escalier *staircase*
un ascenseur *elevator*
le toit *roof*
le grenier *attic*
le sous-sol *basement*
la cave *cellar*

T194

D. Ma maison

J'habite dans une maison.

How to describe one's home:

J'habite dans | **une maison** *(house).*
| **un appartement**
| **un immeuble** *(apartment building)*

Ma maison / mon appartement est | **moderne.**
| **confortable**

Ma chambre est | **en haut** *(upstairs).*
| **en bas** *(downstairs)*

La maison

le garage
le jardin
une chambre
une salle de bains
une chambre
les toilettes
une salle de bains
une chambre
la cuisine
les toilettes
la salle à manger
le salon

194 Unité 6

TPR **The house**

PROPS: Transparency 28; magazine pictures of various rooms

Identify the new words on the transparency.
Voici le salon. Voilà la cuisine. …
X, viens ici et montre-nous le jardin. …

Place the magazine pictures on the desk. Have students pick up specific pictures and place themselves around the room.
X, prends le salon et mets-toi près de la porte.
Y, prends la salle à manger et mets-toi devant le tableau noir.

6 Ma maison

Describe your home by completing the following sentences.

1. J'habite dans . . . (une maison? un appartement?)
2. Mon appartement est . . . (grand? petit? confortable? joli?)
   Ma maison est . . . (grande? petite? confortable? jolie?)
3. La cuisine est . . . (grande? petite? moderne?)
4. La cuisine est peinte *(painted)* en . . . (jaune? vert? gris? blanc?   ??)
5. Ma chambre est peinte en . . . (bleu? rose?   ??)
6. Dans le salon, il y a . . . (une télé? un sofa? des plantes vertes?   ??)
7. En général, nous dînons dans . . . (la cuisine? la salle à manger?)
8. Ma maison / mon appartement a . . . (un jardin? un garage?   ??)

APPARTEMENTS PARIS

VUE SUR PARIS
Beau studio avec séj., cuis., s. de b., w-c, cave. 440 000F.

M° ST-PAUL
Exceptionnel dans imm. historique, refaits neufs. 2 p. 75 m

7 En haut ou en bas?

Imagine you live in a two-story house. Indicate where the following rooms are located.

▶ ma chambre

Ma chambre est en haut.

Ma chambre est en bas.

1. la cuisine
2. la salle à manger
3. les toilettes
4. la salle de bains
5. la chambre de mes *(my)* parents
6. le salon

8 Où sont-ils?

From what the following people are doing, guess where they are — in or around the house.

▶ Madame Martin répare *(is repairing)* la voiture.
   Elle est dans le garage.

1. Nous dînons.
2. Tu regardes la télé.
3. Antoine et Juliette jouent au frisbee.
4. J'étudie le français.
5. Monsieur Martin prépare le dîner.
6. Henri se lave *(is washing up)*.
7. Ma soeur téléphone à son copain.

CHAMBRE 2 408 x 290 | CHAMBRE 1 419 x 311
PL.
S. de B 300 x 170 | PL. | SÉJOUR 467 x 436
ENTRÉE
W.-C. | PL. | CUISINE 601 x 170

COMMUNICATION: describing your home

■ **Realia note:** Help students read the ads.
séj. = un séjour *(living room)*
cuis. = une cuisine
s. de b. = salle de bains
w-c *(pronounced /vese/: toilet)*
cave = une cave *(cellar storage area)*
imm. = un immeuble
refaits neufs *(completely remodeled)*
2 p. = 2 pièces *(two rooms)*
75 m² = 75 mètres carrés *(75 square meters or 810 square feet)*

DESCRIPTION: indicating where rooms are located

■ **Language note:** Be sure students use the plural in item 3: Les toilettes **sont...**

COMPREHENSION: describing where people are

■ **Realia note:** Ask questions about the floor plan:
Trouvez l'entrée, le séjour, les deux chambres, la cuisine, la salle de bains, les toilettes (les W-C).
Est-ce qu'il y a aussi des toilettes dans la salle de bains?
Combien de placards *(closets)* y a-t-il?

Once the layout of the house has been set, have other students go to various rooms.
Z, tu as faim. Va à la cuisine.
Qui est dans la cuisine? [Z]
W, tu veux regarder la télé. Va au salon.
V, tu dois te laver les mains [gesture].
Va dans la salle de bains. ...

Cooperative pair practice Activity 7

1 COMPREHENSION

1-e   4-a
2-c   5-b
3-d

🔊 **Leçon 21, Section 6**

2 GUIDED ORAL EXPRESSION

1. Il y a un café avenue de Bordeaux. / C'est près.
2. Il y a un restaurant boulevard de la République. / C'est près (c'est loin).
3. Il y a une église rue Saint-Louis. / C'est près.
4. Il y a un supermarché rue Pascal. / C'est près (c'est loin).
5. Il y a une bibliothèque avenue de Bordeaux. / C'est très près.
6. Il y a un stade avenue de Bordeaux. / C'est loin.
7. Il y a une piscine rue Jean Moulin. / C'est loin.
8. Il y a un cinéma rue Danton. / C'est près.
9. Il y a un hôpital avenue de Bordeaux. / C'est loin.

🔊 **Leçon 21, Section 7**

3 GUIDED ORAL EXPRESSION

🔊 **Leçon 21, Section 8**

À votre tour!

1 La bonne réponse

Match the questions on the left with the appropriate answers on the right.

1. Pardon, mademoiselle, où est le supermarché?
2. Est-ce que Jacques est à la bibliothèque?
3. Ta voiture est au garage?
4. Est-ce que vous dînez dans la salle à manger?
5. Est-ce qu'il y a une piscine dans la ville où tu habites?

a. Non, dans la cuisine.
b. Non, mais il y a une belle plage.
c. Oui, il regarde des magazines anglais.
d. Non, elle est dans la rue.
e. C'est tout droit!

2 Créa-dialogue

You have just arrived in Villeneuve, where you will spend the summer. Ask a pedestrian where you can find the places represented by the symbols. He (She) will give you the location of each place, according to the map on page 197.

▶ —Pardon, monsieur (madame). Où est-ce qu'il y a un hôtel?
—Il y a un hôtel avenue de Bordeaux.
—Est-ce que c'est loin?
—Non, c'est près.
—Merci beaucoup!

3 Où est-ce?

Now you have been in Villeneuve for several weeks and are familiar with the city. You meet a tourist on the avenue de Bordeaux at the place indicated on the map. The tourist asks you where certain places are and you indicate how to get there.

▶ l'hôpital Sainte Anne

Pardon, monsieur. Où est l'hôpital Sainte Anne?

C'est tout droit, mademoiselle.

Merci bien, monsieur.

196 Unité 6

À votre tour

Select those activities which are most appropriate for your students.

🔊 Cooperative practice
In Act. 2 and 3, you may want to have students work cooperatively in trios, with two performing and one consulting the Answer Key and acting as monitor.

■ Portfolio assessment

You will probably select only one speaking activity and one writing activity to go into the students' portfolios for Unit 6.

In this lesson, Act. 5 offers an excellent writing portfolio topic.

Villeneuve

musée La Salle

piscine municipale

magasin de sport

boulevard de la République

rue Jean Moulin

rue du Commerce

restaurant Le Matador

stade

avenue de Bordeaux

rue Danton

rue Jean Moulin

Ciné-Rex

Café Dupont

hôtel Armor

hôpital Sainte Anne

rue Danton

rue Pascal

boulevard de la République

bibliothèque municipale

avenue de Bordeaux

Église St-Louis

supermarché Casino

rue Saint-Louis

rue Danton

parc de la ville

Vous êtes ici.

 4 **Mon quartier**

Describe your neighborhood, listing five places and giving their names.

▶ **Dans mon quartier, il y a un supermarché. C'est le supermarché Casino.**

1. le musée La Salle
2. le supermarché Casino
3. l'hôtel Armor
4. le restaurant Le Matador
5. l'église Saint Louis

 5 **Composition: La maison idéale**

Briefly describe your dream house. You may use the following adjectives to describe the various rooms: **grand, petit, moderne, confortable, joli,** as well as colors. If you wish, sketch and label a floor plan.

Modernes et confortables . . .
SUPERBES VILLAS
à partir de 995.000 F
Près toutes commodités
Écoles, lycées, commerces, R.E.R. à 10 mn.

Leçon 21 **197**

4 WRITTEN SELF-EXPRESSION

5 WRITTEN SELF-EXPRESSION

■ **Realia notes**
- **Une villa** is a newer house built in the suburbs of the larger cities. It usually has a small yard or garden.
- **Le R.E.R. (Réseau Express Régional** or Regional Express Network) is a rapid train system that connects Paris and its suburbs.
- Vocabulary:
  à partir de 995.000F *prices begin at 995,000 francs*
  commerces *shops*
  à 10 mn. *10 minutes away*

Challenge activities: Villeneuve

If appropriate, you can introduce additional challenge activities using the map of Villeneuve.

Have students give more complex directions, using **continuez tout droit, tournez à gauche dans la rue Pascal, ...**

Getting around: Have students give directions from one place to the next, e.g., from **l'hôtel Armor** to **le musée La Salle**, from **le musée** to **le supermarché**, etc.

Mystery destination: Tell students that they are at place "x" on the map. Give them instructions in French to get to a new location. **Maintenant, où êtes-vous?**

T197

Leçon 22

MAIN TOPICS:

**Going to places
Talking about future plans**

MODULE 22:
Une promenade en ville
Total time: 6:35 min.
(Counter: 8:04 min.)

■ **Comprehension practice:** Play the entire module through as an introduction to the lesson.

⊡⊡ Leçon 22, Section 1

■ **Teaching strategy**
• Have students read the cultural notes and look at the photographs.
• Then have students close their books and play the cassette recording of the opening text.
• Ask them to try to remember words and phrases from the text they just heard. Write these on the board.

LEÇON 22

Weekend à Paris

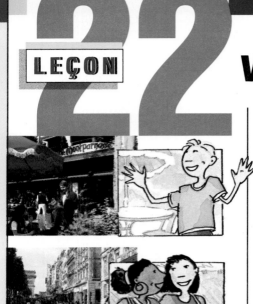

Aujourd'hui c'est samedi.
Les élèves <u>ne vont pas</u> en classe.   *are not going*
Où est-ce qu'ils vont alors?
Ça dépend!

Thomas <u>va</u> au café.   *is going*
Il a un <u>rendez-vous</u> avec une copine.   *date*

Florence et Karine vont aux
Champs-Élysées.
Elles vont regarder les magasins
de <u>mode</u>.   *fashion*
<u>Après</u>, elles vont <u>aller</u> au cinéma.   *Afterward / to go*

Daniel va <u>chez son</u> copain Laurent.   *to the house of / M*
Les garçons vont jouer au ping-pong.
Après, ils vont aller au musée des
sciences de la Villette.
Ils vont jouer avec les machines
électroniques.

Béatrice a un grand sac et des
<u>lunettes de soleil</u>.   *sunglasses*
Est-ce qu'elle va à un rendez-vous
secret?
Non! Elle va au Centre Pompidou.
Elle va regarder les acrobates.
Et après, elle va écouter un concert.

Et Jean-François? Qu'est-ce qu'il va
faire aujourd'hui?
Est-ce qu'il va visiter le Centre Pompidou?
Est-ce qu'il va regarder les acrobates?
Est-ce qu'il va écouter un concert?
<u>Hélas</u>, non!   *Alas (Unfortunat*
Il va <u>rester</u> à la maison.   *to stay*
Pourquoi? Parce qu'il est <u>malade</u>.   *sick*
<u>Pauvre</u> Jean-François!   *Poor*
Il fait <u>si</u> beau <u>dehors</u>!   *so / outside*

198 Unité 6

Talking about past events

Let's talk about where you have been recently. Note that the past participle of **être** is **été**.

▶ **Est-ce que tu as été en ville le
weekend dernier?
Oui, j'ai été en ville.
(Non, je n'ai pas été en ville.)**

• **Est-ce que tu as été à la piscine samedi?**
• **Est-ce que tu as été à la bibliothèque?**
• **Est-ce que tu as été au centre commercial? au musée? au parc?**
• **Est-ce que tu as été au théâtre samedi soir?**
• **Est-ce que tu as été à l'hôpital?**
• **Où est-ce que tu as été dimanche dernier?**

Compréhension

1. Quel jour est-ce aujourd'hui?
2. Pourquoi est-ce que Thomas va au café?
3. Avec qui est-ce que Florence va au cinéma?
4. Où va Daniel?
5. Qu'est-ce que Daniel et Laurent font d'abord *(first)*?
6. Où va Béatrice?
7. Pourquoi est-ce que Jean-François ne va pas en ville?
8. Quel temps fait-il aujourd'hui?

■ NOTE ■ CULTURELLE

À Paris

Paris offers many attractions for people of all ages. Here are some places particularly popular with young people.

Le parc de la Villette

This spacious park on the outskirts of Paris is home to a new modern science museum with its hundreds of hands-on exhibits. Also located on the grounds is Le Zénith, a large music hall that frequently features rock concerts.

Le Centre Pompidou

This immense cultural center, also known as Beaubourg, is dedicated to modern art. It has a large media library where young people have access to all types of audio-visual equipment. On the large plaza in front of the building, one can listen to reggae and jazz bands or watch mimes, jugglers, and acrobats.

Les Champs-Élysées

The Champs-Élysées is a wide avenue with elegant shops, movie theaters, and popular cafés.

199

COMPREHENSION

1. samedi
2. Il a un rendez-vous avec une copine.
3. avec Karine
4. chez son copain Laurent
5. Ils jouent au ping-pong.
6. au Centre Pompidou
7. Il est malade.
8. Il fait très beau.

Critical thinking activity
Write on the chalkboard:
Elles vont aux Champs-Élysées.
Elles vont regarder les magasins.
Ask: How would you express these sentences in English?
In which sentence does **vont** mean that the girls are actually going to *a place?* Is the place mentioned?
In which sentence does **vont** mean that the girls are going to *do something?* Is the activity mentioned?
Read the opening text and look for examples of **va** and **vont**.
Which ones refer to movement?
Which ones refer to future activities?

Note culturelle

■ **Photo culture notes**
À Paris
- **La Cité des Sciences** in the **parc de la Villette.** In the background you see a large steel sphere, **La Géode**, which houses the Omni theater and its circular panoramic screen.
- **Le Centre Pompidou**, seen in the background, was named in honor of Georges Pompidou who was President of France (1969–1974).
In the foreground is the **Fontaine Igor Stravinski.** Note the colorful sculptures which Niki de Saint-Phalle designed to evoke Stravinsky's music such as "The Firebird" (**L'Oiseau de feu**).
- The Champs-Élysées is also the scene of the **Défilé** *(parade)* **du Quatorze Juillet** and the **Arrivée** *(finish)* **du Tour de France** bicycle race.

TPR ⚡ Visiting Paris
PROPS: 3 signs that read
"Le Parc de la Villette"
"Le Centre Pompidou"
"Les Champs-Élysées"

Place the signs around the classroom.
Voici le Parc de la Villette. etc.
(Pronunciation: Villette /vilɛt/)

Have students go to these places.
X, lève-toi et va aux Champs-Élysées.
Où va X? Il va aux Champs-Élysées
Y et Z, allez au Centre Pompidou.
Où vont Y et Z? aux Champs-Élysées?
[non] **Ils vont au Centre Pompidou. ...**
Follow-up questions:
Où est X? Qu'est-ce qu'il va visiter?

■ **Language note:** Remind students of the elision (with **ne**) in the negative forms:
nous n'allons pas
vous n'allez pas

■ **Language usage:** The verb **aller** is usually accompanied by a word or phrase indicating a place. (After the verb *to go* in English, the place is often left out.) Compare:
Quand est-ce que tu vas à Paris?
When are you going to Paris?
Je vais à Paris en mai.
I am going (to Paris) in May.

■ **Pronunciation:** Be sure that students use liaison in **vas-y** and **allons-y.**

■ **Vocabulary expansion**
When speaking to several people:
Allez-y!
Allez-vous-en!

Note also:
On y va! *Let's go!*

A. Le verbe *aller*

Aller *(to go)* is the only IRREGULAR verb that ends in **-er.** Note the forms of **aller** in the present tense.

aller	to go	J'aime **aller** au cinéma.
je **vais**	*I go, I am going*	Je **vais** à un concert.
tu **vas**	*you go, you are going*	**Vas**-tu à la boum?
il/elle **va**	*he/she goes, he/she is going*	Paul **va** à l'école.
nous **allons**	*we go, we are going*	Nous **allons** au café.
vous **allez**	*you go, you are going*	Est-ce que vous **allez** là-bas?
ils/elles **vont**	*they go, they are going*	Ils ne **vont** pas en classe.

→ Remember that **aller** is used in asking people how they feel.

Ça **va?**   Oui, ça **va.**
Comment **vas**-tu?   Je **vais** bien, merci.
Comment **allez**-vous?   Très bien.

→ **Aller** is used in many common expressions.

To encourage someone to do something: To tell someone to go away:
Vas-y! *Come on! Go ahead! Do it!*   **Va-t'en!** *Go away!*

To tell friends to start doing something:
Allons-y! *Let's go!*

Teaching note: Listening activities

A. Review gestures for the subject pronouns (see Lesson 15, TPR activity, p. 110). Make statements about where people are going; have students identify the subject.
   Il va au stade.
   [signal **il/elle**]
   Elles vont au cinéma.
   [signal **ils/elles**] …

B. On the board, write **aller/avoir/être/faire.** Make statements using the four verbs. Students say which one they heard.
   Mes amis sont à Tours. [être]
   Ils ont des vélos. [avoir]
   Ils font une promenade. [faire]
   Ils vont à la piscine. [aller]
   Ils vont nager. [aller] …

1 Les vacances

The following students at a boarding school in Nice are going home for vacation. Indicate to which of the cities they are going, according to the luggage tags shown below.

▶ Jean-Michel est canadien.

an-Michel va à Québec.

1. Je suis suisse.
2. Charlotte est américaine.
3. Nous sommes italiens.
4. Tu es français.
5. Vous êtes espagnols.
6. Michiko est japonaise.
7. Mike et Shelley sont anglais.
8. Ana et Carlos sont mexicains.

2 Jamais le dimanche!
(Never on Sunday!)

On Sundays, French students do not go to class. They all go somewhere else. Express this according to the model.

▶ Philippe/au cinéma
Le dimanche, Philippe ne va pas en classe.
Il va au cinéma.

1. nous / au café
2. vous / en ville
3. Céline et Michèle / à un concert
4. Jérôme / au restaurant
5. je / à un match de foot
6. tu / à la piscine

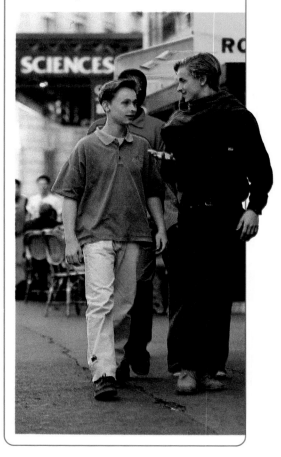

Leçon 22 201

1 COMPREHENSION: telling people what cities to go to

1. Genève
2. Chicago
3. Rome
4. Lyon
5. Madrid
6. Tokyo
7. Londres
8. Acapulco

↩ **Re-entry and review:** Adjectives of nationality (from Lesson 19).

■ **Challenge:** Let students name another city in the appropriate country.
Jean-Michel va à Montréal.

2 PRACTICE: describing where people are going/not going

Classroom Notes

☀ Warm-up: Cities and nationalities

Review nationalities, with books closed.
Indicate where people live, and have students give their nationalities. First use masculine singular subjects.
Henri habite à Paris. [Il est français.]
Bill habite à Boston. [Il est américain.]
Practice with the cities of Act. 1.

Then continue with feminine singular subjects.
Marie habite à Genève. [Elle est suisse.]
Finally practice with plural subjects.
Tatsuo et Michiko habitent à Kyoto. [Ils sont japonais.]
Sally et Susie habitent à Liverpool. [Elles sont anglaises.]

22.1 Mini-scenes: Où allez-vous?
22.2 Mini-scenes: Où est-ce que tu vas?
(8:34–9:30 min.)

🔲 **Leçon 22, Sections 2, 3**

■ **Teaching note:** Be sure students realize that the words in heavy print in the three columns on the right correspond to *the, at the,* and *to the.*

■ **Teaching note:** You may want to point out the use of **à** with certain verbs.
téléphoner à:
Je téléphone à Pierre.
Je téléphone au professeur.
jouer à:
Je joue au tennis.
Nous jouons à la balle.

EXCHANGES: asking where
3 people are going

1. au stade/à la piscine
2. au cinéma/au théâtre
3. à l'hôtel/au supermarché
4. à la bibliothèque/au musée
5. à l'école/au parc

B. La préposition *à; à* + l'article défini

The preposition **à** has several meanings:

in	Patrick habite **à** Paris.	*Patrick lives **in** Paris.*
at	Nous sommes **à** la piscine.	*We are **at** the pool.*
to	Est-ce que tu vas **à** Toulouse?	*Are you going **to** Toulouse?*

CONTRACTIONS

Note the forms of **à** + DEFINITE ARTICLE in the sentences below.

Voici **le** café.	Marc est **au** café.	Corinne va **au** café.
Voici **les** Champs-Élysées.	Tu es **aux** Champs-Élysées.	Je vais **aux** Champs-Élysées.
Voici **la** piscine.	Anne est **à la** piscine.	Éric va **à la** piscine.
Voici **l'**hôtel.	Je suis **à l'**hôtel.	Vous allez **à l'**hôtel.

The preposition **à** contracts with **le** and **les,** but not with **la** and **l'.**

CONTRACTION	NO CONTRACTION		
à + le → **au**	à + la = **à la**	**au** cinéma	**à la** piscine
à + les → **aux**	à + l' = **à l'**	**aux** Champs-Élysées	**à l'**école

→ There is liaison after **aux** when the next word begins with a vowel sound.
Le professeur parle **aux élèves.** Je téléphone **aux amis** de Claire.

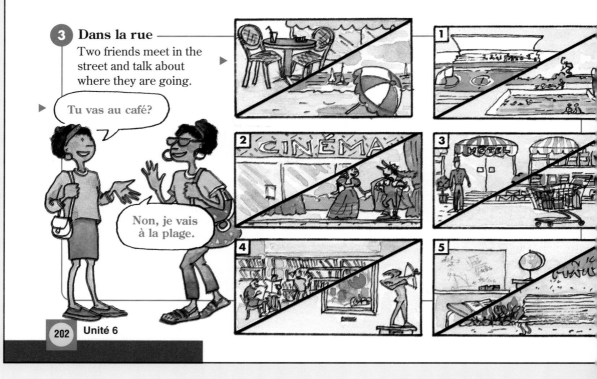

3 **Dans la rue**
Two friends meet in the street and talk about where they are going.

▶ Tu vas au café?

Non, je vais à la plage.

202 **Unité 6**

Cooperative pair practice
Activities 3, 4, 5

Teaching note: Additional practice

Although contractions are not hard to learn, students often fail to use them in conversation. Sometimes extra drill practice helps them internalize the patterns.

Je suis au café.
(le cinéma) **Je suis au cinéma.**

(la piscine)	**Je suis à la piscine.**
(l'hôpital)	**Je suis à l'hôpital.**
(le stade)	**Je suis au stade.**
(l'appartement)	**Je suis à l'appartement.**
(le musée)	**Je suis au musée.**
(la maison)	**Je suis à la maison.**
(le restaurant)	**Je suis au restaurant.**

4 Préférences

Ask your classmates about their preferences. Be sure to use contractions when needed.

▶ aller à (le concert ou le théâtre?)

1. dîner à (la maison ou le restaurant)?
2. étudier à (la bibliothèque ou la maison)?
3. nager à (la piscine ou la plage)?
4. regarder un match de foot à (la télé ou le stade)?
5. aller à (le cinéma ou le musée)?

Tu préfères aller au concert ou au théâtre?

Je préfère aller au concert.

(Je préfère aller au théâtre.)

5 À Paris

You are living in Paris. A friend asks you where you are going and why. Act out the dialogues with a classmate.

▶ —Où vas-tu?
—Je vais à l'Opéra.
—Pourquoi?
—Parce que j'aime le ballet classique.

OÙ?	POURQUOI?
▶ l'Opéra	J'aime le ballet classique.
1. l'Alliance Française	J'ai une classe de français.
2. le Centre Pompidou	J'aime l'art moderne.
3. le musée d'Orsay	C'est un musée intéressant.
4. les Champs-Élysées	J'ai un rendez-vous là-bas.
5. la tour Eiffel	Il y a une belle vue *(view)* sur Paris.
6. le Zénith	Il y a un concert de rock.
7. la Villette	Il y a une exposition *(exhibit)* intéressante.
8. le stade de Bercy	Il y a un match de foot.

6 Où vont-ils?

Read what the following people like to do. Then say where each one is going by choosing the appropriate place from the list.

▶ Daniel aime danser.
Il va à la discothèque.

1. Corinne aime l'art moderne.
2. Jean-François aime manger.
3. Delphine aime les westerns.
4. Marina aime nager.
5. Éric aime regarder les magazines.
6. Denise aime faire des promenades.
7. Philippe aime la musique.
8. Alice aime le football.
9. Cécile aime le shopping.

le stade
la bibliothèque
le cinéma
le centre commercial
la discothèque
le musée
le parc
le restaurant
la plage
le concert

ENTRÉE MUSEE   R1 20-06   14F0 004635
Réunion des musées nationaux
LOUVRE
droit d'entrée

Leçon 22   **203**

COMMUNICATION: expressing preferences

4

■ **Expansion:** Additional cues:
aller à (le musée ou la bibliothèque)?
aller à (le café ou le restaurant)?
aller à (l'école ou le parc)?

EXCHANGES: explaining why one goes somewhere

5

■ **Teaching note:** Have students find these places on the map of Paris in the photo essay on p. 237.

■ **Cultural background: L'Opéra**
There are two opera buildings in Paris:
L'Opéra Garnier, the old opera house, now home of the Paris ballet.
L'Opéra de la Bastille, concert hall built in 1989, home of the Paris opera. (See ticket on p. 204.)

COMPREHENSION: concluding where people are going

6

 22.3 Mini-scenes: Où vont-ils? (9:31–10:35 min.)

 Leçon 22, Section 4

T203

■ **Language note:** The word **rendez-vous** includes all types of appointments with friends, teachers, as well as professional appointments with doctors, dentists, etc. The term means that people have arranged to meet somewhere.

Supplementary vocabulary

---

une exposition *exhibit*

22.7 Vignette culturelle:
Le métro
(13:14–14:36 min.)

Transparency 33
Means of transportation

■ **Language notes**
• **Un bus (un autobus)** is a city bus that follows a regular route.
• An intercity or tour bus is **un car** or **un autocar.**
• A school bus is **un car scolaire.**

■ **Realia note**
Have the students look at the Opera ticket (**le billet**).
Quelle est la date du concert?
[le 19 mai]
Quel jour de la semaine est-ce?
[samedi]
À quelle heure est le concert?
[20 heures = 8 heures du soir]
Qui chante? [Montserrat Caballé]
Combien coûte le billet? [170 F]

Vocabulaire:
la porte *door*   **le rang** *row*
l'allée *aisle*   **la place** *seat*
parterre *orchestra (seating)*

COMMUNICATION:
answering personal
questions

■ **Photo culture note**
Le Lycée Corot
The students are at the entrance to the lycée. (For more on this school, see pages 76–81.)

T204

Vocabulaire: En ville

Quelques endroits où aller

un endroit	place	une boum	party
un concert	concert		
un film	movie		
un pique-nique	picnic		
un rendez-vous	date, appointment		

VERBES

arriver	to arrive, come	J'arrive à l'école à 9 heures.
rentrer	to go back, come back	À quelle heure **rentres**-tu à la maison?
rester	to stay	Les touristes **restent** à l'hôtel.

EXPRESSIONS

à pied	on foot	en voiture	by car	en métro	by subway
à vélo	by bicycle	en bus	by bus	en taxi	by taxi
		en train	by train		

faire une promenade à pied	to go for a walk
faire une promenade à vélo	to go for a ride (by bike)
faire une promenade en voiture	to go for a drive

7 Questions personnelles

1. En général, à quelle heure est-ce que tu arrives à l'école?
2. À quelle heure est-ce que tu rentres à la maison? Qu'est-ce que tu fais quand tu rentres à la maison?
3. Comment vas-tu à l'école? à pied, à vélo, en voiture ou en bus?
4. Le weekend, est-ce que tu restes à la maison? Où vas-tu?
5. Comment vas-tu à la piscine? à la plage? au cinéma?
6. Est-ce que tu aimes faire des promenades à pied? Où vas-tu? avec qui?
7. Est-ce que tu aimes faire des promenades à vélo? Où vas-tu?
8. En général, est-ce que tu aimes regarder les films à la télé? Quels films est-ce que tu préfères? (films d'action? films de science-fiction? comédies?)
9. Quand tu as un rendez-vous avec un copain ou une copine, où allez-vous?
10. Est-ce que tu fais *(go on)* des pique-niques? où?

Talking about past events

Let's talk about where you went yesterday. We will use the passé composé of **aller**:

> present of **être** + **allé(e)**

(Note: since the focus is on spoken French, there is no need to introduce the agreement of the past participle at this time.)

▶ **Est-ce que tu es allé(e) en ville hier?**
Oui, je suis allé(e) en ville.
(Non, je ne suis pas allé(e) en ville.)

• **X, est-ce que tu es allé(e) au cinéma hier? à l'école? au supermarché?**

C. La préposition *chez*

Note the use of **chez** in the following sentences.

Paul est **chez Céline**.	*Paul is **at Céline's (house)**.*
Je dîne **chez un copain**.	*I am having dinner **at a friend's (home)**.*
Nathalie va **chez Juliette**.	*Nathalie is going **to Juliette's (apartment)**.*
Tu vas **chez ta cousine**.	*You are going **to your cousin's (place)**.*

The French equivalent of *to* or *at someone's (house, home)* is the construction:

chez + PERSON	**chez** Béatrice	**chez** ma cousine

➡ Note the interrogative expression: **chez qui?**

    Chez qui vas-tu?   ***To whose house** are you going?*

---

8 En vacances

When we are on vacation, we often like to visit friends and relatives. Say where the following people are going.

▶ Claire / Marc
   Claire va chez Marc.

1. Hélène / Jérôme
2. Jean-Paul / Lucie
3. tu / un copain
4. Corinne / une cousine
5. vous / des copines à Québec
6. nous / un cousin à Paris

Chez nous... l'argent va plus loin avec le train!

SNCF

9 Weekend

On weekends, we often like to visit friends and do things together. Say how the following people are spending Sunday afternoon.

▶ Cécile / jouer au ping-pong / Robert

Cécile joue au ping-pong chez Robert.

1. Nathalie / aller / Béatrice
2. Claire / dîner / des cousins
3. Éric / jouer au croquet / Sylvie
4. Marc / écouter des disques / un copain
5. Jean-Pierre / regarder la télé / une copine
6. Catherine / jouer au Monopoly / François

Leçon 22 205

22.4 Mini-scenes: Qu'est-ce que vous allez faire?

22.5 Mini-scenes: Tu vas nager?
(10:26–12:22 min.)

Leçon 22, Sections 5, 6

■ **Casual speech:** One can also say: **Vous allez rentrer quand?** Note that **Tu vas faire quoi?** is less common than **Qu'est-ce que tu vas faire?**

10 DESCRIPTION: describing destinations and plans

■ **Cultural notes**
- The coliseum (**la Colisée**) is a large stadium built by the Romans.
- The **Vieux Carré** is the part of the French Quarter known for its jazz clubs and its picturesque old buildings with wrought iron balconies.
- Historically, Kyoto was the capital of Japan; one can still visit the many Buddhist temples there as well as the Emperor's palace.

■ **Realia note:** These are two folding brochures (**un dépliant**), one for **Le Louvre** (the famous Paris art museum), and the other for the Mediterranean village of **Sanary**.

Cooperative pair practice
Activity 11

T206

D. La construction *aller* + l'infinitif

The following sentences describe what people are *going to do*. Note how the verb **aller** is used to describe these FUTURE events.

Nathalie **va nager.** *Nathalie is going to swim.*
Paul et Marc **vont jouer** au tennis. *Paul and Marc are going to play tennis.*
Nous **allons rester** à la maison. *We are going to stay home.*
Je **vais aller** en ville. *I am going to go downtown.*

To express the NEAR FUTURE, the French use the construction:

> PRESENT of **aller** + INFINITIVE

→ In negative sentences, the construction is:

SUBJECT	+ **ne** +	PRESENT of **aller**	+ **pas** +	INFINITIVE . . .
Sylvie	**ne**	va	**pas**	écouter le concert avec nous.

→ Note the interrogative forms:

Qu'est-ce que tu vas faire? ***What are you going** to do?*
Quand est-ce que vous allez rentrer? ***When are you going** to come back?*

Learning about language
To talk about FUTURE plans and intentions, French and English frequently use similar verbs: **aller** *(to be going to).*

10 **Tourisme**
Say where the following people are going this summer and what they are going to visit.

▶ Monique (à Paris / le Louvre)
Monique va à Paris. Elle va visiter le Louvre.

1. Alice (à New York / la statue de la Liberté)
2. nous (en Égypte / les pyramides)
3. vous (à Rome / le Colisée)
4. tu (à la Nouvelle Orléans / le Vieux Carré)
5. je (à San Francisco / Chinatown)
6. les élèves (à San Antonio / l'Alamo)
7. Madame Lambert (à Beijing / la Cité interdite [*Forbidden City*])
8. les touristes (à Kyoto / les temples)

11 **Qu'est-ce que tu vas faire?**

Ask your classmates if they are going to do the following things this weekend.

▶ étudier

Est-ce que tu vas étudier?

Oui, je vais étudier.

(Non, je ne vais pas étudier.)

1. travailler
2. écouter la radio
3. regarder la télé
4. nager
5. inviter des amis
6. aller à une boum
7. jouer au tennis
8. rester à la maison
9. faire une promenade à vélo

12 **Un jeu: Descriptions**

Choose a person from Column A and say where the person is, what he or she has, and what he or she is going to do. Use the verbs **être, avoir,** and **aller** with the phrases in columns B, C, and D. How many logical descriptions can you make?

A	B (être)	C (avoir)	D (aller)
tu	sur le court	des livres	chanter
Monique	à la bibliothèque	un vélo	manger un sandwich
je	au salon	30 francs	étudier
les amis	en vacances	une télé	faire une promenade
nous	à la boum	une chaîne stéréo	regarder un film
vous	à la maison	une guitare	faire un match
	au café	une raquette	écouter des cassettes

▶ Monique est en vacances. Elle a un vélo. Elle va faire une promenade.

Prononciation	/w/	/j/

Les semi-voyelles /w/ et /j/

In French, the semi-vowels /w/ and /j/ are pronounced very quickly, almost like consonants.

Répétez:

/w/ **oui chouette Louise**

/wa/, /wɛ̃/ **moi toi pourquoi voiture loin**
Chouette! La voiture de Louise n'est pas loin.

/j/ **bien chien radio piano Pierre Daniel violon pied étudiant**
Pierre écoute la radio avec Daniel.

oui

très bien

Leçon 22 **207**

---

11 EXCHANGES: talking about weekend plans

■ **Variation** (with **vous** and **nous**):
– Est-ce que vous allez étudier?
– Oui, nous allons étudier.
  (Non, nous n'allons pas étudier.)

■ **Teaching strategy:** Act. 11 may be conducted as a classroom survey. See *Game: Getting acquainted* on p. T122.

22.6 Dialogue: Julien travaille (12:23–13:13 min.)

Leçon 22, Section 7

12 DESCRIPTION: describing people and their plans

↺ **Re-entry and review:** This activity reviews the forms of **être, avoir,** and **aller.**

Prononciation

Leçon 22, Section 8

■ **Pronunciation notes**
• Be sure students pronounce the /j/ very quickly.
  The following words should sound like two (and not three) syllables:
  pia-no   Da-niel
  ra-dio   vio-lon
  These words are pronounced in one syllable:
  Pierre /pjɛr/
  pied /pje/
• You may want to present the other French semi vowel /ɥ/, which is not formally introduced at this level: It is spelled **u** + vowel, as in **lui, suis, juillet** and **aujourd'hui.**

Game: Un jeu

Act. 12 can be done as a team game. Divide the class into groups of 3 or 4 students. Have each group take out a sheet of paper and choose a recorder (**un/une secrétaire**). As the group creates a description, the recorder will write it down.

Give a signal for the groups to start. At the end of the time limit, stop the groups.

Have them exchange papers (Group 1 passes its paper to Group 2, Group 2 to Group 3, etc.).

Each group checks the paper it received for accuracy and records the number of correct and logical descriptions. The group with the highest score wins.

À votre tour!

1 COMPREHENSION

1-d   3-b
2-c   4-a

Leçon 22, Section 9

2 GUIDED ORAL EXPRESSION

1. au café / manger une pizza
2. au parc / faire une promenade
3. au stade / jouer au foot
4. à la piscine / nager
5. à la plage / jouer au volley
6. au supermarché / travailler
7. au centre commercial /
   (answers will vary)

■ **Teaching strategy:** If students have difficulty with item 7, you may wish to suggest possible activities: **rencontrer des amis, aller dans les magasins, manger un hot-dog,** etc.
(The verb **acheter** is introduced in Lesson 25.)

Leçon 22, Section 10

1 Allô!

Anne is calling Jérôme. Match Jérôme's answers with Anne's questions. Then act out the dialogue with a friend.

1 Tu restes chez toi samedi?

2 Qu'est-ce que vous allez faire?

3 Est-ce que vous allez aller au cinéma?

4 À quelle heure est-ce que tu vas rentrer?

a À dix heures.

b Peut-être! Il y a un très bon film au Rex.

c Nous allons faire une promenade en ville.

d Non, j'ai un rendez-vous avec Christine.

2 Créa-dialogue

As you are going for a walk in town, you meet several friends. Ask them where they are going and what they are going to do there.

OÙ?	ACTIVITÉ
	dîner avec un copain

► —Salut, Alison. Ça va?
—Oui, ça va!
—Où vas-tu?
—Je vais au restaurant.
—Ah bon? Qu'est-ce que tu vas faire là-bas?
—Je vais dîner avec un copain.
—Avec qui?
—Avec Chris.

	OÙ?	ACTIVITÉ
1	CAFÉ	manger une pizza
2		faire une promenade
3		jouer au foot
4		nager
5		jouer au volley
6		travailler
7		??

À votre tour

Select those activities which are most appropriate for your students.

Cooperative practice
Act. 1–3 lend themselves well to cooperative pair practice. For preparation, have the class listen to the corresponding cassette recordings.

■ Portfolio assessment

You will probably select only one speaking activity and one writing activity to go into the students' portfolios for Unit 6.

In this lesson, Act. 2 can be the basis for an oral portfolio dialogue. Act. 5 can be used as a writing portfolio topic.

3 Conversation libre

Have a conversation with a classmate. Ask your classmate questions about what he / she plans to do on the weekend. Try to find out as much as possible, using yes / no questions.

▶

> Est-ce que tu vas rester à la maison?

> Non, je ne vais pas rester à la maison.

> Est-ce que tu vas aller en ville?

> Oui, je vais aller en ville.

> Est-ce que tu vas au cinéma?

> Oui, je vais au cinéma.

(Non, je ne vais pas au cinéma.)

4 Qu'est-ce que vous allez faire?

Leave a note for your friend Jean-Marc, telling him three things that you and your friends are going to do tonight and three things that you are going to do this weekend.

Jean-Marc

Ce soir (Tonight)
1. Nous allons....
2.
3.
Ce weekend
1.
2.
3.

5 Bonnes résolutions

Imagine that it is January 1 and you are making up New Year's resolutions. On a separate sheet of paper, describe six of your resolutions by saying what you are going to do and what you are not going to do in the coming year.

▶

1 JANVIER

1. Je vais toujours parler français en classe.
2. Je ne vais pas être pénible avec mes copains...

Leçon 22 **209**

3 CONVERSATION

4 WRITTEN SELF-EXPRESSION

5 WRITTEN SELF-EXPRESSION

Classroom Notes

👥 Cooperative reading and writing practice

Have all students prepare Act. 5 as homework. Then, divide the class into groups of 4.

Ask students to share their lists of resolutions with those in their group. Then have each group compare the 4 lists and vote on the 6 best resolutions.

The recorder (**le/la secrétaire**) rewrites the 6 resolutions in the **nous**-form.
1. **Nous allons toujours parler français en classe.**
2. **Nous n'allons pas être pénibles avec nos copains.** etc.

The reporter (**le reporter**) will read the group's list to the rest of the class.

T209

MODULE 23:
Sports et musique
Total time: 5:11 min.
(Counter: 14:59 min.)

23.1 Mini-scenes: Listening — Quels sports est-ce que vous pratiquez? (15:25–15:45 min.)

23.2 Mini-scenes: Listening — Tu veux jouer au volley? (15:46–16:10 min.)

23.3 Mini-scenes: Speaking — Est-ce que Paul joue au tennis? (16:11–17:00 min.)

23.4 Mini-scenes: Listening — De quel instrument est-ce que tu joues? (17:01–17:59 min.)

23.5 Dialogue: Interview avec Éric (18:00–18:33 min.)

23.6 Vignette culturelle: À la Maison des jeunes (18:34–19:56 min.)

■ **Comprehension practice:** Play the entire module through as an introduction to the lesson.

▭▭ Leçon 23, Section 1

LEÇON 23 Au Café de l'Univers

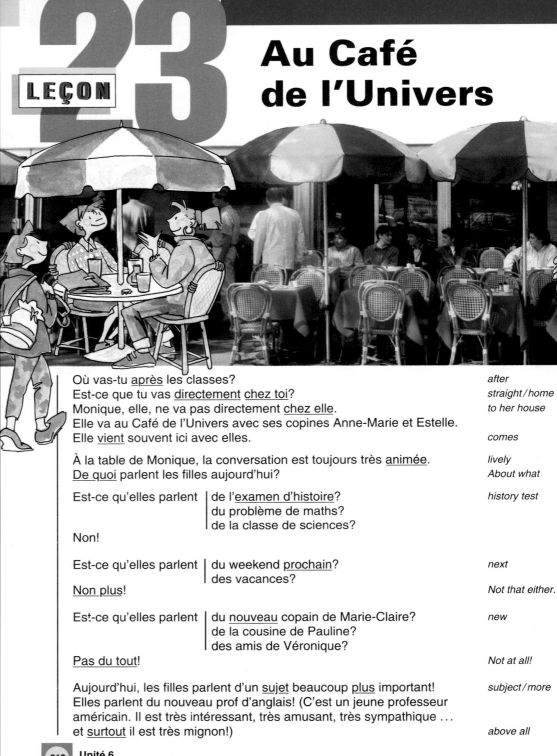

Où vas-tu <u>après</u> les classes?	*after*
Est-ce que tu vas <u>directement</u> <u>chez toi</u>?	*straight/home*
Monique, elle, ne va pas directement <u>chez elle</u>.	*to her house*
Elle va au Café de l'Univers avec ses copines Anne-Marie et Estelle.	
Elle <u>vient</u> souvent ici avec elles.	*comes*
À la table de Monique, la conversation est toujours très <u>animée</u>.	*lively*
<u>De quoi</u> parlent les filles aujourd'hui?	*About what*

Est-ce qu'elles parlent	de l'<u>examen d'histoire</u>?	*history test*
	du problème de maths?	
	de la classe de sciences?	
Non!		

Est-ce qu'elles parlent	du weekend <u>prochain</u>?	*next*
	des vacances?	
<u>Non plus</u>!		*Not that either.*

Est-ce qu'elles parlent	du <u>nouveau</u> copain de Marie-Claire?	*new*
	de la cousine de Pauline?	
	des amis de Véronique?	
<u>Pas du tout</u>!		*Not at all!*

Aujourd'hui, les filles parlent d'un <u>sujet</u> beaucoup <u>plus</u> important!	*subject/more*
Elles parlent du nouveau prof d'anglais! (C'est un jeune professeur américain. Il est très intéressant, très amusant, très sympathique ...	
et <u>surtout</u> il est très mignon!)	*above all*

210 Unité 6

Setting the stage

With books closed, ask students what they talk about when they get together. List the topics (in English) on the board.

Then play the cassette recording of the above text. Have students listen to see what topics of conversation are mentioned in the text.

Which of the topics on the students' list are the same as those mentioned by the speaker? Which are new?

Play the cassette again, and ask them to try to get additional information.

Finally have them open their books and follow along as you play the cassette once more.

Compréhension

1. Où va Monique après les classes?
2. Avec qui est-ce qu'elle va au café?
3. Qu'est-ce que les filles font au café?
4. Est-ce qu'elles parlent de l'école?
5. Est-ce qu'elles parlent des activités du weekend?
6. De quelle *(which)* personne parlent-elles aujourd'hui?
7. De quelle nationalité est le professeur d'anglais?
8. Comment est-il?

Et toi?

Describe what you do by completing the following sentences.

1. En général, après les classes,
   je vais . . .
   je ne vais pas . . .

   - à la bibliothèque
   - chez mes *(my)* copains
   - au café
   - directement chez moi

2. Avec mes copains,
   je parle . . .
   je ne parle pas . . .

   - de la classe de français
   - du prof de français
   - des examens
   - du weekend

3. Avec mes parents,
   je parle . . .
   je ne parle pas . . .

   - de l'école
   - de la classe de français
   - de mes notes *(grades)*
   - de mes copains

4. Avec mon frère ou ma soeur,
   je parle . . .
   je ne parle pas . . .

   - de mes copains
   - du weekend
   - de mes problèmes
   - des vacances

■ NOTE ■ CULTURELLE

Au café

For French teenagers, the café is much more than just a place to have a soft drink or a sandwich. Some go there to study, others go to listen to music, to play electronic games (**le flipper**), or to make a phone call. Most students, however, go to their favorite café after class or on weekends to meet their friends and simply talk.

A French café usually consists of two parts: **l'intérieur** (the indoor section) and **la terrasse** (the outdoor section which often occupies part of the sidewalk). In spring and summer, **la terrasse** is the ideal spot to enjoy the sun and to watch the people passing by.

Leçon 23 211

 COMPREHENSION

1. au Café de l'Univers
2. avec Anne-Marie et Estelle
3. Elles parlent.
4. non
5. non
6. du nouveau prof d'anglais
7. Il est américain.
8. Il est intéressant, amusant, sympathique et... mignon.

COMMUNICATION: describing what one does

■ **Teaching strategy:** Have students raise their hands as you read through the items in **Et toi?** (Note: Read only the affirmative sentences.)
En général, après les classes, qui va à la bibliothèque?
Qui va chez ses copains? etc.

💡 **Critical thinking activity**
Have students give the English equivalents of the following phrases in the dialogue on p. 210.
le nouveau copain de Marie-Claire
[Marie-Claire's new boyfriend]
la cousine de Pauline
[Pauline's cousin]

Ask: Is the word order the same in French and English?
Does French use an apostrophe to express relationship?
What is a word-for-word translation of the French construction?

■ **Looking ahead:** Possession with **de** is formally introduced in Lesson 24.

Talking about past events

Let's talk about where you went Saturday.

▶ **X et Y, est-ce que vous êtes allé(e)s au cinéma samedi soir?**
  Oui, nous sommes allé(e)s au cinéma.
  (Non, nous ne sommes pas allé(e)s au cinéma.)
- **Est-ce que vous êtes allé(e)s en ville? chez des amis? à un concert?**
- **Où êtes-vous allé(e)s samedi matin? samedi après-midi?**

Let's say where others went last weekend.

▶ **Est-ce que X et Y sont allé(e)s au cinéma samedi soir?**
  Oui, ils/elles sont allé(e)s au cinéma.
  (Non, ils/elles ne sont pas allé(e)s au cinéma.)

COMMUNICATIVE FUNCTION:
Saying who is coming

■ **Pronunciation note:** Be sure that students pronounce the third person plural form correctly: **viennent** /vjɛn/.

■ **Language note:** If someone is waiting for you and calls out: **Tu viens?** the usual French response is: **J'arrive** (which means *I'm just about ready and I'm coming*). However, if the person is simply asking if you are planning to join them, the French response is: **Oui, je viens** (which means *Yes I'm coming along with you*).

① EXCHANGES: inviting friends to come along

■ **Challenge:** For negative answers, explain why you cannot come.
Non, je ne viens pas.
Je dois dîner avec Michelle.

② PRACTICE: saying who is coming to an event

A. Le verbe *venir*

The verb **venir** *(to come)* is irregular. Note the forms of **venir** in the present tense.

venir	Nous allons **venir** avec des amis.
je **viens**	Je **viens** avec toi.
tu **viens**	Est-ce que tu **viens** au cinéma?
il / elle **vient**	Monique ne **vient** pas avec nous.
nous **venons**	Nous **venons** à cinq heures.
vous **venez**	À quelle heure **venez**-vous à la boum?
ils / elles **viennent**	Ils **viennent** de Paris, n'est-ce pas?

➡ **Revenir** *(to come back)* is conjugated like **venir**.
   —À quelle heure **revenez**-vous?
   —Nous **revenons** à dix heures.

➡ Note the interrogative expression: **d'où?** *(from where?)*
   D'où viens-tu?   *Where do you come from?*

① Tu viens?

Tell a friend where you are going and ask him or her to come along.

▶ au restaurant

Je vais au restaurant. Tu viens avec moi?

D'accord, je viens.

(Non, je ne viens pas.)

1. au café
2. à la bibliothèque
3. à la piscine
4. au supermarché
5. au centre commercial
6. au magasin de disques
7. au stade
8. en classe

② Le pique-nique de Monique

Monique has invited friends to a picnic. Say who is coming and who is not.

▶ Philippe (non)
Philippe ne vient pas.

1. Alice (oui)
2. Jean-Pierre (non)
3. Paul et Caroline (oui)
4. vous (non)
5. je (oui)
6. nous (non)
7. tu (non)
8. les copines d'Alice (oui)
9. le prof d'anglais (oui)

You may think French verbs are hard to learn because they have several forms. French students, on the other hand, have a hard time with English verbs because so many are made up of two words. For example, they may know the words *get* and *keep*, but then they have to learn the meanings of *get up*, *get out*, *get on*, and these meanings are different from *keep up*, *keep out*, *keep on*, etc.

Cooperative pair practice
Activity 1

Touring Paris

PROPS: Paper and pencils or crayons

Name and sketch on the board four Paris sites:
1. **le Louvre**
2. **la Tour Eiffel**
3. **les Champs-Élysées**
4. **l'Arc de Triomphe**

Have the class count off by four's. Then have each student draw and label a site.
   Si vous avez le numéro 1, dessinez le Louvre.
   Si vous avez le numéro 2, dessinez...
Ask about tourist plans.
   Qui va visiter la Tour Eiffel aujourd'hui?
   Levez le dessin.

B. La préposition *de; de* + l'article défini

The preposition **de** has several meanings:

from	Nous venons **de** la bibliothèque.	*We are coming **from** the library.*
of	Quelle est l'adresse **de** l'école?	*What is the address **of** the school?*
about	Je parle **de** mon copain.	*I am talking **about** my friend.*

CONTRACTIONS

Note the forms of **de** + DEFINITE ARTICLE in the sentences below.

Voici **le** café.	Marc vient **du** café.
Voici **les** Champs-Élysées.	Nous venons **des** Champs-Élysées.
Voici **la** piscine.	Tu reviens **de la** piscine.
Voici **l'**hôtel.	Les touristes arrivent **de l'**hôtel.

The preposition **de** contracts with **le** and **les,** but not with **la** and **l'.**

CONTRACTION	NO CONTRACTION			
de + le → **du**	de + la = **de la**	**du** café	**de la** plage
de + les → **des**	de + l' = **de l'**	**des** magasins	**de l'**école

➡ There is liaison after **des** when the next word begins with a vowel sound.
   Où sont les livres **des** étudiants?
   ‿z

3 **Rendez-vous**

The following students live in Paris. On a Saturday afternoon they are meeting in a café. Say where each one is coming from.

▶ Jacques: le musée d'Orsay

1. Sylvie: le Louvre
2. Isabelle: le parc de la Villette
3. Jean-Paul: le Centre Pompidou
4. François: le Quartier latin
5. Cécile: l'avenue de l'Opéra
6. Nicole: la tour Eiffel
7. Marc: le jardin du Luxembourg
8. André: les Champs-Élysées
9. Pierre: les Galeries Lafayette
10. Corinne: la rue Bonaparte

Jacques vient du musée d'Orsay.

Leçon 23 **213**

Section B

COMMUNICATIVE FUNCTION:
Talking about where people are coming from

■ **Teaching strategy:** Be sure students realize that the words in heavy print in the sentences on the left correspond to *the* and that those in the sentences on the right correspond to *from the.*

 3 PRACTICE: saying where people are coming from

■ **Cultural background:** The **Quartier latin** is the historical students' quarter on the Left Bank. One of the streets is **la rue Bonaparte,** named in honor of Napoleon.
Le jardin du Luxembourg is also in that part of Paris.
Les Galeries Lafayette is a well-known Paris department store.

■ **Teaching strategy:** This exercise should be done quickly with the rhythm of a practice drill. Be sure to read the cues aloud, carefully modeling the pronunciation of the new place names.

■ **Variation:** Repeat the drill, changing the subjects orally.
nous: le musée d'Orsay
Nous venons du musée d'Orsay.

↩ **Re-entry and review:** Say that the people are going to these places.
Jacques va au musée d'Orsay.

Review **aller** and contractions with **à.** Ask each group where they are going.
  Qui va au Louvre?
  [Nous, nous allons au Louvre.]
  Vous allez à l'Arc de Triomphe?
  [Non, nous allons au Louvre!]...
On the board write: **au Louvre, aux Champs-Élysées, à la Tour Eiffel, à l'Arc de Triomphe.**

Practice **venir** and contractions with **de.**
  Qui vient des Champs-Élysées?
  [Moi, je viens des Champs-Élysées.]
  Et X, est-ce qu'il vient des Champs-Élysées?
  [Non, il vient de la Tour Eiffel.] ...
On the board write: **du Louvre, des Champs-Élysées, de la Tour Eiffel, de l'Arc de Triomphe.**

ROLE PLAY: finding out where people are coming from

4

▷ Vocabulaire

Module 23
Sports et musique
(14:59–19:57 min.)

▭ **Leçon 23, Sections 2–6**

Language notes
- **Le foot (le football)** is soccer; American football is **le football américain.**
- **Language note:** In the expressions **jouer du piano** and **jouer de la flûte, du** and **de la** represent the preposition **de** plus a definite article. Therefore, in the negative one does not use **de.** Compare:
  Je n'ai pas de clarinette.
  Je ne joue pas de la clarinette.

Supplementary vocabulary

SPORTS
le croquet   le golf
le frisbee   le rugby
le hockey sur glace, sur gazon

INSTRUMENTS
le cor anglais *French horn*
le synthé *synthétiseur*
le trombone
le tuba
la flûte à bec *recorder*
la guitare électrique
la trompette
la violoncelle *cello*

5 COMMUNICATION: talking about leisure activities

1. de la guitare, 2. de la flûte
3. au basket[ball], 4. de la clarinette, 5. de la batterie, 6. aux échecs, 7. aux dames, 8. aux cartes, 9. du violon, 10. au tennis

Cooperative pair practice

Activities 4, 5

---

4 **D'où viens-tu?**

During vacation, Philippe goes out every day. When he gets home, his sister Cécile asks him where he is coming from.

▶ mardi

D'où viens-tu?

Je viens du théâtre.

1. lundi
2. mercredi
3. vendredi
4. dimanche
5. samedi
6. jeudi

▶

LUNDI	le restaurant
MARDI	le théâtre
MERCREDI	la bibliothèque
JEUDI	l'opéra
VENDREDI	le concert
SAMEDI	le pique-nique de Monique
DIMANCHE	la boum de Christine

Vocabulaire: Les sports, les jeux et la musique

Les sports		**Les instruments de musique**	
le foot(ball)	**le volley(ball)**	**le piano**	**la flûte**
le basket(ball)	**le tennis**	**le violon**	**la guitare**
le ping-pong	**le baseball**	**le saxo(phone)**	**la clarinette**
		le clavier (keyboard)	**la batterie** (drums)

Les jeux (games)	
les échecs (chess)	**les dames** (checkers)
le Monopoly	**les cartes** (cards)

VERBES

jouer à + **le, la, les** + SPORT or GAME	*to play*	Nous **jouons au** tennis.
jouer de + **le, la, les** + INSTRUMENT	*to play*	Alice **joue du** piano.

---

5 **Activités**

Ask your classmates if they play the following instruments and games.

▶ —Est-ce que tu joues au ping-pong?
—Oui, je joue au ping-pong.
(Non, je ne joue pas au ping-pong.)

▶ —Est-ce que tu joues du piano?
—Oui, je joue du piano.
(Non, je ne joue pas du piano.)

214 Unité 6

⌨ **Using the video**

The entire video module for this lesson develops the themes of sports and music, and utilizes the expressions **jouer à** and **jouer de.**

If you do not want to present the whole module at once, you can show some of the segments at the end of the lesson for review.

C. Les pronoms accentués

In the answers to the questions below, the nouns in heavy print are replaced by pronouns. These pronouns are called STRESS PRONOUNS. Note their forms.

—François dîne avec **Florence?**   *Is François having dinner with **Florence?***
—Oui, il dîne avec **elle.**   *Yes, he is having dinner with **her.***

—Tu parles de **Jean-Paul?**   *Are you talking about **Jean-Paul?***
—Non, je ne parle pas de **lui.**   *No, I'm not talking about **him.***

FORMS

(SUBJECT PRONOUNS)	STRESS PRONOUNS	(SUBJECT PRONOUNS)	STRESS PRONOUNS
(je)	**moi**	(nous)	**nous**
(tu)	**toi**	(vous)	**vous**
(il)	**lui**	(ils)	**eux**
(elle)	**elle**	(elles)	**elles**

USES

Stress pronouns are used:

- to reinforce a subject pronoun
  Moi, je parle français.   *__I__ speak French.*
  Vous, vous parlez anglais.   *__You__ speak English.*

- after **c'est** and **ce n'est pas**
  —C'est Paul là-bas?
  —Non ce n'est pas **lui.**   *No, it's not **him.***

- in short sentences where there is no verb
  —Qui parle français ici?
  —**Moi!**   *I do!*

- before and after **et** and **ou**
  Lui et moi, nous sommes copains.   *He and I, (we) are friends.*

- After prepositions such as **de, avec, pour, chez**
  Voici Marc et Paul. Je parle souvent **d'eux.**   *I often talk **about them.***
  Voici Isabelle. Je vais au cinéma **avec elle.**   *I go to the movies **with her.***
  Voici M. Mercier. Nous travaillons **pour lui.**   *We work **for him.***

  ➡ Note the meaning of **chez** + STRESS PRONOUN:
  Je vais **chez moi.**   *I am going **home.***
  Paul étudie **chez lui.**   *Paul is studying **at home.***

  Tu viens **chez nous?**   *Are you coming **to our house?***
  Je suis chez Alice. Je dîne **chez elle.**   *I am having dinner **at her place.***

C'EST MOI QUI POSE LES QUESTIONS!
TF1
VENDREDI 29 MARS
20.50

Leçon 23   **215**

Section C

COMMUNICATIVE FUNCTION:
Referring to people

■ **Language notes**
- One can also reinforce the subject as follows:
  Je parle français, moi.
  Vous parlez anglais, vous.
- The stress form of **que** *(what)* is **quoi**.
  It is used:
  – alone: **Quoi?**
  – after a preposition:
  De quoi est-ce que tu parles?
  – in casual questions:
  Tu fais **quoi?**

⌨ **Transparency 16**
Subject pronouns

■ **Teaching strategy**
- Use Transparency 16 to introduce stress pronouns, writing the corresponding pronoun in the box below each drawing.
- Erase the words from the transparency. As you make statements, have a student volunteer point to the corresponding pronouns.
  Qui vient? Lui! Toi! Nous!
  Qui joue au tennis? Eux! Vous! etc.
- Then point to the pronouns and let the students respond.
  Qui parle français?
  [point to "je"] **Moi.**
  Qui parle anglais?
  [point to "il"] **Lui.** etc.

■ **Photo culture note**
Une chambre
In the photograph of Act. 4 on the left page, note the position of the bed above the bookcase.
Because city apartments are often small, it is important to use space as efficiently as possible.

Talking about past events

Let's talk about what sports and games you and your friends played last weekend.

▶ **X et Y, est-ce que vous avez joué au tennis le weekend dernier?**
Oui, nous avons joué au tennis.
(Non, nous n'avons pas joué au tennis.)

- **Est-ce que vous avez joué au football? au baseball? au ping-pong? au volley? aux échecs? aux cartes? aux dames? au Monopoly?**

Additional challenge questions:
- **Où est-ce que vous avez joué?**
- **Avec qui est-ce que vous avez joué?**
- **Qui a gagné?** *(Who won?)*

Expression pour la conversation

How to contradict someone:

Pas du tout!   *Not at all!*   —Vous êtes français?
   Definitely not!   —**Pas du tout!** Nous sommes italiens!

6 Mais, pas du tout!

You are not good at guessing the identities of the following people. A classmate will indicate that you are wrong.

▶ —C'est Tarzan?
   —Mais, pas du tout!
     Ce n'est pas lui!

Tarzan?

1. Batman?	**2. Superman?**	**3. Wonder Woman?**
4. Big Bird?	**5. Dustin Hoffman?**	**6. la princesse Diana?**

7 Samedi soir *(Saturday night)*

On Saturday night, some people stay home and others do not. Read what the following people are doing and say whether or not they are at home.

▶ Alice étudie.
   Elle est chez elle.

▶ Paul va au cinéma.
   Il n'est pas chez lui.

1. François regarde la télé.
2. Jacqueline va au café.
3. Marc et Pierre dînent au restaurant.
4. Hélène et Pauline écoutent des disques.
5. Les voisins font une promenade.
6. Je travaille avec mon père.
7. Tu vas au théâtre.
8. Nous allons à la bibliothèque.
9. Tu prépares le dîner.

Expression pour la conversation

How to express surprise:

Vraiment?!   *Really?!*   —C'est Batman.
   —**Vraiment?**

C'EST BATMAN!   VRAIMENT?

8 Commérage *(Gossip)*

Thomas likes to gossip. Act out the dialogues between him and his friend Sandrine.

▶ Marina dîne avec Jean-Pierre.

Marina dîne avec Jean-Pierre.
Vraiment?
Mais oui!
Elle dîne avec lui!

1. Éric dîne avec Alice.
2. Thérèse va chez Paul.
3. Jérôme est au cinéma avec Delphine.
4. Monsieur Mercier travaille pour Mademoiselle Duval.
5. Philippe travaille pour le voisin.
6. Marc et Vincent dansent avec Mélanie et Juliette.

9 Questions personnelles

Use stress pronouns in your answers.

1. Est-ce que tu étudies souvent avec tes *(your)* copains?
2. Est-ce que tu vas souvent chez ta cousine?
3. Est-ce que tu travailles pour les voisins?
4. Est-ce que tu parles français avec ton père?
5. Est-ce que tu vas souvent au cinéma avec tes copines?
6. Est-ce que tu restes chez toi le weekend?
7. Est-ce que tu restes chez toi pendant *(during)* les vacances?

D. La construction: nom + *de* + nom

Compare the word order in French and English.

J'ai une raquette.   C'est une **raquette de tennis.**   *It's a tennis racket.*
Paul a une voiture.   C'est une **voiture de sport.**   *It's a sports car.*

When one noun is used to modify another noun, the French construction is:

MAIN NOUN + **de** + MODIFYING NOUN ↓ **d'** (+ VOWEL SOUND)	une classe de français une classe d'espagnol

➡ In French, the main noun comes *first*. In English, the main noun comes second.
➡ There is no article after **de**.

10 Précisions

Complete the following sentences with an expression consisting of **de** + underlined noun.

▶ J'aime le <u>sport</u>. J'ai une voiture . . .

> J'ai une voiture de sport!

1. Claire aime le <u>ping-pong</u>. Elle a une raquette . . .
2. Nous adorons le <u>jazz</u>. Nous écoutons un concert . . .
3. Jacques aime la <u>musique</u> <u>classique</u>. Il écoute un programme . . .
4. Vous étudiez l'<u>anglais</u>. Vous avez un livre . . .
5. Tu étudies le <u>piano</u>. Aujourd'hui, tu as une leçon . . .
6. Thomas et Paul aiment l'<u>espagnol</u>. Ils ont une bonne prof . . .
7. Je regarde mes <u>photos</u>. J'ai un album . . .

Prononciation

Les voyelles /ø/ et /œ/

/ø/   **d<u>eu</u>x**   /œ/   **n<u>eu</u>f**

The letters "**eu**" and "**oeu**" represent vowel sounds that do not exist in English but that are not very hard to pronounce.

Répétez:
/ø/ d<u>eu</u>x <u>eu</u>x je v<u>eu</u>x je p<u>eu</u>x un p<u>eu</u> j<u>eu</u>x il pl<u>eu</u>t Tu p<u>eu</u>x aller chez <u>eu</u>x.
/œ/ n<u>eu</u>f s<u>oeu</u>r h<u>eu</u>re prof<u>eu</u>sseur j<u>eu</u>ne Ma s<u>oeu</u>r arrive à n<u>eu</u>f h<u>eu</u>res.

COMMUNICATION: answering personal questions

Section D

COMMUNICATIVE FUNCTION: Describing objects and people

Critical thinking: Point out that in English, the main noun comes second: *tennis <u>racket</u>, sports <u>car</u>.* In French, the main noun comes first: **une <u>raquette</u> de tennis, une <u>voiture</u> de sport.** How do the French say: *orange juice* [**un jus d'orange**] *tomato salad* [**une salade de tomates**] *bathroom* [**une salle de bains**]

PRACTICE: describing objects using **de** + noun

■ **Pronunciation:** Item 7: **album** /albɔm/

Prononciation

 Leçon 23, Section 7

À votre tour!

1 COMPREHENSION

1-b   3-d
2-c   4-a

🔊 **Leçon 23, Section 8**

2 GUIDED ORAL EXPRESSION

1. chez Françoise / regarder la télé
2. chez Corinne et Claire / dîner
3. chez Nicolas et Patrick / jouer aux cartes
4. chez mon cousin / jouer aux échecs
5. chez ma cousine / jouer du piano
6. chez des copains / écouter la radio

🔊 **Leçon 23, Section 9**

3 COMPREHENSION

1. de l'école
2. de la bibliothèque
3. du parc
4. du supermarché
5. du stade
6. de la piscine

---

1 Conversation

Saturday afternoon, Henri meets Stéphanie downtown. Match Henri's questions with Stéphanie's answers. Then act out the conversation with a classmate.

1. Salut, Stéphanie! D'où viens-tu?
2. Et où vas-tu maintenant?
3. Tu ne veux pas venir au cinéma avec moi?
4. Ah bon? Pourquoi?

a. J'ai un examen d'anglais lundi.
b. Du supermarché.
c. Je rentre chez moi.
d. Je ne peux pas. Je dois étudier.

2 Créa-dialogue

Ask your classmates whom they are going to visit and what they are going to do. Then decide if you are going to come along.

CHEZ QUI?	Jean–Claude
ACTIVITÉ	

▶ — Où vas-tu?
— Je vais chez <u>Jean-Claude</u>. Tu viens?
— Ça dépend! Qu'est-ce que tu vas faire chez <u>lui</u>?
— Nous allons <u>jouer au ping-pong</u>.
— D'accord, je viens!
  (Non, je ne viens pas.)

CHEZ QUI?	1. Françoise	2. Corinne et Claire	3. Nicolas et Patrick	4. mon cousin	5. ma cousine	6. des copains
ACTIVITÉ						

3 Retour à la maison

This afternoon, the following people went downtown. Say which places they are coming from.

▶ **Nous venons de l'école.**

1 tu	2 vous	3 Madame Simon
nous		

| 4 Monsieur Dupont | 5 Claire et Diane | 6 Daniel et Philipp |

À votre tour

Depending on your goals and objectives, you may or may not wish to assign all of the activities in the **À votre tour** section.

👥 Cooperative practice

Act. 1–4 lend themselves to cooperative pair practice.

For Act. 2 and 4, you may have students work in trios, with two performing while the other holds the Answer Key and acts as monitor.

4 Message illustré

Frédéric likes to use illustrations in his diary. Transcribe what he has written about himself and others, replacing the pictures with the corresponding missing words.

5 Une lettre à Sandrine

In a recent letter, Sandrine, your French pen pal, mentioned various hobbies she enjoys. In a short letter, tell her ...

- which sports you play
- which musical instruments you play
- which games you play

parc
supermarché
stade
école
bibliothèque
piscine

4 READING COMPREHENSION

au volleyball
à la piscine
au tennis
de la clarinette
du violon
aux cartes
du stade
au foot[ball]

■ **Challenge:** You may wish to have the students prepare their own "messages illustrés."
(See *Challenge: De nouveaux messages*, p. T117.)

5 WRITTEN SELF-EXPRESSION

Classroom Notes

■ **Portfolio assessment**

You will probably select only one speaking activity and one writing activity to go into the students' portfolios for Unit 6.

In this lesson, Act. 2 lends itself well to an oral portfolio recording.

Act. 5 offers an excellent writing portfolio topic.

MODULE 24:
Où habitez-vous?
Total time: 5:09 min.
(Counter: 20:07 min.)

24.1 Presentation: Listening — C'est ma maison
(20:57–22:05 min.)

24.2 Mini-scenes: Listening — C'est ta voiture?
(22:06–22:55 min.)

24.3 Dialogue: C'est ta famille?
(22:56–23:55 min.)

24.4 Vignette culturelle: Un immeuble à Paris
(23:56–25:12 min.)

■ **Comprehension practice:** Play the entire module through as an introduction to the lesson.

🔲 Leçon 24, Section 1

🔲 **Transparency 34**
Apartment building

Mes voisins

Bonjour!
Je m'appelle Frédéric Mallet.
J'habite à Versailles avec ma famille.
Nous habitons dans un <u>immeuble</u> de   *building*
six <u>étages</u>.   *floors*
Voici mon immeuble et voici <u>mes</u>   *my*
voisins.

Monsieur Lacroche habite au <u>sixième</u>   *sixth*
étage avec sa femme. Ils sont
musiciens. Lui, il joue du piano et elle,
elle chante. Oh là là, <u>quelle</u> musique!   *what*

Mademoiselle Jolivet habite au
<u>cinquième</u> étage avec <u>son</u> oncle et   *fifth / her*
<u>sa</u> tante.   *her*

Paul, mon <u>meilleur</u> ami, habite au   *best*
<u>quatrième</u> étage avec <u>sa</u> soeur et   *fourth / his*
<u>ses</u> parents.   *his*

Mademoiselle Ménard habite au
<u>troisième</u> étage avec son chien   *third*
Pomme, ses deux chats Fritz et Arthur,
son <u>perroquet</u> Coco et son canari   *parrot*
Froufrou. (Je <u>pense</u> <u>que</u> c'est une *think / that*
personne très intéressante, mais mon
père pense qu'elle est un peu bizarre.)

Monsieur et Madame Boutin habitent
au <u>deuxième</u> étage avec <u>leur</u> <u>fils</u> et   *second / their son*
leurs deux <u>filles</u>.   *daughters*

Et qui habite au premier étage?
C'est un garçon super-intelligent,
super-cool et très sympathique! Et ce
garçon . . . c'est moi!

Setting the stage
PROP: Transparency 34

(Have students keep their books closed.)
Describe the building on the transparency.
  Voici un immeuble.
  Voici le rez-de-chaussée.
  Voici le premier étage, le deuxième étage, ...

On the chalkboard, write the following list:
  Paul
  Frédéric Mallet
  Mademoiselle Jolivet
  Mademoiselle Ménard
  Monsieur et Madame Boutin
  Monsieur et Madame Lacroche

Compréhension

1. Où habite Frédéric?
2. Combien *(How many)* d'étages est-ce qu'il y a dans l'immeuble où il habite?
3. Quelle est la profession des Lacroche?
4. Comment s'appelle le meilleur ami de Frédéric?
5. Combien d'animaux a Mademoiselle Ménard?
6. Qui est Pomme?
7. Qui sont Fritz et Arthur?
8. Selon toi *(In your opinion)*, est-ce que Mademoiselle Ménard est une personne bizarre ou intéressante?
9. Quel est le numéro *(number)* de l'étage où habite Frédéric?
10. Est-ce que Frédéric habite en haut ou en bas de l'immeuble?

COMPREHENSION

1. à Versailles
2. six
3. Ils sont musiciens.
4. Paul
5. cinq animaux
6. C'est un chien.
7. Ce sont des chats.
8. *(answers will vary)*
9. le numéro un
10. en bas

■ NOTES ■
CULTURELLES

1 Versailles

Versailles is a city of about 100,000 inhabitants, located about 15 miles southwest of Paris. Its famous **château,** built for King Louis XIV (1638–1715), welcomes four million visitors every year. It is the third most visited monument in France (after the Pompidou Center and the Eiffel Tower).

2 La vie en appartement

Most French people in urban areas live in apartments. Newer high-rise apartment buildings have been built in the suburbs. In the cities, however, apartment houses are traditionally no more than six or seven stories high. (This is because, historically, there were no elevators.) The ground floor, which often houses stores and shops, is known as **le rez-de-chaussée** (literally, "level with the street"). The next floor, **le premier étage** (or "first" floor above the street), corresponds to the American second floor. Similarly, **le deuxième étage** corresponds to our third floor, etc. The top floor of older buildings used to consist of individual rooms, one per apartment. These original maid's rooms often became student rooms. In recent years, as elevators were installed in these buildings, the top-floor rooms frequently have been combined to form new apartments.

Leçon 24 221

Notes culturelles

 24.4 **Vignette culturelle: Un immeuble à Paris** (23:56–25:12 min.)

■ Photo culture note
Versailles
Visitors to Versailles may visit not only the **château** itself with its magnificent Hall of Mirrors (**la Salle des Glaces**), but they can also walk through the park with its formal gardens and sculptured fountains.

Tell students to listen carefully to the cassette and to determine who lives on which floor. You may want to play the cassette recording more than once.

Then have students open their books and follow along as you play the recording once more.

Answers:
Paul (4e)
Frédéric Mallet (1er)
Mademoiselle Jolivet (5e)
Mademoiselle Ménard (3e)
Monsieur et Madame Boutin (2e)
Monsieur et Madame Lacroche (6e)

■ **Teaching strategy:** To help students remember the word order, have them think of **de** as meaning *of* or *which belongs to.*

PRACTICE: expressing relationships

DESCRIPTION: describing ownership

- Marc a la guitare d'Alice et la radio d'Éric.
- Alice a le vélo de Laure et le walkman de Marc.
- Éric a la raquette de Marc et l'appareil-photo de Laure.
- Laure a le scooter d'Alice et les compacts d'Éric.

A. La possession avec *de*

Note the words in heavy print:

Voici une moto.	C'est la moto **de Frédéric.**	*It's **Frédéric's** motorcycle.*
Voici un vélo.	C'est le vélo **de Sophie.**	*It's **Sophie's** bike.*

To express POSSESSION, French speakers use the construction:

le/la/les + NOUN + **de** + OWNER ↓ **d'** (+ VOWEL SOUND)	la radio **de** Thomas les disques **de** Claire la maison **d'**Émilie

➡ The same construction is used to express RELATIONSHIP:

C'est **le copain de Daniel.** *That's **Daniel's** friend.*
C'est **la mère de Paul.** *That's **Paul's** mother.*

➡ Remember that **de** contracts with **le** and **les**:

Pomme est le chien **du voisin.** *Pomme is **the neighbor's** dog.*
Voici la chambre **des enfants.** *Here is **the children's** room.*

➡ While English often indicates possession with *s,* French always uses **de.**

la copine **de Monique** ***Monique's** friend (the friend **of Monique**)*

1 Présentations *(Introductions)*

Imagine that you are hosting a party in France. Introduce the following people.

▶ Marc (cousin / Sylvie)

Marc est le cousin de Sylvie.

1. Carole (cousine / Jacques)
2. Michel (copain / Caroline)
3. Philippe (camarade / Charles)
4. Robert (frère / Guillaume)
5. Marina (copine / Paul)
6. Pauline (amie / Éric)
7. Thomas (frère / Christine)
8. Alice (soeur / Karine)

2 Échanges

The following friends have decided to trade a few of their possessions. On a separate sheet of paper, write out what each person has, once the exchange has been completed.

Marc   **Alice**   **Éric**   **Laure**

Talking about past events

Let's talk about what you and your friends did last weekend.

(Reminder: If the question contains **tu as...**, students should answer with **j'ai...** or **je n'ai pas...** If it contains **tu es...**, they should answer with **je suis...** or **je ne suis pas...**)

▶ **Est-ce que tu es allé(e) à la plage?**
Oui, je suis allé(e) à la plage.
(Non, je ne suis pas allé(e) à la plage.)
▶ **Est-ce que tu as nagé?**
Oui, j'ai nagé.
(Non, je n'ai pas nagé.)

Vocabulaire: La famille

la famille *(family)*

les grands-parents
  le grand-père   **la grand-mère**

les parents *(parents)*
  le père   **la mère**
  le mari *(husband)* **la femme** *(wife)*

les enfants *(children)*
  un enfant   **une enfant**
  le frère   **la soeur**
  le fils *(son)*   **la fille** *(daughter)*

les parents *(relatives)*
  l'oncle   **la tante** *(aunt)*

  le cousin   **la cousine**

3 La famille de Frédéric

Frédéric has drawn his family tree. Study it and explain the relationships between the people below.

▸ Éric / Isabelle Vidal
  Éric est le fils d'Isabelle Vidal.

1. Véronique / Frédéric
2. Martine Mallet / Véronique
3. Albert et Suzanne Mallet / Frédéric
4. Isabelle Vidal / Frédéric Mallet
5. François Mallet / Martine Mallet
6. Isabelle Vidal / Maurice Vidal
7. François Mallet / Suzanne Mallet
8. Catherine / Maurice Vidal
9. Véronique / Éric
10. Frédéric / Catherine

Albert Mallet **+** Suzanne Mallet

Maurice Vidal **+** Isabelle Vidal

François Mallet **+** Martine Mallet

Catherine Vidal   Éric Vidal   Véronique Mallet   Frédéric Mallet

▸ Marc a la guitare d'Alice et . . .

Marc   Alice   Éric   Laure

Leçon 24 223

▷ Vocabulaire

🔊 Leçon 24, Section 2

🔄 Re-entry and review:
The following words were taught in Lesson 7: père, mère, frère, soeur, cousin, cousine.

▪ Pronunciation: Make sure that students pronounce the following nouns correctly:
fils /fis/
femme /fam/
cousin /kuzẽ/
cousine /kuzin/

Supplementary vocabulary

les petits-enfants *grandchildren*
le petit-fils / la petite-fille
les jumeaux *twins*
un jumeau / une jumelle
un frère aîné / une soeur aînée
  older brother / sister
un frère cadet / une soeur cadette
  younger brother / sister
un enfant unique *only child*
le neveu *nephew* **/ la nièce**
le beau-père / la belle-mère
  stepfather, father-in-law /
  stepmother, mother-in-law
le beau-frère / la belle-soeur
  stepbrother, brother-in-law /
  stepsister, sister-in-law
le demi-frère / la demi-soeur
  half-brother / half-sister
le parrain / la marraine
  godfather / godmother

 COMPREHENSION: describing family relationships

3

1. la soeur
2. la mère
3. les grands-parents
4. la tante
5. le mari
6. la femme
7. le fils
8. la fille
9. la cousine
10. le cousin

 Transparency 8
Family tree

🔊 Leçon 24, Section 3

- **Est-ce que tu es allé(e) à la plage?**
- **Est-ce que tu as nagé?**
- **Est-ce que tu es allé(e) au restaurant?**
- **Est-ce que tu as mangé une pizza?**
- **Est-ce que tu es allé(e) en ville?**
- **Est-ce que tu as acheté des vêtements?**

- **Est-ce que tu es allé(e) au parc?**
- **Est-ce que tu as joué au frisbee?**
- **Où est-ce que tu es allé(e)?**
- **Qu'est-ce que tu as fait?**

↻ **Review and expansion:**
Mon/ma and ton/ta were introduced in Lesson 7.

💡 **Critical thinking:** Point out that just as **ma** becomes **mon** before a vowel sound in French, the article *a* in English also changes form.
Contrast: <u>a</u> pear, <u>an</u> apple.

Classroom Notes

B. Les adjectifs possessifs:
mon, ton, son

Note the forms of the possessive
adjectives in the chart below:

(POSSESSOR)		SINGULAR		PLURAL			
		MASCULINE	FEMININE				
(je)	*my*	**mon**	**ma**	**mes**	**mon** frère	**ma** soeur	**mes** copains
(tu)	*your*	**ton**	**ta**	**tes**	**ton** oncle	**ta** tante	**tes** cousins
(il)	*his*	**son**	**sa**	**ses**	**son** père	**sa** mère	**ses** parents
(elle)	*her*	**son**	**sa**	**ses**	**son** père	**sa** mère	**ses** parents

➡ The feminine singular forms **ma, ta, sa** become **mon, ton, son** before a vowel sound.

| **une** amie | **mon** amie | **ton** amie | **son** amie |
| **une** auto | **mon** auto | **ton** auto | **son** auto |

➡ There is liaison after **mon, ton, son, mes, tes, ses** when the next word begins with a vowel sound.

    mon oncle   **mes** amis

➡ The choice between **son, sa,** and **ses** depends on the gender (masculine or feminine) and the number (singular or plural) of the noun that *follows*. It does NOT depend on the gender of the possessor (that is, whether the owner is male or female). Compare:

	un vélo	une radio	des cassettes
Voici Frédéric.	Voici son vélo. (*his bike*)	Voici sa radio. (*his radio*)	Voici ses cassettes. (*his cassettes*)
Voici Sophie.	Voici son vélo. (*her bike*)	Voici sa radio. (*her radio*)	Voici ses cassettes. (*her cassettes*)

224 Unité 6

PROPS: Books, watches, etc.

Hold up your own textbook, saying:
    Voici un livre de français.
    C'est mon livre.
    X, montre-nous ton livre de français.
Continue with **ma/ta montre.**

Walk around holding up students' items.
    C'est le livre de X [boy]?
    Oui, c'est son livre.
    C'est le livre de Y [girl]?
    Oui, c'est son livre.
    C'est la montre de Z?
    Oui, c'est sa montre.
Follow-up (pointing out items):
    Comment dit-on: *his book? her book?*

4 Marc et Hélène

Marc Pertout never knows where his things are. Fortunately, his friend Hélène Sétout knows. Play both roles.

▶ le vélo / dans le garage

Où est mon vélo?

Ton vélo? Il est dans le garage.

1. les cassettes / ici
2. la raquette / là-bas
3. la montre / sur toi
4. les livres / dans le sac
5. la radio / sur le bureau
6. les tee-shirts / sous le lit
7. le chien / derrière la porte
8. l'appareil-photo / dans la chambre

5 Invitations

Each of the following people is bringing a friend or relative to the school party. Say whom each person is inviting, using the appropriate possessive adjectives.

▶ Michel / la copine
Michel invite sa copine.

1. André / la cousine
2. Jean-Claude / la soeur
3. Marie-Noëlle / les frères
4. Pascal / l'amie Sophie
5. Monique / les cousins
6. Nathalie / l'ami Marc
7. Georges / l'amie Cécile
8. Paul / l'amie Thérèse
9. Isabelle / les copains

6 Chez Marie et Christophe Boutin

Items 1 to 8 belong to Marie. Items 9 to 16 belong to Christophe. Point these things out.

Marie		Christophe	
▶ le vélo **C'est son vélo.**		▶ les disques **Ce sont ses disques.**	
1. le walkman	5. la radiocassette	9. la guitare	13. les livres
2. le sac	6. la guitare	10. la chaîne stéréo	14. la montre
3. le chien	7. les disques	11. le chat	15. les photos
4. l'album	8. les cassettes	12. la mobylette	16. les skis

Expression pour la conversation

C'EST MON PANTALON! **TU ES SÛR?**

How to question a statement or express a doubt:

Tu es sûr(e)? *Are you sure?* —C'est mon pantalon *(pants)!*
—**Tu es sûr?**

7 Après la boum

Last night Frédéric and Paul gave a party. They realize that their friends left certain things behind. Frédéric thinks he knows what belongs to whom.

▶ le sac / Claire
FRÉDÉRIC: **Voici le sac de Claire.**
PAUL: **Tu es sûr?**
FRÉDÉRIC: **Mais oui, c'est son sac!**

1. le sac / Jean-Pierre
2. la guitare / Antoine
3. l'appareil-photo / Cécile
4. le walkman / Stéphanie
5. les livres / Philippe
6. le chapeau *(hat)* / Thomas
7. la cassette / Roger
8. les compacts / Corinne

Leçon 24 225

---

4 ROLE PLAY: finding one's things

■ **Language note:** Be sure students use plural forms in items 1, 4, and 6.
1. Où sont...? Elles sont...
4. Où sont...? Ils sont ...
6. Où sont...? Ils sont...

5 PRACTICE: identifying friends and relatives

6 PRACTICE: identifying possessions

7 ROLE PLAY: identifying ownership

■ **Language note:** Be sure students use the plural **Ce sont** in items 4 and 8.

Talking about past events

Let's talk about a recent party.
Imaginez que vous avez organisé une boum le weekend dernier avec des amis.

▶ **Est-ce que tu as organisé une boum le weekend dernier?**
Oui, j'ai organisé une boum.

• **Avec qui est-ce que tu as organisé la boum?**
• **À qui est-ce que vous avez téléphoné?**
• **Qui est-ce que vous avez invité?**
• **Est-ce que vous avez dansé?**
• **Est-ce que vous avez chanté?**
• **Qu'est-ce que vous avez mangé?**

Cooperative pair practice Activities 4, 7

T225

24.1 Mini-scenes:
  C'est ma maison
24.2 Mini-scenes:
  C'est ta voiture?
24.3 Dialogue: C'est ta
  famille?
  (20:57–23:55 min.)

Leçon 24, Sections 4–6

■ **Language note:** Be sure students note that **notre**, **votre**, and **leur** are used with singular nouns and that **nos**, **vos**, and **leurs** are used with plural nouns. Contrast:
leur frère *their brother*
leurs frères *their brothers*

8 ROLE PLAY: asking for items in a store

9 PRACTICE: pointing out possessions

■ **Challenge:** To practice adjectives, have students make a comment on each thing they are pointing out.
Voici leur maison.
Elle est belle (grande, super, extra, etc.), n'est-ce pas?

10 COMPREHENSION: indicating family relationships

1. son   6. leurs
2. ses   7. leur
3. leur   8. leurs
4. son   9. sa
5. sa

C. Les adjectifs possessifs: *notre, votre, leur*

Note the forms of the possessive adjectives in the chart below:

(POSSESSOR)		SINGULAR	PLURAL		
(nous)	*our*	**notre**	**nos**	**notre** prof	**nos** livres
(vous)	*your*	**votre**	**vos**	**votre** ami	**vos** copains
(ils / elles)	*their*	**leur**	**leurs**	**leur** radio	**leurs** disques

➡ There is liaison after **nos, vos, leurs** when the next word begins with a vowel sound.
  nos amis   **vos** amies   **leurs** ordinateurs

C'est son vélo.

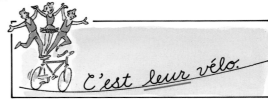

C'est leur vélo.

8 **Aux Galeries Lafayette**

At the Galeries Lafayette department store, a customer is looking for various things. The person at the information desk indicates where they can be found. Play both roles.

▶ les disques / là-bas

1. les livres / à gauche   4. le garage / en bas
2. les affiches / à droite   5. les ordinateurs / ici
3. le restaurant / en haut   6. la cafétéria / tout droit

S'il vous plaît, où sont vos disques?

Nos disques sont là-bas.

9 **Les millionnaires**

Imagine you are showing a millionaire's estate to French visitors.

▶ la maison
  Voici leur maison.

1. la piscine
2. la Cadillac
3. les chiens
4. le parc
5. l'hélicoptère
6. les courts de tennis

10 **En famille**

We often do things with our family. Complete each sentence with a possessive adjective: **son, sa, ses, leur,** or **leurs.**

▶ Pascal joue au tennis avec **sa** cousine.
▶ Éric et Paul jouent au Monopoly avec <u>**leurs**</u> cousins.

1. Frédéric dîne chez … oncle.
2. André dîne chez … grands-parents.
3. Caroline et Paul vont chez … grand-mère.
4. Mlle Vénard fait une promenade avec … chien.
5. Antoine va à la piscine avec … soeur.
6. Stéphanie et Céline vont au cinéma avec … parents.
7. M. et Mme Boutin voyagent avec … fille.
8. Mme Denis visite Paris avec … fils, Marc et Frédéric.
9. M. Mallet est à Québec avec … femme.

Cooperative pair practice
Activities 8, 9

Game: Possessions

PREPARATION: Prepare 2 bags.
Bag A contains 12 sentence cards.
(6 cards with names of single people)
Voici Pierre. Voici Michelle. Voici…
(6 cards with names of two people)
Voici Anne et Paul. Voici Éric et Sylvie. …

Bag B contains 12 sentence cards.
(6 cards with singular nouns)
Voici son crayon, …son stylo, sa montre.
Voici leur crayon, …leur stylo, leur montre.
(6 cards with plural nouns)
Voici ses crayons, …ses stylos, ses montres.
Voici leurs crayons, …leurs stylos, leurs montres.

D. Les nombres ordinaux

Compare the following regular numbers and the ordinal numbers in French:

(2)	deux	**deuxième**	Février est le **deuxième** mois de l'année.
(3)	trois	**troisième**	Mercredi est le **troisième** jour de la semaine.
(4)	quatre	**quatrième**	J'habite au **quatrième** étage *(floor)*.
(12)	douze	**douzième**	Qui habite au **douzième** étage?

To form ordinal numbers, the French use the following pattern:

NUMBER (minus final **-e,** if any) + **-ième**
(6) six : **six** + **-ième** → **sixième**
(11) onze : **onz-** + **-ième** → **onzième**

Quatrième . . .

et pourtant premier.

➡ EXCEPTIONS: **un (une)** → **premier (première)**
 cinq → **cinquième**
 neuf → **neuvième**

➡ Ordinal numbers are adjectives and come BEFORE the noun.

11 La course *(The race)*

Frédéric and his friends are participating in a five-kilometer race. Announce the order of arrival of the following runners.

▶ Paul (6)

Paul est sixième.

1. Frédéric (4)	5. Christine (1)
2. Jérôme (7)	6. Claire (10)
3. Christophe (8)	7. Karine (11)
4. Sophie (2)	8. Olivier (12)

▶▶▶▶▶▶▶▶▶▶▶▶▶▶▶▶▶▶

Prononciation

Les voyelles /o/ et /ɔ/

/o/

/ɔ/

vélo

téléphone

The French vowel /o/ is pronounced with more tension than in English. It is usually the last sound in a word.

Répétez: /o/ **vélo radio nos vos eau château chaud**
 Nos vélos sont au château.

The French vowel /ɔ/ occurs in the middle of a word. Imitate the model carefully.

Répétez: /ɔ/ **téléphone école Nicole notre votre copain prof dommage**
 Comment s'appelle votre prof?

Section D

COMMUNICATIVE FUNCTION: Indicating sequence

■ **Language notes:**
• For **deuxième**, one can also say **second(e)**, pronounced /səgɔ̃(d)/
• 21st = **vingt et unième**
 31st = **trente et unième**, etc.
 Note that the "u" of **unième** is pronounced /y/.

■ **Extra practice:** Write the numbers 1 to 20 on the board. Point to a number and have students give the corresponding ordinal number.
For example:
15 [quinzième], etc.

11 PRACTICE: ranking people

Prononciation

 Leçon 24, Section 7

■ **Pronunciation notes**
• Have students pronounce the /o/ with tension and clip off the ending before the glide /oᵘ/ of the English *go*.
• Be sure students do not pronounce these words with the vowel /o/. The French /ɔ/ is close to the "o" sound of the English *orange*.

PROCEDURE: Divide the class into two teams: **logique** and **illogique**. Each team names a scorekeeper.

Two players (one from each team) come to the front. One reads a card from Bag A, the other reads a card from Bag B.

If the sentences fit logically, the **logique** team earns a point. If not, a point goes to the **illogique** team. For example:

Voici Marc. Voici leur stylo. = illogique

Have students at their seats decide if the sentences are logical or not.

1 COMPREHENSION

1-c   3-b
2-a   4-d

▣ Leçon 24, Section 8

2 GUIDED ORAL EXPRESSION

1. la guitare d'Anne / orange
2. le scooter de Paul et Anne / vert
3. le chien de tes cousins / noir
4. la mobylette d'Isabelle / rouge
5. la maison de M. et Mme Lavoie / blanche
6. la voiture de ton oncle / jaune

▣ Leçon 24, Section 9

Classroom Notes

À votre tour!

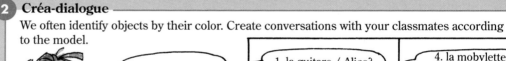

1 Allô!

Émilie is on the phone with Bernard. Match Émilie's questions with Bernard's answers. Then act out the dialogue with a classmate.

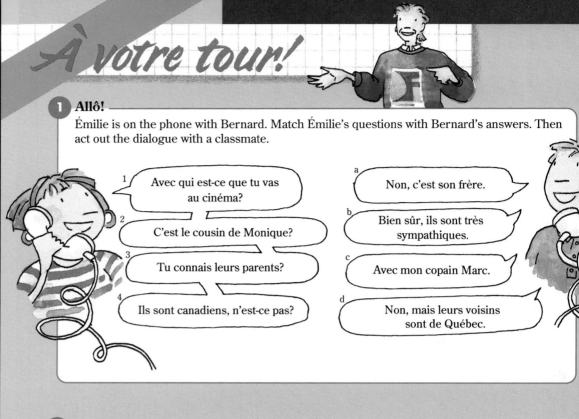

1 Avec qui est-ce que tu vas au cinéma?

2 C'est le cousin de Monique?

3 Tu connais leurs parents?

4 Ils sont canadiens, n'est-ce pas?

a Non, c'est son frère.

b Bien sûr, ils sont très sympathiques.

c Avec mon copain Marc.

d Non, mais leurs voisins sont de Québec.

2 Créa-dialogue

We often identify objects by their color. Create conversations with your classmates according to the model.

le vélo / Paul?

▶ —C'est le vélo de Paul?
—Non, ce n'est pas son vélo.
—Tu es sûr?
—Mais oui. Son vélo est bleu.

1. la guitare / Alice?

2. le scooter / Paul et Anne?

3. le chien / tes cousins?

4. la mobylette / Isabelle?

5. la maison / M. et Mme Lavoie?

6. la voiture / ton oncle?

À votre tour

Depending on your goals and objectives, you may or may not wish to assign all of the activities in the **À votre tour** section.

👥👥 Cooperative practice

Act. 1–3 lend themselves to cooperative pair practice.

3 Faisons connaissance

You want to know more about certain relatives and acquaintances (friends, neighbors, teachers, etc.) of your classmates. Ask a classmate three questions: each question will be about a different person. You may want to use some of the following suggestions:

OUI/NON	INFORMATION
parler français?	où/habiter?
avoir une voiture?	quel âge/avoir?
aimer les sports?	où/travailler?
travailler beaucoup?	à quelle école/étudier?
voyager souvent?	quand/venir chez toi?

Où est-ce que tes grands-parents habitent?

4 Composition: Ma famille

Select five people in your family and write one to three sentences about each person.

Ma cousine s'appelle Barbara. Elle habite à San Francisco. Elle a treize ans.

5 Arbre généalogique *(Family tree)*

On a separate sheet of paper, draw your own (real or imaginary) family tree. Label the people and indicate their relationships to you.

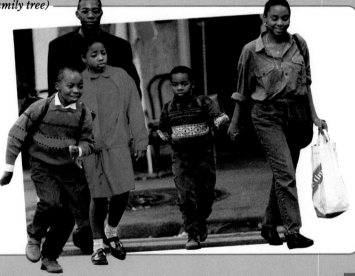

Leçon 24 **229**

3 GUIDED ORAL EXPRESSION

■ **Expansion:** You may wish to have students record their partners' responses in the third person. For example:
Les grands-parents de Sylvie habitent à Miami.
Son père travaille beaucoup.
Ses cousins viennent chez elle en été. etc.

4 WRITTEN SELF-EXPRESSION

5 WRITTEN SELF-EXPRESSION

■ **Teaching strategy:** Some students may prefer preparing the family tree of a TV family or a family in the public eye.

■ **Photo culture note**
French people of African ancestry come principally from the French Carribean islands of **Martinique** and **Guadeloupe**, and from countries of western Africa, especially **Mali, Sénégal, Cameroun, Congo,** and **Côte d'Ivoire.**

Portfolio assessment

You will probably select only one speaking activity and one writing activity to go into the students' portfolios for Unit 6.

In this lesson, Act. 3 lends itself well to an oral portfolio recording.

Act. 4 and 5 are appropriate writing portfolio topics.

OBJECTIVES:
- Reading skills development
- Re-entry of material in the unit
- Development of cultural awarenesss

Les loisirs

OBJECTIVES:
- Rapid reading at the sentence level
- Reading for cultural information about leisure time activities

ENTRACTE 6

Vive la différence!
Les loisirs

Parlons° de vos loisirs.° Répondez aux questions suivantes.° Selon° vous, quelles sont les réponses des jeunes Français en général à ces questions?

1 **Qu'est-ce que vous préférez faire quand vous n'étudiez pas?**
- aller au cinéma
- aller dans les magasins
- pratiquer un sport
- jouer avec les jeux vidéo

Selon vous, qu'est-ce que les jeunes Français préfèrent faire?

2 **Quand vous allez au cinéma, quels films est-ce que vous préférez voir?°**
- les films de science-fiction
- les films d'aventures
- les comédies
- les films d'horreur

Selon vous, quels sont les films préférés des jeunes Français?

3 **Combien de fois° par an° est-ce que vous allez au concert?**
- jamais°
- une fois ou deux
- de trois à six fois
- sept fois ou plus°

Et les jeunes Français, combien de fois vont-ils au concert en moyenne° par an?

4 **Voici quatre acteurs américains très célèbres° en France. Quel est votre acteur préféré?**
- Tom Cruise
- Jack Nicholson
- Robert Redford
- Dustin Hoffman

Selon vous, qui est l'acteur américain préféré des Français?

5 **Quelle musique est-ce que vous préférez écouter?**
- les chansons folkloriques°
- le rock
- le jazz
- la musique classique

Selon vous, quelle est la musique préférée des jeunes Français?

6 **Quels livres est-ce que vous préférez lire?°**
- les biographies
- les livres de science-fiction
- les livres d'aventures
- les albums de bandes dessinées°

Selon vous, quels sont les livres préférés des jeunes Français?

7 **Quelle est votre dépense° principale?**
- Je vais au concert.
- Je vais au cinéma ou au restaurant.
- J'achète° des cassettes ou des compacts.
- J'achète des vêtements.°

Et pour les jeunes Français, quelle est leur dépense principale?

Et les jeunes Français?

1. Ils préfèrent aller au cinéma. 2. Ils préfèrent les comédies. 3. Ils vont au concert en moyenne six fois par an.
4. Leur acteur américain préféré est Dustin Hoffman. 5. Ils préfèrent le rock. 6. Ils préfèrent les albums de bandes dessinées. 7. Ça dépend. Les garçons vont au cinéma ou au restaurant. Les filles achètent des vêtements.

Parlons *Let's talk* **loisirs** *leisure activities* **suivantes** *following* **Selon** *According to* **voir** *to see* **fois** *times* **par an** *per year* **jamais** *never* **plus** *more* **en moyenne** *on the average* **célèbres** *famous* **chansons folkloriques** *folksongs* **lire** *to read* **bandes dessinées** *comics, cartoons* **dépense** *expense* **achète** *buy* **vêtements** *clothes*

230 Unité 6

📖 Cooperative reading practice

Divide the class into groups of 4 or 5, each with a recorder (**secrétaire**).

For each question, have the groups first vote on their own preferences and then on what they imagine the preferences of French young people to be. (Keep answers at the bottom of the page covered.)

Then have the recorders announce their results to the entire class. For example:
1. Quand nous n'étudions pas, nous préférons aller au cinéma.
Selon nous, les jeunes Français préfèrent aller au cinéma aussi.

EN FRANCE

Vive la musique!

Est-ce que vous préférez écouter votre groupe favori à la radio ou dans une salle de concert? Regardez bien ces documents.

Rolling Stones Story à partir du 25 décembre

1° diffusion le mardi à 21 h 30 - 2° diffusion le vendredi à 23 h sur

RADIO 2 EUROPE 1

♪ Quel groupe est-ce qu'on peut écouter à la radio? Quels jours et à quelle heure?

♪ Est-ce que vous connaissez° ce groupe? Est-ce que vous avez leurs disques? Aimez-vous leur musique?

LE PLUS GRAND DES GRANDS CONCERTS

AVEC

Rod STEWART

Stevie WONDER

INXS

Edie BRICKELL

Gipsy KINGS

RTL AVEC

FRÉDÉRIC PARTOUCHE PRÉSENTE

Liberty Show

SAMEDI 24 JUIN DE 12 À 24 HEURES

HIPPODROME DE VINCENNES

PARIS

RÉSERVATIONS : 48 05 10 10

Pour la première fois dans tous les CARREFOUR de France   Carrefour

Cyndi LAUPER

George MICHAEL

Bob DYLAN

Tracy CHAPMAN

Elvis COSTELLO

Boris GREBENSHIKOV

♪ Quand a lieu° le concert? Où?

♪ À quelle heure est-ce que le concert commence?° À quelle heure est-ce qu'il finit?°

♪ Quel est le numéro de téléphone pour réserver les billets?°

♪ Qui sont les «stars» de ce concert? Quelles stars est-ce que vous connaissez? Qui est votre star préférée?

♪ Est-ce que vous aimeriez° aller à ce concert? Pourquoi ou pourquoi pas?

connaissez *know*   **a lieu** *does ... take place*   **commence** *does ... begin*   **finit** *does ... end*   **billets** *tickets*
aimeriez *would like*

Entracte 6   231

Vive la musique!

OBJECTIVES:
• Reading for information
• Understanding authentic documents

■ **Realia notes**
Le rock en France
French young people enjoy all kinds of popular music, especially British and American rock groups. When French teens form their own rock bands, they often give them English names like "The Chelsea Five."

Classroom Notes

Pre-reading

Ask pairs of students to name their favorite music groups.
Quel est votre groupe favori?
Notre groupe favori est [New Kids on the Block].

Post-reading

OPTIONAL: Prepare a poster in French announcing a school event.

Interview avec Karine Legoff

OBJECTIVES:
- Reading a longer text
- Building reading skills

■ Questions sur le texte
1. Est-ce que Karine habite très loin de l'école?
2. À quelle heure est-ce qu'elle arrive à l'école le matin?
3. Est-ce qu'elle rentre chez elle à midi?
4. Quels sports est-ce qu'elle pratique?
5. Combien de fois par mois est-ce qu'elle va au cinéma?
6. Qui est son acteur américain préféré?
7. Quels groupes est-ce qu'elle aime?
8. En général, est-ce qu'elle aime les Américains? Pourquoi?
9. Qu'est-ce qu'elle n'aime pas aux États-Unis?

■ Questions personnelles
1. Comment vas-tu à l'école?
2. Est-ce que tu rentres chez toi à midi?
3. À quelle heure rentres-tu chez toi l'après-midi?
4. Quels sports est-ce que tu pratiques à l'école?
5. Combien de fois par mois vas-tu au cinéma?
6. Qui est ton acteur favori?
7. Qui est ton actrice favorite?
8. Est-ce que tu joues d'un instrument? De quel instrument?

Entre amis: Interview avec Karine Legoff

Karine Legoff est élève dans un lycée° français. En mars, elle a passé° deux semaines aux États-Unis avec un programme d'échange.° Nous avons interviewé° Karine pendant° son séjour.° Voici les réponses de Karine à nos questions.

École
En France, comment vas-tu à l'école? — À pied, généralement.°
À quelle heure arrives-tu le matin? — À huit heures.
À quelle heure rentres-tu chez toi le soir? — Ça dépend des° jours. En général, à 5 heures 30 ou à 6 heures.
Où déjeunes-tu?° — Je déjeune à la cantine° du lycée.

Sports
Quels sports pratiques-tu à l'école? — Je joue au volley.
Et en dehors de° l'école? — Je joue au tennis.
Où? — Au club de la ville.

Loisirs
Est-ce que tu vas au cinéma? — Oui, de temps en temps.°
Combien de fois par mois?° — Une ou deux fois.
Qui sont tes acteurs préférés? — Christophe Lambert, Gérard Depardieu. Aussi Dustin Hoffman.
Et tes actrices préférées? — Isabelle Adjani, Emmanuelle Béart.
Est-ce que tu vas au concert? — Oui, mais pas très souvent.
Où vas-tu? — Ça dépend! Au Zénith, au parc des Princes.
Qui sont tes groupes ou tes chanteurs° préférés? — The Police, U2, Tracy Chapman.
Est-ce que tu joues d'un instrument? — Non.
Est-ce que tu vas à des boums? — Oui, de temps en temps.
Où et quand? — Chez des amis. Généralement le samedi soir.

Les États-Unis
Quelles sont tes impressions des États-Unis? — J'aime le pays° et les gens.
Pourquoi? — C'est un pays très dynamique et très ouvert.° Les gens sont francs, communicatifs et honnêtes avec eux-mêmes.° Les Américains sont très cool!
Qu'est-ce que tu n'aimes pas? — La nourriture.°

lycée *high school* **a passé** *spent* **échange** *exchange* **avons interviewé** *interviewed* **pendant** *during* **séjour** *stay* **généralement** *generally* **Ça dépend des** *It depends on the* **déjeunes-tu** *do you have lunch* **cantine** *cafeteria* **en dehors de** *outside of* **de temps en temps** *from time to time* **fois par mois** *times a month* **chanteurs** *singers* **pays** *country* **ouvert** *open* **eux-mêmes** *themselves* **nourriture** *food*

📖 Pre-reading
Ask the class if they have ever hosted French exchange students in their homes.

If your school has an exchange program, have they met some of the students?

Have they ever spent a week or two in a French-speaking country?

Post-reading
Which of Karine's answers, if any, do they find surprising?

Do they agree with her impressions of the United States?

Comment lire
SOUNDING FRENCH

As you read the interview over, try to think how the new words sound in French.

- Remember to put the accent on the LAST syllable of a word or phrase.

  pro**gramme**   acteur préfé**ré**   communi**catif**

- Remember that many final consonants are silent.

  spor~~t~~ Zéni~~th~~ mat~~hs~~ instrumen~~t~~

If you think of the right French pronunciation as you read, you will be prepared to recognize these words when you hear them spoken.

Enrichissez votre vocabulaire
SUFFIXES

You can expand your reading vocabulary easily by learning to recognize common suffixes (or endings).

	FRENCH	ENGLISH		
(ADJECTIVE +)	**-ment**	*-ly*	**généralement**	*generally*
(VERB STEM +)	**-ant**	*-ing*	**amusant**	*amusing*
(VERB STEM +)	**-é**	*-ed*	**préféré**	*preferred*

Activité

Can you identify the English equivalents of the following French words?

- **normalement   finalement   rarement   rapidement   sûrement**
- **intéressant   alarmant   terrifiant   charmant**
- **importé   occupé   limité   marié**

Activité: Une interview
Interview a classmate about his / her school life and leisure activities. Use Karine's interview as a point of departure.

Activité: Une lettre à Karine
Write Karine a letter about yourself. Using her responses to the interview as a model, tell her about your school, the sports you play, your leisure-time activities, as well as your impressions of France and the French people.

■ **Teaching strategy** (Une lettre à Karine): Since most, if not all, of your students will not yet have had the opportunity to visit France, have them base their impressions on the video.

■ **Les stars du cinéma français**
Some other French movie stars:
actrices Sabine Azéma
          Nathalie Baye
          Sandrine Bonnaire
          Catherine Deneuve
          Isabelle Hupert
          Sophie Marceau
          Miou-Miou
acteurs Jean-Paul Belmondo
          Alain Delon
          Philippe Noiret
          Michel Serrault

Quelques stars du cinéma français

Gérard Depardieu   Christophe Lambert   Isabelle Adjani   Emmanuelle Béart

Entracte 6   233

Quatre stars

NOM	NÉ(E)	FILMS CONNUS
G. Depardieu	1948	Le Dernier Métro, Jean de Florette, Camille Claudel, Cyrano de Bergerac, Green Card
C. Lambert	1957	Le Sicilien, Le Retour
I. Adjani	1955	L'Histoire d'Adèle H., Les Soeurs Brontë, Camille Claudel
E. Béart	1965	Jean de Florette

Variétés

Variétés

Les jeunes Français et le cinéma américain

En général, les jeunes Français aiment beaucoup les films américains. (Quand ils parlent anglais, ils peuvent° voir° ces films en «version originale».) Voici une liste de films qui ont eu° beaucoup de succès en France. Est-ce que vous pouvez° identifier ces films? Lisez° le titre° français de chaque° film. Faites correspondre° le titre de ce film avec le titre américain.

TITRES FRANÇAIS

1. *Blanche-Neige*
2. *Le parrain*
3. *Un prince à New York*
4. *Un poisson nommé Wanda*
5. *E.T. l'extra-terrestre*
6. *Le retour du Jedi*
7. *Les aventuriers de l'arche perdue*
8. *Rencontres du troisième type*
9. *Les dents de la mer*
10. *Danse avec les loups*
11. *La guerre des étoiles*
12. *Indiana Jones et la dernière croisade*
13. *Qui veut la peau de Roger Rabbit?*
14. *Le retour de la panthère rose*

TITRES AMÉRICAINS

A. *Jaws*
B. *Star Wars*
C. *E.T. The Extra Terrestrial*
D. *Close Encounters of the Third Kind*
E. *Indiana Jones and the Last Crusade*
F. *The Return of the Jedi*
G. *Coming to America*
H. *The Godfather*
I. *Raiders of the Lost Ark*
J. *Dances with Wolves*
K. *A Fish Called Wanda*
L. *The Return of the Pink Panther*
M. *Who Framed Roger Rabbit?*
N. *Snow White and the Seven Dwarfs*

peuvent *can* **voir** *see* **ont eu** *had* **pouvez** *can* **Lisez** *Read* **titre** *title* **chaque** *each*
Faites correspondre *Match*

234

UN FILM D'AVENTURES
américain

20.30   DURÉE : 2h00

FILM AMÉRICAIN DE STEVEN SPIELBERG

LES AVENTURIERS DE L'ARCHE PERDUE

SCÉNARIO DE LAWRENCE KASDAN · MUSIQUE DE JOHN WILLIAMS

Indiana Jones	Harrison Ford	Belloq	Paul Freeman
Marion Ravenhood	Karen Allen	Toht	Ronald Lacey
Dietrich	Wolf Kahler	Sallah	John Rhys-Davies

Indiana Jones (Harrison Ford) est en compétition avec Belloq (Paul Freeman)

Ce film américain a eu° beaucoup de succès en France.

- Est-ce que vous avez vu° ce film? Où? à la télévision? au cinéma? sur vidéocassette?
- Quel est le titre anglais du film?
- Qui est le directeur du film?
- Qui est l'acteur principal?
- Qui sont les autres acteurs?
- Qui est le compositeur de la musique?
- Combien de temps dure° le film?

■ NOTE ■
CULTURELLE

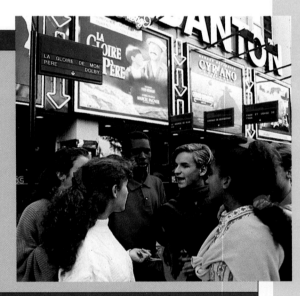

Au cinéma

Le samedi, les jeunes Français adorent aller au cinéma. C'est pour eux l'occasion de voir° un bon film et aussi d'être avec leurs copains. En général, ils vont au cinéma pour voir des films récents. Leurs films préférés sont les films comiques. Ils aiment aussi les films d'aventures, les films de science-fiction et les films policiers.°

Beaucoup de jeunes vont aussi au cinéclub de leur école ou de la ville où ils habitent. Là ils peuvent° voir les «grands classiques» du cinéma. Ces grands classiques sont des films anciens° réalisés° par des cinéastes° français ou étrangers.°

---

a eu *had*   **Est-ce que vous avez vu** *Did you see*   **dure** *does ... last*   **de voir** *to see*   **films policiers** *detective movies*
peuvent *can*   **anciens** *old*   **réalisés** *made*   **cinéastes** *filmmakers*   **étrangers** *foreign*

Entracte 6   235

À Paris

CULTURAL THEME:

Paris

VIDEO ESSAY:
À Paris
Total time: 8:12 min.
(Counter: 25:23 min.)

C.1 **Introduction à Paris**
(25:23–26:36 min.)

C.2 **Interview avec Jean-Marc Lacoste**
(26:37–27:32 min.)

C.3 **Visite de Paris**
(27:33–31:40 min.)

C.4 **Promenade en bateau-mouche**
(31:41–33:30 min.)

■ Photo culture notes
Street signs
• **Concorde:** The **Place de la Concorde,** at the end of the Champs-Élysées, is one of the largest squares in the world. At the center stands **l'obélisque,** a gift to the king of France (Charles X) from the viceroy of Egypt.

• **Invalides: Les Invalides** is a former French military hospital (hence its name). Tourists come to **Les Invalides** to see Napoleon's tomb and visit the military museum.

• **Opéra:** This sign shows the way to the "old" **Opéra Garnier** in the center of Paris. The "new" **Opéra de la Bastille** is also shown on the map at the right.

• **Les Tuileries:** Le jardin des **Tuileries** is a large public park which extends from the **Place de la Concorde** to the **Louvre.**

• **Assemblée nationale:** The French legislature has two houses, **l'Assemblée nationale** (similar to the U.S. House of Representatives) and **le Sénat.**

T236

À PARIS

Bonjour, Paris!

QUELQUES FAITS

■ Paris est la capitale de la France.

■ Paris est une très grande ville. La ville de Paris a deux millions d'habitants. La région parisienne a dix millions d'habitants. Quinze pour-cent (15%) des Français habitent dans la région parisienne.

■ Paris est situé° sur la Seine. Ce fleuve° divise° la ville en deux parties: la rive° droite (au nord) et la rive gauche (au sud).

■ Administrativement, Paris est divisé en vingt arrondissements.°

■ Paris est une ville très ancienne.° Elle a plus de° deux mille° ans.

■ Paris est aussi une ville moderne et dynamique. C'est le centre économique, industriel et commercial de la France.

■ Avec ses musées, ses théâtres, ses bibliothèques, ses écoles d'art, Paris est un centre culturel et artistique très important.

■ Avec ses nombreux° monuments et ses larges avenues, Paris est une très belle ville. Pour beaucoup de gens, c'est la plus° belle ville du monde.° Chaque année,° des millions de touristes visitent Paris.

situé *located* **fleuve** *river* **divise** *divides*
rive *(river)bank* **arrondissements** *districts* **ancienne** *old*
plus de *more than* **mille** *thousand* **nombreux** *many*
la plus *the most* **monde** *world* **Chaque année** *Each year*

236

☐ Using the video
In this Video Essay, **À Paris,** Jean-Marc Lacoste (see p. 243) takes the students around Paris. Play the entire module as an introduction to the photo essay.

FRANCE

PARIS

ÉFENSE

RIVE DROITE

RIVE GAUCHE

PORTE DE
LA VILLETTE

LA VILLETTE:
CITÉ DES SCIENCES
ET DE L'INDUSTRIE

SACRÉ-COEUR

BUTTE MONTMARTRE

boulevard Malesherbes
boulevard des
Batignolles

avenue de Wagram

boulevard de
Rochechouart

boulevard
Magenta

rue de Flandre

ARC DE
TRIOMPHE

boulevard Haussmann

rue La Fayette

avenue Foch

avenue Kléber

avenue des Champs-Élysées

OPÉRA

MADELEINE

avenue de
l'Opéra

PLACE DE LA
CONCORDE

GRAND PALAIS

LOUVRE

rue du
Temple

boulevard Beaumarchais

CENTRE POMPIDOU

rue de Rivoli

INVALIDES

TOUR EIFFEL

Seine

MUSÉE D'ORSAY

boulevard des Invalides

boulevard
Saint-Germain

boulevard Raspail

boulevard Saint-Michel

NOTRE-DAME

OPÉRA DE LA
BASTILLE

avenue Daumesnil

TOUR
MONTPARNASSE

boulevard du
Montparnasse

SORBONNE

QUARTIER
LATIN

Seine

PALAIS
OMNISPORTS

PORTE DE
BERCY

Moulin Rouge   PARIS à la CARTE   TEL. 01 42 42 31 63

Montmartre   Madeleine   Invalides

(237)

■ **Photo culture notes**
(clockwise)
• La tour Eiffel
• La Place du Trocadéro
• Café Kléber at the Place du
  Trocadéro
• Les Champs-Élysées
• L'arc de Triomphe

The tourist bus is decorated with
pictures of various places in Paris.
From left to right:
• **un bateau-mouche**
• **la tour Eiffel**
• **l'arc de Triomphe**
• **les Galeries Lafayette** (department store)
• **Notre Dame**
• **l'Opéra Garnier**
• **le Moulin Rouge** (in
  Montmartre)
• **la Madeleine** (near Place de la
  Concorde)
• **les Invalides**

Le **PARIS** *traditionnel*

Le Paris traditionnel

■ Cultural background

- The Eiffel Tower was built to commemorate the 100th anniversary of the French Revolution which began July 14, 1789 and lasted ten years.
- Napoleon came to power after the French Revolution. He declared himself Emperor in 1804 and was defeated at Waterloo in 1815. In France he is remembered as a military genius and an efficient administrator.

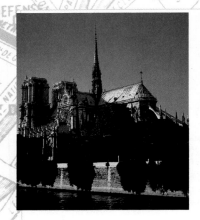

1 Notre-Dame

Notre-Dame est la cathédrale de Paris. Elle est située au centre de Paris sur une île,° l'île de la Cité. Notre-Dame a été construite° aux treizième et quatorzième siècles.°

2 La tour Eiffel

Pour beaucoup de gens, la tour Eiffel est le symbole de Paris. Cette° immense tour de fer° a trois cent mètres de haut.° Elle a été construite en 1889 (dix-huit cent quatre-vingt-neuf) par l'ingénieur Gustave Eiffel. Du sommet de la tour Eiffel, on° a une très belle vue sur Paris.

3 L'Arc de Triomphe et les Champs-Élysées

L'Arc de Triomphe est un monument qui° commémore les victoires de Napoléon (1769–1821). Ce monument est situé en haut° des Champs-Élysées. Les Champs-Élysées sont une très grande et très belle avenue avec beaucoup de cinémas, de cafés, de magasins et de boutiques élégantes.

4 Le Sacré-Coeur

Le Sacré-Coeur est une église de pierre° blanche qui domine Paris. Cette église est située sur la butte° Montmartre. Montmartre est un quartier pittoresque. Les artistes viennent ici pour peindre° et les touristes viennent pour regarder les artistes. Si vous voulez° avoir un souvenir personnel de Paris, allez à Montmartre et demandez à° un artiste de faire votre portrait.

île *island*	**a été construite** *was built*	**siècles** *centuries*	**Cette** *This* **fer** *iron*
a trois cent mètres de haut *is 300 meters high*			**qui** *which* **en haut** *at the top*
pierre *stone* **butte** *hill* **peindre** *to paint*	**voulez** *want*		**demandez à** *ask*

5 **Le Marché aux fleurs**
Ce° marché° est situé près de Notre-Dame. Ici on trouve° toutes° sortes de fleurs° et de plantes vertes. À Paris il y a beaucoup d'autres° marchés spécialisés: marché aux oiseaux,° marché aux timbres° et, bien sûr, le fameux Marché aux puces.°

6 **Le Quartier latin**
Le Quartier latin est le quartier des étudiants. C'est un quartier très animé avec des cafés, des cinémas, des librairies et des restaurants exotiques et bon marché.° Pourquoi est-ce que ce quartier s'appelle «Quartier latin»? Parce qu'autrefois° les étudiants parlaient° latin ici.

ACTIVITÉ CULTURELLE

Imaginez que vous passez une journée° à Paris. Où allez-vous aller le matin? Où allez-vous aller l'après-midi? Choisissez deux endroits à visiter et expliquez° votre choix.°

Ce *This* **marché** *market* **trouve** *finds* **toutes** *all* **fleurs** *flowers* **d'autres** *other* **oiseaux** *birds* **timbres** *stamps* **Marché aux puces** *flea market* **bon marché** *inexpensive* **autrefois** *in the past* **parlaient** *used to speak* **passez une journée** *are spending the day* **expliquez** *explain* **choix** *choice*

239

Le nouveau PARIS

■ **Cultural background**
- Mona Lisa (also known as "la Joconde") was painted by Léonard de Vinci (1452–1519).
- Le Centre Pompidou was named after Georges Pompidou (1911–1974), President of France (1969–1974).
- Claude Monet (1840–1926) and Auguste Renoir (1841–1919), Impressionist painters; Henri de Toulouse-Lautrec (1864–1901).

❶ Le Louvre et la pyramide du Louvre

Le Louvre est une ancienne° résidence royale transformée en musée. C'est dans ce° musée que se trouve° la fameuse «Mona Lisa». On entre dans le Louvre par° une pyramide de verre.° Cette pyramide moderne a été construite° par l'architecte américain I.M. Pei. Avec sa pyramide, le Louvre est le symbole du nouveau° Paris, à la fois° moderne et traditionnel.

❷ Le Centre Pompidou

Le Centre Pompidou est le monument le plus° visité de Paris. C'est un musée d'art moderne. C'est aussi une bibliothèque, une cinémathèque et un centre audio-visuel. À l'extérieur,° sur l'esplanade, il y a des musiciens, des mimes, des acrobates, des jongleurs° . . . Un peu plus loin,° il y a une place° avec des fontaines, un bassin° et des sculptures mobiles.

❸ Le musée d'Orsay

Autrefois,° c'était° une gare.° Aujourd'hui, c'est un musée. On vient ici admirer les chefs-d'oeuvre° des grands peintres° et sculpteurs français du dix-neuvième siècle.° On peut,° par exemple, admirer les oeuvres° de Monet, de Renoir et de Toulouse-Lautrec. À l'extérieur, il y a des sculptures qui représentent les cinq continents.

ancienne *former* **ce** *this* **se trouve** *is located* **par** *by* **verre** *glass* **a été construite** *was built* **nouveau** *new*	
à la fois *at the same time* **le plus** *the most* **À l'extérieur** *Outside* **jongleurs** *jugglers* **plus loin** *farther away*	
place *square* **bassin** *ornamental pool* **Autrefois** *Formerly* **c'était** *it used to be* **gare** *train station*	
chefs-d'oeuvre *masterpieces* **peintres** *painters* **siècle** *century* **peut** *can* **oeuvres** *works*	

5 Le parc de la Villette

Le parc de la Villette est un lieu° de récréation pour les jeunes de tout âge.° On trouve ici des parcs d'enfants,° des terrains de jeu° et différentes° constructions ultra-modernes.

- Le Zénith est une salle de concert où viennent les vedettes du monde° entier.
- Le Géode est un omni-cinéma avec un écran° circulaire géant.
- La Cité des sciences et de l'industrie est un grand musée scientifique où les jeunes peuvent° faire leurs propres° expériences° et jouer avec toutes sortes de gadgets électroniques.

4 Le palais Omnisports de Bercy

Sport ou musique? Bercy est le nouveau stade de Paris. C'est aussi une immense salle° de concert. On vient ici écouter et applaudir les vedettes° de la chanson° française . . . et de la chanson américaine.

6 La Défense et son arche

La Défense est le nouveau centre d'affaires° situé à l'ouest de Paris. Chaque° jour, des milliers° de Parisiens viennent travailler dans ses gratte-ciel° de verre. Il y a aussi des magasins, des cinémas, des restaurants et une patinoire.° Récemment,° une immense arche a été construite pour commémorer le deux centième anniversaire de la Révolution française.

ACTIVITÉ CULTURELLE

Vous êtes à Paris pour une semaine. Pendant votre séjour, vous voulez faire les choses suivantes. Dites où vous allez pour cela.

Quand?	Pourquoi?	Où?
▶ lundi	voir (to see) une exposition d'art moderne	??
mardi	voir une exposition sur les lasers	??
mercredi	voir la «Mona Lisa»	??
jeudi	voir un match de basket	??
vendredi	voir une exposition sur Toulouse-Lautrec	??
samedi	aller dans les magasins et faire du shopping	??

▶ Lundi, je voudrais voir une exposition d'art moderne. Je vais au Centre Pompidou.

salle *hall* **vedettes** *stars* **chanson** *song* **lieu** *place* **de tout âge** *of all ages* **parcs d'enfants** *playgrounds*
terrains de jeu *playing fields* **différentes** *several* **monde** *world* **écran** *screen* **peuvent** *can* **propres** *own*
expériences *experiments* **affaires** *business* **Chaque** *Each* **des milliers** *thousands* **gratte-ciel** *skyscrapers*
patinoire *skating rink* **Récemment** *Recently*

241

Salut, les amis!

C.1 Introduction à Paris
C.2 Interview avec
    Jean-Marc Lacoste
C.3 Visite de Paris
    (25:30–31:40 min.)

*S*alut, *les amis!*

Je m'appelle Jean-Marc Lacoste. Je suis parisien. J'habite rue Racine. C'est une petite rue du Quartier latin. Notre appartement est situé au quatrième étage° d'un vieil° immeuble. L'immeuble est très ancien (il n'y a pas d'ascenseur°), mais notre appartement est moderne et confortable.

Je vais à l'École Alsacienne où je suis élève de seconde. En général, je vais là-bas en bus. Quand il fait beau, je prends° ma mob,° ou bien° je vais à pied. C'est assez loin, mais j'adore marcher.

En semaine, j'ai beaucoup de travail et je n'ai pas le temps° de sortir.° Le weekend, c'est différent. Qu'est-ce que je fais ? Ça dépend ! Quand j'ai de l'argent,° je vais au concert. Le weekend prochain,° j'espère aller au Zénith écouter le groupe Indochine. Quand je n'ai pas d'argent, je vais au Centre Pompidou. Là, au moins,° le spectacle° est gratuit.°

J'aime aussi me promener° dans mon quartier avec mes copains. Il y a toujours quelque chose° à faire au Quartier latin. On° va au cinéma. On va dans les magasins de disques pour écouter les nouveaux albums. On va dans les librairies° pour regarder les vieux livres et les bandes dessinées.° On va au café. Là, on regarde les gens qui passent dans la rue. Parfois,° on rencontre° des filles...

Et vous, quand est-ce que vous allez venir à Paris ? Bientôt,° j'espère. Je vous attends !°

Amitiés,°
Jean-Marc

étage *floor*	**vieil** *old*	**ascenseur** *elevator*	**prends** *take*	**mob** *moped*	**ou bien** *or else*	**temps** *time*

étage *floor* **vieil** *old* **ascenseur** *elevator* **prends** *take* **mob** *moped* **ou bien** *or else* **temps** *time*
sortir *go out* **argent** *money* **prochain** *next* **au moins** *at least* **spectacle** *show* **gratuit** *free*
me promener *to go for walks* **quelque chose** *something* **On** *We* **librairies** *bookstores*
bandes dessinées *comics* **Parfois** *Sometimes* **rencontre** *meet* **Bientôt** *Soon*
Je vous attends! *I'm expecting you!* **Amitiés** *In friendship*

Pre-reading

Replay parts 2 and 3 of the video, so that students get to know Jean-Marc.
    Then have them read his letter.

Post-reading

Have students make a list of the places that Jean-Marc mentions in his letter and then locate them on the map of Paris.
    Which place or places they would like to visit with him?

*P*ARIS *en* BATEAU-MOUCHE

■ **Activité culturelle**
Answers:
• 15 F
• la tour Eiffel
 les Invalides
 l'Assemblé Nationale
 le musée d'Orsay
 l'École Nationale des Beaux Arts
 l'Institut de France
 le Palais de Justice
 Notre Dame
 St-Louis-en-l'Île
 l'Hôtel de Ville
 le Louvre
 le jardin des Tuileries
 le Grand Palais.

*C*omment visiter Paris? On peut° visiter Paris en taxi, mais c'est cher.° On peut prendre° le bus. C'est amusant, mais la circulation° à Paris est souvent difficile. On peut prendre le métro. C'est pratique, rapide et bon marché,° mais on ne voit rien.°

Pourquoi ne pas faire une promenade° en bateau-mouche?° Les bateaux-mouches sont des bateaux modernes et confortables qui circulent sur la Seine. Pendant° la promenade, on peut prendre des photos et admirer les monuments le long de° la Seine. Le soir, on peut voir les monuments illuminés!

ACTIVITÉ CULTURELLE

Vous faites une promenade en bateau-mouche.
• Combien coûte le billet?
• Quels° monuments est-ce que vous pouvez° voir?

On peut *One can*   **cher** *expensive*   **prendre** *take*   **circulation** *traffic*   **bon marché** *inexpensive*
ne voit rien *sees nothing*   **Pourquoi ne pas faire une promenade** *Why not take a ride*
bateau-mouche *sight-seeing boat*   **Pendant** *During*   **le long de** *along*   **Quels** *Which*   **pouvez** *can*

243

🖥 **Using the video**

Play Part 4 of the video, in which students are taken on a bateau-mouche ride. Students may look for **Notre Dame, la tour Eiffel,** and the many beautiful bridges and **quais** along the Seine.

Unité 7

MAIN THEME:

Buying clothes

UNITÉ 7
Modules 25–28

25. Le français pratique:
    L'achat des vêtements
26. Rien n'est parfait!
27. Un choix difficile
28. Alice a un job

UNITÉ 7 Le shopping

LEÇON 25 Le français pratique:
L'achat des vêtements

LEÇON 26 Rien n'est parfait!

LEÇON 27 Un choix difficile

LEÇON 28 Alice a un job

244

Unit overview

COMMUNICATION GOALS: Students will be able to shop for clothing, describe what people are wearing, and make comparisons.
LINGUISTIC GOALS: Students will learn the present tense of **-ir** and **-re** verbs, the imperative, and comparative forms of adjectives.

CRITICAL THINKING GOALS: Students will observe similarities and differences in the ways French and English make commands and express comparisons.
CULTURAL GOALS: Students will become aware of the French concept of style and the ways in which young people earn and spend their money.

■ **Photo culture note**
Chanel
The French design house Chanel, known for its perfumes and women's fashions, was founded by Coco Chanel (1883–1971).

THÈME ET OBJECTIFS

Buying clothes

Are you interested in clothes? When you visit France, you will enjoy going window shopping. In fact, you will probably want to try on a few items and buy something special to bring home.

In this unit, you will learn . . .
- to name and describe the clothes you wear
- to discuss style
- to shop for clothes and other items
- to talk about money

You will also be able . . .
- to point out certain people or objects to your friends
- to make comparisons
- to make suggestions and tell others what to do

MODULE 25:
Le français pratique:
L'achat des vêtements
Total time: 7:52 min.
(Counter: 33:43 min.)

■ **Comprehension practice:** Play the entire module through as an introduction to the lesson.

■ **Photo culture note**
In 1991, the Galeries Lafayette opened a store in New York City.

T246

LEÇON 25

L'achat des vêtements

LE FRANÇAIS PRATIQUE

246 Unité 7

Accent sur . . . L'élégance française

French people like to look good. Young people are generally well-informed about fashions and trends. They like to be in style, even if their clothes are casual and not too expensive. Many well-known fashion design houses started in Paris: Christian Dior, Chanel, Yves Saint-Laurent, Pierre Cardin, Sonia Rykiel.

Depending on their budgets, French young people may buy their clothes at:

- **une boutique de soldes** *(discount shop)*
- **un grand magasin** *(department store)*
- **une boutique de vêtements** *(clothing store)*
- **le Marché aux puces** *(flea market)*

● **Un grand magasin**
A large Parisian department store, the **Galeries Lafayette** has branches in other French cities. It offers a wide variety of clothing, from modestly priced items to more expensive designer labels.

Setting the stage

Ask your students if they like to shop for clothes and where they go.

Est-ce que vous aimez faire du shopping? Où allez-vous?

Allez-vous dans un grand magasin? Comment s'appelle-t-il?

Allez-vous dans une boutique de vêtements? Comment s'appelle-t-elle?

Allez-vous dans une boutique de soldes? Comment s'appelle-t-elle?

Est-ce qu'il y a une marché aux puces dans notre ville?

Tell students that in the video they will observe French young people shopping for clothes. In the *Vignette culturelle*, they will see various types of clothing stores.

- **Une boutique de vêtements**
  There are several **Céline** shops in Paris. They sell relatively expensive designer clothes.

25.7 Vignette culturelle: Où acheter les vêtements?
(40:00–41:31 min.)

■ **Language notes**
un mouton = sheep
une patte = foot (of an animal)

- **Une boutique de soldes**
  At a discount store called the **Mouton à cinq pattes,** you can find jeans and casual clothes at good prices.

Classroom Notes

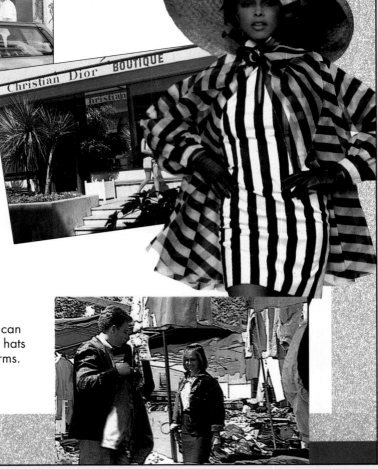

- **Une maison de couture**
  One of the most famous French fashion design houses is that of **Christian Dior.** Every season it presents a new collection which influences fashion trends all over the world. Christian Dior sells original designer dresses at very high prices, but also markets a more affordable line of clothes under its ready-to-wear label.

- **Le Marché aux puces**
  At the **Marché aux puces,** you can find all types of used clothes, from hats of the 1930's to old military uniforms.

Critical thinking skills

English has borrowed many words pertaining to clothing and fashion: **boutique, eau de cologne, haute couture.**

Ask students to list other borrowed French words relating to fashion and clothes.

For example:

chemise	**crêpe**
culottes	**maillot**
chic	

Section A

COMMUNICATIVE FUNCTION:
Talking about clothing

 25.1 Mini-scenes: Qu'est-ce que vous cherchez?
(36:42–37:39 min.)

 Leçon 25, Section 1

 Transparency 35
Les vêtements

▪ **Looking ahead:** Students will learn the forms of **acheter** in Lesson 26.

▪ **Language notes**
- **Un pull** is a shortened form of **un pull-over**, which is a borrowed word from English. It is used for any sweater which is pulled over the head. French has also borrowed the word **un sweater** /swɛtɛr/.
- In Quebec, **un chandail** /ʃɑ̃daj/ is used for **un pull**.

▪ **Pronunciation:** Be sure students say **pull** /pyl/ with the /y/ of **tu**.

Supplementary vocabulary

faire les magasins *to go shopping (browsing from store to store)*
un anorak *ski jacket*
un costume *man's suit*
un tailleur *woman's suit*

A. Les vêtements

Je vais dans un magasin.

How to talk about shopping for clothes:

Où vas-tu?
Je vais | dans **une boutique** *(shop)*.
| dans **un magasin** *(store)*
| dans **un grand magasin** *(department store)*
Qu'est-ce que tu vas **acheter** *(to buy)*?
Je vais acheter **des vêtements** *(clothes)*.

Les vêtements

Pour hommes et femmes

un chapeau
une veste
un blouson
un manteau
un pull
un imper (un imperméable)
un pantalon
un jean
une chemise
un polo
des chaussettes (une chaussette)

➡ Nouns that end in **-eau** in the singular end in **-eaux** in the plural.
un chap**eau**   des chap**eaux**   un mant**eau**   des mant**eaux**

T248

TPR 🏃 Clothes

PROPS: A bag of old clothes in large sizes

Give students various items of clothing.
   X, montre-nous le pull.
   Y, montre-nous la cravate. ...
   Qui a le pull? [X]...
If appropriate, have students try items on.

Z, mets le chapeau. Ah, c'est très joli!
   Qui porte le chapeau? [Z]
Have students move the clothing around.
   X, mets le pull sur la chaise de Z.
   Où est le pull? [sur la chaise de Z]
   Z, donne le pull à W.
   Qui a le pull maintenant? [W]

Pour hommes		Pour femmes		
une cravate	un chemisier	une jupe	une robe	des collants (un collant)

acheter	*to buy*	Je vais **acheter** une cravate.
porter	*to wear*	Qu'est-ce que tu vas **porter** demain?
mettre	*to put on, wear*	Oh là là, il fait froid. Je vais **mettre** un pull.

➡ **Mettre** is irregular. (Its forms are presented in Leçon 26.)

1 Shopping

Below are the names of several Paris stores. Using the illustrations as a guide, talk to a classmate about where you are going shopping and what you plan to buy.

▶ —Où vas-tu?
—Je vais au Monoprix.
—Qu'est-ce que tu vas acheter?
—Je vais acheter une chemise.

(au) MONOPRIX

1. (au) PRINTEMPS

2. (au) BON MARCHÉ

3. (au) PRISUNIC

4. (chez) CÉLINE

5. (aux) GALERIES LAFAYETTE

6. (chez) BURBERRY

7. (chez) DIOR

8. (à) LA SAMARITAINE

2 Quels vêtements?

What we wear often depends on the circumstances: where we are, what we will be doing, what the weather is like. Complete the following sentences with the appropriate items of clothing.

1. Aujourd'hui, je porte...
2. Le professeur porte...
3. L'élève à ma gauche porte...
4. L'élève à ma droite porte...
5. Quand je vais à une boum, je porte...
6. Quand je vais dans un restaurant élégant, je porte...
7. S'il pleut *(If it rains)* demain, je vais mettre...
8. S'il fait chaud demain, je vais mettre...
9. Si *(If)* je vais en ville samedi, je vais mettre...
10. Si je vais à un concert dimanche, je vais mettre...

Leçon 25 249

1 EXCHANGES: talking about shopping plans

1. au Printemps / un pantalon
2. au Bon Marché / une robe
3. au Prisunic / des chaussettes
4. chez Céline / une jupe
5. aux Galeries Lafayette / un blouson
6. chez Burberry / un imper[méable]
7. chez Dior / un chemisier
8. à la Samaritaine / un manteau

2 COMMUNICATION: talking about clothes

■ Expansion
Quand il neige, je porte...
Quand je vais en ville, je porte...
Quand je vais à un match de football américain, je porte...
Quand je vais au cinéma avec mes copains, je porte...

Supplementary listening practice

You can build listening comprehension skills by talking about the clothing that students are wearing. Students respond with gestures or one-word answers. Repeat each item of clothing in several different questions and responses.

For example:
Qui porte un polo aujourd'hui?
W et X portent un polo.
Y ne porte pas de polo.
Et toi, Z, tu portes un polo? [oui]
De quelle couleur est le polo de Z? [bleu]
Mais oui, il est bleu...

Cooperative pair practice
Activity 1

COMMUNICATIVE FUNCTION:
Talking about clothing
and accessories

25.4 Mini-scenes: Vous désirez?
(37:40–38:37 min.)

Leçon 24, Section 2

Transparency 36
Vêtements et accessoires

■ **Pronunciation:** Un swea**t** is
pronounced /swit/.

■ **Casual speech:** Un maillot de
bain is often referred to as **un
maillot.**

■ **Language note:** Point out that
des lunettes (de soleil) is feminine.

Supplementary vocabulary

LES ACCESSOIRES
des gants (m.) *gloves*
un foulard *(silk) scarf*
un mouchoir *handkerchief*
une casquette *cap*
des verres (m.) **de contact**
    contact lenses
une écharpe *(winter) scarf*

LES BIJOUX
un bijou *piece of jewelry*
un collier *necklace*
un bracelet
une bague *ring*
une chaîne *chain*
des boucles (f.) **d'oreille** *earrings*

③ DESCRIPTION: indicating
what people are wearing

1. des lunettes de soleil, un polo,
   un short, des sandales
2. un maillot de bain, des tennis
3. un survêtement, des baskets
4. un sweat, un short, des lunettes
   de soleil
5. (answers will vary)

■ **Challenge:** Students say what
each person is NOT wearing,
using **pas de.**
Paul ne porte pas de tee-shirt.

T250

Je vais mettre
des lunettes de soleil.

B. D'autres vêtements et accessoires

Les chaussures

les chaussures
(une chaussure)

des tennis
(une tennis)

des sandales
(une sandale)

des bottes
(une botte)

des baskets
(une basket)

**Les vêtements
de sport**

un sweat

un short

un tee-shirt

un survêtement
(un jogging)

un maillot de bain

Les accessoires

une ceinture

des lunettes

des lunettes
de soleil

---

③ **À la plage de Deauville**

You are spending the summer vacation in Deauville, a popular ocean resort in Normandy.
Describe what you and your friends are wearing.

▶ **Paul**   **1. Anne**   **2. Sophie**   **3. Michel**   **4. Catherine**   **5. moi**

▶ Paul porte un maillot de bain ...

Talking about past events

Let's talk about what you wore yesterday.
Remember to use **pas de** in negative
answers.

▶ **Est-ce que tu as porté un manteau
hier?**
  Oui, j'ai porté un manteau.
  (Non, je n'ai pas porté de manteau.)

• **Est-ce que tu as porté un manteau hier?**
• **Est-ce que tu as porté un chapeau hier?**
• **Est-ce que tu as porté un survêtement?**
• **Est-ce que tu as porté des lunettes de
  soleil?**
• **Est-ce que tu as porté des tennis?**
• **Est-ce que tu as porté une cravate?**

4 **Qu'est-ce que tu portes?**

Ask your classmates what they wear in the following circumstances. Let them use their imagination.

▶ jouer au tennis

1. aller à la piscine
2. aller à la plage
3. jouer au basket
4. travailler dans le jardin
5. aller au gymnase *(gym)*
6. faire une promenade dans la forêt *(forest)*
7. faire une promenade dans la neige *(snow)*

> Qu'est-ce que tu portes quand tu joues au tennis?

> Je porte un tee-shirt, un short et des tennis.

5 **Un jeu**

When you see what people are wearing, you can often tell what they are going to do. How many different logical sentences can you make in five minutes? Follow the model below.

A	B	C
André	un maillot de bain	nager
Sylvie	des lunettes de soleil	aller à la plage
Paul et Éric	un short	aller à un concert
Michèle et Anne	des chaussettes blanches	jouer au tennis
	un sweat	jouer au volley
	un pantalon très chic	jouer au football
	des chaussures noires	aller à la campagne *(country)*
	des bottes	faire du jogging *(to jog)*
	un costume *(suit)*	dîner en ville
	une robe	

> Sylvie porte un short. Elle va jouer au football.

6 **Joyeux anniversaire!**

The following people are celebrating their birthdays. Find a present for each person by choosing an item of clothing from pages 248, 249, or 250.

1. Pour mon père (ma mère), je vais acheter, …
2. Pour ma grand-mère (mon grand-père), …
3. Pour ma petite cousine Chantal (10 ans), …
4. Pour mon grand frère Guillaume (18 ans), …
5. Pour le professeur, …
6. Pour mon meilleur *(best)* ami, …
7. Pour ma meilleure amie, …

4 COMMUNICATION: talking about what one wears when

■ **Challenge:** Have students ask questions using **si** *(if)* and **mettre**.
– Qu'est-ce que tu vas mettre si tu vas à la plage samedi?
– Je vais mettre…

5 COMPREHENSION: describing clothes and related activities

■ **Variation** (conversation format): Student 1 states what someone is wearing. Student 2 asks why. Student 3 gives the reason.
– Sylvie porte un short.
– Pourquoi?
– Elle va jouer au football.

■ **Variation:** Have students reverse columns B and C, using **mettre**.
André va nager.
Il va mettre un maillot de bain.

6 COMMUNICATION: selecting gifts

- **Est-ce que tu as porté une robe?**
- **Qu'est-ce que tu as porté hier?**
- **Qu'est-ce que tu as porté vendredi soir? samedi après-midi? dimanche matin?**

Follow-up:
- **Qu'est-ce que X a porté hier?**
- **Qu'est-ce que Y a porté vendredi soir?**
- **Qu'est-ce que Z a porté dimanche matin?**

Cooperative pair practice
Activity 4

25.1 Introduction: Le shopping
25.2 Dialogue: Aux Galeries Lafayette (33:55–36:41 min.)
25.6 Mini-scenes: Comment trouves-tu ma robe? (39:23–39:59 min.)

 Leçon 25, Sections 3, 6

Transparency 37
Comparing clothing

Classroom Notes

C. Dans un magasin

Pardon, madame.

Vous désirez, mademoiselle?

Je cherche un pantalon.

▶ *How to get help from a salesperson:*

Pardon, monsieur (madame).
Vous désirez *(May I help you)*, | **monsieur?**
| **madame**
| **mademoiselle**

Je cherche *(I'm looking for)* . . .
un pantalon.
Quel est le prix *(What is the price)* du pantalon?
Combien *(How much)* **coûte** le pantalon?
Combien est-ce qu'il coûte?
Il coûte 200 francs.

Je cherche . . .
une veste.
Quel est le prix de la veste?
Combien coûte la veste?
Combien est-ce qu'elle coûte?
Elle coûte 300 francs.

▶ *How to discuss clothes with a friend:*

Qu'est-ce que tu penses du pantalon vert?
(What do you think of . . . ?)
Comment trouves-tu le pantalon vert?
(What do you think of . . . ?)

Qu'est-ce que tu penses de
la veste verte?
Comment trouves-tu
la veste verte?

Comment trouves-tu le pantalon vert?

Il est trop petit.

Il est	**joli.**		Elle est	**jolie.**
	élégant			**élégante**
	super			**super**
	chouette *(terrific)*			**chouette**
	à la mode *(in style)*			**à la mode**
Il est	**moche** *(plain, ugly).*		Elle est	**moche.**
	démodé *(out of style)*			**démodée**
Il est **trop** *(too)*	**petit.**		Elle est **trop**	**petite.**
	grand *(big)*			**grande**
	court *(short)*			**courte**
	long *(long)*			**longue**
Il est	**cher** *(expensive).*		Elle est	**chère.**
	bon marché *(cheap)*			**bon marché**

➡ **Super** and **bon marché** are INVARIABLE. They do not take adjective endings.
La robe rouge est **super.**   Les chaussures blanches sont **bon marché.**

VERBES
chercher | *to look for* | Je **cherche** un jean.
coûter | *to cost* | Les chaussures **coûtent** 300 francs.
penser | *to think* | Qu'est-ce que tu **penses** de cette *(this)* robe?
penser que | *to think (that)* | Je **pense qu'**elle est super!
trouver | *to find* | Je ne **trouve** pas ma veste.
| *to think of* | Comment **trouves**-tu mes lunettes de soleil?

➡ The verb **penser** is often used alone.
   Tu **penses?**   *Do you think so?*   Je **ne pense pas.**   *I don't think so.*

Game: Prices

PROP: Transparency 12

Using the menu on the transparency, have each student write an addition problem with an answer that is under 100 francs. For example:
Combien coûtent 2 steak-frites et 2 thés? [86 francs]

Place the problems into a hat. Divide the class into two teams. Draw a problem from the hat and read it aloud. Player A-1 plays against player B-1. The first player from either team to stand and answer correctly wins a point. If the response is incorrect, the other player tries to answer. Continue with players A-2 and B-2, etc.

Les nombres de 100 à 1000

100	cent	200	deux cents	500	cinq cents	800	huit cents
101	cent un	300	trois cents	600	six cents	900	neuf cents
102	cent deux	400	quatre cents	700	sept cents	1000	mille

7 Au Marché aux puces

You are at the Paris flea market looking for clothes with a French friend. Explain why you are not buying the following items. Use your imagination ... and expressions from the **Vocabulaire.**

▶ — Tu vas acheter le blouson?
— Non, je ne pense pas.
— Pourquoi pas?
— Il est trop grand.

8 C'est combien?

You are at the Printemps, a department store in Paris. Ask a salesperson how much the various items cost.

Pardon, mademoiselle, combien coûte le polo?

Il coûte 200 francs.

Merci.

▷ **Les nombres de 100 à 1000**

 Leçon 25, Section 4

■ **Language notes**
• When used with a noun, as in **200 francs — deux cent francs** — there is no "s" on **cent**.
• The word **mille** never takes an "s": **deux mille, trois mille**, etc. Note: at this level, students are not expected to spell the numbers.

7 EXCHANGES: explaining why one is not buying certain items

1. une cravate
2. un pull
3. un jean
4. un chapeau
5. une veste
6. un imper[méable]
7. des bottes (Elles sont ...)

8 ROLE PLAY: asking about prices

1. la veste
2. l'imper[méable]
3. la ceinture
4. les lunettes de soleil
5. les chaussures

 25.5 Mini-scenes: Combien coûte la veste? (38:39–39:22 min.)

 Leçon 25, Section 5

Challenge activity: Une idole

Une idole is a music superstar. Have students bring in a picture of an American **idole** and describe what he/she is wearing. They can give the approximate prices and comment on the style. For example:

Mon idole est Michael Jackson. Ici il porte un blouson qui (which) **coûte $150 et un pantalon qui coûte $75. Le blouson est trop grand mais le pantalon est très élégant. Il porte aussi des lunettes de soleil. Elles sont chouettes mais chères: elles coûtent $200!**

Cooperative pair practice
Activities 7, 8

T253

À votre tour!

1 COMPREHENSION

1-c   4-b
2-d   5-a
3-e

🔊 Leçon 25, Section 7

■ Photo culture note
Au grand magasin
Note the signs in the store:
- **Caisse** (cashier)
- **Sortie** (exit)

2 GUIDED ORAL EXPRESSION

1. un pull rouge
2. un imper[méable] bleu
3. une veste jaune
4. un tee-shirt blanc
5. une cravate orange
6. une ceinture blanche

🔊 Leçon 25, Section 8

■ Cultural note
Place Bonaventure is part of Montreal's unique underground city. Various underground neighborhoods are linked by metro and climate-controlled corridors, a feature which Montrealers greatly appreciate in the wintertime. Between **Place Bonaventure** and **Place du Canada** one can find supermarkets, banks, boutiques, beauty salons, cinemas, theaters, hotels, and two railway stations.

1 La bonne réponse

You are in a French department store. Match the questions on the left with the appropriate answers on the right.

1. Vous désirez, monsieur?	a. Mon pantalon gris et ma veste bleue.
2. Est-ce que tu vas acheter le survêtement bleu?	b. 900 francs.
3. Comment trouves-tu les lunettes de soleil?	c. Je cherche une cravate.
4. Combien coûte l'imper?	d. Non, il est trop cher.
5. Qu'est-ce que tu vas mettre pour aller au restaurant?	e. Elles sont chouettes.

2 Créa-dialogue

You are at Place Bonaventure in Montreal looking at clothes in various shops. You like what the salesperson shows you and ask how much each item costs. React to the price.

joli/$60

1. élégant/$30

2. joli/$150

3. à la mode/$50

4. super/$15

5. chouette/$10

6. ??/??

▸ —Vous désirez, monsieur (mademoiselle)?
—Je cherche <u>un pantalon</u>.
—Comment trouvez-vous <u>le pantalon gris</u>?
—Il est <u>joli</u>. Combien est-ce qu'<u>il</u> coûte?
—<u>Soixante</u> dollars.
—Oh là là, <u>il</u> est cher!
(Il est bon marché.)

254   Unité 7

À votre tour
Depending on your goals and objectives, you may or may not wish to assign all of the activities in the **À votre tour** section.

👥 Cooperative practice
Act. 1–4 lend themselves to cooperative pair practice.

T254

③ Conversation dirigée

Sophie and Christophe are shopping in a department store. Act out their conversation in French.

Sophie			Christophe
asks Christophe what he is looking for	→ ←	answers that he is looking for a tie	
asks him what he thinks of the yellow tie	→ ←	says that it is pretty but adds that he is going to buy the blue tie	
asks how much it costs	⇄	answers 25 francs	
says that it is inexpensive but adds that the tie is out of style			

④ Qu'est-ce qui ne va pas? *(What's wrong?)*

The people in the pictures below are not very good shoppers. Describe what is wrong with each of the items they bought.

Monsieur Dupont   **Édouard**

▶ Le chapeau de Monsieur Dupont est trop grand.

⑤ Les valises

Imagine that you are spending a year in Paris. On two different weekends, you have been invited by families of your classmates to visit their homes. On the first weekend, you will visit Nice and go sailing in the Mediterranean. For the second weekend, you have been invited to go skiing at Chamonix in the French Alps. Prepare your suitcases for the two trips, listing the items you will take with you.

▶ *un maillot de bain / deux shorts* — *un jean / un pull*

⑥ À l'aéroport

Next week you are going to Paris for the first time on an exchange program. At the airport, you will be met by your host family. They do not have a picture of you. Describe yourself in a short note, telling what you look like and what you are going to wear.

▶

Je vais arriver à Paris par le vol (Flight) Air France 070. Je suis... Je vais porter...

---

③ GUIDED ORAL EXPRESSION

S: Qu'est-ce que tu cherches?
C: Je cherche une cravate.
S: Comment trouves-tu la cravate jaune?
C: Elle est jolie, mais je vais acheter la cravate rouge.
S: Combien est-ce qu'elle coûte?
C: Elle coûte 25 francs.
S: Elle est bon marché (elle n'est pas chère), mais elle est démodée.

🔊 Leçon 25, Section 9

④ COMPREHENSION

Monsieur Dupont:
La veste est trop grande.
Le pantalon est trop court.
Édouard:
La chemise est trop petite.
La cravate est trop longue (grande).
Le pantalon est trop long (grand).

⑤ WRITTEN SELF-EXPRESSION

⑥ WRITTEN SELF-EXPRESSION

📖 Portfolio assessment

You will probably select only one speaking activity and one writing activity to go into the students' portfolios for Unit 7.

In this lesson, Act. 2 lends itself well to an oral portfolio recording.

Act. 6 offers a good writing portfolio topic.

T255

MODULE 26:
Rien n'est parfait!
Total time: 5:22 min.
(Counter: 41:41 min.)

26.1 Dialogue: Rien n'est parfait!
(42:08–43:11 min.)

26.2 Mini-scenes: Listening — Comment trouves-tu ce pull?
(43:12–44:26 min.)

26.3 Mini-scenes: Listening — Quel café?
(44:27–44:54 min.)

26.4 Mini-scenes: Speaking — Quelle veste désirez-vous?
(44:55–45:38 min.)

26.5 Vignette culturelle: Un grand magasin
(45:39–46:59 min.)

■ **Comprehension practice:** Play the entire module through as an introduction to the lesson.

 26.1 Dialogue: Rien n'est parfait!
(42:08–43:11 min.)

 Leçon 26, Section 1

 Transparency 38
Dans un grand magasin

LEÇON 26
Rien n'est parfait!

<u>Cet</u> après-midi, Frédéric et Jean-Claude vont acheter des vêtements. Ils vont acheter <u>ces</u> vêtements dans un grand magasin. <u>Ce</u> magasin s'appelle Le Bon Marché.

This

these / This

Scène 1.
Frédéric et Jean-Claude regardent les pulls.

FRÉDÉRIC:	Regarde! Comment trouves-tu ce pull?	
JEAN-CLAUDE:	Quel pull?	*Which*
FRÉDÉRIC:	Ce pull bleu.	
JEAN-CLAUDE:	Il est chouette.	
FRÉDÉRIC:	C'est vrai, il est très chouette.	
JEAN-CLAUDE:	*(qui regarde le prix)* Il est aussi très cher.	
FRÉDÉRIC:	Combien est-ce qu'il coûte?	
JEAN-CLAUDE:	Six cents francs.	
FRÉDÉRIC:	Six cents francs! Quelle horreur!	*What a scandal!*

NOTE CULTURELLE

Le grand magasin

Many people consider the department store **(le grand magasin)** to be a typically American institution. However, it is a Frenchman, Aristide Boucicaut (1810–1877), who is generally credited with its creation. Monsieur Boucicaut's idea was to satisfy his Paris customers by offering them a large selection of good quality items at inexpensive prices. When he opened his new store in 1852, he appropriately named it Au Bon Marché. His success was soon imitated, leading to the creation in Paris of more department stores: Printemps, Galeries Lafayette, Samaritaine. These well-known stores still exist today and have branches in cities across France.

 256 Unité 7

☀ Warm-up and review

PROP: Transparency 38

Using a transparency marker, fill in prices up to 1000 francs in the price tags on the transparency. Then ask questions about the items of clothing and their prices.

Qu'est-ce que c'est?
C'est un pantalon noir.
Combien coûte le pantalon?
Il coûte [six cent cinquante] francs.
C'est cher?
Mais oui, c'est très cher.

Scène 2.

Maintenant Frédéric et Jean-Claude regardent les vestes.

FRÉDÉRIC: Quelle veste est-ce que tu préfères?

JEAN-CLAUDE: Je préfère cette veste jaune. Elle est très élégante et elle n'est pas très chère.

FRÉDÉRIC: Oui, mais elle est trop grande pour toi!

JEAN-CLAUDE: Dommage!

 26.5 **Vignette culturelle: Un grand magasin** (45:39–46:59 min.)

Scène 3.

Marc est au rayon des chaussures. Quelles chaussures est-ce qu'il va acheter?
department

JEAN-CLAUDE: Alors, quelles chaussures est-ce que tu achètes?

FRÉDÉRIC: J'achète ces chaussures noires. Elles sont très confortables . . . et elles ne sont pas chères. Regarde, elles sont en solde.
on sale

JEAN-CLAUDE: C'est vrai, elles sont en solde . . . mais elles ne sont plus à la mode.
are no longer

FRÉDÉRIC: Hélas, rien n'est parfait!
too bad/nothing is perfect

COMPREHENSION

1. dans un grand magasin (au Bon Marché)
2. acheter des vêtements
3. les pulls
4. 600 francs
5. Il pense que le pull est trop cher. (Il ne va pas acheter le pull.)
6. Elle est élégante. Elle n'est pas chère.
7. Elle est trop grande.
8. Elles sont confortables. (Elles ne sont pas chères.)
9. Elles ne sont pas à la mode.

 Compréhension

1. Où vont Frédéric et Jean-Claude cet après-midi?
2. Qu'est-ce qu'ils vont faire?
3. Qu'est-ce qu'ils regardent d'abord *(first)*?
4. Combien coûte le pull bleu?
5. Quelle *(What)* est la réaction de Frédéric?
6. Qu'est-ce que Jean-Claude pense de la veste jaune?
7. Pourquoi est-ce qu'il n'achète pas la veste?
8. Qu'est-ce que Frédéric pense des chaussures noires?
9. Pourquoi est-ce qu'il n'achète pas les chaussures?

Note culturelle

■ In 1989, **Au Bon Marché** changed its name to **Le Bon Marché.**

■ **Photo culture note**
La Samaritaine
The Samaritaine Department store in Paris faces the Seine River. On the top floor is a restaurant which is especially popular because of its panoramic view of the city.

Leçon 26 257

Leçon 26, Section 2

Teaching strategies

- Point out that the stem changes occur only in those forms of the verb where the ending is not pronounced. There is no stem change before **-ons** and **-ez.**
- For your visually-minded students you can present stem-changing verbs as "boot verbs." Within the "boot" the verb endings are not pronounced and there is the same change in the stem. Outside the boot, the endings are pronounced, and there is no stem change.

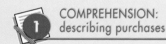

j'achète	nous achetons
tu achète	vous achetez
il achète	ils achètent

COMPREHENSION:
describing purchases

A. Les verbes *acheter* et *préférer*

Verbs like **acheter** *(to buy)* end in: **e** + CONSONANT + **-er.**
Verbs like **préférer** *(to prefer)* end in: **é** + CONSONANT + **-er.**

Note the forms of these two verbs in the chart, paying attention to:
- the **e** of the stem of **acheter**
- the **é** of the stem of **préférer**

INFINITIVE	acheter	préférer
PRESENT	J' ach**è**te une veste. Tu ach**è**tes une cravate. Il/Elle ach**è**te un imper.	Je préf**è**re la veste bleue. Tu préf**è**res la cravate jaune. Il/Elle préf**è**re l'imper gris.
	Nous achetons un jean. Vous achetez un short. Ils/Elles ach**è**tent un pull.	Nous préférons le jean noir. Vous préférez le short blanc. Ils/Elles préf**è**rent le pull rouge.

→ Verbs like **acheter** and **préférer** take regular endings and have the following changes in the stem:

> acheter e → è } in the **je, tu, il,** and **ils**
> préférer é → è } forms of the present

1 **Achats** *(Purchases)*

What we buy depends on how much money we have. Complete the sentences below with **acheter** and one or more of the items from the list.

1. Avec dix dollars, tu …
2. Avec quinze dollars, j' …
3. Avec trente dollars, nous …
4. Avec cinquante dollars, Jean-Claude …
5. Avec cent dollars, vous …
6. Avec quinze mille dollars, mes parents …
7. Avec ?? dollars, mon cousin …
8. Avec ?? dollars, j' …

une voiture

des chaussures

un survêtement

une cravate

des lunettes de soleil

un polo

une veste

un compact

un jean

??

Talking about past events

Let's talk about what clothes you bought last summer.

▶ **Est-ce que tu as acheté un jean l'été dernier?**
Oui, j'ai acheté un jean.
(Non, je n'ai pas acheté de jean.)
- **Est-ce que tu as acheté un polo?**

- **Est-ce que tu as acheté des sandales?**
- **Est-ce que tu as acheté un maillot de bain?**
- **Est-ce que tu as acheté une veste?**
- **Qu'est-ce que tu as acheté?**
Follow-up:
   Est-ce que X a acheté un jean?

Vocabulaire: Verbes comme (like) *acheter* et *préférer*

acheter	*to buy*	Qu'est-ce que tu **achètes?**
amener	*to bring (a person)*	François **amène** sa copine à la boum.
préférer	*to prefer*	**Préfères**-tu le manteau ou l'imper?
espérer	*to hope*	J'**espère** visiter Paris en été.

➡ In French, there are two verbs that correspond to the English *to bring:*
amener + PEOPLE — J'**amène** une copine au pique-nique.
apporter + THINGS — J'**apporte** des sandwichs au pique-nique.

2 **Pique-nique**

Everyone is bringing someone or something to the picnic. Complete the sentences below with the appropriate forms of **amener** or **apporter.**

▶ Nous amenons un copain.   Marc apporte des sandwichs.

1. Tu . . . ta guitare.
2. Philippe . . . sa soeur.
3. Nous . . . nos voisins.
4. Vous . . . un dessert.
5. Michèle . . . des sodas.
6. Antoine et Vincent . . . leur cousine.
7. Raphaël . . . ses cassettes.
8. Mon cousin . . . sa copine.
9. J' . . . ma radiocassette.

3 **Expression personnelle**

Complete the sentences below with one of the suggested options or an expression of your choice. Note: You may wish to make some of the sentences negative.

1. Quand je vais à un pique-nique, j'amène . . . (ma petite soeur, mes voisins, mon chien, ??) J'apporte . . . (mon walkman, mon livre de français, des sandwichs, ??)
2. Quand je vais à une boum, j'amène . . . (des copains, une copine, ma grand-mère, ??) J'apporte . . . (des sandwichs, ma guitare, mes cassettes, ??)
3. Le weekend, je préfère . . . (étudier, aller au cinéma, rester à la maison, ??) Ce *(This)* weekend, j'espère . . . (travailler, avoir un rendez-vous avec un copain ou une copine, jouer au volley, ??)

Quand je vais à un pique-nique, j'amène mon chat.

Et moi, j'amène mon chien.

4. Pendant *(During)* les vacances, j'espère . . . (rester à la maison, trouver un job, voyager, ??) Un jour, j'espère . . . (visiter la France, parler français, aller à l'université, être millionnaire, ??)

Leçon 26 (259)

Talking about past events

Let's talk about what things you brought to a recent party.

▶ Tu es allé(e) à une boum récemment.
Est-ce que tu as apporté des cassettes?
Oui, j'ai apporté des cassettes.
(Non, je n'ai pas apporté de cassettes.)

- Est-ce que tu as apporté des compacts?
- Est-ce que tu as apporté des disques?
- Est-ce que tu as apporté une guitare?
- Est-ce que tu as apporté des pizzas?
- Est-ce que tu as apporté des sodas?
- Qu'est-ce que tu as apporté?

■ **Teaching strategy:** Using subject pronoun cue cards, have students conjugate **amener** and **espérer** orally and in writing.

COMPREHENSION: describing what and whom people are bringing to a picnic

2

1. apportes
2. amène
3. amenons
4. apportez
5. apporte
6. amènent
7. apporte
8. amène
9. apporte

COMMUNICATION: describing what one does and hopes to do

3

■ **Expansion:** In trios, have students discuss and vote on the choices. The recorder (**secrétaire**) then writes the sentences in the **nous**-form.
1. **Quand nous allons à un pique-nique, nous amenons [nos voisins]. Nous apportons [des sandwiches].**
Answers:
2. nous allons..., nous amenons..., nous apportons...
3. nous préférons..., nous espérons...
4. nous espérons..., nous espérons...

■ **Variation** (with **amener**):
Est-ce que tu as amené
un copain?
une copine?
des amis français?
des cousins?

Section B

COMMUNICATIVE FUNCTION:
Pointing out people and things

 26.2 Mini-scenes:
Comment trouves-tu
ce pull?
(43:12–44:26 min.)

▭ **Leçon 26, Section 3**

■ **Teaching strategies**
• Point out that **ces** (like **les, des, mes**) is used with both masculine and feminine plural nouns. (There is no **cettes**.)
• Tell students that the masculine singular form **cet** is derived from the feminine singular form **cette** minus **-te**: **cette → cet.**

■ **Language note:** The tag **-ci** is related to **ici** *(here)* and **-là** means *there.* The expression **voici** has evolved from **vois ici** *(see here)* and **voilà** from **vois là** *(see there).*

4 ROLE PLAY: commenting on items in a store

■ **Expansion:** Now Nathalie is with Jérôme who is critical of everything. Have students use an expression of their choice in Jérôme's responses.
N: **Regarde cette robe!**
 Elle est jolie!
J: **Cette robe-là?**
 Elle est moche.
 (Elle n'est pas à la mode. etc.)

5 ROLE PLAY: discussing preferences

 Cooperative pair practice Activities 4, 5, 6

B. L'adjectif démonstratif *ce*

Note the forms of the demonstrative adjective **ce** in the chart below.

	SINGULAR *(this, that)*	PLURAL *(these, those)*		
MASCULINE	**ce** ↓ **cet** (+ VOWEL SOUND)	**ces**	**ce** blouson **cet** homme	**ces** blousons **ces** hommes
FEMININE	**cette**	**ces**	**cette** veste **cette** amie	**ces** vestes **ces** amies

➡ There is liaison after **cet** and **ces** when the next word begins with a vowel sound.

➡ To distinguish between a person or an object that is close by and one that is further away, the French sometimes use **-ci** or **-là** after the noun.

Philippe achète **cette chemise-ci.** *Philippe is buying **this shirt** (over here).*
François achète **cette chemise-là.** *François is buying **that shirt** (over there).*

4 À la Samaritaine

Marc and Nathalie are at the Samaritaine department store. Marc likes everything that Nathalie shows him. Play both roles.

▶ une robe (jolie)   NATHALIE: **Regarde cette robe!**
            MARC: **Elle est jolie!**

1. un imper (élégant)   4. un survêtement (super)   7. une télé (moderne)
2. des bottes (à la mode)   5. des livres (amusants)   8. une ceinture (jolie)
3. une cravate (chouette)   6. un ordinateur (super)   9. des sandales (jolies)

Expression pour la conversation

How to emphasize a question or remark:

Eh bien! *Well!* —**Eh bien,** est-ce que tu viens en ville avec nous?
              —**Eh bien,** non!

5 Différences d'opinion

Whenever they go shopping together, Éric and Brigitte cannot agree on what they like. Play both roles.

▶ un short

J'aime ce short-ci.

Eh bien, moi, je préfère ce short-là.

1. une chemise   5. des disques
2. un blouson   6. une affiche
3. des chaussures 7. un stylo
4. des lunettes   8. un ordinateur

C. L'adjectif interrogatif *quel?*

The interrogative adjective **quel** *(what? which?)* is used in questions. It agrees with the noun it introduces and has the following forms:

	SINGULAR	PLURAL		
MASCULINE	quel	quels	**Quel** garçon?	**Quels** cousins?
FEMININE	quelle	quelles	**Quelle** fille?	**Quelles** copines?

➡ Note the liaison after **quels** and **quelles** when the next word begins with a vowel sound.
Quelles affiches est-ce que tu préfères?

6 Vêtements d'été

You are shopping for the following items before going on a summer trip to France. A friend is asking you which ones you are buying. Identify each item by color.

J'achète une jupe.

Cette jupe jaune.

Quelle jupe est-ce que tu achètes?

une jupe/ jaune

1. un maillot de bain/ bleu

2. des chaussettes/ vertes

3. un pantalon/ noir

4. une veste/ bleue

5. des chaussures/ blanches

6. des sandales/ brunes

7. un sweat/ gris

8. une chemise/ orange

9. un pull/ rouge

7 Questions personnelles

1. À quelle école vas-tu?
2. Dans quel magasin achètes-tu tes vêtements?
3. Dans quel magasin achètes-tu tes chaussures?
4. Quels disques aimes-tu écouter?
5. Quels programmes aimes-tu regarder à la télé?
6. Quel est ton restaurant préféré?

Leçon 26 **261**

Section C

COMMUNICATIVE FUNCTION:
Asking for clarification

 26.3 Mini-scenes: Quel café?
26.4 Mini-scenes: Quelle veste désirez-vous? (44:27–45:38 min.)

 Leçon 26, Sections 4, 5

■ **Language notes**
• Point out that all four forms of **quel** sound the same.
• **Quel** may be separated from its noun by **être**.
Quelle est la date?

■ **Teaching strategy:** Ask students if they can remember any questions they learned that use **quel**.
Quelle est la date?
Quelle heure est-il?
Quel temps fait-il?
Quel jour est-ce?
De quelle couleur est...?

6 ROLE PLAY: discussing purchases

↩ Re-entry and review: This activity reviews colors from Lesson 20.

7 COMMUNICATION: answering personal questions

Listening activity: Préférences

PROPS: One red and one blue index card for each student

On the board, write **QUEL(S)** in blue chalk and **QUELLE(S)** in red chalk. Then read aloud questions containing forms of **quel**. If the form is spelled **quel(s)**, students hold up the blue card. If it is spelled **quelle(s)**, they hold up the red card.

1. **Quel sweat préfères-tu?** [B]
2. **Quels appareils...?** [B]
3. **Quelle jupe...?** [R]
4. **Quel blouson...?** [B]
5. **Quelles affiches...?** [R]
6. **Quelles chaussettes...?** [R]
7. **Quel pull...?** [B]
8. **Quelle école...?** [R]

Supplementary vocabulary

VERBS LIKE **METTRE**
mettre la table   *to set the table*
   (introduced in Lesson 33)
permettre   *to permit, allow, let*
promettre   *to promise*

COMPREHENSION:
describing where people
put things

■ **Variation:** Have students give
illogical answers.
**Mme Arnaud met la voiture dans
le salon.**

■ **Realia note**
Ask students:
**Comment s'appelle le grand
   magasin?** [les Galeries
   Lafayette]
**À quel étage sont les meubles et
   les lampes?** [au 4ème étage]
**Quelles choses est-ce qu'on peut
   mettre dans ce meuble?** [des
   vêtements, des livres et des
   cartes]

T262

D. Le verbe *mettre*

The verb **mettre** *(to put, place)* is irregular. Note its forms in the chart below.

INFINITIVE	**mettre**	
PRESENT	je **mets**	nous **mettons**
	tu **mets**	vous **mettez**
	il/elle **met**	ils/elles **mettent**

➡ In the singular forms, the "**t**" of the stem is silent. The "**t**" is pronounced in the plural forms.

➡ The verb **mettre** has several English equivalents:

to put, place	Je **mets** mes livres sur la table.
to put on, wear	Caroline **met** une robe rouge.
to turn on	Nous **mettons** la télé.

8 **Où?**

Say where the people of Column A put the
objects of Column B, by choosing a place from
Column C. Be logical!

> Madame Arnaud met la voiture
> dans le garage.

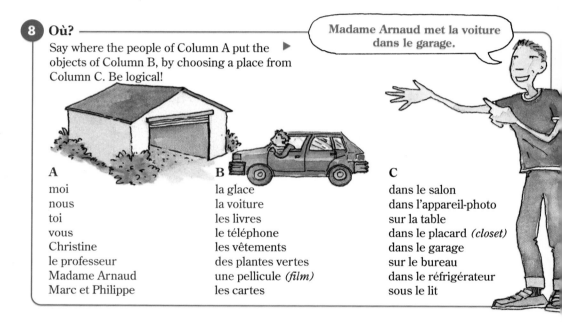

A	B	C
moi	la glace	dans le salon
nous	la voiture	dans l'appareil-photo
toi	les livres	sur la table
vous	le téléphone	dans le placard *(closet)*
Christine	les vêtements	dans le garage
le professeur	des plantes vertes	sur le bureau
Madame Arnaud	une pellicule *(film)*	dans le réfrigérateur
Marc et Philippe	les cartes	sous le lit

Où mettre...
   vos vêtements?
   vos livres?
   les cartes?

G A L E R I E S
Lafayette

Nouveau!

Meubles et lampes: 4ème étage

⊞ **Teaching note: Un jeu**

Divide the students into pairs. Have each
student take a sheet of paper. At a given
signal, students write a phrase using elements from columns A and B (e.g., **Je
mets la glace...**). As soon as they finish,
they exchange papers and complete their
partner's sentence using an element from
column C (**...dans le réfrigérateur**).

Then, they write another phrase using
columns A and B, exchange papers, and
again complete their partner's sentence
using column C.

After you have called time, have the
pairs exchange papers for peer correction.
The winner is the pair with the most
correct sentences.

9 **Questions personnelles**

1. Est-ce que tu mets la radio quand tu étudies?
2. Chez vous, est-ce que vous mettez la télé quand vous dînez?
3. Est-ce que tu mets des lunettes de soleil quand tu vas à la plage?
4. Où est-ce que tes parents mettent leur voiture? (dans le garage? dans la rue?)
5. Quels programmes de télé est-ce que tu mets le dimanche? le samedi?
6. Quels disques (ou quelles cassettes) est-ce que tu mets quand tu vas à une boum?
7. Quels vêtements est-ce que tu mets quand il fait froid?
8. Quels vêtements est-ce que tu mets quand tu joues au basket?

COMMUNICATION:
answering personal
questions

Prononciation

Les lettres «e» et «è»

e = /ə/	e = /ɛ/	è = /ɛ/
chemise	**chaussette**	**chère**

Richard: Pls add special "E" phonetic symbol from Symbol font.

Practice pronouncing "**e**" within a word:

• /ə/ (as in **je**) [. . . "e" + *one* CONSONANT + VOWEL]

Répétez: **chemise regarder Denise Renée petit venir**

Note that in the middle of a word the /ə/ is sometimes silent.

acheter achetons amener samedi rarement avenue

• /ɛ/ (as in **elle**) [. . . "e" + *two* CONSONANTS + VOWEL]

Répétez: **chaussette veste quelle cette rester professeur raquette**

Now practice pronouncing "**è**" within a word:

• /ɛ/ (as in **elle**) [. . . "è" + *one* CONSONANT + VOWEL]

Répétez: **chère père mère achète amènent espère deuxième**

Prononciation

🔊 Leçon 26, Section 6

■ **Pronunciation notes**
• The sound /ə/ is called a *mute e* because it is sometimes mute or silent.
• The sound /ɛ/ is called an *open e* because when you say it your mouth is more open than when you say /e/ as in **café**.

NOS CHEMISES

MONOPRIX
UNIPRIX

Leçon 26 **263**

■ **Realia note**
Monoprix
Monoprix is a moderately priced chain store that sells clothing, cosmetics, stationery supplies, toys, and housewares. Many of the stores also have a supermarket section.
Ask: **Combien coûtent les chemises au Monoprix?**

À votre tour!

1 COMPREHENSION

1-d   3-b
2-a   4-b

🔲 Leçon 26, Section 7

1 La bonne réponse

Alice is talking to her cousin Jérôme. Match Alice's questions with Jérôme's answers. Act out the dialogue with a classmate.

Alice

1 Je vais à la boum de Delphine. Et toi?

2 Tu amènes une copine?

3 Qu'est-ce que vous allez apporter?

4 Qu'est-ce que tu vas mettre?

a Oui, Christine.

b Mon pull jaune et mon blouson marron.

c Nous allons acheter des pizzas.

d Moi aussi.

Jérôme

2 GUIDED ORAL EXPRESSION

1. ces livres
2. ce monsieur
3. cette cravate
4. cette jupe
5. cette cravate
6. ces chaussures
7. ces lunettes de soleil
8. ce manteau

🔲 Leçon 26, Section 8

2 Créa-dialogue

Ask your classmates what they think about the following. They will answer affirmatively or negatively.

▶ — Comment trouves-tu <u>cette fille</u>?
— <u>Quelle fille</u>?
— <u>Cette fille-là</u>!
— Eh bien, je pense qu'<u>elle</u> est <u>jolie</u>.
(<u>Elle</u> n'est pas <u>jolie</u>.)

▶ jolie?

1. intéressants?

2. sympathique?

3. courte?

4. moche?

5. bon marché?

6. ??

7. ??

À votre tour

Depending on your goals and objectives, you may or may not wish to assign all of the activities in the **À votre tour** section.

👥 Cooperative practice

Act. 1–3 lend themselves to cooperative pair practice.

3 Shopping

You and a friend are shopping by catalog. Choose an object and tell your friend what you are buying. Identify it by color and explain why you like it.

GRANDES TAILLES

vert vif

jaune vif

A — depuis 32f50

B — 119f le pull

159f

C

D

85f le chemisier

E

COLORAMA
LES COULEURS DE LA VIE

225f l'imper

F — depuis 119f

▶ — Je vais acheter un sac.
— Quel sac?
— Ce sac noir.
— Pourquoi?
— Parce qu'il est joli.

4 Composition: La boum

You have been invited to a party by a French friend. In a short paragraph, describe ...

• what clothes you are going to wear
• whom you are going to bring along
• what things (food? records? cassettes?) you are going to bring

Leçon 26   265

3 CONVERSATION

A. un tee-shirt (vert, jaune)
B. un pull (gris)
C. un sac (noir)
D. un chemisier (blanc)
E. un imper (rouge)
F. des chaussures (bleues)

■ Language note
depuis 32F50 = *prices begin at 32F50*

4 WRITTEN SELF-EXPRESSION

Classroom Notes

Portfolio assessment

You will probably select only one speaking activity and one writing activity to go into the students' portfolios for Unit 7.

Act. 4 offers a good writing portfolio topic.

■ **Comprehension practice:** Play the entire module through as an introduction to the lesson.

27.1 Dialogue: Un choix difficile
(47:45–48:55 min.)

Leçon 27, Section 1

Un choix difficile

Dans un mois, Delphine va aller au mariage de sa cousine. Elle va acheter une <u>nouvelle</u> robe pour cette occasion. Pour cela, elle va dans une boutique de mode avec sa copine Véronique. Il y a beaucoup de jolies robes dans cette boutique.
　Delphine <u>hésite</u> <u>entre</u> une robe jaune et une robe rouge. Quelle robe est-ce que Delphine va <u>choisir</u>? Ah là là, le <u>choix</u> n'est pas facile.

new

is hesitating/between
to choose/choice

Scène 1.

VÉRONIQUE: Alors, quelle robe est-ce que tu choisis?
　DELPHINE: Eh bien, <u>finalement</u> je choisis la robe rouge. Elle est <u>plus jolie que</u> la robe jaune.
VÉRONIQUE: C'est vrai, elle est plus jolie ... mais la robe jaune est <u>moins</u> chère et elle est <u>plus grande</u>. Regarde. La robe rouge est trop petite pour toi.
　DELPHINE: Mais non, elle n'est pas trop petite.
VÉRONIQUE: Bon, écoute, <u>essaie-la</u>!

finally
prettier than

less/larger

■ **N O T E** ■
CULTURELLE

Le choix de vêtements

Since clothes are more expensive in France than in the United States and because budgets are limited, French teenagers are very careful when buying clothes. They spend a lot of time window shopping, comparing (brands, labels, and prices), and discussing with their friends what is in or out of fashion, before finally deciding what to buy. In general, French teenagers would rather buy one item of good quality than several of lesser quality. Of course, this item has to be the right one!

Setting the scene

Have the class imagine they have all been invited to a wedding. What will they wear?
Imaginez que nous sommes invités à un mariage ce weekend.
Moi, je vais mettre ... [describe the outfit you would plan to wear]

Have various students describe what they are going to wear.
Et toi, X, qu'est-ce que tu vas mettre?
Y, est-ce que tu vas mettre [...] aussi?
Introduce Section 27.1 of the video:
Ce weekend Delphine va à un mariage.
Qu'est-ce qu'elle va mettre?

Scène 2.

Delphine <u>sort</u> de la <u>cabine d'essayage</u>.

		comes out / fitting room
DELPHINE:	C'est vrai, la robe rouge est <u>plus petite</u> mais ce n'est pas un problème.	*smaller*
VÉRONIQUE:	Pourquoi?	
DELPHINE:	Parce que j'ai un mois pour <u>maigrir</u>.	*to lose weight*
VÉRONIQUE:	Et <u>si</u> tu <u>grossis</u>?	*if / gain weight*
DELPHINE:	Toi, <u>tais-toi</u>!	*be quiet*

Compréhension

1. Où vont Delphine et Véronique?
2. Qu'est-ce que Delphine va acheter?
3. Pourquoi?
4. Delphine hésite entre deux robes. De quelle couleur sont-elles?
5. Quelle robe est-ce qu'elle choisit?
6. Pourquoi est-ce qu'elle préfère la robe rouge?
7. Selon (*According to*) Véronique, quel est le problème de la robe rouge?
8. Qu'est-ce que Delphine doit (*must*) faire pour porter la robe?

COMPREHENSION

1. dans une boutique de mode
2. une nouvelle robe
3. parce qu'elle va aller au mariage de sa cousine
4. jaune et rose
5. la robe rouge
6. parce qu'elle est plus jolie que la robe jaune
7. Elle est trop petite.
8. Elle doit maigrir.

Note culturelle

■ **Cultural note:** In France, window displays almost always include the prices of the items shown. Only the most expensive designer boutiques do not indicate prices.

27.4 **Vignette culturelle: Dans un centre commercial** (51:25–53:00 min.)

Talking about past events

Let's talk about where you went yesterday and what you wore. Note that the past participle of **mettre** is **mis**.

▶ **Imagine que tu es allé(e) à la plage hier. Qu'est-ce que tu as mis? J'ai mis un maillot de bain et des sandales.**

- **Imagine que tu es allé(e) à une boum hier. Qu'est-ce que tu as mis?**
- **Imagine que tu es allé(e) en ville hier. Qu'est-ce que tu as mis?**
- **Imagine que tu es allé(e) au stade hier. Qu'est-ce que tu as mis?**
- **Imagine que tu es allé(e) à un pique-nique hier. Qu'est-ce que tu as mis?**

Transparency 39
-ir verbs

Leçon 27, Section 2

■ **Teaching strategy:** Using subject pronoun cue cards, have students conjugate other **-ir** verbs orally and in writing (e.g., **choisir**, **réussir**).

① PRACTICE: saying who finishes a race

| **Supplementary vocabulary** |

a) Some **-ir** verbs correspond to English verbs in **-ish**
finir *to finish*
établir *to establish*
abolir *to abolish*

b) Verbs derived from adjectives often end in **-ir**
COLORS:
(rouge) rougir *to blush, to turn red*
(blanc, blanche) blanchir
   to blanche, to turn white
(jaune) jaunir *to turn yellow*
(brun) brunir *to turn brown, to tan*

SIZE:
(grand) grandir *to grow tall*
Note:
(gros, grosse–*fat***) grossir**
(maigre–*thin***) maigrir**

COMPREHENSION: indicating who is gaining or losing weight

②

A. Les verbes réguliers en *-ir*

Many French verbs end in *-ir*. Most of these verbs are conjugated like **finir** *(to finish)*. Note the forms of this verb in the present tense, paying special attention to the endings.

INFINITIVE	finir		STEM (infinitive minus **-ir**)	ENDINGS
PRESENT	Je **finis** à deux heures. Tu **finis** à une heure. Il/Elle **finit** à cinq heures. Nous **finissons** à midi. Vous **finissez** à une heure. Ils/Elles **finissent** à minuit.		fin-	-is -is -it -issons -issez -issent

➡ Note that all final consonants are silent.

① **Le marathon de Paris**

Not everyone who enters the Paris marathon finishes. Say which of the following runners finish the marathon and which do not.

▶ Philippe (non)   *Philippe ne finit pas.*

1. moi (oui)   3. nous (oui)   5. Éric (oui)   7. Frédéric et Marc (non)
2. toi (non)   4. vous (non)   6. Stéphanie (non)   8. Anne et Cécile (oui)

Vocabulaire: Verbes réguliers en *-ir*

choisir	*to choose*	Quelle veste **choisis**-tu?
finir	*to finish*	Les classes **finissent** à midi.
grossir	*to gain weight, get fat*	Marc **grossit** parce qu'il mange beaucoup.
maigrir	*to lose weight, get thin*	Je **maigris** parce que je ne mange pas beaucoup.
réussir	*to succeed*	Tu vas **réussir** parce que tu travailles!
réussir à un examen	*to pass an exam*	Nous **réussissons à nos examens.**

② **Le régime** *(Diet)*

Read about the following people. Then say whether they are gaining weight or losing weight. Use the verbs **grossir** and **maigrir**.

1. Vous faites des exercices.
2. Nous allons souvent au gymnase.
3. Vous êtes inactifs.
4. Je mange des carottes.
5. Monsieur Moreau adore la bonne cuisine.

▶ Philippe mange beaucoup de pizzas.
  Il grossit.

6. Vous n'êtes pas très sportifs.
7. Ces personnes mangent trop *(too much).*
8. Je nage, je joue au volley et je fais des promenades.

☀ **Warm-up and review: Telling time**

PROPS: Clock with movable hands or Transparency 6

Review times by changing the hands on the clock.
Quelle heure est-il?
Il est deux heures vingt-cinq. ...

Have students practice forms of the verb **finir** together with clock times.
[moi: 1h30] **Je finis à une heure et demie.**
[vous: 8h45] **Vous finissez à neuf heures moins le quart.**
[X: 3h10] **X finit à trois heures dix.**

3 Questions personnelles

1. À quelle heure finissent les classes aujourd'hui?
2. À quelle heure finit la classe de français?
3. Quand finit l'école cette année *(year)*?
4. Tu es invité(e) au restaurant ou au cinéma. Où choisis-tu d'aller?
5. Quand tu vas au cinéma avec ta famille, qui choisit le film?
6. En général, est-ce que tu réussis à tes examens? Est-ce que tu vas réussir à l'examen de français?
7. Est-ce que tes copains réussissent aussi?

B. Les adjectifs *beau, nouveau* et *vieux*

The adjectives **beau** *(beautiful, good-looking)*, **nouveau** *(new)*, and **vieux** *(old)* are irregular. Note their forms and their position.

		beau	nouveau	vieux
SINGULAR	**MASC.**	le **beau** manteau (le **bel** imper)	le **nouveau** manteau (le **nouvel** imper)	le **vieux** manteau (le **vieil** imper)
	FEM.	la **belle** veste	la **nouvelle** veste	la **vieille** veste
PLURAL	**MASC.**	les **beaux** manteaux	les **nouveaux** manteaux	les **vieux** manteaux
	FEM.	les **belles** vestes	les **nouvelles** vestes	les **vieilles** vestes

➡ The adjectives **beau, nouveau,** and **vieux** usually come BEFORE the noun. If the noun begins with a vowel sound, there is liaison between the adjective and the noun.

    les **nouveaux** ordinateurs   les **belles** affiches   les **vieux** impers

➡ In the masculine singular, the liaison forms **bel, nouvel,** and **vieil** are used before a vowel sound. Note that **vieil** is pronounced like **vieille:**

    un **vieil** imper   une **vieille** robe

4 La collection de printemps

Mod Boutique is presenting its spring collection. You are impressed by the new clothes and accessories. Point them out to a French friend, using the appropriate forms of **beau.**

▶ une chemise
   Regarde la belle chemise!

1. une robe
2. un pantalon
3. des jeans
4. des blousons
5. un imper
6. des sandales
7. un manteau
8. un chapeau

5 Différences d'opinion

François is showing the new things he bought to his sister Valérie. She prefers his old things. Play both roles.

▶ des chaussures

1. un polo
2. des lunettes de soleil
3. un imper
4. des affiches
5. une veste
6. une montre
7. un ordinateur
8. des baskets
9. un survêtement

Tu aimes mes nouvelles chaussures?

Eh bien, non, je préfère tes vieilles chaussures.

Leçon 27 **269**

Section B

COMMUNICATIVE FUNCTION: Describing people and things (new, beautiful, old)

Transparency 40
Beau, nouveau, vieux

■ **Pronunciation notes**
• Remind students that in liaison "x" is pronounced /z/; the "il" of **vieil** is pronounced /j/.
• Point out that all three masculine singular liaison forms sound like the corresponding feminine singular forms.

3 COMMUNICATION: answering personal questions

4 PRACTICE: saying things are beautiful

■ **Expansion** (dialogue format):
– Regarde la belle chemise!
– C'est vrai. Elle est belle.

5 ROLE PLAY: discussing preferences between old and new items

---

Talking about past events

Let's talk about what you ordered when you ate out the last time. Note that the past participle of **-ir** verbs ends in **-i.**

▶ **Est-ce que tu as choisi une pizza?**
   Oui, j'ai choisi une pizza.
   (Non, je n'ai pas choisi de pizza.)
• **Est-ce que tu as choisi une salade?**

• **Est-ce que tu as choisi un steak?**
• **Est-ce que tu as choisi une glace?**
• **Est-ce que tu as choisi un soda?**
• **Est-ce que tu as choisi un café?**
• **Qu'est-ce que tu as choisi?**

Follow-up:
• **Est-ce que X a choisi une pizza? ...**

Cooperative pair practice
Activity 5

27.2 Mini-scenes:
Comparaisons
27.3 Mini-scenes:
Comparaisons
(48:56–51:24 min.)

Leçon 27, Sections 3, 4

■ **Language notes**
• In French as in English, the second part of the comparison may be left out:
Cette robe est plus chère.
• The comparative form of **bon marché** is **meilleur marché.** This form is not actively presented at this time.

COMMUNICATION:
expressing one's opinion
about relative prices

C. La comparaison avec les adjectifs

Note how COMPARISONS are expressed in French.

Cet imper est **plus cher que** ce manteau.	... *more expensive than* ...
Cette jupe est **plus jolie que** cette robe.	... *prettier than* ...
Paul est **moins sportif que** Patrick.	... *less athletic than* ...
Il est **moins amusant que** lui.	... *less amusing than* ...
Je suis **aussi grand que** toi.	... *as tall as* ...
Tu **n'**es **pas aussi timide que** moi.	... *not as timid as* ...

To make comparisons with adjectives, the French use the following constructions:

+	**plus**			**plus cher (que)**	*more expensive (than)*
–	**moins**	+ ADJECTIVE (+ **que** . . .)		**moins cher (que)**	*less expensive (than)*
=	**aussi**			**aussi cher (que)**	*as expensive (as)*

➡ Note the irregular **plus**-form of **bon** *(good)*:

plus + **bon(ne)** → **meilleur(e)** *(better)*

    Ta cassette est **bonne,** mais ma cassette est **meilleure.**

    But: Cette cassette est **moins bonne que** ce disque.
             Est-ce que les Red Sox sont **aussi bons que** les Yankees?

➡ There is liaison after **plus** and **moins** when the next word begins with a vowel sound.
    Cette robe-ci est **plus élégante.**   Ce livre-là est **moins intéressant.**

➡ In comparisons, the adjective always agrees with the noun (or pronoun) it describes.

    La jupe est plus **chère** que le chemisier.

    Les vestes sont moins **chères** que les manteaux.

➡ In comparisons with people, STRESS PRONOUNS are used after **que.**
    Paul est plus petit **que moi.**   Je suis plus grand **que lui.**

6 **Comparaisons**

How much do you think the following pairs of items cost? Give your opinion, saying whether the first one is more expensive, less expensive, or as expensive as the second one.

▶ une guitare/une raquette   **Une guitare est plus (moins, aussi) chère qu'une raquette.**

1. un vélo/un scooter
2. une mobylette/une moto
3. une pizza/un sandwich   7. des bottes/des tennis
4. une télé/un ordinateur   8. un sweat/un maillot de bain
5. des chaussures/des sandales   9. des chaussettes/des collants
6. un pantalon/une robe   10. des lunettes de soleil/une montre

---

Cooperative
pair practice
Activity 8

TPR Comparisons

PROPS: Plastic bag with 30 "money cards" (labelled with amounts from $50–$1000)

Have students come up and draw a "prize."
    Vous êtes tous riches.
    Vous avez gagné à la loterie hier.
    Venez chercher vos prix!

Review numbers by asking what they drew.
    X, montre-nous ton prix. [holds up $100]
    Combien d'argent as-tu? [cent dollars]
    Est-ce que X est riche aujourd'hui? [oui!]
    Y, montre-nous ton prix. ...
Call up two students with different "prizes."
    X et Y, venez ici.
    Combien d'argent a X? [$100] **Et Y?** [$500]

T270

Expression pour la conversation

How to introduce a personal opinion:

à mon avis ...   *in my opinion ...*   **À mon avis,** le français est facile.

7 Expression personnelle

Compare the following by using the adjectives suggested. Give your personal opinion.

▶ le tennis/intéressant/le ping-pong

À mon avis, le tennis est plus intéressant que le ping-pong.

(moins, aussi)

1. le basket/intéressant/le foot
2. l'anglais/facile/le français
3. la classe de français/amusant/ la classe d'anglais
4. la ville de New York/beau/ la ville de Chicago
5. la Floride/beau/la Californie
6. les Yankees/bon/les Red Sox
7. les Celtics/bon/les Lakers
8. les Cowboys/bon/les Saints
9. la cuisine américaine/bon/ la cuisine française
10. les voitures japonaises/bon/ les voitures américaines
11. les filles/intelligent/les garçons
12. les Américains/intelligent/ les Français

▶▶▶▶▶▶▶▶▶▶▶▶▶▶▶▶▶▶▶▶

8 Et toi?

Use the appropriate stress pronouns in answering the questions below.

▶ —Es-tu plus grand(e) que ton copain?
—Oui, je suis plus grand(e) que lui.
(Non, je suis moins grand(e) que lui.)
(Je suis aussi grand(e) que lui.)

1. Es-tu plus grand(e) que ta mère?
2. Es-tu aussi riche que Donald Trump?
3. Es-tu plus sportif (sportive) que tes cousins?
4. Es-tu plus intelligent(e) qu'Einstein?

Prononciation

Les lettres «ill»   ill /j/

maillot

In the middle of a word, the letters "**ill**" almost always represent the semi-vowel /j/ which is like the "**y**" of *yes*.

Répétez: **maillot travaillez oreille vieille fille famille juillet**
En juillet, Mireille va travailler pour sa vieille tante.

At the end of a word, the sound /j/ is sometimes spelled **il.**

Répétez: **appareil-photo vieil travail** *(job)*
Mon oncle a un vieil appareil-photo.

EXCEPTION: The letters **ill** are pronounced /il/ in the following words:

Répétez: **ville village mille Lille**

COMMUNICATION:
comparing people and things
7

■ **Teaching strategies**
• Remind students that the adjective must agree with the subject.
• For items 6–10, remind students that **plus + bon(ne)** → **meilleur**; as in English, there is no change for **moins bon(ne)** and **aussi bon(ne).**

COMMUNICATION:
comparing oneself to others
8

Prononciation

Lecon 27, Section 5

■ **Pronunciation:** Note that **tranquille** *(quiet)* also contains the sound /il/: /trãnkil/

Place Y next to the chalkboard to the left, and place X to the right.
Mais Y est plus riche que X.
Between the two, write: **plus riche que.**
Call on other students to demonstrate the other comparisons, also writing them.
Z est moins riche que B. [$300 < $650]
A est aussi riche que C. [$400 = $400]

Ask all students to hold up their cards.
Montrez-nous vos prix. Qui a $200? [M]
Qui est plus riche que M? Qui est moins riche que lui/elle? Qui est aussi riche?
Have students hand around their "prizes."
En ce moment, Z est moins riche que M.
S'il te plaît, D, va donner tes $1000 à Z.
Maintenant Z est plus riche que B. etc.

À votre tour!

1 COMPREHENSION

1-c   3-d
2-a   4-b

🔊 **Leçon 27, Section 6**

2 GUIDED ORAL EXPRESSION

1. la chaîne stéréo :: le walkman
2. les bottes :: les chaussures
3. le chien jaune :: le chien blanc
4. Alice :: Anne
5. Paul :: Philippe

🔊 **Leçon 27, Section 7**

1 La bonne réponse

François and Stéphanie are shopping. Match François's questions with Stéphanie's answers. You may act out the dialogue with a friend.

François

Stéphanie

1. Tu aimes cette veste verte?
2. Combien est-ce qu'elle coûte?
3. Alors, qu'est-ce que tu vas choisir?
4. Et qu'est-ce que tu penses de cette veste rouge?

a. 600 francs.
b. À mon avis, elle est moins jolie.
c. Oui, mais elle est très chère.
d. La veste bleue. Elle est meilleur marché et elle est aussi élégante.

2 Créa-dialogue

With a classmate, prepare a dialogue comparing the items in one of the following pictures. Use the suggested verb and some of the suggested adjectives.

▶ —Tu <u>choisis</u> <u>la voiture rouge</u> ou <u>la voiture noire</u>?
—Je <u>choisis</u> <u>la voiture rouge</u>.
—Pourquoi?
—Parce qu'<u>elle</u> est <u>plus petite</u> et <u>moins chère</u>.

choisir
petit/grand/confortable/rapide/cher

1. acheter
petit/grand/cher/bon

2. préférer
joli/confortable/cher/bon

3. choisir
petit/grand/mignon/joli

4. amener
ALICE / ANNE
mignon/amusant/intelligent intéressant/sympathique

5. inviter
PAUL / PHILIPPE
??

272   Unité 7

À votre tour

Depending on your goals and objectives, you may or may not wish to assign all of the activities in the **À votre tour** section.

🧠🧠 Cooperative practice

Act. 1–3 lend themselves to cooperative pair practice.

3 Choix personnels

Select two people or two items in each of the following categories and ask a classmate to indicate which one he / she prefers. You may ask your classmate to explain why.

▶ *2 actors*

> Tu préfères Tom Cruise ou Dustin Hoffman?
>
> Je préfère Tom Cruise.

> Pourquoi?
>
> Parce que Tom Cruise est plus mignon que Dustin Hoffman.

(plus beau, plus jeune . . .)

CATEGORIES:
▶ *2 actors*
- *2 actresses*
- *2 singers (male)*
- *2 singers (female)*
- *2 baseball teams*
- *2 cities*
- *2 restaurants in your town*
- *2 stores in your town*

4 Composition: Portrait comparatif

Write a description of yourself, comparing yourself to six other people (your friends, your family, well-known personalities, etc.) You may use some of the following adjectives:

> grand petit jeune vieux amusant
> intelligent bête sportif sympathique
> timide élégant beau joli mignon

▶ *Je suis moins sportif (sportive) que Michael Jordan (Steffi Graff).*

5 Composition: Comparaisons personnelles

Choose a friend or relative about your age. Give this person's name and age. Then, in a short paragraph, compare yourself to that person in terms of physical appearance and personality traits.

> *Mon cousin s'appelle Patrick. Il a quinze ans. Je suis plus jeune que lui, mais il est moins grand que moi...*

Classroom Notes

▉ Portfolio assessment

You will probably select only one speaking activity and one writing activity to go into the students' portfolios for Unit 7.

In this lesson, Act. 2 lends itself well to an oral portfolio recording.

Act. 4 and 5 are good writing portfolio topics.

MODULE 28:
Alice a un job
Total time: 5:53 min.
(Counter 53:11 min.)

28.1 Dialogue: Alice a un job
(53:54–54:26 min.)
28.2 Mini-scenes: Listening — Qu'est-ce qu'on vend?
(54:27–55:13 min.)
28.3 Mini-scenes: Speaking — Qu'est-ce qu'on vend ici?
(55:14–55:56 min.)
28.4 Mini-scenes: Listening — On dîne?
(55:57–56:33 min.)
28.5 Mini-scenes: Speaking — On joue au tennis?
(56:34–57:31 min.)
28.6 Vignette culturelle: Au magasin hifi
(57:32–59:02 min.)

■ **Comprehension practice:** Play the entire module through as an introduction to the lesson.

 28.1 Dialogue: Alice a un job
(53:54–54:26 min.)

 Leçon 28, Section 1

LEÇON 28 Alice a un job

Alice a un nouveau job. Elle travaille dans un magasin hifi. Dans ce magasin, <u>on</u> <u>vend</u> <u>toutes</u> sortes de choses: des chaînes stéréo, des <u>mini-chaînes</u>, des radiocassettes . . . On vend aussi des cassettes et des compacts.

one, they / sell(s) / all compact stereos

Un jour, son cousin Jérôme <u>lui rend visite</u>.

comes to visit her

JÉRÔME:	Salut, ça va?
ALICE:	Oui, ça va.
JÉRÔME:	Et ce nouveau job?
ALICE:	C'est super.
JÉRÔME:	Qu'est-ce qu'on vend dans ton magasin?
ALICE:	Eh bien, tu <u>vois</u>, on vend toutes sortes de matériel hifi. . . Moi, je vends des mini-chaînes.
JÉRÔME:	Tu es bien <u>payée</u>?
ALICE:	Non, on n'est pas très bien payé, mais on a des réductions sur l'équipement stéréo et sur les compacts.
JÉRÔME:	Qu'est-ce que tu vas faire avec ton <u>argent</u>?
ALICE:	Je ne sais pas . . . <u>J'ai envie de</u> voyager cet été.
JÉRÔME:	Tu <u>as de la chance</u>. Moi aussi, j'ai envie de voyager, mais je n'ai pas d'argent.
ALICE:	Écoute, Jérôme, si tu as <u>besoin</u> d'argent, <u>fais comme moi.</u>
JÉRÔME:	<u>Comment</u>?
ALICE:	<u>Cherche</u> un job!

see

paid

money
feel like

are lucky

need / do as I do
What?
Find

274 **Unité 7**

T274

Compréhension

1. Où travaille Alice?
2. Qu'est-ce qu'elle vend?
3. Qu'est-ce qu'elle espère faire cet été?
4. Pourquoi est-ce que Jérôme ne va pas voyager?
5. Qu'est-ce que Jérôme doit *(must)* faire pour avoir de l'argent?

COMPREHENSION

1. dans un magasin hifi /ifi/
2. des mini-chaînes
3. voyager
4. Il n'a pas d'argent.
5. Il doit chercher un job.

■ NOTE ■
CULTURELLE

L'argent des jeunes

Do you have a job? Do you have an older brother or sister who works in a supermarket or a restaurant? In the United States, many teenagers work to earn money. Because French labor laws restrict the type of work that young people can do, few French teenagers have regular jobs. (In addition, during the school year most families expect their children to concentrate on their studies.)

It is, however, more and more common for young people in France to earn money by babysitting or doing odd jobs in the neighborhood, such as washing cars or walking dogs. Some (lucky ones) work a few hours a week in stores owned by a relative or a friend of the family.

On the whole, most French teenagers must rely on the generosity of their parents for their spending money. How much they receive depends on particular circumstances, such as how well they do in school, how much they help at home, and obviously, how much their parents can afford. On the average, the allowance of a fifteen-year-old is about 200 francs (or $35) per month.

Classroom Notes

■ Photo culture note
Ask students how many ice cream flavors (**un parfum**) they recognize. Note also:
menthe *mint*
noix *hazelnut*
cassis *black currant*
fraise de bois *wild strawberry*
goyave *guava*

Talking about past events

Let's about what you and your family did during a recent vacation.

▶ **Toi et ta famille, est-ce que vous avez voyagé pendant les vacances?**
Oui, nous avons voyagé.
(Non, nous n'avons pas voyagé.)

• **Où êtes-vous allés?**

• **Est-ce que vous êtes allés à Disneyland?**

• **Est-ce que vous avez trouvé un bon hôtel?**

• **Est-ce que vous avez dîné au restaurant?**

• **Qu'est-ce que vous avez visité?**

◼ **Language notes**
• Point out that **payer** is also a "boot" verb (see p. 258).
• Some students may understand the **avoir** idioms better if they think of them as *I have need of...* and *I have desire of...*

◼ **Casual speech:**
One can also say:
Ce disque coûte combien?
Tu as combien d'argent?
Tu as combien de disques?

Supplementary vocabulary

l'argent de poche *allowance, pocket money*
la monnaie *change*
un job *(part-time) job*
économiser *to save money*
par jour *per day, a day*
par semaine *per week, a week*
par heure *per hour, an hour*

---

1 EXCHANGES: asking how many things people have

◼ **Pronunciation:** Be sure students pronounce the **de** of **combien de** correctly with a mute "e" so that it does not sound like **des.**

◼ **Language note:** There is no elision before **un** when it represents the number *one:*
un billet de un dollar. (cf. item 7)

◼ **Variation** (using casual speech):
Tu as combien de disques?

Cooperative
pair practice
Activities 1, 2

T276

Vocabulaire: L'argent

NOMS

l'argent *(m.)*	money	**une pièce**	coin
un billet	bill, paper money		

ADJECTIFS

riche ≠ **pauvre**   *rich ≠ poor*

VERBES

dépenser	*to spend*	Je n'aime pas **dépenser** mon argent.
gagner	*to earn, to win*	Je **gagne** 10 dollars par *(per)* jour.
		Tu joues bien. Tu vas **gagner** le match.
payer	*to pay, pay for*	Qui va **payer** aujourd'hui?

EXPRESSIONS

combien + VERB	*how much*	**Combien** coûte ce disque?
combien de + NOUN	*how much*	**Combien d'**argent as-tu?
	how many	**Combien de** disques as-tu?
avoir besoin de + NOUN	*to need*	J'**ai besoin de** 5 dollars.
+ INFINITIVE	*to need to, have to*	J'**ai besoin d'**étudier.
avoir envie de + NOUN	*to want*	J'**ai envie d'**une pizza.
+ INFINITIVE	*to feel like, want to*	J'**ai envie de** manger.

➡ Verbs like **payer** that end in **-yer,** have the following stem change:
    y → i in the **je, tu, il, ils** forms of the verb
        je **paie**   tu **paies**   il/elle **paie**   ils/elles **paient**
  But: nous payons   vous payez

> L'ARGENT NE FAIT PAS LE BONHEUR

Money does not buy happiness.

1 Combien? ————————

Ask your classmates how many of the following they have.

▶ des disques   —Combien de disques as-tu?
               —J'ai vingt disques.
                  (Je n'ai pas de disques.)

1. des frères	3. des compacts	5. des tee-shirts	7. des billets de un dollar
2. des soeurs	4. des affiches	6. des jeans	8. des pièces de dix cents

2 Qu'est-ce que tu as envie de faire?

Ask your classmates if they feel like doing the following things.

► aller au cinéma

Est-ce que tu as envie d'aller au cinéma?

Oui, j'ai envie d'aller au cinéma.

Et toi?

Non, je n'ai pas envie d'aller au cinéma.

1. aller au restaurant
2. manger une pizza
3. aller à la piscine
4. parler français
5. étudier
6. visiter Paris
7. jouer au Frisbee
8. acheter une moto
9. faire une promenade
10. aller à la bibliothèque

3 Au restaurant

The following students are in a restaurant in Quebec. Say what they feel like buying and estimate how much money they need.

► Hélène / une pizza
  **Hélène a envie d'une pizza.
  Elle a besoin de cinq dollars.**

1. Marc / un sandwich
2. nous / une glace
3. moi / un soda
4. toi / un jus d'orange
5. vous / une salade
6. mes copains / un steak

4 Questions personnelles

1. Est-ce que tu as un job? Où est-ce que tu travailles? Combien est-ce que tu gagnes par *(per)* heure? par semaine?
2. Quand tu vas au cinéma, qui paie? toi ou ton copain (ta copine)?
3. Combien est-ce que tu paies quand tu achètes un hamburger? une pizza? une glace?
4. Est-ce que tu as des pièces dans ta poche *(pocket)*? quelles pièces?
5. Qui est représenté sur le billet de un dollar? sur le billet de cinq dollars? sur le billet de dix dollars?
6. Est-ce que tu préfères dépenser ou économiser *(to save)* ton argent? Pourquoi?
7. Est-ce que tu espères être riche un jour? Pourquoi?

Le Vendôme
36. Côte de la Montagne
Québec
tél 692.0557

CANADA
QUÉBEC
ÉTATS-UNIS
MEXIQUE

LE VENDOME

EXCHANGES: discussing what one feels like doing

COMPREHENSION: describing what people in a restaurant want and what it costs

■ **Expansion:** Have students discuss their wants and needs by completing the following open-ended sentences.
J'ai envie de (d')... (réussir en français.)
J'ai besoin de (d')... (étudier souvent.)

COMMUNICATION: answering personal questions

■ **Notes:**
• Item 5:
  $1 – George Washington
  $5 – Abraham Lincoln
  $10 – Alexander Hamilton

■ **Realia note**
Ask students:
Comment s'appelle ce restaurant?
  [Le Vendôme]
Quelle est l'adresse du restaurant?
  [36, Côte de la Montagne]
Quel est son numéro de téléphone?
  [692.0557]
NOTE: Remind students that in Quebec telephone numbers are given digit by digit.

■ **Cultural note:** The **Château Frontenac** (a four-star hotel) is located in upper town (**la Haute Ville**) and **Le Vendôme** restaurant is located in lower town (**la Basse Ville**) The oldest part of Quebec City is located around the **Place Royale** in lower town. Here one finds historic houses, restaurants, boutiques, antique stores, and art galleries. A **funiculaire** and the Breakneck Stairs (**l'Escalier Casse-Cou**) connects lower town with upper town.

Section A

COMMUNICATIVE FUNCTION:
Talking about people in general

28.2 Mini-scenes: Qu'est-ce qu'on vend?

28.3 Mini-scenes: Qu'est-ce qu'on vend ici?

28.4 Mini-scenes: On dîne?

28.5 Mini-scenes: On joue au tennis?
(54:27–57:31 min.)

 Leçon 28, Sections 3, 4, 5, 6

■ **Looking ahead:** The forms of **vendre** are presented in section B of this lesson.

COMPREHENSION:
discussing what languages
⑤ are spoken in certain cities

1. français (ou anglais)
2. anglais
3. espagnol
4. français
5. français
6. japonaise
7. espagnol
8. anglais
9. italien
10. chinois

■ **Variation** (using the negative in many responses):
– **Est-ce qu'on parle français à Acapulco?**
– **Non, on ne parle pas français.**

■ **Challenge:** Have students turn to the world map on pp. R2–R3. They can ask additional questions: **Est-ce qu'on parle français à Dakar?** etc.

Cooperative pair practice
Activities 6, 7

A. Le pronom *on*

Note the use of the subject pronoun **on** in the sentences below.

Qu'est-ce qu'**on** vend ici?	*What do **they** (do **you**) sell here?*
Où est-ce qu'**on** achète ce magazine?	*Where does **one** (do **people**) buy that magazine?*
En France, **on** parle français.	*In France, **people** (**you**, **they**) speak French.*

The pronoun **on** is used in GENERAL statements, according to the construction:

on + **il/elle-** form of verb	**On** travaille beaucoup.	**One** works a lot. **They** work a lot. **You** work a lot. **People** work a lot.

➡ There is liaison after **on** when the next word begins with a vowel sound.
  Est-ce qu'**on** invite Stéphanie à la boum?

➡ In conversation, **on** is often used instead of **nous**:
  —Est-ce qu'**on** dîne à la maison? *Are **we** having dinner at home?*
  —Non, on **va** au restaurant. *No, **we** are going to the restaurant.*

⑤ **Ici on parle . . .**

Imagine you have won a grand prize of a world tour. Say which of the following languages is spoken in each of the cities that you will be visiting.

▶ Acapulco

À Acapulco, on parle espagnol.

1. Québec
2. Boston
3. Madrid
4. Bruxelles
5. Genève
6. Tokyo
7. Buenos Aires
8. Londres *(London)*
9. Rome
10. Beijing

anglais   français   espagnol   italien   japonais   chinois

Did you know that more and more French companies are investing in the United States? There may be places where you can use French right in your home state!

Expression pour la conversation

How to indicate approval:
C'est une bonne idée!   *That's a good idea!*

6 Projets de weekend

Suggest possible weekend activities to your classmates. They will let you know whether they think each idea is a good one or not.

▶ jouer au baseball?

1. étudier?
2. aller à la bibliothèque?
3. aller à la plage?
4. téléphoner au professeur?
5. faire une promenade à vélo?
6. aller dans les magasins?
7. acheter des vêtements?
8. écouter des disques?

> On joue au baseball?

> Oui, c'est une bonne idée!

> Non, ce n'est pas une bonne idée.

7 En Amérique et en France

A French student and an American student are comparing certain aspects of life in their own countries. Play both roles.

▶ jouer au baseball (au foot)

> En Amérique, on joue au baseball.

> En France, on joue au foot.

1. parler anglais (français)
2. étudier le français (l'anglais)
3. dîner à six heures (à huit heures)
4. manger des hamburgers (des omelettes)
5. voyager souvent en avion *(by plane)* (en train)
6. skier dans le Colorado (dans les Alpes)
7. aller à l'école le mercredi après-midi (le samedi matin)
8. chanter «la Bannière étoilée» *("The Star-Spangled Banner")* («la Marseillaise»)

8 Expression personnelle

Describe what you, your friends, and your relatives generally do. Complete the following sentences according to your personal routine.

1. À la maison, on dîne . . . (à quelle heure?)
2. À la télé, on regarde . . . (quel programme?)
3. À la cafétéria de l'école, on mange . . . (quoi?)
4. En été, on va . . . (où?)
5. Le weekend, avec mes copains, on va . . . (où?)
6. Avec mes copains, on joue . . . (à quel sport?)
7. On a une classe de français . . . (quels jours?)
8. On a un examen de français . . . (quel jour?)

Leçon 28 279

T279

Transparency 41
-re verbs

Leçon 28, Section 7

■ **Teaching strategy:** Point out that the plural endings of -re verbs are the same as those of -er verbs: **nous vendons, vous vendez,** and **ils vendent.**

■ **Language note:** You may indicate that **vendre** is a REGULAR verb since many verbs follow the same pattern. However, **mettre** is IRREGULAR since the pattern applies only to verbs that have **mettre** as a root: **permettre, promettre,** etc.

↶ **Re-entry and review:** The verb chart reviews possessive adjectives (Lesson 24).

■ **Realia note**
Ask students:
How do you say *whale* in French? [la baleine]
In which river can one go whale watching? [the St. Lawrence: **le St. Laurent**]

■ **Cultural note:** Observing the seasonal migration of whales up and down the St. Lawrence River is a major tourist attraction. One of the favorite tours in Quebec is **la route des baleines.**

9 PRACTICE: describing who's waiting for whom

B. Les verbes réguliers en -re

Many French verbs end in **-re**. Most of these are conjugated like **vendre** *(to sell)*. Note the forms of this verb in the present tense, paying special attention to the endings.

INFINITIVE	vendre		STEM (infinitive minus **-re**)	ENDINGS
PRESENT	Je **vends** ma raquette. Tu **vends** ton scooter. Il/Elle/On **vend** son ordinateur.		**vend-**	-s -s —
	Nous **vendons** nos disques. Vous **vendez** vos cassettes. Ils/Elles **vendent** leur voiture.			-ons -ez -ent

→ The "**d**" of the stem is silent in the singular forms, but it is pronounced in the plural forms.

Vocabulaire: Verbes réguliers en -re

attendre	*to wait, wait for*	Pierre **attend** Michèle au café.
entendre	*to hear*	Est-ce que tu **entends** la radio?
perdre	*to lose, waste*	Jean-Claude **perd** le match.
rendre visite à	*to visit (a person)*	Je **rends visite à** mon oncle.
répondre à	*to answer*	Nous **répondons à** la question du prof.
vendre	*to sell*	À qui **vends**-tu ton vélo?

→ There are two French verbs that correspond to the English verb *to visit*.
visiter (+ PLACES)   Nous **visitons** Québec.
rendre visite à (+ PEOPLE)   Nous **rendons visite à** nos cousins canadiens.

Visitez Québec ...
et la route des baleines.

Société écologique
des baleines
du St. Laurent

9 **Rendez-vous**

The following people have been shopping and are now waiting for their friends at a café. Express this, using the appropriate forms of the verb **attendre**.

▶ Jérôme (Michèle)   Jérôme **attends** Michèle.

1. nous (nos copains)
2. vous (vos cousines)
3. moi (Christophe)
4. toi (Anne)
5. Olivier et Éric (Claire et Sophie)

6. les étudiants (les étudiantes)
7. Jacques et moi, nous (Pauline et Hélène)
8. Annette et toi, vous (Jean-Marc)
9. on (notre copine)

Talking about past events

Let's talk about whom you visited last summer. (Note that the past participle of -re verbs ends in **-u**.)
▶ **Est-ce que tu as rendu visite à ta tante l'été dernier?**
Oui, j'ai rendu visite à ma tante.
(Je n'ai pas rendu visite à ma tante.)

• **Est-ce que tu as rendu visite à ton oncle l'été dernier?**
• **As-tu rendu visite à tes cousins?**
• **As-tu rendu visite à tes grands-parents?**
• **Et le weekend dernier, à qui est-ce que tu as rendu visite?**

10 Qui

Who is doing what? Answer the following questions, using the suggested subjects.

1. Qui perd le match? (toi, vous, Alice)
2. Qui rend visite à Pierre? (Patrick, Corinne et Hélène, toi)
3. Qui entend l'avion *(plane)?* (moi, vous, les voisins)
4. Qui vend des disques? (on, ce magasin, ces boutiques, moi)
5. Qui attend le bus? (les élèves, le professeur, on, vous)
6. Qui répond au professeur? (toi, nous, les élèves)

11 Qu'est-ce qu'ils font?

Read about the following people. Then complete each sentence with the appropriate form of one of the verbs from the list. Be logical!

1. Guillaume est patient. Il … ses amis.
2. Vous êtes à Paris. Vous … à vos cousins français.
3. Tu joues mal. Tu … le match.
4. Je suis dans ma chambre. J' … un bruit *(noise)* curieux.
5. Les élèves sont en classe. Ils … aux questions du professeur.
6. Jacqueline travaille dans une boutique. Elle … des robes.
7. On est au café. On … nos copains.

attendre **entendre** perdre rendre visite **répondre** vendre

C. L'impératif

Compare the French and English forms of the imperative in the sentences below.

Écoute ce disque!   ***Listen*** to this record!
Ne vendez pas votre voiture!   ***Don't sell*** your car!
Allons au cinéma!   ***Let's go*** to the movies!

> **Learning about language**
> The IMPERATIVE is used to make suggestions and to give orders and advice. The commands or suggestions may be affirmative or negative.

Note the forms of the imperative in the chart below.

INFINITIVE	parler	finir	vendre	aller
IMPERATIVE (tu) (vous) (nous)	**parle** **parlez** **parlons**	**finis** **finissez** **finissons**	**vends** **vendez** **vendons**	**va** **allez** **allons**

For regular verbs and most irregular verbs, the forms of the imperative are the same as the corresponding forms of the present tense.

➡ EXCEPTION: For all **-er** verbs, including **aller,** the **-s** of the **tu**- form is dropped in the imperative. Compare.

     Tu **parles** anglais.   **Parle** français, s'il te plaît!
     Tu **vas** au café.   **Va** à la bibliothèque!

➡ The negative imperative is formed as follows:

ne + VERB + **pas** …	**Ne choisis pas** ce blouson.

Leçon 28   **281**

---

10 PRACTICE: describing what people are doing

11 COMPREHENSION: describing people and activities

1. attend
2. rendez visite à
3. perds
4. entends
5. répondent
6. vend
7. attend

Section C

COMMUNICATIVE FUNCTION: Giving commands

■ **Extra practice:** Have students give the **tu, vous,** and **nous** command forms of the following irregular verbs.
faire une promenade:
   fais une promenade
   faites une promenade
   faisons une promenade
revenir demain:
   reviens demain
   revenez demain
   revenons demain

■ **Language note:** The irregular imperative forms of **avoir** and **être** are not presented at this level because they are used in only a few phrases. If students ask, you can mention them:
avoir: aie, ayez, ayons
   N'aie pas peur.
   Don't be afraid.
être: sois, soyez, soyons
   Ne sois pas bête.
   Don't be silly.

Follow-up:
- **Est-ce que X a rendu visite à son oncle l'été dernier?**
- **Est-ce que Y a rendu visite à ses cousins?**
- **À qui est-ce que Z a rendu visite le week-end dernier?**

Left margin column

12 ROLE PLAY: offering and accepting assistance

■ **Challenge:** Have students invent suggestions that are turned down. They can use the same verb and change the rest of the sentence.
J'amène mes parents?
Mais non, n'amène pas tes parents!
Remind students to use **pas de** where needed.

13 ROLE PLAY: giving good and bad advice

■ **Teaching strategy:** Have the girls respond as the demons and the boys as the angels; then change roles.

■ **Realia note**
Ask students:
To whom is this advertisement addressed? [to students and their parents]
What does **Réussissez au bac!** mean? [pass the "bac"!]

■ **Cultural note:** The **bac (le bac-calauréat)** is the final comprehensive exam that lycée students must pass before continuing on to the university.

14 COMPREHENSION: giving logical advice

■ **Variation** (using the **nous** form):
N'étudions pas! Voyageons!

■ **Challenge:** For each situation, have students invent additional advice. Encourage them to be creative.
Visitez Québec!
Faites "la route des baleines".
Dînez au Vendôme!

Main content

12 Mais oui!

You have organized a party at your home. Juliette offers to do the following. You accept.

▶ apporter une pizza?

J'apporte une pizza?

Mais oui, apporte une pizza!

1. faire une salade?
2. inviter nos copains?
3. acheter des croissants?
4. apporter des cassettes?
5. choisir des disques de danse?
6. venir à huit heures?

13 L'ange et le démon
(The angel and the devil)

Véronique is wondering whether she should do certain things. The angel gives her good advice. The devil gives her bad advice. Play both roles.

▶ étudier les verbes
 Étudie les verbes.
 N'étudie pas les verbes.

1. téléphoner à ta tante
2. attendre tes copains
3. faire attention en classe
4. aller à l'école
5. finir la leçon
6. écouter tes professeurs
7. mettre *(set)* la table
8. inviter tes amis
9. rendre visite à ta grand-mère
10. choisir des copains sympathiques
11. acheter un cadeau *(gift)* pour ton frère
12. réussir à l'examen

ÉTUDIANTS
ET
PARENTS D'ÉTUDIANTS

Réussissez au bac!

14 Oui ou non?

For each of the following situations, give your classmates advice as to what to do and what not to do. Be logical.

▶ Nous sommes en vacances. (étudier? voyager?)
 N'étudiez pas! Voyagez!

1. Nous sommes à Paris. (parler anglais? parler français?)
2. C'est dimanche. (aller à la bibliothèque? aller au cinéma?)
3. Il fait beau. (rester à la maison? faire une promenade?)
4. Il fait froid. (mettre un pull? mettre un tee-shirt?)
5. Il est onze heures du soir. (rester au café? rentrer à la maison?)
6. Il fait très chaud. (aller à la piscine? regarder la télé?)

Cooperative pair practice
Activities 12, 13, 15

Game: Drilling with dice

PROPS: Dice (one for every pair of students); transparency with the verb list at right

INSTRUCTIONS (students play in pairs):
Student A rolls the die. For example, 5 spots = **vous**. Student B writes the corresponding form of the first verb: **vous cherchez.**

Then Student B rolls the die and Student A writes the corresponding form of the next verb: 2 spots + **gagner** → **tu gagnes**.

Keep track of pairs as they finish. Then have teams exchange their papers for peer correction. The first pair with the most correct answers is the winning team.

15 L'esprit de contradiction *(Disagreement)*

Make suggestions to your friends about things to do. Your friends will not agree and will suggest something else.

▶ aller au cinéma (à la plage)

Allons au cinéma!

Non, n'allons pas au cinéma! Allons à la plage!

1. jouer au tennis (au volley)
2. écouter la radio (des disques)
3. regarder la télé (un film vidéo)
4. dîner au restaurant (à la maison)
5. inviter Michèle (Sophie)
6. organiser un pique-nique (une boum)
7. faire des sandwichs (une pizza)
8. aller au musée (à la bibliothèque)
9. faire une promenade à pied (en voiture)
10. rendre visite à nos voisins (à nos copains)

Prononciation   an, en /ɑ̃/

Les lettres «an» et «en»

The letters "**an**" and "**en**" represent the nasal vowel /ɑ̃/. Be sure not to pronounce the sound "**n**" after the vowel.

enfa**nt**

Répétez:

/ɑ̃/ **enf**a**nt** **an** **m**a**nteau coll**a**nts gr**a**nd élég**a**nt**

André ma**nge un gr**a**nd s**a**ndwich.**

/ɑ̃/ **enf**a**nt** **en** **arg**e**nt dép**e**nser att**e**nds ent**e**nd**

ve**nd** **en**vie

Vince**nt dép**e**nse rarem**e**nt son arg**e**nt.**

André mange un grand sandwich.

Leçon 28 **283**

---

15 EXCHANGES: making plans

■ **Challenge:** Expand the conversation to include three people. The third one does not like the second suggestion and has another idea.
– **Allons au cinéma!**
– **Non, n'allons pas au cinéma! Allons à la plage.**
– **Mais non, n'allons pas à la plage. Restons à la maison!**

Prononciation

▭ Leçon 28, Section 8

■ **Pronunciation notes**
• Exception: the "**en**" in **examen** represents the sound /ɛ̃/ as in **pain**: **examen** /egzamɛ̃/
• In the combination **ien**, the letters "**en**" also represent the sound /ɛ̃/: **italien** /italjɛ̃/

Classroom Notes

Drilling with dice

1. chercher
2. gagner
3. acheter
4. amener
5. finir
6. grossir
7. maigrir
8. réussir
9. attendre
10. entendre
11. perdre
12. répondre
13. aller
14. avoir
15. être
16. faire
17. mettre
18. permettre *(permit)*
19. revenir
20. venir

1 = je
2 = tu
3 = elle
4 = nous
5 = vous
6 = ils

1 COMPREHENSION

1-d 3-b
2-c 4-a

🔲 **Leçon 28, Section 9**

2 GUIDED ORAL EXPRESSION

🔲 **Leçon 28, Section 10**

1 La bonne réponse

Anne is talking to Jean-François. Match Anne's questions with Jean-François's answers. You may act out the conversation with a classmate.

Anne

Jean-François

1. Est-ce que tu rends visite à tes cousins ce weekend?

2. Tu veux aller dans les boutiques avec moi?

3. Est-ce que tu as envie d'aller au cinéma?

4. Et après *(afterwards)* qu'est-ce qu'on fait?

a. Eh bien, allons au restaurant!

b. Bonne idée! Il y a un nouveau film au «Majestic».

c. Écoute! Je n'ai pas besoin de vêtements.

d. Non, je reste ici.

2 Créa-dialogue

When we are with our friends, it is not always easy to agree on what to do. With your classmates, discuss the following possibilities.

Qu'est-ce qu'on fait samedi?

Allons au cinéma.

Je n'ai pas envie d'aller au cinéma.

Eh bien, rendons visite à nos amis. D'accord?

Oui, c'est une bonne idée.

Quand?	Première suggestion	Deuxième suggestion
▶ samedi	aller au cinéma	rendre visite à nos amis
1. ce soir *(tonight)*	étudier	regarder la télé
2. dimanche	aller au café	dîner au restaurant
3. après *(after)* les classes	jouer au basket	faire une promenade
4. cet été	trouver un job	voyager
5. ce weekend	faire un pique-nique	??
6. demain	aller à la bibliothèque	??

284 Unité 7

À votre tour

Depending upon your goals and objectives, you may or may not wish to assign all of the activities in the **À votre tour** section.

👥 Cooperative practice

Act. 1–4 lend themselves to cooperative pair practice.

3 Conseils

Your friends tell you what they would like to do. Give them appropriate advice, either positive or negative. Use your imagination.

▶ Je voudrais maigrir.   Alors, mange moins.
                          (Alors, ne mange pas de pizza.)

1. Je voudrais avoir un «A» en français.
2. Je voudrais gagner beaucoup d'argent.
3. Je voudrais organiser une boum.
4. Je voudrais préparer un pique-nique.

3 GUIDED ORAL EXPRESSION

4 Que faire?

Give a classmate advice about what to do or not to do in the following circumstances.

Pendant *(During)* la classe	Après *(After)* la classe	Ce weekend	Pendant les vacances
écouter le prof parler à tes copains regarder les bandes dessinées *(comics)* manger un sandwich répondre en français ??	étudier aller au cinéma préparer tes leçons rentrer chez toi regarder la télé ??	rester à la maison aller en ville dépenser ton argent organiser une boum faire une promenade à pied ??	voyager travailler grossir oublier *(forget)* ton français ??

4 COMPREHENSION

5 WRITTEN SELF-EXPRESSION

▶ Pendant la classe, écoute le prof.
    Ne parle pas à tes copains.

5 Bon voyage!

Your French friend Ariane is going to visit the United States next summer with her cousin. They are traveling on a low budget and are asking you for advice as to how to save money. Make a list of suggestions, including five things they could do and five things they should not do. You may want to use some of the following ideas:

- voyager (comment?)
- rester (dans quels hôtels?)
- dîner (dans quels restaurants?)
- visiter (quelles villes?)
- aller (où?)
- acheter (quelles choses?)
- apporter (quelles choses?)

▶

Voyagez en bus.
Ne voyagez pas
en train.

Classroom Notes

📁 Portfolio assessment

You will probably select only one speaking activity and one writing activity to go into the students' portfolios for Unit 7.

In this lesson, Act. 2 lends itself well to an oral portfolio recording.

Act. 5 offers a good writing portfolio topic.

Entracte 7

La mode et les vêtements

Petit test culturel
La mode et les vêtements

Aujourd'hui la mode° est internationale. Les jeunes Français adoptent le «look» américain ou anglais. Les Américains achètent des vêtements de style français ou italien.

Imaginez que vous habitez en France. Est-ce que vous pouvez° répondre aux questions suivantes?° Vérifiez° vos réponses au bas° de la page.

1 Vincent va en ville pour acheter des «tennis». Qu'est-ce qu'il va acheter?
a. une raquette
b. un short
c. des chaussures
d. des chemises

2 Monique habite à Paris. Elle a envie d'acheter un blouson. Où va-t-elle?
a. à la Villette
b. aux Galeries Lafayette
c. au Zénith
d. au Centre Pompidou

3 Dans ce magasin on vend des vêtements de marques° différentes. Voici quatre marques. Quelle est la marque qui n'est *pas* française?
a. Benetton
b. Christian Dior
c. Pierre Cardin
d. Yves Saint-Laurent

4 René Lacoste est un champion français de tennis. Aujourd'hui son nom° est associé° avec une marque de . . .
a. vêtements de sport
b. chaussures de ski
c. chocolats
d. vitamines

5 Jean Vuarnet est un champion olympique de ski. À quels produits° est-ce que son nom est associé?
a. des skis
b. des chaussures
c. des vêtements de sport
d. des lunettes de soleil

6 Coco Chanel est le nom d'une couturière° française très célèbre.° Son nom est aussi associé avec . . .
a. un parfum
b. un festival de cinéma
c. une compétition sportive
d. une eau minérale°

7 Les jeans sont faits° avec un coton spécial appelé° «denim». Ce mot vient du français «de Nîmes». Nîmes est le nom . . .
a. d'un textile
b. d'un vêtement
c. d'un couturier° français
d. d'une ville française

mode *fashion* **pouvez** *can* **suivantes** *following* **Vérifiez** *Check*
au bas *at the bottom* **marques** *designer labels* **nom** *name* **associé** *associated*
produits *products* **couturière** *fashion designer* **célèbre** *famous*
eau minérale *mineral water* **faits** *made* **appelé** *called* **couturier** *fashion designer*

286 Unité 7

 Cooperative reading practice

Divide the class into groups of 4 or 5, each with a **secrétaire.**

For each question, have the groups first vote on the correct answer (keeping the box at the bottom of the page covered).

Then have the recorders check the right answers and announce their group score to the entire class.

Nous avons six réponses correctes.

EN FRANCE

Les Trois Suisses

La compagnie Les Trois Suisses vend des vêtements par corresponance. Voici une page de son catalogue.

PRÈS DE CHEZ VOUS
VOTRE RELAIS

GUADELOUPE
1 bis, rue de nozieres
97110 POINTE-A-PITRE.
Tel : 82.03.91.

MARTINIQUE
96, rue Moreau de Jonnes
97200 FORT DE FRANCE.
Tel : 63.82.00.

GUYANE
78, rue du lieutenant Becker
97300 CAYENNE.
Tel : 30.20.78.

RÉUNION
73, rue Monseigneur de Beaumont
97400 SAINT-DENIS.
Tel : 21.67.39.
202, rue M. et Ary Leblond
97410 SAINT PIERRE.
Tel : 35.01.78.

SAINT-PIERRE ET MIQUELON
17 bis, rue M° Delamont
B.P. 256
97500 SAINT-PIERRE ET MIQUELON.
Tel : 41.46.36.

NOUVELLE CALEDONIE
11, rue du dr. Lescour
Quartier latin B.P. 4285
NOUMEA.
Tel : 27.57.76.

OBJECTIVES s/b/ BF-COMP

CARACO PAGE 17
PANTALON PAGE 4
ACCESSOIRES PAGES 14 ET 20

catalogue printemps-été

3 SUISSES
le Chouchou

Prix garantis jusqu'au 15 août

Promo!
depuis
89ᶠ
le sweat

noir
jaune vif
blanc
gris chiné
pêche
rouge vif
vert vif
bleu vif

Promo!
depuis
59'90ᶠ
les tennis

Promo!
depuis
99ᶠ
le pantalon
jogging

vert menthe

DU
34
AU
52

 Sur cette page, trois articles sont en «promo».° Quels sont ces trois articles?

Combien coûte le pantalon jogging?

Combien coûtent les tennis en francs? et en dollars? (un dollar = 6 francs) Est-ce que c'est cher? Quelles couleurs est-ce qu'on peut choisir? Quelle couleur préférez-vous?

Combien coûte le sweat? Quelles couleurs est-ce qu'on peut° choisir? Quelle couleur préférez-vous?

promo = promotion *special sale*
peut *can*

3 SUISSES 113

Entracte 7 287

Les Trois Suisses

OBJECTIVES:
• Reading for information
• Understanding authentic documents

■ **Vocabulary notes**
depuis 89F *prices start at 89F*
uni *solid (color)*
jaune vif *bright yellow*
chiné *woven with threads of different colors (here gray and white)*
verte menthe *mint green*
caraco *halter top*

■ **Expansion:** Have students look at the map on pp. 4–5 and locate the French-speaking departments (**DOM**) and territories (**TOM**) mentioned on the cover of the catalogue.

📖 Pre-reading
Ask students if they sometimes order clothes from catalogues.
Which catalogues do they like best?

Post-reading
Have students each select an item they plan to buy (for themselves or as a gift for a friend). In pairs, have students describe their intended purchases to one another.
– Moi, je vais acheter un sweat.
– Ah bon? Pour qui? ...

Les jeunes Français et la mode

OBJECTIVES:
- Reading at the paragraph level
- Building reading skills

■ **Pronunciation: Chloé** /kloe/

■ **Cultural note:** The literal translation of **l'habit ne fait pas le moine** is *the habit (monk's attire) does not make the monk.* Compare to the English: *Clothes do not make the man.*

■ **Questions sur le texte**
1. Comment est-ce que Florence gagne son argent?
2. Où est-ce qu'elle achète ses vêtements?
3. Est-ce que Jean-Marc aime être bien habillé?
4. Est-ce qu'il achète beaucoup de vêtements?
5. Est-ce que Chloé achète beaucoup de vêtements?
6. Qu'est-ce qu'elle fait pour être à la mode?
7. Qui achète les vêtements d'Antoine?
8. Où est-ce que la mère d'Antoine achète les vêtements de son fils?
9. Est-ce que Julien aime être à la mode?
10. Qu'est-ce qu'il fait avec son argent?

■ **Cultural note (Les grandes surfaces):** Larger stores of this type (a combination supermarket plus discount chain store) are also called **hypermarchés.**

Entre amis: **Les jeunes Français et la mode**

Est-ce que vous aimez être à la mode?° Où est-ce que vous achetez vos vêtements? Et qu'est-ce qui compte° le plus° pour vous? le style? la qualité? le prix? Nous avons posé° ces questions à cinq jeunes Français. Voilà leurs réponses.

Florence (16 ans)
J'aime être à la mode. Malheureusement,° mon budget est limité. La solution? Le samedi après-midi je travaille dans une boutique de mode. Là, je peux acheter mes jupes et mes pulls à des prix très avantageux.° Pour le reste, je compte sur la générosité de mes parents.

Jean-Marc (15 ans)
Aujourd'hui la présentation extérieure° est très importante. Mais il n'est pas nécessaire d'être à la mode pour être bien habillé.° Pour moi, la qualité des vêtements est aussi importante que leur style. En général, j'attends les soldes.° J'achète peu de° vêtements mais je fais attention à la qualité.

Chloé (15 ans)
Pour moi, le style, c'est tout.° Hélas, la mode n'est pas bon marché. Heureusement° j'ai une cousine qui a une machine à coudre° et qui est très très adroite.° Alors, nous faisons nos propres° robes! Nous choisissons le tissu,° la couleur, le style ... Ainsi, nous sommes toujours à la mode. C'est chouette, non?

Antoine (12 ans)
Moi, je n'ai pas le choix!° C'est ma mère qui choisit mes vêtements. En ce qui concerne° la mode, elle n'est pas dans le coup.° Elle achète tout dans les grandes surfaces. C'est pas° drôle!

Julien (14 ans)
Vous connaissez° le proverbe: «L'habit ne fait pas le moine».° Eh bien, pour moi les vêtements n'ont aucune° importance. Avec mon argent je préfère acheter des compacts. Quand j'ai besoin de jeans ou de tee-shirts, je vais aux Puces.* C'est pas cher et c'est marrant!°

*Marché aux puces *flea market*

à la mode *in style*   **compte** *counts*   **le plus** *the most*
avons posé *asked*   **Malheureusement** *Unfortunately*
avantageux *reasonable*
présentation extérieure *outward appearance*   **habillé** *dressed*
soldes *sales*   **peu de** *few*   **tout** *everything*
Heureusement *Fortunately*   **machine à coudre** *sewing machine*
adroite *skillful*   **propres** *own*   **tissu** *fabric*   **choix** *choice*
En ce qui concerne *As for*   **dans le coup** *"with it"*
C'est pas = Ce n'est pas   **connaissez** *know*   **moine** *monk*
aucune *no*   **marrant** *fun*

288 Unité 7

■ **NOTES** ■
CULTURELLES

1 Les grandes surfaces

Les grandes surfaces sont des magasins en libre-service° où on peut acheter toutes° les marchandises nécessaires à la vie quotidienne.° En général les prix ne sont pas très élevés,° mais la qualité est moyenne.°

📖 **Pre-reading**
Have students glance over the reading quickly. What are the questions that were asked in the interview?

Post-reading
Ask each student to decide which of the five people he/she would most want to be introduced to and why.
Imaginez que vous pouvez faire la connaissance d'un de ces jeunes Français. Qui voulez-vous rencontrer? Pourquoi?

Comment lire

DIFFERENCES IN SPOKEN AND WRITTEN LANGUAGE

The interviews you read were conducted orally. Notice how casual speech is different from standard written language.

- Spoken language often contains slang expressions.

    Elle n'est pas dans le coup!   **C'est marrant!**   **C'est chouette!**

- Spoken French sometimes drops the **ne** in **ne . . . pas.**

    C'est pas cher. = Ce n'est pas cher.

Enrichissez votre vocabulaire

MORE COGNATE PATTERNS

Here are a few common cognate patterns to help you recognize new words more easily.

FRENCH	ENGLISH	FRENCH	ENGLISH
-x	*-ce*	**le prix**	*price*
-eux	*-ous*	**avantageux**	*advantageous, reasonable*
-eur	*-or*	**la couleur**	*color*
-aire	*-ary*	**nécessaire**	*necessary*

Activité

Can you identify the English equivalents of the following French words?

- **le choix**   **la voix**   • **courageux**   **sérieux**   **dangereux**   **curieux**
- **un acteur**   **une odeur**   **un docteur**   **supérieur**   **une erreur**
- **un salaire**   **le vocabulaire**   **un commentaire**   **un anniversaire**

Activité: Et toi?

Voici ce que disent° les jeunes Français. Est-ce que c'est vrai pour vous aussi?

Oui, c'est vrai pour moi.

Non, ce n'est pas vrai pour moi.

OUI OU NON?
- ▶ ? 1. J'aime être à la mode.
- ? 2. Mon budget est limité.
- ? 3. J'attends les soldes.
- ? 4. Je fais attention à la qualité.

OUI OU NON?
- ? 5. J'achète le tissu et je fais mes vêtements.
- ? 6. Ma mère choisit mes vêtements.
- ? 7. Je préfère acheter des compacts.
- ? 8. J'achète mes vêtements aux Puces.

2 Les soldes

En général, les boutiques de vêtements ont des soldes° deux ou trois fois° par an. On peut alors acheter des vêtements de bonne qualité à des prix avantageux. Certaines boutiques ont des soldes toute l'année.°

libre-service *self-service*   **toutes** *all*   **quotidienne** *daily*   **élevés** *high*
moyenne *average*   **soldes** *sales*   **fois** *times*   **toute l'année** *all year long*

■ Questions personnelles

1. Comment est-ce que tu gagnes ton argent?
2. Est-ce que tu travailles? Où?
3. Où est-ce que tu achètes tes vêtements?
4. Est-ce que tu attends les soldes pour acheter tes vêtements?
5. Qu'est-ce que tu achètes dans les grandes surfaces?
6. Jean-Marc dit: "La présentation extérieure est très importante." Est-ce que tu es d'accord avec cette opinion?
7. Julien dit: "L'habit ne fait pas le moine." Est-ce que tu es d'accord avec ce proverbe?

Classroom Notes

Variétés

OBJECTIVES:
- Reading for fun
- Taking a French self-test

Variétés

L'argent et vous

Nous avons tous° besoin d'argent. L'argent est nécessaire, mais l'argent crée° aussi des problèmes. Quelle est votre attitude envers° l'argent? Répondez aux questions suivantes.°

1 Que représente l'argent pour vous?
a. l'indépendance
b. la possibilité d'acheter beaucoup de choses
c. la possibilité d'aider vos amis

2 Selon vous, quel est le rapport° entre l'argent et le bonheur?°
a. L'argent est nécessaire.
b. L'argent est utile.°
c. Il n'y a pas de rapport.

3 Vous avez trois possibilités de job ce weekend. Qu'est-ce que vous choisissez?
a. faire du baby-sitting (3 dollars par l'heure pour 4 heures)
b. laver° la voiture des voisins (5 dollars au total)
c. vendre des hot dogs à un match de football (un pourcentage de 10% sur les ventes°)

4 C'est votre anniversaire. Vos grands-parents vous donnent° cinquante dollars. Qu'est-ce que vous faites?
a. J'invite mes copains à un concert.
b. J'achète des vêtements.
c. Je mets mon argent à la banque.°

5 Pendant les vacances vous avez le choix entre les trois possibilités suivantes. Qu'est-ce que vous choisissez?
a. faire un grand voyage avec la famille
b. travailler comme volontaire° dans un hôpital
c. travailler dans un supermarché

6 Selon vous, quel est l'aspect le plus° important quand on cherche un travail?°
a. avoir un bon salaire
b. avoir un travail intéressant
c. avoir la possibilité de travailler avec des gens sympathiques

tous all **crée** creates **envers** toward **suivantes** following
rapport relationship **bonheur** happiness **utile** useful
laver wash **ventes** sales **vous donnent** give you **banque** bank
comme volontaire as a volunteer **le plus** the most **travail** job

■ **Photo culture note**
Banking
The **Crédit Lyonnais**, one of the largest French banks, has branches throughout the country. Note the line of customers waiting their turn at the automatic teller (**le guichet automatique** or **le distributeur de billets automatique**).

Pre-reading
Ask students to look at these two pages and decide what type of reading it is. [a personality quiz]

Post-reading
Once students have read the questions and selected their answers, have them get together in pairs to analyze their scores. Do they agree with the interpretation? **Êtes-vous d'accord avec l'interprétation?**

INTERPRÉTATION

Comptez° vos points en utilisant° la grille° suivante.

Questions		1	2	3	4	5	6
Options	a	3	3	2	1	1	3
	b	2	2	1	2	2	1
	c	1	1	3	3	3	2

Combien de points avez-vous?

15 points ou plus:

Vous avez beaucoup d'énergie. Pour vous, l'argent est important et vous êtes prêt(e)° à travailler dur° pour gagner votre argent.

entre 9 et 14 points:

Vous êtes réaliste. Pour vous l'argent est un moyen° et pas un but.°

8 points ou moins:

Vous êtes idéaliste et généreux (généreuse). Entre l'amitié° et l'argent, vous préférez l'amitié.

Comptez Count   **en utilisant** by using
grille grid   **prêt(e)** ready   **dur** hard   **moyen** means
but end   **amitié** friendship

NIVEAU **C**

Le monde

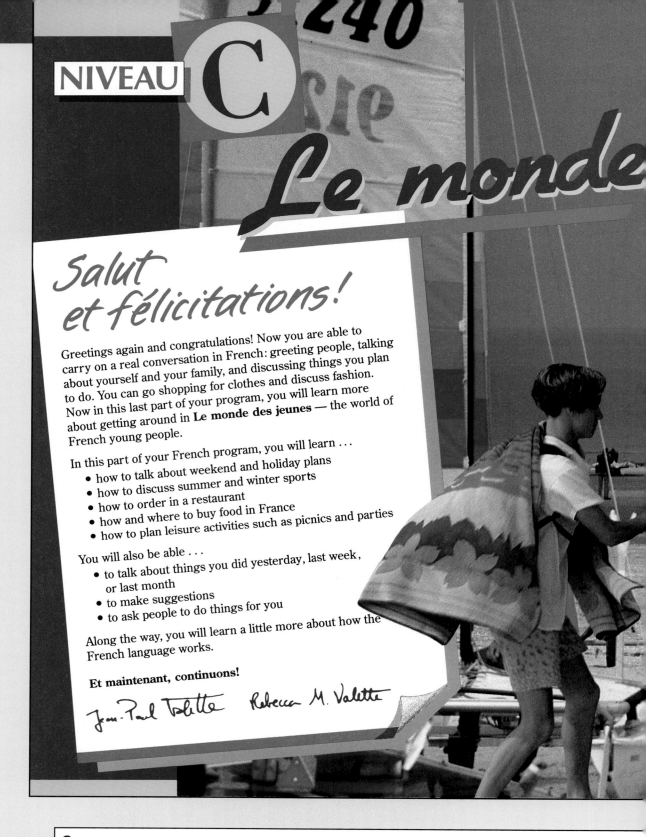

Salut et félicitations!

Greetings again and congratulations! Now you are able to carry on a real conversation in French: greeting people, talking about yourself and your family, and discussing things you plan to do. You can go shopping for clothes and discuss fashion. Now in this last part of your program, you will learn more about getting around in **Le monde des jeunes** — the world of French young people.

In this part of your French program, you will learn . . .
- how to talk about weekend and holiday plans
- how to discuss summer and winter sports
- how to order in a restaurant
- how and where to buy food in France
- how to plan leisure activities such as picnics and parties

You will also be able . . .
- to talk about things you did yesterday, last week, or last month
- to make suggestions
- to ask people to do things for you

Along the way, you will learn a little more about how the French language works.

Et maintenant, continuons!

Jean-Paul Valette   Rebecca M. Valette

Overview of Niveau C
Niveau C takes students beyond the core of Niveau B, and introduces them to somewhat more complex language functions: object pronouns, the partitive, and a formal presentation of the **passé composé** (which they have been using informally).

Although it is desirable to present these units, it is not critical to finish them, since the material is re-entered and expanded in the first part of **Discovering French —Blanc.**

In format, Niveau C is similar to Niveau B, with an emphasis on a four-skills

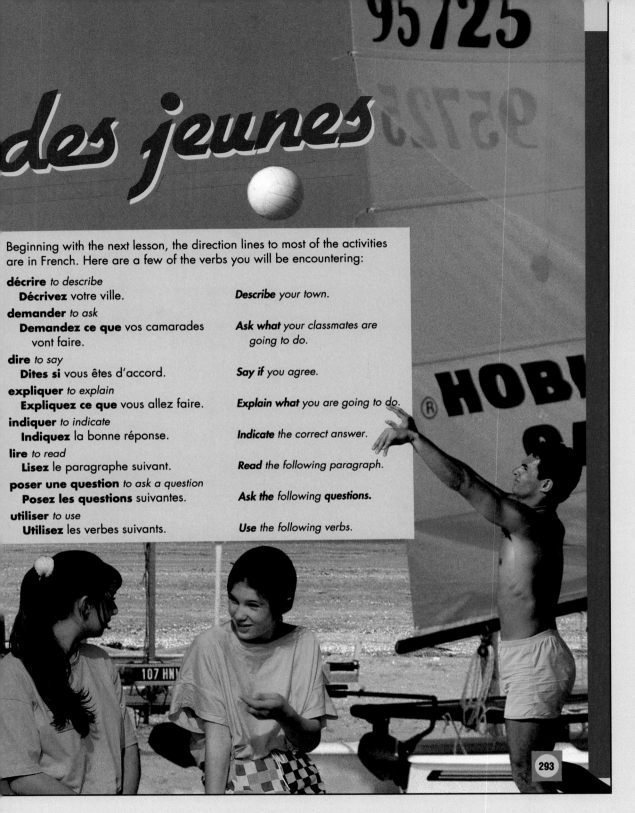

des jeunes

Beginning with the next lesson, the direction lines to most of the activities are in French. Here are a few of the verbs you will be encountering:

décrire *to describe*
  Décrivez votre ville.

Describe your town.

demander *to ask*
  Demandez ce que vos camarades vont faire.

Ask what your classmates are going to do.

dire *to say*
  Dites si vous êtes d'accord.

Say if you agree.

expliquer *to explain*
  Expliquez ce que vous allez faire.

Explain what you are going to do.

indiquer *to indicate*
  Indiquez la bonne réponse.

Indicate the correct answer.

lire *to read*
  Lisez le paragraphe suivant.

Read the following paragraph.

poser une question *to ask a question*
  Posez les questions suivantes.

Ask the following questions.

utiliser *to use*
  Utilisez les verbes suivants.

Use the following verbs.

293

approach and a focus on linguistic interaction, as well as activities designed for Cooperative Practice.

UNITÉ 8

Le temps libre

294

Unit overview

COMMUNICATION GOALS: Students will be able to talk about individual sports, helping out at home, and what they did over the weekend or during vacation.

LINGUISTIC GOALS: Students will learn to describe and narrate past events using the passé composé.

CRITICAL THINKING GOALS: Students will observe the similarities and differences between the passé composé in French and the past tense in English.

CULTURAL GOALS: Students will learn about weekend and sports activities popular in France and the importance of leisure time to the French people.

T294

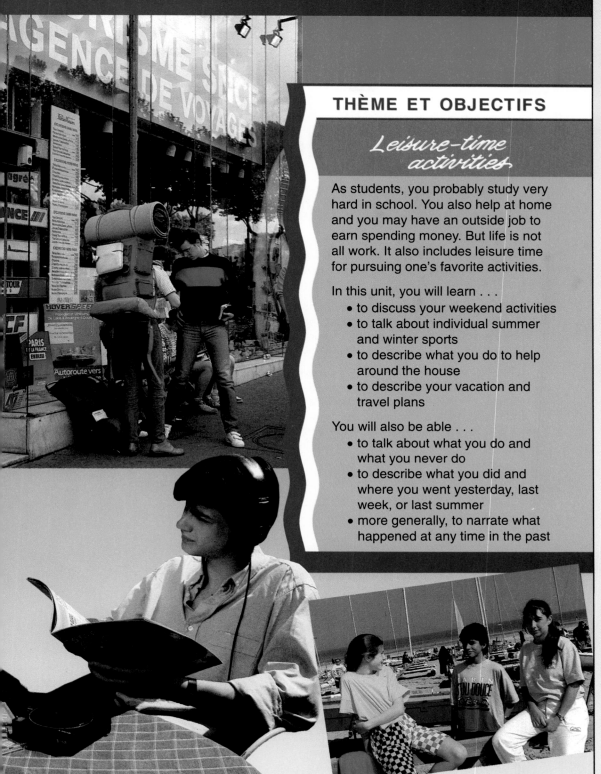

■ **Photo culture note**
À l'agence de voyage
Note the signs in the window:
- **Air France** and **UTA (Union des Transports Aériens)** are French airlines.
- **SNCF (Société Nationale des Chemins de fer Français)** is the French national railroad system.
- **Hoverspeed** offers rapid ferryboat crossings between France and England via hovercraft.

THÈME ET OBJECTIFS

Leisure-time activities

As students, you probably study very hard in school. You also help at home and you may have an outside job to earn spending money. But life is not all work. It also includes leisure time for pursuing one's favorite activities.

In this unit, you will learn . . .
- to discuss your weekend activities
- to talk about individual summer and winter sports
- to describe what you do to help around the house
- to describe your vacation and travel plans

You will also be able . . .
- to talk about what you do and what you never do
- to describe what you did and where you went yesterday, last week, or last summer
- more generally, to narrate what happened at any time in the past

Classroom Notes

Pacing

Your pacing of Units 8 and 9 depends on what point in the academic year you begin Niveau C.

Since this material is reintroduced in **Discovering French—blanc,** you may wish to present the material of Units 8 and 9 primarily for student recognition.

Or you may wish to focus on Unit 8 so that the students have a solid introduction to the passé composé.

For further suggestions on pacing, see the general discussion in the Front Matter.

MODULE 29:
Le français pratique:
Le weekend et les vacances
Total time: 6:11 min.
(Counter: 00:40 min.)

■ **Comprehension practice:** Play the entire module through as an introduction to the lesson.

LE FRANÇAIS
PRATIQUE

LEÇON 29

Le weekend et les vacances

Accent sur ... Les loisirs

I f you had to decide between earning more money or having more free time, what would you choose? When asked this question on a survey, French people indicated their overwhelming preference for more leisure time.

For the French, leisure plays an important role in what they call **la qualité de la vie** *(quality of life)*. In fact, they consider leisure time to be not only a necessity but a right. By law, French workers are entitled to five weeks of paid vacation, as compared to two weeks for the average American.

French teenagers also place great value on their leisure time. Because they have so much homework and need to study so hard for their exams, they have no real time — and also little opportunity — to take an outside job. Instead, they try to make the most of their leisure hours. What are their favorite activities? Here is how French young people answered the question "What do you do when you have a free evening?"

Qu'est-ce que tu aimes faire le soir?	GARÇONS	FILLES
Je regarde la télé.	24%	18%
Je sors° avec mes copains.	20%	18%
Je vais au cinéma.	16%	14%
Je lis.°	14%	20%
Je vais au concert ou au théâtre.	10%	12%
Je vais danser.	8%	12%
Je fais un sport.	6%	4%
Je bricole.°	2%	2%

sors *go out* **lis** *read*
bricole *do things around the house*

 Je regarde la télé.

296 **Unité 8**

📺 Using the video

The main focus of Video Module 29 is on what French people do in their leisure time, both on weekends and on vacation. As students watch, have them look for similarities and differences in the ways the French and Americans spend their leisure time.

The *Vignette culturelle* introduces students to the sport of windsurfing **(la planche à voile),** which is very popular throughout metropolitan France, as well as in the overseas departments of Martinique and Guadeloupe.

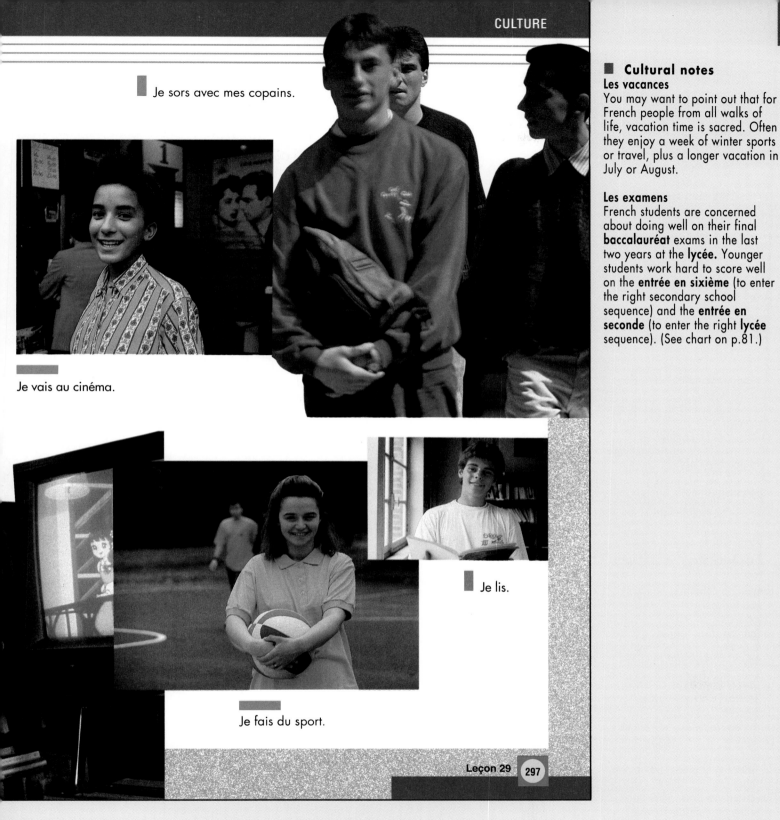

Je sors avec mes copains.

Je vais au cinéma.

Je lis.

Je fais du sport.

Leçon 29 | 297

■ Cultural notes
Les vacances
You may want to point out that for French people from all walks of life, vacation time is sacred. Often they enjoy a week of winter sports or travel, plus a longer vacation in July or August.

Les examens
French students are concerned about doing well on their final **baccalauréat** exams in the last two years at the **lycée.** Younger students work hard to score well on the **entrée en sixième** (to enter the right secondary school sequence) and the **entrée en seconde** (to enter the right **lycée** sequence). (See chart on p.81.)

⊕ Cross-cultural comparisons

Ask your students what they like to do when they have a free evening, using the suggestions in the **sondage** on p. 296. Then analyze your results and compare them to those in the reading.

You can review numbers by tallying the results in French, using a calculator.

Dans la classe, il y a [12] garçons et [16] filles.
[4] garçons regardent la télé.
Ça fait [25% – vingt-cinq pour cent].
[4] filles regardent la télé.
Ça fait [33 % – trente-trois pour cent].

A. Le weekend

▶ *How to plan your weekend activities:*

Qu'est-ce que tu vas faire samedi?

Je vais rester chez moi pour réparer mon vélo.

Qu'est-ce que tu vas faire	samedi?	
	samedi **matin**	**le matin** *morning*
	dimanche **après-midi**	**l'après-midi** *afternoon*
	demain **soir**	**le soir** *evening*
	ce **weekend**	
	le weekend **prochain** *(next)*	

Je vais rester chez moi **pour** *(in order to)*
  faire mes **devoirs** *(homework)*.
  réparer *(to fix)* mon vélo
  préparer le dîner
  aider *(to help)* mes parents
  laver *(to wash)* ma mobylette
  nettoyer *(to clean)* ma chambre

Je vais aller ...   pour ...
  en ville   **faire des achats**
  dans les magasins   *(go shopping)*.
  au **centre commercial** *(mall)*

Moi, je vais aller en ville pour faire des achats.

  au cinéma   **voir** *(to see)* **un film**
  au café   **rencontrer** *(to meet)* mes copains
  au stade   **assister à** *(to go to, attend)*
                             un match de foot

  à la campagne *(countryside)*   **faire un pique-nique** *(to have a picnic)*

Je vais aller à une boum.
  Avant *(Before)* la boum, je vais faire des achats.
  Pendant *(During)* la boum, je vais écouter des cassettes.
  Après *(After)* la boum, je vais faire mes devoirs.

➡ The verb **nettoyer** is conjugated like **payer:**
  je **nettoie**   tu **nettoies**   il/elle/on **nettoie**   ils/elles **nettoient**
  but: nous nettoyons   vous nettoyez

298 **Unité 8**

1 Et toi?

Décris tes activités. Pour cela, complète les phrases suivantes.

1. En général, je vais
au cinéma . . .
- le vendredi soir
- le samedi soir
- le dimanche après-midi
- . . . ?

2. En général, je rencontre
mes copains . . .
- chez moi
- chez eux
- dans un café
- . . . ?

3. En général, je fais
mes devoirs . . .
- avant le dîner
- après le dîner
- pendant la classe
- . . . ?

4. Je préfère assister à . . .
- un match de foot
- un match de baseball
- un concert de rock
- . . . ?

5. En général, je préfère faire
mes achats . . .
- seul(e) *(by myself)*
- avec mes copains
- avec mes frères et mes soeurs
- . . . ?

6. En général, quand je rentre
chez moi après les classes, . . .
- je fais mes devoirs
- je regarde la télé
- j'aide ma mère ou mon père
- . . . ?

7. En été, je préfère faire
un pique-nique . . .
- dans mon jardin
- à la campagne
- à la plage
- . . . ?

8. Si *(If)* je dois aider mes
parents à la maison et si j'ai
le choix *(choice)*, je préfère . . .
- nettoyer le salon
- laver la voiture
- faire la vaisselle *(dishes)*
- . . . ?

2 Qu'est-ce qu'ils font?

Informez-vous sur les personnes suivantes. Décrivez
ce qu'elles font ou ce qu'elles vont faire. Pour cela,
complétez les phrases avec une expression du
vocabulaire à la page 298.

▶ Sandrine est au garage.
Elle <u>répare son vélo</u> (<u>sa mobylette</u>).

1. Mme Jolivet est dans la cuisine. Elle . . .
2. Vincent Jolivet est aussi dans la cuisine. Il . . .
3. Anne et Sylvie sont au Bon Marché. Elles . . .
4. Je suis dans ma chambre et je regarde mon livre
de français. Je . . .
5. Olivier et ses copains achètent des billets *(tickets)*
de cinéma. Ils vont . . .
6. Mes amis vont à Yankee Stadium. Ils vont . . .
7. Tu vas au café. Tu vas . . .
8. Vous faites des sandwichs. Vous allez . . . à la campagne.

3 Mon calendrier personnel

Décrivez ce que vous allez faire.

MERCREDI

1. Après la classe, je vais . . .
2. Avant le dîner, . . .
3. Après le dîner, . . .
4. Demain soir, . . .
5. Vendredi soir, . . .
6. Samedi après-midi, . . .
7. Samedi soir, . . .
8. Dimanche après-midi, . . .
9. Pendant les vacances, . . .

299

1 COMMUNICATION:
describing leisure activities

■ **Variations**
- In pairs:
Have students work in pairs,
sharing their answers.
- In small groups:
(See suggested actvity on
p. T91.)

2 COMPREHENSION: describ-
ing what people are doing

3 COMMUNICATION:
describing future plans

 **29.4 Mini-scenes:
Samedi**
(2:39–3:41 min.)

 Leçon 29, Section 3

Teaching note: Directions to activities

From now on, direction lines for the
activities are given in French. You may
want to present the key verbs listed on
p. 293. Encourage your students to guess
the meanings of other new words and
expressions from context.

With more challenging activities, you may
wish to have a volunteer paraphrase the
instructions in English.

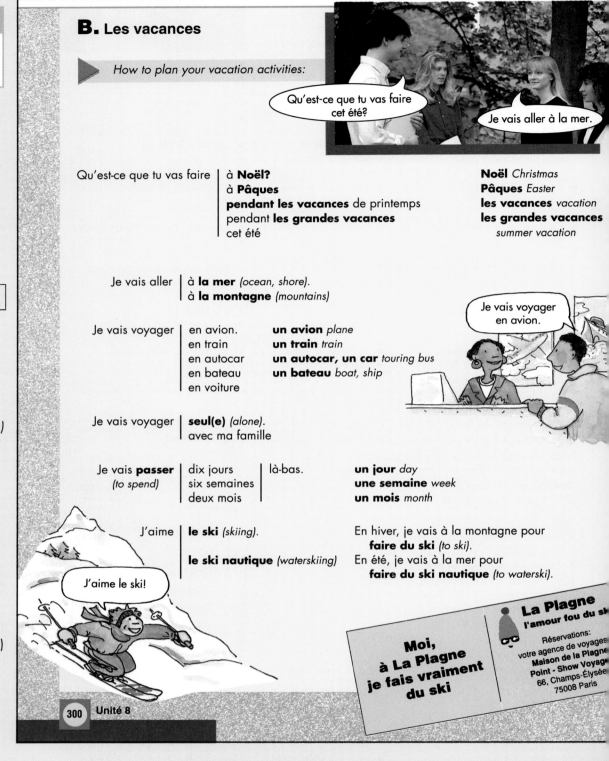

B. Les vacances

How to plan your vacation activities:

Qu'est-ce que tu vas faire cet été?

Je vais aller à la mer.

Qu'est-ce que tu vas faire	à **Noël?**	**Noël** Christmas
	à **Pâques**	**Pâques** Easter
	pendant les vacances de printemps	**les vacances** vacation
	pendant **les grandes vacances**	**les grandes vacances** summer vacation
	cet été	

| Je vais aller | à **la mer** (ocean, shore). |
| | à **la montagne** (mountains) |

Je vais voyager en avion.

Je vais voyager	en avion.	**un avion** plane
	en train	**un train** train
	en autocar	**un autocar, un car** touring bus
	en bateau	**un bateau** boat, ship
	en voiture	

| Je vais voyager | **seul(e)** (alone). |
| | avec ma famille |

Je vais **passer** (to spend)	dix jours	là-bas.	**un jour** day
	six semaines		**une semaine** week
	deux mois		**un mois** month

| J'aime | **le ski** (skiing). |
| | **le ski nautique** (waterskiing) |

En hiver, je vais à la montagne pour **faire du ski** (to ski).
En été, je vais à la mer pour **faire du ski nautique** (to waterski).

J'aime le ski!

Moi, à La Plagne je fais vraiment du ski

La Plagne
l'amour fou du ski
Réservations:
votre agence de voyages
Maison de la Plagne
Point - Show Voyage
66, Champs-Élysées
75008 Paris

300 Unité 8

Activités sportives

le sport	*sport(s)*	Je **fais du sport.**	*I practice sports.*
le jogging	*jogging*	Nous **faisons du jogging.**	*We jog.*
le ski	*skiing*	Tu **fais du ski?**	*Do you ski?*
le ski nautique	*waterskiing*	Anne **fait du ski nautique.**	*Anne waterskis.*
la voile	*sailing*	Paul **fait de la voile.**	*Paul sails.*
la planche à voile	*windsurfing*	Vous **faites de la planche à voile?**	*Do you windsurf?*
la natation	*swimming*	Tu **fais de la natation** en été?	*Do you go swimming in (the) summer?*
l'alpinisme *(m.)*	*mountain climbing*	J'aime **faire de l'alpinisme.**	*I like to go mountain climbing.*

➡ To describe participation in individual sports or other activities, the French use the construction:

$$\text{faire} \begin{cases} \text{du} \\ \text{de la} \\ \text{de l'} \end{cases} + \begin{matrix} \text{SPORT} \\ \text{or} \\ \text{ACTIVITY} \end{matrix}$$

le camping	→	**faire du camping**
la voile	→	**faire de la voile**
l'alpinisme	→	**faire de l'alpinisme**

NOTE CULTURELLE

Le calendrier des fêtes françaises

Voici les principales fêtes *(holidays)* en France:

le jour de l'An	*New Year's Day*
Mardi Gras	*Shrove Tuesday*
Pâques	*Easter*
le premier mai	*Labor Day*
la Pentecôte	*Pentecost*
le 14 juillet	*Bastille Day (French National Holiday)*
la Toussaint	*All Saints' Day (November 1)*
le 11 novembre	*Armistice Day*
Noël	*Christmas (December 25)*

Mardi Gras

Le 14 juillet

Leçon 29 **301**

▷ **Vocabulaire**

Transparency 43
Activités sportives

Language note: The word **alpinisme** comes from **les Alpes,** which are the highest mountain range of France and Western Europe.

Note culturelle

■ **Photo culture notes**

• Mardi Gras is the last Tuesday before Lent (**le Carême**), which begins on Ash Wednesday (**le mercredi des cendres**). Traditionally, Lent (the 40 days before Easter) was a period of penance and fasting, and so **Mardi gras** — or fat Tuesday — was the last day to eat and be merry. In France (and areas with historic ties to France: **le Québec, Haïti, la Nouvelle Orléans,** etc.), this day is known as **Carnaval** and is celebrated with parades, floats, and masked balls.

• French people celebrate **la Pentecôte,** which is the seventh Sunday after Easter, with a long weekend since the following Monday is a national holiday.

• **Le 14 juillet** commemorates the beginning of the French Revolution (1789–1799). The holiday is celebrated with fireworks (**des feux d'artifice**) and dancing in the streets (**des bals populaires**).
Note that the poster proclaims the motto (**la devise**) of France: **Liberté, égalité, fraternité.** This motto was adopted during the French Revolution.

• **La Toussaint** is a Catholic holiday on which French people remember their dead and visit their family cemetery.

• **Le onze novembre** commemorates the 1918 signing of the Armistice ending World War I. It is the day on which the French remember their veterans and those who died for their country.

🎲 Game: Activités

PROP: Transparency 43
With the overhead projector turned off, have one student come to the front and write an "X" by one of the activities on the transparency. Students at their desks try to guess which activity the student has chosen.

Tu fais de la natation? [Non, je ne fais pas de natation.]
Tu fais du ski? [Oui, je fais du ski.]
The student at the front verifies the correct guess by turning on the overhead projector. The student who guesses then comes forward, turns off the projector, erases the "X," chooses another activity, and the game continues.

COMMUNICATION:
describing one's vacation
preferences

■ **Expansion** (question 2):
Pendant les fêtes de Hanoukka, je préfère ...

■ **Variation:** See variation for Act. 1, p. T299.

■ **Challenge:** Have students give an original completion for each sentence. For example:
1. **Mes vacances préférées sont [les vacances de "Thanks-giving".]**

COMPREHENSION:
describing people's
activities

 29.8 Vignette culturelle:
La planche à voile
(5:28–6:47 min.)

■ **Photo culture note**
La planche à voile
The sport of windsurfing (**la planche à voile**) originated in California and was introduced in the the early 1970s. It has become one of the favorite sports of French young people. In international competition, the French windsurfers (**un véliplan-chiste**) are among the world's best.

4 Et toi?

Indique tes préférences personnelles en complétant les phrases suivantes.

1. Mes vacances préférées sont . . .

- les vacances de Noël
- les vacances de printemps
- les grandes vacances
- . . . ?

2. Pendant les vacances de Noël, je préfère . . .

- rester avec ma famille
- rendre visite à mes grands-parents
- faire du ski
- . . . ?

3. Pendant les grandes vacances, je préfère . . .

- aller à la mer
- aller à la montagne
- aller à la campagne
- . . . ?

4. Quand je voyage pendant les vacances, je préfère voyager . . .

- seul(e)
- avec mes copains
- avec ma famille
- . . . ?

5. Quand je vais loin, je préfère voyager . . .

- en train
- en avion
- en car
- . . . ?

5 Leurs activités favorites

Les personnes suivantes ont certaines activités favorites. Lisez où elles sont et dites ce qu'elles font. Pour cela choisissez une activité appropriée de la liste à droite.

▶ Je suis à la plage.

1. Jean-Pierre est au stade.
2. Anne et Marie sont dans un studio de danse.
3. En juillet, nous allons dans le Colorado.
4. Tu passes les vacances de Noël en Suisse.
5. Mes copains passent les vacances à la campagne.
6. Pauline est à la salle *(room)* de gymnastique.
7. Vous êtes à la mer.
8. Nous sommes à Tahiti.
9. Avant le dîner, nous allons au parc municipal.
10. Je suis à la Martinique.

Je fais de la planche à voile

 Cooperative group practice

For Act. 4, divide the class into groups of 4 or 5 students. Name one person as recorder (**secrétaire**).

For each question, members of the group each state their preferences, by selecting one of the completions.

The **secrétaires** tally the responses of their groups and report back to the entire class or hand results to the teacher.

La majorité préfère les grandes vacances.
Pendant les vacances de Noël, la majorité préfère rester avec la famille. ...

5. En été, je vais à la plage spécialement *(especially)* pour . . .

- nager
- faire du ski nautique
- bronzer *(to get a tan)*
- . . . ?

7. Je voudrais être un champion (une championne) de . . .

- ski
- ski nautique
- planche à voile
- . . . ?

8. Je voudrais aller à la Guadeloupe principalement *(mainly)* pour . . .

- nager
- parler français
- faire de la planche à voile
- . . . ?

9. Je voudrais aller dans le Colorado pour . . .

- faire du ski
- faire des promenades à pied
- faire de l'alpinisme
- . . . ?

10. Je voudrais aller à Paris et rester là-bas pendant . . .

- dix jours
- trois semaines
- six mois
- . . . ?

■ **Cultural note:** Remind students that Guadeloupe is a French island in the Caribbean.

 COMMUNICATION: answering personal questions

- la gymnastique
- la danse moderne
- le sport
- le jogging
- le camping
- la voile
- la planche à voile
- le ski
- le ski nautique
- l'alpinisme

6 **Questions personnelles**

1. En général, qu'est-ce que tu fais pendant les vacances de Noël?
2. Est-ce que tu vas voyager pendant les grandes vacances? Où vas-tu aller? Combien de temps *(How long)* est-ce que tu vas rester là-bas?
3. Qu'est-ce que tu aimes faire quand tu es à la plage?
4. Est-ce que tu voyages souvent? Comment voyages-tu?

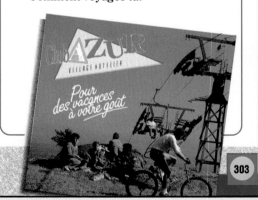

303

Classroom Notes

Cooperative pair practice Activity 6

1 COMPREHENSION

1. à la campagne / faire une promenade à vélo
2. à la campagne / faire un pique-nique
3. à Aspen / faire du ski
4. à la Floride / faire du ski nautique
5. à la mer (plage) / faire de la voile
6. à la montagne / faire de l'alpinisme
7. (answers will vary) / faire du jogging
8. (answers will vary)
9. (answers will vary)

[▭▭] Leçon 29, Section 6

2 GUIDED ORAL EXPRESSION

JP: Qu'est-ce que tu vas faire cet été?

H: Je vais à la mer avec des amis.

JP: Est-ce que vous allez voyager en voiture?

H: (Non,) nous allons voyager en train parce que nous n'avons pas de voiture.

JP: Est-ce que tu vas faire de la voile?

H: Oui, et je vais faire de la planche à voile aussi.

JP: Au revoir, Hélène. Bonnes vacances!

H: Au revoir!

[▭▭] Leçon 29, Section 7

---

1 Créa-dialogue

Des amis parlent de leurs projets. Avec un(e) camarade de classe, choisissez une scène et composez le dialogue correspondant.

▶ —Où vas-tu vendredi?
—Je vais en ville.
—Qu'est-ce que tu vas faire là-bas?
—Je vais faire des achats.

▶ | vendredi | en ville |

1. samedi matin		2. samedi après-midi		3. à Noël	à Aspen
4. pendant les vacances de printemps	à la Floride	5. en juillet		6. en août	
7. demain matin		8. dimanche après-midi		9. cet été	

2 Conversation dirigée

Avec un(e) camarade, composez un dialogue basé sur les instructions suivantes. Jean-Pierre demande à Hélène si elle a des projets de vacances.

Jean-Pierre

		Hélène
asks Hélène where she is going this summer	↘	says that she is going to the ocean with friends
asks her if they are going to travel by car	↗	answers that they are going to travel by train because they do not have a car
asks her if she is going to go sailing	↘	answers yes and says that she is also going to windsurf
says good-bye to Hélène and wishes her a good vacation (**Bonnes vacances!**)	→	answers good-bye

---

À votre tour

Depending on your goals and objectives, you may or may not wish to assign all of the activities in the **À votre tour** section.

👥 Cooperative practice

In Act. 1 and 2, you may want to have students work cooperatively in trios, with two performing and one consulting the Answer Key and acting as monitor.

3 Composition: Le weekend prochain

Make plans for next weekend. Prepare a list of activities describing . . .

- four things that you are going to do at home
- four things that you are going to do outside

4 Au club de vacances

Avec qui passez-vous vos vacances? On peut passer ses vacances avec sa famille ou avec des copains. On peut aussi aller dans un club de vacances. Là on peut faire du sport et rencontrer d'autres jeunes.

Lisez le document suivant.

Ce club de vacances offre la possibilité d'aller dans différents «villages de mer». Choisissez un des villages de mer proposés par le club.

- Dans quel pays est situé ce village?
- Quels sports est-ce qu'on peut pratiquer *(participate in)* dans ce village?
- Pourquoi est-ce que vous choisissez ce village?
- En général, quels sports pratiquez-vous?

VILLAGES DE MER

	AGADIR MAROC	LES ALMADIES SÉNÉGAL	ASSINIE CÔTE D'IVOIRE	BORA-BORA TAHITI-POLYNÉSIE FR.SE	LES BOUCANIERS MARTINIQUE	CANCÚN MEXIQUE	CAP SKIRRING SÉNÉGAL	LA CARAVELLE GUADELOUPE	LES CORAUX EILAT-ISRAËL	DJERBA LA DOUCE TUNISIE
Village-hôtel, bungalow										
Ski nautique, planche à voile										
Voile										
Plongée libre										
Plongée scaphandre										
Piscine										
Équitation										
Tennis										
Tir à l'arc										
Promenades en mer										
Pêche en haute mer										
Arts appliqués										

Leçon 29 **305**

Portfolio assessment

You will probably select only one speaking activity and one writing activity to go into the students' portfolios for Unit 8.

In this lesson, you might suggest that students do their own variations of Act. 2 as an oral portfolio recording.

You may also want to use the Challenge activities in the margin, above.

---

3 WRITTEN SELF-EXPRESSION

■ **Follow-up activity:** Have students in pairs compare their compositions. How many similar activities did they choose?

4 READING COMPREHENSION

■ **Challenge**
Conversational role play: At the challenge level, students might want to prepare one of the following conversations.

1. Curious Thomas is trying to find out what Nathalie is going to do this weekend. Nathalie, who is a quiet person, knows what she plans to do but answers only with oui or non.
(Roles: Thomas and Nathalie)

2. Two close friends are arguing about what they are going to do this weekend. One wants to go out and the other wants to stay in.
(Roles: two friends)

3. Shortly before vacation, Carole calls her cousin Olivier. They discuss their summer plans. Carole is going to go to the ocean with her family. Olivier is going to spend some time in the mountains with a friend.
(Roles: Carole and Olivier)

■ **Realia note**
Students may be able to guess these terms from the icons:
la plongée libre *snorkeling*
la plongée scaphandre *scuba diving*
(**un scaphandre** *diving tank*)
l'équitation *horseback riding*
le tir à l'arc *archery*
une promenade en mer *ocean cruise*
une pirogue *pirogue (native boat hollowed out from the trunk of a tree)*
la pêche en haute mer *deep-sea fishing*
les arts appliqués *arts and crafts*

■ **Comprehension practice:** Play the entire module through as an introduction to the lesson.

⬛ **Leçon 30, Section 1**

LEÇON 30 Vive le weekend!

Le weekend, nous avons nos occupations préférées. Certaines personnes aiment aller en ville et rencontrer leurs amis. <u>D'autres</u> préfèrent rester à la maison et <u>bricoler</u>. Qu'est-ce que les personnes suivantes <u>ont fait</u> le weekend <u>dernier</u>?

Others / do things around the house did . . . do / last

Le weekend	**Le weekend dernier**
J'aime acheter des vêtements.	J'<u>ai acheté</u> des vêtements. *boug*
Tu aimes réparer ton vélo.	Tu <u>as réparé</u> ton vélo. *fixed*
M. Lambert aime travailler dans le jardin.	Il <u>a travaillé</u> dans le jardin. *work*
Nous aimons organiser des boums.	Nous <u>avons organisé</u> une boum. *orga*

306 Unité 8

Setting the scene

In this lesson, the video module is independent of the opening text. However, the opening scenes are narrated in Section 1 of the audiocassette.

The video first shows how Jean-Claude and Nathalie spent the day on Wednesday. Then it shows them talking on Thursday morning when Jean-Claude realizes that he has forgotten about his math test.

To set the scene, ask students if they have ever forgotten about a test (**oublier la date d'un examen**). If so, how did they perform on the exam?

Le weekend

Vous aimez jouer au foot.

Pluton et Philibert aiment rencontrer leurs amis.

Le weekend dernier

Vous <u>avez joué</u> au foot. *played*

Ils <u>ont rencontré</u> leurs amis. *met*

■ **Expansion:** Ask for more information. Have students give only short answers unless they have been practicing the passé composé.
1. où? quels vêtements?
2. quand?
3. quel jour? avec qui?
4. quand? où?
5. où?
6. où?

Et toi?

Indique si oui ou non tu as fait les choses suivantes le weekend dernier. Pour cela complète les phrases suivantes.

1. (J'ai / Je n'ai pas) … acheté des vêtements.
2. (J'ai / Je n'ai pas) … réparé mon vélo.
3. (J'ai / Je n'ai pas) … travaillé dans le jardin.
4. (J'ai / Je n'ai pas) … organisé une boum.
5. (J'ai / Je n'ai pas) … joué au foot.
6. (J'ai / Je n'ai pas) … rencontré mes amis.

■ NOTE ■ CULTURELLE

Le weekend

Le weekend ne commence pas° le vendredi soir pour tout le monde.° Dans beaucoup d'écoles françaises, les élèves ont classe le samedi matin. Pour eux, le weekend commence seulement° le samedi à midi.

Que font les jeunes Français le samedi? Ça dépend. Beaucoup° vont en ville. Ils vont dans des magasins pour écouter les nouveaux disques ou pour regarder, essayer° et parfois° acheter des vêtements. Ils vont au café ou au cinéma avec leurs copains. Certains° préfèrent rester chez eux ou aller chez des copains. Parfois ils vont à une boum. Là on écoute de la musique, on mange des sandwichs et on danse …

En général, le dimanche est réservé aux activités familiales.° Un weekend, on invite des cousins. Un autre° weekend, on rend visite aux grands-parents … Le dimanche, on déjeune° et on dîne en famille.° Le soir, on regarde la télé et souvent on fait ses devoirs pour les classes du lundi matin.

ne commence pas *does not begin* **tout le monde** *everyone* **seulement** *only* **Beaucoup** *Many* **essayer** *try on* **parfois** *sometimes* **Certains** *Some of them* **activités familiales** *family activities* **Un autre** *Another* **déjeune** *has lunch* **en famille** *at home (with the family)*

Leçon 30 **307**

Cross-cultural observation

The *Vignette culturelle* of the video presents one of the favorite pastimes of French young people: going to the movies.

Have students watch to see whether they have the same taste in films as the students who were interviewed in Paris.

The *Vignette* shows two short interviews, the first with two young boys and the second with a girl. The boys like going to see "L'Ours." The first boy likes **les films d'adventures;** his friend's favorite actress is Kim Basinger in "Batman." The girl's favorite actress is Marilyn Monroe.

Section A

COMMUNICATIVE FUNCTION:
Expressing thirst, hunger,
and other feelings

🔊 Leçon 30, Section 2

🔄 **Re-entry and review:** The
purpose of this section is to have
students review **avoir** before
practicing the passé composé.
Students have already learned
avoir faim/soif (Lesson 18).

■ **Teaching strategy:** Introduce
the **avoir** expressions using
appropriate gestures. For
example:
avoir chaud (fanning self)
avoir froid (shivering)
avoir faim (pointing to stomach)
avoir soif (pointing to throat)
avoir tort (wagging index finger
 back and forth)
avoir de la chance (extending
 arms in a "youpie!" manner)
See TPR activity, p. T90.

Supplementary vocabulary

avoir sommeil *to be (feel) sleepy*
avoir peur *to be scared, afraid*

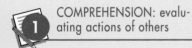 COMPREHENSION: evalu-
ating actions of others

 COMPREHENSION: asking
logical questions

A. Les expressions avec *avoir*

Note the use of **avoir** in the following sentences:

J'ai **faim**.   *I am **hungry**.*
Brigitte **a soif**.   *Brigitte **is thirsty**.*

French speakers use **avoir** in many expressions where English speakers use the verb *to be*.

Vocabulaire: Expressions avec *avoir*

avoir chaud	to be (feel) warm	Quand j'**ai chaud** en été, je vais à la plage.
avoir froid	to be (feel) cold	Est-ce que tu **as froid**? Voici ton pull.
avoir faim	to be hungry	Tu **as faim**? Est-ce que tu veux une pizza?
avoir soif	to be thirsty	J'**ai soif**. Je voudrais une limonade.
avoir raison	to be right	Est-ce que les profs **ont** toujours **raison**?
avoir tort	to be wrong	Marc n'étudie pas. Il **a tort**!
avoir de la chance	to be lucky	J'**ai de la chance**. J'ai des amis sympathiques.

1 **Tort ou raison?**

Informez-vous sur les personnes
suivantes et dites si, à votre avis, elles
ont tort ou raison.

▶ Les élèves n'étudient pas.
 Ils ont tort!

▶ Tu écoutes le prof.
 Tu as raison!

1. Catherine est généreuse avec ses
 copines.
2. Nous aidons nos parents.
3. Tu fais tes devoirs.
4. Vous êtes très impatients avec vos
 amis.
5. Mes copains étudient le français.
6. Jean-François dépense son argent
 inutilement *(uselessly)*.
7. M. Legros mange trop *(too much)*.
8. Alain et Nicolas sont impolis *(impolite)*.
9. Vous nettoyez votre chambre.

2 **De bonnes questions**

Étudiez ce que font les personnes
suivantes. Ensuite, posez une question
logique sur chaque personne. Pour
cela, utilisez l'une des expressions
suivantes:

avoir faim	avoir soif	avoir chaud
avoir froid	avoir de la chance	

▶ Philippe va au restaurant.
 Est-ce que Philippe a faim?

1. Tu veux un soda.
2. Jean-Pierre mange une pizza.
3. Cécile porte un manteau.
4. Vous gagnez à la loterie.
5. Vous faites des sandwichs.
6. Tu mets ton blouson.
7. Mes copains vont aller à la piscine.
8. Ces élèves n'étudient pas beaucoup,
 mais ils réussissent toujours à leurs
 examens.
9. Tu as des grands-parents très
 généreux.

☀ **Warm-up: Quel âge as-tu?**

Quickly review the forms of **avoir** by asking students how old they are.

Quel âge as-tu, X? [J'ai [treize] ans.]
Dis, Y, quel âge a X? [X a treize ans.]
Et Z, quel âge as-tu? [J'ai treize ans.]
**Comme X! Alors, Z et X, quel âge
 avez-vous?** [Nous avons treize ans.]

**Eh bien, tout le monde, quel âge ont
X et Z?** [Ils ont treize ans.]

EXPANSION: Hold up magazine ads and
have the class estimate the people's ages.

B. Le passé composé des verbes en -er

The sentences below describe past events. In the French sentences, the verbs are in the PASSÉ COMPOSÉ. Note the forms of the passé composé and its English equivalents.

Hier j'**ai réparé** mon vélo.   *Yesterday I **fixed** my bicycle.*
Le weekend dernier, Marc **a organisé** une boum.   *Last weekend, Marc **organized** a party.*
Pendant les vacances, nous **avons visité** Paris.   *During vacation, we **visited** Paris.*

FORMS

The PASSÉ COMPOSÉ is composed of two words. For most verbs, it is formed as follows:

> PRESENT of **avoir** + PAST PARTICIPLE

Note the forms of the passé composé for **visiter.**

PASSÉ COMPOSÉ	PRESENT of **avoir** + PAST PARTICIPLE	
J'**ai visité** Québec.	j' **ai**	
Tu **as visité** Paris.	tu **as**	
Il/Elle/On **a visité** Montréal.	il/elle/on **a**	
Nous **avons visité** Genève.	nous **avons**	**visité**
Vous **avez visité** Strasbourg.	vous **avez**	
Ils/Elles **ont visité** Fort-de-France.	ils/elles **ont**	

➡ For all -er verbs, the past participle is formed by replacing the -er of the infinitive by -é.

jou|er| → jou|é| Nous **avons joué** au tennis.
parl|er| → parl|é| Éric **a parlé** à Nathalie.
téléphon|er| → téléphon|é| Vous **avez téléphoné** à Cécile.

Learning about language

The PASSÉ COMPOSÉ, as its name indicates, is a "past" tense "composed" of two parts. It is formed like the present perfect tense in English.

AUXILIARY VERB + PAST PARTICIPLE of the main verb

Nous **avons**   **travaillé.**
We have   worked.

Bonjour de MONTRÉAL

USES

The passé composé is used to describe past actions and events. It has several English equivalents.

J'ai visité Montréal. { *I **visited** Montreal.*
{ *I **have visited** Montreal.*
{ *I **did visit** Montreal.*

Leçon 30   **309**

TPR 🏃 **Past activities**

Review the gestures your class developed for the verbs on pp. 108–109.
Tout le monde: dansez.
Chantez. Téléphonez. Nagez.
Have an individual act out an activity.
X, joue au tennis. C'est bien. Merci.
Then describe what the student did.

Qu'est-ce que X a fait?
Il a joué au tennis.
Then have two students act out an activity.
Y et Z, dansez. Voilà, c'est très bien.
Describe what the students did.
Qu'est-ce que Y et Z ont fait?
Ils ont dansé.

3 DESCRIPTION: saying what people bought

1. un jean
2. une montre
3. une guitare
4. des chemises
5. une chaîne stéréo
6. des chaussures
7. des livres
8. une voiture

4 ROLE PLAY: talking about past activities

5 ROLE PLAY: asking about past actions

■ **Variation:** Have students ask and answer questions in the plural.
– **Vous avez acheté des sodas?**
– **Mais oui, nous avons acheté des sodas.**

6 COMPREHENSION: making logical statements about past events

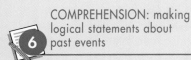

■ **Realia note**
Le Jazz en France
The poster reads **"Nice, l'arène du jazz"** (Nice, the arena of jazz). When said aloud, it could be interpreted as **"Nice, la reine du jazz"** (Nice, the queen of jazz). Jazz has always been popular in France, especially after the creation of the **Hot Club de France** in 1932. Festivals are regularly organized in many cities, attracting both French and American musicians.

3 Achats

Samedi dernier *(Last Saturday)*, les personnes suivantes ont fait des achats. Dites ce que chaque personne a acheté.

▶ Philippe (des compacts)
Philippe a acheté des compacts.

Philippe		
	1. Pauline	2. moi

4 Vive la différence!

Caroline et Jean-Pierre sont des copains, mais ils aiment faire des choses différentes. Ils parlent de ce qu'ils ont fait ce weekend.

▶ jouer au volley (au tennis)

J'ai joué au volley.

Eh bien, moi, j'ai joué au tennis.

1. acheter des disques (des magazines)
2. dîner au restaurant (chez moi)
3. inviter mon cousin (un ami)
4. téléphoner à ma tante (à mon grand-père)
5. aider ma mère (mon père)
6. nettoyer ma chambre (le garage)
7. réparer ma mobylette (mon vélo)
8. assister à un match de foot (à un concert de rock)
9. laver mes tee-shirts (mes jeans)

5 La boum

Anne et Éric organisent une boum ce weekend. Florence demande à Philippe s'il a fait les choses suivantes. Il répond que oui.

▶ acheter des sodas?

Tu as acheté des sodas?

Mais oui, j'ai acheté des sodas.

1. acheter des jus de fruit
2. préparer les sandwichs
3. nettoyer le salon
4. réparer la chaîne stéréo
5. apporter des disques
6. inviter nos copains

6 Un jeu

Décrivez ce que certaines personnes ont fait samedi dernier. Pour cela, faites des phrases logiques en utilisant les éléments des Colonnes A, B et C. Combien de phrases est-ce que vous pouvez *(can)* faire en cinq minutes?

▶ **Vous avez assisté à un concert de jazz.**

A	B	C
nous	acheter	une boum
vous	assister	un musée
Marc	dîner	des vêtements
Hélène et Juliette	jouer	un film à la télé
Éric et Stéphanie	organiser	au Monopoly
mes copains	regarder	dans le jardin
les voisins	travailler	dans un restaurant vietnamien
	visiter	à un concert de jazz

NICE, L'ARÈNE DU JAZZ

 Cooperative pair practice
Activities 4, 5

✕ ◻ Game: Samedi dernier

You can treat Act. 6 as a team game. Divide the class into teams of three. Each team picks a person from column A and decides what that subject did last Saturday. All three team members must then write the same sentence down correctly.

Then the team formulates another sentence using elements of columns A, B, and C, and again all three members write it down.

The game is played against the clock. The team whose three members have written the greatest number of correct sentences in five minutes is the winner.

3. toi	4. vous	5. nous	6. Stéphanie et Isabelle	7. Patrick et Jean-Paul	8. M. et Mme Dupont

Expressions pour la conversation

How to indicate the order in which actions take place:

d'abord	*first*	**D'abord,** nous avons invité nos copains à la boum.
après	*after, afterwards*	**Après,** tu as préparé des sandwichs.
ensuite	*then, after that*	**Ensuite,** Jacques a acheté des jus de fruit.
enfin	*at last*	**Enfin,** vous avez décoré le salon.
finalement	*finally*	**Finalement,** j'ai apporté mes cassettes.

7 **Dans quel ordre?**

Décrivez ce que les personnes suivantes ont fait dans l'ordre logique.

▶ nous (manger / préparer la salade / acheter des pizzas)
 D'abord, nous avons acheté des pizzas.
 Après, nous avons préparé la salade.
 Ensuite, nous avons mangé.

1. Alice (travailler / trouver un job / acheter une moto)
2. les touristes canadiens (voyager en avion / visiter Paris / réserver les billets [*tickets*])
3. tu (assister au concert / acheter un billet / acheter le programme)
4. vous (danser / apporter des disques / inviter des copains)
5. nous (payer l'addition [*check*] / dîner / trouver un restaurant)

D' **abord, la protection des ressources naturelles . . .**

Ensuite, la jouissance des générations futures . . .

Parcs Canada

Classroom Notes

7 COMPREHENSION: narrating past events in logical sequence

■ **Teaching strategy:** Note that several logical sequences are sometimes possible.

■ **Realia note**
Like the United States, Canada has developed a park system (**Parcs Canada**) to protect natural resources for the enjoyment of future generations.

T311

30.1 Introduction:
Mercredi après-midi
30.2 Dialogue: L'examen
de maths
(7:06–8:51 min.)

 Leçon 30, Section 6

■ **Learning hint:** Point out to students that if the English sentence contains *did not* or *didn't*, the equivalent French sentence will use the negative passé composé.

8 ROLE PLAY: talking about what one did not do

■ **Teaching strategy:** Students should be able to produce quickly the form: **je n'ai pas...**

■ **Cultural note:** *Paris-Match* is a French magazine.

C. Le passé composé: forme négative

Compare the affirmative and negative forms of the passé composé in the sentences below.

AFFIRMATIVE	NEGATIVE	
Alice **a travaillé**.	Éric **n'a pas travaillé**.	*Éric has not worked.* *Éric did not work.*
Nous **avons visité** Paris.	Nous **n'avons pas visité** Lyon.	*We have not visited Lyon.* *We did not visit Lyon.*

In the negative, the passé composé follows the pattern:

> negative form of **avoir** + PAST PARTICIPLE

Note the negative forms of the passé composé of **travailler**.

PASSÉ COMPOSÉ (NEGATIVE)	PRESENT of **avoir** (NEGATIVE) + PAST PARTICIPLE	
Je **n'ai pas travaillé**. Tu **n'as pas travaillé**. Il/Elle/On **n'a pas travaillé**.	je **n'ai pas** tu **n'as pas** il/elle/on **n'a pas**	**travaillé**
Nous **n'avons pas travaillé**. Vous **n'avez pas travaillé**. Ils/Elles **n'ont pas travaillé**.	nous **n'avons pas** vous **n'avez pas** ils/elles **n'ont pas**	

8 **Oublis** *(Things forgotten)*

Éric a décidé de faire certaines choses, mais il a oublié *(forgot)*. Sabine demande s'il a fait les choses suivantes.

▶ nettoyer ta chambre?

1. réparer ta chaîne stéréo?
2. apporter tes livres?
3. étudier?
4. téléphoner à ta tante?
5. inviter tes copains?
6. acheter *Paris-Match*?
7. laver tes chemises?

Tu as nettoyé ta chambre?

Euh, non . . .
Je n'ai pas nettoyé
ma chambre.

9 Quel mauvais temps!

Le weekend, il a fait mauvais et les personnes suivantes sont restées *(stayed)* chez elles. Dites qu'elles n'ont pas fait les choses suivantes.

▶ nous / nager
  Nous n'avons pas nagé.

1. vous / jouer au tennis
2. Philippe / rencontrer ses copains à la plage
3. Nathalie / dîner en ville
4. les voisins / travailler dans le jardin
5. Mlle Lacaze / laver sa voiture
6. mes copains / organiser un pique-nique
7. nous / assister au match de foot
8. toi / visiter le musée

LA MÉTÉO au Québec — dimanche — PLUIE

10 Une question d'argent

Les personnes suivantes n'ont pas beaucoup d'argent. Décrivez leur choix. Pour cela, dites ce qu'elles ont fait et ce qu'elles n'ont pas fait.

▶ nous / dîner au restaurant ou chez nous?
  Nous avons dîné chez nous. Nous n'avons pas dîné au restaurant.

1. Philippe / acheter un tee-shirt ou une chemise?
2. vous / manger un steak ou un sandwich?
3. nous / assister au concert ou au match de foot?
4. les touristes / voyager en car ou en avion?
5. mes voisins / acheter une Mercedes ou une Ford?
6. Marc / passer dix jours ou trois semaines à Paris?

11 Impossibilités

Sans *(Without)* certaines choses il n'est pas possible de faire certaines activités. Expliquez cela logiquement en choisissant une personne de la Colonne A, un objet de la Colonne B et une activité de la Colonne C.

▶ **Je n'ai pas d'aspirateur. Je n'ai pas nettoyé le salon.**

A	B	C
je	une raquette	écouter les disques
vous	un billet *(ticket)*	voyager en Europe
nous	un passeport	nettoyer le salon
Frédéric	une chaîne stéréo	regarder la comédie
Éric et Olivier	une télé	assister au concert
Claire et Caroline	un aspirateur *(vacuum cleaner)*	jouer au tennis

TORNADO — **Nettoie tout dans la maison.**

TORNADO
Aspirateur "Las'Air", variateur électronique linéaire, accessoires intégrés, dépression 3 000 mm, 1300 W*, 1445 F.

Leçon 30 313

9 PRACTICE: describing what people didn't do

■ **Teaching note:** Be sure students use **pas de** in item 6.

■ **Realia note**
La météo (short for **météorologie**) is the French word for weather report.

10 COMPREHENSION: describing what did and did not happen

■ **Teaching note:** Be sure students use **pas de** in items 1, 2, and 5.

11 COMPREHENSION: drawing conclusions about what did not happen

■ **Teaching note:** Remind students to use **pas de** with the items in Column B.

■ **Variation** (game format): See how many logical sentences teams of students can construct within a given time limit. See **Game: Samedi dernier** on p. T310.

■ **Realia note**
Comment s'appelle cet aspirateur? [Tornado]
Combien coûte-t-il? [mille quatre cent quarante-cinq (1445) francs]

■ **Teaching strategy:** Remind students that in French, unlike English, interrogative expressions cannot be separated. Compare:
Pour qui as-tu travaillé?
For whom did you work?
Who(m) did you work for?

■ **Expansion:** You may want to present inversion with **il/elle/on** for recognition.
A-t-il téléphoné?
A-t-elle téléphoné?
A-t-on téléphoné?

EXCHANGES: discussing past activities

■ **Teaching note:** Remind students to use **pas de** in items 3, 5, and 8.

■ **Variation:** Have students ask and answer the questions in the plural.
– **Est-ce que vous avez visité Paris?**
– **Oui, nous avons visité Paris. (Non, nous n'avons pas visité Paris.)**

PRACTICE: asking questions about past events

D. Les questions au passé composé

Compare the statements and questions in the passé composé.

STATEMENT	QUESTION	
Tu as travaillé.	Tu as travaillé?	*Did you work?*
	Est-ce que tu as travaillé?	
Philippe a voyagé cet été.	**Quand est-ce que** Philippe a voyagé?	*When did Philippe travel?*
	Où est-ce qu'il a voyagé?	*Where did he travel?*

For most verbs, questions in the passé composé are formed as follows:

PRESENT of **avoir** (interrogative form) + PAST PARTICIPLE

	YES/NO QUESTIONS	INFORMATION QUESTIONS
WITH INTONATION	Tu as voyagé? Paul a téléphoné?	— —
WITH **est-ce que**	**Est-ce que** tu as voyagé? **Est-ce qu'**Alice a téléphoné?	**Avec qui est-ce que** tu as voyagé? **À qui est-ce qu'**Alice a téléphoné?

➡ When the subject is a pronoun, questions in the passé composé can also be formed by inversion.

As-tu assisté au match de foot?   *Did you go to the soccer game?*
Avec qui **avez-vous joué** au foot?   *With whom did you play soccer?*
                             Who(m) did you play soccer with?

12 Expériences personnelles
Demandez à vos camarades s'ils ont déjà *(already)* fait les choses suivantes.

▶ visiter Paris?

Est-ce que tu as visité Paris?

Oui, j'ai visité Paris.

(Non, je n'ai pas visité Paris.)

1. visiter le Tibet?
2. voyager en Alaska?
3. piloter un avion?
4. dîner dans un restaurant vietnamien?
5. manger des escargots *(snails)*?
6. gagner à la loterie?
7. assister à un match de catch *(wrestling)*?
8. rencontrer un fantôme *(ghost)*?

13 Curiosité
Lisez ce que les personnes suivantes ont fait et posez des questions sur leurs activités.

▶ Paul a joué au tennis. (avec qui?)
Avec qui est-ce qu'il a joué au tennis?

1. Thomas a visité Québec. (quand?)
2. Corinne a téléphoné. (à quelle heure?)
3. Nathalie a voyagé en Italie. (comment?)
4. Marthe a acheté une robe. (où?)
5. Michèle a visité Genève. (avec qui?)
6. Philippe a trouvé un job. (où?)
7. Éric et Véronique ont dîné en ville. (dans quel restaurant?)
8. Les voisins ont téléphoné. (quand?)

Cooperative pair practice
Activities 12, 14, 15

Casual French

Information questions using intonation may be formed by placing the interrogative expression in the same position in the sentence as the corresponding answer. Usually, but not always, this is at the end.

Paul a voyagé <u>avec qui</u>?
   Paul a voyagé <u>avec ses parents</u>.
Vous avez téléphoné <u>quand</u>?
   J'ai téléphoné à <u>cinq heures</u>.
Claire a amené <u>qui</u> à la boum?
   Elle a invité <u>Bruno</u> à la boum.

14 Jérôme et Valérie

Jérôme est très curieux. Il veut toujours savoir ce que Valérie a fait. Valérie répond à ses questions.

▶ où/ dîner? (dans un restaurant italien)
JÉRÔME: **Où est-ce que tu as dîné?**
VALÉRIE: **J'ai dîné dans un restaurant italien.**

1. avec qui/ jouer au tennis? (avec Marc)
2. quand/ assister au concert? (samedi après-midi)
3. qui/ inviter au café? (ma copine Nathalie)
4. où/ rencontrer Pierre? (dans la rue)
5. où/ acheter ta veste? (au Bon Marché)
6. combien/ payer ce disque? (50 francs)
7. à qui/ téléphoner? (à ma grand-mère)
8. chez qui/ passer le weekend? (chez une amie)

15 Conversation

Demandez à vos camarades ce qu'ils ont fait hier.

▶ à quelle heure/ dîner?

J'ai dîné à six heures.

Dis, Hélène, à quelle heure est-ce que tu as dîné?

1. avec qui/ dîner?
2. à qui/ téléphoner?
3. quel programme/ regarder à la télé?
4. quel programme/ écouter à la radio?
5. qui/ rencontrer après les classes?
6. quand/ étudier?

Prononciation

Les lettres «ain» et «in»

ain /ɛ̃/	aine /ɛn/	in /ɛ̃/	ine /in/
sa m<u>ain</u>	sem<u>aine</u>	magas<u>in</u>	maga<u>zine</u>

When the letters "**ain**", "**aim**", "**in**", "**im**" are at the end of a word or are followed by a *consonant*, they represent the nasal vowel /ɛ̃/.

REMEMBER: Do not pronounce an /n/ after the nasal vowel /ɛ̃/.

Répétez: /ɛ̃/ dem<u>ain</u> f<u>aim</u> tr<u>ain</u> m<u>ain</u> vois<u>in</u> cous<u>in</u> jard<u>in</u> magas<u>in</u>
m<u>ain</u>tenant <u>in</u>telligent <u>in</u>téressant <u>im</u>portant

When the letters "**ain**", "**aim**", "**in(n)**", "**im**" are followed by a *vowel*, they do NOT represent a nasal sound.

Répétez: /ɛn/ sem<u>aine</u> améric<u>aine</u>
/ɛm/ j'<u>aime</u>

/in/ vois<u>ine</u> cous<u>ine</u> cu<u>in</u>e maga<u>zine</u> c<u>in</u>éma Cor<u>inn</u>e f<u>in</u>ir
/im/ t<u>im</u>ide d<u>im</u>anche M<u>im</u>i cent<u>im</u>e

Al<u>ain</u> M<u>in</u>ime a un rendez-vous <u>im</u>portant dem<u>ain</u> mat<u>in</u>, avenue du M<u>aine</u>.

Leçon 30 **315**

ROLE PLAY: asking and answering questions about
14 past events

■ **Variation** (with inversion):
Où as-tu dîné?

EXCHANGES: talking about
15 yesterday

■ **Teaching strategy:** Encourage students to give only affirmative answers, since they have not yet learned the negative forms **ne...rien, ne...personne**. These forms will be introduced in Lesson 32.

Prononciation

Leçon 30, Section 7

■ **Teaching strategy:** Before doing the **prononciation** section, have students practice minimal pairs containing /ɛ̃/, /ɛn/ and /ɛ̃/, /in/.

/ɛ̃/	/ɛn/
certain	**certaine**
américain	**américaine**
musicien	**musicienne**

/ɛ̃/	/in/
cousin	**cousine**
voisin	**voisine**
Martin	**Martine**

■ **Pronunciation:** Point out that **maintenant, intelligents,** etc. all end in the sound /ã/. Be sure students do not pronounce the final "n" or "t."

T315

COMPREHENSION

1-e   4-b
2-d   5-c
3-a

Leçon 30, Section 8

2 ORAL EXPRESSION

■ **Teaching strategy:** If students want to use some of the expressions listed in the text, encourage them to vary them in some way.

■ **Expansion:** Last Saturday I was in town with your friends but we did not see you. You probably were busy at home. Answer my questions in French. Please tell me ...
• Did you help your parents?
• Did you clean your room?
• Did you wash the car?
• Did you phone your friends?
• What else did you do?

3 GUIDED ORAL EXPRESSION

1. joué au tennis
2. joué au volley(ball)
3. nettoyé ta chambre
4. rencontré des amis
5. dansé

■ **Teaching strategy:** Have pairs of students each choose and prepare one of the dialogues and present it to the class.

T316

À votre tour!

1 Allô!

Reconstituez la conversation entre Alain et Christine. Pour cela, faites correspondre les réponses de Christine avec les questions d'Alain.

1 À quelle heure est-ce que tu as dîné hier soir?
2 Et après, tu as regardé la télé?
3 Qu'est-ce que tu as regardé après?
4 Qui a gagné?
5 Dis, tu as préparé la leçon pour demain?

a Le match Marseille–Nice.
b Nice. Par un score de trois à un.
c Mais oui! J'ai étudié avant le dîner.
d Oui, mais d'abord j'ai aidé ma mère.
e À sept heures et demie.

2 Dis-moi ...

I will tell you a few things that I did yesterday after school and a few things that I did not do, then you will tell me what you did and did not do.

• J'ai étudié.
• J'ai dîné avec mes parents.
• J'ai téléphoné à une copine.

• Je n'ai pas nettoyé ma chambre.
• Je n'ai pas rencontré mes copains.
• Je n'ai pas regardé la télé.

Et maintenant, dis-moi ...

3 Créa-dialogue

Demandez à vos camarades s'ils ont fait les choses suivantes le weekend dernier. En cas de réponse affirmative, continuez la conversation.

▶ — Est-ce que tu as <u>dîné au restaurant</u>?
— Oui, j'ai <u>dîné au restaurant</u>.
— <u>Avec qui</u>?
— <u>Avec mes cousins</u>.
— <u>Où</u> est-ce que <u>vous avez dîné</u>?
— <u>Nous avons dîné Chez Tante Lucie</u> (à McDonald's, etc.).

avec qui? où?

1 avec qui? quand?

2 quand? où?

3 quand? pourquoi?
4 quand? où?
5 quand? avec qui?

316 Unité 8

À votre tour

Depending on your goals and objectives, you may or may not want to assign all of the activities in the **À votre tour** section.

👥 Cooperative practice

In Act. 1 and 3, you may want to have students work cooperatively in trios, with two performing and one consulting the Answer Key and acting as monitor.

4 Situation

Avec un(e) camarade, composez un dialogue correspondant à la situation suivante. Jouez ce dialogue en classe.

You are spending a week in Paris with your best friend. Up to now you have been touring the city together, but today you both decided to go out on your own. At the end of the day, you both meet back at your hotel room. Discuss . . .
• what monuments you visited
• what things you bought
• whom you met
• what you ate at noon
• where you had dinner

5 Conversation libre *(free)*

Avec un(e) camarade analysez la situation suivante. Composez un dialogue original basé sur cette situation. Jouez le dialogue en classe.

Last weekend, you stayed home and your friend went into town. Now you are both trying to find out what the other one did. Ask each other questions, using the passé composé of **-er** verbs that you know. (Do not use **aller** or **rester,** since they have special passé composé forms that you have not learned yet.)

▶ — Moi, j'ai nettoyé ma chambre. Et toi?
— J'ai assisté à un concert, mais d'abord j'ai dîné avec des copains.

6 Composition: Vive les vacances!

Vacations are for fun, not for work. Write a brief composition in the passé composé about what you did on a recent vacation, describing . . .
• four things that you did • four things that you did not do
You may want to use some of the verbs in the box. (Do not use **aller** or **rester.**)

jouer	inviter	nager	parler	travailler	voyager	visiter
téléphoner	rencontrer	acheter	trouver	dépenser	gagner	

Comment dit-on . . . ?

How to wish somebody a nice time:

Bon weekend! *(Have a nice weekend!)*

Bonnes vacances! *(Have a good vacation!)*

Bonne journée! *(Have a nice day!)*

Bon voyage! *(Have a good trip!)*

317

---

4 GUIDED ORAL EXPRESSION

■ **Challenge:**
Conversational role play
Note: for suggestions on how to use the Challenge activities, see p. T305.
1. Your friend Corinne went shopping. She meets you at your favorite café, loaded down with packages. You want to know...
• what she bought
• where she bought each item
• how much she spent

2. Yesterday your French friend Sylvie went out for dinner. You phone Sylvie to find out...
• with whom she had dinner
• where they had dinner
• what they ate
• who paid
• if they spoke English or French

5 CONVERSATION

6 WRITTEN SELF-EXPRESSION

Supplementary vocabulary

Amuse-toi bien! *Have a good time*
Amusez-vous bien!

■ **Language note:** In Quebec, the traditional term for *weekend* is **fin de semaine: Bonne fin de semaine!** *(Have a nice weekend!)*

📓 Portfolio assessment

You will probably select only one speaking activity and one writing activity to go into the students' portfolios for Unit 8.

In this lesson, Act. 6 offers an excellent writing portfolio topic. Act. 4 and 5 are good oral portfolio conversation topics.

At the challenge level, students might want to prepare one of the conversational role plays suggested to the right.

l'inspecteur Leflic

LEÇON 31 L'alibi

Êtes-vous bon (bonne) détective? <u>Pouvez</u>-vous trouver la solution du mystère <u>suivant</u>?

Can
following

Samedi dernier à deux heures de l'après-midi, <u>il y a eu</u> une <u>panne</u> d'électricité dans la petite ville de Marcillac-le-Château. La panne <u>a duré</u> une heure. <u>Pendant</u> la panne, un <u>cambrioleur a pénétré</u> dans la Banque Populaire de Marcillac-le-Château. Bien sûr, l'alarme n'a pas fonctionné et c'est <u>seulement</u> lundi matin que le directeur de la banque <u>a remarqué</u> le <u>cambriolage</u>: un million de francs.

there was / powe
failure
lasted / During /
burglar / entere

only
noticed / burglary

Lundi après-midi, l'<u>inspecteur</u> Leflic a interrogé quatre suspects, mais <u>chacun</u> a un alibi.

police detective
each one

Sophie Filou

Euh, . . . excusez-moi, Monsieur l'Inspecteur.
Ma mémoire n'est pas très bonne.
<u>Voyons</u>, qu'est-ce que <u>j'ai fait</u> samedi après-midi?
Ah oui, <u>j'ai fini</u> un livre.
Le <u>titre</u> du livre? *Le crime ne paie pas!*

Let's see / did I d
I finished
title

Marc Laroulette

Qu'est-ce que j'ai fait samedi?
<u>J'ai rendu visite</u> à mes copains.
Nous avons joué aux cartes.
C'est moi qui ai gagné!

visited

Patrick Lescrot

Voyons, samedi dernier . . .
Ah oui . . . J'ai invité des amis chez moi.
Nous avons regardé la télé.
Nous <u>avons vu</u> le match de foot France-<u>Allemagne</u>.
Quel match! <u>Malheureusement</u>, c'est la France qui <u>a perdu</u>!
Dommage!

saw / Germany
Unfortunately / lo

Pauline Malin

Ce n'est pas moi, Monsieur l'Inspecteur!
Samedi j'ai fait un pique-nique à la campagne avec une copine.
Nous <u>avons choisi</u> un <u>coin</u> près d'une rivière.
Ensuite, nous avons fait une promenade à vélo.
Nous <u>avons eu de la chance</u>!
Il a fait un temps extraordinaire!

chose / spot

were lucky
The weather was
great!

Lisez <u>attentivement</u>° les quatre déclarations. À votre avis, qui est le cambrioleur ou la cambrioleuse? Pourquoi? (Vous pouvez comparer votre réponse avec la réponse de l'inspecteur à la page 325.)

carefully

MODULE 31:
Pas de chance!
Total time: 5:10 min.
(Counter: 13:06 min.)

3.1 **Dialogue: Pas de chance!**
(13:20–14:43 min.)
3.2 **Mini-scenes: Listening — Qu'est-ce que vous avez fait?**
(14:44–15:23 min.)
3.3 **Mini-scenes: Speaking — Est-ce qu'ils ont perdu?**
(15:24–16:33 min.)
3.4 **Vignette culturelle: La télé**
(16:34–18:04 min.)

■ **Comprehension practice:** Play the entire module through as an introduction to the lesson.

 Leçon 31, Section 1

■ **Challenge activity:** Have students consult a French-English dictionary and try to find out the meanings of the suspects' last names.
filou *(dishonest person, thief)*
la roulette *(roulette wheel)*
l'escroc *(crook)*
malin *(shrewd, cunning)*

🗣️ Cooperative reading

Since this is a longer story, you may want to use it as a recapitulation at the end of the lesson.

Divide the class into groups of three or four. Have each group read the story, without turning to p. 325 to see the solution.

The recorder (**secrétaire**) of each group writes down the solution: who is the guilty one and why. **Qui est le coupable et pourquoi?**

After all the recorders have given their reports to the class, the students may read the solution in the text.

Compréhension

Certains événements ont eu lieu *(took place)* samedi dernier. Indiquez si oui ou non les événements suivants ont eu lieu.

1. Le directeur de la banque a vu *(saw)* le cambrioleur.
2. Un cambriolage a eu lieu *(took place)* à Marcillac-le-Château.
3. L'inspecteur Leflic a arrêté *(arrested)* le cambrioleur.
4. Sophie Filou a vu le film *Le crime ne paie pas* à la télé.
5. Marc Laroulette a perdu un million de francs.
6. L'Allemagne a gagné un match de foot.
7. Pauline Malin a fait une promenade à vélo à la campagne.
8. Il a fait beau.

Et toi?

Dis si oui ou non tu as fait les choses suivantes le weekend dernier.

1. (J'ai / Je n'ai pas) … rendu visite à mes copains.
2. (J'ai / Je n'ai pas) … vu un match de foot à la télé.
3. (J'ai / Je n'ai pas) … fini un livre.
4. (J'ai / Je n'ai pas) … fait une promenade à vélo.
5. (J'ai / Je n'ai pas) … fait un pique-nique.

TF1
MARDI 20.35
FOOTBALL - COUPE DE FRANCE:
SEIZIÈME DE FINALE

NOTE CULTURELLE

CANAL+ **LA CINQ 5**

Les jeunes Français et la télé

Combien d'heures par° jour est-ce que tu regardes la télé? Une heure? deux heures? trois heures? plus? moins? En général, les jeunes Français regardent la télé moins souvent et moins longtemps° que les jeunes Américains: en moyenne° 1 heure 15 les jours d'école et 2 heures 15 les autres° jours (mercredi, samedi et dimanche). Dans beaucoup de familles, les parents contrôlent l'usage° de la télé. Souvent ils exigent° que leurs enfants finissent leurs devoirs avant de regarder la télé. Ainsi,° beaucoup de jeunes regardent la télé seulement° après le dîner.

Quels sont leurs programmes favoris? Les jeunes Français aiment surtout° les films, les programmes de sport, les variétés et les jeux télévisés,° comme «La roue° de la fortune» et «Le prix est juste».° Les séries américaines (comme «Deux flics° à Miami» et «Santa Barbara») sont aussi très populaires.

par *per* **moins longtemps** *for a shorter time* **en moyenne** *on an average of* **autres** *other* **usage** *use* **exigent** *insist* **Ainsi** *Thus* **seulement** *only* **surtout** *especially* **jeux télévisés** *TV games* **roue** *wheel* **juste** *right* **flics** *cops*

Leçon 31 319

COMPREHENSION

1. non 5. non
2. oui 6. oui
3. oui 7. oui
4. non 8. oui

COMMUNICATION: describing what one did last weekend

■ **Realia note**
La Coupe de France
The French national soccer tournament is called **La Coupe de France.**
This TV ad is for a game early in the playoffs where 32 teams are in competition and playing in 16 games around the country (**les seizièmes de finale**).

Note culturelle

 31.4 Vignette culturelle: La télé
(16:34–18:04 min.)

■ **Teaching strategy:** For more information on French TV channels, see p. 129.

Setting the scene

Video Module 31 opens with **Pas de chance** *(out of luck)*, a humorous series of dialogues. Philippe has had a bad day, and in these conversations he explains what happened.

The *Vignette culturelle* focuses on French television and expands on the cultural note in the student text.

Leçon 31, Section 2

■ **Pronunciation:** Be sure students maintain the sound /vwa/ in all forms of the verb, especially in:
nous voyons /vwajɔ̃/
vous voyez /vwaje/

1 PRACTICE: seeing sights in Paris

■ **Teaching strategy:** Tell students that **voir** is another "boot" verb.

je vois	nous voyons
tu vois	vous voyez
il voit	ils voient

 COMMUNICATION: answering personal questions
2

A. Le verbe *voir*

The verb **voir** *(to see)* is irregular. Note the forms of **voir** in the present tense.

INFINITIVE	voir	
PRESENT	Je **vois** Marc. Tu **vois** ton copain. Il/Elle/On **voit** un accident.	Nous **voyons** un film. Vous **voyez** un match de baseball. Ils/Elles **voient** le professeur.

1 **Weekend à Paris**

Les personnes suivantes passent le weekend à Paris. Décrivez ce que chacun voit.

▶ Olivier   Olivier voit Notre-Dame.

▶ **Notre-Dame**

1. le musée d'Orsay	**2. l'Arc de Triomphe**	**3. le Centre Pompidou**

4. le Quartier latin	**5. la pyramide du Louvre**	**6. le musée Picasso**

1. nous	3. moi	5. vous
2. toi	4. Sophie	6. les touristes japonais

2 **Questions personnelles**

1. Est-ce que tu vois bien? Est-ce que tu portes des lunettes?
2. Est-ce que tu vois tes amis pendant les vacances? Est-ce que tu vois tes professeurs?
3. Est-ce que tu vois souvent tes cousins? Est-ce que tu vois tes cousins pendant les vacances? à Noël?
4. Qu'est-ce que tu préfères voir à la télé? un match de football ou un match de baseball?
5. Quand tu vas au cinéma, quels films aimes-tu voir? les comédies? les films d'aventures? les films policiers *(detective movies)*?

320 Unité 8

B. Le passé composé des verbes réguliers en *-ir* et *-re*

Note the passé composé of the verbs below, paying special attention to the ending of the past participle.

choisir	J'**ai choisi** ce disque.	Je **n'ai pas choisi** cette cassette.
finir	Nous **avons fini** le magazine.	Nous **n'avons pas fini** le livre.
vendre	Tu **as vendu** ton vélo.	Tu **n'as pas vendu** ta moto.
attendre	Jacques **a attendu** Paul.	Il **n'a pas attendu** François.
répondre	J'**ai répondu** au professeur.	Tu **n'as pas répondu** à la question.

The past participle of regular **-ir** and **-re** verbs is formed as follows:

-ir → -i	-re → -u
chois[ir] → chois[i]	vend[re] → vend[u]
fin[ir] → fin[i]	attend[re] → attend[u]

---

3 Besoins d'argent *(Money needs)*

Parce qu'elles ont besoin d'argent, les personnes suivantes ont vendu certains objets. Dites ce que chaque personne a vendu.

▶ Philippe/sa guitare
Philippe a vendu sa guitare.

1. M. Roche/sa voiture
2. mes copains/leur chaîne stéréo
3. moi/mon appareil-photo
4. toi/ton vélo
5. les voisins/leur piano
6. nous/nos livres
7. vous/votre ordinateur
8. François et Victor/leurs disques

4 Bravo!

Les personnes suivantes méritent *(deserve)* des félicitations *(congratulations)*. Expliquez pourquoi.

▶ les élèves/réussir à l'examen
Les élèves ont réussi à l'examen.

1. M. Bedon/maigrir
2. Mlle Legros/perdre dix kilos
3. Florence/gagner le match de tennis
4. ces enfants/finir leur soupe
5. nous/choisir une classe difficile
6. toi/finir les exercices
7. Marc/rendre visite à un copain à l'hôpital
8. vous/attendre vos copains
9. les élèves/répondre en français

— À vendre —
INSTRUMENTS DE MUSIQUE

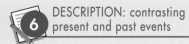

5 ROLE PLAY: talking about past events

6 DESCRIPTION: contrasting present and past events

7 ROLE PLAY: explaining why one did not do certain things

Classroom Notes

---

5 **Non!**

Jean-Louis répond négativement aux questions de Béatrice. Jouez les deux rôles.

▶ gagner le match / perdre

Tu as gagné le match?

Non! J'ai perdu.

1. étudier ce weekend / rendre visite à un copain
2. acheter une cassette / choisir un compact
3. finir ce livre / regarder la télé
4. vendre ta guitare / vendre mon appareil-photo
5. téléphoner à Marc / rendre visite à son cousin
6. maigrir / grossir
7. répondre à la lettre / téléphoner

6 **Aujourd'hui et hier**

Dites ce que les personnes suivantes font aujourd'hui et ce qu'elles ont fait hier.

▶ Paul / acheter un blouson / un pantalon
Aujourd'hui, Paul achète un blouson.
Hier, il a acheté un pantalon.

1. moi / téléphoner à mon cousin / à mes copains
2. toi / finir ce livre / ce magazine
3. nous / manger des sandwichs / une pizza
4. Mélanie / choisir une jupe / un chemisier
5. les élèves / réussir à l'examen de français / à l'examen d'anglais
6. Philippe / vendre sa chaîne stéréo / ses disques
7. Philippe et Jean-Pierre / rendre visite à leurs cousins / à leur grand-mère
8. les touristes / attendre le train / le car

7 **Excuses**

Quand Olivier ne fait pas une chose, il a toujours une excuse. Jouez le dialogue entre Olivier et sa soeur Caroline.

▶ étudier / perdre mon livre

Tu as étudié?

Non, je n'ai pas étudié.

Pourquoi est-ce que tu n'as pas étudié?

Parce que j'ai perdu mon livre.

1. jouer au tennis / perdre ma raquette
2. acheter une veste / choisir un blouson
3. finir le livre / regarder la télé
4. rendre visite à Marc / étudier
5. réussir à l'examen / perdre mes notes
6. écouter tes disques / vendre ma chaîne stéréo

322 Unité 8

Cooperative pair practice
Activities 5, 7, 8, 9

TPR Past and present

Teach students gestures for present and past.
Montrez-moi le présent. [index finger pointing to floor]
Montrez-moi le passé. [thumb pointing back over shoulder]
Now read sentences aloud containing the present or the passé composé and have students identify the tense by using the appropriate gesture.
Est-ce que c'est le présent ou le passé?
• **Tu finis la leçon de natation.** [P]
• **J'ai fini la leçon de ski nautique.** [PC]
• **Paul a eu un accident de ski.** [PC]

C. Le passé composé des verbes *être, avoir, faire, mettre* et *voir*

The verbs **être, avoir, faire, mettre,** and **voir** have irregular past participles.

être	→	été	Nous **avons été** à Paris.
avoir	→	eu	M. Lambert **a eu** un accident.
faire	→	fait	Qu'est-ce que tu **as fait** hier?
mettre	→	mis	Nous **avons mis** des jeans.
voir	→	vu	J'**ai vu** un bon film.

"On n'a jamais fait quelque chose d'aussi appétissant avec des petits pois."

MONOPRIX
UNIPRIX

→ In the passé composé, the verb **être** has two different meanings:

Mme Lebrun **a été** malade.   *Mme Lebrun **has been** sick.*
Elle **a été** à l'hôpital.   *She **was** in the hospital.*

8 Dialogue

Demandez à vos camarades s'ils ont fait les choses suivantes récemment *(recently)*.

▶ faire une promenade.
   —Est-ce que tu as fait une promenade récemment?
   —Oui, j'ai fait une promenade. (Non, je n'ai pas fait de promenade.)

1. faire un pique-nique?
2. faire une promenade en voiture?
3. être malade *(sick)*?
4. avoir la grippe *(flu)*?
5. avoir une dispute *(fight)* avec ton copain?

6. avoir une bonne surprise?
7. avoir un «A» en français?
8. voir un film?
9. voir tes cousins?
10. mettre des posters dans ta chambre?

9 Pourquoi?

Avec vos camarades de classe,
parlez des personnes suivantes.

▶ Éric est content.
   (avoir un «A» à l'examen)

1. Mes copains sont furieux.
   (avoir un «F» à l'examen)
2. Pauline est très contente. (voir son copain)
3. Mon père n'est pas content. (avoir une dispute
   avec son chef [*boss*])
4. Philippe est pâle. (voir un accident)
5. Juliette est fatiguée *(tired)*. (faire du jogging)
6. Alice et Laure sont bronzées *(tanned)*. (être à la mer)
7. Mon frère est fatigué. (faire des exercices
   de gymnastique)
8. Patrick et Marc sont contents. (voir un bon film)
9. Isabelle est très élégante. (mettre une jolie robe)

Éric est content.

Ah, bon? Pourqoui?

Il a eu un «A» à l'examen.

Leçon 31   323

Section C

COMMUNICATIVE FUNCTION:
Talking about the past

 31.2 Mini-scenes:
   Qu'est-ce que vous
   avez fait?
31.3 Mini-scenes:
   Est-ce qu'ils ont
   perdu?
   (14:44–16:33 min.)

 Leçon 31, Sections 3, 4

■ **Language note:** Point out that
the passé composé of most irregular verbs is formed with **avoir.**

■ **Pronunciation:** Be sure students pronounce the past participle **eu** /y/, as in **tu.**

8 COMMUNICATION: asking
about past activities

■ **Pronunciation:**
récemment /resamã/

■ **Teaching note:** Remind
students to use **pas de** in items 1,
2, 5, 6, 7, and 8 if they choose to
answer in the negative.

9 EXCHANGES: explaining
people's looks and moods

- **Nous sommes à la mer.** [P]
- **Sophie fait de l'alpinisme.** [P]
- **Marc a fait de la planche à voile.** [PC]
- **Vous avez acheté un vélo.** [PC]
- **J'ai grossi cet été.** [PC]

- **Nous passons les vacances à la
mer.** [P]
- **Mes cousins ont vu un match de
tennis.** [PC]
- **Stéphanie met son maillot de bain.** [P]

31.1 Dialogue: Pas de chance!
(13:20–14:43 min.)

Leçon 31, Section 5

COMPREHENSION: describing what people did and did not do

10

■ **Realia note**
Villages vacances
Most French employees get at least five weeks of paid vacation. One popular option is to go to a "vacation village" (**un village vacances**).
In this ad, the Viva group announces that they have a network (**un réseau**) of such "villages" and that, in addition to room and board, they offer sports instruction and numerous social events (**les villages sont "animés"**).

Supplementary vocabulary

cette année *this year*
l'année dernière
l'année prochaine

COMMUNICATION: finding out when past events took place

11

---

10 Vive les vacances!

Dites où les personnes suivantes ont été pendant les vacances. Dites aussi si oui ou non elles ont fait les choses entre parenthèses. Soyez logique *(Be logical)*.

▶ Christophe: à la piscine (étudier / nager)
  Christophe a été à la piscine. Il n'a pas étudié. Il a nagé.

1. Sylvie: à la montagne (nager / faire de l'alpinisme)
2. nous: à la campagne (visiter des monuments / faire du camping)
3. vous: à Paris (parler italien / voir la tour Eiffel)
4. moi: à la mer (faire de la planche à voile / travailler)
5. mes parents: en Égypte (voir les pyramides / visiter Paris)
6. vous: dans un club de sport (faire de la gymnastique / grossir)
7. Christine: à la plage (mettre des lunettes de soleil / jouer au tennis)

VIVE LES VACANCES
viva
RÉSEAU DE VILLAGES
VACANCES ANIMÉS

Vocabulaire: *Quand?*			
	maintenant	**avant**	**après**
le jour	**aujourd'hui**	**hier**	**demain**
le matin	**ce matin**	**hier matin**	**demain matin**
l'après-midi	**cet après-midi**	**hier après-midi**	**demain après-midi**
le soir	**ce soir**	**hier soir**	**demain soir**
le jour	**samedi**	**samedi dernier** *(last)*	**samedi prochain** *(next)*
le weekend	**ce weekend**	**le weekend dernier**	**le weekend prochain**
la semaine	**cette semaine**	**la semaine dernière**	**la semaine prochaine**
le mois	**ce mois-ci**	**le mois dernier**	**le mois prochain**

---

11 Quand?

Demandez à vos camarades quand ils ont fait les choses suivantes. Ils vont répondre en utilisant une expression du **Vocabulaire**.

▶ faire tes devoirs?

1. faire des achats?
2. nettoyer ta chambre?
3. rencontrer tes voisins?
4. voir ton copain?
5. voir un film?
6. avoir un examen?
7. faire une promenade à pied?
8. être en ville?
9. mettre *(set)* la table?

Quand est-ce que tu as fait tes devoirs?

J'ai fait mes devoirs hier après-midi.

(vendredi soir, le weekend dernier, . . .)

Cooperative pair practice
Activity 11

 Game: Moi aussi

For homework, have students write out their answers to Act. 12.

In class, students share their responses with one another. The object of the game is to find ten classmates who wrote the same answers.

One student reads the first statement, without showing the text to his/her partner.

The partner then reads his/her first statement.

   X: Ce matin, j'ai regardé la télé. Et toi?
   Y: Moi aussi. Ce matin, j'ai regardé la télé.

12 Le passé et le futur

Décrivez ce que vous avez fait (phrases 1 à 5) et ce que vous allez faire (phrases 6 à 10). Dites la vérité ... ou utilisez votre imagination!

1. Ce matin, j'ai ...	✓
2. Hier matin, j'ai ...	✓
3. Samedi après-midi, j'ai ...	✓
4. La semaine dernière, j'ai ...	✓
5. Le mois dernier, j'ai ...	✓

6. Ce soir, je vais ...	___
7. Demain soir, je vais ...	___
8. Vendredi soir, je vais ...	___
9. Le weekend prochain, je vais ...	___
10. La semaine prochaine, je vais ...	___

13 Questions personnelles

1. En général, est-ce que tu étudies avant ou après le dîner?
2. En général, est-ce que tu regardes la télé avant ou après le dîner?
3. À quelle heure est-ce que tu as dîné hier soir?
4. Quel programme de télé est-ce que tu as regardé hier après-midi?
5. Qu'est-ce que tu vas faire le weekend prochain?
6. Où vas-tu aller le weekend prochain?

COMMUNICATION: describing past events and future plans

COMMUNICATION: answering personal questions

Prononciation

Les lettres «gn»

gn /ɲ/

The letters "**gn**" represent a sound similar to the "**ny**" in *canyon*. First, practice with words you know.

Répétez: **espagnol   gagner   mignon
la montagne   la campagne
un magnétophone**

Now try saying some new words. Make them sound French!

Répétez: **Champagne   Espagne** (Spain)   **un signe
la vigne** (vineyard)   **la ligne** (line)   **un signal
la dignité   ignorer   magnétique   magnifique   Agnès**

Agnès Mignard a gagné son match. C'est magnifique!

espagnol

Prononciation

(L'alibi, p. 318)

La réponse de l'inspecteur:

C'est Patrick Lescrot le cambrioleur. Samedi après-midi, il y a eu une panne d'électricité. Patrick Lescrot n'a pas pu *(was not able to)* regarder la télé. Son alibi n'est pas valable *(valid)*.

Leçon 31, Section 6

The answers match, so each one writes the other's name next to #1. Then they both read their responses to the next item.

Often the answers will not be the same:

X: Hier matin, j'ai étudié. Et toi?
Y: Hier matin, j'ai joué au tennis.

Here the answers do not match, so they continue with #3. If time remains when they have shared the ten responses with one another, they may talk to another partner to try to find the missing matches.

At the end of the time limit, the student who has found the most matches wins.

1 COMPREHENSION

1-b	4-c
2-d	5-e
3-a	

▸ Leçon 31, Section 7

2 GUIDED ORAL EXPRESSION

3 GUIDED ORAL EXPRESSION

▸ Leçon 31, Section 8

■ **Realia note**
Le tennis
The French not only love to play tennis, they are avid tennis fans. It was a national event when France won the Davis Cup in 1991.
Roland Garros is the tennis stadium near Paris which hosts the annual French Open (**Les Internationaux de France**). The stadium was named in memory of Roland Garros (1888–1918), a World War I fighter pilot and the first aviator to cross the Mediterranean (1913).

À votre tour!

1 Allô!

Reconstituez la conversation entre Robert et Julien. Pour cela, faites correspondre les réponses de Julien avec les questions de Robert.

1. Tu as fini tes devoirs de français?
2. Qu'est-ce que tu as fait alors?
3. Tu as gagné?
4. Mais d'habitude (*usually*) tu joues bien?
5. Peut-être que Caroline a joué mieux (*better*) que toi?

a. Non, j'ai perdu!
b. Non, je n'ai pas étudié cet après-midi.
c. C'est vrai, mais aujourd'hui, je n'ai pas eu de chance . . .
d. J'ai joué au tennis avec Caroline.
e. Tu as raison. Elle a joué comme une championne.

2 Dis-moi . . .

I will tell you about some nice things that happened to me recently; then you will tell me about three nice things that happened to you.

- J'ai réussi à mon examen d'anglais. (J'ai eu un «A».)
- J'ai eu un rendez-vous avec une personne très intéressante.
- J'ai vu un très bon film.

Et maintenant, dis-moi . . .

3 Créa-dialogue

Avec vos camarades, discutez de ce que vous avez fait récemment (*recently*). Vous pouvez utiliser les expressions et les activités suggérées. Continuez la conversation avec des questions supplémentaires.

Quand?		Quoi?	
dimanche après-midi	lundi dernier	jouer au tennis	dîner au restaurant
hier soir	la semaine dernière	faire des achats	voir un film
samedi soir	le mois dernier	faire une promenade	avoir un rendez-vous
le weekend dernier		à la campagne	rendre visite à un
		voir mes cousins	copain

▸ —Qu'est-ce que tu as fait dimanche après-midi?
—J'ai joué au tennis avec ma soeur.
—Est-ce que tu as gagné?
—Non, j'ai perdu.
—Dommage!

tennis de France

ROLAND GARROS

À votre tour
Depending on your goals and objectives, you may or may not wish to assign all of the activities in the **À votre tour** section.

👥 **Cooperative practice**
In Act. 1 and 3, you may want to have students work cooperatively in trios, with two performing and one consulting the Answer Key and acting as monitor.

4 Situation

Avec un(e) camarade, composez un dialogue original correspondant à la situation suivante. Jouez ce dialogue en classe.

Your friend Michèle (played by a classmate) went to Canada for spring vacation.

Ask Michèle . . .

- how she traveled (by plane? by car?)
- if she visited Montreal
- whom she visited **(rendre visite à)**
- if she saw Quebec City **(Québec)**
- if she went skiing and with whom
- if she went shopping and what she bought

5 Conversation libre

Avec un(e) camarade, composez un dialogue basé sur la situation suivante. Jouez ce dialogue en classe.

Philippe spent spring vacation in Nice, on the French Riviera **(la Côte d'Azur).** Juliette spent her vacation in a small village high in the Alps **(les Alpes).** They meet and compare what they did. (In your dialogue, try to use several expressions with **faire.**)

▶ PHILIPPE: J'ai été à Nice. J'ai fait de la voile.
 JULIETTE: Moi, j'ai été dans les Alpes. J'ai fait du ski.

6 Composition: Quand?

Describe two things that you or people you know have done at each of the times indicated below:

| *La semaine dernière, . . .* | *Le mois dernier, . . .* | *L'an dernier* (Last year), . . . |

▶ La semaine dernière, mon père a vendu sa voiture.
 La semaine dernière, mes cousins ont acheté une moto.

Comment dit-on . . . ?

How to wish someone good luck or give encouragement:

Bonne chance!

Bon courage!

Leçon 31 327

4 GUIDED ORAL EXPRESSION

■ **Challenge activity**
Have students prepare an original dialogue on this model where they talk about a real or imaginary trip to a destination of their choice.

5 CONVERSATION

6 WRITTEN SELF-EXPRESSION

Classroom Notes

📁 Portfolio assessment

You will probably select only one speaking activity and one writing activity to go into the students' portfolios for Unit 8.

In this lesson, Act. 4 and 5 lend themselves well to oral portfolio recordings.

MODULE 32:
Samedi / Weekend
Total Time: 6:36 min.
(Counter: 18:15 min.)

32.1 Dialogue: Un bon weekend
(18:22–20:00 min.)
32.2 Mini-scenes: Listening — Où êtes-vous allé? Et qu'est-ce que vous avez fait?
(20:01–21:48 min.)
32.3 Mini-scenes: Speaking — Où est-ce qu'ils sont allés?
(21:49–23:00 min.)
32.4 Vignette culturelle: La musique
(23:01–24:47 min.)

■ **Comprehension practice:** Play the entire module through as an introduction to the lesson.

 Leçon 32, Section 1

■ **Photo culture note**
Le métro
Valérie and Anne are standing in front of an entrance to the Paris subway (**le métro**, or **métropolitain** as it was originally called). The architecture is typical of the **Art Nouveau** style.

LEÇON 32 Qui a de la chance?

Vendredi après-midi

Anne et Valérie parlent de leurs projets pour le weekend.

ANNE: Qu'est-ce que tu vas faire samedi soir?
VALÉRIE: Je vais aller au cinéma avec Jean-Pierre.
ANNE: Tu as de la chance! Moi, je dois rester à la maison.
VALÉRIE: Mais pourquoi?
ANNE: Les amis de mes parents viennent chez nous ce weekend. Mon père insiste <u>pour que</u> je reste pour le dîner. <u>Quelle barbe!</u>   *that / What a pain!*
VALÉRIE: C'est vrai! Tu n'as pas de chance!

Lundi matin

Anne et Valérie parlent de leur weekend.

ANNE: Alors, tu as passé un bon weekend?
VALÉRIE: Euh non, pas très bon.
ANNE: Mais tu <u>es sortie</u> avec Jean-Pierre!   *went out*
VALÉRIE: C'est vrai. Je <u>suis allée</u> au cinéma avec lui . . .   *went*
Nous avons vu un très, très mauvais film! Après le film, j'ai eu une <u>dispute</u> avec Jean-Pierre. Et, <u>en plus</u>, j'ai perdu mon <u>porte-monnaie</u> . . . et je <u>suis rentrée</u> chez moi à pied! Et toi, tu <u>es restée</u> chez toi?   *quarrel / in addition / wallet / went back / stayed*
ANNE: Non.
VALÉRIE: Comment? Les amis de tes parents <u>ne sont pas venus</u>?   *didn't come*
ANNE: Si, si, ils sont venus . . . avec leur fils!
VALÉRIE: Et alors?
ANNE: Eh bien, c'est un garçon très <u>sympa</u> et très amusant . . .   *sympa = sympathique*
Après le dîner, nous <u>sommes allés</u> au Zénith.* Nous avons assisté à un concert de rock absolument extraordinaire. Après, nous sommes allés dans un café et nous avons fait des projets pour le weekend prochain.   *went*
VALÉRIE: Qu'est-ce que vous allez faire?
ANNE: Nous allons faire une promenade à la campagne dans la nouvelle voiture de sport de Thomas. (C'est le nom de mon nouveau copain!)
VALÉRIE: Toi, vraiment, tu as de la chance!

* Une salle *(hall)* de concert à Paris, parc de la Villette.

 Cooperative reading

Since this is a longer story, you may want to use it as a recapitulation at the end of the lesson.

Have students read the title. Then, in pairs, have them read the story and write out brief answers to the following questions:

Qui a de la chance? Pourquoi?
Qui n'a pas de chance? Pourquoi?

Compréhension

1. Qu'est-ce que Valérie va faire samedi soir?
2. Pourquoi est-ce qu'Anne doit *(must)* rester à la maison?
3. Est-ce que Valérie a aimé le film?
4. Qu'est-ce qu'elle a perdu?
5. Comment est-ce qu'elle est rentrée chez elle?
6. Où et avec qui est-ce qu'Anne a dîné?
7. Où est-ce qu'elle est allée après le dîner?
8. Qu'est-ce qu'elle va faire le weekend prochain?
9. Comment s'appelle son nouveau copain?

Et toi

Dis si oui ou non tu as fait les choses suivantes samedi dernier.

1. (Je suis / Je ne suis pas) … allé(e) en ville.
2. (Je suis / Je ne suis pas) … allé(e) au cinéma.
3. (Je suis / Je ne suis pas) … allé(e) à un concert.
4. (Je suis / Je ne suis pas) … rentré(e) chez moi pour le dîner.
5. (Je suis / Je ne suis pas) … resté(e) chez moi le soir.

■ NOTE ■
CULTURELLE

Les jeunes Français et la musique

«Pour moi, la musique c'est tout!»° déclare Anne, une jeune Française de quinze ans. Sa copine Hélène est d'accord:° «Aujourd'hui, on ne peut pas° vivre° sans° musique.»

Comme les jeunes Américains, les jeunes Français sont des «fanas»° de musique. Quel type de musique est-ce qu'ils préfèrent? D'abord le rock. Ils aiment aussi la chanson° française et la chanson étrangère,° la musique classique, la musique folk et le jazz.

PARIS BERCY

Les jeunes Français ont l'équipement nécessaire pour écouter leur musique favorite: 70% ont une radio, 58% une chaîne stéréo, 42% une radiocassette et 39% un walkman. Dans les grandes villes, les jeunes vont au concert. À Paris, ils vont à Bercy ou au Zénith écouter les grandes vedettes° de la chanson française et de la musique anglaise et américaine.

Les jeunes Français ne se contentent pas° d'écouter la musique. Beaucoup jouent d'un instrument. Ils jouent du piano, de la flûte, de la guitare et du synthétiseur° . . . Et toi, est-ce que tu peux vivre sans musique? Est-ce que tu joues d'un instrument? De quel instrument joues-tu?

tout *everything* **est d'accord** *agrees* **ne peut pas** *cannot* **vivre** *live* **sans** *without* **fanas = fanatiques** **chanson** *song* **étrangère** *foreign* **vedettes** *stars* **ne se contentent pas** *do not limit themselves* **synthétiseur** *keyboard*

Leçon 32 **329**

COMPREHENSION

1. Elle va aller au cinéma avec Jean-Pierre.
2. Des amis de ses parents viennent chez eux.
3. non
4. son porte-monnaie
5. à pied
6. à la maison avec ses parents
7. au Zenith (dans un concert de rock) et dans un café
8. Elle va faire une promenade à la campagne.
9. Thomas.

COMMUNICATION: describing what one did last weekend

Note culturelle

 32.4 Vignette culturelle: La musique (23:01–24:47 min.)

 Leçon 32, Section 5

■ **Realia note**
Bercy is a large modern sports complex at the edge of Paris along the Seine. It is also used for rock concerts and other large-scale events.

Setting the scene

The opening scene of Video Module 32 presents two girls who are at a café talking about where they went last Saturday. At the end, the conversation takes an unexpected twist.

The *Vignette culturelle* of the video expands on the culture note in the text. French young people are interviewed about their tastes in music.

32.2 Mini-scenes:
Où êtes-vous allé?
Et qu'est-ce que
vous avez fait?
32.3 Où est-ce qu'ils
sont allés?
(20:01–23:00 min.)

 Leçon 32, Sections 2, 3

■ **Pronunciation:** In spoken French, the four forms of **allé** sound the same.

A. Le passé composé avec *être*

Note the forms of the passé composé of **aller** in the sentences below, paying attention to the endings of the past participle **(allé).**

Jean-Paul **est allé** au cinéma.	*Jean-Paul **went** to the movies.*
Mélanie **est allée** à la plage.	*Mélanie **went** to the beach.*
Éric et Patrick **sont allés** en ville.	*Éric and Patrick **went** downtown.*
Mes copines **sont allées** à la campagne.	*My friends **went** to the country.*

The passé composé of **aller** and certain verbs of motion is formed with **être** according to the pattern:

> PRESENT of **être** + PAST PARTICIPLE

➡ When the passé composé of a verb is conjugated with **être** (and not with **avoir**), the PAST PARTICIPLE *agrees* with the SUBJECT in gender and number.

INFINITIVE	aller	
PASSÉ COMPOSÉ	je **suis** **allé** tu **es** **allé** il **est** **allé** nous **sommes** **allé**s vous **êtes** **allé**s ils **sont** **allé**s	je **suis** **allé**e tu **es** **allé**e elle **est** **allé**e nous **sommes** **allé**es vous **êtes** **allé**es elles **sont** **allé**es
NEGATIVE	je **ne suis pas** **allé**	je **ne suis pas** **allé**e
INTERROGATIVE	est-ce que tu **es** **allé**? tu **es** **allé**? (**es**-tu **allé?**)	est-ce que tu **es** **allé**e? tu **es** **allé**e? (**es**-tu **allé**e?)

➡ When **vous** refers to a single person, the past participle is in the singular:
Mme Mercier, est-ce que vous êtes **allée** au concert hier soir?

☀ **Warm-up and review**

As a preparation for the passé composé of **aller,** have students review the forms of **être,** together with the expression **chez.**

You will indicate what people are doing, and the students will let you know whether those people are at home or not.

Paul joue au foot. [Il n'est pas chez lui.]
Je regarde la télé. [Je suis chez moi.]
Nous étudions. [Nous sommes chez nous.]
Mes copains dînent. [Ils sont chez eux.]
Tu fais de la voile. [Tu n'es pas chez toi.]

1. À Paris

Des amis sont allés à Paris samedi dernier.
Chacun est allé à un endroit différent.
Dites qui est allé aux endroits suivants.
Complétez chaque phrase avec le sujet
approprié et la forme correspondante
du verbe **aller.**

Olivier   Claire   Éric et Jacques   Anne et Monique

▶ **Anne et Monique** sont allées au
Louvre.

1. ... allée à la tour Eiffel.
2. ... allé au Centre Pompidou.
3. ... allés à l'Opéra.
4. ... allées aux Galeries Lafayette.
5. ... allé à la Villette.
6. ... allés au Zénith.
7. ... allé au musée d'Orsay.
8. ... allées au Quartier latin.

Musée
d'Orsay
petit
guide

2. Conversation

Demandez à vos camarades s'ils sont
allés aux endroits suivants.

▶ ce matin / à la bibliothèque?

Ce matin, est-ce que
tu es allé à la bibliothèque?

Oui, je suis allé à la bibliothèque.

(Non, je ne suis pas allé à la bibliothèque.)

1. hier matin/à l'école?
2. hier soir/au cinéma?
3. dimanche dernier/au restaurant?
4. samedi dernier/dans les magasins?
5. l'été dernier/chez tes cousins?
6. le weekend dernier/à la campagne?
7. le mois dernier/à un concert?
8. la semaine dernière/chez
   le coiffeur *(barber, hairdresser)*?
9. les vacances dernières/à la mer?

3. Le weekend dernier

Dites ce que les personnes de la Colonne A ont fait en choisissant une activité de la Colonne B.
Puis dites où ces personnes sont allées en choisissant un endroit de la Colonne C.
Soyez logiques!

A	B	C
je	voir des clowns	à la campagne
tu	nager	au zoo
nous	dîner en ville	dans un magasin de chaussures
Catherine	regarder les éléphants	à la bibliothèque
vous	choisir des livres	à la plage
mon petit frère	faire une promenade	au restaurant
André et Thomas	acheter des sandales	au cirque *(circus)*
les filles		

▶ **J'ai nagé. Je suis allé(e) à la plage.**

Leçon 32   331

PRACTICE: describing who
went where

1. Claire est
2. Olivier est
3. Éric et Jacques sont
4. Anne et Monique sont
5. Olivier est
6. Éric et Jacques sont
7. Olivier est
8. Anne et Monique sont

COMMUNICATION: finding
out where people went

COMPREHENSION: describing where people went to do
certain things

■ **Pronunciation**
clown /klun/
zoo /zo/ or /zoo/

■ **Teaching note:** This activity
may be done in a game format.
See **Teaching note,** p. T262.

Sophie nettoie sa chambre. [Elle est
chez elle.]
Elles font du ski. [Elles ne sont pas chez
elles.]
Vous voyagez. [Vous n'êtes pas chez
vous.]

Cooperative
pair practice
Activity 2

4 Weekend

Des amis parlent de leur weekend.
Jouez ces dialogues.

▶ en ville / acheter des vêtements

1. au stade / regarder un match de foot
2. à la plage / jouer au volley
3. à une boum / danser
4. à la campagne / faire une promenade à pied
5. au Bon Marché / acheter des cassettes
6. dans un restaurant italien / manger des spaghetti

Où est-ce que tu es allée?

Je suis allée en ville.

Ah bon! Qu'est-ce que tu as fait?

J'ai acheté des vêtements.

Vocabulaire: Quelques verbes conjugués avec *être* au passé composé

INFINITIVE	PAST PARTICIPLE		
aller	**allé**	*to go*	Nous **sommes allés** en ville.
arriver	**arrivé**	*to arrive*	Vous **êtes arrivés** à midi.
rentrer	**rentré**	*to return, go back, come back*	Nous **sommes rentrés** à la maison à onze heures.
rester	**resté**	*to stay*	Les touristes **sont restés** à l'hôtel Ibis.
venir	**venu**	*to come*	Qui **est venu** hier?

---

5 Qui est resté à la maison?

Samedi après-midi, les personnes suivantes ont fait certaines choses. Dites si oui ou non elles sont restées à la maison.

▶ Paul a regardé la télé.   **Il est resté à la maison.**
▶ Mélanie a fait des achats.   **Elle n'est pas restée à la maison.**

1. Mlle Joly a lavé sa voiture.
2. Nous avons fait une promenade à vélo.
3. Tu as nettoyé le garage.
4. Éric et Olivier ont joué au volley.
5. Christine et Isabelle ont travaillé dans le jardin.
6. Vous avez fait une promenade en voiture.
7. Mes cousins ont fait de la voile.
8. J'ai fait du jogging.

JOGGING

TPR Destinations and arrival times

PROPS: Map (or transparency) of France, clock with movable hands

Imagine that the class is visiting France.
Je suis allé(e) à Nice. [point to Nice]
Je suis arrivé(e) à midi. [move clock to 12]

Have pairs of students come up to show where they went and when they arrived.
X et Y, vous êtes allé(e)s à Lyon.
Vous êtes arrivé(e)s à 1h20.
Venez nous montrer la ville et l'heure.

6 La journée de Nathalie

Pendant les vacances, Nathalie travaille dans une agence de tourisme. Le soir, elle raconte *(tells about)* sa journée à son père.

Je suis allée au bureau.

▶ aller au bureau *(office)*

1. arriver à neuf heures
2. téléphoner à un client anglais
3. parler avec des touristes japonais
4. aller au restaurant à midi et demi
5. rentrer au bureau à deux heures
6. copier des documents
7. préparer des billets *(tickets)* d'avion
8. rester jusqu'à *(until)* six heures
9. dîner en ville
10. rentrer à la maison à neuf heures

7 Une question de circonstances *(A matter of circumstances)*

Nos activités dépendent souvent des circonstances. Dites si oui ou non les personnes suivantes ont fait les choses indiquées.

▶ On est mardi aujourd'hui.
  • les élèves / rester à la maison?
  Les élèves ne sont pas restés à la maison.

1. On est dimanche.
  • M. Boulot / travailler?
  • nous / aller à l'école?
  • vous / dîner à la cantine *(school cafeteria)*?

2. Il fait très beau aujourd'hui.
  • moi / aller à la campagne?
  • mes copines / regarder la télé?
  • toi / venir à la piscine avec nous?

3. Il fait très mauvais!
  • Marc / faire un pique-nique?
  • Hélène et Juliette / rester à la maison?
  • ma mère / rentrer à la maison à pied?

4. Mes copains et moi, nous n'avons pas beaucoup d'argent.
  • toi / aller dans un restaurant cher?
  • mes copains / venir chez moi en taxi?
  • moi / acheter des vêtements?

Leçon 32 333

ROLE PLAY: narrating the day's events (6)

■ **Variation** (using other subjects):
[elle] Elle est allée au bureau.
[nous] Nous sommes allés au bureau.
[Élisabeth et sa soeur Alice (elles)] Elles sont allées au bureau.

COMPREHENSION: drawing conclusions about past actions (7)

■ **Teaching note:** Remind students to use **pas de** in items 3 and 4:
3. Marc n'a **pas** fait **de** pique-nique.
4. Je n'ai **pas** acheté **de** vêtements.

■ **Expansion:** Have students write an original affirmative and negative sentence for each item.
▶ Nous avons eu un examen de français.
Je n'ai pas regardé la télé ce matin.

Follow-up questions:
Où est-ce que X et Y sont allé(e)s?
À quelle heure sont-ils(elles) arrivé(e)s?

T333

■ **Teaching strategy:** Point out
that the pattern with **ne... jamais**
in the passé composé is the same
as with **ne... pas.**

8 PRACTICE: talking about
what one never does

9 COMMUNICATION:
answering personal
questions

B. La construction négative *ne ... jamais*

Compare the following negative constructions.

Éric **ne** parle **pas** à Paul.	*Éric does **not** speak to Paul.*
Éric **ne** parle **jamais** à Paul.	*Éric **never** speaks to Paul.*
Nous **n'**étudions **pas** le dimanche.	*We do **not** study on Sundays.*
Nous **n'**étudions **jamais** le dimanche.	*We **never** study on Sundays.*

To say that one NEVER does something, French speakers use the construction **ne ... jamais,**
as follows:

SUBJECT	+	**ne**	+	VERB	+	**jamais** ...
Nous		**ne**		regardons		**jamais** la télé.

➡ **Ne** becomes **n'** before a vowel sound.

Nous **n'**allons **jamais** à l'opéra.

➡ Note the use of **ne ... jamais** in the passé composé:

Nous **n'**avons **jamais** visité Québec.	*We **never** visited Quebec.*
Je **ne** suis **jamais** allé à Genève.	*I **never** went to Geneva.*

---

8 **Jamais le dimanche**

Le dimanche les personnes suivantes
ne font jamais ce qu'elles font pendant
la semaine. Exprimez cette situation.

▶ François va à l'école.
**Le dimanche, il ne va jamais à
l'école.**

1. Anne étudie.
2. Marc travaille.
3. Nous parlons français.
4. Vous allez à la bibliothèque.
5. M. Bernard va en ville.
6. Les élèves mangent à la cantine.
7. Tu rends visite à tes copains.
8. Vous dînez chez vous.
9. Je nettoie ma chambre.
10. Je lave la voiture.

---

9 **Questions personnelles**

Dans tes réponses, utilise les
expressions **souvent, rarement** ou
ne ... jamais.

▶ Est-ce que tu vas souvent au zoo?
Oui, je vais souvent au zoo.
(Non, je vais rarement au zoo.)
(Non, je ne vais jamais au zoo.)

1. Est-ce que tu parles souvent français
à la maison?
2. Est-ce que tu mets *(set)* la table?
3. Est-ce que tu fais souvent ton lit?
4. Est-ce que tu téléphones souvent au
professeur?
5. Est-ce que tu nages souvent en hiver?
6. Est-ce que tu vas souvent à l'opéra?
7. Est-ce que tu vois souvent des matchs
de boxe?
8. Est-ce que tu voyages souvent en
limousine?

Do you like cars? Then you must know about
Michelin radial tires. But did you know that
Michelin employs over 16,000 people in its
North American plants in South Carolina,
Alabama, and Nova Scotia?

**Cooperative
pair practice
Activity 10**

C. Les expressions *quelqu'un, quelque chose* et leurs contraires

Compare the affirmative and negative constructions in heavy print.

—Tu attends **quelqu'un?**   *Are you waiting for **someone (anyone)?***
—Non, je **n'**attends **personne.**   *No, I'm **not** waiting for **anyone.***

—Vous faites **quelque chose** ce soir?   *Are you doing **something (anything)** tonight?*
—Non, nous **ne** faisons **rien.**   *No, we're **not** doing **anything.***
                                       *No, we're doing **nothing.***

To refer to unspecified people or things, French speakers use the following expressions:

quelqu'un	someone, anyone somebody, anybody	**ne … personne**	no one, not anyone nobody, not anybody
quelque chose	something, anything	**ne … rien**	nothing, not anything

➡ Like all negative expressions, **personne** and **rien** require **ne** before the verb. Remember that **ne** becomes **n'** before a vowel sound.

➡ In short answers, **personne** and **rien** may be used alone.
     Qui est là? **Personne.**
     Qu'est-ce que tu fais? **Rien.**

10 **Florence est malade**

Florence est malade *(sick)* aujourd'hui. Elle répond négativement aux questions de Paul.

     ▶ dîner avec quelqu'un?

1. inviter quelqu'un?
2. faire quelque chose ce soir?
3. manger quelque chose à midi?
4. regarder quelque chose à la télé?
5. attendre quelqu'un ce matin?
6. voir quelqu'un cet après-midi?
7. préparer quelque chose pour le dîner?
8. rencontrer quelqu'un après le dîner?

Tu dînes avec quelqu'un?

Non, je ne dîne avec personne.

Prononciation   qu /k/

Les lettres «qu»

The letters "**qu**" represent the sound /k/. First, practice with words you know.

un bouquet

Répétez: **qui quand quelque chose quelqu'un quatre quatorze Québec Monique Véronique sympathique un pique-nique le ski nautique**

Now try reading some new words. Make them sound French!

Répétez: **un bouquet un banquet la qualité la quantité la conséquence une équipe** *(team)* **l'équipement fréquent la séquence**

     Véronique pense que Monique aime la musique classique.

Leçon 32   **335**

Section C

COMMUNICATIVE FUNCTION: Identifying people and things

 32.1 Dialogue: Un bon weekend (18:22–20:00 min.)

 Leçon 32, Section 1

■ **Language note:** Word order with **ne… personne** and **ne… rien** is presented in Book Two. In general, **personne** and **rien** have the same position in the sentence as **quelqu'un** and **quelque chose**:
Quelqu'un a téléphoné?
Non, **personne** n'a téléphoné.
EXCEPTION: In the passé composé **rien** comes between the auxiliary and the past participle:
Tu as acheté **quelque chose**?
Non, je n'ai **rien** acheté.

■ **Teaching strategy:** Point out that **pas** is never used together with **personne** or **rien**.

10 ROLE PLAY: giving negative responses

Prononciation

Leçon 32, Section 6

1 COMPREHENSION

1-e   4-a
2-c   5-b
3-d

[□=□] **Leçon 32, Section 7**

2 GUIDED ORAL EXPRESSION

■ **Expansion:** I did not see you last weekend. Please answer my questions in French. Tell me:
• Did you stay home Saturday morning?
• What did you do?
• Where did you go Saturday afternoon?
• What did you do there?
• Did you meet your friends?
• If so, what did you do together?

3 GUIDED ORAL EXPRESSION

[□=□] **Leçon 32, section 8**

À votre tour!

1 Allô!

Reconstituez la conversation entre Sophie et Charlotte. Pour cela, faites correspondre les réponses de Charlotte avec les questions de Sophie.

1 Tu es restée chez toi samedi soir?

2 Qu'est-ce que vous avez vu?

3 Qu'est-ce que vous avez fait ensuite?

4 Vous avez mangé quelque chose?

5 À quelle heure es-tu rentrée chez toi?

a Oui, des sandwichs.

b À onze heures et demie.

c Un vieux western avec Gary Cooper.

d Nous sommes allées dans un café sur le boulevard Saint Michel.

e Non! J'ai téléphoné à une copine et nous sommes allées au cinéma.

2 Dis-moi ...

I will tell you a few things that I did Saturday; then you will tell me where you went on Saturday and what you did.

• Le matin, je suis resté(e) à la maison. J'ai nettoyé ma cham[...]
• L'après-midi, je suis allé(e) au cinéma avec mon copain Jean-Claude. Nous avons vu une comédie. Après, je suis rentré(e) chez moi.
• Le soir, j'ai dîné avec mes parents. Après, je suis resté(e) dans ma chambre et j'ai écouté mes cassettes.

Et maintenant, dis-moi ...

3 Créa-dialogue

Avec vos copains, discutez de ce que vous avez fait récemment *(recently)*. Utilisez les suggestions suivantes.

▶ —Tu es resté(e) chez toi hier matin?
—Oui, je suis resté(e) chez moi.
—Qu'est-ce que tu as fait?
—J'ai nettoyé ma chambre.

▶ —Tu es resté(e) chez toi hier matin?
—Non, je ne suis pas resté(e) chez moi.
—Qu'est-ce que tu as fait?
—Je suis allé(e) à l'école.

hier matin	1. samedi après-midi	2. vendredi soir	3. m[...]
rester chez toi	aller en ville	rentrer chez toi	re[...] à m[...]
??	??	??	?[...]

À votre tour

Depending on your goals and objectives, you may or may not wish to assign all of the activities in the **À votre tour** section.

👥 Cooperative practice

In Act. 1 and 3, you may want to have students work cooperatively in trios, with two performing and one consulting the Answer Key and acting as monitor.

4 Situation

Avec un(e) camarade, composez un dialogue correspondant à la situation suivante. Jouez ce dialogue en classe.

Your French friend Marie-Hélène (played by your classmate) has just come back from a vacation with a great suntan. Try to find out . . .
- where she went
- how long **(combien de temps)** she stayed there
- what she did
- when she came back

5 Conversation libre

Avec un(e) camarade, composez un dialogue original basé sur la situation suivante.

You and your cousin Valérie have not seen each other for a while. Talk about what you did either . . .
- last night **(hier soir),** or
- during spring vacation **(pendant les vacances de printemps),** or
- during summer vacation **(pendant les vacances d'été)**

You will each ask the other at least three different questions to find out where your cousin went and what she saw or did, etc.

6 Composition: Un voyage

Write a short paragraph describing a trip you took — real or imaginary! You may want to use some of the following suggestions.

aller (où?)
voyager (comment?)
arriver (quel jour?)
rester (où? combien de temps?)
visiter (quoi?)

voir (quoi?)
rencontrer (qui?)
acheter (quoi?)
faire (quoi?)
rentrer (quel jour?)

▶ **L'été dernier, je suis allé(e) à Montréal . . .**

che r	5. le weekend dernier	6. la semaine dernière	7. le mois dernier	8. l'été dernier
la	aller à la campagne	aller à une boum	faire un voyage	travailler
	??	??	??	??

Comment dit-on . . . ?

How to celebrate a happy occasion:

Bon anniversaire!

Bonne année!

Leçon 32 337

4 GUIDED ORAL EXPRESSION

■ **Challenge:**
Conversational role play
Note: For suggestions on how to use the Challenge activities, see p. T305.
Your cousin Annette has just come back from two weeks in Paris. Ask her about her trip. You may want to find out:
- when she arrived in Paris
- where she stayed (in a hôtel? with friends?)
- if she visited a museum (which museum?)
- what she saw
- whom she met
- what she bought
- when she came back

5 CONVERSATION

6 WRITTEN SELF-EXPRESSION

📁 Portfolio assessment

You will probably select only one speaking activity and one writing activity to go into the students' portfolios for Unit 8.

In this lesson, Act. 6 offers an excellent writing portfolio topic. Act. 4 and 5 lend themselves well to oral recordings.

Entracte 8

Sports, vacances et tourisme

■ **Photo culture note**
The photo is of Port-Camargue, a small resort town on the Mediterranean, near Montpellier and Nîmes.

Petit test culturel
Sports, vacances et tourisme

Quand on est en vacances, on aime voyager. Est-ce que vous pouvez répondre aux questions suivantes? Vérifiez vos réponses au bas° de la page.

1 Christèle habite à Paris. Elle va passer les vacances à Nice chez des cousins. Où est-ce qu'elle va passer les vacances?
a. à la mer
b. à la montagne
c. à la campagne
d. chez elle

2 Les Dupont adorent passer les vacances à la montagne. Cette année ils ont réservé une chambre d'hôtel. Dans quelle ville?
a. à Bordeaux
b. à Marseille
c. à Grenoble
d. à Tours

3 En hiver, beaucoup de touristes vont à la Martinique. Quel sport est-ce qu'on ne peut° pas pratiquer là-bas?
a. le ski
b. le ski nautique
c. la voile
d. la planche à voile

4 Nous sommes en février. Un copain revient de vacances bien bronzé.° Il dit:° «J'ai passé d'excellentes vacances dans une île° où on parle français.» Où est-il allé?
a. aux Bermudes
b. à Tahiti
c. à Puerto Rico
d. à la Jamaïque

5 Madame Gilbert travaille pour une agence de tourisme. Samedi dernier, elle est allée de Paris à New York. Elle dit: «J'ai fait la traversée° de l'Atlantique en trois heures!» Quel avion est-ce qu'elle a pris?°
a. un Boeing 747
b. un DC-10
c. un Airbus
d. un Concorde

6 Quand il est rentré de vacances, Jean-François a dit:° «J'ai passé un mois magnifique chez mon oncle en Bretagne.» Dans quelle partie de la France est-ce qu'il est allé?
a. à l'ouest°
b. à l'est
c. au sud
d. au nord

nord

ouest

sud

au bas *at the bottom* **peut** *can* **bronzé** *tanned* **dit** *says* **île** *island* **traversée** *crossing* **a pris** *did . . . take*
a dit *said* **ouest** *west*

 Cooperative reading practice

Divide the class into groups of 4 or 5, each with a **secrétaire.**

Keeping the box at the bottom of the page covered, have the groups vote on the correct answer for each question.

Then have the recorders check the right answers. If appropriate, have recorders announce their group score to the entire class.

Nous avons six réponses correctes.

Follow-up: Have the students find all the places mentioned on the maps in the Reference section, pp. R2–R3.

EN FRANCE

Vive le sport!

Quels sports pratiquez-vous pendant les vacances? Où allez-vous pour pratiquer votre sport favori? Voici plusieurs possibilités:

◩ Quels sports est-ce qu'on peut pratiquer dans ce club?

◩ En quelle saison?

◩ Quel est le numéro de téléphone du club?

⚠ Comment s'appelle ce club?

⚠ Quels sports est-ce qu'on peut pratiquer dans ce club?

◳ Comment s'appelle ce centre de loisirs?°

◳ Quels sports est-ce qu'on peut pratiquer?

◳ Quelles autres° activités sont offertes?

LE STADIUM CENTRE DE LOISIRS
VACANCES DE PÂQUES

PATINAGE
SKATE
NATATION

SAMEDI SOIR - Animation
SPÉCIALE AVEC L'ORCHESTRE
SQUAD - 21 h à 24 h

BOWLING
JUDO et
sports de combat
DANSE

66, AVENUE D'IVRY (M° PORTE D'IVRY) 45.83.11.00

Vous avez la possibilité d'aller dans un des endroits mentionnés plus haut.° Quel endroit est-ce que vous allez choisir? Pourquoi?

loisirs *leisure activities*   **autres** *other*   **plus haut** *above*

Vive le sport!

OBJECTIVES:
- Reading for information
- Understanding authentic documents

◼ Realia notes
un stage *organized instruction or class*
PLM *a French hotel chain*
la location *rental*
le tarif *rates, price*
un abonnement *membership (subscription)*
une animation spéciale *special entertainment*
skate = **le skateboard** (**la planche à roulettes**)
M° = **métro**

◼ Answers to questions
Tennis action
- le tennis et le golf
- en été
- 47.34.36.36

Sports loisirs
- Sports loisirs
- le ski nautique et la planche à voile

Le stadium
- le patinage, le skate et la natation
- le bowling, le judo et les sports

📖 Pre-reading

Ask students if they sometimes go to sports clubs or take sports lessons. Which sports do they prefer?
Quels sports préférez-vous?

Post-reading

As students answer the last questions about which club they prefer, tally their responses on the board.
La majorité préfère ...
Ensuite, il y a [9] élèves qui préfèrent...
Il y a seulement [3] élèves qui préfèrent...

Entre amis: Le weekend

Qu'est-ce que vous faites le weekend? Qu'est ce que vous avez fait le weekend dernier? Voici les réponses de cinq jeunes du monde° francophone.°

Carole, 15 ans, France
Le weekend dernier, j'ai fait une promenade en mobylette avec une copine. Nous sommes allées à la campagne. À midi, on a fait un pique-nique. Après, on a visité un vieux château en ruines. Malheureusement,° j'ai eu une crevaison.° Je suis rentrée chez moi seulement° pour le dîner. Après le dîner, j'ai regardé la télé et j'ai fait mes devoirs pour lundi.

Élisabeth, 15 ans, Belgique
Samedi matin, j'ai fait des achats. J'ai choisi un cadeau° pour l'anniversaire de mon père. (J'ai acheté une cravate en soie.°) L'après-midi, je suis allée au ciné-club avec un copain. Nous avons vu *Les Temps modernes*, un vieux film de Charlie Chaplin. Après, nous sommes allés dans un café et nous avons rencontré d'autres° copains. J'ai passé la soirée° en famille.

Pierre, 16 ans, la Martinique
Le samedi, je joue généralement au foot. Je fais partie de° l'équipe° junior de mon village. Le weekend dernier, nous avons fait un match. Nous avons bien joué, mais nous avons perdu! Après le match, je suis allé à la plage. Le soir, je suis allé chez des copains. Nous avons mis de la musique et nous avons dansé.

Djemila, 16 ans, Algérie
Samedi dernier, nous avons eu une grande réunion de famille chez mon oncle Karim. Une centaine° de personnes sont venues. Nous avons fait un «méchoui». (C'est un repas° où on rôtit° un mouton° entier à la broche.°) J'ai eu l'occasion° de voir tous° mes cousins et cousines. On s'est bien amusé!°

Yvan, 14 ans, Québec
Le matin, je suis allé à la patinoire° avec des copains, mais je ne suis pas resté très longtemps.° À midi, je suis rentré chez moi. L'après-midi, j'ai aidé mes parents à repeindre° la cuisine. Pour le dîner, nous sommes allés au restaurant.

monde *world* **francophone** *French-speaking*
Malheureusement *Unfortunately* **crevaison** *flat tire*
seulement *just* **cadeau** *present* **soie** *silk* **d'autres** *other*
soirée *evening* **fais partie de** *am a member of* **équipe** *team*
Une centaine *About a hundred* **repas** *meal* **rôtit** *roasts*
mouton *sheep* **à la broche** *on the spit* **occasion** *chance*
tous *all* **On s'est bien amusé!** *We had a good time!*
patinoire *skating rink* **très longtemps** *for a very long time*
repeindre *to repaint*

■ **NOTES**
CULTURELLES

Alger

1 L'Algérie
L'Algérie est un pays° d'Afrique du Nord. C'est une ancienne° colonie française. Aujourd'hui beaucoup de familles d'origine algérienne habitent en France. Dans ces familles, on parle généralement français et arabe.

Comment lire
WORDS WITH SEVERAL MEANINGS

Sometimes a word may have several meanings. For example, the French word **temps** can mean:

weather	Quel beau **temps**!
time	Je n'ai pas le **temps** d'aller au cinéma.

Enrichissez votre vocabulaire
MORE COGNATE PATTERNS

Here are two important cognate patterns that will help you read French more easily.

- French verbs in **-er** sometimes correspond to English verbs in *-ate*.
situer	*situate*

  Note also how this pattern works in past participles:
situé	*situated*

- The circumflex accent on a vowel often indicates that the English cognate contains an *"s"*.
rôtir	*to roast*
coûter	*to cost*

Activité

Can you identify the English equivalents of the following French words?

- **séparer   indiquer   associer   apprécier   opérer
  décoré   créé   libéré   illustré   agité   animé**

- **un hôpital   une forêt   honnête   en hâte   une hôtesse   une île**

2 La Belgique

La Belgique est un petit pays situé au nord-est° de la France. Sa capitale, Bruxelles, est un centre européen important. La Belgique est un pays bilingue. Les langues officielles sont le français et le flamand.°

pays *country* **ancienne** *former*
nord-est *northeast* **flamand** *Flemish*

Activité: Une lettre

Imaginez que vous avez passé le weekend avec l'une des cinq personnes. Choisissez cette personne (Carole, Élisabeth, Pierre, Djemila ou Yvan). Dans une lettre, décrivez ce weekend de votre point de vue personnel.

▶

Chers amis,
J'ai passé le weekend avec Carole.
Nous avons . . .

Entracte 8 341

■ **Vocabulary note:** Other words with several meanings:
passer *to pass [by], to spend*
gagner *to earn, to win*
l'anniversaire *anniversary, birthday*

■ **Vocabulary note:** Other cognates with a circumflex accent:
un mât, arrêter, un hôte, la pâte

Notes culturelles

■ **Les Algériens en France**
The Algerians represent the largest group of foreigners living in France. Young French people of Algerian origin often refer to themselves as **Beurs.**

■ **Bruxelles**
Brussels is an important center for the 12-member European Community (**la Communauté Européenne**). It is the seat of the Council of Ministers and houses the working committees of the European Parliament.

Variétés

Variétés

OBJECTIVES:
- Reading for fun
- Logical thinking: finding errors of fact

■ Photo culture notes
Paris
This postcard shows a **bateau mouche** passing in front of Notre Dame. These double-deckered boats offer tourists a spectacular view of Paris, especially in the evening when the monuments are illuminated.
(For more information, see p. 243.)

Normandie
This postcard shows a section of Omaha Beach. On June 6, 1944, D-Day, allied troups landed on the beaches in Normandy (code-named Omaha, Utah, Juno and Sword). In the ensuing months, the Allies liberated France and the rest of Europe from German occupation. The American military cemetery at Omaha Beach is maintained by the U.S. Government and is considered as part of U.S. territory.

■ Cultural note: Une marmite is
a covered stewing pot with small handles on each side. It is a symbol of home-cooked food.

Les quatre erreurs d'Hélène

Pendant les vacances, Hélène Ladoucette, une jeune étudiante québécoise, est allée en France. Là, elle a voyagé et elle a visité beaucoup d'endroits différents. Pendant son voyage, elle a écrit des cartes postales à ses copains. Dans chaque° carte postale, Hélène a fait une erreur.° (Les erreurs d'Hélène concernent l'histoire ou la géographie.) Pouvez-vous° trouver ces erreurs? Lisez° attentivement chaque carte et découvrez° l'erreur qui s'y trouve.°

PARIS

Paris, le 2 juillet

Cher Alain,
　Je suis arrivée à Paris samedi dernier. Avant hier,° j'ai visité Notre-Dame et le musée d'Orsay. Hier, j'ai rendu visite à une copine parisienne. Nous avons fait une promenade sur la Saône en bateau-mouche.° Après, nous sommes allées dans un restaurant qui s'appelle la "Petite Marmite". J'ai mangé des escargots!°
　Amitiés,
　Hélène

NORMANDIE

Deauville, le 8 juille

Ma chère Pauline,
　Je suis maintenant en Normandie. Je suis venue ici avec Véronique, ma copine parisienne. Il y a beaucoup de choses à faire ici. Hier, nous avons visité le Havre, un grand port sur l'Atlantique. Aujourd'hui, nous sommes allées sur les plages où les soldats° canadiens et américains ont débarqué° en 1844. C'est très impressionnant!°
　Amicalement, Hélène

chaque *each*　**erreur** *mistake*
Pouvez-vous *Can you*　**Lisez** *Read*　**découvrez** *discover*
qui s'y trouve *that is there*　**Avant hier** *The day before yesterday*
bateau-mouche *sight-seeing boat*　**escargots** *snails*
soldats *soldiers*　**ont débarqué** *landed*　**impressionnant** *impressive*

342　Unité 8

📖 **Pre-reading activity**
Have students look at each of the post-cards and read the descriptions of the places pictured. Then have them locate the four cities on a map of France.

Post-reading activity
Have students imagine that they had been able to accompany Hélène on one part of her trip. Which part would they have chosen and why?

Lyon, le 10 juillet

Mes chers cousins,

Un grand bonjour de Lyon! Je suis arrivée ici hier matin. J'ai voyagé en TGV. Le TGV est un train très confortable et très rapide. (Je suis allée de Paris à Lyon en moins de° deux heures!) Lyon est une ville très moderne et très ancienne aussi. Elle a été fondée en 43 avant Jésus-Christ°. Ce matin, j'ai visité le musée du Louvre. Là, j'ai admiré les antiquités romaines°.

Affectueusement, Hélène

LYON

Toulon, le 15 juillet

Ma chère Michèle,

Je suis arrivée ici hier, 14 juillet, pour la fête nationale française. Le matin, j'ai vu un défilé° militaire. Le soir, j'ai assisté aux feux d'artifices° et j'ai dansé dans les rues. Toulon est situé sur la Méditerranée. Demain, je vais aller en Corse° en bateau. La Corse est une île italienne très célèbre° parce que c'est là que Napoléon est né.°

Je t'embrasse, Hélène

LES QUATRE ERREURS D'HÉLÈNE:

1. Paris est situé sur la Seine, et non sur la Saône.   2. Les soldats canadiens et américains ont débarqué en Normandie en 1944, et non en 1844.   3. Le musée du Louvre est à Paris, pas à Lyon.   4. La Corse est une île française, et non italienne.

moins de *less than*   43 avant Jésus-Christ *43 B.C.*   romaines *Roman*
défilé *parade*   feux d'artifices *fireworks*   Corse *Corsica*   célèbre *famous*
est né *was born*

Entracte 8   343

LON

Photo culture notes

Lyon

This postcard shows **l'amphithéâtre des Trois Gaules** in Lyon. Lyon, which is the third largest city of France, is located at the junction of two rivers, **le Rhône** and **la Saône**. It was founded by the Romans in 43 B.C. Because of its strategic location, it became the capital of Gaul (**la Gaule**), as France was called in Roman times.

Toulon

This postcard shows the harbor of Toulon as viewed from the mountains to the north of the city. Toulon, with a population of 400,000, is an important French naval base and also a port of call for the U.S. fleet in the Mediterranean.

👥👥 Cooperative writing practice

Ask students to bring in local postcards. Divide the class into small groups.

Each group of students writes a postcard in French. In the text, however, they introduce an error of history or geography.

Then let groups exchange cards and try to find the errors.

■ **Photo culture notes**

À la cantine
At the school cafeteria in Savigny-sur-Orge, food is served at the table, family style.

Un déjeuner dehors
In the summer, French people prefer to eat outside (**dehors**) on their terrace or in their garden.
In the picture, the meal is almost finished. After the cheese will come fruit.

UNITÉ 9 Les repas

Unit overview

COMMUNICATION GOALS: Students will be able to buy food and order a meal.
LINGUISTIC GOALS: Students will learn to express quantities and use object pronouns.
CRITICAL THINKING GOALS: Students will begin to understand the concept of the partitive and to observe the differences between object pronouns in French and English.
CULTURAL GOALS: Students will learn about French meals, restaurants, and cafeterias as well as grocery shopping habits in France.

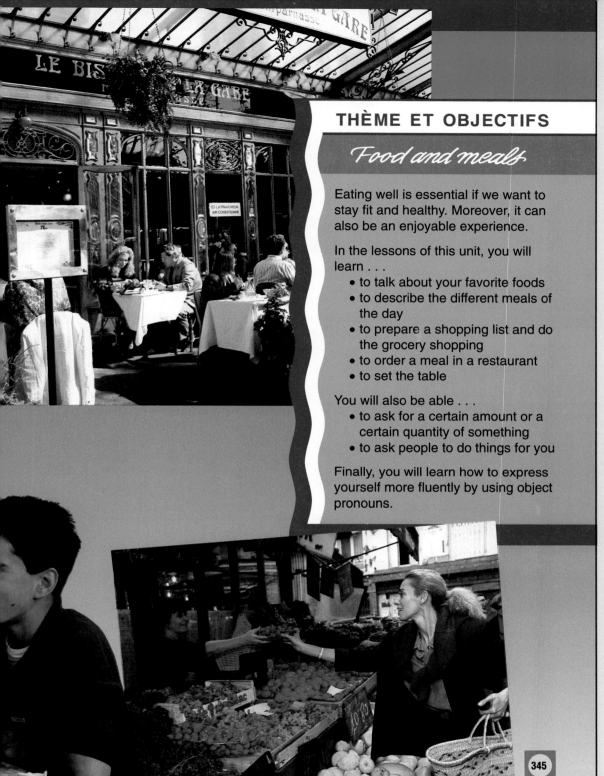

THÈME ET OBJECTIFS

Food and meals

Eating well is essential if we want to stay fit and healthy. Moreover, it can also be an enjoyable experience.

In the lessons of this unit, you will learn . . .
- to talk about your favorite foods
- to describe the different meals of the day
- to prepare a shopping list and do the grocery shopping
- to order a meal in a restaurant
- to set the table

You will also be able . . .
- to ask for a certain amount or a certain quantity of something
- to ask people to do things for you

Finally, you will learn how to express yourself more fluently by using object pronouns.

345

■ **Photo culture notes**

Déjeuner au café
In spring and summer, weather permitting, city cafés and restaurants often serve meals on the sidewalk (**la terrasse**). French people do not mind (and in fact enjoy) the constant flow of pedestrians passing their tables.
For clients who do not like the summer heat, the sign on the door indicates that inside the café is air-conditioned (**la fraîcheur** = coolness).
Note that the menu (**le menu**) is posted outside the café.
This restaurant is called **Le bistrot de la gare**. The name **bistrot** is often given to small café-restaurants.

Le marché
French people prefer buying fruits and vegetables at outdoor markets (**le marché**). Many foodstores also have a sidewalk stand (**un étal**) where passersby can buy these products.
Notice how the prices for the various items are written in chalk on small signs.
Note that the shopper in the picture has her own shopping basket (**un sac à provisions**). This is important in France, because many merchants at open-air markets do not provide shopping bags.

Pacing

Your pacing of Unit 9 will depend on where you are in the academic year.

Since this material is reintroduced in **DISCOVERING FRENCH—BLANC**, you may want to present the material primarily for student recognition. However, if you have the time, present all four lessons of Unit 9 so that students have a solid introduction to object pronouns.

For further suggestions on pacing, see the general discussion in the Front Matter.

MODULE 33:
Le français pratique:
Les repas et la
nourriture
Total time: 6:32 min.
(Counter: 25:01 min.)

33.1 **Introduction: Listening — Où allez-vous quand vous avez faim?** (25:16–26:04 min.)

33.2 **Mini-scenes: Listening — Qu'est-ce que vous aimez manger?** (26:05–27:04 min.)

33.3 **Mini-scenes: Listening — Vous préférez les frites ou les spaghetti?** (27:05–27:30 min.)

33.4 **Mini-scenes: Speaking — Qu'est-ce que vous préférez?** (27:31–28:22 min.)

33.5 **Dialogue: Au marché** (28:23–29:40 min.)

33.6 **Vignette culturelle: Les courses** (29:41–31:29 min.)

■ **Comprehension practice:** Play the entire module through as an introduction to the lesson.

■ **Cultural note:** Biscottes are dried slices of toasted bread that have been baked in the oven. They don't get stale and can be stored easily.

T346

LEÇON 33

Les repas et la nourriture

LE FRANÇAIS PRATIQUE

Accent sur ... Les repas français

For French people, a meal is more than just food served on a plate. It is a social occasion in which family and friends sit down together to enjoy one another's company. French meals are different from American meals not only in terms of the foods and beverages that are served, but also in the way these foods are presented and in the order in which they are served.

• **Le petit déjeuner** (*Breakfast*)
The French **petit déjeuner** is simpler and not as abundant as the American breakfast. Usually it consists of bread, warm toast (**du pain grillé**) or dry toast (**des biscottes**), eaten with butter and jam. Children drink hot milk with coffee (**du café au lait**) or hot chocolate served in deep bowls. On Sundays or special occasions, the first person up may go out to buy fresh croissants.

• **Le déjeuner** (*Lunch*)
The French **déjeuner** is traditionally the main meal of the day. It begins with one or several appetizers (**les hors d'oeuvre**), such as salami, cucumber salad, radishes, and grated carrots. Next, comes the main course (**le plat principal**), which may be a meat or fish dish accompanied by vegetables. This is followed by a green salad, a cheese course, and a dessert. Children drink water, mineral water, apple cider, or carbonated fruit juices. Adults drink mineral water and sometimes may enjoy a glass of wine. When coffee is served, it always comes at the very end of the meal.

346 **Unité 9**

📺 ## Using the video

Ask students whether they prefer to eat in restaurants, cafés, of fast-food places. What do they usually order there? What kinds of foods do they eat at home? Where do their families shop for groceries?

Then show the Video Module 33 and have students look for similarities and differences in eating and grocery shopping habits in France and the U.S.

In the first part, French people are eating out in cafés and resataurants. Then diners express their preferences for various foods in an interview situation. The *Vignette culturelle* shows French shoppers purchasing fruits and vegetables at an open-air market.

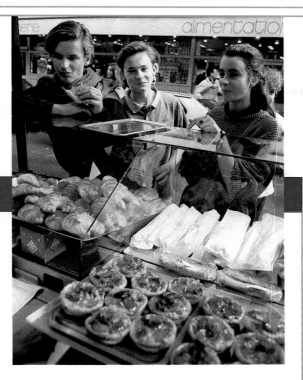

Le petit déjeuner
This French breakfast mixes traditional elements (**des biscottes, du pain, du beurre, de la confiture**) with modern foods (**des céreales**). Note that the coffee is served in deep bowls (**un bol**).
Note also the open cupboard (**le buffet**) in the back of the room. It is used to display decorative dishes.

Le déjeuner
In summer, lunches are lighter and may consist of cold cuts (**des viandes froides**), salad, and fruit. Note the bottle of mineral water which is almost always present on a French table.

Le goûter
Many department stores have snack counters where one can buy sandwiches, croissants, mini-pizzas, and light pastries.

Le dîner
Note the basket of fruit on the table. In France, it is typical to serve fruit at the end of the meal. Note also the wardrobe (**l'armoire**) against the wall.

- **Le goûter** (*Afternoon snack*)
  When children come back from school, they often have a light snack which traditionally consists of bread and a piece of chocolate. Some days they may stop at the pastry shop (**la pâtisserie**) for a **pain au chocolat** (a croissant-like pastry with chocolate inside).

- **Le dîner** (*Supper*)
  In France, supper is served between seven and eight o'clock. It is traditionally a simpler meal than lunch, consisting of soup, a light main course (such as a slice of ham, an omelet, pasta, or a light meat dish), and then a green salad and a simple dessert (yogurt or fruit).
  Supper is a sit-down meal, served once everyone is home. This is the occasion for parents and children to spend time together and talk about the events of the day. (In France, children are not allowed to go to the refrigerator and fix their own meals. They are expected to sit down at the table and are not excused until everyone is finished.)

■ **Cultural note:** Eating habits in Quebec are a blend between those in France and English-speaking Canada. Like other Canadians, the **Québécois** have bacon, eggs, toast, and cereal for breakfast. But, like the French, they enjoy wine, mineral water, and croissants at a sidewalk café. Ethnic food, particularly in Montreal, is also very popular. People eat out in cafés, restaurants, and fast-food places. **Le casse-croûte** (*snack bar*) is a favorite place for a quick lunch.

COMMUNICATIVE FUNCTION:
Discussing meals and food

 33.1 Introduction: Où allez-vous quand vous avez faim?
(25:16–26:04 min.)

🔲 Leçon 33, Section 1

■ **Looking ahead:** The verb **prendre** is formally presented in Lesson 34. Here students will be using only the **je** and **tu** forms.

■ **Language note:** Remind students that **la cuisine** is also *the kitchen*.

■ **Language note:** In Quebec, meals of the day are:
le déjeuner *(breakfast)*
le dîner *(lunch)*
le souper *(dinner)*

📇 **Transparency 45**
Table setting

■ **Cultural note:** In setting the table in France, the spoon is usually placed above the plate.

T348

A. Les repas et la table

▶ *How to talk about meals:*

—En général, à quelle heure est-ce que tu **prends le petit déjeuner** *(have breakfast)*?
—Je prends le petit déjeuner à sept heures et demie.
—Où est-ce que tu vas **déjeuner** *(to have lunch)* aujourd'hui?
—Je vais déjeuner à **la cantine de l'école** *(school cafeteria)*.

> À quelle heure est-ce que tu prends le petit déjeuner?

> Je prends le petit déje... à sept heures et dem...

Les repas et la nourriture

NOMS		VERBES	
un repas	meal		
le petit déjeuner	breakfast	**prendre le petit déjeuner**	to have breakfast
le déjeuner	lunch	**déjeuner**	to have lunch
le dîner	dinner	**dîner**	to have dinner
la nourriture	food		
la cuisine	cooking, cuisine		

—Tu peux **mettre** *(set)* la table?
—D'accord. Je vais mettre la table.

- un verre
- une tasse
- une cuillère
- une assiette
- une serviette
- une fourchette
- un couteau

348

1 Et toi?

Exprime tes préférences. Pour cela complète les phrases suivantes.

1. Mon repas préféré est …
- • le petit déjeuner
- • le dîner
- • le déjeuner

2. Je préfère déjeuner …
- • chez moi
- • à la cantine de l'école
- • dans un fast food
- • … ?

3. En général, la nourriture de la cantine de l'école est …
- • excellente
- • bonne
- • mauvaise
- • … ?

4. Je préfère dîner …
- • chez moi
- • chez mes copains
- • au restaurant
- • … ?

5. Je préfère la nourriture …
- • mexicaine
- • italienne
- • chinoise
- • … ?

6. Quand je dois aider avec le dîner, je préfère …
- • préparer la salade
- • mettre la table
- • laver les assiettes
- • … ?

2 Questions personnelles

1. À quelle heure est-ce que tu prends ton petit déjeuner le lundi? Et le dimanche?
2. En général, à quelle heure est-ce que tu dînes?
3. Où est-ce que tu déjeunes pendant la semaine? le samedi? le dimanche?
4. Où est-ce que tu as déjeuné hier? Avec qui?
5. Où est-ce que tu vas dîner ce soir? Avec qui?
6. Est-ce que tu vas souvent au restaurant? Quand? Avec qui? Quel est ton restaurant préféré?
7. Est-ce que tu as jamais *(ever)* déjeuné dans un restaurant français? (dans un restaurant mexicain? dans un restaurant italien? dans un restaurant chinois? dans un restaurant vietnamien?) Quand et avec qui?
8. Est-ce que tu mets la table chez toi? Qui a mis la table pour le petit déjeuner? Et pour le dîner?

3 Au restaurant

Vous êtes dans un restaurant français. Vous avez commandé *(ordered)* les choses suivantes. Le serveur a oublié *(forgot)* d'apporter le nécessaire (les ustensiles, etc.).

▶ pour le jus d'orange

Monsieur, je voudrais une verre pour le jus d'orange.

Pardon. Voici une verre.

1. pour l'eau minérale *(mineral water)*
2. pour le thé
3. pour la soupe
4. pour les frites
5. pour le steak
6. pour le gâteau *(cake)*

Leçon 33   **349**

COMMUNICATION: expressing opinions about food

■ **Language note: Un fast-food** (in official French, **un restaurant rapide**) is a restaurant that serves hamburgers, pizza, etc.

COMMUNICATION: answering personal questions

ROLE PLAY: asking for missing utensils

Cooperative pair practice Activity 3

COMMUNICATIVE FUNCTION:
Talking about food and beverages

33.2 Mini-scenes: Qu'est-ce que vous aimez manger?
33.3 Mini-scenes: Vous préférez les frites ou les spaghetti?
33.4 Mini-scenes: Qu'est-ce que vous préférez?
(26:05–28:22 min.)

Transparencies 46A, 46B
La nourriture et les boissons

Leçon 33, Sections 2, 3, 4

Pronunciation
• l'oeuf /lœf/
• les oeufs /lezø/

Supplementary vocabulary

LE PETIT DÉJEUNER
les oeufs brouillés scrambled eggs
les oeufs sur le plat fried eggs
le beurre de cacahuète peanut butter

LA VIANDE
le rôti roast
l'agneau lamb
le boeuf beef
le porc pork
une côtelette chop, cutlet

LE POISSON
le saumon salmon
la morue cod
la perche perch

B. La nourriture et les boissons

How to express food preferences:

— Est-ce que tu aimes **le poisson** (fish)?
— Oui, j'aime le poisson mais je préfère **la viande** (meat).
— Quelle viande est-ce que tu aimes?
— J'aime **le rosbif** (roast beef) et **le poulet** (chicken).

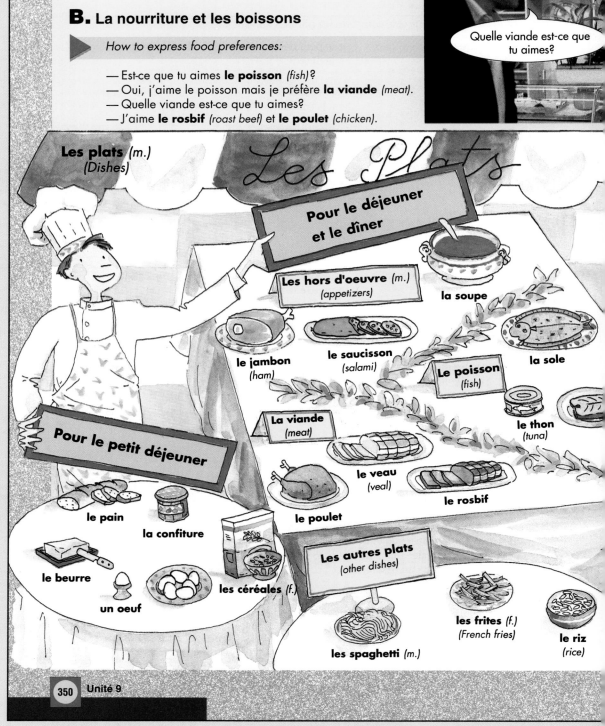

Quelle viande est-ce que tu aimes?

Les plats (m.) (Dishes)

Les Plats

Pour le déjeuner et le dîner

Les hors d'oeuvre (m.) (appetizers)

la soupe

le jambon (ham) le saucisson (salami)

Le poisson (fish)

la sole

le thon (tuna)

La viande (meat)

Pour le petit déjeuner

le veau (veal)

le rosbif

le pain

la confiture

le poulet

le beurre

Les autres plats (other dishes)

un oeuf

les céréales (f.)

les spaghetti (m.)

les frites (f.) (French fries)

le riz (rice)

Teaching strategy: Foods and beverages

Use Transparencies 46A and B to present the various foods and beverages. Since the partitive will not be introduced until Lesson 34, ask questions about students' likes and dislikes using the definite article.

X, est-ce que tu préfères le poulet ou le jambon?
Y, est-ce que tu aimes les céréales?
Z, est-ce que W aime la confiture? etc.

J'aime le rosbif et le poulet.

aimer	to like	Alice **aime** le poulet.
préférer	to prefer	Philippe **préfère** le rosbif.
détester	to hate	Paul **déteste** le poisson.

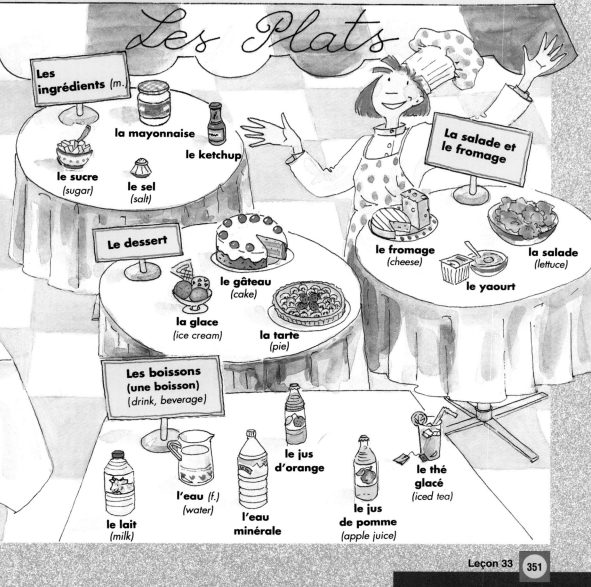

Les Plats

Les ingrédients (m.)

la mayonnaise

le ketchup

le sucre *(sugar)*

le sel *(salt)*

La salade et le fromage

le fromage *(cheese)*

la salade *(lettuce)*

le yaourt

Le dessert

le gâteau *(cake)*

la glace *(ice cream)*

la tarte *(pie)*

Les boissons (une boisson) *(drink, beverage)*

le jus d'orange

l'eau *(f.)* *(water)*

l'eau minérale

le lait *(milk)*

le jus de pomme *(apple juice)*

le thé glacé *(iced tea)*

Leçon 33 **351**

■ **Photo culture note**
Le rayon de charcuterie
Many French supermarkets have a deli counter (**un rayon de charcuterie**) where one can buy salami (**du saucisson**), sausages (**des saucisses**), slices of ham (**des tranches de jambon**), and all types of **pâtés**.

■ **Looking ahead:** Vegetables and fruits are activated in the next section of this lesson.

■ **Pronunciation**
• **le yaourt** /jaurt/
• **la mayonnaise** /majɔnɛz/
• **le ketchup** /kɛtʃœp/

Supplementary vocabulary

LES INGRÉDIENTS
le poivre *pepper*
l'huile *oil*
le vinaigre *vinegar*
la moutarde *mustard*
la sauce tomate
la margarine

At your discretion, you may want to introduce some common adult beverages:
le vin *wine*
la bière *beer*
le cidre *cider*

■ **Cultural note:** Soft drinks are usually ordered by brand name. All are masculine: **un Orangina, un Coca-cola,** etc.

■ **Language note**
In Quebec:
le yogourt /yogurt/ *yogurt*
un breuvage *beverage*
la crème glacée *ice cream*

💡 Critical Thinking: The French connection

Ask students: Which of the above food names have English cognates?

dessert < **dessert**	juice < **jus**;
salad < **salade**	sole < **sole**;
poultry < **poule**t	soup < **soupe**;
tart < **tarte**	

Which food names has English borrowed from French? [hors d'oeuvre, mayonnaise]

Which food names has French borrowed from English? [**le rosbif**, **le ketchup**]

COMMUNICATION:
expressing food preferences

4

1. le poulet
2. les frites
3. l'eau minérale
4. les oeufs
5. le yaourt
6. le fromage
7. le jambon
8. le thon
9. le gâteau
10. le thé glacé
11. le poisson
12. le riz
13. les céréales
14. le veau

↪ **Re-entry and review:** You
may wish to review the use of the
definite article in the general
sense; see page 156.

ROLE PLAY: asking a friend
5 to pass you food

1. le sel
2. le sucre
3. le beurre
4. le lait
5. le fromage
6. la confiture
7. l'eau

6 ROLE PLAY: choosing food

4 **Vous aimez ça?**

Dites si oui ou non vous
aimez les choses suivantes.

- J'aime …
- J'aime beaucoup …
- Je n'aime pas …
- Je déteste …

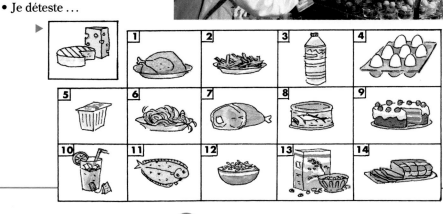

Je n'aime pas
le fromage.

J'aime le fromage.

5 **Dîner avec André**

Vous dînez avec André, un
ami canadien. Demandez
à André de passer les
choses suivantes.

▶ —S'il te plaît, André,
passe-moi le pain.
—Tiens. Voilà
le pain.
—Merci.

6 **La Petite Marmite**

Vous dînez au restaurant français La Petite Marmite. Le
garçon demande ce que vous préférez. Répondez-lui.

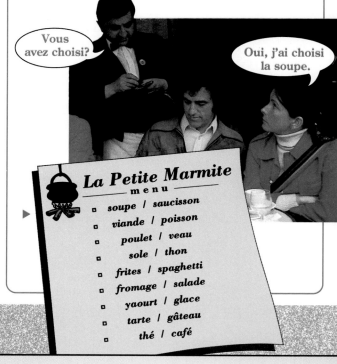

Vous
avez choisi?

Oui, j'ai choisi
la soupe.

La Petite Marmite
menu

□ soupe / saucisson
□ viande / poisson
□ poulet / veau
□ sole / thon
□ frites / spaghetti
□ fromage / salade
□ yaourt / glace
□ tarte / gâteau
□ thé / café

**Cooperative
pair practice**
Activities 5, 6, 7

T352

7 **Dans le réfrigérateur ou sur la table?**

Choisissez un produit et demandez à vos camarades où est le produit. Ils vont dire si le produit est dans le réfrigérateur ou sur la table.

▶ Où est la confiture?

Elle est sur la table.

- **Dans le réfrigérateur:**
  les oeufs
  le yaourt
  le beurre
  le jambon
  la mayonnaise,
  le gâteau
  le lait
- **Sur la table:**
  le poulet
  l'eau minérale
  les céréales
  le sel
  le riz
  le pain
  le ketchup
  la confiture

◼ **Language note:** In France, a refrigerator is often referred to as **un frigo** or **un frigidaire**.

8 **Les préférences**

Indiquez les préférences culinaires des personnes suivantes en complétant les phrases.

1. J'aime . . .
2. Je déteste . . .
3. Ma mère aime . . .
4. Mon petit frère (ma petite soeur) déteste . . .
5. Mon copain aime . . .
6. Ma copine déteste . . .
7. Les enfants aiment . . .
8. En général, les Italiens aiment . . .
9. En général, les Japonais aiment . . .

9 **Les courses** *(Food shopping)*

Vous passez les vacances en France avec votre famille. Faites la liste des courses pour les repas suivants.

▶ un repas végétarien

LISTE

▶ *Un repas*
végétarien:
— oeufs
— salade
— fromage
— pain
— yaourt
— eau minérale

1. un pique-nique à la campagne
2. un bon petit déjeuner
3. un repas d'anniversaire
4. le dîner de ce soir
5. le déjeuner de demain
6. un repas de régime *(diet)*

8 COMMUNICATION: expressing preferences

9 COMMUNICATION: writing shopping lists

Cooperative group practice

Have groups of 3 or 4 students work together to compose a shopping list for one of the meals suggested in Act. 9.

Each recorder (**secrétaire**) then reads aloud the shopping list that the group has prepared. The rest of the class tries to guess the corresponding menu.

Section C

COMMUNICATIVE FUNCTION:
Talking about fruits and
vegetables

33.5 Dialogue: Au
marché
33.6 Vignette culturelle:
Les courses
(28:23–31:29 min.)

Leçon 33, Section 5

■ **Pronunciation:** There is no
liaison (or elision) before **haricot**:
des haricots (le haricot)

COMMUNICATION:
10 indicating food preferences

■ **Variation:** This activity may be
done in pairs. See *Variation* to
Act. 1, p. T299.

EXCHANGES: describing
11 food purchases

1. des bananes et des poires
2. des carottes et des pommes de
   terre
3. des petits pois et des pample-
   mousses
4. des oranges et des pommes
5. des fraises et des cerises
6. des haricots verts et des
   carottes

C. **Les fruits et les légumes** *(Fruits and vegetables)*

▶ *How to shop for food:*

À la maison	Au marché
— Où vas-tu?	— Pardon, madame. Combien
— Je vais au **marché**.	coûtent les **pommes?**
Je vais **faire les courses** *(to do*	— Elles coûtent dix francs le kilo.
the food shopping).	— Donnez-moi deux **kilos de** pommes,
— Qu'est-ce que tu vas acheter?	s'il vous plaît.
— Je vais acheter des **tomates**	— Voilà. Ça fait vingt francs.
et des **oranges.**	

Où vas-tu?

Je vais au marché.

Pardon, madame. Combien coûtent les pommes?

Elles coûtent dix francs le kilo.

10 **Qu'est-ce que vous préférez?**
Indiquez vos préférences.

▶ pour le petit déjeuner: un oeuf ou des céréales?   **Je préfère des céréales.**

1. pour le petit déjeuner: un pamplemousse ou une banane?
2. après le déjeuner: une pomme ou une poire?
3. avec le poulet: des haricots verts ou des petits pois?
4. avec le steak: des pommes de terre ou des carottes?
5. comme *(as)* salade: une salade de tomates ou une salade de
   concombres *(cucumbers)*?
6. pour le dessert: une tarte aux cerises ou une tarte aux poires?
7. comme glace: une glace à la vanille ou une glace à la fraise?

11 **Les achats**
Vos copains reviennent du marché.
Demandez ce qu'ils ont acheté.

▶ —Qu'est-ce que tu as acheté au marché?
— J'ai acheté des carottes et des tomates.

**Cooperative
pair practice**
Activities 11, 12

TPR **Fruits and vegetables**

PROPS: Plastic fruits and vegetables

Place the items on a desk ("market stand").
Have students "buy" and distribute them.
**X, viens au marché et achète une
pomme.**
Maintenant, donne la pomme à Y.

Frequently ask who has what.
Qui a la pomme? [Y]   **Qui a l'orange?** [Z]

Les fruits (un fruit)

- une orange
- une banane
- une pomme
- une poire
- une fraise
- une cerise
- un pamplemousse

Les légumes (un légume *vegetable*)

- une tomate
- une pomme de terre
- une carotte
- une salade
- des petits pois (m.) *(peas)*
- des haricots verts (m.)

NOTE CULTURELLE

Le marché

In France, as in the United States, most people do their food shopping at the supermarket (**le supermarché**). However, to have fresher fruits and vegetables, many people still go to the local open-air market (**le marché**) where farmers come to sell their produce.

LES QUANTITÉS

une livre (de)	*pound*	**Donnez-moi**
un kilo (de)	*kilo (2.2 pounds)*	
une douzaine (de)	*dozen*	

une livre de tomates.
un kilo de pommes.
une douzaine d'oeufs.

---

12 **Au marché**

Vous êtes au marché. Demandez au vendeur combien coûtent certaines choses. Dites aussi quelle quantité vous voulez acheter.

Pardon, monsieur. Combien coûtent [les] pommes de terre?

Elles coûtent dix francs le kilo.

Alors, donnez-moi deux kilos de pommes de terre, s'il vous plait.

Voici. Ça fait vingt francs.

10 francs le kilo	18 francs la douzaine	12 francs la livre	16 francs la douzaine	15 francs la livre	14 francs le livre	12 francs le kilo	13 francs le kilo	20 francs la livre

| 1 douzaine | 1 livre | 2 douzaines | 3 livres | 1 livre | 3 kilos | 1 kilo | 1 livre |

Leçon 33 **355**

Cultural notes

- In general, farmers come to sell their produce on a given day of the week (**le jour du marché**). These open-air markets exist in large cities as well as in small villages.
- French people often buy food in speciality shops, such as:
  la boulangerie *(bakery)*
  la pâtisserie *(pastry shop)*
  la boucherie *(butcher shop)*
  la charcuterie *(delicatessen)*
  la crémerie *(dairy shop)*
  l'épicerie *(grocery store)*
- In the metric system, a pound (**une livre**) equals 500 grams or 1.1 U.S. pounds.

Supplementary vocabulary

LES FRUITS
un ananas /anana/ or /ananas/
un citron
un melon
le raisin *grapes*
une cerise
une pastèque *watermelon*
une pêche

LES LÉGUMES
un champignon *mushroom*
un choufleur *cauliflower*
un concombre
des épinards (m.) *spinach*
un oignon *onion*
un poivron *pepper*
une aubergine *eggplant*
une laitue
une salade

12 ROLE PLAY: Purchasing food at the market

■ **Teaching note:** The cues for this activity are written on the ends of the "boxes" at the bottom of the illustration.
- les oeufs / ça fait 18 F
- les fraises / ça fait 12 F
- les oranges / ça fait 32 F
- les haricots verts / ça fait 45 F
- les petits pois / ça fait 14 F
- les pommes / ça fait 36 F
- les poires / ça fait 13 F
- les cerises / ça fait 20 F

OPTIONAL: If the fruits and vegetables are light in weight and if the class is well behaved, manipulate the props as follows:
Y, donne-moi la pomme, s'il te plaît.
Attention, je vais lancer la pomme à X.
[Toss the apple to X.]

Qui a l'orange? X? Bien, lance l'orange à Y.

1 COMPREHENSION

■ Photo culture note
La Marine
"La Marine" is a seafood restaurant located in the harbor section of Deauville, an Atlantic Ocean resort on the coast of Normandy.

■ Teaching strategy: As a preparation for Act. 1, have students name the types of foods that might be on the menu in each of the restaurants. This list of foods could function as a point of departure for the dialogues.

🔲 Leçon 33, Section 6

2 GUIDED ORAL EXPRESSION

M: Est-ce que tu as faim?
J: Oui, j'ai très faim.
M: Est-ce que tu veux déjeuner?
J: Oui.
M: (Est-ce que) tu aimes la cuisine italienne?
J: Je préfère la cuisine française.
M: Tu aimes la viande?
J: Oui, mais j'aime aussi les légumes.
M: On déjeune à La Campagne?
J: D'accord.

🔲 Leçon 33, Section 7

---

1 Créa-dialogue

Vous êtes à Deauville avec un(e) ami(e). Essayez de découvrir *(try to discover)* ce que votre ami(e) aime manger. Proposez à votre ami(e) de déjeuner dans le restaurant correspondant à ses préférences.

▶ —Tu aimes <u>la viande</u>?
—Non, je n'aime pas <u>la viande</u>.
—Tu aimes <u>les légumes</u>?
—Non, je n'aime pas <u>les légumes</u>.
—Tu aimes <u>le poisson</u>?
—Oui, j'aime beaucoup <u>le poisson</u>.
—On déjeune <u>à La Marine</u>?
—D'accord.

la marine
spécialités de la mer

CHEZ RIGOLETTO
spécialités italiennes
1

AU PALAIS DES GLACES
spécialités de glaces
2

À la Normandie
spécialités de fromages
3

À LA CAMPAGNE
Restaurant végétarien
4

L'Auvergnat
spécialités de jambon
5

CHEZ OBÉLIX
spécialités de bonnes viandes
6

Au petit gourmand
ses glaces et ses gâteau
7

2 Conversation dirigée

Avec un(e) camarade, composez un dialogue basé sur les instructions suivantes. C'est samedi aujourd'hui. Ce matin Marc et Juliette ont fait des achats en ville. Il est midi et demi maintenant.

Marc			**Juliette**
asks Juliette if she is hungry	⇄	says she is very hungry	
asks her if she wants to have lunch	→ ↙	answers yes	
asks if she likes Italian cooking (**la cuisine italienne**)	→ ↙	says that she prefers French cooking	
asks her if she likes meat	→ ↙	says she does, but that she also likes vegetables	
suggests they go to La Campagne	→	accepts	

À votre tour

Depending on your goals and objectives, you may or may not wish to assign all of the activities in the **À votre tour** section.

🗣🗣 Cooperative practice

Act. 1 and 4 lend themselves to cooperative pair practice. They can also be done in trios, with two students performing and the third acting as monitor and following along in the Answer Key.

3 Composition: À la pension

This summer you are going to spend two weeks in France with your family. There are five people in your family and you are going to stay in a **pension** *(an inn offering a room and all meals)*. Write a letter to the owner saying what each family member likes or does not like to eat. Use your imagination.

> *le 18 mai*
> *Chère Madame,*
> *J'aime . . .*
> *Je n'aime pas . . .*
> *Mon père aime . . .*
> *Il n'aime pas . . .*
> *Ma mère . . .*
> *Mon frère . . .*
> *Ma sœur . . .*

4 Au «Départ»

Vous êtes à Paris avec des copains. Il est une heure et vous avez faim. Vous allez déjeuner dans le café suivant.

Regardez bien les illustrations.
- Comment s'appelle le café?
- Où est-il situé?

Regardez le menu et choisissez un sandwich ou une salade et un dessert (crêpe ou pâtisserie).
- Qu'est-ce que vous avez choisi?
- Combien coûte le sandwich ou la salade? le dessert?
- Quel est le prix total de votre repas?

1, Place Saint-Michel
75005 PARIS

3 WRITTEN SELF-EXPRESSION

4 READING COMPREHENSION

■ Realia notes

Le Départ
"Le Départ" is a small Parisian café-restaurant on the Left Bank (**la rive gauche**). The name of the restaurant recalls the nineteenth century when there used to be a train station across the street (**la gare Saint Michel**).
Note that in addition to mixed salads, sandwiches and pastries, one can also order **crêpes**.

Tarte Tatin
Tarte Tatin is an upside-down apple tart which is usually served warm.

Salades Composées

SALADE NIÇOISE 38,00
Salade, thon, olives, tomates, oeuf dur, anchois, poivron
Lettuce, tuna, olives, tomatoes, hard-boiled egg, anchovies, sweet pepper

SALADE 4 SAISON 30,00
Crudités de saison
Vegetables in season

SALADE SAINT-MICHEL 35,00
Salade, jambon épaule, comté, pomme fruit
Lettuce, ham, Comté cheese, apples

SALADE MIXTE 28,00
Salade, tomates, oeuf dur
Lettuce, tomatoes, hard-boiled egg

SALADE DE POULET 38,00
Salade, poulet, comté, mayonnaise
Lettuce, chicken, Comté cheese, mayonnaise

SALADE CAMPAGNARDE 38,00
Salade, pommes de terre à l'huile, cantal, jambon cru
Lettuce, potato salad, Cantal cheese, country ham

SALADE VERTE 17,00
Green salad

Sandwichs

Rillettes paysannes 14,00
Country minced potted pork

Paté du Quercy 14,00
Quercy style meat pie

Jambon de Paris 14,00
Paris ham

Saucisson d'Auvergne ... 14,00
Dry sausage from Auvergne

Le Végétarien 26,00
Salade, tomate, oeuf dur
Lettuce, tomato, hard-boiled egg

Fromage 14,00
Cheese

Mixte (jambon et gruyère) 26,00
Combination (ham and Gruyère cheese)

Club Sandwich 35,00
Poulet, tomate, oeuf dur, salade, mayonnaise
Chicken, tomato, hard-boiled egg, lettuce, mayonnaise

Saucisses chaudes 21,00
Hot sausages

Crêpes Maison

Crêpe au sucre 14,00
Pancake sprinkled with sugar

Crêpe à la confiture 18,00
Groseille, abricot, fraise
Pancake with red currant, apricot, or strawberry jam

Crêpe aux noix et crème de cassis 27,00
Pancake with nuts and black currant cream

Crêpe aux marrons et Chantilly 27,00
Pancake with chestnuts and whipped cream

Crêpe au miel 23,00
Pancake with honey

Crêpe au Grand-Marnier 27,00
Pancake with Grand-Marnier

Crêpe Belle-Époque 37,00
Banane fruit, glace vanille, noisettes, Chantilly
Pancake with bananas, vanilla ice cream, chestnuts, whipped cream

Crêpe au chocolat 23,00
Pancake with chocolate sauce

Pâtisseries

Tarte du jour 25,00
Tart of the day

Tarte aux pommes 22,00
Apple tart

Tarte aux fraises (selon saison) 29,00
Strawberry tart (in season)

Salade de fruits rafraîchis 21,00
Cold fruit salad

Gâteau du jour 25,00
Cake of the day

Tarte Tatin chaude 29,00
Hot Tatin tart

Tarte Tatin chaude, crème fraîche 33,00
Hot Tatin tart with cream

PRIX SERVIS COMPRIS (15%)

Portfolio assessment

You will probably select only one speaking activity and one writing activity to go into the students' portfolios for Unit 9.

In this lesson, Act. 1 can be used as an oral portfolio recording. Act. 3 is an excellent topic for a written portfolio piece.

À la cantine

Il est midi et demi. Sophie va à la cantine. Elle rencontre Jean-Paul.

MODULE 34:
Les courses
Total time: 7:02 min.
(Counter: 31:40 min.)

34.1 Dialogue: Le pique-nique
(31:49–34:17 min.)
34.2 Mini-scenes: Listening — Voici du pain
(34:18–35:40 min.)
34.3 Mini-scenes: Listening — Je prends du beurre?
(35:41–36:07 min.)
34.4 Mini-scenes: Speaking — Tu veux du pain?
(36:08–37:33 min.)
34.5 Vignette culturelle: Le petit déjeuner
(37:34–38:39 min.)

■ **Comprehension practice:** Play the entire module through as an introduction to the lesson.

 Leçon 34, Section 1

 COMPREHENSION

1. à midi et demi
2. Jean-Paul
3. non
4. Il aime le gâteau et la glace.
5. Oui. Il aime les desserts au menu (le gâteau et la glace).

SOPHIE:	Est-ce que tu veux déjeuner avec moi?
JEAN-PAUL:	Ça dépend. Qu'est-ce qu'il y a aujourd'hui?
SOPHIE:	Il y a du poisson!
JEAN-PAUL:	Du poisson?
SOPHIE:	Oui, du poisson.
JEAN-PAUL:	<u>Quelle horreur</u>! Bon, aujourd'hui, je ne veux pas déjeuner.
SOPHIE:	Il y a aussi du gâteau.
JEAN-PAUL:	Du gâteau! Hm . . .
SOPHIE:	Et de la glace!
JEAN-PAUL:	Une minute . . . je vais <u>prendre</u> un <u>plateau</u>.

How disgusting!

to take/tray

● Compréhension

1. À quelle heure est-ce que Sophie va déjeuner?
2. Qui est-ce qu'elle rencontre?
3. Est-ce que Jean-Paul aime le poisson?
4. Qu'est-ce qu'il aime?
5. Est-ce qu'il va déjeuner avec Sophie? Pourquoi?

Setting the scene

Ask questions about the school cafeteria.
Est-ce que vous déjeunez à la cantine de l'école? Si oui, levez la main.
Est-ce que vous aimez la nourriture?
Qu'est-ce que vous aimez particulière-ment?
Qu'est-ce que vous détestez?

Then have students read the opening text and the *Note culturelle* to find out what foods and beverages French students are served at school and what their reactions are.

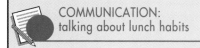
COMMUNICATION:
talking about lunch habits

Et toi?

1. En général, où est-ce que tu déjeunes?
2. À quelle heure est-ce que tu déjeunes?
3. En général, est-ce que tu aimes la nourriture de la cantine?
4. Qu'est-ce que tu fais quand tu n'aimes pas la nourriture de la cantine?

■ NOTE ■ CULTURELLE

À la cantine

Où est-ce que tu déjeunes pendant la semaine? Quand on habite près de l'école, on peut° rentrer à la maison. Quand on habite loin, on déjeune à la cantine. À midi, beaucoup de jeunes Français déjeunent à la cantine de leur école.

À la cantine, chacun° prend° un plateau et va chercher° sa nourriture. Cette nourriture est généralement bonne, abondante° et variée. Le menu change chaque° jour de la semaine. Un repas typique inclut° les plats suivants:

- **un hors d'oeuvre**
  salade de concombres,
  salade de pommes de terre,
  carottes râpées,° jambon ...
- **un plat principal° chaud**
  poulet, steak, côtelette de porc°
- **une garniture°**
  spaghetti, frites, petits pois,
  purée de pommes de terre°
- **une salade verte**
- **du fromage**
- **un dessert**
  glace ou fruit
- **une boisson**
  eau minérale, limonade, jus de fruit

Où est-ce que tu préférerais° déjeuner?
À ton école ou dans une école française?

peut *can* **chacun** *each one* **prend** *takes* **chercher** *to get* **abondante** *plentiful* **chaque** *each*
inclut *includes* **râpées** *grated* **principal** *main* **côtelette de porc** *pork chop* **garniture** *side dish*
purée de pommes de terre *mashed potatoes* **est-ce que tu préférerais** *would you prefer*

Leçon 34 **359**

Note culturelle

■ **Cultural notes**
- **une salade de concombres:** thinly sliced cucumbers served with an oil and vinegar dressing
- **une salade verte:** lettuce and vinaigrette, served after the main course
- **du fromage:** cheese is served as a separate course, after the salad

■ **Photo cultural note**
À la cantine
In school cafeterias in France, there are two ways of serving meals:
- family style (as shown in the top photo): the cafeteria personnel brings the dishes to the table and students serve themselves. There is no choice of menu.
- cafeteria style (as shown on the bottom photo): students take a tray (**un plateau**) and select what they want to eat.

🖵 Using the video

In the opening segment of Video Module 34, a father and son are sent to the supermarket to get food for a picnic. Students will see what a French supermarket looks like.

In the middle segments, people talk about various foods, often in contexts where they naturally use the partitive article.

The *Vignette culturelle* is filmed at Nathalie Aubin's house. The family members each explain what they usually have for breakfast.

Leçon 34, Section 2

↩ **Review and expansion:** The
je and **tu** forms of **vouloir** were
presented in Lessons 9 and 13.
Remind students that **vouloir** can
be followed by a noun or an
infinitive.

■ **Looking ahead:** The verbs
pouvoir and **devoir** are presented
in Lesson 35.

■ **Realia note:** Air Canada offers
an express package service similar to that provided by Federal
Express and UPS.

Supplementary vocabulary

vouloir dire *to mean*
Qu'est-ce que vous voulez dire?
What do you mean?
Qu'est-ce que ce mot veut dire?
What does that word mean?

 PRACTICE: describing
1 people's eating preferences

 COMPREHENSION:
indicating what people
2 want to do

 COMMUNICATION:
describing what one wants
3 and does not want to do

A. Le verbe *vouloir*

Note the forms of the irregular verb **vouloir** *(to want)*.

INFINITIVE	**vouloir**	
PRESENT	Je **veux** aller au café.	Nous **voulons** une glace.
	Tu **veux** déjeuner.	Vous **voulez** des spaghetti.
	Il/Elle/On **veut** dîner.	Ils/Elles **veulent** des frites.
PASSÉ COMPOSÉ	J'**ai voulu** dîner chez Maxim's.	

➡ When making a request, French people often use
je voudrais *(I would like)*, which is more polite than **je veux** *(I want)*.

　　Je voudrais un café.　　　**I would like** a cup of coffee.
　　Je voudrais dîner.　　　　**I would like** to have dinner.

➡ When accepting an offer, the French often use the expression **je veux bien.**
　　— Est-ce que tu veux déjeuner avec moi?　　*Do you want to have lunch with me?*
　　— Oui, **je veux bien.**　　　　　　　　　*Yes, **I do.** (Yes, I want to.)*

Où vous voulez.
Quand vous voule.
EXPRESS
AIR CANADA ⊛ CARGO

---

1 **Vive la différence!**

Nous sommes samedi. Des amis
vont en ville. Pour le déjeuner,
chacun veut faire des choses
différentes.

▶ Cécile / aller dans un café
　Cécile veut aller dans un café.

1. nous / manger des frites
2. toi / manger une pizza
3. vous / aller dans un restaurant
　italien
4. moi / aller dans un restaurant
　chinois
5. Patrick et Alain / déjeuner à midi
6. Isabelle / déjeuner à une heure

---

2 **Oui ou non?**

Dites si oui ou non les personnes entre
parenthèses veulent faire les choses indiquées.

▶ Il est midi. (nous / déjeuner?)
　Oui, nous voulons déjeuner.

▶ C'est samedi. (les élèves / étudier?)
　Non, les élèves ne veulent pas étudier.

1. Il fait froid. (Éric / jouer au foot?)
2. Il fait beau. (mes copains / aller à la plage?)
3. La nourriture est mauvaise. (vous / déjeuner
　à la cantine?)
4. Il y a des spaghetti. (moi / dîner?)
5. Il y a une excellente comédie. (toi / regarder
　la télé?)
6. C'est dimanche. (nous / travailler)

---

3 **Expression personnelle**

Complétez les phrases suivantes avec une expression personnelle.

1. Ce weekend, je voudrais …
　Je ne veux pas …
2. Cet été, je voudrais …
　Je ne veux pas …
3. Après l'école, je voudrais …
　Je ne veux pas …
4. Dans la vie *(life)*, je voudrais …
　Je ne veux pas …

B. Le verbe *prendre*

Note the forms of the irregular verb **prendre** *(to take)*.

INFINITIVE	prendre	
PRESENT	Je **prends** une pizza.	Nous **prenons** le train.
	Tu **prends** un sandwich.	Vous **prenez** l'avion.
	Il / Elle / On **prend** une salade.	Ils / Elles **prennent** des photos.
PASSÉ COMPOSÉ	J'**ai pris** un steak.	

➡ The singular forms of **prendre** follow the pattern of regular **-re** verbs. The plural forms are irregular.

Vocabulaire: Verbes comme *prendre*

prendre	*to take*	Nous **prenons** le métro.
	to have (food)	Est-ce que tu **prends** un café?
apprendre	*to learn*	Nous **apprenons** le français.
apprendre à + *inf.*	*to learn how to*	Sophie **apprend à** jouer de la guitare.
comprendre	*to understand*	Est-ce que vous **comprenez** quand le professeur parle français?

4 **Qu'est-ce qu'ils prennent?**

Dites ce que les personnes suivantes prennent. Pour cela, choisissez une expression logique de la liste.

▶ Philippe a faim.
Il prend un steak et des frites.

1. J'ai très soif.
2. Vous n'avez pas très faim.
3. Hélène a un nouvel appareil-photo.
4. Tu vas à l'aéroport.
5. Nous allons à l'école.
6. Les touristes vont à la Statue de la Liberté.

un bateau	une salade
un taxi	une limonade
le bus	un steak et des frites
des photos	

5 **Questions personnelles**

1. À quelle heure est-ce que tu prends le petit déjeuner le lundi? Et le dimanche?
2. Est-ce que tu prends le bus pour aller à l'école? Et tes copains?
3. Est-ce que tu prends des photos? Avec quel appareil?
4. Quand tu fais un grand voyage, est-ce que tu prends l'autocar? le train? l'avion?
5. Est-ce que tu apprends le français? l'italien? l'espagnol? Et ton copain?
6. Est-ce que tu apprends à jouer du piano? à jouer de la guitare? à faire du ski? à faire de la planche à voile?
7. Où est-ce que tu as appris à nager? À quel âge?
8. Est-ce que tu comprends bien quand le professeur parle français? Et les autres *(other)* élèves?
9. À ton avis, est-ce que les adultes comprennent les jeunes? Est-ce que les jeunes comprennent les adultes?

Leçon 34 **361**

Section B

COMMUNICATIVE FUNCTION:
Describing daily activities

■ **Pronunciation:** You may point out that **prendre** has three stems, all pronounced differently:
prend- /prã/
  je prends, tu prends, il prend
pren- /prən/
  nous prenons, vous prenez
prenn- /prɛn/
  ils prennent
Note: The "d" is silent in all the singular forms, and is dropped in the plural forms.

■ **Language note:** Remind students that *to take* a person somewhere is **amener**. (Also: *to take* a test is **passer** un examen.)

4 COMPREHENSION: describing what people are doing

1. Je prends une limonade.
2. Vous prenez une salade.
3. Elle prend des photos.
4. Tu prends un taxi.
5. Nous prenons le bus.
6. Ils prennent un bateau.

5 COMMUNICATION: answering personal questions

■ **Teaching strategy:** Help students with answer for item 7: **à l'âge de [huit] ans**

TPR 🏃 **Choosing foods**

PROPS: Pictures of various foods: salad, hamburger, sandwich, ice cream, etc.

Hold up the foods and pick one.
J'ai faim. Qu'est-ce que je vais prendre?
Bien, je prends un hamburger.

Have individual students select foods.
X, viens ici. Qu'est-ce que tu prends?
[X picks ice cream] **Ah, X prend une glace.**

Similarly present plural forms of **prendre**.
Y et Z, qu'est-ce que vous prenez?
[salad] **Ah bon, ils prennent une salade.**

Section C

COMMUNICATIVE FUNCTION:
Discussing quantities

**34.1 Dialogue: Le pique-
nique**

**34.2 Mini-scenes:
Listening — Voici du
pain**

**34.3 Mini-scenes:
Listening — Je
prends du beurre?**

**34.4 Mini-scenes:
Speaking — Tu veux
du pain?**
(31:49–37:33 min.)

Leçon 34, Section 3–6

Transparency 49
Le partitif

■ **Looking ahead:** This section
introduces the forms and basic
uses of the partitive article. This
concept is further developed in
Book Two.

C. L'article partitif: *du, de la*

Learning about language

The pictures on the left represent *whole*
items: a whole chicken, a whole cake, a
whole head of lettuce, a whole fish. The
nouns are introduced by INDEFINITE
ARTICLES: **un, une.**

The pictures on the right represent a *part*
or *some quantity* of these items: a serving
of chicken, a slice of cake, some leaves
of lettuce, a piece of fish. The nouns are
introduced by PARTITIVE ARTICLES: **du, de la.**

Voici . . .

un poulet	**du poulet**
un gâteau	**du gâteau**
une salade	**de la salade**
une sole	**de la sole**

Voilà . . .

FORMS

The PARTITIVE ARTICLE is used to refer to A CERTAIN QUANTITY or A CERTAIN AMOUNT OF SOMETHING and
corresponds to the English *some* or *any.* It has the following forms:

MASCULINE	**du**	*some*	**du** fromage, **du** pain
FEMININE	**de la**	*some*	**de la** salade, **de la** limonade

➡ Note that **du** and **de la** become **de l'** before a vowel sound.
   de l'eau minérale

Mangez chaque jour...
**du fromage, de la viande,
des fruits et du pain.**
Santé et Bien-être social
Canada
Health and Welfare
Canada

362 Unité 9

Teaching strategy

PROP: Transparency 49

Use Transparency 49 to present the differences between the indefinite article and
the partitive article.

Help students notice the difference
between *a whole item* (**un/une**) and *a part
or amount of something* (**du/de la**).

Voici un poulet. [pointing to transparency]
Voici du poulet. [pointing to transparency]
    Then have various students come up and
point to the corresponding items as you
mention them randomly in sentences. Mean-
while, students at their desks point to the
illustrations in their books. Begin slowly,
and then speak more rapidly.

USES

Note how the partitive article is used in the sentences below.

Philippe mange **du** fromage.	*Philippe is eating (some) cheese.*
Nous prenons **de la** salade.	*We are having (some) salad.*
—Est-ce que tu veux **du** lait?	*Do you want (any, some) milk?*
—Non, mais je voudrais **de l'**eau.	*No, but I would like some water.*

➡ While the words *some* or *any* are often omitted in English, the articles **du** and **de la** must be used in French.

➡ Partitive articles may also be used with nouns designating things other than foods and beverages. For example:

Tu as **de l'**argent?	*Do you have (any) money?*

Partitive articles are often, but not always, used after the following expressions and verbs.

voici	**Voici du** pain.	*Here is (some) bread.*
voilà	**Voilà de la** mayonnaise.	*Here is (some) mayonnaise.*
il y a	Est-ce qu'**il y a de la** salade?	*Is there (any) salad?*
acheter	Nous **achetons du** fromage.	*We are buying (some) cheese.*
avoir	Est-ce que tu **as de la** limonade?	*Do you have (any) lemon soda?*
manger	Marc **mange du** rosbif.	*Marc is eating (some) roast beef.*
prendre	Est-ce que vous **prenez du** café?	*Are you having (any) coffee?*
vouloir	Est-ce que tu **veux de la** glace?	*Do you want (any) ice cream?*

Voici un gâteau.

Voici du gâteau.

6 Le menu

Vous avez préparé un dîner pour le Club Français. Dites à un(e) camarade ce qu'il y a au menu.

▶ la viande — **Il y a de la viande.**

1. le rosbif	3. la salade	5. la glace	7. l'eau minérale
2. le poulet	4. le fromage	6. la tarte	8. le jus d'orange

Voici un poulet.
Je voudrais du gâteau.
Nous achetons du poulet.
Voilà une sole.

Tu prends de la sole?
Il y a une salade sur la table.
Je vais prendre de la salade.
Maman va faire un gâteau.

Cooperative pair practice
Activity 6

T363

7 EXCHANGES: offering food and beverages

■ **Photo culture note**
À table
Note the typically French checkered tablecloth (**une nappe à carreaux**).

8 COMPREHENSION/
PRACTICE: using the partitive

1. du sucre (du lait, de la crème)
2. du sucre (du lait, de la crème)
3. du sel
4. de la mayonnaise (de la moutarde, du jambon
5. du ketchup
6. de la moutarde (du ketchup)
7. du lait (du sucre)
8. du beurre (de la confiture)

■ **Variation** (dialogue format):
– Qu'est-ce que tu mets sur le pain?
– Je mets du beurre (de la confiture).

9 DESCRIPTION: describing food purchases

1. de la confiture 2. de l'eau minérale 3. du beurre 4. du café 5. du fromage 6. du poisson 7. du lait

10 DESCRIPTION: describing food purchases

■ **Expansion:** Have students say how much was paid for each item.
Jacqueline a pris une salade de tomates. Elle a payé 10 francs.

■ **Variation:** Have students choose only three items at the **Cochon d'Or** and say how much they paid.
J'ai pris du jambon, de la salade et de l'eau minérale. J'ai payé 32 francs.

Cooperative pair practice
Activities 7, 11

---

7 Au choix

Vous déjeunez avec votre famille. Offrez aux membres de votre famille le choix entre les choses suivantes. Ils vont indiquer leurs préférences.

▶ le lait ou l'eau minérale?

Tu veux du lait ou de l'eau minérale?

Je voudrais de l'eau minérale.

1. la soupe ou la salade?
2. le poisson ou la viande?
3. le rosbif ou le poulet?
4. le ketchup ou le mayonnaise?
5. le fromage ou la yaourt?
6. le beurre ou la margarine?
7. le gâteau ou la tarte?
8. le jus d'orange ou le jus de pomme?

9 Les courses

M. Simon a fait les courses. Dites ce qu'il a acheté.

▶ Il a acheté de la viande.

---

8 Qu'est-ce qu'on met?

Dites quels produits de la liste on met dans ou sur les choses suivantes.

▶ On met du beurre (de la confiture) sur le pain.

1. On met … dans le café.
2. On met … dans le thé.
3. On met … dans la soupe.
4. On met … dans un sandwich.
5. On met … sur un hamburger.
6. On met … sur un hot dog.
7. On met … dans les céréales.
8. On met … sur un toast.

le fromage
le jambon
le beurre
la confiture
le ketchup
la mayonnaise
le sel
la crème
le sucre
la moutarde (mustard)
le lait

10 Le cochon d'or

Jacqueline est allée au restaurant. Voici l'addition. Dites ce qu'elle a pris.

▶ Jacqueline a pris de la salade de tomates.

RESTAURANT
Le Cochon d'Or

salade de tomates	10F
jambon	12F
poulet	20F
salade	10F
fromage	12F
glace	15F
eau minérale	10F
café	8F
	97

Teaching project: Les repas

PROPS: One larger paper plate per student
Have students illustrate their paper plates with drawings or pictures of at least five food items for one meal of the day. (They should write their names on the back of the plate.) Then in smaller groups, students take turns telling what they have for the particular meal.

As a follow-up activity, collect the plates and redistribute them so that each student has another student's plate. Then have them write what this person is having. For example:
Pierre prend un hotdog, des frites avec du ketchup et de la salade. Comme dessert, il prend du gâteau et de la glace.

Au café

Au café, une cliente demande les choses suivantes. Le serveur apporte ces choses.

> S'il vous plaît, monsieur, je voudrais du café.

> Voici du café, mademoiselle.

ROLE PLAY: asking for **11** things in a restaurant

1. du pain
2. du sucre
3. du beurre
4. du yaourt
5. du thé
6. de l'eau
7. du jus d'orange
8. du sel
9. de la glace

 Menus

Préparez des menus pour les personnes suivantes. Dites ce que vous allez acheter pour chaque personne.

▶ une personne qui aime manger
  Je vais acheter du rosbif, du fromage, de la glace ...

1. une personne malade *(sick)*
2. un(e) athlète
3. un petit enfant
4. un végétarien (une végétarienne)

5. une personne qui veut maigrir
6. un invité *(guest)* japonais
7. une invitée française

COMPREHENSION:
12 preparing special menus

D. L'article partitif dans les phrases négatives

Note the forms of the partitive articles in the negative sentences below.

AFFIRMATIVE	NEGATIVE	
Tu manges **du jambon?**	Non, je **ne** mange **pas de** jambon.	*No, I don't eat ham.*
Tu veux **de la salade?**	Merci, je **ne** veux **pas de** salade.	*Thanks, I don't want any salad.*
Est-ce qu'il y a **de l'eau minérale?**	Non, il **n'**y a **pas d'eau** minérale.	*No, there is no mineral water.*

In negative sentences, the PARTITIVE ARTICLE follows the pattern:

du, de la (de l')	→	ne ... pas de (d')
Marc prend **du** café.		Éric **ne** prend **pas de** café.
Sophie prend **de la** limonade.		Alain **ne** prend **pas de** limonade.
Anne prend **de l'**eau.		Nicole ne prend **pas d'**eau.

Section D

COMMUNICATIVE FUNCTION:
Making negative statements

■ **Language note:** The same pattern occurs with **ne... jamais.**
Je **ne** prends **jamais de** sucre avec le café.

 Game: Menus

Prepare slips of paper numbered 1 to 7. Divide the class into seven groups, and distribute the numbered slips.

Each group prepares a menu for the corresponding guest in Act. 11 (e.g., group 2 sets up a menu for **un(e) athlète**).

The recorder (**secrétaire**) of each group then reads the menu:
Nous allons servir du rosbif, ...
The rest of the class tries to identify the guest.

ROLE PLAY: explaining one
doesn't have certain foods

PRACTICE: negative
sentences with the partitive

EXCHANGES: talking about
what one does and does not
eat

■ Photo culture note
À la cantine
In the cafeteria, French students
eat directly from the tray. On the
table you will note a pitcher of
water (**un pichet**).

EXCHANGES: describing
which foods are available-
and which are not

1. oui	6. non
2. non	7. oui
3. oui	8. non
4. non	9. non
5. oui	10. non

■ Variation: Ask students
whether these items are in their
refrigerators at home.
– **Et chez toi, est-ce qu'il y a du**
lait dans le réfrigérateur?
– **Oui, il y a du lait. (Non, il n'y a**
pas de lait.)

---

13 Un mauvais restaurant

Une cliente demande au serveur s'il y a
certaines choses au menu. Le serveur répond
négativement.

▶ le rosbif

Est-ce que vous avez
du rosbif?

Je regrette mademoiselle,
mais nous n'avons pas
de rosbif.

1. le jambon	6. le yaourt
2. le melon	7. le jus de pamplemousse
3. le thon	8. l'eau minérale
4. la sole	9. le champagne
5. le veau	

14 Au régime (On a diet)

Les personnes suivantes sont au
régime parce qu'elles veulent
maigrir. Répondez négativement
aux questions suivantes.

▶ — Est-ce qu'Anne mange
du pain?
— Non, elle ne mange pas
de pain.

1. Est-ce que Marc prend
de la mayonnaise?
2. Est-ce que Pauline veut
du gâteau?
3. Est-ce que Jean-Pierre mange
de la glace?
4. Est-ce qu'Alice prend du beurre?
5. Est-ce que Monsieur Ledodu
veut de la tarte?
6. Est-ce que Mademoiselle Poix
met de la crème dans son café?

15 Conversation

Demandez à vos camarades s'ils
mangent souvent les choses suivantes.

▶ du poisson

Est-ce que vous mangez
souvent du poisson?

Oui, je mange
souvent du poiss

Non, je ne mange pas
souvent de poisson.

1. de la glace	6. de la soupe
2. du veau	7. du rosbif
3. du pain français	8. du poulet
4. du fromage français	9. du thon
5. de la tarte aux fraises	

16 Dans le réfrigérateur

Vous préparez le dîner. Demandez à un(e)
camarade s'il y a les choses suivantes
dans le réfrigérateur.

▶ le lait —Est-ce qu'il y a du lait?
—Non, il n'y a pas de lait.

1. le jus d'orange?	6. l'eau minérale?
2. le pain?	7. le jus de pomme?
3. la glace?	8. le fromage?
4. le beurre?	9. la mayonnaise?
5. le jambon?	10. le ketchup?

Cooperative
pair practice
Activities 13, 14,
15, 16

⊞ Game: Qu'est-ce qu'il y a?
PROPS: Vocabulary cards and food items

Divide the class in half—Team A and
Team B. Place 5 cards backwards on the
chalkledge so that students cannot see the
pictures. Player A-1 guesses a food item:
Est-ce qu'il y a du pain?
[Oui, il y a du pain. (Non, ...)]

If A-1 guesses correctly, his/her team wins
a point. The teacher replaces the appropriate card with another one and the student guesses again. If not, player B-1 gets
a chance to guess, etc. The team with the
most points at the end of the game wins.
NOTE: It is easier to remember the position
of the cards if you alphabetize them as
you place them on the chalkledge.

E. Le verbe *boire*

Note the forms of the irregular verb **boire** *(to drink)*.

INFINITIVE	**boire**	
PRESENT	Je **bois** du lait.	Nous **buvons** du café.
	Tu **bois** de l'eau.	Vous **buvez** du thé glacé.
	Il/Elle/On **boit** du soda.	Ils/Elles **boivent** du jus d'orange.
PASSÉ COMPOSÉ	J'**ai bu** du jus de tomate.	

17 Pique-nique

Philippe a organisé un pique-nique avec ses amis. Chacun *(Each person)* boit quelque chose de différent.

▶ Philippe boit de l'eau.

| Philippe | 1. nous | 2. toi | 3. vous | 4. Cécile | 5. mes copains | 6. moi |

18 Expression personnelle

Complétez les phrases suivantes avec la forme appropriée du verbe **boire** et une expression de votre choix. Attention: utilisez le passé composé dans les phrases 6 à 8.

1. Au petit déjeuner, je …
2. Au petit déjeuner, mes parents …
3. À la cantine de l'école, nous …
4. Quand il fait chaud, on …
5. Quand il fait froid, on …
6. Hier soir au dîner, j' …
7. Hier matin, au petit déjeuner, ma mère …
8. À la dernière boum, nous …

Prononciation   ou /u/   u /y/

Les lettres «ou» et «u»

la p<u>ou</u>le   **le p<u>u</u>ll**

The letters "**ou**" always represent the sound /u/.

Répétez: /u/ **v<u>ou</u>s n<u>ou</u>s p<u>ou</u>let s<u>ou</u>pe
f<u>ou</u>rchette c<u>ou</u>teau d<u>ou</u>zaine**

The letter "**u**" always represents the sound /y/.

Répétez: /y/ **t<u>u</u> d<u>u</u> <u>u</u>ne lég<u>u</u>me j<u>u</u>s
s<u>u</u>cre bien s<u>û</u>r aven<u>u</u>e m<u>u</u>sée**

Now distinguish between the two vowel sounds:

Répétez: /u/ – /y/ **p<u>ou</u>le** *(hen)* – **p<u>u</u>ll**
r<u>ou</u>e *(wheel)* – **r<u>u</u>e**   **v<u>ou</u>s** – **v<u>u</u>e** *(view)*
je j<u>ou</u>e – **le j<u>u</u>s**

V<u>ou</u>s b<u>u</u>vez d<u>u</u> j<u>u</u>s de pamplem<u>ou</u>sse.
Je v<u>ou</u>drais de la s<u>ou</u>pe, d<u>u</u> p<u>ou</u>let et d<u>u</u> j<u>u</u>s de raisin.

Leçon 34 367

Section E

COMMUNICATIVE FUNCTION:
Talking about what one is drinking

17 PRACTICE: describing what people are drinking

1. du jus de raisin
2. de la limonade
3. du thé glacé
4. de l'eau minérale
5. du jus de pomme
6. de l'Orangina

■ **Variation:** Have students give sentences in the negative.
Philippe ne boit pas d'eau.

18 COMMUNICATION: describing beverage choices

Prononciation

🔲 Leçon 34, Section 8

■ **Teaching strategy:** If your students still have trouble pronouncing /y/, be sure they pronounce the vowel as /i/. Then have them repeat the word, rounding their lips as if to whistle. For example, to pronounce **du**, first say **di**. Then repeat **di** with rounded lips. The resulting word will be quite close to **du**.

TPR 🏃 Drinking beverages

PROPS: Vocabulary cards of beverages

Hold up the beverages and pick one.
J'ai soif. Qu'est-ce que je vais boire? [gesture "drinking" milk]
Normalement je bois du lait.
Have individual students select beverages.
X, viens ici. Qu'est-ce que tu bois?

[X picks water] **Ah, X boit de l'eau.**
Similarly present plural forms of **boire**.
Y et Z, qu'est-ce que vous buvez? [coffee]
Tiens, Y et Z boivent du café.
Moi aussi, je vais boire du café.
Nous trois, nous buvons du café.

À votre tour!

1 COMPREHENSION

1-d   4-e
2-a   5-c
3-b

🎧 Leçon 34, Section 9

2 GUIDED ORAL EXPRESSION

💻 **34.5 Vignette culturelle: Le petit déjeuner** (37:34–38:39 min.)

🎧 Leçon 34, Section 7

3 GUIDED ORAL EXPRESSION

1. du rosbif, de la salade et de la glace
2. du poulet, du fromage et du yaourt
3. du fromage, du lait et du thon
4. de l'eau minérale et du jus de raisin
5. de la glace et du jus d'orange
6. (answers will vary)
7. (answers will vary)

🎧 Leçon 34, Section 10

1 Allô!

Reconstituez la conversation entre Frédéric et Sandrine. Pour cela, faites correspondre les réponses de Sandrine avec les questions de Frédéric.

1. Tu dînes au restaurant ce soir?

2. Tu as fait les courses?

3. Qu'est-ce que tu as acheté?

4. Tu n'as pas acheté de viande?

5. C'est vrai. Et pour le dessert, tu as acheté de la glace?

a. Oui, je suis allée au supermarché ce matin.
b. Du riz, des oeufs, de la salade et du fromage.
c. Non, j'ai pris un gâteau au chocol
d. Non, j'ai invité mon copain Fabie à dîner chez moi.
e. Mais non, tu sais (know) bien que Fabien est végétarien.

2 Dis-moi …

I will tell you about my breakfast this morning.

- J'ai pris le petit déjeuner à sept heures.
- J'ai mangé du pain avec du beurre et de la confiture.
- J'ai bu du café noir.

Now choose one of the meals you had yesterday and tell me …
- *at what time you had that meal*
- *what you ate*
- *what you drank*

3 Créa-dialogue

Avec vos camarades, décrivez où vous êtes allés et ce que vous avez fait aux endroits suivants.

**au supermarché
acheter**

Où est-tu allée?

Qu'est-ce que tu as acheté?

Je suis allée au supermarch

J'ai acheté du pain, du lait et de la confiture.

À votre tour

Depending on your goals and objectives, you may or may not wish to assign all of the activities in the **À votre tour** section.

👥 Cooperative practice

Act. 1 and 3 lend themselves to cooperative pair practice. Act. 3 can also be done in trios, with two students performing and the third acting as monitor and following along in the Answer Key.

4 Situation

Avec un(e) camarade, composez un dialogue correspondant à la situation suivante et jouez ce dialogue en classe.

You are talking to Florence, a French friend (played by your classmate). You have just invited her for dinner, but you understand she is on a special diet. Try to find out:

• what she eats
• what she does not eat
• what she drinks
• what she does not drink

5 Conversation libre

Avec un(e) camarade, composez un dialogue original basé sur la situation suivante.

You and your friend Caroline are in charge of the French Club picnic. Now you are walking up and down the aisles of a supermarket, discussing what things to buy or not to buy. For example:

▶ —Est-ce qu'on achète du pain?
—Oui, achetons du pain.
(Non, n'achetons pas de pain. J'ai du pain à la maison.)

6 Composition: Un bon repas

Think of a nice meal you had not too long ago — perhaps for a birthday or special holiday. Using the passé composé, write a short paragraph in which you describe . . .

• when, where, and with whom you had that meal
• what you ate and drank

Comment dit-on . . . ?

How to show your appreciation for good food:

Hm. . . C'est délicieux!   C'est exquis!   C'est fameux!

1. à la cantine manger	2. au restaurant manger	3. au marché acheter	4. à la boum boire

5. à la cuisine prendre	6. au café boire	7. dans un restaurant chinois ??

Leçon 34   369

---

4 GUIDED ORAL EXPRESSION

5 CONVERSATION

6 WRITTEN SELF-EXPRESSION

■ **Teaching strategy:** You may suggest supplementary vocabulary, such as:
la dinde *(turkey)*
le maïs /mais/ *(corn)*
le homard *(lobster)*
le rôti *(roast)*

Classroom Notes

▮ Portfolio assessment

You will probably select only one speaking activity and one writing activity to go into the students' portfolios for Unit 9.

In this lesson, Act. 2 and 3 can be adapted as oral portfolio recordings.

Act. 6 is an excellent topic for a written portfolio piece.

MODULE 35:
Un client difficile
Total time: 7:40 min.
(Counter: 34:48 min.)

35.1 Dialogue: Un client difficile
(39:09–41:25 min.)
35.2 Mini-scenes: Listening — Apportez-moi du poulet
(41:26–42:54 min.)
35.3 Mini-scenes: Speaking — Qu'est-ce que tu veux?
(42:55–43:47 min.)
35.4 Vignette culturelle: La recette des crêpes
(43:48–46:21 min.)

■ **Comprehension practice:** Play the entire module through as an introduction to the lesson.

 35.1 Dialogue: Un client difficile
(39:09–41:25 min.)

▭▭ **Leçon 35, Section 1**

LEÇON 35 Un client difficile

M. Ronchon a beaucoup d'appétit . . . mais pas beaucoup de patience. <u>En fait</u>, M. Ronchon est rarement <u>de bonne humeur</u>. Et quand il est de mauvaise humeur, c'est un client difficile. Aujourd'hui, <u>par exemple</u>, au restaurant . . .

As a matter of fa[ct]
a good mood
for instance

—<u>Garçon!</u> — *Waiter!*
— J'arrive! — *I'm coming!*
— Qu'est-ce que vous avez <u>comme</u> hors d'oeuvre? — *as, for*
— Nous avons du jambon et du saucisson.
— Apportez-moi <u>tout ça</u> . . . avec du pain et du beurre! — *all of that*
— Bien, monsieur.

—Et comme boisson, qu'est-ce que je vous apporte?
—Donnez-moi de l'eau minérale . . . <u>Dépêchez-vous!</u> J'ai soif! — *Hurry up!*

—Apportez-moi du poulet et des frites. . . <u>Vite!</u> J'ai très faim! — *Fast!*
—Je vous apporte ça <u>tout de suite</u>. — *right away*

—Et apportez-moi aussi du fromage, de la glace, de la tarte aux pommes et de la tarte aux <u>abricots</u>. . . Mais, qu'est-ce que vous attendez? — *apricots*
—Tout de suite, monsieur, tout de suite.

—Mais qu'est-ce que vous m'apportez?
—Je vous apporte l'<u>addition</u>! — *check*

370

Setting the scene

This comic scene is much more effective if presented by video. If this is not possible, play the corresponding cassette segment which has been taken from the video soundtrack.

Making crêpes

The *Vignette culturelle*, Part 4 of Video Module 35, shows how to make **crêpes**. If students ask, a **crêpe** recipe can be found at the end of Entracte 9, pp. 396–397.

Compréhension

1. En général, est-ce que M. Ronchon est de bonne humeur ou de mauvaise humeur?
2. Qu'est-ce qu'il va prendre comme hors d'oeuvre?
3. Qu'est-ce qu'il va prendre comme plat principal *(main course)*?
4. Qu'est-ce qu'il va boire?
5. Qu'est-ce qu'il va manger comme dessert?
6. Qu'est-ce que le garçon apporte après le dessert?
7. Quelle est la réaction de M. Ronchon? Est-ce qu'il est de bonne humeur ou de mauvaise humeur?

Et toi?

1. En général, est-ce que tu es de bonne humeur?
2. Et aujourd'hui, est-ce que tu es de bonne humeur ou de mauvaise humeur?
3. En général, est-ce que tu as beaucoup d'appétit?
4. Est-ce que tu es une personne patiente?
5. Quand tu vas au restaurant avec un copain (une copine), qui paie l'addition?

■ NOTE ■ CULTURELLE

Les restaurants français et la cuisine française

Les Français aiment manger chez eux, mais ils aiment aussi aller au restaurant. Pour les gens pressés,° il y a les «self-service», les «fast foods» et les pizzerias.

Pour les gens qui veulent faire un bon repas, il y a toutes° sortes de restaurants spécialisés: auberges,° restaurants régionaux, restaurants de poisson, . . . Il y a aussi les «grands restaurants» où la cuisine est extraordinaire . . . et très chère!

La cuisine française a une réputation internationale. Pour beaucoup de personnes, c'est la meilleure° cuisine du monde.°

Les Américains ont emprunté° un grand nombre de mots° au vocabulaire de la cuisine française. Est-ce que tu connais les mots suivants: **soupe, sauce, mayonnaise, omelette, filet mignon, tarte, purée, soufflé?** Est-ce que tu aimes **les croissants? les crêpes? la mousse au chocolat?**

pressés *in a hurry*   toutes *all*   auberges *country inns*
meilleure *best*   du monde *in the world*
ont emprunté *have borrowed*   mots *words*

Leçon 35   371

COMPREHENSION

1. Il est de mauvaise humeur.
2. du jambon, du saucisson, du pain et du beurre
3. du poulet et des frites
4. de l'eau minérale
5. du fromage, de la glace, de la tarte aux pommes et de la tarte aux abricots
6. l'addition
7. Il est furieux.

COMMUNICATION: describing one's personality

Note culturelle

■ **Teaching strategy:** First, have the students pronounce the borrowed French words in boldface type as we do in English. The have them try to pronounce the words "sounding French."

■ **Photo culture notes**
Le Procope
This photo was taken in the **Café Procope** which was founded in 1689 and is the oldest café in Paris. Its walls are decorated with portraits of some of its most famous patrons: Voltaire, Robespierre, Napoléon Bonaparte, Musset, etc.

La cuisine française
Most people who appreciate fine cooking consider French cuisine to be the best in the world. French chefs (**un chef**) like to create new dishes that will enhance their reputations. In France the top chefs enjoy the status of superstars.

Section A

COMMUNICATIVE FUNCTION:
Referring to oneself and to
those one is addressing

A. Les pronoms compléments *me, te, nous, vous*

In the sentences below, the pronouns in heavy print are called OBJECT PRONOUNS. Note the form and the position of these pronouns in the sentences below.

Anne **me** parle.	Elle **m'**invite.	*Anne talks to me.*	*She invites me.*
Mes amis **te** parlent.	Ils **t'**invitent.	*My friends talk to you.*	*They invite you.*
Tu **nous** parles.	Tu **nous** invites.	*You talk to us.*	*You invite us.*
Je **vous** parle.	Je **vous** invite.	*I am talking to you.*	*I invite you.*

FORMS

The OBJECT PRONOUNS that correspond to the subject pronouns **je, tu, nous, vous** are:

me ↓ m' (+ VOWEL SOUND)	me, to me	**nous**	us, to us
te ↓ t' (+ VOWEL SOUND)	you, to you	**vous**	you, to you

Cette carte **vous** donne l'accès à 60 musées.

CARTE
MUSÉES ET MONUMENTS

POSITION

In French, object pronouns usually come *before* the verb, according to the following patterns:

AFFIRMATIVE			NEGATIVE				
SUBJECT + OBJECT PRONOUN + VERB …			SUBJECT + **ne** + OBJECT PRONOUN + VERB + **pas** …				
Paul	**nous**	invite.	Éric	**ne**	**nous**	invite	**pas.**

1 EXCHANGES: asking
friends to do things for you

■ **Variation** (response in the negative):
Non, je ne te téléphone pas.

■ **Variation** (in the plural):
– Tu nous téléphones?
– Oui, je vous téléphone.

■ **Photo culture note**
Les vélos
Note the different types of cycles used by students:
• mountain bikes (**un VTT** or **un vélo tout terrain**)
• racing bicycles (**un vélo de course**)
• mopeds (**une mobylette**)

1 D'accord!

Demandez à vos camarades de faire les choses suivantes pour vous.
Ils sont d'accord pour faire ces choses.

▶ téléphoner ce soir?

1. téléphoner demain?
2. attendre après la classe?
3. inviter à ta boum?
4. inviter à dîner?
5. rendre visite ce weekend?
6. rendre visite cet été?
7. acheter une glace?
8. apporter un sandwich?
9. vendre ta raquette?
10. écouter?

Tu me téléphones ce soir?

D'accord, je te téléphone ce soir.

Cooperative
pair practice
Activities 1, 2

Teaching strategy: Object pronouns

The introduction of **me, te, nous, vous** before **le, la, les, lui, leur** serves two purposes:
• These pronouns are very useful in conversation.
• Students can practice sentence word order with these pronouns without

having to make the distinction between direct and indirect objects.
The third person pronouns are presented in Lesson 36.

2 Pauvre Nathalie!

Stéphanie a de la chance. Sa copine Nathalie n'a pas de chance. Jouez les deux rôles.

▶ mon copain/inviter

1. ma tante/inviter au restaurant
2. mes cousins/téléphoner souvent
3. mon frère/écouter
4. mes parents/comprendre
5. mes voisins/inviter à dîner
6. ma copine/aider avec mes devoirs
7. mon grand-père/acheter des cadeaux *(gifts)*
8. mes amis/attendre après la classe

Mon copain m'invite.

Tu as de la chance. Mon copain ne m'invite pas.

Vocabulaire: Les services personnels

aider quelqu'un	to help	J'**aide** mes copains avec les devoirs.
amener quelqu'un	to bring	Le taxi **amène** les touristes à la gare *(train station)*.
apporter quelque chose à quelqu'un	to bring	Le serveur **apporte** le menu **aux** clients.
donner quelque chose à quelqu'un	to give	Mme Marin **donne** 10 francs **à** sa fille.
montrer quelque chose à quelqu'un	to show	Est-ce que tu **montres** tes photos **à** ton copain?
prêter quelque chose à quelqu'un	to lend, loan	Est-ce que tu **prêtes** tes disques **à** tes amis?

---

3 Questions personnelles

Réponds affirmativement ou négativement aux questions suivantes.

1. Est-ce que tes copains t'aident avec tes devoirs?
2. Est-ce que ta mère ou ton père t'aide avec les devoirs de français?
3. Est-ce que ton père ou ta mère te prête sa voiture?
4. Est-ce que ton frère ou ta soeur te prête ses disques?
5. Est-ce que tes profs te donnent des conseils *(advice)*?
6. Est-ce que ton copain te montre ses photos?
7. Est-ce que tes cousins t'apportent des cadeaux *(gifts)* quand ils viennent chez toi?
8. Est-ce que tes parents t'amènent au restaurant pour ton anniversaire?

SAMEDI leçons et devoirs

MATIÈRES	pour le	TEXTES
histoire	lundi	questions 1-15 page 475
français	mardi	examen chapitre 8

Leçon 35 373

---

2 ROLE PLAY: describing others' actions

■ **Teaching note:** Remind students to use **pas de** in item 7.

■ **Variation** (with ne... jamais): Mon copain ne m'invite jamais.

▷ **Vocabulaire**

■ **Language note:** The verbs **donner**, **montrer**, and **prêter** are new.

↩ **Re-entry and review:** You may want to review the conjugation of **amener**:
j'amène, nous amenons, etc.
Remind students of the distinction between **amener** *(to bring people)* and **apporter** *(to bring things)*.

🔊 Leçon 35, Section 2

3 COMMUNICATION: answering personal questions

■ **Realia note**
Le cahier de texte
French students are often required to buy special notebooks of the type pictured here (**un cahier de texte**) in which they write down their daily homework assignments.

4 Bons services

Informez-vous sur les personnes suivantes. Dites ce que leurs amis ou leurs parents font pour eux. Pour cela, complétez les phrases avec les pronoms **me (m')**, **te (t')**, **nous** ou **vous**.

▶ J'organise une boum.   **Ma soeur me prête ses cassettes.**
▶ Nous avons faim.   **Cécile nous apporte des sandwichs.**

1. Nous organisons un pique-nique. Nos copains … aident.
2. Tu as soif. Je … apporte un soda.
3. Vous préparez l'examen. Le prof … donne des conseils *(advice)*.
4. J'ai besoin d'argent. Mon cousin … prête cent francs.
5. Tu es chez les voisins. Ils … montrent leur appartement.
6. Nous sommes à l'hôpital. Nos amis … rendent visite.
7. Vous êtes sympathiques. Je … invite chez moi.
8. Nous allons prendre l'avion. Le taxi … amène à l'aéroport.
9. Je nettoie le garage. Mon frère … aide.

"QUAND ON ME CHERCHE, ON ME TROUVE."
EUROSIGNAL
TELECOMMUNICATIONS

B. Les pronoms compléments à l'impératif

Compare the position and the form of the object pronouns when the verb is in the imperative.

AFFIRMATIVE	NEGATIVE
Téléphone-**moi** ce soir!	Ne **me** téléphone pas demain!
Invite-**moi** samedi!	Ne **m'**invite pas dimanche!
Apporte-**nous** du thé!	Ne **nous** apporte pas de café!

When the IMPERATIVE verb is AFFIRMATIVE, the object pronouns come *after* the verb.
➡ **me** becomes **moi**
When the imperative verb is negative, the object pronouns come *before* the verb.

5 Prêts *(Loans)*
Demandez à vos copains de vous prêter les choses suivantes. Ils vont accepter.

Prête-moi ta raquette!

Tiens, voilà ma raquette.

Merci.

374 Unité 9

TPR ⚡ **Showing and distributing things**

PROPS: Miscellaneous objects from Lesson 33 (plastic fruits and vegetables; picnicware)

Place the objects on a table. Show and give the class certain items but not others.
Je vous montre une tasse. [hold up cup]
Je ne vous montre pas le verre. [hide glass]

Then call on students.
X, viens ici. Montre-nous la pomme.
Ne nous montre pas l'orange.
Y, viens ici et donne-moi le couteau.
Ne me donne pas la fourchette.
Donne la fourchette à Z.
Z, ne me montre pas la fourchette.
Passe la fourchette à W. …

6 À Paris

Vous visitez Paris. Demandez certains services aux personnes suivantes.

▶ au garçon de café *(waiter)*
  • apporter un sandwich
  S'il vous plaît, apportez-moi un sandwich.

1. au garçon de café
  • apporter de l'eau
  • apporter une limonade
  • donner un croissant

2. à la serveuse *(waitress)* du restaurant
  • montrer le menu
  • donner du pain
  • apporter l'addition *(check)*
3. au chauffeur de taxi *(cab driver)*
  • amener au musée d'Orsay
  • montrer Notre-Dame
  • aider avec les bagages
4. à un copain parisien
  • téléphoner ce soir
  • donner ton adresse
  • prêter ton plan *(map)* de Paris

7 Quel service?

Demandez à vos camarades certains services. Pour cela complétez les phrases en utilisant ces verbes.

aider	amener	apporter
donner	montrer	prêter

▶ J'ai soif. … de la limonade.
  S'il te plaît, <u>apporte-moi</u> (<u>donne-moi</u>) de la limonade.

1. Je ne comprends pas les devoirs de maths.
2. Je voudrais téléphoner à ta cousine.
3. Je n'ai pas d'argent pour aller au cinéma.
4. Je voudrais voir tes photos.
5. J'ai soif.
6. J'organise une boum.
7. Je vais peindre *(to paint)* ma chambre.
8. Je vais à l'aéroport.
9. Je ne sais pas où tu habites.

▶ J'ai faim. … un sandwich
  S'il te plaît, <u>apporte-moi</u> (<u>donne-moi</u>) un sandwich.

… avec le problème.
… son numéro de téléphone.
… six dollars.
… tes photos.
… de l'eau minérale.
… tes disques.
… avec ce projet.
… là-bas avec ta voiture.
… ton adresse.

8 Non!

Proposez à vos camarades de faire les choses suivantes pour eux. Ils vont refuser et donner une explication.

▶ téléphoner ce soir (Je ne suis pas chez moi.)

1. téléphoner demain soir (Je dois faire mes devoirs.)
2. inviter ce weekend (Je vais à la campagne.)
3. inviter dimanche (Je dîne chez mes cousins.)
4. attendre après la classe (Je dois rentrer chez moi.)
5. prêter mes disques (Je n'ai pas de chaîne stéréo.)
6. acheter un sandwich (Je n'ai pas faim.)
7. rendre visite ce soir (Je vais au cinéma.)

Je te téléphone ce soir?

Non, ne me téléphone pas. Je ne suis pas chez moi.

Leçon 35 **375**

ROLE PLAY: asking for services
6

■ **Teaching note:** Have students use the **vous** form in items 1, 2, and 3; and the **tu** form in item 4.

■ **Expansion:** Have students make original requests to the people in items 1–4. Sample answers:
1. S'il vous plaît, apportez-moi le menu.
2. S'il vous plaît, apportez-moi (donnez-moi) du buerre.
3. S'il vous plaît, amenez-moi au musée du Louvre.
4. S'il te plaît, montre-moi la tour Eiffel.

COMPREHENSION: asking for appropriate services
7

1. Aide-moi…
2. Donne-moi (Montre-moi)…
3. Prête-moi…
4. Montre-moi…
5. Donne-moi (Apporte-moi)…
6. Prête-moi…
7. Aide-moi…
8. Amène-moi…
9. Donne-moi…

EXCHANGES: asking friends not to do things
8

■ **Teaching note:** Remind students to use **pas de** in item 6.

T375

[cassette] **Leçon 35, Section 5**

🔄 **Review and expansion:** The **je** form of **devoir** and the **je** and **tu** forms of **pouvoir** were introduced in Lesson 13.

■ **Teaching strategy:** Have students note how the forms of **pouvoir** are similar to those of **vouloir**.

■ **Language notes:**
• In writing, the accent circonflexe appears on the past participle **dû** to distinguish it from the partitive article **du**.
• **Devoir** + noun means *to owe*. **Je dois** dix francs à Hélène.

9 COMPREHENSION: determining shopping options

1. Ils peuvent acheter un disque.
2. Je peux acheter une veste.
3. Tu peux acheter des chaussures.
4. Vous pouvez acheter un appareil-photo.
5. Elle peut acheter un pantalon.
6. Nous pouvons acheter une raquette.
7. Il peut acheter des livres.

[icon] **Cooperative pair practice**
Activity 10

C. Les verbes *pouvoir* et *devoir*

FORMS

Note the forms of the irregular verbs **pouvoir** *(can, may, be able)* and **devoir** *(must, have to)*.

INFINITIVE	pouvoir	devoir
PRESENT	Je **peux** venir. Tu **peux** travailler. Il / Elle / On **peut** voyager. Nous **pouvons** dîner ici. Vous **pouvez** rester. Ils / Elles **peuvent** aider.	Je **dois** rentrer avant midi. Tu **dois** gagner de l'argent. Il / Elle / On **doit** visiter Paris. Nous **devons** regarder le menu. Vous **devez** finir vos devoirs. Ils / Elles **doivent** mettre la table.
PASSÉ COMPOSÉ	J'**ai pu** étudier.	J'**ai dû** faire mes devoirs.

USES

• **Pouvoir** has several English equivalents.

can	Est-ce que tu **peux** venir au pique-nique?	*Can you come to the picnic?*
may	Est-ce que je **peux** prendre la voiture?	*May I take the car?*
to be able	Jacques ne **peut** pas réparer sa mobylette.	*Jacques is not able to fix his moped.*

• **Devoir** is used to express an OBLIGATION.

must	Vous **devez** faire vos devoirs.	*You must do your homework.*
to have to	Est-ce que je **dois** nettoyer ma chambre?	*Do I have to clean my room?*

➡ **Devoir** is usually followed by an infinitive. It cannot stand alone.

Est-ce que tu **dois étudier** ce soir?   *Do you have to study tonight?*
Oui, je **dois étudier.**   *Yes, I have to (study).*
Non, je **ne dois pas étudier.**   *No, I don't have to (study).*

9 **Le coût de la vie** *(The cost of living)*
Décrivez ce que les personnes suivantes peuvent acheter avec leur argent.

▶ Philippe a quatre-vingts francs.
  Il peut acheter des lunettes de soleil.

1. Alice et Françoise ont cinquante francs.
2. J'ai cinq cents francs.
3. Tu as trois cent cinquante francs.
4. Vous avez trois cents francs.
5. Ma copine a deux cent cinquante francs.
6. Nous avons deux cents francs.
7. Mon petit frère a trente francs.

10 Obligations?

Demandez à vos camarades s'ils doivent faire les choses suivantes.

▶ étudier?

1. étudier ce soir?
2. nettoyer ta chambre?
3. mettre la table?
4. réussir à l'examen?
5. aller chez le dentiste cette semaine?
6. parler au professeur après la classe?

Est-ce que tu dois étudier?

Oui, je dois étudier.

(Non, je ne dois pas étudier.)

7. être poli(e) *(polite)* avec tes voisins?
8. rentrer chez toi après la classe?

11 Excuses

Thomas demande à ses amis de repeindre *(to repaint)* sa chambre avec lui, mais chacun a une excuse. Dites que les personnes suivantes ne peuvent pas aider Thomas. Dites aussi ce qu'elles doivent faire.

▶ Hélène (étudier)
Hélène ne peut pas aider Thomas. Elle doit étudier.

1. nous (faire les courses)
2. Lise et Rose (acheter des vêtements)
3. moi (aider ma mère)
4. toi (nettoyer le garage)
5. Alice (rendre visite à sa grand-mère)
6. vous (déjeuner avec vos cousins)
7. mon frère et moi (laver la voiture)
8. Nathalie et toi (préparer l'examen)

12 Expression personnelle

Complétez les phrases suivantes avec vos idées personnelles.

1. Chez moi, je peux …
   Je ne peux pas …
2. À l'école, nous devons …
   Nous ne devons pas …
3. À la maison, je dois …
   Mes frères (Mes soeurs) doivent …
4. Quand on est riche, on peut …
   On doit …
5. Quand on est malade *(sick)*, on doit …
   On ne doit pas …
6. Quand on veut maigrir, on doit …
   On ne peut pas …

Prononciation — s /z/   ss /s/

Les lettres «s» et «ss»

Be sure to distinguish between "**s**" and "**ss**" in the middle of a word.

Répétez: /z/   **mauvai̲se cui̲sine frai̲se mayonnai̲se
quelque cho̲se   maga̲sin**

poi̲son   poi̲sson

/s/   **poi̲sson saucisson dessert boisson assiette pamplemousse**

/z/ – /s/   **poi̲son – poi̲sson   dé̲sert** *(desert)* **– dessert**

Comme dessert nous choisissons une tarte aux frai̲ses.

Leçon 35 **377**

10 EXCHANGES: finding out what friends have to do and don't have to do

11 PRACTICE: making excuses

■ **Teaching note:** Help students choose correct pronouns for items 7 and 8:
nous lavons…, vous préparez…

12 COMMUNICATION: talking about what one can and should do

Prononciation

🔊 Leçon 35, Section 6

À votre tour!

1 COMPREHENSION

1-e 4-c
2-d 5-a
3-b

🔊 **Leçon 35, Section 7**

2 GUIDED ORAL EXPRESSION

3 GUIDED ORAL EXPRESSION

1. ta raquette
2. tes cassettes
3. ton appareil-photo
4. un dollar
5. cinq dollars

🔊 **Leçon 35, Section 8**

---

1 Allô!

Reconstituez la conversation entre Corinne et Philippe. Pour cela, faites correspondre les réponses de Philippe avec ce que dit Corinne.

Corinne

Philip

1 Dis, Philippe, j'ai besoin d'un petit service.

a C'est vrai . . . Bon, je t'achète tout ça *(all that)*.

2 Prête-moi ta mobylette, s'il te plaît.

b D'accord! Je vais aller à la librairie *(bookstore)* Duchemin.

3 Dans ce cas, apporte-moi *Paris-Match*.

c Écoute, je n'ai pas assez d'argent.

4 Alors, achète-moi aussi le nouvel album d'Astérix.

d Ah, je ne peux pas. Je dois aller en ville cet après-midi.

5 Je t'ai prêté cent francs hier!

e Qu'est-ce que je peux faire pour toi?

---

2 Dis-moi . . .

I am going to spend a month living in your city and studying at your school. Since you are my friend, I will ask you a few favors, for instance:

- Prête-moi ton livre d'anglais.
- Montre-moi où est la cantine.
- Amène-moi à la bibliothèque.
- Invite-moi à ton club.
- Donne-moi le plan *(map)* de la ville.
- Téléphone-moi ce weekend.

Now imagine that you are visiting me in France. I am ready to help you. Ask me three or four favors.

---

3 Créa-dialogue

Demandez certains services à vos camarades. Ils vont vous demander pourquoi. Répondez à leurs questions. Ils vont accepter le service.

▶ —S'il te plaît, prête-moi ton vélo!
—Pourquoi?
—Parce que je voudrais faire une promenade à la campagne.
—D'accord, je te prête mon vélo.

▶ prêter	1. prêter	2. prêter	3. apporter	4. prêter	5. donner	6. donner
QUEL SERVICE?						
POURQUOI? faire une promenade à la campagne	jouer au tennis	organiser une boum	prendre des photos	acheter une glace	??	??

378 **Unité 9**

À votre tour

Depending on your goals and objectives, you may or may not wish to assign all of the activities in the **À votre tour** section.

👥 Cooperative practice

Act. 1 and 3 lend themselves to cooperative pair practice. They can also be done in trios, with two students performing and the third acting as monitor and following along in the Answer Key.

T378

4 Situation

Avec un(e) camarade, préparez un dialogue original correspondant à la situation suivante.

You are having dinner at a French restaurant called Sans-Souci. You have a friendly but inexperienced waiter/waitress (played by your classmate) who forgets to bring you what you need. Whenever you mention something however, he/she agrees to bring it right away **(tout de suite).** Tell your waiter/waitress . . .

- to please show you the menu **(le menu)**
- to please give you some water
- to bring you a napkin
- to give you a beverage (of your choice)
- to bring you a dessert (of your choice)
- to bring you the silverware that you need for eating the dessert

6 Composition: Bonnes relations

Select a person you like (a friend, a neighbor, a relative, a teacher) and write a short paragraph mentioning at least four things this person does for you. You may want to use some of the following verbs:

acheter amener aider donner inviter montrer prêter rendre visite téléphoner

> J'ai une bonne copine. Elle s'appelle Stéphanie. Elle est très sympathique. Elle me téléphone souvent et le weekend, elle m'invite chez elle. Elle est très intelligente et quand je ne comprends pas, elle m'aide avec mes devoirs de français. Elle me donne toujours des conseils (advice) excellents.

Now tell me about a friend of yours and let me know some of the things this friend does for you.

5 Conversation libre

Avec un(e) camarade, composez une conversation basée sur la situation suivante.

Imagine you are looking for someone to help you out. Ask a classmate to do you five favors. He/she will accept or refuse. In case of refusal, he/she will give you a reason. You may want to use some of the following verbs:

aider, amener, apporter, inviter, donner, montrer, prêter, vendre, acheter

For example, your conversation might begin like this:

▶ —S'il te plaît, invite-moi chez toi samedi après-midi.
—Je regrette, mais je ne peux pas.
—Pourquoi?
—Je dois faire les courses.

Comment dit-on . . . ?

How to show your reaction to bad food:

Pouah! . . . C'est infect! C'est dégoûtant! C'est infâme!

Leçon 35 379

4 GUIDED ORAL EXPRESSION

- Montrez-moi le menu, s'il vous plaît.
- Donnez-moi (Apportez-moi) de l'eau minéral, s'il vous plaît.
- Apportez-moi une serviette, s'il vous plaît.
- Apportez-moi [du jus de pomme], s'il vous plaît.
- Apportez-moi [du gâteau].
- Donnez-moi (Apportez-moi) [une fourchette] pour le dessert, s'il vous plaît.

5 CONVERSATION

6 WRITTEN SELF-EXPRESSION

Classroom Notes

Portfolio assessment

You will probably select only one speaking activity and one writing activity to go into the students' portfolios for Unit 9.

In this lesson, Act. 4 and 5 can be used as the basis for oral portfolio recordings. Act. 6 could be used as written portfolio topic.

T379

MODULE 36:
Sur la plage
Total time: 5:35 min.
(Counter: 46:34 min.)

36.1 Dialogue: Sur la plage
(47:42–48:55 min.)
**36.2 Mini-scenes: Listening
— Tu le connais?**
(48:57–50:00 min.)
**36.3 Mini-scenes: Listening
— On va lui parler?**
(50:01–50:50 min.)
**36.4 Vignette culturelle: À
la plage de Deauville**
(50:51–52:06 min.)

■ **Comprehension practice:** Play the entire module through as an introduction to the lesson.

▭▭ Leçon 36, Section 1

■ **Photo culture notes**
Deauville
On the coast of Normandy, **Deauville** is one of the oldest and most fashionable ocean resorts of France.
This photo shows the boardwalk (**la promenade des planches**), a very popular place for walking and people-watching.

Un pique-nique
On the left, French youngsters are having a picnic on the grass (**un pique-nique sur l'herbe**) in a park. On the right, French teenagers are having a picnic at the beach. Note that they have simply spread a tablecloth (**une nappe**) on the ground.
In France, public picnic grounds with tables are mainly found at the rest areas along the super-highways (**les autoroutes**).

LEÇON 36 Pique-nique

Florence et Jérôme organisent un pique-nique ce weekend. Ils préparent la liste des <u>invités</u>. *guests*
Qui vont-ils inviter?

FLORENCE: Tu connais Stéphanie?
JÉRÔME: Oui, je la connais. C'est une copine.
FLORENCE: Je l'invite au pique-nique?
JÉRÔME: Bien sûr. Invite-la.
FLORENCE: Et son cousin Frédéric, tu le connais?
JÉRÔME: Oui, je le connais un peu.
FLORENCE: Je l'invite aussi?
JÉRÔME: Non, ne l'invite pas. Il est trop snob.

■ NOTE ■ CULTURELLE

Un pique-nique français

Quand ils vont à la campagne, les Français adorent faire des pique-niques. Un pique-nique est un repas froid assez simple. Il y a généralement du poulet froid et des oeufs durs° et aussi du jambon, du saucisson ou du pâté* pour les sandwichs. Quand on a l'équipement nécessaire, on peut aussi faire des grillades° sur un barbecue. Comme dessert, il y a des fruits (bananes, oranges, pommes, poires, raisin°). Comme boisson, il y a de l'eau minérale ou du cidre.

* The French have created dozens of varieties of **pâté**, ranging from the expensive and refined **pâté de foie gras** (made from the livers of fattened geese) to the everyday **pâté de campagne** (a type of cold meat loaf served in thin slices with bread).

durs *hard-boiled* **grillades** *grilled meat* **raisin** *grapes*

 380 Unité 9

Setting the scene

1. Ask students if they go on picnics with family or friends.

2. Where do they go? What do they do?

3. And what do they eat and drink?

1. **Est-ce que vous faites des pique-niques avec votre famille /vos copains?**

2. **Où allez-vous? Qu'est-ce que vous faites?**

3. **Qu'est-ce que vous mangez? Qu'est-ce que vous buvez?**

36.4 **Vignette culturelle: À la plage de Deauville** (50:51–52:06 min.)

■ **Photo culture note**
La plage à Deauville
On the beach, you can see:
• sailboats (**un bateau à voile**)
• beach cabanas (**une cabine**)
• beach umbrellas (**un parasol**)
• beach chairs (**un transat**)
(The word **transat** /trãzat/ is a shortened form of **transatlantique**; this type of deck chair was so named because it was used on ocean crossings.)

FLORENCE: <u>Comment</u>? Tu le trouves snob? Moi, je le trouve intelligent et sympathique. Et <u>puis</u>, il a une voiture et nous avons besoin d'une voiture pour transporter <u>tout le monde</u>...

JÉRÔME: Florence, tu es <u>géniale</u>... C'est vrai, Frédéric n'est pas <u>aussi snob que</u> ça... Téléphonons-lui <u>tout de suite</u> et invitons-le au pique-nique!

What?
also
everyone
brilliant
that snobbish / right away

Compréhension

1. Qui est Stéphanie?
2. Qui est Frédéric?
3. Est-ce que Jérôme a une bonne ou une mauvaise opinion de Frédéric? Pourquoi?
4. Et Florence, comment est-ce qu'elle trouve Frédéric?
5. Finalement, est-ce que Jérôme va inviter Frédéric au pique-nique? Pourquoi?

Et toi?

1. Est-ce que tu aimes faire des pique-niques?
2. Quand tu fais un pique-nique avec des copains, où allez-vous?
3. Qui invites-tu?
4. En général, qu'est-ce qu'on mange à un pique-nique américain?
5. Qu'est-ce qu'on boit?
6. Dans ta famille, est-ce qu'on fait des barbecues? Où? Qui est le «chef»? Qu'est-ce qu'on mange et qu'est-ce qu'on boit?

Leçon 36 381

COMPREHENSION

1. C'est une copine de Jérôme.
2. C'est le cousin de Stéphanie.
3. Il a une mauvaise opinion de Frédéric. Il pense qu'il est trop snob.
4. Elle le trouve intelligent et sympathique.
5. Oui, parce qu'il a une voiture.

COMMUNICATION: talking about picnics

■ **Pronunciation:** The expression **un barbecue** /barbəkju/ has been borrowed from the English. It refers to the meal as well as to the grill on which it was cooked.

Supplementary vocabulary

PICNIC FOODS
un steak
du poulet frit *fried chicken*
du poulet rôti *roast chicken*
une côtelette de porc *pork chop*
une côtelette d'agneau *lamb chop*
des côtes de porc *spare ribs*
de la salade de pommes de terre *potato salad*

▢ Using the video

Video Module 36 was filmed in Normandy at the resort town of Deauville. In the dialogue scenes, two boys on vacation are trying to figure out how to introduce themselves to a girl at the beach.

In the *Vignette culturelle,* other young people are interviewed about their vacation activities. The theme of the module provides an appropriate point for wishing your students a relaxing summer vacation.

COMMUNICATIVE FUNCTION:
Talking about whom one knows

 Leçon 36, Section 2

■ **Spelling hint:** The circumflex appears on the "î" of **connaître** only when the next letter is a "t."

■ **Supplementary vocabulary:** The verb **reconnaître** (to recognize) is conjugated like **connaître**.

■ **Teaching strategies**
• This is a simplified explanation of the distinction between **connaître** and **savoir**. The more complex differences are presented formally in Book Two, e.g., **Je connais la leçon** (I know which one it is) vs. **Je sais la leçon** (I know it because I have studied it).
• You may wish to present the complete conjugation of **savoir**. See Appendix, p. R10.

PRACTICE: describing whom or what people know

COMMUNICATION: answering personal questions

■ **Language note:** In item 5, **connaître** means to know in the sense of to know of or to know by reputation. Students should be able to name one person in each category.

A. Le verbe *connaître*

Note the forms of the irregular verb **connaître** (to know).

INFINITIVE	**connaître**	
PRESENT	Je **connais** Stéphanie.	Nous **connaissons** Paris.
	Tu **connais** son cousin?	Vous **connaissez** Montréal?
	Il / Elle / On **connaît** ces garçons.	Ils / Elles **connaissent** ce café.
PASSÉ COMPOSÉ	J'**ai connu** ton frère pendant les vacances.	

➡ In the passé composé, **connaître** means *to meet for the first time.*

➡ The French use **connaître** to say that they *know* or *are acquainted with people or places.* To say that they *know information,* they use **je sais, tu sais.** Compare:

PEOPLE/PLACES
Je **connais** Éric.
Tu **connais** Frédéric.
Je **connais** un bon restaurant.

INFORMATION
Je **sais** où il habite.
Tu **sais** à quelle heure il vient?
Je **sais** qu'il est près du théâtre.

Je connais Éric.

Je sais où il habite.

1 On ne peut pas connaître tout
Les personnes suivantes connaissent la première personne ou la première chose entre parenthèses. Elles ne connaissent pas la deuxième.

▶ Philippe (Isabelle/sa soeur)
Philippe connaît Isabelle.
Il ne connaît pas sa soeur.

1. nous (Paul / ses copains)
2. vous (le prof d'anglais / le prof de maths)
3. moi (les voisins / leurs amis)
4. toi (Paris / Bordeaux)
5. les touristes (le Louvre / le musée d'Orsay)
6. mon copain (ce café / ce restaurant)

2 Questions personnelles
1. Est-ce que tu connais New York? Chicago? San Francisco? Montréal? Quelles villes est-ce que tu connais bien?
2. Dans ta ville est-ce que tu connais un bon restaurant? Comment est-ce qu'il s'appelle? Est-ce que tu connais un supermarché? un centre commercial? un magasin de disques? Comment est-ce qu'ils s'appellent?
3. Est-ce que tu connais des monuments à Paris? Quels monuments?
4. Est-ce que tu connais bien tes voisins? Est-ce qu'ils sont sympathiques? Est-ce que tu connais personnellement le directeur (la directrice) de ton école? Est-ce qu'il (elle) est strict(e)?
5. Quels acteurs de cinéma est-ce que tu connais? Quelles actrices? Quels musiciens? Quels athlètes professionnels?

TPR **Direct object pronouns**
PROPS: 3 pictures of known personalities: a man, a woman, a couple

Tape the 3 pictures on the chalkboard.
Point to the picture of the man:
Vous le connaissez? [write **le** on board]
Bien sûr, vous le connaissez. C'est ...

Present the other 2 pictures (writing **la, les**).
Have students point to the right picture.
X, tu le connais? [X points to man]
Tu ne la connais pas? [X points to woman]
Tu les connais? [X points to couple]

Vary the verbs (beginning with consonants).
Y, tu la vois souvent? [Y points to woman]
Tu les trouves intéressants? [points to couple]

B. Les pronoms compléments: *le, la, les*

In the questions below, the nouns in heavy type follow the verb directly. They are the DIRECT OBJECTS of the verb. Note the forms and position of the DIRECT OBJECT PRONOUNS which are used to replace those nouns in the answers.

Tu connais **Éric?**	Oui, je **le** connais.	*Yes, I know **him**.*
	Je **l'**invite souvent.	*I invite **him** often.*
Tu connais **Stéphanie?**	Oui, je **la** connais.	*Yes, I know **her**.*
	Je **l'**invite aussi.	*I invite **her** also.*
Tu connais **mes copains?**	Je **les** connais bien.	*I know **them** well.*
	Je **les** invite.	*I invite **them**.*
Tu connais **mes amies?**	Je **les** connais aussi.	*I know **them** too.*
	Je **les** invite souvent.	*I invite **them** often.*

FORMS AND USES

Direct object pronouns have the following forms:

	SINGULAR		PLURAL
MASCULINE	**le** ↓ *him, it* **l'** (+ VOWEL SOUND)		**les** *them*
FEMININE	**la** ↓ *her, it* **l'** (+ VOWEL SOUND)		

Qui le vend?
Qui le répare?

On le trouve
dans les pages
jaunes!

TELECOMMUNICATIONS

➡ The direct object pronouns **le, la, l', les** can refer to either people or things.

Tu vois **Nicole?**	Oui, je **la** vois.	*Yes, I see **her**.*
Tu vois **ma voiture?**	Oui, je **la** vois.	*Yes, I see **it**.*
Tu comprends **le professeur?**	Oui, je **le** comprends.	*Yes, I understand **him**.*
Tu comprends **ce mot** *(word)*?	Oui, je **le** comprends.	*Yes, I understand **it**.*

POSITION

Direct object pronouns generally come *before* the verb according to the following patterns:

	AFFIRMATIVE			NEGATIVE				
	SUBJECT + **le/la/les** + VERB ...			SUBJECT + **ne** + **le/la/les** + VERB + **pas** ...				
Éric?	Je	**le**	connais bien.	Tu	**ne**	**le**	connais	**pas.**
Ces filles?	Nous	**les**	invitons.	Vous	**ne**	**les**	invitez	**pas.**

Leçon 36 **383**

Section B

COMMUNICATIVE FUNCTION:
Talking about people and things

🖥 **36.2 Mini-scenes: Tu le connais?**
(48:57–50:50 min.)

📼 Leçon 36, Sections 3, 4

■ **Pronunciation:** Be sure students make the liaison when the next word begins with a vowel sound.

■ **Language notes**
• Point out that direct object pronouns, in French as in English, replace the entire noun group: article (possessive, demonstrative, number), noun, adjective.
• Direct object pronouns are NOT used to replace nouns introduced by **un, une, des, du, de la.**
• The pronoun **en** is introduced in Book Two.

■ **Teaching strategy:** The following common verbs take direct objects in French. You may want to write them on the board.
WITH PEOPLE:
   aider
   inviter
   rencontrer
WITH THINGS:
   acheter
   avoir
   laver
   nettoyer
   prendre
   vendre
WITH PEOPLE OR THINGS:
   aimer
   connaître
   trouver
   voir
Point out that while **attendre**, **écouter**, and **regarder** take direct objects in French, the English equivalents have prepositions: *to wait <u>for</u>, to listen <u>to</u>, to look <u>at</u>.*

Once students are comfortable with **le, la, les**, you may wish to introduce verbs beginning with vowels.
Z, tu les admires? [Z points to couple]
Tu l'admires aussi? [Z is confused]

Point to the man, addressing the entire class:
Cet homme, est-ce que vous l'admirez?
Write **l'** under the man's picture.

Et cette femme, vous l'admirez? Oui?
Write **l'** under the woman's picture.

3 ROLE PLAY: indicating whether one knows people

4 EXCHANGES: answering questions using pronouns

5 ROLE PLAY/ COMPREHENSION: asking about activities

■ **Photo culture note**
Fontaine Igor Stravinski
The students in the photo are seated along the **Fontaine Igor Stravinski** which is behind the **Centre Pompidou** in Paris. (See TE note, page T199.)

Classroom Notes

3 À la boum de Delphine

Pierre connaît tous les invités *(all the guests)* à la boum de Delphine, mais Lise ne les connaît pas. Jouez les trois rôles.

▶ ces garçons?

Tu connais ces garçons?

Et toi, Lise?

Oui, je les connais.

Non, je ne les connais pas.

1. Christophe
2. Jacqueline?
3. Anne et Valérie?
4. Jérôme et Jean-François?
5. la fille là-bas?
6. cette étudiante?
7. ma cousine?
8. les cousins de Véronique?
9. la copine de Jacques?
10. ses frères?

4 Un choix difficile

Vous allez passer le mois de juillet en France. Vous êtes limité(e) à 20 kilos de bagages. Un(e) camarade demande si vous allez prendre les choses suivantes. Répondez affirmativement ou négativement.

▶ ta raquette?
—Tu prends ta raquette?
— Oui, je la prends.
(Non, je ne la prends pas.)

1. tes cassettes?
2. ton livre de français?
3. ta guitare?
4. ton walkman?
5. ta chaîne stéréo?
6. ton maillot de bain?
7. ton vélo?
8. tes tee-shirts?
9. tes sandales?

5 Questions et réponses

Michèle pose des questions à Jérôme en utilisant les éléments des Colonnes A et B. Jérôme répond logiquement en utilisant les éléments des Colonnes B et C et un pronom complément. Avec un(e) camarade, jouez les deux rôles.

A	B	C
où	rencontrer tes copains	le samedi matin
quand	voir ta cousine	à 8 heures du matin
à quelle heure	regarder la télé	à 9 heures du soir
	nettoyer ta chambre	à la Boîte à Musique
	faire les courses	à Mod' Shop
	acheter tes disques	au café Le Pont Neuf
	acheter tes vêtements	dans un supermarché
	prendre le petit déjeuner	le weekend
		pendant les vacances
		dans la cuisine
		dans le salon

Où est-ce que tu rencontres tes copains?

Je les rencontre au café Le Pont Neuf.

Quand est-ce que tu rencontres tes copains?

Je les rencontre le weekend.

Cooperative pair practice
Activities 3, 4, 5, 7, 8

C. La place des pronoms à l'impératif

Note the position of the object pronoun when the verb is in the imperative.

	AFFIRMATIVE COMMAND	NEGATIVE COMMAND
J'invite **Frédéric?**	Oui, invite-**le**!	Non, ne **l'**invite pas!
Je prends **la guitare?**	Oui, prends-**la**!	Non, ne **la** prends pas!
J'achète **les cassettes?**	Oui, achète-**les**!	Non, ne **les** achète pas!

In AFFIRMATIVE COMMANDS, the object pronoun comes *after* the verb and is joined to it by a hyphen.

In NEGATIVE COMMANDS, the object pronoun comes *before* the verb.

6 Invitations

Vous préparez une liste de personnes à inviter à une boum. Vous êtes limité(e)s à quatre *(4)* des personnes suivantes. Faites vos suggestions d'après les modèles.

▶ Caroline est sympathique.
  Invitons-la!

▶ Jean-Louis est pénible.
  Ne l'invitons pas!

1. Sylvie est très sympathique.
2. Cécile et Anne aiment danser.
3. Jacques est stupide.
4. Robert joue bien de la guitare.
5. Ces filles sont intelligentes.
6. Martin et Thomas sont snobs.
7. Nicolas n'est pas mon ami.
8. Ces garçons sont pénibles.
9. Cette fille est gentille.
10. Tes copains sont méchants.

7 Le pique-nique

Olivier demande à Claire s'il doit prendre certaines choses pour le pique-nique.

▶ ma guitare (oui)

Est-ce que je prends ma guitare?

Oui, prends-la!

1. la limonade (oui)
2. les sandwichs (non)
3. la salade (oui)
4. le lait (non)
5. le gâteau (non)
6. mon appareil-photo (oui)
7. mes lunettes de soleil (oui)
8. les impers (non)

8 Oui ou non?

Votre petit cousin de Québec passe deux semaines chez vous. Il vous demande s'il doit ou peut faire les choses suivantes. Répondez affirmativement ou négativement.

1. Je fais les courses?
2. Je regarde tes photos?
3. Je nettoie ma chambre?
4. J'achète le journal *(newspaper)*?
5. J'invite les voisins à déjeuner?
6. Je prépare le dîner?
7. Je prends ton vélo?
8. J'écoute tes disques?
9. J'aide ta mère?
10. Je mets la télé?

Je fais les devoirs?

Oui, fais-les.

(Non, ne les fais pas.)

Section C

COMMUNICATIVE FUNCTION:
Giving orders

COMPREHENSION: making suggestions about whom to invite
6

■ **Variation** (dialogue format):
With a classmate, decide if you will invite the following people.
▶ Caroline est sympathique.
– **J'invite Caroline?**
– **Oui, invite-la.**
▶ Jean-Louis est pénible.
– **J'invite Jean-Louis?**
– **Non, ne l'invite pas.**

ROLE PLAY: offering and accepting or refusing services
7

ROLE PLAY: telling a friend what to do and not to do
8

T385

36.4 Mini-scenes: On va lui parler?
(50:01–50:50 min.)

 Leçon 36, Section 5

■ **Realia note**
This is a French **télécarte** or telephone "smart card." Most public telephones in the larger cities now take **télécartes** rather than coins. At the end of your phone conversation, the cost of the call is automatically deducted from the card. You can buy a **télécarte** at any post office or tobacco shop (**bureau de tabac**).

9 EXCHANGES: asking friends whom they're telephoning

■ **Variation** (in the plural):
– Vous téléphonez à votre copine?
– Oui, nous lui téléphonons.
(Non, nous ne lui téléphonons pas.)

D. Les pronoms compléments *lui, leur*

In the questions below, the nouns in heavy type are INDIRECT OBJECTS. These nouns represent PEOPLE and are introduced by **à**.

Note the forms and position of the corresponding INDIRECT OBJECT PRONOUNS in the answers on the right.

Tu téléphones **à Philippe?**	Oui, je **lui** téléphone.
Tu parles **à Juliette?**	Non, je ne **lui** parle pas.
Tu téléphones **à tes amis?**	Oui, je **leur** téléphone.
Tu prêtes ton vélo **à tes cousines?**	Non, je ne **leur** prête pas mon vélo.

FORMS

INDIRECT OBJECT PRONOUNS replace **à** + <u>noun representing people</u>. They have the following forms:

	SINGULAR		PLURAL	
MASCULINE/FEMININE	**lui**	*to him, to her*	**leur**	*to them*

POSITION

Like other object pronouns, **lui** and **leur** come *before* the verb, *except* in affirmative commands.

Voici Henri. Parle-**lui!** Prête-**lui** ton vélo!

➡ In negative sentences, **lui** and **leur,** like other object pronouns, come *between* **ne** and the verb.

Voici Éric.	Je ne **lui** téléphone pas.
Voici mes voisins.	Je ne **leur** parle pas.

9 Au téléphone

Demandez à vos camarades s'ils téléphonent aux personnes suivantes.

▶ ta copine

Tu téléphones à ta copine?

Oui, je lui téléphone.

(Non, je ne lui téléphone pas.)

1. ton copain
2. tes cousins
3. ta grand-mère
4. ton prof de français
5. tes voisins
6. ta tante favorite

 Cooperative pair practice Activity 9

Vocabulaire: Verbes suivis (followed) d'un complément indirect

parler à	to speak, talk (to)	Je **parle à** mon copain.
rendre visite à	to visit	Nous **rendons visite à** nos voisins.
répondre à	to answer	Tu **réponds au** professeur.
téléphoner à	to phone, call	Jérôme **téléphone à** Juliette.
demander à	to ask	Je ne **demande** pas d'argent **à** mes frères.
donner à	to give (to)	Tu **donnes** ton adresse **à** ta copine.
montrer à	to show (to)	Nous **montrons** nos photos **à** nos amis.
prêter à	to lend, loan (to)	Je ne **prête** pas mon walkman **à** ma soeur.

➡ **Répondre** is a regular **-re** verb.

   Je réponds à François.   **J'ai répondu** à Catherine.

➡ The verbs **téléphoner, répondre,** and **demander** take indirect objects in French, but not in English. Compare:

téléphoner	Nous **téléphonons**	à	Paul.	Nous **lui téléphonons.**
	*We **are calling***	. . .	*Paul.*	*We **are calling him.***

répondre	Tu **réponds**	à	tes parents.	Tu **leur réponds.**
	*You **answer***	. . .	*your parents.*	*You **answer them.***

demander	Je **demande**	à	Sylvie	. . .	ses disques.	Je **lui demande** ses disques.
	*I **am asking***	. . .	*Sylvie*	*for*	*her records.*	*I **am asking her** for her records.*

10 **Les copains de Dominique**

Dominique a beaucoup de copains. Décrivez ce que chacun fait pour elle. Complétez les phrases avec **Dominique** ou **à Dominique.**

▶ Françoise invite <u>Dominique</u>.
  Patrick rend visite <u>à Dominique</u>.

1. Marc téléphone . . .
2. Jean-Paul voit . . . samedi prochain.
3. Sophie prête son vélo . . .
4. Corinne écoute . . .
5. François donne son adresse . . .
6. Philippe regarde . . . pendant la classe.
7. Delphine attend . . . après la classe.
8. Nathalie parle . . .
9. Pauline invite . . . au concert.
10. Pierre répond . . .
11. Isabelle montre ses photos . . .
12. Thomas demande . . . son numéro de téléphone.

Leçon 36   **387**

▷ Vocabulaire

◻ **Language note:** Point out that **rendre visite** takes an indirect object because the expression literally means *render a visit <u>to</u> someone.*

◻ **Extra practice:** Have students reword the sample sentences using object pronouns.
Je lui parle.
Nous leur rendons visite. etc.

PRACTICE: distinguishing between direct and indirect objects

10

1. à Dominique
2. Dominique
3. à Dominique
4. Dominique
5. à Dominique
6. Dominique
7. Dominique
8. à Dominique
9. Dominique
10. à Dominique
11. à Dominique
12. à Dominique

◻ **Expansion** (using object pronouns):
Dominique, C'est une fille!
Françoise l'invite.
Patrick lui rend visite.

T387

11 **Joyeux anniversaire!**

Choisissez un cadeau d'anniversaire pour les personnes suivantes. Un(e) camarade va vous demander ce que vous donnez à chaque personne.

▶ à ton copain

Qu'est-ce que tu donnes à ton copain?

Je lui donne un livre.

Cadeaux

un pull
des compacts
une cravate
un livre
des billets (tickets) de théâtre
un magazine
ma photo
une boîte (box) de chocolats
un gâteau
??

1. à ton petit frère
2. à ta mère
3. à ta grand-mère
4. à ta copine
5. à tes cousins
6. à ton (ta) prof
7. à tes copains

12 **Questions personnelles**

Réponds aux questions suivantes. Utilise **lui** ou **leur** dans tes réponses.

1. Le weekend, est-ce que tu rends visite à tes copains? à ton oncle?
2. Est-ce que tu prêtes tes disques à ta soeur? à ton frère? à tes copains?
3. Est-ce que tu demandes de l'argent à ton père? à ta mère?
4. Est-ce que tu demandes des conseils *(advice)* à tes parents? à tes professeurs?
5. Est-ce que tu donnes de bons conseils à tes copains?
6. Est-ce que tu montres tes photos à ton frère? à ta soeur? à ta copine? à ton copain? à tes cousins?
7. En classe, est-ce que tu réponds en français à ton professeur?
8. Quand tu as un problème, est-ce que tu parles à tes copains? à ton professeur? à tes grands-parents? à tes parents?

Section E

COMMUNICATIVE FUNCTION: Describing what people say and write

⟳ **Re-entry and review:** Ask students which two other verbs have **vous** forms ending in **-tes**: **vous êtes, vous faites.**

■ **Looking ahead:** The verb **lire** is not introduced until Book Two. If you wish to present the forms quickly for recognition, have students turn to the Appendix, page R9.

E. Les verbes *dire* et *écrire*

Note the forms of the irregular verbs **dire** *(to say, tell)* and **écrire** *(to write)*.

INFINITIVE	dire	écrire
PRESENT	je **dis** tu **dis** il/elle/on **dit** nous **disons** vous **dites** ils/elles **disent**	j' **écris** tu **écris** il/elle/on **écrit** nous **écrivons** vous **écrivez** ils/elles **écrivent**
PASSÉ COMPOSÉ	j'**ai dit**	j'**ai écrit**

➡ Note the use of **que/qu'** *(that)* after **dire** and **écrire**.

Florence **dit que** Frédéric est sympathique.   *Florence **says (that)** Frédéric is nice.*
Alain **écrit qu'**il est allé à un pique-nique.   *Alain **writes (that)** he went on a picnic.*

➡ **Décrire** *(to describe)* follows the same pattern as **écrire**.

388 Unité 9

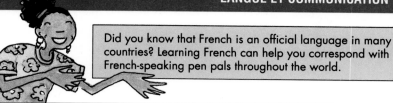

Did you know that French is an official language in many countries? Learning French can help you correspond with French-speaking pen pals throughout the world.

13 Correspondance

Pendant les vacances, on écrit beaucoup de lettres. Dites à qui les personnes suivantes écrivent.

▶ Juliette / à Marc
Juliette écrit à Marc.

1. nous / à nos copains
2. toi / à ta cousine
3. moi / à ma grand-mère
4. Nicolas / à ses voisins
5. vous / à vos parents
6. les élèves / au professeur

14 La boum

Des amis sont à une boum. Décrivez ce que chacun dit.

▶ toi / la musique est super
Tu dis que la musique est super.

1. Nicole / les sandwichs sont délicieux
2. nous / les invités *(guests)* sont sympathiques
3. Pauline / Jérôme danse bien
4. moi / ces garçons dansent mal
5. vous / vous n'aimez pas cette cassette
6. mes copains / ils vont organiser une boum le weekend prochain

15 Questions personnelles

1. Est-ce que tu aimes écrire?
2. Pendant les vacances, est-ce que tu écris à tes copains? à tes voisins? à ton(ta) meilleur(e) *(best)* ami(e)?
3. À Noël, est-ce que tu écris des cartes *(cards)*? À qui?
4. À qui as-tu écrit récemment *(recently)*?
5. Est-ce que tu dis toujours la vérité *(truth)*?
6. À ton avis, est-ce que les journalistes disent toujours la vérité? Et les politiciens?

Prononciation

Les lettres «on» et «om»

Be sure to distinguish between the nasal and non-nasal vowel sounds.

REMEMBER: Do not pronounce an /n/ or /m/ after the nasal vowel /ɔ̃/.

on /ɔ̃/   on(n)e /ɔn/

lion   **lionne**

Répétez: /ɔ̃/   **m<u>on</u> t<u>on</u> s<u>on</u> b<u>on</u> avi<u>on</u> m<u>on</u>trer répondre invit<u>on</u>s blous<u>on</u>**

/ɔn/   **télép<u>hone</u> Sim<u>one</u> d<u>onn</u>er c<u>onn</u>ais may<u>onn</u>aise pers<u>onn</u>e b<u>onn</u>e**

/ɔm/   **fr<u>om</u>age pr<u>om</u>enade t<u>om</u>ate p<u>omm</u>e d<u>omm</u>age c<u>omm</u>ent**

/ɔ̃/–/ɔn/   **li<u>on</u>–li<u>onn</u>e b<u>on</u>–b<u>onn</u>e Sim<u>on</u>–Sim<u>one</u> Yv<u>on</u>–Yv<u>onn</u>e**

M<u>on</u>ique d<u>onn</u>e une p<u>omm</u>e à Raym<u>on</u>d.
Sim<u>one</u> c<u>onn</u>aît m<u>on</u> <u>on</u>cle Lé<u>on</u>.

Leçon 36   **389**

---

13 PRACTICE: telling whom people are writing

■ **Variation** (dialogue format, reviewing lui, leur):
– Est-ce que Juliette écrit à Marc?
– Oui, elle lui écrit.

■ **Variation** (in the passé composé):
Juliette a écrit à Marc.

14 PRACTICE: describing what people are saying

15 COMMUNICATION: answering personal questions

Prononciation

🔲 **Leçon 36, Section 7**

■ **Pronunciation:** Remind students that the letters "on" and "om" represent a nasal vowel when they occur at the end of a word or when they are followed by a consonant. When these letters are followed by a vowel, they do not represent a nasal sound.

■ **Additional practice**
/ɔ̃/	/ɔn/
champion	championne
mignon	mignonne

1 COMPREHENSION

1-d   4-f
2-c   5-b
3-e   6-a

🔊 Leçon 36, Section 8

2 GUIDED ORAL EXPRESSION

3 GUIDED ORAL EXPRESSION

🔊 Leçon 36, Section 9

1 Allô!

Reconstituez la conversation entre Jacques et Florence. Pour cela, faites correspondre les réponses de Florence avec les questions de Jacques.

1 Qu'est-ce que tu fais ce weekend?

2 Tu m'invites?

3 Et Catherine? Tu l'invites aussi?

4 C'est ma nouvelle copine.

5 Tu veux son numéro de téléphone?

6 C'est le 44.32.28.50.

a. Je lui téléphone tout de suite (right away)
b. Oui, je ne l'ai pas.
c. Bien sur, je t'invite.
d. J'organise une boum.
e. Catherine? Je ne la connais pas. Qui est-c
f. Ah oui, je vois qui c'est maintenant.
   Eh bien, d'accord! Je l'invite.

2 Dis-moi ...

I met your cousin at a party last weekend. She is a very bright and pleasant person. I would like to see her again. Tell me ...

- Comment est-ce qu'elle s'appelle?
- Où est-ce qu'elle habite?
- Est-ce que tu la vois souvent?
- Est-ce que je lui téléphone? Quand?
- Est-ce que je l'invite au restaurant?
  À quel restaurant?

3 Créa-dialogue

Avec vos camarades, discutez de certaines choses que vous faites. Posez plusieurs questions sur chaque activité.

Tu regardes la télé?

À quelle heure est-ce que tu la regardes?

Oui je la regarde.

À huit heures.

▶ regarder la télé? à quelle heure?	1. inviter tes amis? quand? à quelle occasion?	2. voir tes cousins? quand? où?
	5. faire tes devoirs? quand? où?	6. téléphone à tes copains? quand? pourquoi

À votre tour

Depending on your goals and objectives, you may or may not wish to assign all of the activities in the **À votre tour** section.

🧠🧠 Cooperative practice

Act. 1 and 3 lend themselves to cooperative pair practice. They can also be done in trios, with two students performing and the third acting as monitor and following along in the Answer Key.

4 Situation

Avec un(e) camarade, composez un dialogue original correspondant à la situation suivante. Jouez ce dialogue en classe.

You and another classmate know a very nice Canadian girl by the name of Catherine. Next weekend is her birthday and you want to do something special. With your friend discuss . . .
- whether to invite her to your house or to a restaurant
- what small gift *(petit cadeau)* you may buy for her
- what else you may do for her

5 Conversation libre

Avec un(e) camarade, composez un dialogue basé sur la situation suivante. Jouez ce dialogue en classe.

A group of French students are going to visit your town next week. As members of the Foreign Students Club, you and a classmate discuss what kinds of activities you will organize for them. You may want to use the following verbs:

> **inviter (où?), montrer (quels endroits?), amener (où?), donner (quels petits cadeaux [gifts]?)**

4 GUIDED ORAL EXPRESSION

5 CONVERSATION

6 Composition: Les personnes dans ma vie (life)

Make a list of two or three people you know well. Give the name of each person and describe one thing you do for this person and one thing you don't do.
You may want to select:

- un cousin/une cousine
- un frère/une soeur
- un copain/une copine
- un voisin/une voisine
- un ami/une amie
- un professeur de français (d'anglais, de maths, d'histoire)

6 WRITTEN SELF-EXPRESSION

Ma cousine s'appelle Denise. Je la vois pendant les vacances de Noël. Je ne lui rends pas souvent visite.

3. faire les courses?	4. aider ta mère?
quand? où?	quand? comment?
7. rendre visite à ta grand-mère?	8. écrire à ton cousin?
quand? pourquoi?	pourquoi?

Comment dit-on . . . ?

How to tell someone to leave you alone:

Laisse-moi tranquille!

Fiche-moi la paix!

Leçon 36 **391**

Classroom Notes

Portfolio assessment

You will probably select only one speaking activity and one writing activity to go into the students' portfolios for Unit 9.

In this lesson, Act. 4 and 5 can be used as the basis for oral portfolio recordings.

Petit test culturel

Bon appétit!

Répondez aux questions suivantes. Vérifiez vos réponses au bas° de la page.

1 Dans un repas français, quand est-ce qu'on mange la salade en général?
a. comme° premier plat
b. avec la viande
c. après le plat principal
d. après le dessert

2 En général, avec quel repas est-ce qu'on mange des croissants en France?
a. avec le petit déjeuner
b. avec le déjeuner
c. avec le dîner
d. avec les trois repas

3 Dans un restaurant français typique, qu'est-ce qu'on mange généralement avec un steak?
a. du riz
b. des spaghetti
c. des frites
d. des épinards°

Réponses:

1. c; 2. a; 3. c; 4. d; 5. b;
6. b; 7. b

au bas *at the bottom* comme *as*
épinards *spinach* fin *end*
vin *wine* célèbre *famous*

4 Quand est-ce que les Français boivent le café?
a. avant le repas
b. pendant le repas
c. avec le fromage
d. à la fin° du repas

5 Le «camembert» est une spécialité qui vient originairement de Normandie. Qu'est-ce que c'est?
a. un gâteau
b. un fromage
c. une glace
d. un jus de fruit

6 La «bouillabaisse» est le plat traditionnel de Marseille, un grand port français sur la Méditerranée. Qu'est-ce que c'est?
a. une salade de fruits
b. une soupe de poisson
c. une tarte aux bananes
d. une omelette au jambon

7 Quelle province française a donné son nom à un vin° célèbre?°
a. la Savoie
b. la Champagne
c. la Bretagne
d. la Picardie

Entracte 9

OBJECTIVES:
• Reading skills development
• Re-entry of material in the unit
• Development of cultural awareness

Bon appétit!

OBJECTIVES:
• Rapid reading at the sentence level
• Reading for cultural information about French foods and eating habits

■ Photo culture note
La Champagne
The photo shows the Champagne region in eastern France. This area is known around the world for its vineyards (**les vignobles**) and its famous sparkling wine (**le champagne**).

Cooperative reading practice

Divide the class into group of 4 or 5, each with a **secrétaire.**

For each question, have the groups first vote on the correct answer (keeping the box at the bottom of the page covered).

Then have the recorders check the right answers and announce their group score to the entire class.

Nous avons six réponses correctes.

Follow-up: Have students find all the places mentioned on the maps in the reference section, pages R2–R3.

Le Château Frontenac

(De 6h30 à midi) **PETIT DÉJEUNER CONTINENTAL**	(From 6:30 to noon) **CONTINENTAL BREAKFAST** $7.75
☐ Jus d'orange ou ☐ Jus de tomate ou ☐ Jus de pamplemousse	☐ Orange juice or ☐ Tomato juice or ☐ Grapefruit juice
☐ Café ou ☐ Thé ou ☐ Lait	☐ Coffee or ☐ Tea or ☐ Milk
avec ☐ rôties, ou ☐ croissant, ou ☐ danoise, beurre et confitures	served with ☐ toast, or ☐ croissant, or ☐ sweet roll, butter and preserves

LE COMTE DE FRONTENAC
$11.25

☐ Jus d'orange ou ☐ Jus de tomate ou ☐ Jus de pamplemousse ou ☐ 1/2 pamplemousse ou ☐ Pruneaux	☐ Orange juice or ☐ Tomato juice or ☐ Grapefruit juice or ☐ 1/2 grapefruit or ☐ Stewed prunes
☐ Café ou ☐ Thé ou ☐ Lait	☐ Coffee or ☐ Tea or ☐ Milk
☐ Deux oeufs frits ou ☐ Oeufs brouillés ou ☐ Deux oeufs à la coque ou ☐ Crêpes canadiennes ou ☐ Crêpes françaises	☐ Two fried eggs or ☐ Scrambled eggs or ☐ Two boiled eggs or ☐ Canadian pancakes or ☐ French pancakes
☐ Jambon ou ☐ Bacon ou ☐ Saucisses	☐ Ham or ☐ Bacon or ☐ Sausages

avec
☐ rôties ou
☐ croissant ou
☐ danoise
beurre et confitures ☐ Fraises
          ☐ Framboises
          ☐ Orange
          ☐ Miel
	served with
	☐ toast or
	☐ croissant or
	☐ sweet roll
	butter and preserves ☐ Strawberry
	          ☐ Raspberry
	          ☐ Orange
	          ☐ Honey

LE CAFÉ CANADIEN Pour un petit déjeuner léger ou complet service à la carte ou buffet de 07h00 à 11h00.	**LE CAFÉ CANADIEN** Light and full course breakfast à la carte or buffet from 7 to 11:00 a.m.

Petit déjeuner au Château Frontenac

Vous voyagez au Canada avec votre famille. Cette semaine vous êtes à Québec. Vous restez au Château Frontenac, un célèbre hôtel de la ville. Regardez bien le menu.

 À quelle heure est servi° le petit déjeuner?

Vous avez le choix entre deux menus. Quel menu allez-vous choisir? Combien coûte-t-il?

Vous avez décidé de choisir le menu «Le Comte de Frontenac».

Quel jus de fruit allez-vous choisir?

Quelle boisson allez-vous choisir?

Quels oeufs allez-vous prendre?

Est-ce que vous allez prendre du jambon, du bacon ou des saucisses?

Est-ce que vous allez choisir des rôties, un croissant ou une danoise? Et qu'est-ce que vous allez prendre comme° confiture?

servi *served*   **comme** *as, for*

OBJECTIVES:
- Reading authentic documents
- Vocabulary expansion

■ **Photo culture note**
Le Château Frontenac
The landmark hotel of Quebec City, **le Château Frontenac**, was named after Louis de Frontenac (1620-1698), Governor of **la Nouvelle France**, the former French territory which is now part of Canada.

■ **Language note:** In France, one would say:
des toasts (rather than **des rôties**)
une pâtisserie (rather than **une danoise**)

Pre-reading
Have students look quickly at the menu and decide what meal is presented. How can they tell?

Post-reading
Have students pretend that they are on a student tour to Quebec City and are staying at the Château Frontenac. They have assembled in the reception area and are talking in pairs about what they each had for breakfast.
Moi, j'ai pris le Continental. J'ai choisi …

Entre amis: Le petit déjeuner

«Qu'est-ce que vous prenez au petit déjeuner?» Aux États-Unis, le petit déjeuner est généralement un repas abondant.° En France, c'est un repas simple.

Fabrice (13 ans)

Chez nous, nous sommes très traditionnels. Je mange du pain avec du beurre et de la confiture. Je bois un grand bol° de café au lait.

Sylvie (14 ans)

Je mange des tartines de pain grillé° et je bois du lait chaud ou du chocolat avec beaucoup de sucre. Le dimanche, il y a parfois° des croissants. (Ça dépend si quelqu'un veut faire les courses!)

Daniel (12 ans)

Chez nous, nous prenons le petit déjeuner «à l'américaine». Je mange des céréales et je bois du jus d'orange.

Marie-Hélène (16 ans)

Je ne veux pas grossir. Alors, je mange une ou deux biscottes.° Sans° beurre, bien sûr. Et je bois du thé.

Chantal (13 ans)

Je suis martiniquaise. En général, je mange du pain et de la confiture comme° tout le monde.° Parfois ma mère prépare un petit déjeuner martiniquais typique. On mange du blaff de poisson° et des bananes vertes cuites.° On mange aussi des ananas,° des papayes et de la gelée de goyave.° C'est délicieux!

abondant *copious, large*   **bol** *deep bowl*   **pain grillé** *buttered toast*   **parfois** *sometimes*
biscottes *dried toast*   **Sans** *Without*   **comme** *like*   **tout le monde** *everybody*
blaff de poisson *fish stew*   **cuites** *cooked*   **ananas** *pineapples*   **gelée de goyave** *guava jelly*

■ NOTE ■
CULTURELLE

La cuisine créole

La cuisine créole est une cuisine régionale typique de la Martinique et de la Guadeloupe. C'est une cuisine assez épicée° qui utilise les produits locaux,° principalement les produits de la mer et les fruits exotiques.

épicée *hot (spiced)*   **locaux** *local*

LA VILLA CRÉOLE

La Bonne Cuisine Française et Créole

ANSE-MITAN TROIS-ILETS
☎ 66.05.53

Le petit déjeuner

OBJECTIVES:
- Reading at the paragraph level
- Building reading skills

■ Questions sur le texte
1. Qu'est-ce que Fabrice met sur son pain?
2. Qu'est-ce qu'il boit?
3. Qu'est-ce que Sylvie boit au petit déjeuner?
4. Quel jour est-ce qu'elle mange des croissants?
5. Pourquoi est-ce que Daniel dit qu'il prend le petit déjeuner à l'américaine?
6. Pourquoi est-ce que Marie-Hélène ne mange pas beaucoup au petit déjeuner?
7. Qu'est-ce qu'elle boit?
8. Où habite Chantal?
9. En général, qu'est-ce qu'elle mange au petit déjeuner?
10. Qu'est-ce qu'elle mange avec le blaff de poisson?

■ Questions personnelles
1. Est-ce que tu bois du jus de fruit le matin? Quel jus de fruit?
2. Est-ce que tes parents boivent du café? Sinon, qu'est-ce qu'ils boivent?
3. Est-ce que tu manges souvent des croissants? Quand?
4. Est-ce que tu aimes la confiture? Quelle est ta confiture préférée?
5. Est-ce que tu manges des céréales? De quelles sortes?
6. Est-ce que tu préfères le petit déjeuner français ou le petit déjeuner américain? Pourquoi?

■ Realia note
La Villa Créole is a small Martinique restaurant on the beach at Anse-Mitan (**anse** = bay) in the town of Trois Ilets (**îlet** = small island).

Pre-reading
Have students glance over the reading quickly.
   What is the question that was asked in the interview?

Post-reading
Ask each student to decide which of the five people they would like to have breakfast with and why.
Chez qui veux-tu prendre le petit déjeuner?
Pourquoi?

Comment lire
MORE GUESSING FROM CONTEXT

When you are reading, the context is not only the printed word. Sometimes there are illustrations to help you understand the text. As you read the recipe for **crêpes** on the next page, try guessing what the new words mean by studying the pictures. (You can check how well you are doing by looking at the English equivalents at the bottom of the page.)

Enrichissez votre vocabulaire
INCREASING YOUR ENGLISH VOCABULARY

Learning French will also help you increase your English vocabulary. Sometimes a French word you know will help you guess the meaning of an unfamiliar English word. For example:

a repast   looks like **un repas**   and is an old word for *meal*

Activité
Match these English words with their corresponding definitions.

1. to blanch a. painfully difficult work
2. facile b. easily done
3. travail c. very hungry
4. famished d. to whiten, to bleach

Activité: **Mon petit déjeuner**
Décrivez le petit déjeuner chez vous.
- pendant la semaine
- le dimanche matin

DÉCOUVREZ
LA MARTINIQUE
au
TYPIC BELLEVUE
LE PLUS TYPIQUE DES RESTAURANTS
UN CHOIX UNIQUE DE SPÉCIALITÉS CRÉOLES
Boulevard de la Marne   Tél. 71.68.87
FORT-DE-FRANCE
Parking Boulevard de Verdun

—— RELAIS CRÉOLE ✳ ✳
Menu du jour   et à la carte
Ouvert midi et soir sauf Dimanche

Voici certaines spécialités:

boudin créole	hot sausage, creole style	**bifteck de tortue**	turtle steak
blaff de poisson	fish stew	**matoutou crabes**	stewed crabs served
crabes farcis	stuffed crabs		with rice
langoustes grillées	(small) lobsters, grilled		

Entracte 9 **395**

■ Realia note
Le menu
At the **Typic Bellevue** one can either select the **prix fixe** menu (**le menu du jour**) or order dishes from the main menu (**à la carte**).

OBJECTIVES:
• Reading for information
• Understanding and following instructions

35.4 **Vignette culturelle: La recette des crêpes**
(43:48–46:21 min.)

■ **Photo culture note**
Une cuisine française
French kitchens are smaller than American kitchens, but they are usually equipped in the same way. Note in the background:
• the counter (**le comptoir**)
• the cabinets (**les placards**)
• the sink (**l'évier**)
• pots and pans (**les casseroles**)
• the microwave oven (**le four à micro-ondes**)

■ **Realia note**
Crêpes bretonnes
The area of Brittany (**la Bretagne**) in western France is known for its **crêpes**. For festive occasions, the women of Brittany have traditionally won starched lace head-dresses (**une coiffe bretonne**).

Variétés

Les crêpes

Les crêpes sont d'origine bretonne.° Aujourd'hui, on vend les crêpes dans les «crêperies». On peut aussi faire des crêpes à la maison. Voici une recette° très simple.

LES INGRÉDIENTS
3 oeufs
3 cuillères à soupe de sucre
une pincée° de sel
2 tasses de lait
1 tasse de farine°
1 cuillère à soupe d'huile°
du beurre

LES USTENSILES

 un petit bol

 un grand bol

un fouet

une poêle

D'abord: Pour faire la pâte°

Mettez les oeufs dans le petit bol. Battez-les° bien avec le fouet.

Ajoutez° le sucre, le sel et un peu de lait.

Mettez la farine dans le grand bol. Versez° le contenu° du petit bol dans le grand bol.

Ajoutez l'huile et le reste du lait. Mélangez° bien la pâte. Attendez deux heures.

AU PETIT COIN BRETON LTÉE
Spécialités
CRÊPES BRETONNES

La Crêperie Québécoise
1775 St-Hubert, Montréal H2L 3Z1
(Métro Berri-de-Montigny)
Tél: 521-8362

bretonne *from Brittany*   **recette** *recipe*   **pincée** *pinch*   **farine** *flour*   **huile** *oil*   **pâte** *batter*
Battez-les *Beat them*   **Ajoutez** *Add*   **Versez** *Pour*   **contenu** *contents*   **Mélangez** *Mix, Stir*

 Pre-reading

Have students identify the type of reading. [a recipe: **une recette**]
   What kinds of verb forms are used in this recipe? [commands]

OPTIONAL: Show the *Vignette culturelle* of Video Module 35 which demonstrates the making of crêpes.

Ensuite: Pour faire les crêpes ───────────────────

Chauffez° la poêle. Mettez du beurre dans la poêle.

Mettez une cuillère de pâte dans la poêle.

Agitez° la poêle pour étendre° la pâte.

Retournez° la crêpe quand elle est dorée.°

Si vous êtes adroit(e), faites sauter° la crêpe en l'air. Si vous n'êtes pas adroit(e), abstenez-vous!°

Enfin: Pour servir les crêpes ───────────────────

Mettez la crêpe sur une assiette chaude. Faites les autres° crêpes.

Mettez du sucre ou de la confiture sur chaque° crêpe.

Au choix, roulez-la° ou pliez-la° en quatre.

Chauffez *Heat* **Agitez** *Shake* **étendre** *spread*
Retournez *Turn over* **dorée** *golden brown* **faites sauter** *flip*
abstenez-vous *don't try* **autres** *other* **chaque** *each*
roulez-la *roll it* **pliez-la** *fold it*

Bon appétit!

Entracte 9 397

Teaching strategy: Les crêpes

You might want to cooperate with the home economics department and let the students learn to make **crêpes** in the school kitchen.

REFERENCE SECTION

CONTENTS

The French-Speaking World

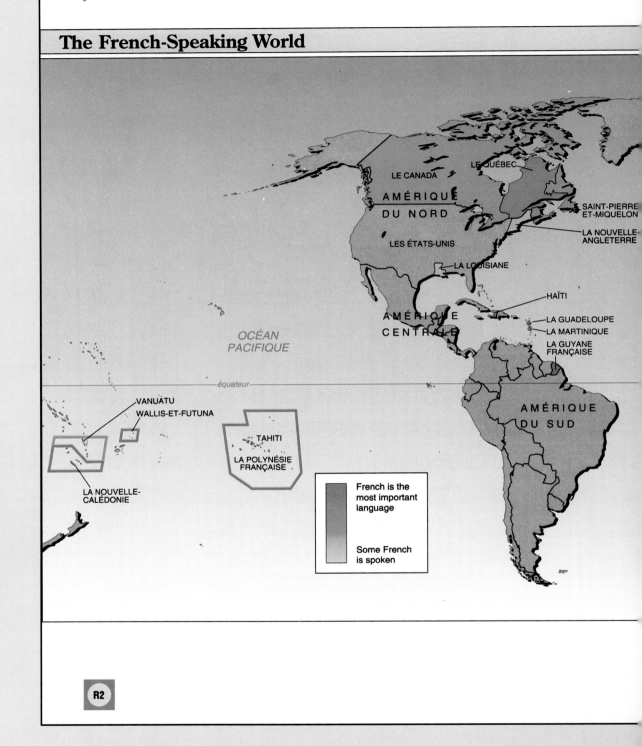

LE QUÉBEC

LE CANADA

AMÉRIQUE
DU NORD

SAINT-PIERRE
ET-MIQUELON

LA NOUVELLE-
ANGLETERRE

LES ÉTATS-UNIS

LA LOUISIANE

HAÏTI

AMÉRIQUE
CENTRALE

LA GUADELOUPE
LA MARTINIQUE

LA GUYANE
FRANÇAISE

OCÉAN
PACIFIQUE

équateur

AMÉRIQUE
DU SUD

VANUATU
WALLIS-ET-FUTUNA

TAHITI

LA POLYNÉSIE
FRANÇAISE

French is the
most important
language

Some French
is spoken

LA NOUVELLE-
CALÉDONIE

R2

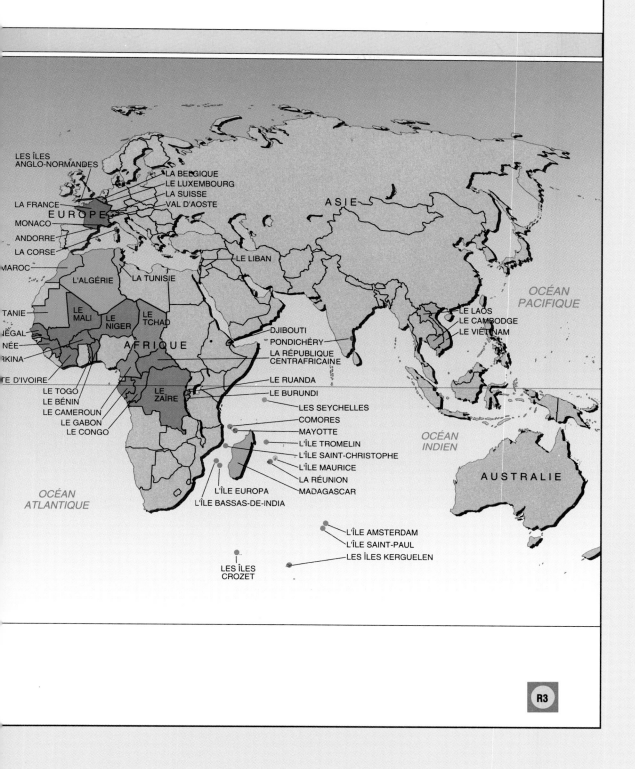

LES ÎLES
ANGLO-NORMANDES
LA BELGIQUE
LE LUXEMBOURG
LA SUISSE
VAL D'AOSTE
LA FRANCE
EUROPE
MONACO
ANDORRE
LA CORSE
MAROC
L'ALGÉRIE
LA TUNISIE
TANIE
LE MALI
LE NIGER
LE TCHAD
ÉGAL
NÉE
AFRIQUE
RKINA
TE D'IVOIRE
LE TOGO
LE BÉNIN
LE CAMEROUN
LE GABON
LE CONGO
LE ZAÏRE

ASIE

LE LIBAN

LE LAOS
LE CAMBODGE
LE VIÊT-NAM

OCÉAN
PACIFIQUE

DJIBOUTI
PONDICHÉRY
LA RÉPUBLIQUE
CENTRAFRICAINE
LE RUANDA
LE BURUNDI
LES SEYCHELLES
COMORES
MAYOTTE
L'ÎLE TROMELIN
L'ÎLE SAINT-CHRISTOPHE
L'ÎLE MAURICE
LA RÉUNION
MADAGASCAR
L'ÎLE EUROPA
L'ÎLE BASSAS-DE-INDIA

OCÉAN
INDIEN

AUSTRALIE

OCÉAN
ATLANTIQUE

L'ÎLE AMSTERDAM
L'ÎLE SAINT-PAUL
LES ÎLES KERGUELEN

LES ÎLES
CROZET

France

L'ANGLETERRE

LA MANCHE

LA BELGIQUE

L'ALLEMAGNE

LE LUXEMBOURG

Lille•
NORD [2]

Le Havre• •Rouen
HAUTE-
NORMANDIE
Caen•
BASSE-
NORMANDIE

PICARDIE

LORRAINE

Nancy•

LES VOSGES

ALSACE
Strasbourg
•

•Paris
Versailles•
RÉGION
PARISIENNE [1]

CHAMPAGNE-
ARDENNE

Colmar•

Rhin

BRETAGNE

Seine

Meuse

Rennes•

PAYS DE
LA LOIRE

Loire

CENTRE

Dijon•

FRANCHE-
COMTÉ

LA SUISSE

•Nantes

•Tours

BOURGOGNE

Saône

OCÉAN
ATLANTIQUE

POITOU-
CHARENTES

AUVERGNE

Vichy•

Annecy•

LIMOUSIN

Clermont-
Ferrand•

•Lyon
RHÔNE-ALPES

LES ALPES

L'ITALIE

Grenoble•

•Bordeaux

Garonne

LE MASSIF

CENTRAL

Rhône

AQUITAINE

•Albi

Nîmes• Avignon
•

•MONAC

MIDI-PYRÉNÉES

Montpellier•

PROVENCE-
CÔTE D'AZUR [3]

•Nice
Cannes

Toulouse•

LANGUEDOC-
ROUSSILLON

Marseille•
Toulon•

•Saint-
Tropez

LES PYRÉNÉES

L'ESPAGNE

LA MÉDITERRANÉE

LA CORSE

[1] Also known as Île-de-France
[2] Also known as Nord-Pas-de-Calais
[3] Also known as Provence-Alpes-Côte d'Azur *(Bottin 1989)*

APPENDIX 2
Sound-Spelling Correspondences

Vowels

Sound	Spelling	Examples
/a/	a, à, â	Madame, là-bas, théâtre
/i/	i, î	visite, Nice, dîne
	y (initial, final, or between consonants)	Yves, Guy, style
/u/	ou, où, oû	Toulouse, où, août
/y/	u, û	tu, Luc, sûr
/o/	o (final or before silent consonant)	piano, idiot, Margot
	au, eau	jaune, Claude, beau
	ô	hôtel, drôle, Côte-d'Ivoire
/ɔ/	o	Monique, Noël, jolie
	au	Paul, restaurant, Laure
/e/	é	Dédé, Québec, télé
	e (before silent final z, t, r)	chez, et, Roger
	ai (final or before final silent consonant)	j'ai, mai, japonais
/ɛ/	è	Michèle, Ève, père
	ei	seize, neige, tour Eiffel
	ê	tête, être, Viêt-nam
	e (before two consonants)	elle, Pierre, Annette
	e (before pronounced final consonant)	Michel, avec, cher
	ai (before pronounced final consonant)	française, aime, Maine
/ə/	e (final or before single consonant)	je, Denise, venir
/ø/	eu, oeu	deux, Mathieu, oeufs
	eu (before final se)	nerveuse, généreuse, sérieuse
/œ/	eu (before final pronounced consonant except /z/)	heure, neuf, Lesieur
	oeu	soeur, coeur, oeuf
	oe	oeil

Nasal vowels

Sound	Spelling	Examples
/ɑ̃/	an, am	France, quand, lampe
	en, em	Henri, pendant, décembre
/ɔ̃/	on, om	non, Simon, bombe
/ɛ̃/	in, im	Martin, invite, impossible
	yn, ym	syndicat, sympathique, Olympique
	ain, aim	Alain, americain, faim
	(o) + in	loin, moins, point
	(i) + en	bien, Julien, viens
/œ̃/	un, um	un, Lebrun, parfum

Semi-vowels

Sound	Spelling	Examples
/j/	**i, y** (before vowel sound)	b<u>i</u>en, p<u>i</u>ano, L<u>y</u>on
	-il, -ill (after vowel sound), **-ll**	oe<u>il</u>, trava<u>ill</u>e, Marse<u>ill</u>e, f<u>ill</u>e
/ɥ/	**u** (before vowel sound)	l<u>u</u>i, S<u>u</u>isse, j<u>u</u>illet
/w/	**ou** (before vowel sound)	<u>ou</u>i, L<u>ou</u>is, j<u>ou</u>er
/wa/	**oi, oî**	v<u>oi</u>ci, Ben<u>oî</u>t
	oy (before vowel)	v<u>oy</u>age

Consonants

Sound	Spelling	Examples
/b/	**b**	<u>B</u>arbara, <u>b</u>anane, <u>B</u>elgique
/k/	**c** (before **a, o, u,** or consonant)	<u>C</u>oca-<u>C</u>ola, <u>c</u>uisine, <u>c</u>lasse
	ch(r)	<u>Ch</u>ristine, <u>Ch</u>ristian, <u>Ch</u>ristophe
	qu, q (final)	<u>Qu</u>ébec, <u>qu</u>'est-ce <u>qu</u>e, cin<u>q</u>
	k	<u>k</u>ilo, <u>K</u>iki, <u>k</u>etchup
/ʃ/	**ch**	<u>Ch</u>arles, blan<u>ch</u>e, <u>ch</u>ez
/a/	**d**	<u>D</u>idier, <u>d</u>ans, mé<u>d</u>ecin
/f/	**f**	<u>F</u>élix, <u>f</u>ranc, neu<u>f</u>
	ph	<u>Ph</u>ilippe, télé<u>ph</u>one, <u>ph</u>oto
/g/	**g** (before **a, o, u,** or consonant)	<u>G</u>abriel, <u>g</u>orge, lé<u>g</u>umes, <u>g</u>ris
	gu (before **e, i, y**)	va<u>gu</u>e, <u>Gu</u>illaume, <u>G</u>uy
/ɲ/	**gn**	mi<u>gn</u>on, champa<u>gn</u>e, Allema<u>gn</u>e
/ʒ/	**j**	<u>j</u>e, <u>J</u>érôme, <u>j</u>aune
	g (before **e, i, y**)	rou<u>g</u>e, <u>G</u>igi, <u>g</u>ymnastique
	ge (before **a, o, u**)	oran<u>ge</u>ade, <u>Ge</u>orges, na<u>ge</u>ur
/l/	**l**	<u>L</u>ise, e<u>ll</u>e, cheva<u>l</u>
/m/	**m**	<u>M</u>aman, <u>m</u>oi, to<u>m</u>ate
/n/	**n**	ba<u>n</u>ane, <u>N</u>ancy, <u>n</u>ous
/p/	**p**	<u>p</u>eu, <u>P</u>apa, <u>P</u>ierre
/r/	**r**	a<u>rr</u>ive, <u>r</u>ent<u>r</u>e, <u>P</u>aris
/s/	**c** (before **e, i, y**)	<u>c</u>e, <u>C</u>écile, Nan<u>c</u>y
	ç (before **a, o, u**)	<u>ç</u>a, gar<u>ç</u>on, dé<u>ç</u>u
	s (initial or before consonant)	<u>s</u>ac, <u>S</u>ophie, re<u>s</u>te
	ss (between vowels)	boi<u>ss</u>on, de<u>ss</u>ert, Sui<u>ss</u>e
	t (before **i** + vowel)	atten<u>t</u>ion, Na<u>t</u>ions Unies, nata<u>t</u>ion
	x	di<u>x</u>, si<u>x</u>, soi<u>x</u>ante
/t/	**t**	<u>t</u>rop, <u>t</u>élé, <u>T</u>ours
	th	<u>Th</u>érèse, <u>th</u>é, Mar<u>th</u>e
/v/	**v**	<u>V</u>iviane, <u>v</u>ous, nou<u>v</u>eau
/gz/	**x**	e<u>x</u>amen, e<u>x</u>emple, e<u>x</u>act
/ks/	**x**	Ma<u>x</u>, Me<u>x</u>ique, e<u>x</u>cellent
/z/	**s** (between vowels)	dé<u>s</u>ert, Loui<u>s</u>e, télévi<u>s</u>ion
	z	Su<u>z</u>anne, <u>z</u>ut, <u>z</u>éro

APPENDIX 3
Numbers

A. Cardinal numbers

0	zéro	18	dix-huit	82	quatre-vingt-deux
1	un (une)	19	dix-neuf	90	quatre-vingt-dix
2	deux	20	vingt	91	quatre-vingt-onze
3	trois	21	vingt et un (une)	100	cent
4	quatre	22	vingt-deux	101	cent un (une)
5	cinq	23	vingt-trois	102	cent deux
6	six	30	trente	200	deux cents
7	sept	31	trente et un (une)	201	deux cent un
8	huit	32	trente-deux	300	trois cents
9	neuf	40	quarante	400	quatre cents
10	dix	41	quarante et un (une)	500	cinq cents
11	onze	50	cinquante	600	six cents
12	douze	60	soixante	700	sept cents
13	treize	70	soixante-dix	800	huit cents
14	quatorze	71	soixante et onze	900	neuf cents
15	quinze	72	soixante-douze	1.000	mille
16	seize	80	quatre-vingts	2.000	deux mille
17	dix-sept	81	quatre-vingt-un (une)	1.000.000	un million

Notes:
1. The word **et** occurs only in the numbers 21, 31, 41, 51, 61, and 71: **vingt et un**, **soixante et onze**
2. **Un** becomes **une** before a feminine noun: **trente et une filles**
3. **Quatre-vingts** becomes **quatre-vingt** before another number: **quatre-vingt-cinq**
4. **Cents** becomes **cent** before another number: **trois cent vingt**
5. **Mille** never adds an **-s**: **quatre mille**

B. Ordinal numbers

1er (ère)	premier (première)	5e	cinquième	9e	neuvième
2e	deuxième	6e	sixième	10e	dixième
3e	troisième	7e	septième	11e	onzième
4e	quatrième	8e	huitième	12e	douzième

Note: **Premier** becomes **première** before a feminine noun: **la première histoire**

C. Metric equivalents

1 gramme	= 0.035 ounces	**1 ounce**	=	**28,349 grammes**
1 kilogramme	= 2.205 pounds	**1 pound**	=	**0,453 kilogrammes**
1 litre	= 1.057 quarts	**1 quart**	=	**0,946 litres**
1 mètre	= 39.37 inches	**1 foot**	=	**30,480 centimètres**
1 kilomètre	= 0.62 miles	**1 mile**	=	**1,609 kilomètres**

R7

Appendix 3 Numbers

APPENDIX 4
Verbs

A. Regular verbs

Infinitive	Present		Passé composé	
parler *(to talk, speak)*	je **parle** tu **parles** il **parle**	nous **parlons** vous **parlez** ils **parlent**	j'ai **parlé** tu **as parlé** il **a parlé**	nous **avons parlé** vous **avez parlé** ils **ont parlé**

IMPERATIVE: **parle, parlons, parlez**

finir *(to finish)*	je **finis** tu **finis** il **finit**	nous **finissons** vous **finissez** ils **finissent**	j'ai **fini** tu **as fini** il **a fini**	nous **avons fini** vous **avez fini** ils **ont fini**

IMPERATIVE: **finis, finissons, finissez**

vendre *(to sell)*	je **vends** tu **vends** il **vend**	nous **vendons** vous **vendez** ils **vendent**	j'ai **vendu** tu **as vendu** il **a vendu**	nous **avons vendu** vous **avez vendu** ils **ont vendu**

IMPERATIVE: **vends, vendons, vendez**

B. *-er* verbs with spelling changes

Infinitive	Present		Passé composé
acheter *(to buy)*	j'**achète** tu **achètes** il **achète**	nous **achetons** vous **achetez** ils **achètent**	j'ai **acheté**

Verb like **acheter**: amener *(to bring, take along)*

espérer *(to hope)*	j'**espère** tu **espères** il **espère**	nous **espérons** vous **espérez** ils **espèrent**	j'ai **espéré**

Verbs like **espérer**: célébrer *(to celebrate)*, préférer *(to prefer)*

commencer *(to begin, start)*	je **commence** tu **commences** il **commence**	nous **commençons** vous **commencez** ils **commencent**	j'ai **commencé**

manger *(to eat)*	je **mange** tu **manges** il **mange**	nous **mangeons** vous **mangez** ils **mangent**	j'ai **mangé**

Verbs like **manger**: nager *(to swim)*, voyager *(to travel)*

payer *(to pay, pay for)*	je **paie** tu **paies** il **paie**	nous **payons** vous **payez** ils **paient**	j'ai **payé**

C. Irregular verbs

Infinitive	Present		Passé composé
avoir *(to have, own)*	j'**ai** tu **as** il **a**	nous **avons** vous **avez** ils **ont**	j'ai **eu**
	IMPERATIVE: **aie, ayons, ayez**		
être *(to be)*	je **suis** tu **es** il **est**	nous **sommes** vous **êtes** ils **sont**	j'ai **été**
	IMPERATIVE: **sois, soyons, soyez**		
aller *(to go)*	je **vais** tu **vas** il **va**	nous **allons** vous **allez** ils **vont**	je suis **allé(e)**
boire *(to drink)*	je **bois** tu **bois** il **boit**	nous **buvons** vous **buvez** ils **boivent**	j'ai **bu**
connaître *(to know)*	je **connais** tu **connais** il **connaît**	nous **connaissons** vous **connaissez** ils **connaissent**	j'ai **connu**
devoir *(to have to, should, must)*	je **dois** tu **dois** il **doit**	nous **devons** vous **devez** ils **doivent**	j'ai **dû**
dire *(to say, tell)*	je **dis** tu **dis** il **dit**	nous **disons** vous **dites** ils **disent**	j'ai **dit**
dormir *(to sleep)*	je **dors** tu **dors** il **dort**	nous **dormons** vous **dormez** ils **dorment**	j'ai **dormi**
écrire *(to write)*	j'**écris** tu **écris** il **écrit**	nous **écrivons** vous **écrivez** ils **écrivent**	j'ai **écrit**
	Verb like **écrire:** décrire *(to describe)*		
faire *(to make, do)*	je **fais** tu **fais** il **fait**	nous **faisons** vous **faites** ils **font**	j'ai **fait**
lire *(to read)*	je **lis** tu **lis** il **lit**	nous **lisons** vous **lisez** ils **lisent**	j'ai **lu**
mettre *(to put, place)*	je **mets** tu **mets** il **met**	nous **mettons** vous **mettez** ils **mettent**	j'ai **mis**
	Verb like **mettre:** promettre *(to promise)*		

Appendix 4 Verbs

Infinitive	Present		Passé composé
ouvrir *(to open)*	j'**ouvre** tu **ouvres** il **ouvre**	nous **ouvrons** vous **ouvrez** ils **ouvrent**	j'ai ouvert

Verbs like **ouvrir**: découvrir *(to discover)*, offrir *(to offer)*

partir *(to leave)*	je **pars** tu **pars** il **part**	nous **partons** vous **partez** ils **partent**	je suis parti(e)
pouvoir *(to be able, can)*	je **peux** tu **peux** il **peut**	nous **pouvons** vous **pouvez** ils **peuvent**	j'ai pu
prendre *(to take)*	je **prends** tu **prends** il **prend**	nous **prenons** vous **prenez** ils **prennent**	j'ai pris

Verbs like **prendre**: apprendre *(to learn)*, comprendre *(to understand)*

savoir *(to know)*	je **sais** tu **sais** il **sait**	nous **savons** vous **savez** ils **savent**	j'ai su
sortir *(to go out, get out)*	je **sors** tu **sors** il **sort**	nous **sortons** vous **sortez** ils **sortent**	je suis sorti(e)
venir *(to come)*	je **viens** tu **viens** il **vient**	nous **venons** vous **venez** ils **viennent**	je suis venu(e)

Verb like **venir**: revenir *(to come back)*

voir *(to see)*	je **vois** tu **vois** il **voit**	nous **voyons** vous **voyez** ils **voient**	j'ai vu
vouloir *(to want)*	je **veux** tu **veux** il **veut**	nous **voulons** vous **voulez** ils **veulent**	j'ai voulu

D. Verbs with *être* in the *passé composé*

aller *(to go)*	je **suis allé(e)**	**passer** *(to go by, through)*	je **suis passé(e)**
arriver *(to arrive, come)*	je **suis arrivé(e)**	**rentrer** *(to go home)*	je **suis rentré(e)**
descendre *(to go down)*	je **suis descendu(e)**	**rester** *(to stay)*	je **suis resté(e)**
entrer *(to enter, go in)*	je **suis entré(e)**	**revenir** *(to come back)*	je **suis revenu(e)**
monter *(to go up)*	je **suis monté(e)**	**sortir** *(to go out, get out)*	je **suis sorti(e)**
mourir *(to die)*	Il/elle **est mort(e)**	**tomber** *(to fall)*	je **suis tombé(e)**
naître *(to be born)*	je **suis né(e)**	**venir** *(to come)*	je **suis venu(e)**
partir *(to leave)*	je **suis parti(e)**		

FRENCH-ENGLISH VOCABULARY

R13

VOCABULARY
French-English

The French-English vocabulary contains active and passive words from the text, as well as the important words of the illustrations used within the units. Obvious passive cognates have not been listed.

The numbers following an entry indicate the lesson in which the word or phrase is activated. (**B** stands for the photo essay that precedes **Niveau B; C** stands for the list of phrases and expressions that precedes **Niveau C;** and **E** stands for **Entracte.**)

Nouns: If the article of a noun does not indicate gender, the noun is followed by *m.* (*masculine*) or *f.* (*feminine*). If the plural (*pl.*) is irregular, it is given in parentheses.

Adjectives: Adjectives are listed in the masculine form. If the feminine form is irregular, it is given in parentheses. Irregular plural forms (*pl.*) are also given in parentheses.

Verbs: Verbs are listed in the infinitive form. An asterisk (*) in front of an active verb means that it is irregular. (For forms, see the verb charts in Appendix 4C.) Irregular present tense forms are listed when they are used before the verb has been activated. Irregular past participle (*p.p.*) forms are listed separately.

Words beginning with an **h** are preceded by a bullet (•) if the **h** is aspirate; that is, if the word is treated as if it begins with a consonant sound.

A

a: il y a there is, there are **17**
à at, in, to **14, 22**
  à côté next door
  à demain see you tomorrow **8**
  à droite on (to) the right **21**
  à gauche on (to) the left **21**
  à la mode popular; in fashion; fashionable **25**
  à mon avis in my opinion **27**
  à partir de as of, beginning
  à pied on foot **22**
  à samedi! see you Saturday! **8**
  à vélo by bicycle **22**
abolir to abolish
abondant plentiful, copious, large
abord: d'abord (at) first **30**
un **abricot** apricot
absolument absolutely
un **accent** accent mark, stress
accepter to accept
des **accessoires** *m.* accessories **25**

un **accord** agreement
  d'accord okay, all right **13**
  être d'accord to agree **14**
un **achat** purchase
  faire des achats to go shopping **29**
  acheter to buy **25, 26**
  acheter + du, de la (*partitive*) to buy (some) **34**
un **acteur, une actrice** actor, actress
une **activité** activity
l' **addition** *f.* check
  adorer to love
une **adresse** address **21**
  quelle est ton adresse? what's your address? **21**
  adroit skilled, skillful
un **adulte** adult
  aéronautique aeronautic, aeronautical
un **aéroport** airport
  affectueusement affectionately (*at the end of a letter*)
une **affiche** poster **17**
  affirmativement affirmatively
l' **Afrique** *f.* Africa
l' **âge** *m.* age

  quel âge a-t-il/elle? how old is he/she? **17**
  quel âge as-tu? how old are you? **7**
  quel âge a ton père/ta mère? how old is your father/your mother? **7**
  âgé old
une **agence** agency
  une agence de tourisme tourist office
  une agence de voyages travel agency
  agiter to shake
  agité agitated
  ah! ah!, oh!
  ah bon? oh? really? **16**
  ah non! ah, no!
ai (*see* **avoir**): **j'ai** I have **17**
  j'ai... ans I'm . . . (years old) **7**
  aider to help **29, 35**
une **aile** wing
  aimer to like **15, 33**
  est-ce que tu aimes...? do you like . . .? **13**
  j'aime... I like . . . **13**
  j'aimerais I would like
  je n'aime pas... I don't like . . . **13**

ainsi thus
aîné older
  un frère aîné older
    brother
  une soeur aînée older
    sister
ajouter to add
l' **Algérie** *f.* Algeria *(country in North Africa)*
algérien (algérienne) Algerian
l' **Allemagne** *f.* Germany
allemand German
* **aller** to go **22**
  aller + *inf.* to be going to + *inf.* **22**
  allez *(see* **aller***):* **allez-vous-en** go away!
  allez-y come on!, go ahead!, do it!
  comment allez-vous? how are you? **3**
allô! hello! *(on the telephone)*
allons *(see* **aller***):* **allons-y** let's go! **22**
alors so, then **19**
une **alouette** lark
les **Alpes** *f.* (the) Alps
l' **alphabet** *m.* alphabet
l' **alpinisme** *m.* mountain climbing **29**
  faire de l'alpinisme to go mountain climbing **29**
l' **Alsace** *f.* Alsace *(province in eastern France)*
amener to bring *(a person)* **26, 35**
américain American **2, 19**
  à l'américaine American-style
un **Américain, une Américaine** American person
l' **Amérique** *f.* America
un **ami, une amie** (close) friend **5**
amicalement love *(at the end of a letter)*
l' **amitié** *f.* friendship
  amitiés best regards *(at the end of a letter)*
amusant funny, amusing **19**
amuser to amuse
  s'amuser to have fun
  on s'est bien amusé! we had a good time!
un **an** year

avoir... ans to be ... (years old) **18**
  il/elle a... ans he/she is ... (years old) **7**
  j'ai... ans I'm ... (years old) **7**
  l'an dernier last year
  par an per year
un **ananas** pineapple
ancien (ancienne) former, old, ancient
un **âne** donkey
un **ange** angel
anglais English **2, 19**
un **Anglais, une Anglaise** English person
un **animal** *(pl.* **animaux***)* animal
une **animation** live entertainment
animé animated, lively
une **année** year **8**
  bonne année! Happy New Year! **32**
  toute l'année all year long
un **anniversaire** birthday **8**
  bon anniversaire! happy birthday! **32**
  c'est quand, ton anniversaire? when is your birthday? **8**
  mon anniversaire est le (2 mars) my birthday is (March 2nd) **8**
un **annuaire** telephone directory
un **anorak** ski jacket
les **antiquités** *f.* antiquities, antiques
août *m.* August **8**
un **appareil-photo** *(pl.* **appareils-photo***)* (still) camera **17**
un **appartement** apartment **21**
s' **appeller** to be named, called
  comment s'appelle...? what's ...'s name? **6**
  comment s'appelle-t-il/elle? what's his/her name? **17**
  comment t'appelles-tu? what's your name? **1**
  il/elle s'appelle... his/her name is ... **6**
  je m'appelle... my name is ... **1**
apporter to bring *(things)* **26**

apporter quelque chose à quelqu'un to bring something to someone **35**
  apporte-moi (apportez-moi) bring me **B**
* **apprendre (à)** + *inf.* to learn (to) **34**
apprécier to appreciate
approprié appropriate
après after **29**; after, afterwards **30, 31**
  d'après according to
l' **après-midi** *m.* afternoon **29**
  cet après-midi this afternoon **31**
  de l'après-midi in the afternoon, P.M. **4**
  demain après-midi tomorrow afternoon **31**
  hier après-midi yesterday afternoon **31**
l' **arabe** *m.* Arabic *(language)*
un **arbre** tree
  un arbre généalogique family tree
l' **arche** *f.* **de Noé** Noah's Ark
l' **argent** *m.* money **28**
  l'argent de poche allowance, pocket money
arrêter to arrest
arriver to arrive, come **22**
  j'arrive! I'm coming!
une **arrivée** arrival
un **arrondissement** district
un **artifice: le feu d'artifice** fireworks
un **artiste, une artiste** artist
as *(see* **avoir***):* **est-ce que tu as...?** do you have ...? **17**
un **ascenseur** elevator
un **aspirateur** vacuum cleaner
asseyez-vous! sit down! **B**
assez rather **19**; enough
assieds-toi! sit down! **B**
une **assiette** plate **33**
assister à to go to, attend **29**
associer to associate
l' **Atlantique** *m.* Atlantic Ocean
attendre to wait, wait for **28**
attention *f.:* **faire attention** to be careful, pay attention **16**
attentivement carefully

au (à + le) to (the), at (the), in (the) **14, 22**
au revoir! good-bye! **3**
une auberge inn
une auberge de campagne country inn **30**
aucun: ne... aucun none, not any
aujourd'hui today **8, 31**
aujourd'hui, c'est... today is . . . **8**
aussi also, too **2, 15**
aussi... que as . . . as **27**
une auto (automobile) car, automobile **17**
une auto-école driving school
un autobus bus
un autocar touring bus **29**
l' automne m. autumn, fall
en automne in (the) autumn, fall **12**
autre other **33**
d'autres others
un(e) autre another
aux (à + les) to (the), at (the), in (the) **22**
avant before **29, 31**
avant hier the day before yesterday
en avant let's begin
avantageux (avantageuse) reasonable, advantageous
avec with **14**
avec moi, avec toi with me, with you **13**
avec qui? with who(m)? **16**
une avenue avenue **21**
un avion airplane, plane **29**
en avion by airplane **29**
un avis opinion
avis de recherche missing person's bulletin
à mon avis in my opinion **27**
à votre avis in your opinion
* avoir to have **18**
avoir... ans to be . . . (years old) **18**
avoir besoin de to need **28**
avoir chaud to be warm, hot **30**

avoir de la chance to be lucky **30**
avoir envie de to feel like, want **28**
avoir faim to be hungry **18**
avoir froid to be cold **30**
avoir lieu to take place
avoir raison to be right **30**
avoir soif to be thirsty **18, 30**
avoir tort to be wrong **30**
avril m. April **8**

B

le babyfoot tabletop soccer game
le babysitting: faire du babysitting to baby-sit
les bagages m. bags, baggage
bain: un maillot de bain bathing suit **25**
une banane banana **33**
une bande reel-to-reel tape **B**
une bande dessinée comic strip
des bandes dessinées comics
la Bannière étoilée Star-Spangled Banner
une banque bank
une barbe: quelle barbe! what a pain! (colloq.)
bas: en bas downstairs **21**
au bas at the bottom
le baseball baseball **23**
basé based
le basket (basketball) basketball **23**
jouer au basket to play basketball **13**
des baskets m. hightops (sneakers) **25**
bateau boat, ship **29**
un bateau-mouche sightseeing boat
la batterie drums **23**
battre to beat
bavard talkative
beau (bel, belle; m.pl. beaux) handsome, good-looking, beautiful **17, 20, 27**

il est beau he is good-looking, handsome **17**
il fait beau it's beautiful (nice) out **12**
un beau-frère stepbrother, brother-in-law
un beau-père stepfather, father-in-law
beaucoup (de) much, very much, many, a lot **15**
la beauté beauty
un bec beak
bel (see beau) beautiful, handsome **27**
la Belgique Belgium
belle (see beau) beautiful **17, 20, 27**
elle est belle she is beautiful **17**
une belle-mère stepmother, mother-in-law
une belle-soeur stepsister, sister-in-law
les Bermudes f. Bermuda
le besoin need
avoir besoin de to need, to have to **28**
des besoins d'argent money needs
bête dumb, silly **19**
le beurre butter **33**
une bibliothèque library **21**
une bicyclette bicycle **17**
bien well, very well, carefully **15**
bien sûr of course **13**
ça va bien everything's fine (going well) **3**
ça va très bien I'm (everything's) very well **3**
c'est bien that's good (fine) **20**
eh bien! well! **26**
je veux bien (...) I'd love to (. . .), I do, I want to **13, 34**
oui, bien sûr... yes, of course . . . **14**
très bien very well **15**
bientôt: à bientôt! see you soon!
bienvenue welcome
le bifteck steak
un biftek de tortue turtle steak

bilingue bilingual

un billet bill, paper money 28; ticket

la biologie biology

une biscotte dry toast

blaff de poisson *(m.)* fish stew

blanc (blanche) white 20

Blanche-Neige *f.* Snow White

blanchir to blanch, turn white

bleu blue 20

blond blonde 17
  il/elle est blond(e) he/she is blond 17

un blouson jacket 25

* boire to drink 34

une boisson drink, beverage 10, 33

une boîte box

un bol deep bowl

bon (bonne) good 20
  bon marché *(inv.)* inexpensive 25
  ah bon? oh, really? 16
  de bonne humeur in a good mood
  il fait bon the weather's good (pleasant) 12

le bonheur happiness

bonjour hello 1, 3

une botte boot 25

une bouche mouth E3

une boucherie butcher shop

le boudin sausage

une boulangerie bakery

un boulevard boulevard 21

une boum party *(colloq.)* 22

une boutique boutique, shop 25

boxe: un match de boxe boxing match

un bras arm E3

brésilien (brésilienne) Brazilian

la Bretagne Brittany *(province in northwestern France)*

bricoler to do things around the house

broche: à la broche on the spit

bronzé tan

un bruit noise

brun brown, dark-haired 17
  il/elle est brun(e) he/she has dark hair 17

brunir to turn brown

Bruxelles *f.* Brussels

le bulletin des notes report card

un bureau desk B, 17; office

un bus bus
  en bus by bus 22

un but goal; end

C

ça that, it
  ça fait combien? ça fait... how much is that (it)? that (it) is ... 11
  ça, là-bas that (one), over there 17
  ça va? how's everything? how are you? 3
  ça va everything's fine, I'm OK 3
  ça va (très) bien, ça va bien everything's going very well, everything's fine (going well) 3
  ça va comme ci, comme ça everything's (going) so-so 3
  ça va (très) mal things are going (very) badly 3
  regarde ça look at that 17

une cabine d'essayage fitting room

les cabinets *m.* toilet

un cadeau *(pl. cadeaux)* gift, present

cadet (cadette) younger
  un frère cadet (a) younger brother
  une soeur cadette (a) younger sister

le café coffee 10, 21
  un café au lait coffee with hot milk

un café café *(French coffee shop)* 14
  au café to (at) the café 14

un cahier notebook B

une calculatrice calculator 17

un calendrier calendar

un camarade, une camarade classmate 17

le Cambodge Cambodia *(country in Asia)*

un cambriolage burglary

un cambrioleur burglar

une caméra movie camera

la campagne countryside 29
  à la campagne to (in) the countryside 29
  une auberge de campagne country inn
  camping: faire du camping to go camping 29

le Canada Canada
  canadien (canadienne) Canadian 2, 19

un Canadien, une Canadienne Canadian person

un canard duck

une cantine de l'école school cafeteria 33

un car touring bus 29
  un car scolaire school bus

une carotte carrot 33
  des carottes rapées grated carrots

un carré square
  le Vieux Carré *the French Quarter in New Orleans*

une carte map B; card
  une carte postale postcard
  les cartes *f.* (playing) cards 23
  jouer aux cartes to play cards 23

un cas case
  en cas de in case of

une cassette cassette tape B, 17

le catch wrestling

une cathédrale cathedral

une cave cellar

ce (c') this, that, it
  ce n'est pas that's/it's not 20
  ce que what C
  ce sont these are, those are, they are 20
  c'est it's, that's 5, 17, 20
  c'est + *day of the week* it's ... 8
  c'est + *name or noun* it's ... 5
  c'est bien/mal that's good/bad 20
  c'est combien? how much is that/it? 11
  c'est le (12 octobre) it's (October 12) 8

qu'est-ce que c'est? what
is it? what's that? **17**
qui est-ce? who's
that/this? **17**
ce (cet, cette; ces) this, that,
these, those **26**
ce... -ci this . . . (over
here) **26**
ce mois-ci this month **31**
ce n'est pas it's (that's)
not **20**
ce soir this evening,
tonight **31**
une **cédille** cedilla
une **ceinture** belt **25**
cela that
célèbre famous
cent one hundred **6, 25**
cent un, cent deux 101,
102 **25**
**deux cents, trois cents,
... neuf cents** 200, 300,
. . . 900 **25**
une **centaine** about a hundred
un **centime** centime *(1/100 of a
franc)*
un **centre** center
un centre commercial
shopping center **21**
les **céréales** *f.* cereal **33**
une **cerise** cherry **33**
certain certain
certains some of them
ces *(see* **ce)** these, those **26**
c'est *(see* **ce)**
cet *(see* **ce)** this, that **26**
cette *(see* **ce)** this, that **26**
chacun each one, each
person
une **chaise** chair **B, 17**
une **chaîne** (TV) channel
une **chaîne stéréo** stereo set **17**
une mini-chaîne compact
stereo
la **chaleur** heat, warmth
une **chambre** bedroom **17, 21**
un **champion, une championne**
champion
la **chance** luck
avoir de la chance to be
lucky **30**
bonne chance! good luck!
31
une **chanson** song
chanter to sing **13, 15**

un **chanteur, une chanteuse**
singer
un **chapeau** *(pl.* **chapeaux)** hat
25
chaque each, every
charmant charming
un **chat** cat **7, E5**
un **château** *(pl.* **châteaux)** castle
chaud warm, hot
avoir chaud to be warm
(hot) *(people)* **30**
il fait chaud it's warm
(hot) *(weather)* **12**
chauffer to warm, heat up
un **chauffeur, une chauffeuse**
driver
une **chaussette** sock **25**
une **chaussure** shoe **25**
un **chef** boss; chef
une **chemise** shirt **25**
un **chemisier** blouse **25**
cher (chère) expensive; dear
25
chercher to look for, to get,
to find **25**
je cherche... I'm looking
for . . . **25**
un **cheval** *(pl.* **chevaux)** horse
E5
les **cheveux** *m.* hair **E3**
chez + *person* at (to)
someone's house **22;** at
(to) the office of
chez moi (toi, lui...) (at)
home **23**
chic *(inv.)* nice; elegant, in
style
une chic fille a great girl
un **chien** dog **7**
la **chimie** chemistry
chinois Chinese **19**
le **chinois** Chinese *(language)*
le **chocolat** hot chocolate, cocoa
10
une glace au chocolat
chocolate ice cream
choisir to choose **27**
un **choix** choice
au choix choose one, your
choice
une **chorale** choir
une **chose** thing **17**
quelque chose something
32
chouette great, terrific **20, 25**

le **cidre** cider
un **cinéaste, une cinéaste** film
maker
un **cinéma** movie theater **21**
le cinéma the movies
au cinéma to (at) the
movies, movie theater
14
cinq five **1**
cinquante fifty **3**
cinquième fifth **24**
une **circonstance** circumstance
cité: la Cité Interdite
Forbidden City
une **clarinette** clarinet **23**
une **classe** class
en classe in class **14**
classique classical
un **clavier** keyboard **23**
un **client, une cliente** customer
un **clip** music video
un **cochon** pig
un **coiffeur, une coiffeuse**
hairdresser
un **coin** spot
une **coïncidence** coincidence
le **Colisée** the Coliseum *(a large
stadium built by the
Romans)*
des **collants** *m.* (pair of) tights,
pantyhose **25**
un **collège** junior high school
une **colonie** colony
une **colonne** column
combien how much **28**
combien coûte...? how
much does . . . cost? **11,
25**
combien de how much,
how many **28**
combien de temps? how
long?
combien d'heures? how
many hours?
ça fait combien? how
much is this (it)? **11**
c'est combien? how
much is this (it)? **11**
commander to order
comme like, as, for
comme ci, comme ça
so-so
**ça va comme ci, comme
ça** everything's so-so **3**
commencer to begin, start

comment? how? **16**; what?

comment allez-vous? how are you? **3**

comment est-il/elle? what's he/she like? what does he/she look like? **17**

comment dit-on... en français? how do you say . . . in French? **B**

comment lire reading hints

comment s'appelle...? what's . . .'s name? **6**

comment s'appelle-t-il/elle? what's his/her name? **17**

comment t'appelles-tu? what's your name? **1**

comment trouves-tu...? what do you think of . . .? **25**

comment vas-tu? how are you? **3**

un commentaire comment, commentary

commercial: un centre commercial shopping center **21**

le commérage gossip

communiquer to communicate

un compact disque compact disc **17**

complément object

compléter to complete

* **comprendre** to understand **34**

je (ne) comprends (pas) I (don't) understand **B**

compter to count (on); to expect, intend

concerne: en ce qui concerne as for

un concert concert **22**

un concombre cucumber

la confiture jam **33**

confortable comfortable **21**

une connaissance acquaintance

faire connaissance (avec) to become acquainted (with)

* **connaître** to know, be acquainted with; *(in passé composé)* to meet for the first time **36**

tu connais...? do you know . . .? are you acquainted with . . .? **6**

connu *(p.p. of* **connaître)** knew, met **36**

un conseil piece of advice, counsel

des conseils *m.* advice

un conservatoire conservatory

une consonne consonant

se contenter to limit oneself

le contenu contents

continuer to continue **21**

une contradiction disagreement

une contravention (traffic) ticket

cool cool, neat

un copain, une copine friend, pal **5**

un petit copain, une petite copine boyfriend, girlfriend

copier to copy

une copine friend **5**

coréen (coréenne) Korean

un corps body

correspondant corresponding

correspondre to correspond, agree

la Corse Corsica *(French island off the Italian coast)*

un costume man's suit

la Côte d'Azur Riviera *(southern coast of France on the Mediterranean)*

la Côte d'Ivoire Ivory Coast *(French-speaking country in West Africa)*

côté: à côté (de) next door; next to

une côtelette de porc pork chop

le cou neck **E3**

une couleur color **20**

de quelle couleur ...? what color . . .? **20**

un couloir hall, corridor

coup: dans le coup with it

courage: bon courage! good luck! **31**

courageux (courageuse) courageous

une course race

faire les courses to go shopping *(for food)* **33**

court short **25**

un cousin, une cousine cousin **7, 24**

le coût: le coût de la vie cost of living

un couteau *(pl.* **couteaux)** knife **33**

coûter to cost

combien coûte...? how much does . . . cost? **11, 25**

il (elle) coûte... it costs . . . **11**

un couturier, une couturière fashion designer

un couvert place setting **33**

un crabe crab

des matoutou crabes stewed crabs with rice

la craie chalk

un morceau de craie piece of chalk **B**

une cravate tie **25**

un crayon pencil **B, 17**

créer to create

un crétin idiot

une crêpe crepe (pancake) **9**

une crêperie crepe restaurant

une crevaison flat tire

une croisade crusade

un croissant crescent (roll) **9**

une cuillère spoon **33**

une cuillère à soupe soup spoon

la cuisine cooking **33**

une cuisine kitchen **21**

cuit cooked

culturel (culturelle) cultural

curieux (curieuse) curious, strange

la curiosité curiosity

un cyclomoteur moped

D

d'abord (at) first **30**

d'accord okay, all right

être d'accord to agree **14**

oui, d'accord yes, okay **13**

une dame lady, woman *(polite term)* **5**

les dames *f.* checkers *(game)* **23**

dangereux (dangereuse) dangerous

R19

Reference Section **R19**

French-English Vocabulary

dans in **17**
danser to dance **13, 15**
la **date** date **8**
    quelle est la date? what's the date? **8**
de (d') of, from, about **14, 23**
    de l'après-midi in the afternoon **4**
    de quelle couleur... ? what color . . . ? **20**
    de qui? of whom? **16**
    de quoi? about what?
    de temps en temps from time to time
    pas de not any, no **18, 34**
débarquer to land
décembre *m.* December **8**
décider (de) to decide (to)
une **déclaration** statement
décoré decorated
  * **découvrir** to discover
  * **décrire** to describe **C**
    décrivez... describe. . . **C**
un **défaut** shortcoming
un **défilé** parade
dégoûtant: c'est dégoûtant! it's (that's) disgusting **35**
dehors outside
    en dehors de outside of
déjà already; ever
déjeuner to eat (have) lunch **33**
le **déjeuner** lunch **33**
    le petit déjeuner breakfast **33**
délicieux (délicieuse) delicious **34**
demain tomorrow **8**
    à demain! see you tomorrow! **8**
    demain, c'est... (jeudi) tomorrow is . . . (Thursday) **8**
demander (à) to ask **C, 36**
    demandez ... ask . . . **C**
un **demi-frère** half-brother
une **demi-soeur** half-sister
demi: ... heures et demie half past . . . **4**
    midi et demi half past noon **4**
    minuit et demi half past midnight **4**

démodé out of style, unfashionable **25**
un **démon** devil
une **dent** tooth
un **départ** departure
se **dépêcher: dépêchez-vous!** hurry up!
dépend: ça dépend that depends
une **dépense** expense
dépenser to spend (money) **28**
dernier (dernière) last **31**
derrière behind, in back of **17**
des some, any **18;** of (the), from (the), about (the) **23**
le **désert** desert
désirer to wish, want
    vous désirez? what would you like? may I help you? **10, 25**
désolé sorry
le **dessert** dessert **33**
le **dessin** art, drawing
    un dessin animé cartoon
détester to hate, detest **3**
deux two **1**
deuxième second **24**
    le deuxième étage third floor
devant in front of **17**
développer to develop
deviner to guess
  * **devoir** to have to, should, must **35**
un **devoir** homework assignment **B**
les **devoirs** *m.* homework
    faire mes devoirs to do my homework **29**
d'habitude usually
différemment differently
différent different
difficile hard, difficult **20**
la **dignité** dignity
dimanche *m.* Sunday **8**
dîner to have dinner **15, 33**
    dîner au restaurant to have dinner at a restaurant **13**
le **dîner** dinner, supper **33**
  * **dire** to say, tell **C, 36**
    que veut dire...? what does . . . mean? **B**

directement straight
un **directeur, une directrice** director, principal
dirigé directed, guided
dis! (*see* **dire**) say!, hey! **20**
    dis donc! say there!, hey there! **20**
discuter to discuss
une **dispute** quarrel, dispute
un **disque** record **17**
    un compact disque compact disc **17**
dit (*p.p. of* **dire**) said
dit (*see* **dire**): **comment dit-on... en français?** how do you say . . . in French? **B**
dites... (*see* **dire**) say . . ., tell . . . **C**
dix ten **1, 2**
dix-huit eighteen **2**
dixième tenth **24**
dix-neuf nineteen **2**
dix-sept seventeen **2**
un **docteur** doctor
dois (*see* **devoir**): **je dois** I have to (must) **13**
domestique domestic
    les animaux *m.* **domestiques** pets **7**
dommage! too bad! **15**
donner (à) to give (to) **35, 36**
    donne-moi... give me . . . **9, B**
    donnez-moi... give me **10, B**
    s'il te plaît, donne-moi... please, give me . . . **10**
doré golden brown
  * **dormir** to sleep
le **dos** back **E3**
une **douzaine** dozen **33**
douze twelve **2**
douzième twelfth **24**
droit: tout droit straight **21**
droite right
    à droite to (on) the right **21**
drôle funny **20**
du (de + le) of (the), from (the) **23;** some, any **34**
    du matin in the morning, A.M. **4**

du soir in the evening, P.M. 4
dû (*p.p. of* **devoir**) had to 35
dur hard
   des oeufs durs hard-boiled eggs
durer to last
dynamique dynamic

E

l' **eau** *f.* (*pl.* **eaux**) water 33
   l'eau minérale mineral water 33
un **échange** exchange
des **échecs** *m.* chess 23
une **éclosion** hatching
une **école** school 21
   économiser to save money
   écouter to listen to B, 15
      écouter la radio to listen to the radio 13
      écouter des cassettes to listen to cassettes 29
* **écrire** to write 36
l' **éducation** *f.* education
   l'éducation civique civics
   l'éducation physique physical education
une **église** church 21
   égyptien (égyptienne) Egyptian
   eh bien! well! 26
   électronique: une guitare électronique electric guitar
   élégant elegant 25
un **éléphant** elephant E5
un **élève, une élève** pupil, student 17
   élevé high
   elle she, it 11, 14, 18; her 23
      elle coûte... it costs ... 11
      elle est (canadienne) she's (Canadian) 6
      elle s'appelle... her name is ... 6
   embrasser: je t'embrasse love and kisses (*at the end of a letter*)
un **emploi du temps** time-table (*of work*)
   emprunter à to borrow from

en in, on, to, by
   en avion by airplane, plane 29
   en bas (haut) downstairs (upstairs) 21
   en bus (métro, taxi, train, voiture) by bus (subway, taxi, train, car) 22
   en ce qui concerne as for
   en face opposite, across (the street)
   en fait in fact
   en famille at home
   en plus in addition
   en scène on stage
   en solde on sale
   va-t'en! go away! 22
un **endroit** place 22
un **enfant, une enfant** child 24
   enfin at last 30
   ensuite then, after that 30
   entendre to hear 28
   entier (entière) entire
l' **entracte** *m.* interlude
   entre between
une **entrée** entry (*of a house*)
un **entretien** discussion
   envers toward
l' **envie** *f.* envy; feeling
   avoir envie de to want; to feel like, want to 28
   épicé hot (spicy)
une **épicerie** grocery store
les **épinards** *m.* spinach
une **équipe** team
une **erreur** error, mistake
   es (*see* **être**)
      tu es + nationality you are ... 2
      tu es + nationality? are you ...? 2
      tu es de... ? are you from ...? 2
un **escalier** staircase
un **escargot** snail
l' **Espagne** *f.* Spain
   espagnol Spanish 19
      parler espagnol to speak Spanish 13
   espérer to hope 26
un **esprit** spirit
   essayer to try on, to try
l' **essentiel** *m.* the important thing

   est (*see* **être**)
      est-ce que (qu')...? *phrase used to introduce a question* 14
      c'est... it's ..., that's ... 5, 7, 20
      c'est le + *date* it's ... 8
      il/elle est + *nationality* he/she is ... 6
      n'est-ce pas...? isn't it? 14
      où est...? where is ... ? 14
      quel jour est-ce? what day is it? 8
      qui est-ce? who's that (this)? 5, 17
l' **est** *m.* east
   et and 2, 14
      et demi(e), et quart half past, quarter past 4
      et toi? and you? 1
   établir to establish
un **étage** floor of a building, story
les **États-Unis** *m.* United States
   été (*p.p. of* **être**) been, was 31
l' **été** *m.* summer
      en été in (the) summer 12
      l'heure d'été daylight savings time
   étendre to spread
une **étoile** star
   étrange strange
   étranger (étrangère) foreign
* **être** to be 14
      être à to belong to
      être d'accord to agree 14
une **étude** study
un **étudiant, une étudiant** (college) student 17
   étudier to study 13, 15
   eu (*p.p. of* **avoir**) had 31
      il y a eu there was
   euh... er ..., uh ...
      euh non... well, no
   européen (européenne) European
   eux they, them 23
      eux-mêmes themselves
un **événement** event
un **examen** exam, test
      réussir à un examen to pass an exam, a test

excusez-moi excuse me **21**

un **exemple** example

    par exemple for instance

un **exercice** exercise

    faire des exercices to exercise

exiger to insist

expliquer to explain **C**

    expliquez... explain . . . **C**

exprimer to express

exquis: c'est exquis! it's exquisite! **34**

extérieur: à l'extérieur outside

extra terrific **20**

extraordinaire extraordinary

    il a fait un temps extraordinaire! the weather was great!

F ━━━━━━━━━━━━━━━

face: en face (de) opposite, across (the street) from

facile easy **20**

faible weak

la **faim** hunger

    avoir faim to be hungry **30**

    j'ai faim I'm hungry **9**

    tu as faim? you're hungry **9**

faire to do, make **16**

    faire attention to pay attention, be careful **16**

    faire de + *activity* to do, play, study, participate in **29**

    faire des achats to go shopping **29**

    faire les courses to go shopping **33**

    faire mes devoirs to do my homework **29**

    faire partie de to be a member of

    faire sauter to flip

    faire un match to play a game (match) **16**

    faire un pique-nique to have a picnic **29**

    faire un voyage to take a trip **16**

    faire une promenade to take a walk **16**

    faire une promenade à pied (à vélo, en voiture) to take a walk (a bicycle ride, a drive) **22**

fait (*p.p. of* **faire**) did, done, made **31**

fait: en fait in fact

fait (*see* **faire**)**: ça fait combien?** how much is that (it)? **11**

    ça fait... francs that's (it's) . . . francs **11**

    il fait (beau, etc.) it's (beautiful, etc.) (*weather*) **12**

    quel temps fait-il? what (how) is the weather? **12**

fameux: c'est fameux! it's superb! **34**

familial with the family

une **famille** family **7, 24**

    en famille at home

un **fana,** une **fana** fan

un **fantôme** ghost

la **farine** flour

fatigué tired

faux (fausse) false **20**

favori (favorite) favorite

une **femme** woman **17;** wife **24**

une **fenêtre** window **B, 17**

fermer to close **B**

une **feuille** sheet, leaf **B**

    une feuille de papier sheet of paper **B**

un **feuilleton** series, serial story (*in newspaper*)

le **feu d'artifice** fireworks

les **félicitations** *f.* congratulations

février *m.* February **8**

une **fête** holiday

    fîche-moi la paix! leave me alone! (*colloq.*) **36**

la **fièvre** fever

une **fille** girl **5;** daughter **24**

un **film** movie **22, 29**

    un film policier detective movie

un **fils** son **24**

la **fin** end

finalement finally **30**

fini (*p.p. of* **finir**) over, finished **31**

finir to finish **27**

flamand Flemish

un **flamant** flamingo

une **fleur** flower

un **fleuve** river

un **flic** cop (*colloq.*)

une **flûte** flute **23**

une **fois** time

    à la fois at the same time

la **folie: à la folie** madly

folklorique: une chanson folklorique folksong

fonctionner to work, function

fondé founded

le **foot (football)** soccer **23**

    le football américain football

    jouer au foot to play soccer **13**

une **forêt** forest

formidable great!

fort strong

    plus fort louder **B**

un **fouet** whisk

une **fourchette** fork **33**

la **fourrure** fur

    un manteau de fourrure fur coat

frais: il fait frais it's cool (*weather*) **12**

une **fraise** strawberry **33**

un **franc** franc (*monetary unit of France, Belgium, and Switzerland*) **11**

    ça fait... francs that's (it's) . . . francs **11**

la **France** France **14**

    en France in France **14**

francophone French-speaking

français French **2, 19**

    comment dit-on... en français? how do you say . . . in French? **B**

    parler français to speak French **13**

le **français** French (*language*)

un **Français,** une **Française** French person

un **frère** brother **7, 24**

des **frites** *f.* French fries **33**

    un steak-frites steak and French fries **9**

froid cold

    avoir froid to be (feel) cold (*people*) **30**

    il fait froid it's cold out (*weather*) **12**

le **fromage** cheese **33**
    un sandwich au fromage
       cheese sandwich
un **fruit** fruit **33**
    furieux (furieuse) furious
une **fusée** rocket

G

    gagner to earn, to win **28**
un **garage** garage **21**
un **garçon** boy **5**; waiter
une **gare** train station
une **garniture** side dish
un **gâteau** (*pl.* **gâteaux**) cake **33**
    gauche left
    à gauche to (on) the left
       21
une **gelée** jelly
    généralement generally
    généreux (généreuse)
       generous
la **générosité** generosity
    génial brilliant
des **gens** *m.* people **18**
    gentil (gentille) nice, kind
       19; sweet
la **géographie** geography
une **girafe** giraffe **E5**
une **glace** ice cream **9, 33**;
       mirror, ice
    glacé iced
    un thé glacé iced tea **33**
un **goûter** afternoon snack
une **goyave** guava
    grand tall **17**; big, large **20**;
       big *(size of clothing)* **25**
    un grand magasin
       department store **25**
    une grande surface big
       store, self-service store
    grandir to get tall
une **grand-mère** grandmother **7,**
       24
un **grand-père** grandfather **7,**
       24
les **grands-parents** *m.*
       grandparents **24**
    grec (greque) Greek
un **grenier** attic
une **grillade** grilled meat
une **grille** grid
    grillé: le pain grillé toast
    une tartine de pain grillé
       buttered toast

la **grippe** flu
    gris gray **20**
    gros (grosse) fat, big
    grossir to gain weight, get fat
       27
la **Guadeloupe** Guadeloupe
       (French island in the West
       Indies)
une **guerre** war
une **guitare** guitar **17, 23**
un **gymnase** gym

H

    habillé dressed
    habiter to live **15**
    Haïti Haiti *(French island in*
       the West Indies)
un **hamburger** hamburger **9**
les• **haricots** *m.* **verts** green
       beans **33**
la• **hâte** haste
    en hâte quickly
 • **haut** high
    en haut upstairs **21**
    plus haut above
 • **hélas!** too bad!
    hésiter to hesitate
l' **heure** *f.* time, hour; o'clock **4**
    ... heure(s) (dix) (ten)
       past ... **4**
    ... heure(s) et demie half
       past ... **4**
    ... heure(s) et quart
       quarter past ... **4**
    ... heure(s) moins (dix)
       (ten) of ... **4**
    ... heure(s) moins le
       quart quarter to ... **4**
    à... heures at ... o'clock
       14
    à quelle heure...? at what
       time ... ? **16**
    à quelle heure est...? at
       what time is ... ? **4**
    il est... heure(s) it's ...
       o'clock **4**
    par heure per hour, an
       hour
    quelle heure est-il? what
       time is it? **4**
    heureux (heureuse) happy
    hier yesterday **31**
    avant hier the day before
       yesterday

un **hippopotame** hippopotamus
    E5
une **histoire** story, history
l' **hiver** *m.* winter **12**
    en hiver in (the) winter
       12
 • **hollandais** Dutch
un **homme** man **17**
    honnête honest
un **hôpital** (*pl.* **hôpitaux**)
       hospital **21**
une **horreur** horror
    quelle horreur! what a
       scandal! how awful!
un• **hors-d'oeuvre** appetizer
    33
un• **hot dog** hot dog **9**
un **hôte, une hôtesse** host,
    hostess
un **hôtel** hotel **21**
    un hôtel de police police
       department
l' **huile** *f.* oil
 • **huit** eight **1**
 • **huitième** eighth **24**
l' **humeur** *f.* mood
    de bonne humeur in a
       good mood
un **hypermarché** shopping
    center

I

    ici here **14**
une **idée** idea
    c'est une bonne idée! it's
       (that's) a good idea! **28**
    ignorer to be unaware of
    il he, it **11, 14, 18**
    il est it is **20**
    il/elle est + *nationality*
       he/she is ... **6**
    il y a there is, there are
       17
    il y a + **du, de la**
       (partitive) there is
       (some) **34**
    il y a eu there was
    il n'y a pas de... there
       is/are no ... **18**
    est-ce qu'il y a...? is
       there, are there ...? **17**
    qu'est-ce qu'il y a...?
       what is there ...? **17**
une **île** island

illustré illustrated
un immeuble apartment
    building 21
un imper (imperméable)
    raincoat 25
l' impératif *m.* imperative
    (command) mood
impoli impolite
l' importance *f.* importance
    ça n'a pas d'importance
        it doesn't matter
importé imported
impressionnant impressive
inactif (inactive) inactive
inclure to include
l' indicatif *m.* area code
indiquer to indicate, show C
    indiquez... indicate . . . C
infâme: c'est infâme! that's
    (it's) awful! 35
infecte: c'est infecte! that's
    revolting! *(colloq.)* 35
les informations *f.* news
l' informatique *f.* computer
    science
s' informer to find out about
un ingénieur engineer
un ingrédient ingredient 33
un inspecteur, une inspectrice
    police detective
un instrument instrument 23
intelligent intelligent 19
intéressant interesting 19
l' intérieur *m.* interior, inside
interroger to question
interviewer to interview
inutilement uselessly
un inventaire inventory
un invité, une invitée guest
inviter to invite 15
israélien (israélienne)
    Israeli
italien (italienne) Italian 19
un Italien, une Italienne Italian
    person

J

j' (*see* je)
jamais ever; never
    jamais le dimanche!
        never on Sunday!
    ne... jamais never 32
la Jamaïque Jamaica
une jambe leg E3

un jambon ham 33
janvier *m.* January 8
japonais Japanese 19
un jardin garden 21
jaune yellow 20
jaunir to turn yellow
je I 14
un jean pair of jeans 23
un jeu (*pl.* jeux) game 25
    les jeux télévisés TV
        game shows
jeudi *m.* Thursday 8
jeune young 17
les jeunes *m.* young people
un job (part-time) job
le jogging jogging 29
    faire du jogging to jog 29
un jogging jogging suit 25
joli pretty (*for girls, women*)
    17; (*for clothing*) 25
    plus joli(e) que prettier
        than
jouer to play 15
    jouer à + *game, sport* to
        play a game, sport 23
    jouer au tennis (volley,
        basket, foot) to play
        tennis (volleyball,
        basketball, soccer) 13
    jouer de + *instrument* to
        play a musical instrument
        23
un jour day 8, 29
    le Jour de l'An New
        Year's Day
    par jour per week, a week
    quel jour est-ce? what
        day is it? 8
un journal (*pl.* journaux)
    newspaper
une journée day, whole day
    bonne journée! have a
        nice day!
joyeux (joyeuse) happy
juillet *m.* July 8
    le quatorze juillet Bastille
        Day (*French national
        holiday*)
juin *m.* June 8
un jumeau (*pl.* jumeaux), une
    jumelle twin
une jupe skirt 25
le jus juice
    le jus d'orange orange
        juice 10, 33

le jus de pomme apple
    juice 10, 33
le jus de raisin grape
    juice 10
le jus de tomate tomato
    juice 10
jusqu'à until
juste right, fair
    le mot juste the right
        word

K

un kangourou kangaroo E5
le ketchup ketchup 33
un kilo kilogram
    un kilo (de) a kilogram
        (of) 33

L

l' (*see* le, la)
la the 6, 18; her, it 36
là here, there 14
    là-bas over there 14
    ça, là-bas that (one), over
        there 17
    ce... -là that . . . (over
        there) 26
    oh là là! uh, oh!; oh, dear!;
        wow!; oh, yes!
laid ugly
laisser: laisse-moi
    tranquille! leave me
        alone! 36
le lait milk 33
une langue language
large wide
laver to wash 29
    se laver to wash (oneself),
        wash up
le the 6, 18; him, it 36
    le + *number* + *month*
        the . . . 8
    le (lundi) on (Mondays)
        18
une leçon lesson
un légume vegetable 33
lent slow
les the 18; them 36
une lettre letter
    leur(s) their 24
    leur (to) them 36
se lever: lève-toi! stand up! B
    levez-vous! stand up! B
un lézard lizard E5

le **Liban** Lebanon (*country in the Middle East*)
libanais Lebanese
libéré liberated
une **librairie** bookstore
libre free
un **lieu** place, area
   avoir lieu to take place
une **ligne** line
limité limited
la **limonade** lemon soda **10**
un **lion** lion **E5**
* **lire** to read **C**
   comment lire reading hints
   lisez... (*see* **lire**) read . . . **B, C**
une **liste** list
   une liste des courses shopping list
un **lit** bed **17**
un **living** living room (*informal*)
un **livre** book **B, 17**
une **livre** metric pound **33**
local (*m.pl.* **locaux**) local
une **location** rental
logique logical
logiquement logically
loin far **21**
   loin d'ici far (from here)
le **loisir** leisure, free time
un **loisir** leisure-time activity
Londres London
long (longue) long **25**
longtemps (for) a long time
   moins longtemps que for a shorter time
le **loto** lotto, lottery, bingo
un **loup** wolf **E5**
lui him **23**; (to) him/her **36**
lui-même: en lui-même to himself
lundi *m.* Monday **8**
des **lunettes** *f.* glasses **25**
   des lunettes de soleil sunglasses **25**
le **Luxembourg** Luxembourg
un **lycée** high school

m' (*see* **me**)
M. (monsieur) Mr. (Mister) **3**

ma my **7, 24**
   et voici ma mère and this is my mother **7**
   ma chambre my bedroom **17**
une **machine** machine
   une machine à coudre sewing machine
le **Madagascar** Madagascar (*French-speaking island off of East Africa*)
Madame (Mme) Mrs., ma'am **3**
Mademoiselle (Mlle) Miss **3**
un **magasin** store, shop **21, 25**
   faire les magasins to go shopping (browsing from store to store)
   un grand magasin department store **25**
magnétique magnetic
un **magnétophone** tape recorder **17**
un **magnétoscope** VCR (videocassette recorder) **B**
magnifique magnificent
mai *m.* May **8**
maigre thin, skinny
maigrir to lose weight, get thin **27**
un **maillot de bain** bathing suit **25**
une **main** hand **E3**
maintenant now **15, 31**
mais but **14**
   j'aime..., mais je préfère... I like . . ., but I prefer . . . **13**
   je regrette, mais je ne peux pas... I'm sorry, but I can't . . . **13**
   mais oui! sure! **14**
   mais non! of course not! **14**
une **maison** house **21**
   à la maison at home **14**
mal badly, poorly **3, 15**
   ça va mal things are going badly **3**
   ça va très mal things are going very badly **3**
   c'est mal that's bad **20**
malade sick

malheureusement unfortunately
malin clever
manger to eat **15**
   j'aime manger I like to eat **13**
   manger + du, de la (*partitive*) to eat (some) **34**
   une salle à manger dining room **21**
un **manteau** (*pl.* **manteaux**) overcoat **25**
   un manteau de fourrure fur coat
un **marchand, une marchande** merchant, shopkeeper, dealer
marcher to work, to run (*for objects*) **17**; to walk (*for people*) **17**
   il/elle (ne) marche (pas) bien it (doesn't) work(s) well **17**
   est-ce que la radio marche? does the radio work? **17**
un **marché** open-air market **33**
   un marché aux puces flea market
   bon marché (*inv.*) inexpensive **25**
mardi *m.* Tuesday **8**
   le Mardi gras Shrove Tuesday
un **mari** husband **24**
le **mariage** wedding, marriage
marié married
une **marmite** covered stew pot
le **Maroc** Morocco (*country in North Africa*)
une **marque** brand (name)
une **marraine** godmother
marrant fun
marron (*inv.*) brown **20**
mars *m.* March **8**
martiniquais from Martinique
la **Martinique** Martinique (*French island in the West Indies*)
un **match** game, (sports) match
   faire un match to play a game, (sports) match **16**
les **maths** *f.* math
le **matin** morning **29**

ce matin this morning **31**
demain matin tomorrow morning **31**
du matin in the morning, A.M. **4**
hier matin yesterday morning **31**
le matin in the morning
des **matoutou crabes** *m.* stewed crabs with rice
mauvais bad **20**
c'est une mauvaise idée that's a bad idea
il fait mauvais it's bad *(weather)* **12**
la **mayonnaise** mayonnaise **33**
me (to) me **35**
méchant mean, nasty **19**
un **médecin** doctor
un médecin de nuit doctor on night duty
la **Méditerranée** Mediterranean Sea
meilleur better, best **27**
mélanger to mix, stir
même same; even
une **mémoire** memory
mentionner to mention
la **mer** ocean, shore **29**
à la mer to (at) the sea **29**
merci thank you **3**
oui, merci yes, thank you **13**
mercredi *m.* Wednesday **8**
une **mère** mother **7, 24**
mériter to deserve
mes my **24**
le **métro** subway
en métro by subway **22**
* **mettre** to put on, to wear **25;** to put, to place, to turn on **26**
mettre la table to set the table **33**
mexicain Mexican **19**
midi noon **4**
mieux better
mignon (mignonne) cute **19**
militaire military
mille one thousand **25**
une **mini-chaîne** compact stereo
minuit midnight **4**
minérale: l'eau *f.* **minérale** mineral water **33**

mis *(p.p. of* **mettre***)* put, placed **31**
mixte mixed
Mlle Miss **3**
Mme Mrs. **3**
une **mob (mobylette)** motorbike, moped **17**
moche plain, ugly **25**
la **mode** fashion
à la mode popular; in fashion; fashionable **25**
moderne modern **21**
moi me **1, 23;** (to) me **35**
moi, je m'appelle (Marc) me, my name is (Marc) **1**
avec moi with me **13**
donne-moi give me **9**
donnez-moi give me **10**
excusez-moi... excuse me . . . **21**
prête-moi... lend me . . . **11**
s'il te plaît, donne-moi... please give me . . . **10**
un **moine** monk
moins less
moins de less than
moins... que less . . . than **27**
... heure(s) moins (dix) (ten) of . . . **4**
... heure(s) moins le quart quarter of . . . **4**
un **mois** month **8, 29**
ce mois-ci this month **31**
le mois dernier last month **31**
le mois prochain next month **31**
par mois a month
mon (ma; mes) my **7, 24**
mon anniversaire est le... my birthday is the . . . **8**
voici mon père this is my father **7**
le **monde** world
du monde in the world
tout le monde everyone
la **monnaie** money; change
le **Monopoly** Monopoly **23**
Monsieur (M.) Mr., sir **3**
un **monsieur** *(pl.* **messieurs***)* gentleman, man *(polite term)* **5**

une **montagne** mountain **29**
à la montagne to (at) the montains **29**
une **montre** watch **17**
montrer à to show . . . to **35, 36**
montre-moi (montrez-moi) show me **B**
un **morceau** piece
un morceau de craie piece of chalk **B**
un **mot** word
une **moto** motorcycle **17**
la **moutarde** mustard
un **mouton** sheep
moyen (moyenne) average, medium
en moyenne on the average
un **moyen** means
muet (muette) silent
un **musée** museum **21**
la **musique** music **23**

N ━━━━━━━━━━━━━━

n' *(see* **ne***)*
nager to swim **15**
j'aime nager I like to swim **13**
une **nationalité** nationality **2**
nautique: le ski nautique water-skiing **29**
ne (n')
ne... aucun none, not any
ne... jamais never **32**
ne... pas not **14**
ne... personne nobody **32**
ne... plus no longer
ne... rien nothing **32**
n'est-ce pas? right?, no?, isn't it (so)?, don't you?, aren't you? **14**
né born
nécessaire necessary
négatif (négative) negative
négativement negatively
la **neige** snow
neiger to snow
il neige it's snowing **12**
nettoyer to clean **29**
neuf nine **1**
neuvième ninth **24**

un **neveu** (*pl.* **neveux**) nephew
un **nez** nose **E3**
une **nièce** niece
un **niveau** (*pl.* **niveaux**) level
   Noël *m.* Christmas
      à Noël at Christmas **29**
   noir black **20**
un **nom** name; noun
un **nombre** number
   nombreux (nombreuses)
      numerous
   nommé named
   non no **2, 14**
      non! no! **14**
      non plus neither
      mais non! of course not!
         14
le **nord** north
   le nord-est northeast
   normalement normally
   nos our **24**
une **note** grade
   notre (*pl.* **nos**) our **24**
la **nourriture** food **33**
   nous we **14**; us **23**; (to) us
      35
   nouveau (nouvel, nouvelle;
      m.pl. nouveaux) new **27**
la **Nouvelle-Angleterre** New
      England
la **Nouvelle-Calédonie** New
      Caledonia *(French island*
      in the South Pacific)
   novembre *m.* November **8**
      le onze novembre
         Armistice Day
la **nuit** night
un **numéro** number

O

   objectif (objective) objective
un **objet** object **17**
une **occasion** occasion;
      opportunity
   occupé occupied
un **océan** ocean
   octobre *m.* October **8**
une **odeur** odor
un **oeil** (*pl.* **yeux**) eye **E3**
un **oeuf** egg **33**
   officiel (officielle) official
   offert (*p.p. of* **offrir**) offered
 * **offrir** to offer, to give

   oh là là! uh,oh!, oh, dear!,
      wow!, oh, yes!
un **oiseau** (*pl.* **oiseaux**) bird
une **omelette** omelet **9**
   on one, they, you, people **28**
      on est... today is . . .
      on va dans un café? shall
         we go to a café?
      on y va let's go
      comment dit-on... en
         français? how do you
         say . . . in French? **B**
un **oncle** uncle **7, 24**
   onze eleven **2**
   opérer to operate
l' **or** *m.* gold
   orange *(inv.)* orange *(color)*
      20
une **orange** orange *(fruit)*
      le jus d'orange orange
         juice **10, 33**
un **ordinateur** computer **B, 17**
une **oreille** ear **E3**
   organiser to organize **15**
   originairement originally
l' **origine** *f.* origin, beginning
      d'origine bretonne from
         Brittany
   orthographiques: les signes
      m. **orthographiques**
         spelling marks
   ou or **2, 14**
   où where **14, 16**
      où est...? where is . . .?
         14
      où est-ce? where is it? **21**
      d'où? from where? **23**
   oublier to forget
l' **ouest** *m.* west
   oui yes **2, 14**
      oui, bien sûr... yes, of
         course . . . **13**
      oui, d'accord... yes,
         okay . . . **13**
      oui, j'ai... yes, I
         have . . . **17**
      oui, merci... yes, thank
         you . . . **13**
      mais oui! sure! **14**
un **ouragan** hurricane
un **ours** bear **E5**
   ouvert open
 * **ouvrir** to open
      ouvre... (ouvrez...)
         open . . . **B**

P

le **pain** bread **33**
   pâle pale
un **pamplemousse** grapefruit
      33
une **panne** breakdown
      une panne d'électricité
         power failure
un **pantalon** pants, trousers **25**
une **panthère** panther
une **papaye** papaya
le **papier** paper
      une feuille de papier a
         sheet (piece) of paper **B**
   Pâques *m.* Easter **29**
      à Pâques at Easter **29**
   par per
      par exemple for example
      par jour per day
un **parc** park **21**
      un parc public city park
   parce que (parce qu')
      because **16**
   pardon excuse me **21, 25**
les **parents** *m.* parents, relatives
      24
   paresseux (paresseuse)
      lazy
   parfait perfect
      rien n'est parfait nothing
         is perfect
   parfois sometimes
   parisien (parisienne)
      Parisian
   parler to speak, talk **B, 15**
      parler à to speak (talk) to
         36
      parler (français, anglais,
         espagnol) to speak
         (French, English,
         Spanish) **13**
un **parrain** godfather
une **partie** part
 * **partir** to leave
      à partir de as of,
         beginning
   partitif (partitive) partitive
   pas not
      ne... pas not **14**
      pas de not a, no, not any
         18, 34
      pas du tout not at all,
         definitely not **23**
      pas possible not possible

R27

pas toujours not always **13**

pas très bien not very well

le passé composé compound past tense

passer to spend (time) **29**; to pass by

passionnément passionately

une pâte dough

patient patient

le patinage ice skating, roller skating

une patinoire skating rink

une pâtisserie pastry, pastry shop

une patte foot, paw *(of bird or animal)*

pauvre poor **28**

payer to pay, pay for **28**

un pays country

la peau skin, hide

* **peindre** to paint

peint painted

une pellicule film (camera)

pendant during **29**

pénétrer to enter

pénible bothersome, a pain **20**

penser to think **25**

  penser de to think of **25**

  penser que to think that **25**

  qu'est-ce que tu penses de...? what do you think of . . .? **25**

une pension inn, boarding house

Pentecôte *f.* Pentecost

perdre to lose, to waste **28**

perdu *(p.p. of* **perdre***)* lost

un père father **7, 24**

* **permettre** to permit

un perroquet parrot

personne (de) nobody **32**

  ne... personne nobody, not anybody, not anyone **32**

une personne person **5**

personnel (personnelle) personal

personnellement personally

péruvien (péruvienne) Peruvian

petit small, short **17, 20, 25**

  il/elle est petit(e) he/she is short **17**

un petit copain, une petite copine boyfriend, girlfriend

plus petite smaller

le petit déjeuner breakfast **33**

  prendre le petit déjeuner to have breakfast **33**

le petit-fils, la petite-fille grandson, granddaughter

les petits pois *m.* peas **33**

peu little, not much

  un peu a little, a little bit **15**

  un peu de a few

peut (*see* **pouvoir**)

peut-être perhaps, maybe **14**

peux (*see* **pouvoir**)

  est-ce que tu peux...? can you . . .? **13**

  je regrette, mais je ne peux pas... I'm sorry, but I can't . . . **13**

la photo photography

une phrase sentence **B**

la physique physics

un piano piano **23**

une pie magpie **E5**

une pièce coin **28**; room

un pied foot **E3**

  à pied on foot **22**

  faire une promenade à pied to take a walk **22**

piloter to pilot (a plane)

une pincée pinch

le ping-pong Ping-Pong **23**

un pique-nique picnic **22**

  faire un pique-nique to have a picnic **29**

une piscine swimming pool **21**

une pizza pizza **9**

un placard closet

une plage beach **21**

plaît: s'il te plaît please *(informal)* **9**; excuse me (please)

  s'il te plaît, donne-moi... please, give me . . .**10**

  s'il vous plaît please *(formal)* **10**; excuse me (please)

un plan map

la planche à voile windsurfing **29**

  faire de la planche à voile to windsurf **29**

une plante plant

un plat dish, course *(of a meal)* **33**

  le plat principal main course

un plateau tray

pleut: il pleut it's raining **12**

plier to fold

plumer to pluck

plus more

  plus de more than

  plus joli que prettier than

  plus... que more . . . than, . . .-er than **27**

  en plus in addition

  le plus the most

  ne... plus no longer, no more

  non plus neither

plusieurs several

une poche pocket

  l'argent *m.* **de poche** allowance, pocket money

une poêle frying pan

un point de vue point of view

une poire pear **33**

pois: les petits pois *m.* peas **33**

un poisson fish **E5, 33**

  un poisson rouge goldfish

  blaff de poisson fish stew

poli polite

un politicien, une politicienne politician

un polo polo shirt **25**

une pomme apple

  le jus de pomme apple juice **10, 33**

une pomme de terre potato **33**

  une purée de pommes de terre mashed potatoes

le porc: une côtelette de porc pork chop

une porte door **B, 17**

un porte-monnaie change purse, wallet

porter to wear **25**

portugais Portuguese

poser: poser une question to ask a question **C**

une possibilité possibility

la poste post office

pouah! yuck! yech!

une **poule** hen E5

le **poulet** chicken 33

pour for 14; in order to 29

    pour que so that

    pour qui? for whom? 16

le **pourcentage** percentage

pourquoi why 16

* **pouvoir** to be able, can, may 35

pratique practical

pratiquer to participate in

des **précisions** *f.* details

préféré favorite

préférer to prefer 26; to like (in general)

    je préfère I prefer 13

    tu préférerais? would you prefer?

premier (première) first 24

    le premier de l'an New Year's Day

    le premier étage second floor

    le premier mai Labor Day *(in France)*

    c'est le premier juin it's June first 8

* **prendre** to take, to have *(food)* B, 34

    prendre + du, de la *(partitive)* to have (some) 34

    prendre le petit déjeuner to have breakfast 33

un **prénom** first name

préparer to prepare; to prepare for 29

près nearby 21

    près d'ici nearby, near here

    tout près very close

une **présentation** appearance

    la présentation extérieure outward appearance

des **présentations** *f.* introductions

pressé in a hurry

prêt ready

un **prêt** loan

prêter à to lend to, to loan 35, 36

    prête-moi... lend me . . . 11

principalement mainly

le **printemps** spring 12

    au printemps in the spring 12

pris (*p.p. of* **prendre**) took 34

un **prix** price

    quel est le prix ...? what's the price . . .? 25

un **problème** problem

prochain next 29, 31

    le weekend prochain next weekend 29

un **produit** product

un **prof, une prof** teacher *(informal)* 5, 17

un **professeur** teacher 17

professionnel (professionnelle) professional

un **programme** program

un **projet** plan

une **promenade** walk

    faire une promenade à pied to go for a walk 16, 22

    faire une promenade à vélo to go for a ride (by bike) 22

    faire une promenade en voiture to go for a drive (by car) 22

* **promettre** promise

une **promo** special sale

proposer to suggest

propre own

un **propriétaire, une propriétaire** landlord/landlady, owner

la **Provence** Provence *(province in southern France)*

pu (*p.p. of* **pouvoir**) could, was able to 35

    n'a pas pu was not able to

public: un parc public city park

    un jardin public public garden

la **publicité** commercials, advertising, publicity

une **puce** flea

    un marché aux puces flea market

puis then, also

puisque since

un **pull** sweater, pullover 25

les **Pyrénées** (the) Pyrenees *(mountains between France and Spain)*

Q

qu' (*see* **que**)

une **qualité** quality

quand when 16

    c'est quand, ton anniversaire? when is your birthday? 8

une **quantité** quantity 33

quarante forty 3

un **quart** one quarter

    ... heure(s) et quart quarter past . . . 4

    ... heure(s) moins le quart quarter of . . . 4

un **quartier** district, neighborhood 21

    un joli quartier a nice neighborhood 21

quatorze fourteen 2

quatre four 1

quatre-vingt-dix ninety 6

quatre-vingts eighty 6

quatrième fourth 24

que that, which

    que veut dire...? what does . . . mean? B

    qu'est-ce que (qu') what *(phrase used to introduce a question)* 16

    qu'est-ce que c'est? what is it? what's that? 17

    qu'est-ce que tu penses de...? what do you think of . . .? 25

    qu'est-ce que tu veux? what do you want? 9

    qu'est-ce qu'il y a? what is there? 17; what's the matter?

    qu'est-ce qui ne va pas? what's wrong?

quel (quelle) what, which, what a 26

    quel (quelle)...! what a . . .!

    quel âge a ta mère/ton père? how old is your mother/your father? 7

    quel âge a-t-il/elle? how old is he/she? 17

quel âge as-tu? how old are you? **7**

quel est le prix...? what is the price . . .? **25**

quel jour est-ce? what day is it? **8**

quel temps fait-il? what's (how's) the weather? **12**

quelle est la date? what's the date? **8**

quelle est ton adresse? what's your address? **21**

quelle heure est-il? what time is it? **4**

à quelle heure? at what time? **4**

à quelle heure est...? at what time is . . .? **4**

de quelle couleur...? what color is . . .? **20**

quelqu'un someone **32**

quelque chose something **32**

quelques some, a few **17**

une **question** question

un **Québécois, une Québécoise** person from Quebec

québécois from Quebec

une **queue** tail

qui who, whom **16**

qui est-ce? who's that (this)? **5, 17**

qui se ressemble... birds of a feather . . .

à qui? to whom? **16**

avec qui? with who(m)? **16**

c'est qui? who's that? *(casual speech)*

de qui? about who(m)? **16**

pour qui? for who(m)? **16**

quinze fifteen **2**

quoi? what? **17**

quotidien (quotidienne) daily

la vie quotidienne daily life

R ━━━━━━━━━━

raconter to tell about

une **radio** radio **17**

écouter la radio to listen to the radio **13**

une **radiocassette** boom box **17**

raisin: le jus de raisin grape juice **10**

une **raison** reason

avoir raison to be right **30**

rapidement rapidly

un **rapport** relationship

une **raquette** racket **17**

une raquette de tennis tennis racket **23**

rarement rarely, seldom **15**

un **rayon** department *(in a store)*

réalisé made

récemment recently

une **recette** recipe

recherche: un avis de recherche missing person's bulletin

un **récital** *(pl.* **récitals)** (musical) recital

reconstituer to reconstruct

un **réfrigérateur** refrigerator

refuser to refuse

regarder to look at, watch **B, 15**

regarde ça look at that **17**

regarder la télé to watch TV **13**

un **régime** diet

être au régime to be on a diet

régional *(m.pl.* **régionaux)** regional

regretter to be sorry

je regrette, mais... I'm sorry, but . . . **13**

régulier (régulière) regular

une **reine** queen

rencontrer to meet **29**

une **rencontre** meeting, encounter

un **rendez-vous** date, appointment **22**

j'ai un rendez-vous à... I have a date, appointment at . . . **4**

rendre visite à to visit, come to visit **28, 36**

la **rentrée** first day back at school in fall

rentrer to go back, come back **22**; to return, go back, come back **32**

réparer to fix, repair **29**

un **repas** meal **33**

* **repeindre** to repaint

répéter to repeat **B**

répondre (à) to answer, respond (to) **B, 36**

répondez-lui (moi) answer him (me)

répondre que oui to answer yes

une **réponse** answer

un **reportage** documentary

représenter to represent

réservé reserved

une **résolution** resolution

un **restaurant** restaurant **21**

au restaurant to (at) the restaurant **14**

dîner au restaurant to have dinner at a restaurant **13**

un restaurant trois étoiles three star restaurant

rester to stay **22, 32**

retard: un jour de retard one day behind

en retard late

retourner to return; to turn over

réussir to succeed **27**

réussir à un examen to pass an exam **27**

* **revenir** to come back **23**

revoir: au revoir! good-bye! **3**

le **rez-de-chaussée** ground floor

un **rhinocéros** rhinoceros **E5**

riche rich **28**

rien (de) nothing **32**

rien n'est parfait nothing is perfect

ne... rien nothing **32**

une **rive** (river)bank

une **rivière** river, stream

le **riz** rice **33**

une **robe** dress **25**

romain Roman

le **rosbif** roast beef **33**

rose pink **20**

rosse nasty *(colloq.)*

une **rôtie** toast *(Canadian)*
rôtir to roast
une **roue** wheel
rouge red **20**
rougir to turn red
rouler to roll
roux (rousse) red-head
une **rue** street **21**
dans la rue (Victor Hugo) on (Victor Hugo) street **21**
russe Russian

S

sa his, her **24**
un **sac** bag, handbag **17**
sais *(see* **savoir***)*
je sais I know **B, 17, 36**
je ne sais pas I don't know **B, 17**
tu sais you know **36**
une **saison** season **12**
toute saison all year round (any season)
une **salade** salad **9, 33;** lettuce **33**
un **salaire** salary
une **salle** hall, large room
une salle à manger dining room **21**
une salle de bains bathroom **21**
une salle de séjour informal living room
un **salon** formal living room **21**
salut hi!, good-bye! **3**
une **salutation** greeting
samedi Saturday **8, 31**
samedi soir Saturday night
à samedi! see you Saturday! **8**
le samedi on Saturdays **18**
une **sandale** sandal **25**
un **sandwich** sandwich **9**
sans without
des **saucisses** *f.* sausages
le **saucisson** salami **33**
* **savoir** to know *(information)*
je sais I know **B, 17, 36**
je ne sais pas I don't know **B, 17**
tu sais you know **36**

un **saxo (saxophone)** saxophone **23**
une **scène** scene, stage
les **sciences** *f.* **économiques** economics
les **sciences** *f.* **naturelles** natural science
un **scooter** motorscooter **17**
second second
seize sixteen **2**
un **séjour** stay; informal living room
le **sel** salt **33**
selon according to
selon toi in your opinion
une **semaine** week **8, 29**
cette semaine this week **31**
la semaine dernière last week **31**
la semaine prochaine next week **31**
par semaine per week, a week
semblable similar
le **Sénégal** Senegal *(French-speaking country in Africa)*
sensationnel (sensationnelle) sensational
séparer to separate
sept seven **1**
septembre *m.* September **8**
septième seventh **24**
une **série** series
sérieux (sérieuse) serious
un **serveur, une serveuse** waiter, waitress
servi served
une **serviette** napkin **33**
ses his, her **24**
seul alone, only; by oneself **29**
seulement only, just
un **short** shorts **25**
si if, whether **C**
si! so, yes! *(to a negative question)* **18**
un **signal** *(pl.* **signaux***)* signal
un **signe** sign
un signe orthographique spelling mark
un **singe** monkey **E5**
situé situated
six six **1**

sixième sixth **24**
un **skate** skateboard
le **ski** skiing
le ski nautique waterskiing **29**
faire du ski to ski **29**
faire du ski nautique to go water-skiing **29**
skier to ski
snob snobbish
la **Société Nationale des Chemins de Fer (SNCF)** *French railroad system*
une **société** society
un **soda** soda **10**
une **soeur** sister **7, 24**
la **soie** silk
la **soif** thirst
avoir soif to be thirsty **30**
j'ai soif I'm thirsty **10**
tu as soif? are you thirsty? **10**
un **soir** evening **29**
ce soir this evening, tonight **31**
demain soir tomorrow night (evening) **29, 31**
du soir in the evening, P.M. **4**
hier soir last night **31**
le soir in the evening
une **soirée** (whole) evening, evening party
soixante sixty **3, 5**
soixante-dix seventy **5**
un **soldat** soldier
un **solde** (clearance) sale
en solde on sale
la **sole** sole (fish) **33**
le **soleil** sun
les lunettes *f.* **de soleil** sunglasses **25**
sommes *(see* **être***)*
nous sommes... it is, today is . . . *(date)*
son (sa; ses) his, her **24**
un **sondage** poll
une **sorte** sort, type, kind
* **sortir** to leave, come out
un **souhait** wish
la **soupe** soup **33**
une **souris** mouse
sous under **17**
le **sous-sol** basement

souvent often **15**
soyez (*see* être): **soyez logique** be logical
les **spaghetti** *m.* spaghetti **33**
spécialement especially
spécialisé specialized
une **spécialité** specialty
le **sport** sports **23, 29**
　　faire du sport to play sports **29**
　　des vêtements *m.* **de sport** sports clothing **25**
　　une voiture de sport sports car **23**
sportif (sportive) athletic **19**
un **stade** stadium **21**
un **stage** sports training camp; internship
une **station-service** gas station
un **steak** steak **9**
un **steak-frites** steak and French fries **9**
un **stylo** pen **B, 17**
le **sucre** sugar **33**
le **sud** south
suggérer to suggest
suis (*see* être)
　　je suis + *nationality* I'm... **2**
　　je suis de... I'm from... **2**
suisse Swiss **19**
la **Suisse** Switzerland
suivant following
suivi followed
un **sujet** subject, topic
super terrific **15**; great **20, 25**
un **supermarché** supermarket **21**
supersonique supersonic
supérieur superior
supplémentaire supplementary, extra
sur on **17**; about
sûr sure, certain
　　bien sûr! of course! **14**
　　oui, bien sûr... yes, of course...! **13**
　　tu es sûr(e)? are you sure? **24**
sûrement surely
la **surface: une grande surface** big store, self-service store

surtout especially
un **survêtement** jogging or track suit **25**
un **sweat** sweatshirt **25**
une **sweaterie** shop specializing in sweatshirts and sportswear
sympa nice, pleasant *(colloq.)*
sympathique nice, pleasant **19**
une **synagogue** Jewish temple or synagogue
un **synthétiseur** electronic keyboard, synthesizer

T ━━━━━━━━━━━━

t' (*see* te)
ta your **7, 24**
une **table** table **B, 17**
　　mettre la table to set the table **33**
un **tableau** (*pl.* **tableaux**) chalkboard **B**
Tahiti Tahiti (*French island in the South Pacific*)
une **taille** size
　　de taille moyenne of medium height or size
un **tailleur** woman's suit
se **taire: tais-toi!** be quiet!
une **tante** aunt **7, 24**
la **tarte** pie **33**
une **tasse** cup **33**
un **taxi** taxi
　　en taxi by taxi **22**
te (to) you **35**
un **tee-shirt** T-shirt **25**
un **temple** Protestant church
le **temps** time; weather
　　combien de temps? how long?
　　de temps en temps from time to time
　　quel temps fait-il? what's (how's) the weather? **12**
　　tout le temps all the time
le **tennis** tennis **23**
　　jouer au tennis to play tennis **13**
des **tennis** *m.* tennis shoes, sneakers **25**
un **terrain de sport** (playing) field

une **terrasse** outdoor section of a café, terrace
la **terre** earth
　　une pomme de terre potato **33**
terrifiant terrifying
tes your **24**
la **télé** TV **B, 17**
　　à la télé on TV
　　regarder la télé to watch TV **13**
un **téléphone** telephone **17**
　　téléphoner (à) to call, phone **13, 15, 36**
　　télévisé: des jeux *m.* **télévisés** TV game shows
la **tête** head **E3**
le **thé** tea **10**
　　un thé glacé iced tea **33**
un **théâtre** theater **21**
le **thon** tuna **33**
tiens! look!, hey! **5, 18**
un **tigre** tiger **E5**
timide timid, shy **19**
le **tissu** fabric
un **titre** title
toi you **23**
　　avec toi with you **13**
　　et toi? and you? **1**
la **toilette** bathroom, toilet **21**
un **toit** roof
une **tomate** tomato **33**
　　le jus de tomate tomato juice **10**
un **tombeau** tomb
ton (ta; tes) your **7, 24**
　　c'est quand, ton anniversaire? when's your birthday? **8**
tort: avoir tort to be wrong **30**
une **tortue** turtle **E5**
　　un bifteck de tortue turtle steak
toujours always **15**
　　je n'aime pas toujours... I don't always like ... **13**
un **tour** turn
　　à votre tour it's your turn
la **Touraine** Touraine (*province in central France*)
tourner to turn **21**
la **Toussaint** All Saint's Day (*November 1*)

tout (toute; tous, toutes)
all, every, the whole
   tous les jours every day
   tout ça all that
   tout le monde everyone
   tout le temps all the time
   toutes sortes all sorts, kinds
tout completely, very
   tout droit straight **21**
   tout de suite right away
   tout près very close
tout all, everything
   pas du tout not at all **23**
un **train** train **29**
tranquille quiet
   laisse-moi tranquille! leave me alone! **36**
un **transistor** transistor radio
un **travail** (*pl.* **travaux**) job
travailler to work **13, 15**
une **traversée** crossing
treize thirteen **2**
trente thirty **3**
un **tréma** diaeresis
très very **19**
   très bien very well **15**
   ça va très bien things are going very well **3**
   ça va très mal things are going very badly **3**
trois three **1**
troisième third **24**; *9th grade in France*
trop too, too much **25**
trouver to find, to think of **25**
   comment trouves-tu...? what do you think of ...? how do you find ...? **25**
   s'y trouve is there
tu you **14**
la **Tunisie** Tunisia *(country in North Africa)*

U ━━━━━━

un, une one **1**; a, an **5, 18**
unique only
uniquement only
une **université** university, college
l' **usage** *m.* use
un **ustensile** utensil
utile useful
utiliser to use **C**

en utilisant (by) using
utilisez... use . . . **C**

V ━━━━━━

va (*see* **aller**)
   va-t'en! go away! **22**
   ça va? how are you? how's everything? **3**
   ça va! everything's fine (going well); fine, I'm OK **3**
   on va dans un café? shall we go to a café?
   on y va let's go
les **vacances** *f.* vacation
   bonnes vacances! have a nice vacation!
   en vacances on vacation **14**
   les grandes vacances summer vacation **29**
une **vache** cow
vais (*see* **aller**): **je vais** I'm going **22**
la **vaisselle** dishes
   faire la vaisselle to do the dishes
valable valid
une **valise** suitcase
vanille: une glace à vanille vanilla ice cream
varié varied
les **variétés** *f.* variety show
vas (*see* **aller**)
   comment vas-tu? how are you? **3**
   vas-y! come on!, go ahead!, do it! **22**
le **veau** veal **33**
une **vedette** star
un **vélo** bicycle **17**
   à vélo by bicycle **22**
   faire une promenade à vélo to go for a bicycle ride **22**
un **vendeur, une vendeuse** salesperson
vendre to sell **28**
vendredi *m.* Friday **8**
vendu (*p.p. of* **vendre**) sold **31**
* **venir** to come **23**
le **vent** wind
une **vente** sale

le **ventre** stomach **E3**
venu (*p.p. of* **venir**) came, come **32**
vérifier to check
la **vérité** truth
un **verre** glass **33**
verser to pour
vert green **20**
   les • haricots *m.* **verts** green beans **33**
une **veste** jacket **25**
des **vêtements** *m.* clothing **25**
   des vêtements de sport sports clothing **25**
veut (*see* **vouloir**): **que veut dire...?** what does . . . mean? **B**
veux (*see* **vouloir**)
   est-ce que tu veux...? do you want . . .? **13**
   je ne veux pas... I don't want . . . **13**
   je veux... I want . . . **13, 34**
   je veux bien... I'd love to, I do, I want to . . . **13, 34**
   qu'est-ce que tu veux? what do you want? **9**
   tu veux...? do you want . . .? **9**
la **viande** meat **33**
une **vidéocassette** videocassette **B**
la **vie** life
   la vie quotidienne daily life
viens (*see* **venir**)
   viens... come . . . **B**
   oui, je viens yes, I'm coming along with you
vieux (vieil, vieille; *m.pl.* **vieux)** old **27**
   le Vieux Carré *the French Quarter in New Orleans*
le **Viêt-nam** Vietnam *(country in Southeast Asia)*
vietnamien (vietnamienne) Vietnamese
une **vigne** vineyard
un **village** town, village **21**
   un petit village small town **21**
une **ville** city
   en ville downtown, in town, in the city **14**

une **grande ville** big city, town **21**

le **vin** wine

vingt twenty **2, 3**

un **violon** violin **23**

une **visite** visit

rendre visite à to visit *(a person)* **28, 36**

visiter to visit *(places)* **15, 28**

vite! fast!, quick!

vive: vive les vacances!

* **vivre** to live

le **vocabulaire** vocabulary

voici... here is, this is..., here come(s) . . . **5**

voici + du, de la *(partitive)* here's some **34**

voici mon père/ma mère here's my father/my mother **7**

voilà... there is . . ., there come(s) . . . **5**

voilà + du, de la *(partitive)* there's some **34**

la **voile** sailing **29**

faire de la voile to sail **29**

la planche à voile windsurfing **29**

* **voir** to see **29, 31**

voir un film to see a movie **29**

un **voisin, une voisine** neighbor **17**

une **voiture** car **17**

une voiture de sport sports car **23**

en voiture by car **22**

faire une promenade en voiture to go for a drive by car **22**

une **voix** voice

le **volley (volleyball)** volleyball **23**

jouer au volley to play volleyball **13**

un **volontaire, une volontaire** volunteer

comme volontaire as a volunteer

vos your **24**

votre *(pl. vos)* your **24**

voudrais *(see vouloir)*: **je voudrais** I'd like **9, 10, 13, 34**

* **vouloir** to want **34**

vouloir + du, de la *(partitive)* to want some (of something) **34**

vouloir dire to mean **34**

voulu *(p.p. of vouloir)* wanted **34**

vous you **14**; (to) you **35**

vous désirez? what would you like? may I help you? **10, 25**

s'il vous plaît please **10**

un **voyage** trip

bon voyage! have a nice trip!

faire un voyage to take a trip **16**

voyager to travel **13, 15**

vrai true, right, real **20**

vraiment really **23**

vu *(p.p. of voir)* saw, seen **31**

une **vue** view

un **point de vue** point of view

W

un **walkman** walkman **17**

les **WC** *m.* toilet

un **weekend** weekend **29, 31**

bon weekend! have a nice weekend!

ce weekend this weekend **29, 31**

le weekend on weekends

le weekend dernier last weekend **31**

le weekend prochain next weekend **29, 31**

Y

y there

il y a there is, there are **17**

est-ce qu'il y a...? is there . . .?, are there . . .? **17**

qu'est-ce qu'il y a? what is there? **17**

allons-y! let's go! **22**

vas-y! come on!, go ahead!, do it! **22**

le **yaourt** yogurt **33**

des **yeux** *m.* *(sg. oeil)* eyes **E3**

Z

le **Zaïre** Zaire *(French-speaking country in Central Africa)*

un **zèbre** zebra

zéro zero **1**

zut! darn! **3**

R34 French-English

R34 Reference Section

ENGLISH-FRENCH VOCABULARY

VOCABULARY
English-French

The English-French vocabulary contains only active vocabulary.

The numbers following an entry indicate the lesson in which the word or phrase is activated. (**B** stands for the photo essay that precedes **Niveau B; C** stands for the list of phrases and expressions that precedes **Niveau C;** and **E** stands for **Entracte.**)

Nouns: If the article of a noun does not indicate gender, the noun is followed by *m. (masculine)* or *f. (feminine)*. If the plural (*pl.*) is irregular, it is given in parentheses.

Verbs: Verbs are listed in the infinitive form. An asterisk (*) in front of an active verb means that it is irregular. (For forms, see the verb charts in Appendix 4C.)

Words beginning with an **h** are preceded by a bullet (•) if the **h** is aspirate; that is, if the word is treated as if it begins with a consonant sound.

A

a, an un, une **5, 18**
  a few quelques **17**
  a little (bit) un peu **15**
  a lot beaucoup **15**
able: to be able (to) *pouvoir **35**
about de **23**
  about whom? de qui? **16**
accessories des accessoires *m.* **25**
acquainted: to be acquainted with *connaître **36**
  are you acquainted with . . . ? tu connais...? **6**
address une adresse **21**
  what's your address? quelle est ton adresse? **21**
after après **29, 30**
  after that ensuite **30**
afternoon l'après-midi *m.* **29**
  in the afternoon de l'après-midi **4**
  this afternoon cet après-midi **31**
  tomorrow afternoon demain après-midi **31**
  yesterday afternoon hier après-midi **31**
afterwards après **30**
to **agree** *être d'accord **14**
airplane un avion **29**
  by airplane en avion **29**
all tout
  all right d'accord **13**
  not at all pas du tout **23**
alone seul **29**

leave me alone! laisse-moi tranquille! **36**
also aussi **2, 15**
always toujours **15**
  not always pas toujours **13**
A.M. du matin **4**
am (*see* **to be**)
  I am . . . je suis + *nationality* **2**
American américain **2, 19**
  I'm American je suis américain(e) **2**
amusing amusant **19**
an un, une **5, 18**
and et **2, 14**
  and you? et toi? **1**
annoying pénible **20**
another un(e) autre
to **answer** répondre (à) **36**
any des **18;** du, de la, de l', de **34**
  not any pas de **18, 34**
anybody: not anybody ne... personne **32**
anyone quelqu'un **32**
anything quelque chose **32**
  not anything ne... rien **32**
apartment un appartement **21**
  apartment building un immeuble **21**
appetizer un •hors-d'oeuvre **33**
apple une pomme
  apple juice le jus de pomme **10, 33**
appointment un rendez-vous **22**
  I have an appointment

at . . . j'ai un rendez-vous à... **4**
April avril *m.* **8**
are (*see* **to be**)
  are there? est-ce qu'il y a? **17**
  are you . . . ? tu es + *nationality?* **2**
  there are il y a **17**
  these/those/they are ce sont **20**
arm un bras **E3**
to **arrive** arriver **22**
  as . . . as aussi... que **27**
to **ask** demander (à) **36**
at à **14;** chez **22**
  at (the) au, à la, à l', aux **22**
  at . . .'s house chez... **22**
  at . . . o'clock à... heure(s) **14**
  at home à la maison **14**
  at last enfin **30**
  at the restaurant au restaurant **14**
  at what time? à quelle heure? **4, 16**
  at what time is . . . ? à quelle heure est...? **4**
  athletic sportif (sportive) **19**
to **attend** assister à **29**
  attention: to pay attention *faire attention **16**
August août *m.* **8**
aunt une tante **7, 24**
automobile une auto, une voiture **17**
autumn l'automne *m.*

in (the) autumn en automne 12

avenue une avenue 21

away: go away! va-t'en! 22

B

back le dos E3

back: to come back rentrer 22, 32; *revenir 23

to go back rentrer 22, 32

in back of derrière 17

bad mauvais 20

I'm/everything's (very) bad ça va (très) mal 3

it's bad (weather) il fait mauvais 12

that's bad c'est mal 20

too bad! dommage! 15

badly mal 3

things are going (very) badly ça va (très) mal 3

bag un sac 17

banana une banane 33

banknote un billet 28

baseball le baseball 23

basketball le basket (basketball) 23

bathing suit un maillot de bain 25

bathroom une salle de bains 21

to **be** *être 14

to be . . . (years old) *avoir... ans 18

to be able (to) *pouvoir 35

to be acquainted with *connaître 36

to be active in *faire de + *activity* 29

to be careful *faire attention 16

to be cold (*people*) *avoir froid 30; (*weather*) il fait froid 12

to be going to (*do something*) *aller + *inf.* 22

to be hot (*people*) *avoir chaud 30

to be hungry *avoir faim 18, 30

to be lucky *avoir de la chance 30

to be present at assister à 29

to be right *avoir raison 30

to be supposed to *devoir 35

to be thirsty *avoir soif 18, 30

to be warm (*people*) *avoir chaud 30, 31

to be wrong *avoir tort 30

beach une plage 21

beans: green beans les •haricots *m.* verts 33

beautiful beau (bel, belle; *m.pl.* beaux) 17

it's beautiful (nice) weather il fait beau 12

because parce que (qu') 16

bed un lit 17

bedroom une chambre 17, 21

been été (*p.p. of* *être) 31

before avant 29, 31

behind derrière 17

below en bas 21

belt une ceinture 25

best meilleur 27

better meilleur 27

beverage une boisson 10, 33

bicycle un vélo, une bicyclette 17

by bicycle à vélo 22

take a bicycle ride *faire une promenade à velo 22

big grand 17, 20

bill (*money*) un billet 28

birthday un anniversaire 8

my birthday is (March 2) mon anniversaire est le (2 mars) 8

when is your birthday? c'est quand, ton anniversaire? 8

bit: a little bit un peu 15

black noir 20

blond blond 17

blouse un chemisier 25

blue bleu 20

boat un bateau (*pl.* bateaux) 29

book un livre B, 17

boom box une radiocassette 17

boots des bottes *f.* 25

bothersome pénible 20

boulevard un boulevard 21

boutique une boutique 25

boy le garçon 5, 6

boyfriend un petit copain

bread le pain 33

breakfast le petit déjeuner 33

to have breakfast prendre le petit déjeuner 33

to **bring** (*a person*) amener 26; (*things*) apporter 35

to bring something to someone apporter quelque chose à quelqu'un 35

brother un frère 7, 24

brown brun 17; marron (*inv.*) 20

building: apartment building un immeuble 21

bus un bus

by bus en bus 22

touring bus un autocar, un car 29

but mais 13

butter le beurre 33

to **buy** acheter 25, 26

to buy (some) acheter + du, de la (*partitive*) 34

by: by airplane, plane en avion 29

by bicycle à vélo 22

by bus en bus 22

by car en voiture 22

by oneself seul(e) 29

by subway en métro 22

by taxi en taxi 22

by train en train 22

C

café un café 14

at (to) the café au café 14

cafeteria: school cafeteria une cantine de l'école 33

cake un gâteau (*pl.* gâteaux) 33

calculator une calculatrice 17

to **call** téléphoner 15

came venu (*p.p. of* *venir) 31

camera un appareil-photo (*pl.* appareils-photo) 17

camping le camping 29

to go camping *faire du camping 29

can *pouvoir 35

can you . . .? est-ce que tu peux...? 13

I can't je ne peux pas 13

Canada le Canada

Canadian canadien (canadienne) 2, 19

he's/she's (Canadian) il/elle est (canadien/ canadienne) 6

cannot: I cannot je ne peux pas 13

I'm sorry, but I cannot je regrette, mais je ne peux pas **13**

car une auto, une voiture **17**
   by car en voiture **22**

card une carte
   (playing) cards des cartes *f.* **23**

careful: to be careful *faire attention **16**

carrot une carotte **33**

cassette tape une cassette **B, 17**
   cassette recorder une magnétophone **17**

cat un chat **7**

cereal les céréales *f.* **33**

chair une chaise **B, 17**

chalk la craie **B**
   piece of chalk un morceau de craie **B**

chalkboard un tableau (*pl.* tableaux) **B**

checkers les dames *f.* **23**

cheese le fromage **33**

cherry une cerise **33**

chess les échecs *m.* **23**

chicken le poulet **33**

child un (une) enfant **24**
   children des enfants *m.* **24**

Chinese chinois **19**

chocolate: hot chocolate un chocolat **10**

to **choose** choisir **27**
   chose, chosen choisi (*p.p. of* choisir) **31**

Christmas le Noël **29**
   at Christmas à Noël **29**

church une église **21**

cinema le cinéma **14**
   to the cinema au cinéma **14**

city une ville **21**
   in the city en ville **14**

clarinet une clarinette **23**

class une classe **14**
   in class en classe **14**

classmate un (une) camarade **17**

to **clean** nettoyer **29**

clothing des vêtements *m.* **25**
   sports clothing des vêtements *m.* de sport **25**

coffee le café **10, 21**

coin une pièce **28**

cold le froid

to be (feel) cold *avoir froid **30**

it's cold (*weather*) il fait froid **12**

college student un étudiant, une étudiante **17**

color une couleur **20**
   what color? de quelle couleur? **20**

to **come** arriver **22**; *venir **23**
   come on! vas-y! **22**
   here comes . . . voici... **5**
   to come back rentrer **22, 32**; *revenir **23**
   to come to visit rendre visite à **28, 36**

comfortable confortable **21**

compact disc un compact disque (un CD) **17**

computer un ordinateur **B, 17**

concert un concert **22**

to **continue** continuer **21**

cooking la cuisine **33**

cool: it's cool (*weather*) il fait frais **12**

cost le coût **25**

to **cost** coûter
   how much does . . . cost? combien coûte...? **11, 25**
   it costs . . . il/elle coûte... **11**

country(side) la campagne **29**
   to (in) the country(side) à la campagne **29**

course: of course! bien sûr! **13**; mais oui! **14**
   of course not! mais non! **14**

cousin un cousin, une cousine **7, 24**

crepe une crêpe **9**

croissant un croissant **9**

cuisine la cuisine **33**

cup une tasse **33**

cute mignon (mignonne) **19**

D ━━━━━━━━━

to **dance** danser **13, 15**

dark-haired brun **17**

darn! zut! **3**

date la date **8**; un rendez-vous **22**
   I have a date at . . . j'ai un rendez-vous à... **4**

what's the date? quelle est la date? **8**

daughter une fille **24**

day un jour **8, 29**
   what day is it? quel jour est-ce? **8**
   whole day une journée

December décembre *m.* **8**

dear cher (chère) **25**

department store un grand magasin **25**

to **describe** *décrire **C**
   describe . . . décrivez... **C**

desk un bureau **B, 17**

dessert le dessert **33**

to **detest** détester **33**

did fait (*p.p. of* *faire) **31**

difficult difficile **20**

dining room une salle à manger **21**

dinner le dîner **33**
   to have (eat) dinner dîner **15, 33**
   to have dinner at a restaurant dîner au restaurant **13**

dish (*course of a meal*) un plat **33**

to **do** *faire **16**
   do it! vas-y! **22**
   I do je veux bien **34**
   to do + *activity* *faire de + activity* **29**
   to do my homework *faire mes devoirs **29**

dog un chien **7**

door une porte **B, 17**

done fait (*p.p. of* *faire) **31**

downstairs en bas **21**

downtown en ville **14**

dozen une douzaine **33**

dress une robe **25**

drink une boisson **10, 33**

to **drink** *boire **34**

drive: to take a drive *faire une promenade en voiture **22**

drums une batterie **23**

dumb bête **19**

during pendant **29**

E ━━━━━━━━━

ear une oreille **E3**

to **earn** gagner **28**

Easter Pâques *m.* **29**

at Easter à Pâques 29
easy facile 20
to eat manger 15
    I like to eat j'aime manger 13
    to eat breakfast *prendre le petit déjeuner 33
    to eat dinner dîner 15, 33
    to eat lunch déjeuner 33
    to eat (some) manger + du, de la *(partitive)* 34
egg un oeuf 33
eight •huit 1
eighteen dix-huit 2
eighth •huitième 24
eighty quatre-vingts 6
elegant élégant 25
elephant un éléphant E5
eleven onze 2, 11
eleventh onzième 24
England l'Angleterre *m.*
English anglais(e) 2, 19
errand: to run errands *faire les courses 33
evening un soir 29
    in the evening du soir 4
    this evening ce soir 31
    tomorrow evening demain soir 29, 31
everything tout
    everything's going (very) well ça va (très) bien 3
    everything's (going) so-so ça va comme ci, comme ça 3
    how's everything? ça va? 3
exam un examen
    to pass an exam réussir à un examen 27
excuse me excusez-moi 21
expensive cher (chère) 25
to explain expliquer C
eye un oeil (*pl.* yeux) E3

F

fall l'automne 12
    in (the) fall en automne 12
false faux (fausse) 20
family une famille 7, 24
far (from) loin (de) 21
fashion la mode
    in fashion (fashionable) à la mode 25
fat: to get fat grossir 27
father un père 24

this is my father voici mon père 7
February février *m.* 8
to feel like *avoir envie de + *inf.* 28
few: a few quelques 17
fifteen quinze 2
fifth cinquième 24
fifty cinquante 3
film un film 22, 29
finally finalement 30
to find trouver 25
fine ça va 3
    fine! d'accord 13
    everything's fine ça va bien 3
    that's fine c'est bien 20
to finish finir 27
    finished fini (*p.p. of* finir) 31
first d'abord 30; premier (première) 24
    it's (June) first c'est le premier (juin) 8
fish un poisson 33
five cinq 1
to fix réparer 29
flute une flûte 23
food la nourriture 33
foot un pied E3
    on foot à pied 22
for pour 14
    for whom? pour qui? 16
fork une fourchette 33
forty quarante 3
four quatre 1
fourteen quatorze 2
fourth quatrième 24
franc un franc 11
    that's (it's) . . . francs ça fait... francs 11
France la France 14
    in France en France 14
French français(e) 2, 19
    how do you say . . . in French? comment dit-on... en français? B
French fries des frites *f.* 33
    steak and French fries un steak-frites 9
Friday vendredi *m.* 8
friend un ami, une amie 5; un copain, une copine 5
    boyfriend, girlfriend un petit copain, une petite copine

school friend un (une) camarade 17
from de 14
    from (the) du, de la, de l', des 23
    from where? d'où? 23
    are you from . . .? tu es de...? 2
    I'm from . . . je suis de... 2
front: in front of devant 17
fruit(s) des fruits *m.* 33
funny amusant 19; drôle 20

G

to gain weight grossir 27
game un jeu (*pl.* jeux) 23; un match 16
    to play a game (match) *faire un match 16
    to play a game jouer à + *game* 23
garage un garage 21
garden un jardin 21
gentleman un monsieur (*pl.* messieurs) 5
to get: to get fat grossir 27
    to get thin maigrir 27
girl une fille 15
    girlfriend une petite copine
to give (to) donner (à) 35, 36
    give me donne-moi, donnez-moi 9, 10
    please give me s'il te plâit, donne-moi 10
glass un verre 33
glasses des lunettes *f.* 25
    sunglasses des lunettes *f.* de soleil 25
to go *aller 22
    go ahead! vas-y! 22
    go away! va-t'en! 22
    to go (come) back rentrer 22, 32; *revenir 23
    to go by bicycle *aller en vélo 22
    to go by car, by train . . . *aller en auto, en train... 22
    to go camping *faire du camping 29
    to go food shopping *faire les courses 33
    to go mountain climbing *faire de l'alpinisme 29
    to go shopping *faire des achats 29

English-French Vocabulary

to go to assister à **29**
gone allé (*p.p. of* *aller) **32**
good bon (bonne) **20**
  good morning (afternoon)
    bonjour **1**
  that's good c'est bien **20**
  the weather's good
    (pleasant) il fait bon **12**
good-bye! au revoir!, salut! **3**
good-looking beau (bel, belle;
    m.pl. beaux) **17, 20, 27**
grandfather un grand-père **7,
    24**
grandmother une grand-mère
    7, 24
grandparents les grands-
    parents *m.* **24**
grape juice le jus de raisin **10**
grapefruit un pamplemousse
    33
gray gris **20**
great chouette, super **20, 25**
green vert **20**
  green beans les •haricots
    m. verts **33**
guitar une guitare **17, 23**

H ━━━━━━━━━━━━

had eu (*p.p. of* *avoir) **31**
hair les cheveux *m.* **E3, 23**
  he/she has dark hair
    il/elle est brun(e) **17**
half: half past . . . ... heure(s)
    et demie **4**
  half past midnight minuit et
    demi **4**
  half past noon midi et demi
    4
ham le jambon **33**
hamburger un hamburger **9**
hand une main **E3**
handbag un sac **17**
handsome beau (bel, belle;
    m.pl. beaux) **17, 20, 27**
hard difficile **20**
hat un chapeau (*pl.* chapeaux)
    25
to **hate** détester **33**
to **have** *avoir **18**; *(food)*
    *prendre **34**
  do you have . . .? est-ce que
    tu as...? **17**
  I have j'ai **17**
  I have to (must) je dois **13**

to **have (some)** *avoir + du,
    de la *(partitive)*; *prendre +
    du, de la *(partitive)* **34**
to **have a picnic** *faire un
    pique-nique **29**
to **have breakfast** *prendre
    le petit déjeuner **33**
to **have dinner** dîner **33**
to **have dinner at a
    restaurant** dîner au
    restaurant **13**
to **have to** *avoir besoin de +
    inf. **28**; *devoir **35**
he il **11, 14, 18**; lui **23**
  he/she is . . . il/elle est +
    nationality **6**
head la tête **E3**
to **hear** entendre **28**
hello bonjour **1, 3**
to **help** aider **29, 35**
  may I help you? vous
    désirez? **10, 25**
her elle **23**; son, sa; ses **24**; la
    36
  (to) her lui **36**
  her name is . . . elle
    s'appelle... **6**
  what's her name? comment
    s'appelle-t-elle? **17**
here ici **14**
  here comes, here is voici **5**
  here's my mother/father
    voici ma mère/mon père **7**
  here's some voici + du, de la
    (partitive) **34**
  this . . . (over here) ce...-ci
    26
hey! dis! **20**; tiens! **5, 18**
  hey there! dis donc! **20**
hi! salut! **3**
high school student un (une)
    élève **17**
him lui **23**; le **36**
  (to) him lui **36**
his son, sa; ses **24**
  his name is . . . il s'appelle...
    6
  what's his name? comment
    s'appelle-t-il? **17**
home, at home à la maison **14**;
    chez (moi, toi...) **23**
  to go home rentrer **22, 32**
homework les devoirs *m.* **29**
  homework assignment un
    devoir **B**

to **do my homework** *faire
    mes devoirs **29**
to **hope** espérer **26**
horse un cheval (*pl.* chevaux)
    E5
hospital un hôpital **21**
hot chaud **12, 31**
  hot chocolate un chocolat
    10
  hot dog un •hot dog **9**
  to be hot *(people)* *avoir
    chaud **30**
  it's hot *(weather)* il fait
    chaud **12**
hotel un hôtel **21**
house une maison **21**
  at someone's house chez +
    person **22**
how? comment? **16**
  how are you? comment
    allez-vous?, comment vas-tu?,
    ça va? **3**
  how do you find . . .?
    comment trouves-tu...? **25**
  **how do you say . . . in
    French?** comment dit-on...
    en français? **B**
  how much? combien (de)?
    28
  how much does . . . cost?
    combien coûte...? **11, 25**
  how much is that/this/it?
    c'est combien?, ça fait
    combien? **11**
  how old are you? quel âge
    as-tu? **7**
  how old is he/she? quel âge
    a-t-il/elle? **17**
  **how old is your father/
    mother?** quel âge a ton
    père/ta mère? **7**
  how's everything? ça va?
    3
  how's the weather? quel
    temps fail-il? **12**
  to learn how to *apprendre
    à **34**
hundred cent **6, 25**
hungry faim **9**
  are you hungry? tu as faim?
    9
  I'm hungry j'ai faim **9**
  to be hungry avoir faim **18,
    30**
husband un mari **24**

I

I je 14, moi 23
  I don't know je ne sais pas B, 17
  I have a date/appointment at . . . j'ai un rendez-vous à... 4
  I know je sais B, 17, 36
  I'm fine/okay ça va 3
  I'm (very) well/so-so/(very) bad ça va (très) bien/comme ci, comme ça/(très) mal 3
ice la glace 9, 33
  ice cream une glace 9, 33
iced tea un thé glacé 33
idea une idée 28
  it's (that's) a good idea c'est une bonne idée 28
if si C
in à 14, 22; dans 17
  in (Boston) à (Boston) 14
  in class en classe 14
  in front of devant 17
  in order to pour 29
  in the afternoon de l'après-midi 4
  in the morning/evening du matin/soir 4
  in town en ville 14
  in (the) au, à la, à l', aux 22
to indicate indiquer C
inexpensive bon marché *(inv.)* 25
ingredient un ingrédient 33
instrument un instrument 23
  to play a musical instrument jouer de + *instrument* 23
intelligent intelligent 33
interesting intéressant 19
to invite inviter 15
is *(see* to be*)*
  is there? est-ce qu'il y a? 17
  isn't it (so)? n'est-ce pas? 14
  there is il y a 17
  there is (some) il y a + du, de la *(partitive)* 34
it il, elle 14, 18; le, la 36
  it's . . . c'est... 5
  it's . . . (o'clock) il est... heure(s) 4
  it's . . . francs ça fait... francs 11
  it's fine/nice/hot/cool/ cold/bad *(weather)* il fait beau/bon/chaud/frais/ froid/mauvais 12
  it's (June) first c'est le premier (juin) 8
  it's not ce n'est pas 20
  it's raining il pleut 12
  it's snowing il neige 12
  what time is it? quelle heure est-il? 4
  who is it? qui est-ce? 5, 17
its son, sa; ses 24
Italian italien, italienne 19

J

jacket un blouson, une veste 25
jam la confiture 33
January janvier *m.* 8
Japanese japonais(e) 19
jeans: pair of jeans un jean 25
to jog *faire du jogging 29
jogging le jogging 29
  jogging suit un jogging, un survêtement 25
juice le jus
  apple juice le jus de pomme 10, 33
  grape juice le jus de raisin 10
  orange juice le jus d'orange 10, 33
  tomato juice le jus de tomate 10
July juillet *m.* 8
June juin *m.* 8

K

ketchup le ketchup 33
keyboard un clavier 23
kilogram un kilo (de) 33
kind gentil (gentille) 19
kitchen une cuisine 21
knife un couteau 33
to know *connaître 36
  do you know . . .? tu connais...? 6
  I (don't) know je (ne) sais (pas) B, 17, 36
  you know tu sais 36

L

lady une dame 5
large grand 17, 20
last dernier (dernière) 31
  last month le mois dernier 31
  last night hier soir 31
  last Saturday samedi dernier 31
  at last enfin 30
to learn (how to) *apprendre (à) + *inf.* 34
left gauche
  on (to) the left à gauche 21
leg une jambe E3
lemon soda la limonade 10
to lend prêter (à) 35, 36
  lend me prête-moi 11
  less . . . than moins... que 27
let's go! allons-y! 22
lettuce la salade 33
library une bibliothèque 21
like: what does he/she look like? comment est-il/elle? 17
  what's he/she like? comment est-il/elle? 17
to like aimer 15
  do you like? est-ce que tu aimes? 13
  I also like j'aime aussi 13
  I don't always like je n'aime pas toujours 13
  I don't like je n'aime pas 13
  I like j'aime 13
  I like . . ., but I prefer . . . j'aime..., mais je préfère... 13
  I'd like je voudrais 9, 10, 13
  what would you like? vous désirez? 10, 25
to listen écouter 15
  to listen to cassettes écouter des cassettes 29
  to listen to the radio écouter la radio 13
little petit 17, 20, 25
  a little (bit) un peu 15
to live habiter 15
living room *(formal)* un salon 21
to loan prêter (à) 35, 36
long long (longue) 25
to look (at) regarder 15

look! tiens! **5, 18**
look at that regarde ça **17**
I'm looking for . . . je
cherche... **25**
to look for chercher **25**
what does he/she look
like? comment est-il/elle?
17
to lose perdre **28**
to lose weight maigrir **27**
lot: a lot beaucoup **15**
to love: I'd love to je veux bien
13
luck la chance **30**
to be lucky *avoir de la
chance **30**
lunch le déjeuner **33**
to have (eat) lunch déjeuner
33

M

made fait (*p.p. of* *faire) **31**
to make *faire **16**
man un homme **17;** un
monsieur *(polite term)* **5**
many beaucoup (de) **15**
how many combien de **28**
map une carte **B**
March mars *m.* **8**
match un match **16**
to play a match *faire un
match **16**
May mai *m.* **8**
may *pouvoir **35**
maybe peut-être **14**
mayonnaise la mayonnaise **33**
me moi **1, 35**
excuse me pardon **21, 25**
(to) me me, moi **35**
meal un repas **33**
mean méchant **19**
to mean *vouloir dire **34**
what does . . . mean? que
veut dire...? **B**
meat la viande **33**
to meet rencontrer **29**
to meet for the first time
*connaître *(in passé
composé)* **36**
Mexican mexicain(e) **19**
midnight minuit **4**
milk le lait **33**
mineral water l'eau *f.* minérale
33

Miss Mademoiselle (Mlle) **3**
modern moderne **21**
Monday lundi *m.* **8**
money l'argent *m.* **29**
Monopoly le Monopoly **23**
month un mois **8, 27**
last month le mois dernier
31
next month le mois prochain
31
this month ce mois-ci **31**
moped une mob (mobylette)
17
more . . . than plus... que **27**
morning le matin **29**
good morning bonjour **1**
in the morning du matin **4**
this morning ce matin **29**
tomorrow morning demain
matin **31**
yesterday morning hier
matin **31**
mother une mère **7, 24**
this is my mother voici ma
mère **7**
motorbike une mob
(mobylette) **17**
motorcycle une moto **17**
motorscooter un scooter **17**
mountain une montagne **29**
mountain climbing
l'alpinisme *f.* **29**
to (at/in) the mountain(s) à
la montagne **29**
to do mountain climbing
*faire de l'alpinisme **29**
mouth une bouche **E3**
movie un film **22, 29**
movie theater un cinéma **14**
movies le cinéma **21**
at (to) the movies au
cinéma **14**
Mr. Monsieur (M.) **3**
Mrs. Madame (Mme) **3**
much, very much beaucoup
15
how much? combien? **28**
how much does . . . cost?
combien coûte...? **11, 25**
how much is it? ça fait
combien?, c'est combien? **11**
too much trop **25**
museum un musée **21**
music la musique **23**
must *devoir **35**

I must je dois **13**
my mon, ma; mes **7, 24**
my birthday is (March 2)
mon anniversaire est le (2
mars) **8**
my name is . . . je
m'appelle... **1**

N

name: his/her name is . . .
il/elle s'appelle... **6**
my name is . . . je
m'appelle... **1**
what's . . .'s name?
comment s'appelle...? **6**
what's his/her name?
comment s'appelle-t-il/elle?
17
what's your name?
comment t'appelles-tu? **1**
napkin une serviette **33**
nasty méchant **19**
nationality la nationalité **2**
nearby près **21**
neck le cou **E3**
to need *avoir besoin de **28**
neighbor un voisin, une voisine
17
neighborhood un quartier **21**
a nice neighborhood un joli
quartier **21**
never ne... jamais **32**
new nouveau (nouvel, nouvelle;
m.pl. nouveaux) **27**
next prochain **29, 31**
next week la semaine
prochaine **31**
nice gentil (gentille),
sympathique **19**
it's nice (beautiful) weather
il fait beau **12**
night: tomorrow night demain
soir **4**
last night hier soir **31**
nine neuf **1**
nineteen dix-neuf **2**
ninety quatre-vingt-dix **6**
ninth neuvième **24**
no non **2,14**
no . . . pas de **18, 34**
no? n'est-ce pas? **14**
nobody ne... personne,
personne **32**
noon midi **4**

nose le nez **E3**
not ne... pas **14**
   not a, not any pas de **18, 34**
   not always pas toujours **13**
   not anybody ne... personne **32**
   not anything ne... rien **32**
   not at all pas du tout **23**
   it's (that's) not ce n'est pas **20**
   of course not! mais non! **14**
notebook un cahier **B**
nothing ne... rien, rien **32**
November novembre *m.* **8**
now maintenant **15, 31**

O

o'clock heure(s)
   at . . . o'clock à... heures **4**
   it's . . . o'clock il est... heure(s) **4**
object un objet **17**
ocean la mer **29**; l'océan *m.*
   to (at) the oceanside à la mer **29**
October octobre *m.* **8**
of de **14**
   of (the) du, de la, de l', des **23**
   of course not! mais non! **14**
   of course! bien sûr **13**
   of whom de qui **16**
often souvent **15**
oh: oh, really? ah, bon? **16**
okay d'accord **13**
   I'm okay ça va **3**
old vieux (vieil, vieille; *m.pl.* vieux) **27**
   he/she is . . . (years old) il/elle a... ans **7**
   how old are you? quel âge as-tu? **7**
   how old is he/she? quel âge a-t-il/elle? **17**
   how old is your father/ mother? quel âge a ton père/ta mère? **7**
   I'm . . . (years old) j'ai... ans **7**
   to be . . . (years old) *avoir... ans **18**
omelet une omelette **9**
on sur **17**

on foot à pied **22**
on Monday lundi **18**
on Mondays le lundi **18**
on vacation en vacances **14**
one un, une **1**; *(we, they, people)* on **28**
oneself: by oneself seul **29**
only seul **29**
open *ouvrir
   open . . . ouvre... (ouvrez...) **B**
opinion: in my opinion à mon avis **27**
or ou **2, 14**
orange *(color)* orange *(inv.)* **20**
orange une orange **33**
   orange juice le jus d'orange **10, 33**
order: in order to pour **29**
to organize organizer **15**
other autre **33**
our notre; nos **24**
out of style démodé **25**
over: over (at) . . .'s house chez... **23**
   over there là-bas **14**
   that (one), over there ça, là-bas **17**
overcoat un manteau *(pl.* manteaux) **25**
to own *avoir **18**

P

P.M. du soir **4**
pain: a pain pénible **20**
pants un pantalon **25**
pantyhose des collants *m.* **25**
paper le papier **B**
   sheet of paper une feuille de papier **B**
parents les parents *m.* **24**
park un parc **21**
party *(informal)* une boum **22**
to pass a test (an exam) réussir à un examen **27**
past: half past . . . ... heure(s) et demie **4**
   quarter past . . . ... heure(s) et quart **4**
to pay (for) payer **28**
   to pay attention *faire attention **16**
pear une poire **33**
peas les petits pois *m.* **33**

pen un stylo **B, 17**
pencil un crayon **B, 17**
people des gens *m.* **18**; on **28**
perhaps peut-être **14**
person une personne **5, 17**
pet un animal *(pl.* animaux) domestique **7**
to phone téléphoner **15**
piano un piano **23**
picnic un pique-nique **22**
   to have a picnic *faire un pique-nique **29**
pie une tarte **33**
piece: piece of chalk un morceau de craie **B**
ping-pong le Ping-Pong **23**
pink rose **20**
pizza une pizza **9**
place un endroit **22**
   place setting un couvert **33**
to place *mettre **26**
placed mis *(p.p. of* *mettre) **31**
plain moche **25**
plane un avion **29**
   by plane en avion **29**
plate une assiette **33**
to play jouer **15**
   to play a game jouer à + *game* **23**
   to play a game (match) *faire un match **16**
   to play a musical instrument jouer de + *instrument* **23**
   to play basketball (soccer, tennis, volleyball) jouer au basket (au foot, au tennis, au volley) **13**
pleasant sympathique **19**
   it's pleasant (good) weather il fait bon **12**
please s'il vous plaît *(formal)* **10**; s'il te plaît *(informal)* **9**
   please give me . . . s'il te plâît, donne-moi... **10**
polo shirt un polo **25**
pool: swimming pool une piscine **21**
poor pauvre **28**
poorly mal **3**
popular à la mode **25**
poster une affiche **17**
potato une pomme de terre **33**
pound une livre (de) **33**

to prefer préférer **26, 33**
   I prefer je préfère + *inf.* **13**
   I like . . ., but I prefer . . .
     j'aime..., mais je préfère... **13**
to prepare préparer **29**
   pretty joli **17, 25**
   price un prix **25**
     what's the price? quel est le
     prix? **25**
   pullover un pull **25**
   pupil un (une) éleve **17**
to purchase acheter **29**
to put *mettre **26**
   to put on *mettre **26**

Q

   quantity une quantité **33**
   quarter un quart
     quarter of . . . ... heure(s)
     moins le quart **4**
     quarter past . . . ... heure(s)
     et quart **4**

R

   racket une raquette **17**
   radio une radio **17**
     to listen to the radio
     écouter la radio **13**
   rain: it's raining il pleut **12**
   raincoat un imper
     (imperméable) **25**
   rarely rarement **15**
   rather assez **19**
   really: oh, really? ah, bon? **16**
     really?! vraiment?! **23**
   record un disque **17**
   reel-to-reel tape une bande **B**
   relatives les parents *m.* **24**
to repair réparer **29**
to respond répondre **36**
   restaurant un restaurant **21**
     at (to) the restaurant au
     restaurant **14**
     have dinner at a restaurant
     dîner au restaurant **13**
to return rentrer **32;** *revenir **23**
   rice le riz **33**
   rich riche **28**
   ride: to take a bicycle ride
     *faire une promenade à velo
     22
   right vrai **20;** droite

   right? n'est-ce pas? **14**
   all right d'accord **13**
   to be right *avoir raison **30**
   to (on) the right à droite **21**
   roast beef le rosbif **33**
   room une chambre **17;** une
     salle **21**
     bathroom une salle de bains
     21
     dining room une salle à
     manger **21**
     formal living room un salon
     21
to run *(referring to objects)*
   marcher **17**

S

   sailing la voile **29**
   salad une salade **9, 33**
   salami le saucisson **33**
   salt le sel **33**
   sandal une sandale **25**
   sandwich un sandwich **9**
   Saturday samedi *m.* **8, 31**
     see you Saturday! à samedi!
     8
     last Saturday samedi
     dernier **31**
     next Saturday samedi
     prochain **31**
   saw vu *(p.p. of* *voir*)* **31**
   saxophone un sax (saxophone)
     23
   say *dire **36**
     say . . . dites... **C**
     say! dis (donc)! **20**
     how do you say . . . in
     French? comment dit-on...
     en français? **B**
   school une école **21**
     school cafeteria une cantine
     de l'école **33**
     school friend un (une)
     camarade **17**
   sea la mer **29**
     to (at) the sea à la mer **29**
   season une saison **12**
   second deuxième **24**
to see *voir **29**
     see you tomorrow! à
     demain! **8, 29**
   seen vu *(p.p. of* *voir*)* **31**
   seldom rarement **15**
to sell vendre **28**

   September septembre *m.* **8**
to set the table *mettre la table
   33
   seven sept **1**
   seventeen dix-sept **2**
   seventh septième **24**
   seventy soixante-dix **5**
   she elle **14, 18, 23**
   sheet of paper une feuille de
     papier **B**
   ship un bateau *(pl.* bateaux*)* **29**
   shirt une chemise **25**
   shoe une chaussure **5**
     tennis shoes des tennis *m.*
     25
   shop une boutique **25**
   shopping: shopping center un
     centre commercial **21**
     to go food shopping *faire
     les courses **33**
     to go shopping *faire des
     achats **29**
   shore la mer **29**
   short court **25;** petit **17, 20,**
     25
     he/she is short il/elle est
     petit(e) **17**
   shorts un short **25**
   should *devoir **35**
to show indiquer **C;** montrer à
   35, 36
to shut fermer **B**
   shy timide **19**
   silly bête **19**
to sing chanter **13, 15**
   sir Monsieur (M.) **3**
   sister une soeur **7, 24**
   six six **1**
   sixteen seize **2**
   sixth sixième **24**
   sixty soixante **3, 5**
to ski *faire du ski **29**
     skiing le ski **29**
   skirt une jupe **25**
   small petit **17, 20, 25**
   sneakers des tennis *m.* **25**
     hightop sneakers des
     baskets *m.* **25**
   snow: it's snowing il neige **12**
   so alors **19**
     so-so comme ci, comme ça **3**
     everything's (going) so-so
     ça va comme ci, comme ça **3**
   soccer le foot (football) **23**
   sock une chaussette **25**

soda un soda 10

    lemon soda une limonade 10

sold vendu (*p.p. of* vendre) 31

sole *(fish)* la sole 33

some des 18; du, de la, de l' 34; quelques 17

somebody quelqu'un 32

someone quelqu'un 32

something quelque chose 32

son un fils 24

sorry: to be sorry regretter

    I'm sorry, but (I cannot) je regrette, mais (je ne peux pas) 13

soup la soupe 33

spaghetti les spaghetti *m.* 33

Spanish espagnol(e) 19

to **speak** parler 15

    to speak (French, English, Spanish) parler (français, anglais, espagnol) 13

    to speak to parler à 36

to **spend** *(money)* dépenser 28; *(time)* passer 29

spoon une cuillère 33

sports le sport 29

    to play a sport *faire du sport 29; jouer à + *sport* 23

    sports clothing des vêtements *m.* de sport 25

spring le printemps 12

    in the spring au printemps 12

stadium un stade 21

to **stay** rester 22

steak un steak 9

    steak and French fries un steak-frites 9

stereo set une chaîne stéréo 17

stomach le ventre E3

store un magasin 21, 25

    department store un grand magasin 25

straight tout droit 21

strawberry une fraise 33

street une rue 21

student *(high school)* un (une) éleve 17; *(college)* un étudiant, une étudiante 17

to **study** étudier 13, 15

stupid bête 19

style: in style à la mode 25

    out of style démodé 25

subway le métro 22

by subway en métro 22

to **succeed** réussir 27

sugar le sucre 33

summer l'été *m.* 12

    summer vacation les grandes vacances 29

    in the summer en été 12

sun le soleil 25

Sunday dimanche *m.* 8

sunglasses des lunettes *f.* de soleil 25

supermarket un supermarché 21

supper le dîner 33

    to have (eat) supper dîner 15, 33

sure bien sûr 13

    sure! mais oui! 14

    are you sure? tu es sûr(e)? 24

sweater un pull 25

sweatshirt un sweat 25

to **swim** nager 15

    I like to swim j'aime nager 13

swimming pool une piscine 21

swimsuit un maillot de bain 25

Swiss suisse 19

T ────────────────

table une table B, 17

    to set the table *mettre la table 33

to **take** *prendre B, 34

    to take along amener 26, 35

    to take a bicycle ride *faire une promenade à velo 22

    to take a drive *faire une promenade en voiture 22

    to take a trip *faire un voyage 16

    to take a walk *faire une promenade à pied 22

to **talk** parler 15

    to talk to parler à 36

tall grand 17, 20

tape: tape recorder un magnétophone 17

    cassette tape une cassette B, 17

    reel-to-reel tape une bande B

taxi un taxi 22

by taxi en taxi 22

tea le thé 10

    iced tea un thé glacé 33

teacher un (une) prof 5, 17; un professeur 17

telephone un téléphone 17

to **telephone** téléphoner 15

television la télé B, 17

    to watch television regarder la télé 13

to **tell** *dire 36

ten dix 1, 2

tennis le tennis 23

    tennis racket une raquette de tennis 23

    tennis shoes des tennis *m.* 25

    to play tennis jouer au tennis 13

tenth dixième 24

terrific chouette 20, 25; extra 20; super 20, 25

test un examen

    to pass a test réussir à un examen 27

than que 27

thank you merci 3

that que 25; ce, cet, cette 26

    that is . . . c'est... 17, 20

    that (one), over there ça, là-bas 17

    that's . . . c'est... 5, 17, 20; voilà 5

    that's . . . francs ça fait... francs 11

    that's bad c'est mal 20

    that's a good idea! c'est une bonne idèe! 28

    that's good (fine) c'est bien 20

    that's not . . . ce n'est pas... 20

    what's that? qu'est-ce que c'est? 17

the le, la, l' 6, 18; les 18

theater un théâtre 21

    movie theater un cinéma 21

their leur, leurs 24

them eux, elles 23; les 36

    (to) them leur 36

then alors 19; ensuite 30

there là 14

    there is (are) il y a 17

    there is (here comes someone) voilà 5

there is (some) il y a + du, de la *(partitive)* 34
there's some voilà + du, de la *(partitive)* 34
over there là-bas 14
that (one), over there ça, là-bas 17; ce...-là 26
what is there? qu'est-ce qu'il y a? 17
these ces 26
these are ce sont 20
they ils, elles 14; eux 23; on 28
they are ce sont 20
thin: to get thin maigrir 27
thing une chose
things are going (very) badly ça va (très) mal 3
to think penser 25
to think of penser de, trouver 25
to think that penser que 25
what do you think of . . .? comment trouves-tu...?, qu'est-ce que tu penses de...? 25
third troisième 24
thirsty: to be thirsty *avoir soif 30
are you thirsty? tu as soif? 10
I'm thirsty j'ai soif 10
thirteen treize 2
thirty trente 3
3:30 trois heures et demie 4
this ce, cet, cette 26
this is . . . voici... 5
those ces 26
those are ce sont 20
thousand mille 25
three trois 1
Thursday jeudi *m.* 8
tie une cravate 25
tights des collants *m.* 25
time: at what time is . . .? à quelle heure est...? 4
at what time? à quelle heure? 4
what time is it? quelle heure est-il? 4
to à 14, 22; chez 22, 23
to (the) au, à la, à l', aux 22
in order to pour 29
to class en classe 14

to someone's house chez + *person* 22
to whom à qui 16
today aujourd'hui 8, 31
today is (Wednesday) aujourd'hui, c'est (mercredi) 8
toilet les toilettes 21
tomato une tomate
tomato juice le jus de tomate 10
tomorrow demain 8
tomorrow afternoon demain après-midi 31
tomorrow is (Thursday) demain, c'est (jeudi) 8
tomorrow morning demain matin 31
tomorrow night (evening) demain soir 31
see you tomorrow! à demain! 8, 29
tonight ce soir 31
too aussi 2, 15; trop 25
too bad! dommage! 15
touring bus un autocar, un car 29
town un village 21
in town en ville 14
track suit un survêtement 25
train un train 29
by train en train 22, 29
to travel voyager 13, 15
trip: to take a trip *faire un voyage 16
trousers un pantalon 25
true vrai 20
T-shirt un tee-shirt 25
Tuesday mardi *m.* 8
tuna le thon 33
to turn tourner 21
to turn on *mettre 26
TV la télé B, 17
to watch TV regarder la télé 13
twelfth douzième 24
twelve douze 2
twenty vingt 2, 3
two deux 1

ugly moche 25
uncle un oncle 7, 24

under sous 17
to understand *comprendre 34
I (don't) understand je (ne) comprends (pas) B
unfashionable démodé 25
United States les États-Unis *m.*
upstairs en •haut 21
us nous 23
(to) us nous 35
to use utiliser C

vacation les vacances *f.* 29
on vacation en vacances 14
summer vacation les grandes vacances 29
VCR (videocassette recorder) un magnétoscope B
veal le veau 33
vegetable un légume 33
very très 19
very well très bien 15
very much beaucoup 15
videocassette une vidéocassette B
videocassette recorder un magnétoscope B
violin un violon 23
to visit *(place)* visiter 15, 28; *(people)* rendre visite à 28, 36
volleyball le volley (volleyball) 23

to wait (for) attendre 28
walk une promenade 22
to take (go for) a walk *faire une promenade à pied 16, 22
to walk *aller à pied 22; marcher 17
walkman un walkman 17
to want *avoir envie de 28; *vouloir 34
do you want . . .? tu veux...? 9
do you want to . . .? est-ce que tu veux...? 13
I don't want . . . je ne veux pas... 13
I want . . . je veux... 13, 34
I want to je veux bien 34

what do you want? qu'est-ce que tu veux? **9;** vous désirez? **10, 25**

wanted voulu *(p.p. of *vouloir)* **34**

warm chaud **12, 31**
  to be warm *(people)* *avoir chaud **30**
  it's warm *(weather)* il fait chaud **12**

was été *(p.p. of *être)* **31**

to **wash** laver **29**

to **waste** perdre **28**

watch une montre **17**

to **watch** regarder **15**
  to watch TV regarder la télé **13**

water l'eau *f.* **33**
  mineral water l'eau minérale **33**

to **waterski** *faire du ski nautique **29**
  waterskiing le ski nautique **29**

we nous **14, 23;** on **28**

to **wear** *mettre **26;** porter **25**

weather: how's (what's) the weather? quel temps fait-il? **12**
  it's . . . weather il fait... **12**

Wednesday mercredi *m.* **8**

week une semaine **8, 29**
  last week la semaine dernière **31**
  next week la semaine prochaine **31**
  this week cette semaine **31**

weekend un weekend **29**
  last weekend le weekend dernier **31**
  next weekend le weekend prochain **29, 31**
  this weekend ce weekend **31**

weight: to gain weight grossir **27**

well bien **15**
  well! eh bien! **26**
  well then alors **19**
  everything's going (very) well ça va (très) bien **3**

went allé *(p.p. of *aller)* **32**

what comment? quoi? **17;** qu'est-ce que **16**

what color? de quelle couleur? **20**

what day is it? quel jour est-ce? **8**

what do you think of . . .? comment trouves-tu...?, qu'est-ce que tu penses de...? **25**

what do you want? qu'est-ce que tu veux? **9;** vous désirez? **10, 25**

what does . . . mean? que veut dire...? **B**

what does he/she look like? comment est-il/elle? **17**

what is it? qu'est-ce que c'est? **17**

what is there? qu'est-ce qu'il y a? **17**

what time is it? quelle heure est-il? **4**

what would you like? vous désirez? **10, 25**

what's . . .'s name? comment s'appelle...? **6**

what's he/she like? comment est-il/elle? **17**

what's his/her name? comment s'appelle-t-il/elle? **17**

what's that? qu'est-ce que c'est? **17**

what's the date? quelle est la date? **8**

what's the price? quel est le prix? **25**

what's the weather? quel temps fait-il? **12**

what's your address? quelle est ton adresse? **21**

what's your name? comment t'appelles-tu? **1**

at what time is . . .? à quelle heure est...? **4**

at what time? à quelle heure? **4, 16**

when quand **16**
  when is your birthday? c'est quand, ton anniversaire? **8**

where où **14, 16**
  where is . . .? où est...? **14**
  where is it? où est-ce? **21**
  from where? d'où? **23**

whether si **C**

which quel (quelle) **26**

white blanc (blanche) **20**

who qui **16**
  who's that/this? qui est-ce? **5, 17**
  about whom? de qui? **16**
  for whom? pour qui? **16**
  of whom? de qui? **16**
  to whom? à qui? **16**
  with whom? avec qui? **16**

why pourquoi **16**

wife une femme **24**

to **win** gagner **28**

window une fenêtre **B, 17**

to **windsurf** *faire la planche à voile **29**
  windsurfing la planche à voile **29**

winter l'hiver *m.* **12**
  in the winter en hiver **12**

with avec **14**
  with me avec moi **13**
  with you avec toi **13**
  with whom? avec qui? **16**

woman une dame *(polite term)* **5;** une femme **17**

to **work** travailler **13, 15;** *(referring to objects)* marcher **17**
  does the radio work? est-ce que la radio marche? **17**
  it (doesn't) work(s) well il/elle (ne) marche (pas) bien **17**

would: I'd like je voudrais **9, 10, 13**

to **write** *écrire **36**

wrong faux (fausse) **20**
  to be wrong *avoir tort **30**

Y

year un an, une année **8**
  he/she is . . . (years old) il/elle a... ans **7**
  I'm . . . (years old) j'ai... ans **7**
  to be . . . (years old) *avoir... ans **18**

yellow jaune **20**

yes oui **2, 14;** *(to a negative question)* si! **18**
  yes, of course oui, bien sûr **13**

yes, okay (all right) oui, d'accord 13
yes, thank you oui, merci 13
yesterday hier 31
   yesterday afternoon hier après-midi 31
   yesterday morning hier matin 31

yogurt le yaourt 33
you tu, vous 14, 23; on 28
   you are . . . tu es + *nationality* 2
   and you? et toi? 1
   (to) you te, vous 35
your ton, ta; tes 7; votre; vos 24

what's your name? comment t'appelles-tu? 1
young jeune 17

Z

zero zéro 1

INDEX

à 103, 202   + definite article 202
    vs. **chez** 205   **à demain** 49
    à samedi 49
acheter, and verbs like 258–259
activities, talking about daily 88
adjectives   agreement and
    formation 20, 138–139, 162–163,
    164   **beau, nouveau, vieux**
    269   **bon/meilleur** 252, 270
    comparison with 270
    demonstrative 260
    interrogative 261   invariable
    172, 252   of nationality 19,
    165   ordinal numbers as 227
    position before and after the
    noun 166, 173   possessive 224,
    226
adverbs   ending in **-ment** 233   in
    impersonal expressions 176   of
    quantity 163   position of 114
age   talking about your age and
    asking others 46, 47
agreement   noun-adjective 164
    subject-past participle 330
    subject-verb 98, 108, 110, 112,
    268, 278, 280, 330
aller   in **passé composé** 330
    present 24, 200   to express
    near future 206   expressions
    200
alphabet 16
approval, expressing 114, 279
articles   *see* definite article;
    indefinite article; partitive article
attention, how to get someone's 174
avoir   expressions with 59, 150,
    276, 308   **passé composé**
    formed with 309   past participle
    323   present 150   to tell age 47

beau, belle 269
body, identifying head, neck, etc. 74
boire   past participle 367   present
    367

**ça va (bien; comme çi, comme
    ça; mal)** 24
celebrating, how to celebrate a
    happy occasion 337
ce, cet, cette, ces 260
c'est 37, 49, 50, 67, 140   in

impersonal expressions 176
    vs. **il est** 41, 175   with stress
    pronouns 215
chez 205, 215
classroom expressions 293
clothing, talking about 248, 250, 252
combien 67   **combien de** 276, 289
cognates 32, 131, 183, 233, 289
colors, talking about 172
commands   *see* imperative
compliments, expressing 184
comparison with adjectives 270
conclusion, how to introduce 165
connaître 382   **tu connais** 41   vs.
    savoir 382
contractions   **à** with **le, les** 202   **de**
    with **le, les** 213, 222
contradict, how to contradict
    negative statements or
    questions 155   how to
    contradict someone 216

danser 90
dates   talking about the day and
    date 50, 51
days of week 49   with definite
    article 51
de 103   + definite article 213   in
    expressions of quantity 362   in
    negative sentences 154   in
    noun + **de** + noun 217
    indicating possession 222
definite article 42, 60, 151, 153
    contractions with **à** 202
    contractions with **de** 213   in
    general sense 156   with days of
    week 51, 157
demonstrative adjectives 260
devoir 94, 376
dire 388
direct object pronouns   **le, la, les**
    383   **me, te, nous, vous**
    372   position in present
    tense 383   with commands 374,
    385
directions   asking for
    information/directions 193

écrire 388
encourage, how to wish someone
    luck or encourage 327

elision 46, 103, 120
emphasize   how to emphasize a
    question/remark 260
-er verbs   imperative 281   past
    participle 309   present 109, 112
espérer, and verbs like 259
est-ce que   in information
    questions 120   in **passé
    composé** 314   in "yes-no"
    questions 100–101
être   **être de** 19   in descriptions
    175   **passé composé** formed
    with 330, 332   past participle
    323   present 98

faire   expressions with 66, 71, 124,
    301   past participle 323
    present 124
familiar vs. formal 23
family members, talking about 45,
    223
food and meals, talking about 59, 63,
    348, 350, 354, 360, 361, 362, 367,
    368, 379
future   expressed with **aller** 206

games, talking about 214
gender 20, 37, 38, 60
geographical names   prepositions
    with 19

holidays (French), talking about 301

il est 41   vs. **c'est** 175
il y a 144, 363
imperative 59, 67   forms and uses
    281   position of object
    pronouns with 374   summary
    charts R8–R11
indefinite article 37, 38, 151, 153   in
    negative sentences 154
indirect object pronouns   **lui, leur**
    386   **me, te, nous, vous**
    372   position in present tense
    386   with commands 374, 386
infinitive 108   after certain verbs 90,
    91, 115   in **aller** + infinitive
    206
interrogative constructions
    combien, combien de 252
    est-ce que 100   in **passé**

R50

Photo Credits